CONTACTS® 2004

93rd edition published in October by The Spotlight, 7 Leicester Place, London WC2H 7RJ
Tel: 020-7437 7631 Fax: 020-7437 5881 e-mail: info@spotlightcd.com www.spotlightcd.com

Dear Reader

The Spotlight is pleased to present the 2004 edition of **Contacts**: the essential handbook for anyone involved in the UK entertainment industry.

This year's edition contains more listings than ever before - all verified and updated for the coming year. In response to your suggestions, we have also introduced two new sections: **Health & Wellbeing** and **Role Play Companies / Theatre Skills in Business**.

The next edition will be published in October 2005. If you wish to submit a free, text entry, please call **020 7437 7631** for an application form.

Or if you are interested in advertising please call 020 7440 5025 or email advertising@spotlightcd.com for more information.

We hope that you continue to find **Contacts** an invaluable reference tool.

Should you require additional copies of Contacts 2004, please call 020 7440 5026 or email sales@spotlightcd.com to place your order.

Best Wishes

THE SPOTLIGHT®

Editor: Kate Poynton   Production: Kathy Norrish

CONTENTS

CONTENTS

ABBOT MEAD VICKERS BBDO Ltd
151 Marylebone Road
London NW1 5QE
Fax: 020-7616 3580   Tel: 020-7616 3500

AKA
1st Floor, 115 Shaftesbury Avenue
London WC2H 8AF
Website: www.akauk.com
e-mail: aka@akauk.com
Fax: 020-7836 8787   Tel: 020-7836 4747

BANKS HOGGINS O'SHEA FCB
55 Newman Street, London W1T 3EB
Fax: 020-7947 8001   Tel: 020-7947 8000

BARTLE BOGLE HEGARTY
60 Kingly Street, London W1B 5DS
Fax: 020-7437 3666   Tel: 020-7734 1677

BATES TAVNER RESOURCES INTERNATIONAL Ltd
International House
World Trade Centre
1 St Katherine's Way
London E1W 1UN
Fax: 020-7702 2271   Tel: 020-7481 2000

BATES UK Ltd
121-141 Westbourne Terrace, London W2 6JR
Fax: 020-7258 3757   Tel: 020-7262 5077

BDH/TBWA
St Paul's
781 Wilmslow Road
Didsbury Village, Manchester M20 2RW
Website: www.bdhtbwa.co.uk
e-mail: info@bdhtbwa.co.uk
Fax: 0161-908 8601   Tel: 0161-908 8600

BMP DDB Ltd
12 Bishops Bridge Road
London W2 6AA
Fax: 020-7402 4871   Tel: 020-7258 3979

BURNETT Leo Ltd
60 Sloane Avenue, London SW3 3XB
Fax: 020-7591 9126   Tel: 020-7591 9111

CDP TRAVIS SULLY
9 Lower John Street, London W1F 9DZ
Fax: 020-7437 5445   Tel: 020-7437 4224

CHIA Ltd
85 Barlby Road
Unit 23 Shaftesbury Centre
London W10 6BN
Website: www.chiastudio.com
e-mail: agency@chiastudio.com   Tel: 020-8962 1800

COGENT
Heath Farm
Hampton Lane, Meriden
West Midlands CV7 7LL
Fax: 0121-627 5038   Tel: 0121-627 5040

DEWYNTERS Plc
48 Leicester Square
London WC2H 7QD
Fax: 020-7321 0104   Tel: 020-7321 0488

DONER CARDWELL HAWKINS
26-34 Emerald Street
London WC1N 3QA
Fax: 020-7437 3961   Tel: 020-7734 0511

EURO RSCG WNEK GOSPER
11 Great Newport Street
London WC2H 7JA
Fax: 020-7465 0552   Tel: 020-7240 4111

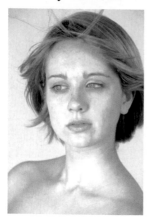

FAULDS ADVERTISING Ltd
Sutherland House
108 Dundas Street
Edinburgh EH3 5DQ
Fax: 0131-557 2261   Tel: 0131-557 6003

GOLLEY SLATER & PARTNERS (LONDON) Ltd
St George's House
3 St George's Place
Church Street, Twickenham TW1 3NE
Fax: 020-8892 4451   Tel: 020-8744 2630

GREY WORLDWIDE
215-227 Great Portland Street
London W1W 5PN
Fax: 020-7637 7473   Tel: 020-7636 3399

HAYMARKET ADVERTISING Ltd
(See M + H COMMUNICATIONS Ltd)

HOLMAN ADVERTISING Ltd
Holman House
30 Maple Street
London W1T 6HA
e-mail: holman.house@lineone.net
Fax: 020-7631 5283   Tel: 020-7637 3533

LEAGAS DELANEY LONDON Ltd
1 Alfred Place
London WC1E 7EB
Website: www.leagusdelaney.com
Fax: 020-7758 1760   Tel: 020-7758 1758

LEITH AGENCY The
37 The Shore
Edinburgh EH6 6QU
Fax: 0131-561 8601   Tel: 0131-561 8600

LEVY McCALLUM ADVERTISING AGENCY The
203 St Vincent Street
Glasgow G2 5NH
Website: www.levymccallum.co.uk
e-mail: ads@levymccallum.co.uk
Fax: 0141-221 5803   Tel: 0141-248 7977

LOWE
Bowater House
68-114 Knightsbridge
London SW1X 7LT
Website: www.loweworldwide.com
Fax: 020-7584 9557   Tel: 020-7584 5033

M + H COMMUNICATIONS Ltd
36 Lexington Street
London W1F 0LJ
Website: www.mandh.co.uk
e-mail: info@mandh.co.uk
Fax: 020-7412 2020   Tel: 020-7412 2000

McCANN-ERICKSON ADVERTISING Ltd
7-11 Herbrand Street
London WC1N 1EX
Fax: 020-7837 3773   Tel: 020-7837 3737

MEDIA ED CIA
1 Paris Garden
London SE1 8NU   Tel: 020-7633 9999

MEDIACOM
180 North Gower Street
London NW1 2NB
Fax: 020-7874 5999   Tel: 020-7874 5500
Fax: 020-7460 9209   Tel: 020-7460 9206

MEDIAJUNCTION
7-8 Apollo House, 18 All Saints Road
Notting Hill, London W11 1HH
Website: www.mediajunction.co.uk
e-mail: mailbox@mediajunction.co.uk
Fax: 020-7460 9209   Tel: 020-7460 9206

MOUNTAIN VIEW Ltd
279 Tottenham Court Road
London W1T 7RJ
Fax: 020-7670 3672   Tel: 020-7670 3670

MUSTOES
2-4 Bucknall Street
London WC2H 8LA
Fax: 020-7379 8487   Tel: 020-7379 9999

OGILVY & MATHER Ltd
10 Cabot Square
Canary Wharf
London E14 4QB
Fax: 020-7345 9000   Tel: 020-7345 3000

PARTNERS BDDH
15 Alfred Place
Cupola House
London WC1E 7EB
Fax: 020-7467 9210   Tel: 020-7467 9200

PUBLICIS Ltd
82 Baker Street
London W1U 6AE
Fax: 020-7487 5351   Tel: 020-7935 4426

RAINEY KELLY CAMPBELL ROALFE Y & R
Greater London House
Hampstead Road
London NW1 7QP
Fax: 020-7611 6011   Tel: 020-7404 2700

RICHMOND TOWERS Ltd
26 Fitzroy Square
London W1T 6BT
Fax: 020-7388 7761   Tel: 020-7388 7421

ROOSE & PARTNERS
102 Sydney Street
London SW3 6NJ
Fax: 020-7349 6801   Tel: 020-7349 6800

RPM 3
William Blake House
8 Marshall Street, London W1V 2AJ
Fax: 020-7439 8884   Tel: 020-7434 4343

SAATCHI & SAATCHI
80 Charlotte Street, London W1A 1AQ
Fax: 020-7637 8489   Tel: 020-7636 5060

SMEE'S ADVERTISING Ltd
3-5 Duke Street, London W1U 3BA
Fax: 020-7935 8588   Tel: 020-7486 6644

SWK & PARTNERS Ltd
27-29 Fitzroy Street, London W1T 6DS
e-mail: firstname.surname@swk.co.uk
Fax: 020-7637 6801   Tel: 020-7637 6800

TBWA LONDON
76-80 Whitfield Street, London W1T 4EZ
Fax: 020-7573 6667   Tel: 020-7573 6666

TBWA/GGT DIRECT
82 Dean Street, London W1D 3HA
Fax: 020-7434 2925   Tel: 020-7439 4282

THOMPSON J Walter CO Ltd
1 Knightsbridge Green, London SW1X 7NW
Website: www.jwt.co.uk
e-mail: firstname.lastname@jwt.com
Fax: 020-7656 7010   Tel: 020-7656 7000

TMP WORLDWIDE
Chancery House, 53-64 Chancery Lane
London WC2A 1QS   Tel: 020-7406 5000

TV MANAGEMENTS
Brink House
Avon Castle, Ringwood
Hants BH24 2BL   Tel: 01425 475544

WCRS
5 Golden Square, London W1F 9BS
Fax: 020-7806 5099   Tel: 020-7806 5000

YOUNG & RUBICAM Ltd
Greater London House
Hampstead Road, London NW1 7QP
Fax: 020-7611 6570   Tel: 020-7387 9366

Bodens Agency
PERSONAL MANAGEMENT OF SELECTED ADULTS
Tel: 020-8447 0909 Fax: 020-8449 5212 E-mail: Bodens2692@aol.com
Michael Throne. 99 East Barnet Road, New Barnet, Herts. EN4 8RF

Key to areas of specialization:
C Cabaret **F** Films **G** General **M** Musicals **Md** Models **PM** Personal Managers **S** Singing **TV** Television **V** Variety
For information regarding membership of the Personal Managers' Association please contact:
Personal Managers' Association Ltd, Rivercroft, 1 Summer Road, East Molesey, Surrey KT8 9LX
Tel: 020-8398 9796 e-mail: info@thepma.com

* Denotes PMA Membership
For information regarding membership of the Co-operative Personal Management Association please contact:
Secretary, CPMA, c/o 1 Mellor Road, Leicester LE3 6HN
Tel: 0116-233 8432 e-mail: cpmauk@yahoo.co.uk **• Denotes CPMA Membership**

1984 PERSONAL MANAGEMENT Ltd•
PM Co-operative
Suite 508, Davina House, 137 Goswell Road
London EC1V 7ET
e-mail: onenine@eightfour.freeserve.co.uk
Fax: 020-7250 3031   Tel: 020-7251 8046

21ST CENTURY ACTORS MANAGEMENT
Co-operative
E10 Panther House, 38 Mount Pleasant
London WC1X 0AN
e-mail: twentyfirstcenturyactors@yahoo.co.uk
Fax: 020-7833 1158   Tel: 020-7278 3438

21ST CENTURY VAUX CASTING
The Corn Exchange
Fenwick Street, Liverpool L2 7QS
e-mail: 21stcenturyvaux@beeb.net
Fax: 0151-231 1068   Tel: 0151-258 1679

2MA
(Sports & Stunts)
Spring Vale, Tutland Road
North Baddesley
Hants SO52 9FL
Website: www.2ma.co.uk
e-mail: mo@2ma.co.uk
Fax: 023-8074 1355   Tel: 023-8074 1354

41 MANAGEMENT*
74 Rose Street, North Lane, Edinburgh EH2 3DX
e-mail: mhunwick@41man.co.uk
Fax: 0131-225 4535   Tel: 0131-225 3585

A-LIST
(Lookalikes & Entertainments)
29 New Line
Greengates, Bradford BD10 9AS
Website: www.alistlookalikes.co.uk
e-mail: info@alistlookalikes.co.uk
Mobile: 07866 583106   Tel: 01274 618309

A & B PERSONAL MANAGEMENT Ltd*
PM Write
Paurelle House, 91 Regent Street
London W1B 4EL
e-mail: billellis@aandb.co.uk
Fax: 020-7734 6318   Tel: 020-7734 6047

A & J MANAGEMENT
551 Green Lanes, London N13 4DR
Website: www.ajmanagement.co.uk
e-mail: ajmanagement@bigfoot.com
Fax: 020-8882 5983   Tel: 020-8882 7716

A PLUS
(16-26 year-olds)
54 Grove Park, London SE5 8LG
Website: www.kidsplus.co.uk
e-mail: janekidsplus@aol.com
Mobile: 07759 944215   Tel/Fax: 020-7737 3901

ABBOTT June ASSOCIATES
The Courtyard
10 York Way, King's Cross
London N1 9AA
Website: www.thecourtyard.org.uk
e-mail: jaa@thecourtyard.org.uk
Fax: 020-7833 0870   Tel: 020-7837 7826

ABSOLUTE MODELS Ltd
(Character & Fashion Models)
4 Hatch Farm Mews, Hatch Farm, Woburn Hill
Weybridge, Surrey KT15 2EH
Website: www.absolutemodels.co.uk
e-mail: enquiries@absolutemodels.co.uk
Fax: 01932 857258   Tel: 01932 857257

ACCESS ASSOCIATES
PO Box 39925, London EC1V 0WN
Website: www.access-associates.co.uk
e-mail: access.mail@virgin.net   Tel: 020-8505 1094

ACROBAT PRODUCTIONS
(Artists & Advisors)
The Circus Space, Coronet Street, London N1 6HD
Website: www.acrobatproductions.co.uk
e-mail: info@acrobatproductions.co.uk
        Tel: 020-7613 5259

ACT ONE DRAMA STUDIO & AGENCY
31 Dobbin Hill, Sheffield S11 7JA
e-mail: info@actonedrama.co.uk
Fax: 07971 112153   Tel: 0114-266 7209

ACT OUT AGENCY
22 Greek Street, Stockport, Cheshire SK3 8AB
e-mail: ab22@supanet.com
        Tel/Fax: 0161-429 7413

ACTING ASSOCIATES
PM
71 Hartham Road, London N7 9JJ
Website: www.actingassociates.co.uk
e-mail: fiona@actingassociates.co.uk
Tel/Fax: 020-7607 3562

ACTIVATE DRAMA SCHOOL
Priestman Cottage, Sea View Road
Sunderland SR2 7UP
e-mail: activate_agcy@hotmail.com
Fax: 0191-551 2051   Tel: 0191-565 2345

ACTORS AGENCY
1 Glen Street
Tollcross, Edinburgh EH3 9JD
Website: www.stivenchristie.co.uk
Fax: 0131-228 4645   Tel: 0131-228 4040

ACTORS ALLIANCE•
Co-operative
Disney Place House, 14 Marshalsea Road
London SE1 1HL
e-mail: actors@actorsalliance.fsnet.co.uk
Tel/Fax: 020-7407 6028

ACTORS' CREATIVE TEAM
Co-operative
Albany House
82-84 South End, Croydon CR0 1DQ
Website: www.actorscreativeteam.co.uk
e-mail: office@actorscreativeteam.co.uk
Fax: 020-8239 8818   Tel: 020-8239 8892

ACTORS DIRECT Ltd
Gainsborough House
109 Portland Street
Manchester M1 6DN
Fax: 0161-237 9993   Tel: 0161-237 1904

ACTORS FILE The
PM Co-operative
Spitfire Studios, 63-71 Collier Street, London N1 9BE
Website: www.theactorsfile.co.uk
e-mail: mail@theactorsfile.co.uk
Fax: 020-7278 0364   Tel: 020-7278 0087

ACTORS' GROUP The (TAG)
PM Co-operative
21-31 Oldham Street, Manchester M1 1JG
e-mail: agent@tagactors.co.uk
Fax: 0161-834 5588   Tel: 0161-834 4466

ACTORS IN SCANDINAVIA
Vuorimiehenkatu 20D, 00150 Helsinki
Finland
Website: www.actors.fi
e-mail: lauram@actors.fi
Fax: 00 358 9 68 404 422   Tel: 00 358 9 68 40440

ACTORS INTERNATIONAL Ltd
Conway Hall, 25 Red Lion Square
London WC1R 4RL
e-mail: actorsinternational@tiscali.co.uk
Fax: 020-7831 8319   Tel: 020-7242 9300

ACTORS IRELAND INCORPORATING ASHDOWN ASSOCIATES
Crescent Arts Centre, 2-4 University Road
Belfast BT7 1NH
e-mail: geraldine@actorsireland.com
Tel/Fax: 028-9024 8861

ACTORUM Ltd
PM Co-operative
3rd Floor, 21 Foley Street, London W1W 6DR
Website: www.actorum.com
e-mail: actorum2@ukonline.co.uk
Fax: 020-7636 6975   Tel: 020-7636 6978

ACTUAL MANAGEMENT
The Studio
63A Ladbroke Road, Notting Hill, London W11 3PD
Website: www.actualmanagement.co.uk
e-mail: agents@actualmanagement.co.uk
Fax: 0870 8741199   Tel: 020-7243 1166

ADAMS Juliet MODELS & TALENT CASTINGS
19 Gwynne House, Challice Way, London SW2 3RB
Website: www.julietadams.co.uk
e-mail: info@julietadams.co.uk
Fax: 020-8671 9314   Tel: 020-8671 7673

AFFINITY MANAGEMENT
Jessops Farm
Tonbridge Road, Bough Beech, Kent TN8 7AU
e-mail: cathy.bird1@btopenworld.com
                                      Tel: 01892 870067

AGENCY The Ltd
(Teri Hayden)
47 Adelaide Road, Dublin 2, Eire
e-mail: info@tagency.ie
Fax: 00 353 1 6760052   Tel: 00 353 1 6618535

AGENCY MODEL & ARTIST MANAGEMENT The
PO Box 4346
London W1A 7US
e-mail: agencymodels@aol.com
                           Tel/Fax: 020-7631 1669

AHA
(See HOWARD Amanda ASSOCIATES Ltd)

**AIM (ASSOCIATED INTERNATIONAL
MANAGEMENT)***
Nederlander House
7 Great Russell Street, London WC1B 3NH
Website: www.a-i-m.net
e-mail: info@aim.demon.co.uk
Fax: 020-7637 8666   Tel: 020-7637 1700

AIR-O-BATS
(Acrobatic & Aerial Agency)
84 Laburnum Avenue
Hornchurch
Essex RM12 4HA
e-mail: kda@air-o-bats.com   Tel: 01708 705601

ALANDER AGENCY
TV F S V
135 Merrion Avenue, Stanmore
Middlesex HA7 4RZ   Tel: 020-8954 7685

ALEXANDER PERSONAL MANAGEMENT Ltd
PO Box 834, Hemel Hempstead
Hertfordshire HP3 9ZP
Website: www.apmassociates.net
e-mail: apm@apmassociates.net
Fax: 01442 241099   Tel: 01442 252907

ALEXANDER Suzanne MANAGEMENT
170 Town Lane, Higher Bebington, Wirral CH63 8LG
e-mail: suzyalex@hotmail.com
                                   Tel/Fax: 0151-608 9655

ALL STAR SPEAKERS
(After Dinner Speakers)
23 Tynemouth Street, Fulham, London SW6 2QS
Fax: 020-7371 7466   Tel: 020-7371 7512

ALLGOOD ASSOCIATES
24 South Road, Bisley
Surrey GU24 9ES   Tel: 01483 487831

ALLSORTS DRAMA FOR CHILDREN
(In Association with Sasha Leslie Management)
2 Pember Road, London NW10 5LP
e-mail: enquiries@allsorts.ltd.uk
                               Tel/Fax: 020-8969 3249

ALPHA PERSONAL MANAGEMENT Ltd
PM Co-operative
Studio B4, 3 Bradbury Street, London N16 8JN
e-mail: alphamanagement3@aol.com
Fax: 020-7241 2410   Tel: 020-7241 0077

ALRAUN Anita REPRESENTATION*
Write, no e-mails
5th Floor
28 Charing Cross Road, London WC2H 0DB
e-mail: anita@cjagency.demon.co.uk
Fax: 020-7379 6865   Tel: 020-7379 6840

ALTARAS Jonathan ASSOCIATES Ltd*
11 Garrick Street
Covent Garden, London WC2E 9AR
e-mail: helen@jaa.ndirect.co.uk
Fax: 020-7836 6066   Tel: 020-7836 8722

ALVAREZ MANAGEMENT
86 Muswell Road, London N10 2BE
e-mail: sga@alvarezmanagement.fsnet.co.uk
Fax: 020-8444 2646   Tel: 020-8883 2206

ALW ASSOCIATES
1 Grafton Chambers, Grafton Place
London NW1 1LN
e-mail: alweurope@onetel.net.uk
Fax: 020-7813 1398   Tel: 020-7388 7018

AMBER PERSONAL MANAGEMENT Ltd
PM
189 Wardour Street, London W1F 8ZD
Website: www.amberltd.co.uk
e-mail: info@amberltd.co.uk
Fax: 020-7734 9883   Tel: 020-7734 7887

28 St Margaret's Chambers, 5 Newton Street
Manchester M1 1HL
Fax: 0161-228 0235   Tel: 0161-228 0236

Sam Kindred

Sally George

Natasha Greenberg

020 8677 8753
07932 618111

AMERICAN AGENCY The
14 Bonny Street
London NW1 9PG
e-mail: americanagency@btconnect.com
Fax: 020-7482 0856   Tel: 020-7485 8883

ANA (Actors Network Agency)•
PM Co-operative
55 Lambeth Walk, London SE11 6DX
Website: www.ana-actors.co.uk
e-mail: info@ana-actors.co.uk
Fax: 020-7735 8177   Tel: 020-7735 0999

ANDREW'S MANAGEMENT
203 Links Road
London SW17 9EP
e-mail: atj@andrewsman.fsnet.co.uk
Fax: 020-8677 8973   Tel: 020-8769 7416

ANDREWS Amanda AGENCY
30 Caverswall Road, Blythe Bridge
Stoke-on-Trent, Staffordshire ST11 9BG
e-mail: amanda.andrews@lineone.net
                              Tel/Fax: 01782 393889

ANGEL Susan & FRANCIS Kevin Ltd*
Write, no e-mails
1st Floor, 12 D'Arblay Street
London W1F 8DU
e-mail: angelpair@freeuk.com
Fax: 020-7437 1712   Tel: 020-7439 3086

ANOTHER FACE
10 D'Arblay Street, London W1F 8DS
Website: www.anotherface.com
e-mail: mia@anotherface.com
Fax: 020-7494 3300   Tel: 020-7494 7001

katie vandyck
london·lewes
01273·475218
www.iphotou.co.uk

antonia bernath

Steve
Lawton

PHOTOGRAPHY

LONDON

Adrian Sarple   Lucianne McAvoy

Student rates

07973 307487 stevelawton@clara.co.uk

A.P.M. ASSOCIATES (Linda French)
(See ALEXANDER PERSONAL MANAGEMENT Ltd)

ARAENA/COLLECTIVE
10 Bramshaw Gardens
South Oxhey, Herts WD1 6XP
e-mail: patricia@araena.watford.net
Tel/Fax: 020-8428 0037

ARCADIA ASSOCIATES
22 Elgin Crescent, London W11 2JR
e-mail: info.arcadia@btopenworld.com
Tel/Fax: 020-7727 8861

ARCH CREATIVE MANAGEMENT Ltd
No. 4, 2 St Stephen's Crescent
London W2 5QT
e-mail: md@arch123.com   Tel/Fax: 020-7727 2910

ARENA ENTERTAINMENT CONSULTANTS
(Corporate Entertainment)
Regent's Court, 39 Harrogate Road, Leeds LS7 3PD
Website: www.arenaentertainments.co.uk
e-mail: stars@arenaentertainments.co.uk
Fax: 0113-239 2016   Tel: 0113-239 2222

ARENA PERSONAL MANAGEMENT Ltd
Co-operative
Room 11
East Block, Panther House
38 Mount Pleasant, London WC1X 0AP
e-mail: arenapmltd@aol.com   Tel/Fax: 020-7278 1661

A R G (ARTISTS RIGHTS GROUP Ltd)
4 Great Portland Street, London W1W 8PA
e-mail: argall@argtalent.com
Fax: 020-7436 6700   Tel: 020-7436 6400

ARGYLE ASSOCIATES
PM (Richard Linford) (SAE for Unsolicited Mail)
St. John's Buildings
43 Clerkenwell Road, London EC1M 5RS
e-mail: argyle.associates@virgin.net
Fax: 020-7608 1642   Tel: 020-7608 2095

ARTISTS INDEPENDENT NETWORK
32 Tavistock Street, London WC2E 7PB
Fax: 020-7240 9029   Tel: 020-7257 8727

ARTSWORLD INTERNATIONAL MANAGEMENT Ltd
1 Farrow Road
Whaplode Drove, Nr Spalding PE12 0TS
e-mail: bob@artsworld.freeserve.co.uk
Fax: 01406 331147   Tel: 01406 330099

ASH PERSONAL MANAGEMENT
3 Spencer Road
Mitcham Common, Surrey CR4 1SG
e-mail: ash_personal_mgmt@yahoo.co.uk
Tel/Fax: 020-8646 0050

ASHCROFT Sharron MANAGEMENT Ltd
Dean Clough, Halifax HX3 5AX
Website: www.sharronashcroft.com
e-mail: info@sharronashcroft.com
Fax: 01422 343417   Tel: 01422 343949

ASIAN TALENT AGENCY The Ltd
(Specialist in Bollywood, UK & India Casting
Artist Management, Events & PR, Research)
43 Colmansmoor Road, Woodley
Reading, Berkshire RG5 4DG
Website: www.ata-uk.com
e-mail: info@ata-uk.com   Tel/Fax: 0118-375 7871

ASQUITH & HORNER
PM Write with SAE
The Studio
14 College Road
Bromley, Kent BR1 3NS
Fax: 020-8313 0443   Tel: 020-8466 5580

ASSOCIATED ARTS
(Directors, Designers, Lighting Designers)
8 Shrewsbury Lane
London SE18 3JF
Website: www.associated-arts.co.uk
e-mail: karen@associated-arts.co.uk
Fax: 020-8856 8189   Tel: 020-8856 4958

ASSOCIATED SPEAKERS
(Lecturers & Celebrity Speakers)
24A Park Road
Hayes
Middlesex UB4 8JN   Tel: 020-8848 9048

AVALON MANAGEMENT GROUP Ltd
4A Exmoor Street
London W10 6BD
Fax: 020-7598 7300   Tel: 020-7598 8000

AVENUE ARTISTES Ltd
C G TV
8 Winn Road, Southampton SO17 1EN
Website: www.avenueartistes.com
e-mail: info@avenueartistes.com
Fax: 023-8090 5703   Tel: 023-8055 1000

AWA - ANDREA WILDER AGENCY
23 Cambrian Drive
Colwyn Bay, Conwy LL28 4SL
Website: www.awagency.co.uk
e-mail: casting@awagency.co.uk
Fax: 07092 249314   Tel: 01492 547542

AWARD COMMUNICATIONS Ltd
PO Box 650, St Albans AL2 3WZ
Website: www.award.co.uk
e-mail: agency@award.co.uk
Fax: 01923 662473   Tel: 01923 662472

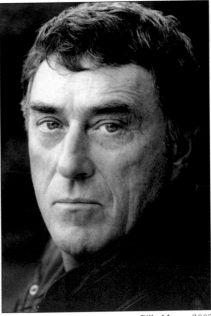

AXM*
Actors' Exchange Management
PM Co-operative
206 Great Guildford Business Square
30 Great Guildford Street, London SE1 0HS
Website: www.axmgt.com
e-mail: info@axmgt.com
Fax: 020-7261 0408   Tel: 020-7261 0400

AZA ARTISTES
(Existing Clients only)
652 Finchley Road
London NW11 7NT   Tel: 020-8458 7288

BaK MANAGEMENT
Linton House, 39-51 Highgate Road
London NW5 1RS
e-mail: bkmanagement@aol.com
Fax: 020-7428 7708   Tel: 020-7428 7707

BALLROOM, LONDON THEATRE OF
(Ballroom/Social Dancers for Film/TV/Theatre)
24 Ovett Close
Upper Norwood, London SE19 3RX
e-mail: paulharrisdance@hotmail.com
Mobile: 07958 784462   Tel: 020-8771 4274

B A M ASSOCIATES
41 Bloomfield Road, Bristol BS4 3QA
e-mail: bamassociates@aol.com
                    Tel/Fax: 0117-971 0636

BARKER Gavin ASSOCIATES Ltd*
(Gavin Barker, Michelle Burke)
2D Wimpole Street, London W1G 0EB
Website: www.gavinbarkerassociates.co.uk
e-mail: rachel@gavinbarkerassociates.co.uk
Fax: 020-7499 3777   Tel: 020-7499 4777

B.A.S.I.C./JD AGENCY
C V S
3 Rushden House
Tatlow Road, Glenfield
Leicester LE3 8ND   Tel/Fax: 0116-287 9594

BECKER Paul Ltd*
223A Portobello Road, London W11 1LU
Fax: 020-7221 5030   Tel: 020-7221 3050

BELCANTO LONDON ACADEMY MANAGEMENT
(Children & Young Adults)
Performance House
20 Passey Place, Eltham, London SE9 5DQ
Fax: 020-8850 9944   Tel: 020-8850 9888

BELFRAGE Julian ASSOCIATES
46 Albemarle Street, London W1S 4DF
Fax: 020-7493 5460   Tel: 020-7491 4400

BELL Olivia Ltd
189 Wardour Street, London W1F 8ZD
e-mail: info@olivia-bell.co.uk
Fax: 020-7439 3485   Tel: 020-7439 3270

BENJAMIN Audrey AGENCY
278A Elgin Avenue, Maida Vale, London W9 1JR
e-mail: aud@elginavenue.fsbusiness.co.uk
Fax: 020-7266 5480   Tel: 020-7289 7180

BETTS Jorg ASSOCIATES
Gainsborough House, 81 Oxford Street
London W1D 2EU
e-mail: jorgbetts@aol.com
Fax: 020-7903 5301   Tel: 020-7903 5300

BIG MANAGEMENT (UK) Ltd
4th Floor, 5 Dean Street, London W1D 3RQ
e-mail: camilla@bigmanagementuk.com
Fax: 020-7287 9934   Tel: 020-7287 9949

SHEILA BURNETT
PHOTOGRAPHY

Paul Freeman

Imelda Staunton

Jackie Clune

Ewan McGregor

020 7289 3058
www.sheilaburnett-photography.com
Student Rates

BILLBOARD PERSONAL MANAGEMENT
Co-operative
The Co-op Centre, 11 Mowll Street
London SW9 6BG
Website: www.billboardpm.com
e-mail: billboardpm@btconnect.com
Fax: 020-7793 0426   Tel: 020-7735 9956

BIRD AGENCY
(Personal Performance Management)
Birkbeck Centre
Birkbeck Road, Sidcup, Kent DA14 4DE
Fax: 020-8308 1370   Tel: 020-8300 6004

BISHOP BURNETT AGENCY & MANAGEMENT
47 Dean Street, London W1D 5BE
e-mail: info@mcs-group.freeserve.co.uk
Fax: 020-7734 9996   Tel: 020-7734 9995

BIZ MANAGEMENT
(In Association with Kidz in The Biz Theatre
Academy)
30 Florence Street, London NW4 1QH
e-mail: thebizmanagement@aol.com
Mobile: 07763 958096   Tel/Fax: 020-8632 9661

BLACKBURN SACHS ASSOCIATES
2-4 Noel Street, London W1F 8GB
Website: www.blackburnsachsassociates.com
e-mail: actors@blackburnsachsassociates.com
Fax: 020-7292 7576   Tel: 020-7292 7555

BLOND Rebecca ASSOCIATES
69A Kings Road, London SW3 4NX
e-mail: rebecca.blond@lineone.net
Fax: 020-7351 4600   Tel: 020-7351 4100

BLUE WAND PRODUCTIONS Ltd
PM TV F G
2nd Floor, 12 Weltje Road, London W6 9TG
e-mail: lino@bluewand.co.uk
Mobile: 07885 528743   Tel/Fax: 020-8741 2038

BMA MODELS
The Stables, 5 Norcott Hall Barns, Norcott Hill
Berkhamsted, Herts HP4 1RB
Website: www.bmamodels.com
e-mail: bmamodels@bmamodels.com
Fax: 01442 879879   Tel: 01442 878878

BODENS AGENCY
PM
99 East Barnet Road, New Barnet, Herts EN4 8RF
Website: www.bodensagency.com
e-mail: bodens2692@aol.com
Fax: 020-8449 5212   Tel: 020-8447 0909

BOOKERS UK
7 Green Avenue, Mill Hill
London NW7 4PX   Tel/Fax: 020-8201 1400

BOOKHOUSE GROUP The
2 Gill's Cottages, Rochester, Kent ME1 1BY
e-mail: mr.barnes@virgin.net   Tel/Fax: 01634 812672

BOSS MODEL MANAGEMENT Ltd
Half Moon Chambers
Chapel Walks, Manchester M2 1HN
e-mail: julie@bossagencies.co.uk
Fax: 0161-832 5219   Tel: 0161-834 3403

BOURNE Sheila MANAGEMENT*
14 Crown Road, Shoreham, Kent TN14 7TL
e-mail: sheila@bourne-uk.freeserve.co.uk
Fax: 01959 524529   Tel: 01959 524528

BOYCE Sandra MANAGEMENT*
1 Kingsway House, Albion Road, London N16 0TA
e-mail: info@sandraboyce.com
Fax: 020-7241 2313   Tel: 020-7923 0606

Heather Peace

Steve McFadden

Yvonne Kaziro

Nyland management

20 School Lane, Heaton Chapel,
Stockport SK4 5DG
Tel: 0161 442 2224
Fax: 0161 432 5406
e-mail: nylandmgmt@freenet.co.uk

BRAIDMAN Michelle ASSOCIATES*
3rd Floor Suite, 10-11 Lower John St, London W1F 9EB
e-mail: info@braidman.com
Fax: 020-7439 3600   Tel: 020-7437 0817

BRAITHWAITE'S THEATRICAL AGENCY
8 Brookshill Avenue, Harrow Weald
Middlesex HA3 6RZ   Tel: 020-8954 5638

BREAK A LEG MANAGEMENT Ltd
Units 2/3 The Precinct
Packington Square, London N1 7UP
Website: www.breakalegman.com
e-mail: agency@breakalegman.com
Fax: 020-7359 3660   Tel: 020-7359 3594

BROADCASTING COMPANY
Unit 23, Canalot Studios, 222 Kensal Road
London W10 5BN
Fax: 020-7460 5223   Tel: 020-7460 5222

BROOD MANAGEMENT
PO Box 21720, London E14 6SU
e-mail: broodmanagement@aol.com
Mobile: 07932 022635   Tel: 020-7531 1810

BROOK Dolly AGENCY
PO Box 5436, Dunmow CM6 1WW
Fax: 01371 875996   Tel: 01371 875767

BROOK Valerie AGENCY
10 Sandringham Road, Cheadle Hulme
Cheshire SK8 5NH
e-mail: colinbrook@freenetname.co.uk
Fax: 0161-488 4206   Tel: 0161-486 1631

BROOKS Claude ENTERTAINMENTS
1 Burlington Avenue, Slough, Berks SL1 2JY
Fax: 01753 520424   Tel: 01753 520717

BROOKS Neil MANAGEMENT
153 Rathgar Road
Rathgar, Dublin 6, Eire
Website: www.neilbrooksmanagement.com
e-mail: nbm2@eircom.net   Tel/Fax: 00 353 1 496 6470

BROWN & SIMCOCKS*
(Barry Brown & Carrie Simcocks) PM Write
1 Bridgehouse Court, 109 Blackfriars Road
London SE1 8HW
e-mail: barryandcarrie@lineone.net
Fax: 020-7928 1909   Tel: 020-7928 1229

BROWNING Malcolm
Room 103, Merchant House
89 Southwark Street, London SE1 0HX
e-mail: info@malcolmbrowning.com
Fax: 0870 4581766   Tel: 020-7960 4669

Tony Curran

Charlotte Comer

Matthew Delamere

ric bacon
07970 970799
www.ricbacon.co.uk

Maxine Peake

Diana Payne Myers

BRUNSKILL MANAGEMENT Ltd*
PM M S TV Write
Suite 8A, 169 Queen's Gate, London SW7 5HE
e-mail: contact@brunskill.com
Fax: 020-7589 9460   Tel: 020-7581 3388

The Courtyard, Edenhall, Penrith
Cumbria CA11 8ST
Website: www.brunskill.com
e-mail: contact@brunskill.fsbusiness.co.uk
Fax: 01768 881850   Tel: 01768 881430

BSA Ltd
(See HARRISON Penny BSA Ltd)

BUCHANAN ASSOCIATES
Nederlander House
7 Great Russell Street, London WC1B 3NH
Website: www.buchanan-associates.co.uk
e-mail: info@buchanan-associates.co.uk
Fax: 020-7631 2034   Tel: 020-7631 2004

BURNETT GRANGER ASSOCIATES*
(Barry Burnett, Lindsay Granger)
3 Clifford Street, London W1S 2LF
e-mail: associates@burnettgranger.co.uk
Fax: 020-7287 3239   Tel: 020-7437 8008

BYRON'S CASTING
(Children & Adults)
North London Performing Arts Centre
76 St James Lane, Muswell Hill, London N10 3DF
Website: www.byronscasting.co.uk
e-mail: byronscasting@aol.com
Fax: 020-8444 4040   Tel: 020-8444 4445

C.A. ARTISTES MANAGEMENT
Md Featured Commercials
153 Battersea Rise, London SW11 1HP
e-mail: casting@caartistes.com
Fax: 020-7924 2334   Tel: 020-7223 7827

C B A INTERNATIONAL
(Cindy Brace)
31 rue Milton, 75009 Paris, France
e-mail: c_b_a@club-internet.fr
Fax: 33 148 74 51 42   Tel: 33 145 26 33 42

166 Waverley Avenue
Twickenham TW2 6DL

CADS MANAGEMENT
209 Abbey Road, Bearwood, Birmingham B67 5NG
Website: www.cadsmanagement.co.uk
e-mail: admin@cadsmanagement.co.uk
Fax: 0121-434 4909   Tel: 0121-420 1996

CAM*
PM Write
19 Denmark Street, London WC2H 8NA
Website: www.cam.co.uk
e-mail: info@cam.co.uk
Fax: 020-7240 7384   Tel: 020-7497 0448

CAMBELL JEFFREY MANAGEMENT
(Set, Costume, Lighting Designers)
11A Greystone Court, South Street
Eastbourne BN21 4LP
e-mail: cambell@theatricaldesigners.co.uk
Fax: 01323 411373   Tel: 01323 411444

CAMPBELL ASSOCIATES
2 Chelsea Cloisters
Sloane Avenue, Chelsea, London SW3 3DW
e-mail: campbell.associates@btopenworld.com
Fax: 020-7584 8799   Tel: 020-7584 5586

Campbell Park, Fernhurst Road
Milland, Nr Liphook
Hants GU30 7LU   Fax: 01428 741648

Mark Lewis Jones

Branca Davies

CAMPBELL Alison MODEL & PROMOTION AGENCY
381 Beersbridge Road, Belfast BT5 5DT
Website: www.alisoncampbellmodels.com
e-mail: info@alisoncampbellmodels.com
Fax: 028-9080 9808   Tel: 028-9080 9809

CAPITAL ARTS THEATRICAL AGENCY
Wyllyotts Centre
Darkes Lane, Potters Bar, Herts EN6 2HN
e-mail: capitalartstheatre@o2.co.uk
Mobile: 07885 232414   Tel/Fax: 020-8449 2342

CAPITAL VOICES
(Anne Skates) Session Singers, Studio, Stage & TV
Brook House, 8 Rythe Rd, Claygate, Surrey KT10 9DF
Website: www.capitalvoices.com
e-mail: capvox@aol.com
Fax: 01372 466229   Tel: 01372 466228

CARDIFF CASTING•
Co-operative Actors Management
Chapter Arts Centre, Market Road, Cardiff CF5 1QE
Website: www.cardiffcasting.co.uk
e-mail: admin@cardiffcasting.co.uk
Fax: 029-2023 3380   Tel: 029-2023 3321

CAREY Roger ASSOCIATES*
PM
Garden Level, 32 Charlwood Street
London SW1V 2DY
e-mail: rogercarey@freeuk.com
Fax: 020-7630 0029   Tel: 020-7630 6301

CARNEY Jessica ASSOCIATES*
PM Write
Suite 90-92, Kent House, 87 Regent Street
London W1B 4EH
e-mail: info@jcarneyassociates.co.uk
Fax: 020-7434 4173   Tel: 020-7434 4143

RICHARD WILSON FOR 'SHELTER'   JULIETTE CHEVELEY   DAVID CONVILLE

**Special Agency Rates
Children's Directories
Theatre Schools
Student Discount**

www.mad-photography.co.uk

020 8363 4182

**CAROUSEL ENTERTAINMENT
& EVENT MANAGEMENT**
(Entertainment for Corporate & Private Events)
18 Westbury Lodge Close
Pinner, Middlesex HA5 3FG
Website: www.carouselentertainments.co.uk
e-mail: info@carouselentertainments.co.uk
Fax: 0870 7518668   Tel: 0870 7518688

CARTEURS
170A Church Road, Hove, East Sussex BN3 2DJ
Website: www.stonelandsschool.co.uk
Fax: 01273 770444   Tel: 01273 770445

CASAROTTO MARSH Ltd
(Film Technicians)
National House, 60-66 Wardour Street
London W1V 4ND
Website: www.casarotto.uk.com
e-mail: casarottomarsh@casarotto.uk.com
Fax: 020-7287 5644   Tel: 020-7287 4450

CASTAWAY ACTORS AGENCY
30-31 Wicklow Street, Dublin 2, Eire
Website: www.irish-actors.com
e-mail: castaway@clubi.ie
Fax: 00 353 1 6719133   Tel: 00 353 1 6719264

CASTCALL & CASTFAX
(Casting & Consultancy Service)
106 Wilsden Avenue, Luton LU1 5HR
Website: www.castcall.co.uk
e-mail: casting@castcall.co.uk
Fax: 01582 480736   Tel: 01582 456213

CASTING COUCH PRODUCTIONS Ltd
97 Riffel Road, London NW2 4PG
e-mail: moiratownsend@yahoo.co.uk
Fax: 020-8208 2373   Tel: 020-8438 9679

CASTING DEPARTMENT The
21H Heathmans Road, London SW6 4TJ
e-mail: jill@thecastingdepartment.com
Fax: 020-7736 2221   Tel: 020-7384 0388

CASTING UK
88-90 Gray's Inn Road, London WC1X 8AA
Website: www.castinguk.com
e-mail: info@castinguk.com
Fax: 020-7430 1155   Tel: 020-7430 1122

C C A MANAGEMENT*
PM Write (Actors and Technicians)
Garden Level, 32 Charlwood St, London SW1V 2DY
e-mail: cca@ccamanagement.co.uk
Fax: 020-7630 7376   Tel: 020-7630 6303

CCM
Co-operative
Panther House, 38 Mount Pleasant
London WC1X 0AP
Website: www.ccmaa.co.uk
e-mail: ccmactors@aol.com
Fax: 020-7813 3103   Tel: 020-7278 0507

CDA
(See DAWSON Caroline ASSOCIATES)

CELEBRITY MANAGEMENT Ltd
12 Nottingham Place, London W1U 5NE
Website: www.celebrity.co.uk
e-mail: info@celebrity.co.uk
Fax: 020-7224 6060   Tel: 020-7224 5050

CELEX CASTING
(Anne Sweeting)
11 Glencroft Drive, Stenson Fields, Derby DE24 3LS
Website: www.celex.co.uk
e-mail: anne@celex.co.uk
Fax: 01332 232115   Tel: 01332 232445

DIRECT LINE

LONDON
St. John's House
16 St. John's Vale
London SE8 4EN
Tel/fax 020 8694 1788

Personal Management
Personal Manager: Daphne Franks

e-mail: daphne.franks@dline.org.uk
website: www.dline.org.uk

LEEDS
Park House
62 Lidgett Lane
Leeds LS8 1PL
Tel/fax 0113 266 4036

CENTRAL AGENCY The
PM
112 Gunnersbury Avenue, London W5 4HB
Website: www.thedormgroup.com
e-mail: info@dorm.co.uk
Fax: 020-8992 9993   Tel: 020-8993 7441

CENTRAL LINE•
PM Co-operative
11 East Circus Street, Nottingham NG1 5AF
Website: www.the-central-line.co.uk
e-mail: mailact@the-central-line.co.uk
Fax: 0115-950 8087   Tel: 0115-941 2937

CENTRE STAGE AGENCY*
7 Rutledge Terrace, South Circular Road
Dublin 8, Eire
e-mail: geraldinecenterstage@eircom.net
                    Tel/Fax: 00 353 1 4533599

Actors
All areas UK

Tel: 01492 547542
Fax: 07092 249314

email: casting@awagency.co.uk
www.awagency.co.uk

N. Wales & North West
based background
artists & children

23 Cambrian Drive, Colwyn Bay,
Conwy, LL28 4SL

CHANCE David A. ASSOCIATES
(See CINEL GABRAN MANAGEMENT)

CHAPMAN AGENCY
The Link Building, Paradise Place
Birmingham B3 3HJ
e-mail: agency@bssd.ac.uk
Fax: 0121-262 6801   Tel: 0121-262 6807

CHARACTERS MANAGEMENT Ltd
28 Fletching Road, Clapton, London E5 9QP
Fax: 020-8533 5554   Tel: 020-8533 5500

CHARLESWORTH Peter & ASSOCIATES
68 Old Brompton Road, London SW7 3LQ
e-mail: petercharlesworth@tiscali.co.uk
Fax: 020-7589 2922   Tel: 020-7581 2478

CHATTO & LINNIT Ltd
123A Kings Road, London SW3 4PL
Fax: 020-7352 3450   Tel: 020-7352 7722

CHILDSPLAY & ALLSORTS
1 Cathedral Street, London SE1 9DE
Website: www.childsplaylondon.co.uk
e-mail: joannaallsorts@aol.com
Fax: 020-7403 1656   Tel: 020-7403 4834

CHURCHILL Hetty PERSONAL MANAGEMENT
9 Daleside Road, London SW16 6SN
e-mail: actors@hettychurchill.com
Fax: 020-8679 2868   Tel: 020-8677 8870

CINEL GABRAN MANAGEMENT*
Tŷ Cefn, 14-16 Rectory Road, Canton
Cardiff, South Wales CF5 1QL
Website: www.cinelgabran.co.uk
e-mail: enquiries@cinelgabran.co.uk
Fax: 029-2066 6601   Tel: 029-2066 6600

CIRCUIT PERSONAL MANAGEMENT Ltd•
Suite 71 S.E.C., Bedford Street, Shelton
Stoke-on-Trent, Staffs ST1 4PZ
Website: www.circuitpm.co.uk
e-mail: mail@circuitpm.co.uk
Fax: 01782 206821   Tel: 01782 285388

CIRCUS MANIACS
(Physical Artistes & Corporate Events)
Office 8A, The Kingswood Foundation
Britannia Road, Kingswood, Bristol BS15 8DB
e-mail: agency@circusmaniacs.com
Mobile: 07977 247287   Tel/Fax: 0117-947 7042

CITY ACTORS' MANAGEMENT Ltd
PM Co-operative
Oval House, 52-54 Kennington Oval
London SE11 5SW
Website: www.city-actors.freeserve.co.uk
e-mail: info@city-actors.freeserve.co.uk
Fax: 020-7793 8282   Tel: 020-7793 9888

Lime

ACTORS AGENCY & MANAGEMENT LIMITED

T 0161 237 3300   F 0161 236 7557

54 Princess Street Manchester M1 6HS

C.K.K. ENTERTAINMENT
PO Box 24550, London E17 9FG
e-mail: ckk.entertainment@virgin.net
Fax: 020-8923 0983   Tel: 020-8923 0977

CLARKE AND JONES Ltd
4B Ainsworth Way, St John's Wood, London NW8 0SR
e-mail: mail@clarkeandjones.plus.com
Fax: 0870 1313391   Tel: 020-7372 3421

CLARKE Jean & BROOK Jeremy MANAGEMENT
International House, 223 Regent Street
London W1R 7DB
Fax: 020-7495 7742   Tel: 020-7495 2424

CLARKE Rose MANAGEMENT
51 Shooters Hill, Blackheath, London SE18 3RL
e-mail: roseclarkemanagement@hotmail.com
                                  Tel/Fax: 020-8856 2536

CLASS ACT
11 Thorn Road, Farnham, Surrey GU10 4TV
e-mail: classact93@hotmail.com
                                  Tel/Fax: 01252 792078

CLAYPOLE MANAGEMENT
PO Box 123 DL3 7WA
e-mail: claypole_1@hotmail.com
Fax: 0870 1334784   Tel: 0845 6501777

CLOUD NINE AGENCY
96 Tiber Gardens, Treaty Street, London N1 0XE
e-mail: cloudnineagency@blueyonder.co.uk
                                  Tel/Fax: 020-7278 0029

CMA (COULTER MANAGEMENT AGENCY)
(Anne Coulter)
74 Victoria Crescent Road, Glasgow G12 9JN
e-mail: cmaglasgow@aol.com
Fax: 0141-579 4700   Tel: 0141-579 1400

Hugh Bonneville   Sarah Ozeke   Tom Burke

SOPHIE BAKER
Photography

0 2 0 - 8 3 4 0   3 8 5 0   *Special rates for students*

DANCERS

1 Charlotte Street, London W1T 1RD
Tel (020) 7636 1473   Fax (020) 7636 1657   Email: info@danceragency.com

CMP MANAGEMENT
Tandy House, 30-40 Dalling Road, London W6 0JB
e-mail: info@ravenscourt.net
Fax: 020-8741 1786   Tel: 020-8741 3400

COHEN MAYER Charlie
(UK and USA Talent) (Incorporating Jimmy D.
Literary/Screenplay Agency)
PM, 121 Brecknock Road, London N19 5AE
Mobile: 07979 856199   Tel: 020-7813 9892

COLLINS Shane ASSOCIATES*
39-41 New Oxford Street
Bloomsbury, London WC1A 1BN
Website: www.shanecollins.co.uk
e-mail: info@shanecollins.co.uk
Fax: 020-7836 9388   Tel: 020-7836 9377

COLLIS MANAGEMENT
182 Trevelyan Road, London SW17 9LW
e-mail: marilyn@collismanagement.co.uk
Fax: 020-8682 0973   Tel: 020-8767 0196

COMEDY CLUB
165 Peckham Rye, London SE15 3HZ
Website: www.comedyclub.org.uk
e-mail: comedyclub@cwcom.net
Fax: 020-7732 9292   Tel: 020-7732 3434

COMMERCIAL AGENCY The
(See TCA)

CONTI Italia AGENCY Ltd
S M TV F Write or Phone
23 Goswell Road, London EC1M 7AJ
e-mail: sca@italiaconti36.freeserve.co.uk
Fax: 020-7253 1430   Tel: 020-7608 7500

CONWAY VAN GELDER Ltd*
PM
3rd Floor, 18-21 Jermyn Street, London SW1Y 6HP
Fax: 020-7287 1940   Tel: 020-7287 0077

COOKE Howard ASSOCIATES*
19 Coulson Street, Chelsea, London SW3 3NA
e-mail: mail@hca1.co.uk
Fax: 020-7591 0155   Tel: 020-7591 0144

CORNER Clive ASSOCIATES
73 Gloucester Road
Hampton, Middlesex TW12 2UQ
e-mail: cornerassociates@aol.com
Fax: 020-8979 4983   Tel: 020-8287 2726

CORNISH Caroline MANAGEMENT Ltd
(Tecnicians Only)
12 Shinfield Street, London W12 0HN
Website: www.carolinecornish.co.uk
e-mail: carolinecornish@btconnect.com
Fax: 020-8743 7887   Tel: 020-8743 7337

COULSON Lou*
1st Floor, 37 Berwick Street, London W1F 8RS
Fax: 020-7439 7569   Tel: 020-7734 9633

CRAWFORDS
6 Brook Street, London W1S 1BB
Website: www.crawfords.tv
e-mail: cr@wfords.com
Fax: 020-7355 1084   Tel: 020-7629 6464

CREATIVE MEDIA
PM Write
22 Kingsbury Avenue, Dunstable
Bedfordshire LU5 4PU   Tel/Fax: 01582 510869

CREATIVE MEDIA MANAGEMENT*
(Film, TV & Theatre Technical Personnel only)
Unit 3B Walpole Court, Ealing Studios
Ealing Green, London W5 5ED
e-mail: enquiries@creativemediamanagement.com
Fax: 020-8566 5554   Tel: 020-8584 5363

CREATIVE SOLUTIONS & EVENTS
21-37 Third Avenue, London E13 8AW
e-mail: info@creativeeventsuk.com
Fax: 020-8471 2111   Tel: 020-8471 3111

CREDITS ACTORS AGENCY Ltd
29 Lorn Road, London SW9 0AB
e-mail: credits@actors29.freeserve.co.uk
          Tel: 020-7737 0735

CRESCENT MANAGEMENT•
PM Co-operative
10 Barley Mow Passage, Chiswick, London W4 4PH
e-mail: jennybenson@crescent-mgemt.demon.co.uk
Fax: 020-8987 0207   Tel: 020-8987 0191

CROUCH ASSOCIATES*
PM Write
9-15 Neal Street, London WC2H 9PW
e-mail: crouchassociates@aol.com
Fax: 020-7379 1991   Tel: 020-7379 1684

CROUCH Sara MANAGEMENT
Suite 1, Ground Floor, 1 Duchess Street
London W1W 6AN
e-mail: sara.crouch@btinternet.com
Fax: 020-7436 4627   Tel: 020-7436 4626

CROWD PULLERS
(Street Performers)
14 Somerset Gardens, London SE13 7SY
e-mail: jhole@crowdpullers.co.uk
Fax: 020-8469 2147   Tel: 020-8469 3900

CRUICKSHANK Harriet*
(Directors, Designers, Choreographers)
97 Old South Lambeth Road, London SW8 1XU
Fax: 020-7820 1081   Tel: 020-7735 2933

Agents & Personal Managers

CS MANAGEMENT
The Croft, 7 Cannon Road, Southgate
London N14 7HE
Website: www.csmanagementuk.com
e-mail: carole@csmanagementuk.com
Fax: 020-8886 7555   Tel: 020-8886 4264

C.S.A.
(Christina Shepherd Advertising)
13 Radnor Walk, London SW3 4BP
e-mail: csa@shepherdmanagement.co.uk
Fax: 020-7352 2277   Tel: 020-7352 2255

CSM (ARTISTES)
PM
St Dunstan's Hall, East Acton Lane, London W3 7EG
e-mail: csm@aol.com
Fax: 020-8740 6542   Tel: 020-8743 9982

CURTIS BROWN GROUP Ltd*
(Actors, Producers, Directors)
Haymarket House, 28-29 Haymarket
London SW1Y 4SP
e-mail: cb@curtisbrown.co.uk
Fax: 020-7393 4404   Tel: 020-7393 4400

CYBER-ARTISTS
In The Can Ltd, The Studio, Kingsway Court
Queen's Gardens, Hove BN3 2LP
Website: www.cyberartists.co.uk
e-mail: cyber.1@btclick.com
Fax: 01273 739984   Tel: 01273 821821

D Lisa MANAGEMENT Ltd
Unit 5, Gun Wharf, 241 Old Ford Road
London E3 5QB
e-mail: casting@lisad.co.uk
Fax: 020-8980 2211   Tel: 020-8980 0117

DALY David ASSOCIATES
586A King's Road, London SW6 2DX
e-mail: agents@daviddaly.co.uk
Fax: 020-7610 9512   Tel: 020-7384 1036

DALY David ASSOCIATES (MANCHESTER)
(Clare Marshall)
16 King Street, Knutsford WA16 6DL
e-mail: clare@daviddaly.co.uk
Fax: 01565 755334   Tel: 01565 631999

DALZELL & BERESFORD Ltd
26 Astwood Mews, London SW7 4DE
Fax: 020-7341 9412   Tel: 020-7341 9411

DANCERS
1 Charlotte Street, London W1T 1RD
e-mail: info@dancersagency.com
Fax: 020-7636 1657   Tel: 020-7636 1473

DARRELL Emma MANAGEMENT
(Producers, Directors & Existing Writers only)
North Vale, Shire Lane, Chorleywood
Herts WD3 5NH
e-mail: emma.mc@virgin.net
Fax: 01923 284064   Tel: 01923 284061

DAVID ARTISTES MANAGEMENT AGENCY Ltd The
F TV Md Write or Phone
153 Battersea Rise, London SW11 1HP
Website: www.davidagency.net
e-mail: casting@davidagency.net
Fax: 020-7924 2334   Tel: 020-7223 7720

DAVIS Dabber PRODUCTIONS
(Write or Phone)
24A Park Road, Hayes
Middlesex UB4 8JN   Tel: 020-8848 9048

DAVIS Lena, JOHN BISHOP ASSOCIATES
Cotton's Farmhouse, Whiston Road
Cogenhoe, Northamptonshire NN7 1NL
Fax: 01604 890405   Tel: 01604 891487

DAWSON Caroline ASSOCIATES*
125 Gloucester Road, London SW7 4TE
e-mail: cda@cdalondon.com
Fax: 020-7373 1110   Tel: 020-7373 3323

D C MANAGEMENT
5 Denmark Street, London WC2H 8LP
e-mail: info@dcmanagementnet.com
Fax: 020-7379 0677   Tel: 020-7240 8490

DEALERS AGENCY BELFAST
22 North Street Arcade
Belfast BT1 1PB
e-mail: patrickduncan609@msn.com
Fax: 028-9023 4072   Tel: 028-9031 1075

the actor's
one-stop
shop

showreels
photographs
CVs

t: 020 8888 7006

www.actorsone-stopshop.com

DENMAN CASTING AGENCY
Burgess House
Main Street, Farnsfield
Notts NG22 8EF   Tel/Fax: 01623 882272

DENMARK STREET MANAGEMENT•
PM Co-operative Write SAE
Packington Bridge Workspace
Unit 11, 1B Packington Square, London N1 7UA
e-mail: mail@denmarkstreet.net
Fax: 020-7354 8558   Tel: 020-7354 8555

DEREK'S HANDS AGENCY
153 Battersea Rise
London SW11 1HP
Website: www.derekshands.com
e-mail: casting@derekshands.com
Fax: 020-7924 2334   Tel: 020-7924 2484

de WOLFE Felix*
PM Write
Garden Offices, 51 Maida Vale, London W9 1SD
e-mail: info@felixdewolfe.com
Fax: 020-7289 5731   Tel: 020-7289 5770

DIAMOND MANAGEMENT*
31 Percy Street, London W1T 2DD
e-mail: agents@diman.co.uk
Fax: 020-7631 0500   Tel: 020-7631 0400

DIESTENFELD Lily
(Personal Manager for 45+ Playing Ages)
(No unsolicited Mail)
28B Alexandra Grove, London N12 8HG
Fax: 020-7485 1005   Tel: 020-8446 5379

DIMPLES MODEL & CASTING ACADEMY
Suite 2, 2nd Floor, Magnum House, 33 Lord Street
Leigh, Lancs WN7 1BY
e-mail: dimples_m_c_a@btinternet.com
Fax: 01942 262232   Tel: 01942 262012

DIRECT LINE•
PM (Personal Manager: Daphne Franks)
St. John's House, 16 St. John's Vale, London SE8 4EN
Website: www.dline.org.uk
e-mail: daphne.franks@dline.org.uk
                             Tel/Fax: 020-8694 1788
Park House, 62 Lidgett Lane
Leeds LS8 1PL   Tel/Fax: 0113-266 4036

DOWNES PRESENTERS AGENCY
96 Broadway, Bexleyheath, Kent DA6 7DE
e-mail: downes@presentersagency.com
Fax: 020-8301 5591   Tel: 020-8304 0541

DQ MANAGEMENT
1st Floor, 115 Church Rd, Hove, East Sussex BN3 2AF
e-mail: info@dqmanagement.com
Fax: 01273 277255   Tel: 01273 721221

DREW Bryan Ltd
PM Write
Mezzanine, Quadrant Hse, 80-82 Regent St W1B 5AU
e-mail: bryan@bryandrewltd.com
Fax: 020-7437 0561   Tel: 020-7437 2293

DUDDRIDGE Paul MANAGEMENT
26 Rathbone Place, London W1T 1JD
Fax: 020-7580 3480   Tel: 020-7580 3580

EARLE Kenneth PERSONAL MANAGEMENT
214 Brixton Road, London SW9 6AP
Website: www.entertainment-kennethearle.co.uk
e-mail: kennethearle@agents-uk.com
Fax: 020-7274 9529   Tel: 020-7274 1219

EARNSHAW Susi MANAGEMENT
PM
5 Brook Place, Barnet, Herts EN5 2DL
Website: www.susiearnshaw.co.uk
e-mail: casting@susiearnshaw.co.uk
Fax: 020-8364 9618   Tel: 020-8441 5010

Lucy Punch

Jamie R Bradley

Elize Du Toit

Daisy Donovan

MAGNUS HASTINGS   t: 020 7700 6475   m: 07905 304 705   *Student Rates*

ECHO THEATRICAL MANAGEMENT
45 Gordon Road, Fareham, Hampshire PO16 7TQ
e-mail: echotm@hotmail.com   Mobile: 07880 701589

EDWARDS REPRESENTATION Joyce
PM Write
275 Kennington Road, London SE11 6BY
e-mail: joyce.edwards@virgin.net
Fax: 020-7820 1845   Tel: 020-7735 5736

E.K.A. MODEL & ACTOR MANAGEMENT
The Warehouse Studios, Glaziers Lane, Culcheth
Warrington WA3 4AQ
Website: www.eka-agency.com
e-mail: info@eka-agency.com
Fax: 01925 767563   Tel: 0871 7501575

ELLIOTT Annie MANAGEMENT
6 Brenchley Close, Chislehurst, Kent BR7 5NQ
e-mail: annieelliottmgmt@aol.com
Tel: 020-8295 1130

ELLIS Bill Ltd
(See A & B PERSONAL MANAGEMENT Ltd)

EMPTAGE HALLETT*
24 Poland Street, London W1F 8QL
e-mail: mail@emptagehallett.co.uk
Fax: 020-7287 4411   Tel: 020-7287 5511

2nd Floor, 3-5 The Balcony
Castle Arcade
Cardiff CF10 1BU
e-mail: gwenprice@emphal.fsnet.co.uk
Fax: 029-2034 4206   Tel: 029-2034 4205

ENGLISH Doreen '95
Write or Phone
4 Selsey Avenue, Aldwick
Bognor Regis
West Sussex PO21 2QZ   Tel/Fax: 01243 825968

Rachel Weisz

Alistair McGowan

CAROLE LATIMER
PHOTOGRAPHY
113 Ledbury Road W11
Tel: 020 7727 9371 Fax: 020 7229 9306

ENTERTAINMENT DIRECTORY The
21-37 Third Avenue
London E13 8AW
Fax: 020-8471 2111   Tel: 020-8471 3111

EPSTEIN June ASSOCIATES
Write
Flat 1, 62 Compayne Gardens, London NW6 3RY
e-mail: june@june-epstein-associates.co.uk
Fax: 020-7328 0684   Tel: 020-7328 0864

ESSANAY*
PM Write
6 Brook Street, London W1S 1BB
e-mail: info@essanay.co.uk
Fax: 020-7355 1084   Tel: 020-7409 3526

ETHNICS ARTISTE AGENCY
86 Elphinstone Road
Walthamstow
London E17 5EX
Fax: 020-8523 4523   Tel: 020-8523 4242

ET-NIK-A PRIME MANAGEMENT & CASTINGS Ltd
Balfour House, 46-54 Great Titchfield Street
London W1W 7QA
Website: www.et-nik-a.co.uk
e-mail: info@et-nik-a.co.uk
Fax: 020-7299 3558   Tel: 020-7299 3555

ETTINGER BROS GROUP
(Representation & Management)
Gladstone House, 2 Church Road
Liverpool L15 9EG
e-mail: ettinger@genie.co.uk
Fax: 0151-733 2468   Tel: 0151-734 2240

**EUROKIDS & ADULTS INTERNATIONAL CASTING
& MODEL AGENCY**
The Warehouse Studios, Glaziers Lane
Culcheth, Warrington WA3 4AQ
Website: www.eka-agency.com
e-mail: info@eka-agency.com
Fax: 01925 767563   Tel: 0871 7501575

EVANS & REISS*
100 Fawe Park Road, London SW15 2EA
e-mail: marcia@evans-reiss.fsnet.co.uk
Fax: 020-8877 0307   Tel: 020-8877 3755

EVANS Jacque MANAGEMENT Ltd
Top Floor Suite, 14 Holmesley Road
London SE23 1PJ
Fax: 020-8699 5192   Tel: 020-8699 1202

EVOLUTION TALENT MANAGEMENT
The Truman Brewery Building
Studio 21, 91 Brick Lane, London E1 6QB
Website: www.evolutionmngt.com
e-mail: info@evolutionmngt.com
Fax: 020-7375 2752   Tel: 020-7053 2128

FACE FACTORY
3 Nottingham Court, Covent Garden
London WC2H 9AY
Website: www.facefactoryuk.com
e-mail: facefactory@btconnect.com
Fax: 020-7240 0565   Tel: 020-7240 2322

FARNES Norma MANAGEMENT
9 Orme Court, London W2 4RL
Fax: 020-7792 2110   Tel: 020-7727 1544

FASTCAST UK
239 Old Street, London EC1V 9EY
Website: www.fastcastuk.co.uk
e-mail: mrblack@fastcastuk.co.uk
Mobile: 07930 612315   Tel/Fax: 020-7553 4470

FAWKES Irene MANAGEMENT
2nd Floor, 91A Rivington Street, London EC2A 3AY
e-mail: irenefawkes@fsbdial.co.uk
Fax: 020-7613 0769   Tel: 020-7729 8559

FBI AGENCY Ltd The
PO Box 250, Leeds LS1 2AZ
Website: www.fbi-agency.ltd.uk
e-mail: j.spencer@fbi-agency.ltd.uk
                              Tel/Fax: 07050 222747

FBI Ltd
4th Floor, 20-24 Kirby Street, London EC1N 8TS
Website: www.fullybooked-inc.com
e-mail: fbi@dircon.co.uk
Fax: 020-7242 8125   Tel: 020-7242 5542

FEAST Sadie MANAGEMENT*
10 Primrose Hill Studios, Fitzroy Road
London NW1 8TR
e-mail: office@feastmanagement.co.uk
Fax: 020-7586 9817   Tel: 020-7586 5502

JONATHAN DOCKAR-DRYSDALE

Tel: 020 8560 1077
Mobile: 07711 006191

E-mail: j.d-d@lineone.net

Student Discount
Studio/Outdoors

| John Virgo | Lisa Maxwell | Simon Russell Beale |

FEATURES
1 Charlotte Street
London W1T 1RD
e-mail: info@features.co.uk
Fax: 020-7636 1657   Tel: 020-7637 1487

FIELD Alan ASSOCIATES
3 The Spinney, Bakers Hill
Hadley Common
Herts EN5 5QJ
e-mail: alanfielduk@aol.com
Fax: 020-8447 0657   Tel: 020-8441 1137

FILM RIGHTS Ltd
PM Write
Mezzanine
Quadrant House
80-82 Regent Street
London W1B 5AU
Fax: 020-7734 0044   Tel: 020-7734 9911

FITZGERALD Sheridan MANAGEMENT
Write with SAE
87 Western Road, Upton Park
London E13 9JE   Tel: 020-8471 9814

FLETCHER ASSOCIATES
(Broadcast & Media)
25 Parkway, London N20 0XN
Fax: 020-8361 8866   Tel: 020-8361 8061

FLETCHER JACOB
(Artist Management)
9 Oman Court, Oman Avenue, London NW2 6AY
e-mail: info@fletcherjacob.co.uk
Tel/Fax: 020-8452 3853

FOX Clare ASSOCIATES
(Designers & Lighting Designers)
9 Plympton Road, London NW6 7EH
e-mail: cimfox@yahoo.co.uk
Fax: 020-7372 2301   Tel: 01483 535818

Rebecca Jones

Nick Moran

Lisa Coleman

Darren Gerrish
Photographer

07770-815-753

gerrishdarren@hotmail.com

FREEHAND PRODUCTIONS Ltd
c/o 97 Clacton Road, London E17 8AP
e-mail: freehanduk@yahoo.com
Tel/Fax: 020-8520 7777

FRENCH Linda
(See ALEXANDER PERSONAL MANAGEMENT Ltd)

FRESH MANAGEMENT
Level 3
3 Stevenson Square, Manchester M1 1DN
e-mail: freshmanagement@btconnect.com
Fax: 0161-237 9938
Tel: 0161-237 9925

FRONTLINE ACTORS' AGENCY DUBLIN
49 North Strand Road, Dublin 3, Eire
Website: www.frontlineactors.org
e-mail: frontlineactors@eircom.net
Fax: 00 353 1 8365252
Tel: 00 353 1 8364777

FRONTLINE MANAGEMENT
PM Co-operative
Colombo Centre, 34-68 Colombo Street
London SE1 8DP
e-mail: frontlineactor@freeuk.com
Tel/Fax: 020-7261 9466

FUNKY BEETROOT CELEBRITY MANAGEMENT Ltd
(Actors, TV Celebrities, Casting & Personal
Management)
PO Box 143, Faversham, Kent ME13 9LP
e-mail: funkbeetr@aol.com
Fax: 01227 752300
Tel: 01227 751549

FUSHION
27 Old Gloucester Street, London WC1N 3XX
Website: www.fushion-uk.com
e-mail: info@fushion-uk.com
Fax: 08700 111020
Tel: 08700 111100

GAGAN Hilary ASSOCIATES*
PM
187 Drury Lane
London WC2B 5QD
e-mail: hilary@hgassoc.freeserve.co.uk
Fax: 020-7430 1869
Tel: 020-7404 8794

GALLIARD'S MANAGEMENT
(Hugh Galliard)
Dunans, Glendaruel, Colintraive, Argyll PA22 3AD
Website: www.galliards.net
e-mail: hugh@galliards.net
Tel: 01369 820116

GALLOWAYS ONE
15 Lexham Mews, London W8 6JW
e-mail: hugh@gallowaysone.com
Fax: 020-7376 2416
Tel: 020-7376 2288

GARDNER Kerry MANAGEMENT*
Douglas House, 16-18 Douglas Street
London SW1P 4PB
e-mail: kerrygardner@freeuk.com
Fax: 020-7828 7758
Tel: 020-7828 7748

GARRETT Michael ASSOCIATES*
23 Haymarket, London SW1Y 4DG
Website: www.michaelgarrett.co.uk
e-mail: enquiries@michaelgarrett.co.uk
Fax: 020-7839 4555
Tel: 020-7839 4888

GARRICKS*
5 The Old School House
The Lanterns, Bridge Lane, London SW11 3AD
e-mail: megan@garricks.net
Fax: 020-7738 1881
Tel: 020-7738 1600

GAY Noel ARTISTS
19 Denmark Street, London WC2H 8NA
Website: www.noelgay.com
Fax: 020-7287 1816
Tel: 020-7836 3941

barry adamson

nan vernon

sarah neville

geraint evans

tina mullaney

shangara singh | PHOTOGRAPHER
studio • location • student rates • all digital workflow

020 8801 3051 | 07860 465 857 • email@shangarasingh.com • www.shangarasingh.com

Michael Garrett Associates
Personal Management

Director	Michael Garrett
Television and Film	Niki Winterson
Musical Theatre	Simon Bashford

Michael Garrett Associates
23 Haymarket
London, SW1Y 4DG

Tel: 020 7839 4888
Fax: 020 7839 4555

E-mail: enquiries@michaelgarrett.co.uk
www.michaelgarrett.co.uk
www.theatricalagent.co.uk

Members of the Personal Managers' Association

Alexandra Reimer

Sophie Lindsay

Photographer

07850 576325

Danny Sapani

GILBERT & PAYNE
Suite 73-74 Kent House
87 Regent Street, London W1B 4EH
e-mail: ee@gilbert&payne.com
Fax: 020-7494 3787   Tel: 020-7734 7505

GJS MANAGEMENT
173 Wellfield Road, London SW16 2BY
Website: www.gjsmanagement.co.uk
e-mail: gjsmgmt@aol.com   Tel/Fax: 020-8769 6788

GLASS Eric Ltd
25 Ladbroke Crescent, Notting Hill, London W11 1PS
e-mail: eglassltd@aol.com
Fax: 020-7229 6220   Tel: 020-7229 9500

GO ENTERTAINMENTS Ltd
(Circus Artistes, Chinese State Circus
Cirque Surreal, Bolshoi Circus "Spirit of The Horse")
The Arts Exchange, Congleton
Cheshire CW12 1JG
Website: www.arts-exchange.com
e-mail: phillipgandey@netcentral.co.uk
Fax: 01260 270777   Tel: 01260 276627

GORDON & FRENCH*
Write
12-13 Poland Street, London W1F 8QB
e-mail: mail@gordonandfrench.net
Fax: 020-7734 4832   Tel: 020-7734 4818

GOSS Gerald Ltd
19 Gloucester Street, London SW1V 2DB
Fax: 020-7592 9301   Tel: 020-7592 9202

G.O.T. PERSONAL MANAGEMENT
1 Balliol Chambers
Hollow Lane, Hitchin, Herts SG4 9SB
Website: www.guild-of-thieves.com
e-mail: cast@guild-of-thieves.com   Tel: 01462 420400

GRANTHAM-HAZELDINE
5 Blenheim Street, London W1S 1LD
Fax: 020-7495 3370   Tel: 020-7499 4011

GRAY Darren MANAGEMENT
(Specializing in representing/promoting Australian Artists)
2 Marston Lane, Portsmouth, Hampshire PO3 5TW
Website: www.darrengraymanagement.co.uk
e-mail: darren.gray1@virgin.net
Fax: 023-9267 7227   Tel: 023-9269 9973

GRAY Joan PERSONAL MANAGEMENT
PM F TV
29 Sunbury Court Island, Sunbury-on-Thames,
Middlesex TW16 5PP   Tel/Fax: 01932 783544

GRAYS MANAGEMENT & ASSOCIATES
PM
Panther House, 38 Mount Pleasant
London WC1X 0AP
Website: www.graysman.com
e-mail: e-mail@graysmanagement.idps.co.uk
Fax: 020-7278 1091   Tel: 020-7278 1054

GREEN & UNDERWOOD
PM Write
6 Brook Street, London W1S 1BB
Website: www.greenandunderwood.com
e-mail: info@greenandunderwood.com
Fax: 020-7355 1084   Tel: 020-7493 0308

GREIG Miranda ASSOCIATES Ltd
41 Beauchamp Road, London SW11 1PG
e-mail: mail@mirandagreigassoc.co.uk
Fax: 020-7228 1400   Tel: 020-7228 1200

GRESHAM Carl GROUP
PO Box 3, Bradford, West Yorkshire BD1 4QN
Website: www.carlgresham.co.uk
e-mail: carl@carlgresham.co.uk
Fax: 01274 827161   Tel: 01274 735880

ROBERT KILROY-SILK

HOWARD SAYER

PHOTOGRAPHER

07860 559891

www.howardsayer.co.uk
howardsayer@btconnect.com

RUTH SHEPHARD

PROFILE PRINTS

B&W or Colour Repros

From negatives, photographs, transparencies, disks or email.
Stickybacked Photos for CVs - Enlargements for Agents.
Photos may be sub-titled.

By-return Mail-Order Service at unbeatable prices.

For an order form and samples, please ring

01736 365 222

PROFILE PRINTS

Courtwood Film Service Limited (Est. 1956)
FREEPOST TO55, Penzance, TR18 2BF
Fax: 01736 350 203   e-mail: people@courtwood.co.uk

01736 365 222

PLA

PAT LOVETT ASSOCIATES

Pat Lovett, Dolina Logan

43 Chandos Place, London, WC2N 4HS Tel: 020 7379 8111 Fax: 020 7379 9111

5 Union Street, Edinburgh, EH1 3LT Tel: 0131 478 7878 Fax: 0131 478 7070 www.pla.uk.com

GRIFFIN Sandra MANAGEMENT
6 Ryde Place
Richmond Road, East Twickenham, Middx TW1 2EH
e-mail: sgmgmt@aol.com
Fax: 020-8744 1812   Tel: 020-8891 5676

GROUP 3 ASSOCIATES
PM (Henry Davies)
35D Newton Road
London W2 5JR   Tel: 020-7221 4989

GURNETT J. PERSONAL MANAGEMENT Ltd
2 New King's Road, London SW6 4SA
Website: www.jgpm.co.uk
e-mail: mail@jgpm.co.uk
Fax: 020-7736 5455   Tel: 020-7736 7828

HALLY WILLIAMS AGENCY The
121 Grange Road, Rathfarnham, Dublin 14, Eire
e-mail: hallywilliams@eircom.net
Fax: 00 353 1 4933076   Tel: 00 353 1 4933685

HAMILTON HODELL Ltd*
24 Hanway Street, London W1T 1UH
e-mail: info@hamiltonhodell.co.uk
Fax: 020-7636 1226   Tel: 020-7636 1221

HARGREAVES Alison MANAGEMEMT
(Directors, Designers, Lighting Designers)
89 Temple Road, London NW2 6PN
e-mail: alisonhargreaves@hotmail.com
Fax: 020-8208 1094   Tel: 020-8438 0112

HARLEY AGENCY The
Regent House
291 Kirkdale, London SE26 4QD
e-mail: mail@theharleyagency.co.uk
Fax: 020-8659 8118   Tel: 020-8659 8147

HARRIS AGENCY Ltd The
52 Forty Avenue
Wembley Park, Middlesex HA9 8LQ
e-mail: sharrisltd@aol.com
Fax: 020-8908 4455   Tel: 020-8908 4451

HARRISON Penny BSA Ltd
Trinity Lodge, 25 Trinity Crescent
London SW17 7AG
e-mail: harrisonbsa@aol.com
Fax: 020-8672 8971   Tel: 020-8672 0136

HARRISPEARSON MANAGEMENT Ltd
64-66 Millman Street, Bloomsbury
London WC1N 3EF
Website: www.harrispearson.co.uk
e-mail: agent@harrispearson.co.uk
Fax: 020-7430 9229   Tel: 020-7430 9890

HARTFIELD MANAGEMENT
16 Hartfield Crescent
West Wickham
Kent BR4 9DN
e-mail: enquiries@hartfieldentertainment.co.uk
                                      Tel: 020-8462 0383

HATSTAND CIRCUS
(Special Skills Pefomers)
39 Old Church Road, Stepney, London E1 0QB
Website: www.hatstandcircus.com
e-mail: helenahatstand@btopenworld.com
                                      Tel/Fax: 020-7791 2541

HATTON McEWAN*
PM Write (Stephen Hatton, Aileen McEwan)
PO Box 37385, London N1 7XF
Website: www.thetalent.biz
e-mail: info@thetalent.biz
Fax: 020-7251 9081   Tel: 020-7253 4770

Lucy Smith ~ photographer

Rachel Mulcahy

David Redgrave

Sabrina Hunter

Tel 020 8521 1347   www.thatlucy.co.uk

HATTON Richard Ltd*
29 Roehampton Gate, London SW15 5JR
Fax: 020-8876 8278   Tel: 020-8876 6699

HAZEMEAD Ltd
(Entertainment Consultants)
Camellia House
38 Orchard Road
Sundridge Park Bromley, Kent BR1 2PS
Fax: 020-8460 5830   Tel: 0870 2402082

H C A
(See COOKE Howard ASSOCIATES)

HEATHCOTE George MANAGEMENT
38 Great Queen Street, London WC2B 5AA
e-mail: gheathcote@freeuk.com
Fax: 020-7404 8681   Tel: 020-7404 8680

HEAVY PENCIL MANAGEMENT
PM Co-operative
BAC, Lavender Hill
London SW11 5TF
e-mail: heavy.pencil@talk21.com
Fax: 020-7924 4636   Tel: 020-7738 9574

HENRIETTA RABITT CHILDREN'S ENTERTAINERS & FACE PAINTERS
(Providing Children's Entertainers, Punch & Judy etc)
The Warren
12 Eden Close, York YO24 2RD
e-mail: info@henriettarabbit.co.uk   Tel: 01904 345404

HENRY'S AGENCY
53 Westbury
Rochford, Essex SS4 1UL
Website: www.henrysagency.co.uk
e-mail: info@henrysagency.co.uk
Fax: 01702 543654   Tel: 01702 541413

HICKS Jeremy ASSOCIATES
11-12 Tottenham Mews
London W1T 4AG
Website: www.jeremyhicks.com
e-mail: hicksworld@aol.com
Fax: 020-7636 8880   Tel: 020-7636 8008

HILL Edward MANAGEMENT
Teddington Film & Television Studios
Broom Road
Twickenham TW11 9NT
e-mail: hill@ehillmanagement.freeserve.co.uk
Fax: 020-8614 2694   Tel: 020-8614 2678

HILLMAN THRELFALL
33 Brookfield, Highgate West Hill
London N6 6AT
e-mail: emma@hillmanthrelfall.net
Fax: 020-8340 9309   Tel: 020-8341 2207

HILTON Elinor ASSOCIATES
PO Box 946, High Wycombe, Bucks HP10 8ZN
e-mail: agent@elinorhilton.co.uk
                          Tel/Fax: 01494 817444

HINDIN Dee ASSOCIATES
9B Brunswick Mews
Great Cumberland Place, London W1H 7FB
Fax: 020-7258 0651   Tel: 020-7723 3706

HIRED HANDS
12 Cressy Road, London NW3 2LY
e-mail: models@hiredhands.freeserve.co.uk
Fax: 020-7267 1030   Tel: 020-7267 9212

HOBBS Liz GROUP Ltd
(Artiste Management)
First Floor, 65 London Road, Newark, Notts NG24 1RZ
Website: www.lizhobbsgroup.com
e-mail: casting@lizhobbsgroup.com
Fax: 0870 3337009   Tel: 08700 702702

HOBSON'S ACTORS
62 Chiswick High Road, Chiswick, London W4 1SY
Website: www.hobsons-international.com
e-mail: actors@hobsons-international.com
Fax: 020-8996 5350   Tel: 020-8995 3628

HOLLAND-FORD Robert
PM Write or Phone
103 Lydyett Lane, Barnton, Northwich
Cheshire CW8 4JT   Tel: 01606 76960

HOLLOWOOD Jane ASSOCIATES Ltd
50 Copperas Street, Manchester M4 1HS
e-mail: janehollowood@ukonline.co.uk
Fax: 0161-834 8333   Tel: 0161-834 8334

HOLLY Dave ARTS MEDIA SERVICES
The Annexe, 23 Eastwood Gardens, Felling
Tyne & Wear NE10 0AH
Fax: 0191-438 2722   Tel: 0191-438 2711

HOPE Sally ASSOCIATES*
108 Leonard Street, London EC2A 4XS
e-mail: casting@sallyhope.biz
Fax: 020-7613 4848   Tel: 020-7613 5353

HOWARD Amanda ASSOCIATES Ltd*
21 Berwick Street, London W1F 0PZ
Website: www.amandahowardassociates.co.uk
e-mail: mail@amandahowardassociates.co.uk
Fax: 020-7287 7785   Tel: 020-7287 9277

HOWE Janet
Studio 1, Whitebridge Estate, Whitebridge Lane
Stone, Staffs ST15 8LQ
Website: www.janethowe.co.uk
e-mail: janet@jhowecasting.fsbusiness.co.uk
Tel/Fax: 01785 818480   Tel/Fax: 01785 816888
40 Princess Street, Manchester M1 6DE
Mobile: 07801 942178   Tel/Fax: 0161-234 0142

HOWELL Philippa
(See PHPM)

HUDSON Nancy ASSOCIATES Ltd
3rd Floor, 50 South Molton Street, London W1K 5SB
Website: www.nancyhudson.cjb.net
e-mail: vilhud@freeuk.com
Fax: 020-7499 0884   Tel: 020-7499 5548

HUGHES Jane MANAGEMENT
The Coach House, PO Box 123, Knutsford
Cheshire WA16 9HX   Tel: 01565 650040

HUNTER Bernard ASSOCIATES
13 Spencer Gardens, London SW14 7AH
Fax: 020-8392 9334   Tel: 020-8878 6308

IAM Ltd
First Floor, 55 Shelbourne Road, Ballsbridge
Dublin 4, Eire
Fax: 00 353 1 6676474   Tel: 00 353 1 6676455

I C M (International Creative Management)*
Oxford House, 76 Oxford Street, London W1D 1BS
e-mail: casting@icmlondon.co.uk
Fax: 020-7323 0101   Tel: 020-7636 6565

I.M.L. •
PM Co-operative
Oval House
52-54 Kennington Oval, London SE11 5SW
Website: www.iml.org.uk
e-mail: imllondon@hotmail.com
          Tel/Fax: 020-7587 1080

ICON
Tanzaro House, Ardwick Green North
Manchester M12 6FZ
Website: www.iconactors.net
e-mail: info@iconactors.net
Fax: 0161-273 4567   Tel: 0161-273 3344

IMPACT INTERNATIONAL MANAGEMENT
2nd Floor, 16-18 Balderton Street, London W1K 6TN
e-mail: info@impactinternationalgroup.com
Fax: 020-8441 4828   Tel: 020-7495 6655

INDEPENDENT THEATRE WORKSHOP The
2 Mornington Road, Ranelagh, Dublin 6, Eire
Website: www.independent-theatre-workshop.com
e-mail: itw@esatclear.ie   Tel/Fax: 00 353 1 4968808

INGMAN T.J.
PM
29 Whitcomb Street, London WC2H 7EP
e-mail: info@tjingman.co.uk
Fax: 020-7930 4441   Tel: 020-7930 4442

INSPIRATION MANAGEMENT
PM Co-operative
Room 227, The Aberdeen Centre
22-24 Highbury Grove, London N5 2EA
Website: www.inspirationmanagement.co.uk
e-mail: agent@inspirationmanagement.freeserve.co.uk
Fax: 020-7704 8497   Tel: 020-7704 0440

HOBSON'S (H)

[actors]
[kids]
[singers]
[voices]
[studio]

62 Chiswick High Road | T. +44 (0)20 8995 3628 | email actors@hobsons-international.com
London W4 1SY | F. +44 (0)20 8996 5350 | www.hobsons-international.com

Charmaine Parsons

Peter Helmer

Daniel Harwood-Stamper

Tel: 020 7930 1372

INTERNATIONAL ARTISTES Ltd*
4th Floor
Holborn Hall, 193-197 High Holborn
London WC1V 7BD
Website: www.intart.co.uk
e-mail: (name)@intart.co.uk
Fax: 020-7404 9865   Tel: 020-7025 0600

INTERNATIONAL ARTISTES MIDLANDS OFFICE
Lapley Hall, Lapley, Staffs ST19 9JR
Fax: 01785 841992   Tel: 01785 841991

INTERNATIONAL THEATRE & MUSIC Ltd
(Piers Chater Robinson)
Shakespeare House, Theatre Street
London SW11 5ND
Website: www.internationaltheatreandmusic.com
e-mail: inttheatre@aol.com
Fax: 020-7801 6317   Tel: 020-7801 6316

INTER-CITY CASTING
PM
Portland Tower, Portland Street
Manchester M1 3LF
Website: www.iccast.co.uk
e-mail: intercity@bigfoot.com   Tel/Fax: 0161-226 0103

IRISH ARTS NETWORK
Victor House, Marlborough Gardens
London N20 0SH
e-mail: rosemaryifbco@aol.com
                                   Tel/Fax: 020-8361 0678

JAA
(See ALTARAS Jonathan ASSOCIATES Ltd)

JAMES Julie
e-mail: juliejames@btclick.com

JAMES Susan
(See SJ MANAGEMENT)

JAMESON Joy Ltd
PM
2.19 The Plaza, 535 Kings Road, London SW10 0SZ
Fax: 020-7352 1744   Tel: 020-7351 3971

JAY Alex PERSONAL MANAGEMENT
Hawthorns, Amberley, Gloucestershire GL5 5AW
e-mail: alex@alex-jay-pm.freeserve.co.uk
                                   Tel/Fax: 01453 872038

JB ASSOCIATES*
First Floor, 3 Stevenson Square
Manchester M1 1DN
Website: www.j-b-a.net
e-mail: info@j-b-a.net
Fax: 0161-237 1809   Tel: 0161-237 1808

JEFFREY & WHITE MANAGEMENT*
PM
9-15 Neal Street, London WC2H 9PW
Fax: 020-7240 0007   Tel: 020-7240 7000

J.G.M.
15 Lexham Mews, London W8 6JW
Website: www.jgmtalent.com
e-mail: mail@jgmtalent.com
Fax: 020-7376 2416   Tel: 020-7376 2414

JLM PERSONAL MANAGEMENT*
(Janet Lynn Malone, Sharon Henry)
259 Acton Lane, London W4 5DG
e-mail: jlm@skynow.net
Fax: 020-8747 8286   Tel: 020-8747 8223

JOHNSON WHITELEY Ltd
25 Villiers Street, London WC2N 6RD
e-mail: jwltd@freeuk.com
Fax: 020-7839 7599   Tel: 020-7839 3977

JOHNSTON & MATHERS ASSOCIATES Ltd
PO Box 3167, Barnet EN5 2WA
e-mail: johnstonmathers@aol.com
Mobile: 07976 961251   Tel/Fax: 020-8449 4968

JPA MANAGEMENT
30 Daws Hill Lane, High Wycombe
Bucks HP11 1PW
Website: www.jackiepalmer.co.uk
e-mail: jackie.palmer@btinternet.com
Fax: 01494 510479   Tel: 01494 520978

KAL MANAGEMENT
Write
95 Gloucester Road, Hampton
Middlesex TW12 2UW
Website: www.kaplan-kaye.co.uk
e-mail: kaplan222@aol.com
Fax: 020-8979 6487   Tel: 020-8783 0039

KANAL Roberta AGENCY
82 Constance Road, Twickenham
Middlesex TW2 7JA
e-mail: roberta@kanal.fsnet.co.uk
Tel/Fax: 020-8894 7952   Tel: 020-8894 2277

KARUSHI MANAGEMENT
Golden Cross House, 8 Duncannon Street
London WC2N 4JF
Website: www.karushi.com
e-mail: lisa@karushi.com
Fax: 020-7484 5151   Tel: 020-7484 5040

KEARNEY Dee MANAGEMENT
Rolekall Casting, 1 Dunwood Bridge
Bridge Street, Shaw OL2 8BG
e-mail: dee@rolekall.fsnet.co.uk
                                   Tel/Fax: 01706 882442

KELLY'S KIND
(Dance Agency & Production Company)
Lower Ground
17-18 Margaret Street, London W1W 8RP
e-mail: office@kellyskind.co.uk   Tel: 0870 8701299

KATRIN RIEDEL
PHOTOGRAPHY

Nora Hartwig

Michael Instone

Helen Coker (*'All or Nothing'*)

FOR INFO AND BOOKING CALL : 07957-790876
OR E-MAIL ME: riedelkatrin@hotmail.com

Anna Tolputt

Carl Prekopp

Remy Hunter
www.remyhunter.co.uk
Tel: 020 7431 8055   Mob: 07766 760724

KENIS Steve & Co*
Royalty House, 72-74 Dean Street
London W1D 3SG
e-mail: sk@sknco.com
Fax: 020-7287 6328   Tel: 020-7434 9055

KENT YOUTH THEATRE & AGENCY
Pinks Hill House, Briton Road
Faversham, Kent ME13 8QH
e-mail: richard@kyt.org.uk   Tel/Fax: 01795 534395

KING Adrian ASSOCIATES
33 Marlborough Mansions
Cannon Hill, London NW6 1JS
e-mail: akassocs@aol.com
Fax: 020-7435 4100   Tel: 020-7435 4600

K M C AGENCIES
PO Box 122, 48 Great Ancoats Street
Manchester M4 5AB
e-mail: casting@kmcagencies.co.uk
Fax: 0161-237 9812   Tel: 0161-237 3009

All postal submissions to Manchester office
e-mail: london@kmcagencies.co.uk
Fax: 0870 4421780   Tel: 0845 6602459

KNIGHT AYTON MANAGEMENT
114 St Martin's Lane, London WC2N 4BE
Website: www.knightayton.co.uk
e-mail: info@knightayton.co.uk
Fax: 020-7836 8333   Tel: 020-7836 5333

KNIGHT Ray CASTING
21A Lambolle Place
London NW3 4PG
Website: www.rayknight.co.uk
e-mail: casting@rayknight.co.uk
Fax: 020-7722 2322   Tel: 020-7722 1551

KREATE PRODUCTIONS
Unit 210, 30 Great Guildford Street
London SE1 0HS
e-mail: kreate@btconnect.com
Fax: 020-7401 3003   Tel: 020-7401 9007

KREMER ASSOCIATES
(See MARSH Billy DRAMA Ltd)

KRUGER Rolf MANAGEMENT Ltd
PM (Rachel & Rolf Kruger)
205 Chudleigh Road, London SE4 1EG
Website: www.krugeractors.com
e-mail: mail@krugeractors.com
Fax: 020-8690 7999   Tel: 020-8690 7666

LADKIN Michael PERSONAL MANAGEMENT
Suite 1, Ground Floor, 1 Duchess Street
London W1W 6AN
e-mail: ladkinm@aol.com
Fax: 020-7436 4627   Tel: 020-7436 4626

LAINE MANAGEMENT Ltd
131 Victoria Road, Salford M6 8LF
e-mail: info@lainemanagement.co.uk
Fax: 0161-787 7572   Tel: 0161-789 7775

LAINE Betty MANAGEMENT
The Studios, East Street, Epsom, Surrey KT17 1HH
e-mail: enquiries@betty-laine-management.co.uk
                                     Tel/Fax: 01372 721815

LAMONT CASTING AGENCY
94 Harington Road, Formby, Liverpool L37 1PZ
Website: www.lamontcasting.co.uk
e-mail: diane@lamontcasting.co.uk
Fax: 01704 872422   Tel: 01704 877024

LANGFORD ASSOCIATES Ltd
17 Westfields Avenue, Barnes, London SW13 0AT
e-mail: langford@ctors.fsnet.co.uk
Fax: 020-8878 7078   Tel: 020-8878 7148

LANGRISHE Millie MANAGEMENT
Highfield, 72 Island Road, Sturry
Canterbury, Kent CT2 0EE
e-mail: millie.langrishe@virgin.net
                                     Tel/Fax: 01227 710804

L'BROOKE PERSONAL MANAGEMENT
7 Malt House Place, High Street, Romford
Essex RM1 1AR
e-mail: lbrooke@btopenworld.com
                                     Tel/Fax: 01708 723883

LEE Bernard MANAGEMENT
20 Howard Place, Reigate Hill, Reigate
Surrey RH2 9NP
e-mail: jon@blm1.freeserve.co.uk
                                     Tel/Fax: 01737 242606

Lindsay Duncan

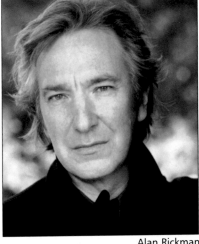

Alan Rickman

Fatimah Namdar   020 8341 1332

Matthew Cottle

Mary Jo Randle

LEE Wendy MANAGEMENT
4th Floor Suite, 40 Langham Street
London W1W 7AS
e-mail: wendylee@wendyleemanagement.fsworld.co.uk
Fax: 020-7580 8700   Tel: 020-7580 4800

LEE'S PEOPLE
60 Poland Street, London W1F 7NT
e-mail: lee@lees-people.co.uk
Fax: 020-7734 3033   Tel: 020-7734 5775

LEHRER Jane ASSOCIATES*
100A Chalk Farm Road
London NW1 8EH
e-mail: janelehrer@aol.com
Fax: 020-7482 4899   Tel: 020-7482 4898

LEIGH MANAGEMENT
14 St David's Drive
Edgware, Middlesex HA8 6JH
e-mail: leighmanagement@aol.com
                              Tel/Fax: 020-8951 4449

LESLIE Sasha MANAGEMENT
(In Association with Allsorts Drama for Children)
2 Pember Road, London NW10 5LP
e-mail: enquiries@allsorts.ltd.uk
                              Tel/Fax: 020-8969 3249

LIME ACTORS AGENCY & MANAGEMENT Ltd
4th Floor
54 Princess Street, Manchester M1 6HS
e-mail: debbie.pine@limemanagement.co.uk
Fax: 0161-236 7557   Tel: 0161-237 3300

LINKS MANAGEMENT
34-68 Colombo Street
London SE1 8DP
e-mail: links@eidosnet.co.uk   Tel/Fax: 020-7928 0806

LINKSIDE AGENCY
21 Poplar Road
Leatherhead, Surrey KT22 8SF
e-mail: linkside_agency@yahoo.co.uk
Fax: 01372 801972   Tel: 01372 802374

LINTON MANAGEMENT
3 The Rock, Bury BN9 0JP
Fax: 0161-761 1999   Tel: 0161-761 2020

LITTLE ACORNS MODELLING AGENCY
London House, 271-273 King Street
Hammersmith, London W6 9LZ
Fax: 020-8408 3077   Tel: 020-8563 0773

LONDON MUSICIANS Ltd
(Orchestral Contracting)
Cedar House, Vine Lane, Hillingdon
Middlesex UB10 0BX
e-mail: mail@londonmusicians.co.uk
Fax: 01895 252556   Tel: 01895 252555

LONGTIME MANAGEMENT
(Existing Clients only)
36 Lord Street
Radcliffe, Manchester M36 3BA
e-mail: longtime_mgt@btinternet.com
                              Tel/Fax: 0161-724 6625

LOOKALIKES (Susan Scott)
26 College Crescent, London NW3 5LH
Website: www.lookalikes.info
e-mail: susan@lookalikes.info
Fax: 020-7722 8261   Tel: 020-7387 9245

LOOKS
12A Manor Court
Aylmer, London N2 0PJ
e-mail: lookslondonltd@btconnect.com
Fax: 020-8442 9190   Tel: 020-8341 4477

LOVETT Pat ASSOCIATES
(See P.L.A.)

LSW PROMOTIONS
181A Faunce House, Doddington Grove
Kennington, London SE17 3TB
Website: www.londonshakespeare.org.uk/promos
e-mail: lswpromos@hotmail.com
Tel/Fax: 020-7735 5911

LYNE Dennis AGENCY*
108 Leonard Street, London EC2A 4RH
e-mail: d.lyne@virgin.net
Fax: 020-7739 4101   Tel: 020-7739 6200

MACFARLANE CHARD ASSOCIATES Ltd*
33 Percy Street, London W1T 2LN
Website: www.macfarlane-chard.co.uk
e-mail: derick@macfarlane-chard.co.uk
Fax: 020-7636 7751   Tel: 020-7636 7750

MACNAUGHTON LORD 2000 Ltd
(Writers, Designers, Directors,
Composers/Lyricists/Musical Directors)
19 Margravine Gardens, London W6 8RL
Website: www.ml2000.org.uk
e-mail: info@ml2000.org.uk
Fax: 020-8741 7443   Tel: 020-8741 0606

MAC-10 MANAGEMENT
Office 69, 2 Hellidon Close
Ardwick, Manchester M12 4AH
Website: www.mac-10.co.uk
e-mail: info@mac-10.co.uk
Fax: 0161-275 9610   Tel: 0161-275 9510

MADELEY Paul PUBLICITY
17 Valley Road, Arden Park, Bredbury
Stockport, Cheshire SK6 2EA
e-mail: madeleypublicity@talk21.com
Tel/Fax: 0161-430 5380

MAGNET PERSONAL MANAGEMENT
310 The Greenhouse
The Custard Factory, Gibb Street
Digbeth, Birmingham B9 4AA
e-mail: magnetagency@talk21.com
Fax: 0121-224 7677   Tel: 0121-224 7676

MAGNOLIA MANAGEMENT*
136 Hicks Avenue, Greenford
Middlesex UB6 8HB
e-mail: jaffreymag@aol.com
Fax: 020-8575 0369   Tel: 020-8578 2899

MAITLAND MANAGEMENT
PM (Anne Skates)
Brook House, 8 Rythe Road
Claygate, Surrey KT10 9DF
Website: www.maitlandmusic.com
e-mail: maitmus@aol.com
Fax: 01372 466229   Tel: 01372 466228

MANAGEMENT 2000
23 Alexandra Road, Mold, Flintshire CH7 1HJ
Website: www.management-2000.co.uk
e-mail: jackey@management-2000.co.uk
Tel/Fax: 01352 771231

MANIC MANAGEMENT
101 Skyline Plaza, 80 Commercial Road
London E1 1NY
Website: www.themanicgroup.com
e-mail: info@themanicgroup.com
Fax: 020-7709 7867   Tel: 020-7709 0637

MANS Johnny PRODUCTIONS Ltd
PO Box 196, Hoddesdon, Herts EN10 7WG
e-mail: real@legend.co.uk
Fax: 01992 470516   Tel: 01992 470907

Kim Medcalf

Todd Carty

MANSON Andrew PERSONAL MANAGEMENT Ltd*
288 Munster Road, London SW6 6BQ
Website: www.talentroom.com
e-mail: post@andrewmanson.com
Fax: 020-7381 8874   Tel: 020-7386 9158

MARCUS & McCRIMMON MANAGEMENT
3 Crouch Hall Road, London N8 8HT
Website: www.marcusandmccrimmon.com
e-mail: mail@marcusandmccrimmon.com
Fax: 020-8347 0006   Tel: 020-8347 0007

MARKHAM & FROGGATT Ltd*
PM Write
4 Windmill Street, London W1T 2HZ
e-mail: admin@markhamfroggatt.co.uk
Fax: 020-7637 5233   Tel: 020-7636 4412

MARKHAM John ASSOCIATES
1A Oakwood Avenue, Purley, Surrey CR8 1AR
e-mail: info@johnmarkhamassociates.co.uk
Fax: 020-8763 8942   Tel: 020-8763 8941

MARSH Billy ASSOCIATES Ltd*
174-178 North Gower Street, London NW1 2NB
e-mail: talent@billymarsh.co.uk
Fax: 020-7388 6848   Tel: 020-7388 6858

MARSH Billy DRAMA Ltd*
174-178 North Gower Street, London NW1 2NB
e-mail: info@billymarshdrama.co.uk
Fax: 020-7383 5514   Tel: 020-7383 5020

MARSH Sandra MANAGEMENT
(Film Technicians)
c/o Casarotto Marsh Ltd, National House
60-66 Wardour Street, London W1V 4ND
e-mail: casarottomarsh@casarotto.uk.com
Fax: 020-7287 5644   Tel: 020-7287 4450

MARSHALL Ronnie AGENCY
S F M PM TV Write or Phone
66 Ollerton Road
London N11 2LA   Tel/Fax: 020-8368 4958

MARSHALL Scott PARTNERS Ltd*
Suite 9, 54 Poland Street, London W1F 7NJ
e-mail: smpm@scottmarshall.co.uk
Fax: 020-7432 7241   Tel: 020-7432 7240

MARTIN Carol PERSONAL MANAGEMENT
19 Highgate West Hill, London N6 6NP
Fax: 020-8340 4868   Tel: 020-8348 0847

MAY John
Garden Flat
6 Westbourne Park Villas
London W2 5EA
e-mail: john@johnmayagent.freeserve.co.uk
Fax: 020-7229 9828   Tel: 020-7221 7917

MAYER Cassie Ltd*
5 Old Garden House
The Lanterns, Bridge Lane, London SW11 3AD
e-mail: info@cassiemayerltd.co.uk
Fax: 020-7350 0890   Tel: 020-7350 0880

MBA (Formerly John Mahoney Management)
Concorde House, 18 Margaret Street
Brighton BN2 1TS
Website: www.mbagency.fsnet.co.uk
e-mail: mba.concorde@virgin.net
Fax: 01273 685971   Tel: 01273 685970

McCORQUODALE Anna PERSONAL MANAGEMENT
43 St Maur Road, London SW6 4DR
e-mail: amc@netcomuk.co.uk
Fax: 020-7371 9048   Tel: 020-7731 1721

McINTOSH RAE MANAGEMENT*
Write SAE
Thornton House
Thornton Road, London SW19 4NG
e-mail: mcinrae@talk21.com
Fax: 020-8944 6624   Tel: 020-8944 6688

McKINNEY MACARTNEY MANAGEMENT Ltd
(Technicians)
The Barley Mow Centre, 10 Barley Mow Passage
London W4 4PH
Website: www.mckinneymacartney.com
e-mail: mail@mckinneymacartney.com
Fax: 020-8995 2414   Tel: 020-8995 4747

McLEAN Bill PERSONAL MANAGEMENT Ltd
PM Write
23B Deodar Road
London SW15 2NP   Tel: 020-8789 8191

Lowri Pritchard

Owen Evans

Photography

07940 700294

London

Special rates for students

Mark McCallum

HUGO SPEER

CATHERINE SHAKESPEARE LANE
PHOTOGRAPHER
020 7226 7694

MK MANAGEMENT
20B Chancellors Street, London W6 9RN
e-mail: catherine.hart@jongleurs.com
Fax: 0870 0111970   Tel: 0870 0111890

M.K.A.
11 Russell Kerr Close, Chiswick, London W4 3HF
e-mail: mka.agency@virgin.net
Fax: 020-8994 2992   Tel: 020-8994 1619

ML 2000 Ltd
(See MACNAUGHTON LORD 2000 Ltd)

MONDI ASSOCIATES Ltd
51 Nevill Court, Edith Terrace, Chelsea
London SW10 0TL
Fax: 020-7439 9301   Mobile: 07817 133349

MONTAGU ASSOCIATES
3 Bretton Hse, 145 Fairbridge Rd, London N19 3HP
Fax: 020-7263 3993   Tel: 020-7263 3883

MOORE ACTORS
71 Buttermere Road
Ashton-under-Lyne, Manchester OL7 9EW
e-mail: mooreactors@btinternet.com
Fax: 0161-330 6626   Tel: 0161-355 7341

MOORE Jakki
146 Cavendish Gardens, Barking, Essex IG11 9DZ
e-mail: jakki@jakkimoore.com
Fax: 07974 406146   Tel: 020-8594 9990

MORE MANAGEMENT
21 Brittany Road, Worthing, West Sussex BN14 7DY
e-mail: kylanik@freeuk.com   Tel/Fax: 01903 538877

MORGAN & GOODMAN
Mezzanine, Quadrant House
80-82 Regent Street, London W1B 5RP
e-mail: mg1@btinternet.com
Fax: 020-7494 3446   Tel: 020-7437 1383

MORRIS Andrew MANAGEMENT
66 Parkhill Road, Belsize Park, London NW3 2YT
e-mail: morrisagent@yahoo.co.uk
Fax: 020-7482 0451   Tel: 020-7485 9748

MOSS Jae ENTERPRISES
Riverside House
Feltham Avenue, Hampton Court, Surrey KT8 9BJ
Website: www.jaemossenterprises.co.uk
e-mail: enquiries@jaemossenterprises.co.uk
Fax: 020-8979 9631   Tel: 020-8979 3459

MOUNTVIEW MANAGEMENT
Ralph Richardson Memorial Studio, Kingfisher Place
Clarendon Road, London N22 6XF
Fax: 020-8829 1050   Tel: 020-8889 8231

MOVIESTYLE ARTIST MANAGEMENT
3 Lefroy Road, Shepherd's Bush, London W12 9LF
Website: www.moviestyle.co.uk
e-mail: mail@moviestyle.co.uk
Fax: 020-8746 2065   Tel: 020-8740 7871

MPC ENTERTAINMENT
Write or Phone
MPC House 15-16 Maple Mews
Maida Vale London NW6 5UZ
Website: www.mpce.com
e-mail: mpc@mpce.com
Fax: 020-7624 4220   Tel: 020-7624 1184

MR.MANAGEMENT
29 Belton Road, Brighton, East Sussex BN2 3RE
e-mail: mr.management@ntlworld.com
Mobile: 07785 341080   Tel/Fax: 01273 232381

MUGSHOTS AGENCY
50 Frith Street, London W1D 4SQ
Fax: 020-7437 0308   Tel: 020-7292 0555

Northern Lights Management

Personal representation of Actors from the North and in the North

Agents: Maureen Magee and Angie Forrest

Dean Clough Mills, Halifax, West Yorkshire HX3 5AX

Tel: 01422 382203
Fax: 01422 330101

email: NLManagement@aol.com

MURPHY Elaine ASSOCIATES
Suite 1
50 High Street
London E11 2RJ
e-mail: emurphy@freeuk.com
Fax: 020-8989 1400   Tel: 020-8989 4122

MUSIC INTERNATIONAL
M
13 Ardilaun Road
London N5 2QR
e-mail: music@musicint.co.uk
Fax: 020-7226 9792   Tel: 020-7359 5183

MW MANAGEMENT*
11 Old School Court
Drapers Road
London N17 6PZ
e-mail: the@gents.co.uk   Tel/Fax: 020-8376 2789

MYERS MANAGEMENT
63 Fairfields Crescent
London NW9 0PR   Tel/Fax: 020-8204 8941

N M MANAGEMENT
16 St Alfege Passage
Greenwich, London SE10 9JS
e-mail: nmmanagement@hotmail.com
Fax: 020-8858 4052   Tel: 020-8853 4337

NARROW ROAD COMPANY The*
22 Poland Street, London W1F 8QH
e-mail: agents@narrowroad.co.uk
Fax: 020-7439 1237   Tel: 020-7434 0406

182 Brighton Road, Coulsdon, Surrey CR5 2NF
e-mail: coulsdon@narrowroad.co.uk
Fax: 020-8763 2558   Tel: 020-8763 9895

4th Floor, Grampian House, 144 Deansgate
Manchester M3 3EE
e-mail: manchester@narrowroad.co.uk
Tel/Fax: 0161-833 1605

NCI MANAGEMENT Ltd
51 Queen Anne Street
London W1G 9HS
Fax: 020-7487 4258   Tel: 020-7224 3960

NCM ASSOCIATES (Nicola Clarkson Associates)
12 Kings Gate, London SW9 6JX
e-mail: nikki.clarkson1@btopenworld.com
Fax: 020-7793 7053   Tel: 020-7582 7343

NEVS AGENCY
Regal House, 198 King's Road, London SW3 5XP
Website: www.nevs.co.uk
e-mail: getamodel@nevs.co.uk
Fax: 020-7352 6068   Tel: 020-7352 4886

NEW CASEY AGENCY
The Annexe, 129 Northwood Way
Middlesex HA6 1RF   Tel: 01923 823182

NICHOLSON Jackie ASSOCIATES
PM
Suite 30, 1st Floor
Kent House, 87 Regent Street
London W1B 4EH
Fax: 020-7434 0445   Tel: 020-7434 0441

NOEL CASTING
(Specializing in Character Actors & Ethnic & Asian Actors)
Suite 501, International House
223 Regent Street, London W1B 2QD
e-mail: noelcasting@yahoo.com
Fax: 020-7544 1090   Tel: 020-7544 1010

NORTH OF WATFORD ACTORS AGENCY
Co-operative
Bridge Mill
Hebden Bridge, West Yorks HX7 8EX
Website: www.northofwatford.com
e-mail: northofwatford@btconnect.com
Fax: 01422 846503   Tel: 01422 845361

NORTH ONE MANAGEMENT•
HG08 Aberdeen Studios
Highbury Grove, London N5 2EA
Website: www.northone.co.uk
e-mail: actors@northone.co.uk
Fax: 020-7359 9449   Tel: 020-7359 9666

NORTHERN DRAMA
PO Box 27, Tadcaster, North Yorkshire LS24 9XS
e-mail: alyson@connew.com   Tel/Fax: 01977 681949

THEATRICAL PHOTOGRAPHY
ACTOR/ACTRESS PORTRAITS
for all your publicity and spotlight needs

on location or in our fully equipped studio in Kilburn 10 minutes from Marble Arch

with special thanks to
the following:

Richard Burton,
Brigitte Bardot,
Sophia Loren,
Kojak,
Peter Sellers,
Judi Dench,
Derek Jacobi,
John Lennon,
Virginia McKenna,
Don Johnson
Grace Jones,
Roger Moore,
Bruce Willis,
Demi Moore,
Patrick Swayze
Sir Richard Branson,
Diana Dors,
David Bellamy
Michael Bolton
Eric Morcambe
Frank Muir
(Dancer) Miyako Yoshida
Soo Soo
Richard O'Sullivan
Marie Helvin
Sam Fox
and all the rest
too many to mention...

**To photograph advanced and
established actors and artists**

30 black and white prints 7x5
30 colour prints 7x5
2 high quality 300 DPI *
- CD of all of the above

£130

**To photograph young actors,
actresses and beginners**

Special beginners pack
30 black and white prints OR
colour photographs your choice
30 prints of the above 7x5
1 high quality 300 DPI * - CD
containing all the photographs

£100

*We can supply a top hair & make-up artist on request. We can also produce one or more high
quality hand printed 10x8 prints of any of the above for £15 each suitable for taking to any repro house

Portraits and Personalities

Tel/Fax: 020 8438 0202
Messages: 020 8438 0303
Mobile: 07712 669 953
Email: billy_snapper@hotmail.com

www.london-photographer.com/
www.theukphotographerexhibition.co.uk
www.theukphotographer.com
www.billysnapper.com

photographer
to the stars

NORTHERN LIGHTS MANAGEMENT
PM
Dean Clough Mills, Halifax, West Yorks HX3 5AX
e-mail: nlmanagement@aol.com
Fax: 01422 330101   Tel: 01422 382203

NORTHERN PROFESSIONALS
(Casting, Technicians, Action Safety, Boat & Diving
Equipment Hire)
21 Cresswell Avenue, North Shields
Tyne & Wear NE29 9BQ
e-mail: bill.gerard@northpro83.freeserve.co.uk
Fax: 0191-296 3243   Tel: 0191-257 8635

NSM
(Natasha Stevenson Management)
85 Shorrolds Road
Fulham, London SW6 7TU
e-mail: nsm@netcomuk.co.uk
Fax: 020-7385 3014   Tel: 020-7386 5333

**NUMBER ONE CASTING & MODEL
MANAGEMENT Ltd**
408F The Big Peg
120 Vyse Street
The Jewellery Quarter, Birmingham B18 6NF
Website: www.numberonemodelagency.co.uk
e-mail: bookings@numberonemodels.globalnet.co.uk
          Tel: 0121-233 2433

NUTOPIA PERSONAL MANAGEMENT
Number 8
132 Charing Cross Road
London WC2H 0LA
Website: www.nutopia.co.uk
Fax: 029-2070 9440   Mobile: 07801 493133

NYLAND MANAGEMENT Ltd
20 School Lane
Heaton Chapel
Stockport SK4 5DG
e-mail: nylandmgmt@freenet.co.uk
Fax: 0161-432 5406   Tel: 0161-442 2224

OAM PROMOTIONS
PO Box 39331
London SE13 6XQ
e-mail: oampromotions@aol.com
          Mobile: 07762 821768

OFF THE KERB PRODUCTIONS
22 Thornhill Crescent, London N1 1BJ
Website: www.offthekerb.co.uk
e-mail: info@offthekerb.co.uk
Fax: 020-7700 4646   Tel: 020-7700 4477

3rd Floor, Hammer House, 113-117 Wardour Street
London W1F 0UN
e-mail: offthekerb@aol.com
Fax: 020-7437 0647   Tel: 020-7437 0607

OPEN DOORS MANAGEMENT Ltd
Les Palmes, No 6, 2 Rathmore Road
Torquay, Devon TQ2 6NY
e-mail: barrygout@hotmail.com
Mobile: 07899 965420   Tel: 01803 200558

OPERA & CONCERT ARTISTS
M Opera
75 Aberdare Gardens, London NW6 3AN
Fax: 020-7372 3537   Tel: 020-7328 3097

ORDINARY PEOPLE Ltd
8 Camden Road, London NW1 9DP
Website: www.ordinarypeople.co.uk
e-mail: info@ordinarypeople.co.uk
Fax: 020-7267 5677   Tel: 020-7267 7007

O'REILLY Dee MANAGEMENT Ltd
PM
112 Gunnersbury Avenue, London W5 4HB
Website: www.thedormgroup.com
e-mail: info@dorm.co.uk
Fax: 020-8992 9993   Tel: 020-8993 7441

ORIENTAL CASTING AGENCY Ltd (Peggy Sirr)
Afro/Asian Artists Write or Phone
1 Wyatt Park Road, Streatham Hill, London SW2 3TN
Website: www.orientalcasting.com
e-mail: peggy.sirr@btconnect.com
Fax: 020-8674 9303   Tel: 020-8671 8538

OTTO PERSONAL MANAGEMENT Ltd•
PM Co-operative
The Printer's Loft
111 Arundel Lane, Sheffield S1 4RF
Website: www.ottopm.freeuk.com
e-mail: ottopm@hotmail.com
Fax: 0114-275 0550   Tel: 0114-275 2592

PAN ARTISTS AGENCY
Ingleby
1 Hollins Grove, Sale, Cheshire M33 6RE
e-mail: bookings@panartists.freeserve.co.uk
Fax: 0161-973 9724   Tel: 0161-969 7419

PANTO PEOPLE
3 Rushden House
Tatlow Road, Glenfield
Leicester LE3 8ND   Tel/Fax: 0116-287 9594

PARAMOUNT INTERNATIONAL MANAGEMENT
Talbot House, 204-226 Imperial Drive
Harrow, Middlesex HA2 7HH
Website: www.ukcomedy.com
e-mail: mail@ukcomedy.com
Fax: 020-8868 6475   Tel: 020-8429 3179

PARK PERSONAL MANAGEMENT Ltd
PM Co-operative
Unit C3, 62 Beechwood Road, London E8 3DY
e-mail: park_management@hotmail.com
    Tel: 020-7923 1498

PARK STREET CASTING
2nd Floor, 46 Park Street, Bristol BS1 5JG
e-mail: parkcasting@btconnect.com
Fax: 0117-929 2933   Tel: 0117-929 2900

PARR & BOND
The Tom Thumb Theatre, Eastern Esplanade
Cliftonville, Kent CT9 2LB   Tel: 01843 221791

PAUL Yvonne MANAGEMENT Ltd
H21 Heathmans Road, London SW6 4TJ
e-mail: yvonne@yvonnepaul.co.uk
Fax: 020-7736 2221   Tel: 020-7384 0300

P B J MANAGEMENT Ltd*
(Comedy)
7 Soho Street, London W1D 3DQ
Website: www.pbjmgt.co.uk
e-mail: general@pbjmgt.co.uk
Fax: 020-7287 1191   Tel: 020-7287 1112

PC THEATRICAL & MODEL AGENCY
(Large Database of Twins)
10 Strathmore Gardens, Edgware
Middlesex HA8 5HJ
Website: www.twinagency.com
e-mail: twinagy@aol.com
Fax: 020-8933 3418   Tel: 020-8381 2229

PELHAM ASSOCIATES
(Peter Cleall)
Pelham Associates, The Media Centre
9-12 Middle Street, Brighton BN1 1AL
Website: www.pelhamassociates.co.uk
e-mail: petercleall@pelhamassociates.co.uk
Fax: 01273 202492   Tel: 01273 323010

PEMBERTON ASSOCIATES Ltd*
193 Wardour Street, London W1F 8ZF
e-mail: general@pembertonassociates.com
Fax: 020-7734 2522   Tel: 020-7734 4144

Suite 35-36 Barton Arcade, Deansgate
Manchester M3 2BH
Fax: 0161-835 3319   Tel: 0161-832 1661

PEPPERPOT PROMOTIONS
(Bands)
Suite 20B, 20-22 Orde Hall Street, London WC1N 3JW
e-mail: chris@pepperpot.co.uk
Fax: 01255 473107   Tel: 020-7405 9108

PERFORMANCE ACTORS AGENCY•
PM Co-operative
137 Goswell Road, London EC1V 7ET
Website: www.p-a-a.co.uk
e-mail: performance@p-a-a.co.uk
Fax: 020-7251 3974   Tel: 020-7251 5716

Edward Hughes

Lee Williams

Paris Jefferson
P H O T O G R A P H E R

020 7404 3219
07876 586601
studio/location

PERFORMERS DIRECTORY
(Actors, Dancers, Models and Extras)
PO Box 29942, London SW6 1FL
Website: www.performersdirectory.co.uk
e-mail: performersdirectory@yahoo.com
Tel: 020-7610 6699

PERFORMING ARTS*
(Directors/Designers/Choreographers/Lighting
Designers)
6 Windmill Street, London W1T 2JB
Website: www.performing-arts.co.uk
e-mail: info@performing-arts.co.uk
Fax: 020-7631 4631   Tel: 020-7255 1362

PERRY George
(See PROFILE MANAGEMENT)

PERSONAL APPEARANCES
20 North Mount, 1147-1161 High Road
Whetstone N20 0PH
e-mail: pers.appearances@talk21.com
Tel/Fax: 020-8343 7748

PETER JOHN INTERNATIONAL*
Suite 7, 23 The Coda Centre, 189 Munster Road
Fulham, London SW6 6AW
e-mail: info@pji.uk.com
Fax: 020-7381 3301   Tel: 020-7381 5525

PFD*
PM
Drury House, 34-43 Russell Street
London WC2B 5HA
Website: www.pfd.co.uk
e-mail: postmaster@pfd.co.uk
Fax: 020-7836 9544   Tel: 020-7344 1010

PHD ARTISTS
24 Ovett Close, Upper Norwood, London SE19 3RX
e-mail: phdartists@hotmail.com
Tel/Fax: 020-8771 4274

PHILLIPS Frances*
Millennium Studios, Elstree Way
Borehamwood, Herts WD6 1SF
e-mail: derekphillips@talk21.com
Fax: 020-8236 1367   Tel: 020-8236 1366

PHPM
(Philippa Howell Personal Management)
184 Bradway Road, Sheffield S17 4QX
e-mail: philippa@phpm.co.uk
Tel/Fax: 0114-235 3663

PHYSICALITY Ltd*
(Physical Skills Specialists)
265-267 Ilford Lane, Ilford, Essex IG1 2SD
Website: www.physicality.co.uk
e-mail: info@physicality.co.uk
Fax: 020-8491 2801   Tel: 020-8491 2800

PHYSICK Hilda
PM Write
78 Temple Sheen Road, London SW14 7RR
Fax: 020-8876 5561   Tel: 020-8876 0073

PICCADILLY MANAGEMENT
PM
23 New Mount Street, Manchester M4 4DE
e-mail: piccadilly.management@virgin.net
Fax: 0161-953 4001   Tel: 0161-953 4057

PICOT Nic ENTERTAINMENT AGENCY
25 Highfield, Carpenders Park WD19 5DY
Website: www.nicpicot.co.uk
e-mail: nic@nicpicot.co.uk
Fax: 020-8421 2700   Tel: 020-8421 2500

PINEAPPLE AGENCY
159-161 Balls Pond Road, London N1 4BG
Fax: 020-7241 3006   Tel: 020-7241 6601

P.L.A.*
(LOVETT Pat ASSOCIATES)
5 Union Street, Edinburgh EH1 3LT
e-mail: edinburgh@pla.uk.com
Fax: 0131-478 7070   Tel: 0131-478 7878

43 Chandos Place, London WC2N 4HS
Website: www.pla.uk.com
e-mail: london@pla.uk.com
Fax: 020-7379 9111   Tel: 020-7379 8111

PLATER Janet MANAGEMENT Ltd
D Floor, Milburn House, Dean Street
Newcastle upon Tyne NE1 1LF
e-mail: magpie@tynebridge.demon.co.uk
Fax: 0191-221 2491   Tel: 0191-221 2490

PLUNKET GREENE ASSOCIATES
(In conjunction with James Sharkey Assocs Ltd)
(Existing Clients only)
PO Box 8365, London W14 0GL
Fax: 020-7603 2221   Tel: 020-7603 2227

POLLYANNA MANAGEMENT Ltd
PO Box 30661, London E1W 3GG
Website: www.eada.demon.co.uk/pollyanna
e-mail: pollyanna-mgmt@yahoo.co.uk
Fax: 020-7480 6761   Tel: 020-7702 1937

POOLE Gordon AGENCY Ltd
The Limes, Brockley, Bristol BS48 3BB
Website: www.gordonpoole.com
e-mail: agents@gordonpoole.com
Fax: 01275 462252   Tel: 01275 463222

POPLAR MANAGEMENT
22 Knightswood, Woking, Surrey GU21 3PY
e-mail: karenfoley@fsmail.net   Tel/Fax: 01483 828056

**POWER MODEL MANAGEMENT CASTING
AGENCY**
Capitol House, 2-4 Heigham Street
Norwich NR2 4TE
Website: www.powermodelmanagement.co.uk
e-mail: powermodelmanagement@btinternet.com
Fax: 01603 621101   Tel: 01603 621100

POWER PROMOTIONS
PO Box 61, Liverpool L13 0EF
Website: www.powerpromotions.co.uk
e-mail: tom@powerpromotions.co.uk
                         Tel/Fax: 0151-230 0070

PPM - ARTISTS MANAGEMENT
9 Kingsway
Ingersoll House, London WC2B 6XF
e-mail: mail@ppmlondon.com
                         Tel/Fax: 020-7240 3432

PREGNANT PAUSE AGENCY
(Pregnant Models, Dancers, Actresses)
11 Matham Road, East Molesey KT8 0SX
Website: www.pregnantpause.co.uk
e-mail: sandy@pregnantpause.co.uk
Fax: 020-8783 0337   Tel: 020-8979 8874

PRICE GARDNER MANAGEMENT
85 Shorrolds Road, London SW6 7TU
Website: www.pricegardner.com
e-mail: info@pricegardner.com
Fax: 020-7381 3288   Tel: 020-7610 2111

**PRICHARD Peter at INTERNATIONAL
ARTISTES Ltd**
4th Floor, Holborn Hall
193-197 High Holborn
London WC1V 7BD
Website: www.intart.co.uk
e-mail: (name)@intart.co.uk
Fax: 020-7404 9865   Tel: 020-7025 0600

John Asquith

Anna Woodside

PRINCIPAL ARTISTES
PM Write
4 Paddington Street, Marylebone
London W1U 5QE
Fax: 020-7486 4668   Tel: 020-7224 3414

PROFILE MANAGEMENT
(George Perry)
2nd Floor, 213 Chalk Farm Road, London NW1 8AB
e-mail: georgeperryprofile@hotmail.com
Fax: 020-7482 1447   Tel: 020-7485 0441

PROSPECTS
The Post Office Theatre, The Malvern
Bevington Road, London W10 5TN
e-mail: hprospects@aol.com   Tel/Fax: 020-8861 5779

PROTOCOL
2/7 Harbour Yard, Chelsea Harbour
London SW10 0XD
e-mail: stars@protocoltalent.com
Fax: 020-7349 1533   Tel: 020-7349 8877

PVA MANAGEMENT Ltd
Hallow Park, Worcester WR2 6PG
e-mail: clients@pva.co.uk
Fax: 01905 641842   Tel: 01905 640663

QDOS ENTERTAINMENT Ltd
8 King Street, Covent Garden, London WC2E 8HN
e-mail: info@qdosentertainment.plc.uk
Fax: 020-7240 4956   Tel: 020-7240 5052

QUICK Nina ASSOCIATES
(See TAYLOR Brian - QUICK Nina ASSOCIATES)

RAGE MODELS
(Young Adults Fashion)
Tigris House, 256 Edgware Road, London W2 1DS
Website: www.ugly.org
e-mail: info@ugly.org
Fax: 020-7402 0507   Tel: 020-7262 0515

RAINBOW REPRESENTATION
45 Nightingale Lane, Crouch End, London N8 7RA
e-mail: rainbowrp@onetel.net.uk
   Tel/Fax: 020-8341 6241

RAMA MANAGEMENT
Huntingdon House, 278-290 Huntingdon High Street
Nottingham NG1 3LY
Website: www.rama-mgt.com
e-mail: admin@rama-mgt.com
Fax: 0115-941 1948   Tel: 0115-952 4333

RAPPORT PROMOTIONS Ltd
(Promotional Staff)
11A Hannell Road, Fulham, London SW6 7RA
e-mail: info@rapportpromotions.com
Fax: 020-7386 8522   Tel: 020-7386 7555

RATTLEBAG ACTORS AGENCY Ltd•
PM
Everyman Theatre Annexe, 13-15 Hope Street
Liverpool L1 9BH
Website: www.rattlebag.co.uk
e-mail: actors@rattlebag.co.uk
Fax: 0151-709 0773   Tel: 0151-708 7273

RAVENSCOURT MANAGEMENT
Tandy House, 30-40 Dalling Road, London W6 0JB
e-mail: ravenscourt@hotmail.com
Fax: 020-8741 1786   Tel: 020-8741 0707

RAY'S NORTHERN CASTING AGENCY
7 Wince Close, Alkrington, Middleton
Manchester M24 1UJ   Tel/Fax: 0161-643 6745

RAZZAMATAZZ MANAGEMENT
Mulberry Cottage, Park Farm
Haxted Road, Lingfield RH7 6DE
e-mail: mcgrogan@tinyworld.co.uk
Fax: 01342 835433   Tel: 01342 835359

RBM
PM (Comedy)
3rd Floor, 18 Broadwick Street, London W1F 8HS
Website: www.rbmcomedy.com
e-mail: info@rbmcomedy.com
Fax: 020-7287 5020   Tel: 020-7287 5010

RDF MANAGEMENT
The Gloucester Building, Kensington Village
Avonmore Road, London W14 8RF
e-mail: debi.allen@rdfmanagement.com
Fax: 020-7013 4101   Tel: 020-7013 4103

REACTORS AGENCY
Co-operative
1 Eden Quay, Dublin 1, Eire
Website: www.reactors.ie
e-mail: reactors@eircom.net
Fax: 00 353 1 8783182   Tel: 00 353 1 8786833

RE.ANIMATOR MANAGEMENT
Wimbledon Theatre, The Broadway
London SW19 1QG
Website: www.reanimator.co.uk
e-mail: management@reanimator.co.uk
Fax: 020-8542 8081   Tel: 020-8542 9763

REDDIN Joan
PM Write
Hazel Cottage, Frogg's Island
Wheeler End Common
Bucks HP14 3NL   Tel: 01494 882729

REDROOFS ASSOCIATES
Room 161, The Admin Building, Iver Heath
Bucks SL0 0NH
Fax: 01753 785443   Tel: 01753 785444

LOOKING FOR AN ACCOUNTANT? SOMEONE YOU CAN RELATE TO AND WHO UNDERSTANDS YOUR BUSINESS?

Our medium-sized accountancy practice based in the heart of London's Soho has a dedicated team offering comprehensive specialist advice to all those operating in and around film, theatre, television and all associated services and industries. Our client list covers the whole spectrum of individuals and companies operating in the media and entertainment sectors including those just starting out to well established industry names.

We pride ourselves in providing a fast and efficient service for all financial needs coupled with a specialist knowledge and understanding developed over many years experience, including:

- **Preparing personal and business accounts and plans.**

- **Raising finance for new business ventures, new homes or simply living.**

- **Specialist tax advice including VAT and also help with investment, pension and mortgage choices.**

- **Bookkeeping and payroll services.**

Call Simon Cryer, José Goumal, Michael Burton or Raef Gregory for a confidential and no obligation free initial discussion.

Registered to carry on audit work by the Institute of Chartered Accountants in England and Wales and regulated to carry on investment business by the Financial Services Authority.

The Quadrangle, 180 Wardour Street, London W1F 8LB
Tel 020 7734 2244 Fax 020 7287 5315
http://www.brebner.co.uk
E-Mail: partners@brebner.co.uk

Brebner **Allen** **Trapp** Chartered Accountants

**REDWAY John ASSOCIATES
(In Association with A.I.M.)**
Nederlander House
7 Great Russell Street, London WC1B 3NH
Website: www.a-i-m.net
e-mail: info@aim.demon.co.uk
Fax: 020-7637 8666   Tel: 020-7637 1700

REGAN RIMMER MANAGEMENT
(Leigh-Ann Regan, Debbie Rimmer)
36-38 Glasshouse Street, London W1B 5DL
e-mail: thegirls@regan-rimmer.co.uk
Fax: 020-7287 9006   Tel: 020-7287 9005

46 Norton Avenue, Birchgrove, Cardiff CF14 4AJ
Fax: 029-2021 3389   Tel: 029-2030 3686

REGARDEZ MODEL MANAGEMENT
89 High Street, West End
Southampton, Hants SO30 3DS
Website: www.regardez.co.uk
e-mail: regardezltd@aol.com
Fax: 023-8065 1856   Tel: 023-8065 1855

REGENCY AGENCY
F TV
25 Carr Road, Calverley
Leeds LS28 5NE   Tel: 0113-255 8980

REPRESENTATION JOYCE EDWARDS
(See EDWARDS REPRESENTATION Joyce)

REYNOLDS Sandra MODEL & CASTING AGENTS
Md F TV
62 Bell Street, London NW1 6SP
Website: www.sandrareynolds.co.uk
e-mail: tessa@sandrareynolds.co.uk
Fax: 020-7387 5848   Tel: 020-7387 5858

35 St Georges Street, Norwich NR3 1DA
Fax: 01603 219825   Tel: 01603 623842

RHINO MANAGEMENT
Oak Porch House
5 Western Road, Nazeing
Essex EN9 2QN
Website: www.rhino-management.com
e-mail: info@rhino-management.co.uk
Mobile: 07901 528988   Tel/Fax: 01992 893259

RICHARDS Lisa
46 Upper Baggot Street, Dublin 4, Eire
e-mail: info@lisarichards.ie
Fax: 00 353 1 6603545   Tel: 00 353 1 6603534

RICHARDS Stella MANAGEMENT
(Existing Clients only)
42 Hazlebury Road, London SW6 2ND
Fax: 020-7731 5082   Tel: 020-7736 7786

RIDGEWAY MANAGEMENT
Fairley House, Andrews Lane
Cheshunt, Herts EN7 6LB
e-mail: info@ridgewaystudios.co.uk
Fax: 01992 633844   Tel: 01992 633775

RK COMMERCIALS
G Md
205 Chudleigh Road, London SE4 1EG
Website: www.rkcommercials.com
e-mail: mail@rkcommercials.com
Fax: 020-8690 7999   Tel: 020-8690 6542

RKM
(See KRUGER Rolf MANAGEMENT Ltd)

ROBSON NEWMAN MANAGEMENT
14 Ritz Buildings, Church Road
Tunbridge Wells, Kent TN1 1HP
Website: www.newmangroup.co.uk
Fax: 01892 514173   Tel: 01892 524122

ROGUE UK Ltd
2nd Floor, Berkeley Square House
Berkeley Square, London W1J 6BD
Website: www.rogueuk.com
e-mail: info@rogueuk.com
Fax: 020-7887 1941   Tel: 020-7887 1942

ROGUES & VAGABONDS MANAGEMENT Ltd
PM Co-operative
The Print House
18 Ashwin Street, London E8 3DL
e-mail: rogues.vagabonds@virgin.net
Fax: 020-7249 8564   Tel: 020-7254 8130

ROLE MODELS
12 Cressy Road, London NW3 2LY
e-mail: models@hiredhands.freeserve.co.uk
Fax: 020-7267 1030   Tel: 020-7284 4337

ROSEBERY MANAGEMENT Ltd•
PM
Diorama Arts Centre, 34 Osnaburgh Street
London NW1 3ND
e-mail: roseberymgt@aol.com
Fax: 020-7692 3065   Tel: 020-7813 1026

ROSEMAN ORGANISATION The
51 Queen Anne Street, London W1G 9HS
Website: www.therosemanorganisation.co.uk
e-mail: info@therosemanorganisation.co.uk
Fax: 020-7486 4600   Tel: 020-7486 4500

ROSS BROWN ASSOCIATES
PM
Rosedale House, Rosedale Road
Richmond, Surrey TW9 2SZ
e-mail: rossbrownassoc@freeuk.com
Fax: 020-8398 3925   Tel: 020-8398 3984

ROSS Frances - CFA MANAGEMENT
East Trevelmond Farm
Trevelmond, Liskeard, Cornwall PL14 4LY
e-mail: frances@cfamanagement.fsnet.co.uk
                    Tel/Fax: 01579 321858

ROSSMORE PERSONAL MANAGEMENT
70-76 Bell Street
London NW1 6SP
e-mail: agents@rossmoremanagement.com
Fax: 020-7258 0124   Tel: 020-7258 1953

ROYCE MANAGEMENT
34A Sinclair Road, London W14 0NH
Fax: 020-7371 4985   Tel: 020-7602 4992

RUBICON MANAGEMENT
27 Inderwick Road, Crouch End
London N8 9LB   Tel/Fax: 020-8374 1836

RUBY TALENT*
Apartment 8, Goldcrest Building
1 Lexington Street, London W1F 9TA
e-mail: tara@ruby-talent.co.uk
Fax: 020-7439 1649   Tel: 020-7439 4554

RUDEYE AGENCY
Website: www.rudeye.com
e-mail: info@rudeye.com   Tel/Fax: 020-8556 7139

RWM MANAGEMENT
The Aberdeen Centre
22-24 Highbury Grove, London N5 2EA
e-mail: rwm.mario-kate@virgin.net
Fax: 020-7226 3371   Tel: 020-7226 3311

SANDERS Loesje*
(Designers, Directors, Choreographers, Lighting
Designers)
Pound Square, 1 North Hill
Woodbridge, Suffolk IP12 1HH
Website: www.loesjesanders.com
e-mail: loesjev@aol.com
Fax: 01394 388734   Tel: 01394 385260

SARABAND ASSOCIATES
(Sara Randall, Bryn Newton)
265 Liverpool Road, London N1 1LX
e-mail: saraband@dna-is.com
Fax: 020-7609 2370   Tel: 020-7609 5313

SAYERS Nicola MANAGEMENT Ltd
2C Admirals Walk
Hoddesdon, Herts EN11 8AA
e-mail: nicki@nsmanagement.fsnet.co.uk
Mobile: 07870 644089   Tel: 01992 442223

SBS Ltd (The Casting Information Service)
Suite 1
16 Sidmouth Road, London NW2 5JX
e-mail: casting@sbsltd.demon.co.uk
Fax: 020-8459 7442   Tel: 020-8459 2781

Caroline Summers

Session includes make up artist

020-7223 7669

Short notice possible

SCA MANAGEMENT
TV F S M Write
77 Oxford Street
London W1D 2ES
e-mail: agency@sca-management.co.uk
Fax: 020-7659 2116   Tel: 020-7659 2027

SCHER Anna THEATRE The
PM
AST Management
70-72 Barnsbury Road, London N1 0ES
e-mail: abby@astm.co.uk
Fax: 020-7833 9467   Tel: 020-7278 2101

SCHNABL Peter
The Barn House, Cutwell, Tetbury
Gloucestershire GL8 8EB
Fax: 01666 502998   Tel: 01666 502133

SCOTT Tim
284 Gray's Inn Road
London WC1X 8EB
e-mail: timscott@btinternet.com
Fax: 020-7278 9175   Tel: 020-7833 5733

SCOT-BAKER AGENCY
35 Caithness Road
Brook Green, London W14 0JA
e-mail: info@scot-baker.com
Fax: 020-7603 7698   Tel: 020-7603 9988

SCOTT-PAUL YOUNG ENTERTAINMENTS Ltd
S.P.Y. Promotions & Productions
Northern Lights House, 110 Blandford Road North,
Langley, Nr Windsor, Berks SL3 7TA
e-mail: sp.young@blueyonder.co.uk
Tel/Fax: 01753 693250

Henry Hargreaves

Sarah Annison

Daniel Coonan

studio and natural light
PHOTOGRAPHER
07974188105
e-mail: casey@caseymoore.com
www.caseymoore.com
STUDENT DISCOUNTS

Josie Hogan

London & Sussex
Portrait & Production Photography

MIKE EDDOWES

Holly Smith

Jason Connery & Tracy Shaw
'The Blue Room'

James Simmons
'Macbeth'

Mike Eddowes
tel: 07970 141005   admin: 01903 882525
email: mike@photo-publicity.co.uk
www.theatre-photography.co.uk

SCREENLITE AGENCY
Shepperton Film Studios
Shepperton, Middlesex TW17 0QD
e-mail: screenlite@dial.pipex.com
Fax: 01932 592507   Tel: 01932 562611 Ext 2271

SCRIMGEOUR Donald ARTISTS AGENCY
(Dance)
49 Springcroft Avenue, London N2 9JH
e-mail: vwest@dircon.co.uk
Fax: 020-8883 9751   Tel: 020-8444 6248

SEARS MANAGEMENT Ltd
Melbury House, 34 Southborough Road
Bickley, Kent BR1 2EB
e-mail: lindasears@btconnect.com
Fax: 01689 862120   Tel: 01689 861859

SECOND SKIN AGENCY
50 Elmwood Road, Chiswick, London W4 3DZ
e-mail: jenny@secondskinagency.com
                                 Tel/Fax: 020-8994 9864

SEDGWICK Dawn MANAGEMENT
3 Goodwins Court, Covent Garden
London WC2N 4LL
Fax: 020-7240 0415   Tel: 020-7240 0404

SHALIT GLOBAL MANAGEMENT
7 Moor Street, Soho, London W1D 5NB
e-mail: info@shalit.co.uk
Fax: 020-7851 9156   Tel: 020-7851 9155

SHAPER Susan MANAGEMENT
Queens House, 1 Leicester Place
London WC2H 7BP
e-mail: shapermg@dircon.co.uk
Fax: 020-7534 3317   Tel: 020-7534 3316

SHAW Vincent ASSOCIATES Ltd
51 Byron Road, London E17 4SN
Website: www.vincentshaw.com
e-mail: info@vincentshaw.com
Fax: 020-8521 1588   Tel: 020-8509 2211

SHEDDEN Malcolm MANAGEMENT
1 Charlotte Street, London W1T 1RD
Fax: 020-7636 1657   Tel: 020-7636 1876

SHEPHERD MANAGEMENT Ltd
13 Radnor Walk, London SW3 4BP
e-mail: info@shepherdmanagement.co.uk
Fax: 020-7352 2277   Tel: 020-7352 2200

SHOWBUSINESS ENTERTAINMENT & TELEVISION CASTING AGENCY
304 College Street, Long Eaton
Nottingham NG10 4GT
Fax: 0115-946 1831   Tel: 0115-973 5445

SHOWSTOPPERS!
(Celebrity Booking Services, Promotions & Entertainments)
42 Foxglove Close, Witham, Essex CM8 2XW
Website: www.showstoppers-group.com
e-mail: mail@showstoppers-group.com
Fax: 01376 510340   Tel: 01376 518486

SILVER FOX ARTIST MANAGEMENT*
8-18 Rampart Street, London E1 2LA
Website: www.silverfoxartist.co.uk
e-mail: enquiries@silverfoxartist.co.uk
Fax: 020-7791 2842   Tel: 020-7791 2952

SILVESTER MANAGEMENT
24 Lake View, Edgware HA8 7RU
e-mail: silvestermgmt@freeuk.com
Fax: 020-8958 7711   Tel: 020-8958 5555

SIMONES INTERNATIONALE
(Artistes Management)
PO Box 15154
London W5 3FW   Tel/Fax: 020-8861 3900

SIMPSON FOX ASSOCIATES Ltd*
(Directors, Designers, Choreographers)
52 Shaftesbury Avenue, London W1D 6LP
e-mail: info@simpson-fox.com
Fax: 020-7494 2887   Tel: 020-7434 9167

SINGER Sandra ASSOCIATES
21 Cotswold Road, Westcliff-on-Sea, Essex SS0 8AA
Website: www.sandrasinger.com
e-mail: sandrasingeruk@aol.com
Fax: 01702 339393   Tel: 01702 331616

SIRR Peggy
(See ORIENTAL CASTING AGENCY Ltd)

SJ MANAGEMENT
15 Maiden Lane, London WC2E 7NG
e-mail: sj@susanjames.demon.co.uk
Fax: 020-7836 5724   Tel: 020-7836 5723

SMILE TALENT
22 The Maltings, Station Road
Newport, Essex CB11 3RN
e-mail: talent.smile@stepc.fsnet.co.uk
Fax: 01799 541658   Tel: 01799 543121

SO DAM TUFF Ltd
(Men Only)
The Coach House
136 Westbridge Road
Battersea Square, London SW11 3PF
Website: www.sodamtuff.com
e-mail: tiger@sodamtuff.com
Fax: 020-7223 7387   Tel: 020-7223 7377

SOLOMON ARTISTES MANAGEMENT INTERNATIONAL
30 Clarence Street
Southend-on-Sea, Essex SS1 1BD
Website: www.solomon-artistes.co.uk
e-mail: info@solomon-artistes.co.uk
Fax: 01702 392385   Tel: 01702 392370

SOPHIE'S PEOPLE
(Dancers and Choreographers)
26 Reporton Road, London SW6 7JR
Website: www.sophiespeople.com
e-mail: sophies.people@btinternet.com
Fax: 0870 7876447   Tel: 0870 7876446

SOUTH WEST MANAGEMENT & CASTING CO Ltd
The Courtyard
Whitchurch, Ross-on-Wye HR9 6DA
Website: www.southwestcasting.co.uk
e-mail: agent@southwestcasting.co.uk
Fax: 01600 891099   Tel: 01600 892005

SPARE PARTS
(Body Parts Specialists)
153 Battersea Rise, London SW11 1HP
Fax: 020-7924 2334   Tel: 020-7924 2484

SPEAK Ltd
140 Devonshire Road
Chiswick, London W4 2AW
Website: www.speak-voices.com
e-mail: info@speak.ltd.uk
Fax: 020-8742 1333   Tel: 020-8742 1001

SPEAKERS CORNER
(Speakers, Presenters, Facilitation and Cabaret for the Corporate Market)
Tigana House, Catlins Lane, Pinner
Middlesex HA5 2AG
Website: www.speakerscorner-uk.com
e-mail: info@speakerscorner-uk.com
Fax: 020-8868 4409   Tel: 020-8866 8967

SPIRE CASTING
PO Box 372, Chesterfield S41 0XW
e-mail: spirecasting@aol.com   Tel: 01246 224798

Verity Hewlett

Joe Brennan

Kika Markham

David Gyasi

SIMON ANNAND
P h o t o g r a p h e r

020-7241 6725
Mobile: 07884 446776
e-mail: simonannand@blueyonder.co.uk

Concessions available

SPLATS ENTERTAINMENT MANAGEMENT
5 Denmark Street
London WC2H 8LP
e-mail: jennifer@splatsentertainment.com
Fax: 020-7240 8409   Tel: 020-7240 8400

SPLITTING IMAGES LOOKALIKES AGENCY
25 Clissold Court
Greenway Close
London N4 2EZ
Website: www.splitting-images.com
e-mail: info@splitting-images.com
Fax: 020-8809 6103   Tel: 020-8809 2327

SPORTABILITY Ltd
(Sporting Personalities)
Unit 2, 23 Green Lane
Dronfield, Derbyshire S18 2LL
Fax: 01246 290520   Tel: 01246 292010

SPORTSMODELS.COM
1A Calton Avenue
Dulwich Village
London SE21 7DE
Website: www.sportsmodels.com
e-mail: info@sportsmodels.com
Fax: 020-8299 8600   Tel: 020-8299 8800

SPORTS WORKSHOP PROMOTIONS Ltd
(Sports Models)
PO Box 878, Crystal Palace
National Sports Centre, London SE19 2BH
e-mail: info@sportspromotions.co.uk
Fax: 020-8776 7772   Tel: 020-8659 4561

SPYKER Paul MANAGEMENT
7 Garrick Street, Covent Garden
London WC2E 9AR
e-mail: info@pspy.com
Fax: 020-7379 8282   Tel: 020-7379 8181

ST. JAMES'S MANAGEMENT
PM Write SAE
19 Lodge Close
Stoke D'Abernon, Cobham
Surrey KT11 2SG
Fax: 01932 860444   Tel: 01932 860666

STACEY Barrie PROMOTIONS
Apartment 8, 132 Charing Cross Road
London WC2H 0LA
Website: www.barriestacey.com
e-mail: hopkinstacey@aol.com
Fax: 020-7836 2949   Tel: 020-7836 4128

STAFFORD Helen MANAGEMENT
14 Park Avenue, Bush Hill Park, Enfield
Middlesex EN1 2HP
e-mail: helen.stafford@blueyonder.co.uk
Fax: 020-8482 0371   Tel: 020-8360 6329

STAGE CENTRE MANAGEMENT Ltd
PM Co-operative
41 North Road, London N7 9DP
e-mail: stagecentre@aol.com
Fax: 020-7609 0213   Tel: 020-7607 0872

STARLINGS THEATRICAL AGENCY
45 Viola Close, South Ockendon, Essex RM15 6JF
Website: www.webspawner.com/users/starlings
e-mail: starlings@blueyonder.co.uk
Mobile: 07941 653463   Tel: 01708 859109

STEVENSON Natasha MANAGEMENT
(See NSM)

STIVEN CHRISTIE MANAGEMENT
(Incorporating The Actors Agency of Edinburgh)
1 Glen Street, Tollcross, Edinburgh EH3 9JD
Fax: 0131-228 4645   Tel: 0131-228 4040

STONE Annette ASSOCIATES*
(See ALTARAS Jonathan ASSOCIATES Ltd/JAA)

STONE Ian ASSOCIATES
4 Masons Avenue, Croydon, Surrey CR0 9XS
Fax: 020-8680 9912   Tel: 020-8667 1627

STONE Richard PARTNERSHIP The*
PM
2 Henrietta Street, London WC2E 8PS
e-mail: all@richstonepart.co.uk
Fax: 020-7497 0869   Tel: 020-7497 0849

STORM ARTISTS MANAGEMENT
4th Floor, 6-10 Lexington Street, London W1F 0LB
Website: www.stormartists.com
e-mail: info@stormartists.co.uk
Fax: 020-7437 4314   Tel: 020-7437 4313

STRALLEN MANAGEMENT
14 Henstal Road, West Hampstead
London NW6 2AN
e-mail: info@strallens.com
Fax: 020-7328 9805   Tel: 020-7692 3154

STREETJAM
(Dancers, Choreographers, Singers, Stylists,
Make-up Artists)
95 Blenheim Gardens, London SW2 5DA
Website: www.streetjamagency.com
e-mail: stjamltd@aol.com   Tel: 020-8671 4618

SUCCESS
Suite 73-74, Kent House, 87 Regent Street
London W1B 4EH
Website: www.successagency.co.uk
e-mail: ee@successagency.co.uk
Fax: 020-7494 3787   Tel: 020-7734 3356

SUCCESSFUL CHOICE
13 Cambridge Drive, Lee Green
London SE12 8AG   Tel: 020-8852 4955

SUMMERS Mark MANAGEMENT
9 Hansard Mews, Kensington, London W14 8BJ
Website: www.marksummers.com
e-mail: mark@marksummers.com
Fax: 0870 4435623   Tel: 0870 4435621

SUMMERTON Michael MANAGEMENT Ltd
PM M C
Mimosa House, Mimosa Street, London SW6 4DS
Fax: 020-7731 0103   Tel: 020-7731 6969

T.A. MANAGEMENT
18 Kingsdale Gardens, Notting Hill, London W11 4TZ
e-mail: tamanagement@hotmail.com
                              Tel/Fax: 020-7603 3471

TALENT ARTISTS Ltd*
59 Sydner Road, London N16 7UF
Fax: 020-7923 2009   Tel: 020-7923 1119

TALENT PARTNERSHIP Ltd The*
Riverside Studios, Crisp Road, Hammersmith
London W6 9RL
e-mail: info@thetalentpartnership.co.uk
Fax: 020-8237 1041   Tel: 020-8237 1040

TALKBACK MANAGEMENT*
20-21 Newman Street, London W1T 1PG
Fax: 020-7861 8061   Tel: 020-7861 8060

TAYLOR Brian - QUICK Nina ASSOCIATES*
50 Pembroke Road, Kensington, London W8 6NX
e-mail: briantaylor@nqassoc.freeserve.co.uk
Fax: 020-7602 6301   Tel: 020-7602 6141

TCA
(The Commercial Agency)
7 Cornwall Crescent, London W11 1PH
e-mail: mail@thecommercialagency.co.uk
Fax: 020-7792 9802   Tel: 020-7243 9844

TCG ARTIST MANAGEMENT
(Rachel Cranmer-Gordon, Kristin Tarry)
6 Langley Street
London WC2H 9JA
Website: www.tcgam.co.uk
e-mail: info@tcgam.co.uk
Fax: 020-7240 3606   Tel: 020-7240 3600

TELFORD Paul MANAGEMENT
PM
23 Noel Street, London W1F 8GT
e-mail: paul@telford-mgt.com
Fax: 020-7434 1200   Tel: 020-7434 1100

T.G.R. DIRECT
88 Recreation Road
Poole, Dorset BH12 2AL
e-mail: tatianaroc.tgrdirect@virgin.net
Fax: 01202 721802   Tel: 01202 721222

KARAM TAKHAR

Mobile: 07950 201035

c/o The Spotlight

THEATRE EXPRESS PERFORMING ARTS AGENCY
PO Box 97
Cleveleys FY5 5XA   Tel: 0870 2430462

THOMAS & BENDA ASSOCIATES Ltd
Top Floor, 15-16 Ivor Place
London NW1 6HS   Tel/Fax: 020-7723 5509

THOMPSON Jim
Herricks, School Lane, Arundel
West Sussex BN18 9DR
e-mail: jim@jthompson42.freeserve.co.uk
Fax: 01903 885887   Tel: 01903 885757

THOMPSON Peggy OFFICE The
PM
1st & 2nd Floor Offices, 296 Sandycombe Road Kew,
Richmond, Surrey TW9 3NG
Fax: 020-8332 1127   Tel: 020-8332 1003

THORNTON AGENCY
(Specialist Agency for Small People)
72 Purley Downs Road, Croydon CR2 0RB
Website: www.dwarfs4hire.com
e-mail: thorntons.leslie@tinyworld.co.uk
Fax: 020-7385 6647   Tel: 020-8660 5588

THRESH Melody MANAGEMENT ASSOCIATES Ltd (MTM)
MTM House, 27 Ardwick Green North
Ardwick, Manchester M12 6FZ
e-mail: melodythreshmtm@aol.com
Fax: 0161-273 5455   Tel: 0161-273 5445

TILDSLEY Janice ASSOCIATES
8 Addison Road, London E17 9LT
e-mail: janice@janicetildsleyassociates.co.uk
Fax: 020-8521 1174   Tel: 020-8521 1888

TIMID ASSOCIATES
44 Summerlee Avenue, Finchley, London N2 9QP
Website: www.timidassociates.com
e-mail: info@timidassociates.com
                    Tel/Fax: 020-8883 1277

TINKER Victoria MANAGEMENT
(Technical, Non-Acting)
Birchenbridge House, Brighton Road
Mannings Heath, Horsham
West Sussex RH13 6HY   Tel/Fax: 01403 210653

TINSEL TOWN TV
44-46 St John Street, London EC1M 4DF
e-mail: info@tinseltown.online.com
                    Tel: 020-7689 7860

TONER CASTING Ltd
Unit E6 Brunswick Business Centre, Brunswick Dock
Brunswick Way, Liverpool L3 4BD
Website: www.tonercasting.com
e-mail: tonercasting@btconnect.com
Fax: 0151-707 8414   Tel: 0151-708 6400

Representing:-

Actors, Dancers, Choreographers, Singers and Children in all aspects of TV Film, Video, Theatre, and Commercial Work.
Full Production Team available for Trade, Fashion & Corporate Events.
Fully Equipped city centre studio for all your audition requirements.

Visit our website: www.kmcagencies.co.uk

London Office:-
t: 0845 660 2459 (local rate)
f: 0870 442 1780
e: london@kmcagencies.co.uk
All postal submissions to head office in Manchester.

PO Box 122,
48 Great Ancoats Street,
Manchester M4 5AB
t: 0161 237 3009 f: 0161 237 9812
e: casting@kmcagencies.co.uk

TOP CATS PROMOTIONS & MODELS
Llantrisant Road
Capel Llanilltern, Cardiff CF5 6JR
Website: www.topcatsmodels.co.uk
e-mail: topcatspromotions@btinternet.com
Tel: 029-2089 0800

TOP LOOK ALIKES/REEL TO REAL PRODUCTIONS
Website: www.toplookalikes.co.uk
e-mail: info@toplooklaikes.co.uk
Tel: 020-8362 1484

TOP MODELS Ltd
57 Holland Park
London W11 3RS
Fax: 020-7243 6046
Tel: 020-7243 6042

TOTS-TWENTIES
Suite 3
Ground Floor, Clements Court
Clements Lane, Ilford, Essex IG1 2QY
Website: www.tots-twenties.co.uk
e-mail: sara@tots-twenties.co.uk
Fax: 020-8553 1880
Tel: 020-8478 1848

TRAIN HOUSE The
27 Prospect Road
Long Ditton
Surrey KT6 5PY
e-mail: agents@trainhouse.demon.co.uk
Fax: 020-8873 2782
Tel: 020-8873 7932

TRENDS AGENCY & MANAGEMENT Ltd
54 Lisson Street
London NW1 5DF
Website: www.trendsgroup.co.uk
e-mail: info@trendsgroup.co.uk
Fax: 020-7258 3591
Tel: 020-7723 8001

TROLAN Gary MANAGEMENT
PM Write
30 Burrard Road, London NW6 1DB
e-mail: garytrolanmgmt@aol.com
Tel/Fax: 020-7794 4429

TROUPERS.COM
3 Shirragh Way, Port Erin, Isle of Man
Website: www.troupers.com
e-mail: info@troupers.com   Mobile: 07624 470123

TUCKER Tommy AGENCY
Suite 66
235 Earl's Court Road, London SW5 9FE
e-mail: tommytucker.agency@yahoo.co.uk
Fax: 020-7370 4784   Tel: 020-7370 3911

TV MANAGEMENTS
Brink House, Avon Castle, Ringwood
Hants BH24 2BL
Fax: 01425 480123   Tel: 01425 475544

TWINS
(See PC THEATRICAL & MODEL AGENCY)

TWINS & TRIPLETS
(Identical Babies, Children, Teenagers & Adults for Film/Television)
Holmhurst Road, Upper Belvedere DA17 6HW
Website: www.twins.triplets.freeuk.com
e-mail: twinsontv@aol.com
Fax: 01322 447250   Tel: 01322 440184

TWIST & FLIC SPORTS AGENCY
(Sports Model Agent)
1A Calton Avenue, Dulwich Village
London SE21 7ED
Website: www.sportsmodels.com
e-mail: info@sportsmodels.com
Fax: 020-8299 8600   Tel: 020-8299 8800

David Creedon

Becky Riggs

Junior Bartlett

JAMES GILL 020 7735 5632 *Photographer with Attitude & Imagination*

TWO'S COMPANY
244 Upland Road
London SE22 0DN
e-mail: 2scompany@britishlibrary.net
Fax: 020-8299 3714   Tel: 020-8299 4593

UGLY MODELS
Tigris House
256 Edgware Road
London W2 1DS
Website: www.ugly.org
e-mail: info@ugly.org
Fax: 020-7402 0507   Tel: 020-7402 5564

UNIQUE MANAGEMENT GROUP
Beaumont House
Kensington Village
Avonmore Road
London W14 8TS
e-mail: celebrities@uniquegroup.co.uk
Fax: 020-7605 1101   Tel: 020-7605 1100

UNITED COLOURS OF LONDON Ltd
4th Floor (FBI)
20-24 Kirby Street
London EC1N 8TS
Fax: 020-7242 8125   Tel: 020-7242 5542

UNITED PRODUCTIONS
(Stylists, Dancers, Choreographers)
6 Shaftesbury Mews
Clapham
London SW4 9BP
Website: www.united-productions.co.uk
                         Tel/Fax: 020-7720 9624

UPBEAT MANAGEMENT
(Theatre Touring & Events - No Actors)
PO Box 63
Wallington, Surrey SM6 9YP
Website: www.upbeat.co.uk
e-mail: info@upbeat.co.uk
Fax: 020-8669 6752   Tel: 020-8773 1223

URBAN TALENT
54 Princess Street
Manchester M1 6HS
Fax: 0161-236 7557   Tel: 0161-228 6444

VACCA Roxane MANAGEMENT*
73 Beak Street
London W1F 9SR
Fax: 020-7734 8086   Tel: 020-7734 8085

VALLÉ ACADEMY THEATRICAL AGENCY The
Wilton House, Delamare Road
Cheshunt, Herts EN8 9SG
Website: www.valleacademy.co.uk
e-mail: agency@valleacademy.co.uk
Fax: 01992 622868   Tel: 01992 622861

VAMP ORGANISATION Ltd The
Ealing House, 33 Hanger Lane, London W5 3HJ
e-mail: info@vampevents.com
Fax: 020-8932 6169   Tel: 020-8997 3355

VIBES UK Ltd
(Choreographers, Dancers, Models & Creative
Directors)
68A Rochester Place, London NW1 9JX
Website: www.vibesuk.com
e-mail: info@vibesuk.com
Fax: 020-7485 2225   Tel: 020-7485 2221

VIDAL-HALL Clare*
(Directors, Designers, Choreographers, Lighting
Designers, Composers)
28 Perrers Road
London W6 0EZ
e-mail: clarevidalhall@email.com
Fax: 020-8741 9459   Tel: 020-8741 7647

VINE Michael ASSOCIATES
(Light Entertainment)
29 Mount View Road
London N4 4SS
e-mail: mpvine@aol.com
Fax: 020-8348 3277   Tel: 020-8348 5899

W6 AGENCY The
Riverside Studios
Crisp Road
Hammersmith
London W6 9RL
e-mail: info@thew6agency.co.uk
Fax: 020-8237 1041   Tel: 020-8237 1046

WALMSLEY Peter ASSOCIATES
(Agent's Locum/Assistant. No Representation)
37A Crimsworth Road
London SW8 4RJ
e-mail: associates@peterwalmsley.net
Mobile: 07778 347312   Tel: 020-7787 6419

WARING & McKENNA*
22 Grafton Street
London W1S 4EX
e-mail: dj@waringandmckenna.com
Fax: 020-7409 7932   Tel: 020-7491 2666

WAVE ENTERTAINMENT
308 Desborough Avenue
High Wycombe
Buckinghamshire HP11 2TJ
Website: www.wave-entertainment.co.uk
e-mail: paul@wave-entertainment.co.uk
Mobile: 07736 309290   Tel/Fax: 0870 7606263

WEEKS Kimberley MANAGEMENT
116 Earlham Grove
Forest Gate
London E7 9AS   Tel: 020-8519 4473

WELCH Janet PERSONAL MANAGEMENT
11 Sunbury Court Island
Lower Hampton Road
Sunbury-on-Thames
Middlesex TW16 5PP
Fax: 01932 766191   Tel: 01932 766190

WESSON Penny*
PM
26 King Henry's Road
London NW3 3RP
Fax: 020-7483 2890   Tel: 020-7722 6607

WEST CENTRAL MANAGEMENT
Co-operative
Room 4
East Block, Panther House
38 Mount Pleasant
London WC1X 0AP
Website: www.westcentralmanagement.co.uk
e-mail: mail@westcentralmanagement.co.uk
Tel/Fax: 020-7833 8134

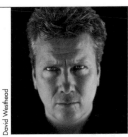

WEST END MANAGEMENT
(Maureen Cairns)
Forsyth House
3rd Floor
111 Union Street
Glasgow G1 3TA
e-mail: info@west-end-management.co.uk
Fax: 0141-226 8983   Tel: 0141-226 8941

WHATEVER ARTISTS MANAGEMENT Ltd
1 York Street, London W1U 6PA
Website: www.wamshow.biz
e-mail: wam@agents-uk.com
Fax: 020-7487 3311   Tel: 020-7487 3111

WHITEHALL ARTISTS
10 Lower Common South, London SW15 1BP
e-mail: mwhitehall@email.msn.com
Fax: 020-8788 2340   Tel: 020-8785 3737

WILD THEATRICAL MANAGEMENT
PO Box 222, Rainham
Essex RM13 7WQ
e-mail: wildtm@lineone.net   Tel: 01708 505543

WILDE Vivien Ltd*
193 Wardour Street
London W1F 8ZF
e-mail: vivien.wilde@virgin.net
Fax: 020-7439 1941   Tel: 020-7439 1940

WILKINSON David ASSOCIATES*
115 Hazlebury Road
London SW6 2LX
Fax: 020-7371 5161   Tel: 020-7371 5188

WILLOW PERSONAL MANAGEMENT
(Specialist Agency for Short Actors)
151 Main Street
Yaxley, Peterborough
Cambridgeshire PE7 3LD
e-mail: info@willowmanagement.co.uk
                    Tel/Fax: 01733 240392

WILLS Newton MANAGEMENT
The Studio
29 Springvale Avenue
Brentford, Middlesex TW8 9QT
e-mail: newtoncttg@aol.com
Fax: 00 33 241 823108   Tel: 07989 398381

WILSON-GOUGH MANAGEMENT
102 Jermyn Street
London SW1Y 6EE
e-mail: info@wilson-gough.com
Fax: 020-7747 8288   Tel: 020-7477 2214

WINSLETT Dave ASSOCIATES
6 Kenwood Ridge
Kenley
Surrey CR8 5JW
Website: www.davewinslett.com
e-mail: info@davewinslett.com
Fax: 020-8668 9216   Tel: 020-8668 0531

WIS
(Welsh, Irish, Scottish)
86 Elphinstone Road
Walthamstow
London E17 5EX   Tel: 020-8523 4234

WYMAN Edward AGENCY
F TV (English & Welsh Language)
67 Llanon Road
Llanishen, Cardiff CF14 5AH
Website: www.wymancasting.fsnet.co.uk
e-mail: edward@wymancasting.fsnet.co.uk
Fax: 029-2075 2444   Tel: 029-2075 2351

X-FACTOR MANAGEMENT
6 Fulham Park Studios
Fulham Park Road, London SW6 4LW
e-mail: natalie@xfactorltd.com
Fax: 020-7371 9953   Tel: 020-7610 6186

YELLOW BALLOON PRODUCTIONS Ltd
Freshwater House, Outdowns
Effingham, Surrey KT24 5QR
e-mail: yellowbal@aol.com
Fax: 01483 281502   Tel: 01483 281500

YEOH Eddie MANAGEMENT
37 Falmouth Gardens, Redbridge, Essex IG4 5JU
Fax: 020-8550 0348   Tel: 020-8550 9994

YOUNG April Ltd
11 Woodlands Road, Barnes
London SW13 0JZ
Fax: 020-8878 7017   Tel: 020-8876 7030

ZAHL Ann PERSONAL MANAGEMENT
57 Great Cumberland Place
London W1H 7LJ
Fax: 020-7262 4143   Tel: 020-7724 3684

ZAHRA & REMICK
F TV Theatre
186 Albert Road
London N22 7AH   Tel/Fax: 020-8889 6225

ZWICKLER Marlene & ASSOCIATES
2 Belgrave Place, Edinburgh EH4 3AN
Website: www.mza-artists.com
                    Tel/Fax: 0131-343 3030

A & J MANAGEMENT
551 Green Lanes, London N13 4DR
Website: www.ajmanagement.co.uk
e-mail: ajmanagement@bigfoot.com
Fax: 020-8882 5983   Tel: 020-8882 7716

ABACUS AGENCY
The Studio
4 Bailey Road, Westcott
Dorking, Surrey RH4 3QS
Website: www.abacusagency.co.uk
e-mail: admin@abacusagency.co.uk
Fax: 01306 877813   Tel: 01306 877144

ACADEMY MANAGEMENT
41 Worcestershire Lea
Warfield
Berks RG42 3TQ
Fax: 01344 426410   Tel: 01344 426313

ACT ONE DRAMA STUDIO & AGENCY
31 Dobbin Hill
Sheffield S11 7JA
Website: www.actonedrama.co.uk
e-mail: casting@actonedrama.co.uk
Fax: 07971 112153   Tel: 0114-266 7209

ACT OUT AGENCY
22 Greek Street
Stockport, Cheshire SK3 8AB
e-mail: ab22@supanet.com Tel/Fax: 0161-429 7413

ACTIVATE DRAMA SCHOOL
(Drama School and Agency)
Priestman Cottage, Sea View Road
Sunderland SR2 7UP
e-mail: activate_agcy@hotmail.com
Fax: 0191-551 2051   Tel: 0191-565 2345

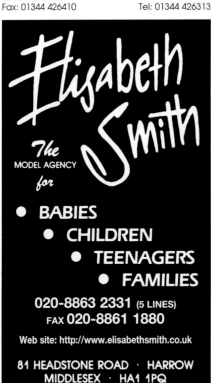

ADAMS Juliet CHILD MODEL & TALENT AGENCY
19 Gwynne House
Challice Way
London SW2 3RB
Website: www.julietadams.co.uk
e-mail: models@julietadams.co.uk
Fax: 020-8671 9314   Tel: 020-8671 7673

AGENCY K-BIS
Clermont Hall
Cumberland Road
Brighton BN1 6SL
e-mail: k-bis@zoom.co.uk   Tel/Fax: 01273 564366

ALEXANDER Suzanne MANAGEMENT
170 Town Lane
Higher Bebington
Wirral CH63 8LG
e-mail: suzyalex@hotmail.com
                                Tel/Fax: 0151-608 9655

ALLSORTS DRAMA FOR CHILDREN
(In Association with Sasha Leslie Management)
2 Pember Road
London NW10 5LP
e-mail: enquiries@allsorts.ltd.uk
                                Tel/Fax: 020-8969 3249

ANNA'S MANAGEMENT
(Formerly of ALADDIN'S CAVE)
25 Tintagel Drive
Stanmore, Middlesex HA7 4SR
Fax: 020-8238 2899   Tel: 020-8958 7636

ARAENA/COLLECTIVE
10 Bramshaw Gardens
South Oxhey
Herts WD1 6XP   Tel/Fax: 020-8428 0037

ARTS ACADEMY The (T.A.A.)
15 Lexham Mews
London W8 6JW
Fax: 020-7376 2416   Tel: 020-7376 0267

ASHCROFT ACADEMY OF DRAMATIC ART
The Studio
28 Beckenham Road, Kent BR3 4LS
Website: www.ashcroftacademy.co.uk
                                Tel/Fax: 020-8693 8088

AWA - ANDREA WILDER AGENCY
23 Cambrian Drive
Colwyn Bay, Conwy LL28 4SL
Website: www.awagency.co.uk
e-mail: casting@awagency.co.uk
Fax: 07092 249314   Tel: 01492 547542

BARDSLEY'S Pamela UNIQUE AGENCY
1 Birkdale Mews, 15A Liverpool Road
Birkdale, Southport, Merseyside PR8 4AS
e-mail: pamelabardsley@hotmail.com
Mobile: 07802 411446   Tel/Fax: 01704 566771

BELCANTO LONDON ACADEMY Ltd
(Stage School & Agency)
Performance House, 20 Passey Place
London SE9 5DQ
e-mail: enquiries@theatretraining.com
Fax: 020-8850 9944   Tel: 020-8850 9888

BIZ MANAGEMENT
(In Association with Kidz in the Biz Theatre
Academy)
30 Florence Street
London NW4 1QH
Website: www.kidzinthebiz.co.uk
e-mail: thebizmanagement@aol.com
Mobile: 07763 958096   Tel: 020-8632 9661

BIZZYKIDZ Ltd
Riverside House
High Street
Crayford, Kent DA1 4HG
Website: www.bizzykidz.com
e-mail: info@bizzykidz.com
Fax: 01322 554897   Tel: 01322 552214

BODENS AGENCY
99 East Barnet Road
New Barnet, Herts EN4 8RF
Website: www.bodensagency.com
e-mail: bodens2692@aol.com
Fax: 020-8449 5212   Tel: 020-8447 0909

BOURNE Michelle ACADEMY & AGENCY
Studio 1, 22 Dorman Walk
Garden Way, London NW10 0PF
Website: www.michellebourneacademy.co.uk
e-mail: info@michellebourneacademy.co.uk
Mobile: 07956 853564   Tel: 020-8451 3261

BOURNEMOUTH YOUTH THEATRE The (BYT)
14 Cooper Dean Drive
Bournemouth BH8 9LN
Website: www.thebyt.com
e-mail: klair@thebyt.com
Fax: 01202 393290   Tel: 01202 854116

BRUCE & BROWN
203 Canalot Studios
222 Kensal Road, London W10 5BN
Fax: 020-8964 0457   Tel: 020-8968 5585

BUBBLEGUM
Ardreigh, Beaconsfield Road
Farnham Royal, Bucks SL2 3BP
Website: www.bubblegummodels.com
e-mail: kids@bubblegummodels.com
Fax: 01753 669255   Tel: 01753 646348

BYRON'S CASTING
(Babies, Children & Adults)
North London Performing Arts Centre
76 St James Lane
Muswell Hill, London N10 3DF
Website: www.byronscasting.co.uk
e-mail: byronscasting@aol.com
Fax: 020-8444 4040   Tel: 020-8444 4445

C.A.L.S. CASTING
(Children & Teenagers)
Unit E2, Bellevale Shopping Centre
Liverpool L25 2RG
Mobile: 07904 551914   Tel/Fax: 0151-487 8500

CAMPBELL ASSOCIATES
2 Chelsea Cloisters, Sloane Avenue
Chelsea, London SW3 3DW
email: campbell.associates@btopenworld.com
Fax: 020-7584 8799   Tel: 020-7584 5586

CAPITAL ARTS
Wyllyotts Centre, Darkes Lane
Potters Bar, Herts EN6 2HN
e-mail: capitalartstheatre@o2.co.uk
Mobile: 07885 232414   Tel/Fax: 020-8449 2342

CARR Norrie MODEL AGENCY
(Babies, Children & Adults)
Holborn Studios
49-50 Eagle Wharf Road, London N1 7ED
Website: www.norriecarr.com
e-mail: info@norriecarr.com
Fax: 020-7253 1772   Tel: 020-7253 1771

CARTEURS THEATRICAL AGENCY
170A Church Road, Hove, East Sussex BN3 2DJ
Website: www.stonelandschool.co.uk
e-mail: info@stonelandsschool.co.uk
Fax: 01273 770444   Tel: 01273 770445

ACT ONE
Drama Studio & Agency

Children & adults up to 40 yrs. available for tv, theatre, radio, films, commercials, voice overs, corporate videos etc.

31 Dobbin Hill, Sheffield, S11 7JA.
tel **0114 2667209** mobile **07971 850617**
fax **07971 112153**
email **casting@actonedrama.co.uk**
web **www.actonedrama.co.uk**

CENTRE STAGE MANAGEMENT
(Children & Young Adults)
The Croft, 7 Cannon Road
Southgate, London N14 7HE
Website: www.csmanagementuk.com
e-mail: carole@csmanagementuk.com
Fax: 020-8886 7555   Tel: 020-8886 4264

CHARACTERS MANAGEMENT Ltd
28 Fletching Road, Clapton
London E5 9QP
Fax: 020-8533 5554   Tel: 020-8533 5500

CHILDREN OF LONDON ACTING & MODEL AGENCY
The Playhouse
273 Malden Road, Surrey KT3 6AH
e-mail: childrenoflondon@aol.com
Fax: 020-8949 0522   Tel: 020-8949 0450

CHILDSPLAY & ALLSORTS
1 Cathedral Street
London SE1 9DE
Website: www.childsplaylondon.co.uk
e-mail: childsplaylondon@aol.com
Fax: 020-7403 1656   Tel: 020-7403 4834

CHRYSTEL ARTS AGENCY
15 Churchill Road, Edgware
Middlesex HA8 6NX
e-mail: chrystelarts@talk21.com
                            Tel: 020-8952 1281

CIRCUS MANIACS
(Circus, Theatre, Dance, Extreme Sports)
Office 8A, The Kingswood Foundation
Britannia Road, Kingswood, Bristol BS15 8DB
e-mail: agency@circusmaniacs.com
Mobile: 07977 247287   Tel/Fax: 0117-947 7042

James Pallister Ant & Dec's Saturday Night Take Away

YOUR IMAGINATION
Drama School and Agency

Actors, Extras, Models, Licensed Chaperones and Tutors with all round training for Theatre, T.V., Film and Commercial work

Contact: Lesley McDonough

Priestman Cottage, Sea View Road,
Sunderland SR2 7UP

Tel: 0191 565 2345   Mob: 07989 365737
Fax: 0191 551 2051

http://www.lineone.net/~lesley.mcdonough
e-mail: activate_agcy@hotmail.com

Connor Doyle
TVC for Comet

Tuesdays Child
Television & Model Agency
(Est. 1976)

Children from many parts of the UK including Manchester, West Midlands, Merseyside & Notts

Tel: 01625 501765 and **612244 (4 lines)**

www.tuesdayschildagency.co.uk
Email: bookings@tuesdayschildagency.co.uk

Amanda Andrews Agency

**Training & Representing
Children & Adults
For TV & Film**

30 Caverswall Road, Blythe Bridge,
Staffordshire ST11 9BG

Tel/Fax: 01782 393889
Email: amanda.andrews@lineone.net

*Academy of
Performing Arts*   *Casting Agency*

CHILDREN - YOUNG ADULTS
TV • FILM • COMMERCIALS • THEATRE • MODELLING
Children Open License • Licensed Chaperones

MAXINE GLASBY - DANIEL HEALD

3, Newgate Lane, Mansfield, Nottingham. NG18 2LB
Phone: 01623 424334 Fax: 01623 474820
e-mail: expressions@route56.co.uk www.expressions-uk.com

CITY LITES
PO Box 29673
London E8 3FH
e-mail: gulcan@freeuk.com
Mobile: 07773 353645   Tel/Fax: 020-7683 9016

CLAPPERBOARD CASTING
(Main Agents for Stagecoach Schools)
PO Box 153, Manchester M7 4YU
Fax: 0161-792 4285   Tel: 0161-792 2277

CLARKE Rose MANAGEMENT & THEATRE SCHOOL
51 Shooters Hill
Blackheath
London SE18 3RL
e-mail: roseclarkemanagement@hotmail.com
    Tel/Fax: 020-8856 2536

COLIN'S PERFORMING ARTS AGENCY & MANAGEMENT
(Colin's Performing Arts Ltd)
The Studios, 219B North Street
Romford, Essex RM1 4QA
Website: www.colinsperformingarts.co.uk
e-mail: agency@colinsperformingarts.co.uk
Fax: 01708 766077   Tel: 01708 766444

COLLINS STUDENT MANAGEMENT
St Dunstan's Hall
East Acton Lane
East Acton, London W3 7EG
e-mail: collinsstudents@aol.com
Fax: 020-8740 6542   Tel: 020-8743 9514

CONTI Italia AGENCY Ltd
23 Goswell Road
London EC1M 7AJ
e-mail: sca@italiaconti36.freeserve.co.uk
Fax: 020-7253 1430   Tel: 020-7608 7500

CYBER-KIDS
(Principal Hilary Wiltshire)
25 Southdown Road
Shoreham-by-Sea, West Sussex BN43 5AL
e-mail: hilliwiltshire@aol.com
Fax: 01273 739984   Tel: 01273 462999

The Studio, Kingsway Court
Queen's Gardens, Hove BN3 2LP
Website: www.cyberartists.co.uk
e-mail: cyber.1@btclick.com
Fax: 01273 739984   Tel: 01273 821821

D & B MANAGEMENT & THEATRE SCHOOL
470 Bromley Road, Bromley, Kent BR1 4PN
Website: www.dandbperformingarts.co.uk
e-mail: bonnie@dandbperformingarts.co.uk
Fax: 020-8697 8100   Tel: 020-8698 8880

DIMPLES MODEL & CASTING ACADEMY
(Adults & Children)
Suite 2, 2nd Floor, Magnum House
33 Lord Street, Leigh, Lancs WN7 1BY
e-mail: dimples_m_c_a@btinternet.com
Fax: 01942 262232   Tel: 01942 262012

DMS AGENCY
30 Lakedale Road
Plumstead, London SE18 1PP
Mobile: 07740 288869   Tel/Fax: 020-8317 6622

DQ MANAGEMENT
1st Floor, 115 Church Road
Hove, East Sussex BN3 2AF
e-mail: info@dqmanagement.com
Fax: 01273 277255   Tel: 01273 721221

DRAGON DRAMA
(Drama for Children)
1B Station Road, Hampton Wick, Kingston KT1 4HG
Website: www.dragondrama.co.uk
e-mail: info@dragondrama.co.uk
    Tel/Fax: 020-8943 1504

DRAMA STUDIO EDINBURGH The
(Previously Juno Casting Agency)
19 Belmont Road, Edinburgh EH14 5DZ
Website: www.thedramastudio.co.uk
e-mail: thedra@thedramastudio.co.uk
Fax: 0131-453 3108   Tel: 0131-453 3284

EARNSHAW Susi MANAGEMENT
5 Brook Place, Barnet, Herts EN5 2DL
Website: www.susiearnshaw.co.uk
e-mail: casting@susiearnshaw.co.uk
Fax: 020-8364 9618   Tel: 020-8441 5010

ENGLISH Doreen '95
(Gerry Kinner)
4 Selsey Avenue, Aldwick, Bognor Regis
West Sussex PO21 2QZ   Tel: 01243 825968

EUROKIDS & ADULTS INTERNATIONAL CASTING & MODELLING AGENCY
The Warehouse Studios, Glaziers Lane
Culcheth, Warrington, Cheshire WA3 4AQ
Website: www.eka-agency.com
e-mail: info@eka-agency.com
Fax: 01925 767563   Tel: 0871 7501575

EXPRESSIONS
3 Newgate Lane, Mansfield
Nottingham NG18 2LB
e-mail: expressions@route56.co.uk
Fax: 01623 474820   Tel: 01623 4242334

EXTRAS UNLIMITED
9 Hansard Mews, Kensington, London W14 8BJ
Fax: 0870 4435621   Tel: 0870 4435622

FBI AGENCY Ltd The
PO Box 250, Leeds LS1 2AZ
e-mail: casting@fbi-agency.ltd.uk
                     Tel/Fax: 07050 222747

FIORENTINI Anna THEATRE & FILM SCHOOL & AGENCY
87 Glyn Road, Hackney, London E5 0JA
Website: www.annafiorentini.co.uk
e-mail: info@annafiorentini.co.uk
                     Tel/Fax: 020-7682 1403

FOOTSTEPS THEATRE SCHOOL CASTING
55 Pullan Avenue, Eccleshill, Bradford BD2 3RP
e-mail: helen@footsteps.fslife.co.uk
Fax: 01274 637429   Tel: 01274 636036

FOX Betty AGENCY
The Friends Institute, 220 Moseley Road
Birmingham B12 0DG
e-mail: bettyfox.school@virgin.net
                     Tel/Fax: 0121-440 1635

GLYNNE Frances MANAGEMENT
12 Stoneleigh Close, Leeds LS17 8FH
e-mail: franandmo@yahoo.co.uk
Fax: 0113-237 1038   Tel: 0113-266 4286

GO FOR IT CHILDREN'S AGENCY
(Children & Teenagers)
47 North Lane
Teddington, Middlesex TW11 0HU
Website: www.goforitts.com
e-mail: info@goforitts.com
Fax: 020-8287 9405   Tel: 020-8943 1120

GOBSTOPPERS MANAGEMENT
50 Bencroft Road
Hemel Hempstead, Herts HP2 5UY
e-mail: chrisgobstoppers@btopenworld.com
Mobile: 07961 372319   Tel: 01442 269543

GOLDMAN'S Shana THEATRICAL SCHOOL & AGENCY
74 Braemore Road
Hove, East Sussex BN3 4HB
Website: www.shana-goldmans.co.uk
e-mail: casting@shana-goldmans.co.uk
                     Tel/Fax: 01273 329916

G. P. ASSOCIATES
4 Gallus Close
Winchmore Hill
London N21 1JR
e-mail: clients@gpassociates.co.uk
Fax: 020-8882 9189   Tel: 020-8886 2263

GRAYSTONS
843-845 Green Lanes
Winchmore Hill, London N21 2RX
e-mail: graystons@btinternet.com
Fax: 020-8364 2009   Tel: 020-8360 5700

GREVILLE Jeannine THEATRICAL AGENCY
Melody House, Gillotts Corner
Henley-on-Thames, Oxon RG9 1QU
Fax: 01491 411533   Tel: 01491 572000

HARLEQUIN CASTING AGENCY
Lee Chapel Centre, Knibcaps
The Knares, Basildon, Essex SS16 5RX
e-mail: harlequincasting@aol.com
Mobile: 07799 761089   Tel: 01268 440184

HARLEQUIN STUDIOS AGENCY FOR CHILDREN
223 Southcoast Road
Peacehaven
East Sussex BN10 8LB   Tel: 01273 581742

HARRIS AGENCY Ltd The
52 Forty Avenue
Wembley Park, Middlesex HA9 8LQ
e-mail: sharrisltd@aol.com
Fax: 020-8908 4455   Tel: 020-8908 4451

HEWITT PERFORMING ARTS
160 London Road
Romford
Essex RM7 9QL
e-mail: hewittcontrol@aol.com Tel: 01708 727784

HINDIN Dee ASSOCIATES
9B Brunswick Mews
Great Cumberland Place
London W1H 7FB
Fax: 020-7258 0651   Tel: 020-7723 3706

HOBSON'S KIDS
62 Chiswick High Road, London W4 1SY
Website: www.hobsons-international.com
e-mail: kids@hobsons-international.com
Fax: 020-8996 5350   Tel: 020-8995 3628

HORNIMANS MANAGEMENT
31 Stafford Street
Gillingham, Kent ME7 5EN
Mobile: 07866 689865   Tel/Fax: 01634 576191

**HOWE Janet CHILDREN'S CASTING &
MODELLING AGENCY**
40 Princess Street, Manchester M1 6DE
Mobile: 07801 942178   Tel/Fax: 0161-233 0700

Studio 1, Whitebridge Estate
Whitebridge Lane
Stone, Staffs ST15 8LQ
Website: www.janethowe.co.uk
e-mail: janet@jhowecasting.fsbusiness.co.uk
Tel/Fax: 01785 816888   Tel/Fax: 01708 818480

INTER-CITY KIDS
Portland Tower, Portland Street
Manchester M1 3LF
Website: www.iccast.co.uk
e-mail: intercity@bigfoot.com
                                       Tel/Fax: 0161-226 0103

JABBERWOCKY AGENCY
(Children & Teenagers 6 Months -18 Years)
Wood Pecker Barn
Wickhurst Farm
Lamberhurst, Kent TN3 8BH
Website: www.jabberwockyagency.com
e-mail: jabberagency@aol.com
Mobile: 07884 431724   Tel/Fax: 01892 890499

JB ASSOCIATES
(Children & Teenagers 6 Months - 18 Years)
3 Stevenson Square
Manchester M1 1DN
Website: www.j-b-a.net   e-mail: info@j-b-a.net
Fax: 0161-237 1809   Tel: 0161-237 1808

Sasha Leslie Management
in association with
allsorts™ drama for children
ages 3-16

t f : 020 8969 3249
e : enquiries@allsorts.ltd.uk

2 Pember Road,
London NW10 5LP

JIGSAW ARTS MANAGEMENT
(Representing Children and Young People from
Jigsaw Performing Arts Schools)
64-66 High Street, Barnet, Hertfordshire EN5 5SJ
Website: www.jigsaw-arts.co.uk/agency
Tel: 020-8447 4530

JOHNSTON & MATHERS ASSOCIATES Ltd
PO Box 3167, Barnet, Hertfordshire EN5 2WA
e-mail: johnstonmathers@aol.com
Tel/Fax: 020-8449 4968

K M C AGENCIES AND THEATRE SCHOOL
PO Box 122, 48 Great Ancoats Street
Manchester M4 5AB
e-mail: kids@kmcagencies.co.uk
Fax: 0161-237 9812   Tel: 0161-237 3009

KASTKIDZ
40 Sunnybank Road, Unsworth, Bury BL9 8HF
e-mail: kastkidz@ntlworld.com
Tel/Fax: 0161-796 7073

KIDS LONDON
67 Dulwich Road, London SE24 0NJ
Website: www.kidslondon.uk.com
e-mail: kidslondon@btconnect.com
Fax: 020-7924 9766   Tel: 020-7924 9595

KIDS PLUS
54 Grove Park, London SE5 8LG
Website: www.kidsplus.co.uk
e-mail: janekidsplus@aol.com
Mobile: 07759 944215   Tel/Fax: 020-7737 3901

KIDZ NATIONAL MODEL & CASTING AGENCY
21 Bolton Road, Manchester M28 3AX
Website: www.kidzltd.com
e-mail: info@kidzltd.com
Tel/Fax: 0870 2416260   Tel: 0870 2414418

KRACKERS KIDS THEATRICAL AGENCY
6/7 Electric Parade
Seven Kings Road, Ilford, Essex IG3 8BY
Website: www.krackerskids.co.uk
e-mail: krackerskids@hotmail.com
Tel/Fax: 01708 502046

LAMONT CASTING AGENCY
94 Harington Road, Formby, Liverpool L37 1PZ
Website: www.lamontcasting.co.uk
e-mail: diane@lamontcasting.co.uk
Fax: 01704 872422   Tel: 01704 877024

LESLIE Sasha MANAGEMENT
(In Association with Allsorts Drama for Children)
2 Pember Road
London NW10 5LP
e-mail: enquiries@allsorts.ltd.uk
Tel/Fax: 020-8969 3249

LINTON MANAGEMENT
3 The Rock, Bury BL9 0JP
Fax: 0161-761 1999   Tel: 0161-761 2020

LITTLE ACORNS
London House
271-273 King Street, London W6 9LZ
e-mail: acorns@dircon.co.uk
Fax: 020-8408 3077   Tel: 020-8563 0773

**LITTLE ADULTS ACADEMY & MODELLING
AGENCY Ltd**
Studio 11
Suite 13, Essex House
375-377 High Street
Stratford, London E15 4QZ
Website: www.littleadults.co.uk
e-mail: donna@littleadults.demon.co.uk
Fax: 020-8519 9797   Tel: 020-8519 9755

LINTON MANAGEMENT
In association with Coral Godby Theatre Workshop providing training to over 1300 members
representing
Child Actors, Adult Actors & Background Artists
available for
TV, Film, Theatre, Radio, Commercials, Voice overs etc.
Complimentary audition facilities and casting workshop available
Licenced Chaperones and Tutors supplied
Photo Directory & full cv's available on request

Established 1991

3 The Rock

Bury BL9 0JP

Tel: 0161 761 2020   Fax: 0161 761 1999
E-mail: Carol@lintonmanagement.freeserve.co.uk

KastKidZ © (Children's and young adult's theatrical agency)
For Castings and Headsheets contact
Tel/Fax: 0161 796-7073 / Mob 07905 646832 (Reece)
40 Sunnybank Road, Unsworth, Bury, BL9 8HF. Or email kastkidz@ntlworld.com
(Affiliated with Drama-Dance-Song School of Performing Arts)

LITTLE GEMS
11 Thorn Rd, Farnham, Surrey GU10 4TU
e-mail: littlegems30@hotmail.com
Mobile: 07960 978439   Tel/Fax: 01252 792078

LIVE & LOUD
The S.P.A.C.E.
188 St Vincents Street, 2nd Floor, Glasgow G2 5SP
e-mail: info@west-end-management.co.uk
Fax: 0141-226 8983   Tel: 0141-222 2942

LIVEWIRES CASTING AGENCY
PO Box 23199, Edinburgh EH7 5AH
e-mail: livewiresscotland@genie.co.uk
Fax: 0131-557 2437   Tel: 0131-557 2647

MOVIEMITES AGENCY
30 Spedan Close, Branch Hill
Hampstead, London NW3 7XF
Website: www.moviemitesagency.com
e-mail: kids@moviemitesagency.com
Fax: 020-7794 0771   Tel: 020-7431 5698

MRS WORTHINGTON'S
(7-16 Years)
16 Ouseley Road
London SW12 8EF   Tel/Fax: 020-8767 6944

NEXT GENERATION
e-mail: nextgeneration27@aol.com
          Tel/Fax: 020-8651 9070

NOEL CASTING
(Specialising in Character Actors and Ethnic and
Asian Actors)
Suite 501, International House
223 Regent Street, London W1B 2QD
e-mail: noelcasting@yahoo.com
Fax: 020-7544 1090   Tel: 020-7544 1010

NORTHERN FILM & DRAMA
PO Box 27, Tadcaster, North Yorks LS24 9XS
Website: www.connew.com/nfd
e-mail: alyson@connew.com
Mobile: 07932 653466   Tel: 01977 681949

NUTOPIA PERSONAL MANAGEMENT
Number 8, 132 Charing Cross Road
London WC2H 0LA
Website: www.nutopia.co.uk
Fax: 029-2070 9440   Mobile: 07801 493133

O'FARRELL STAGE & THEATRE SCHOOL
36 Shirley Street, Canning Town
London E16 1HU   Tel: 020-7511 9444

ORR THEATRE DANCE CENTRE & AGENCY
20 Bembridge Drive, Bolton BL3 1RJ
Website: www.orrdance.co.uk
e-mail: barbara@orrdance.co.uk
          Tel/Fax: 01204 579842

PALMER Jackie AGENCY
30 Daws Hill Lane, High Wycombe
Bucks HP11 1PW
Website: www.jackiepalmer.co.uk
e-mail: jackie.palmer@btinternet.com
Fax: 01494 510479   Tel: 01494 520978

PATMORE Sandra SCHOOL AND AGENCY
(Dancing, Drama & Acrobatic)
173 Uxbridge Road, Rickmansworth
Herts WD3 2DW   Tel/Fax: 01923 772542

PC THEATRICAL & MODEL AGENCY
10 Strathmore Gardens
Edgware, Middlesex HA8 5HJ
Website: www.twinagency.com
e-mail: twinagy@aol.com
Fax: 020-8933 3418   Tel: 020-8381 2229

PHA YOUTH
Tanzaro House, Ardwick Green North
Manchester M12 6FZ
Website: www.pha-agency.co.uk
e-mail: youth@pha-agency.co.uk
Fax: 0161-273 4567   Tel: 0161-273 4444

POLLYANNA MANAGEMENT
PO Box 30661, London E1W 3GG
Website: www.eada.demon.co.uk/pollyanna
e-mail: pollyanna-mgmt@yahoo.com
Fax: 020-7480 6761   Tel: 020-7702 1937

**POWER MODEL MANAGEMENT
CASTING AGENCY**
Capitol House, 2-4 Heigham Street
Norwich NR2 4TE
Website: www.powerchildmodels.co.uk
e-mail: powermodelmanagement@btinternet.com
Fax: 01603 621101   Tel: 01603 621100

RASCALS MODEL AGENCY
13 Jubilee Parade
Snakes Lane East
Woodford Green, Essex IG8 7QG
Website: www.rascals.co.uk
e-mail: kids@rascals.co.uk
Fax: 020-8559 1035   Tel: 020-8504 1111

RAVENSCOURT MANAGEMENT
Tandy House, 30-40 Dalling Road, London W6 0JB
e-mail: mark@ravenscourt.net
Fax: 020-8741 1786   Tel: 020-8741 0707

REDROOFS THEATRE SCHOOL AGENCY
Room 161, First Floor Property Building
Iver, Bucks SL0 0NH
Fax: 01753 785443   Tel: 01753 785444

REFLECTIONS AGENCY
9 Weavers Terrace, Fulham
London SW6 1QE   Tel/Fax: 020-7385 1537

REYNOLDS THEATRICAL AGENCY
Westgate House, Spital Street
Dartford, Kent DA1 2EH
Website: www.reynoldsgroup.co.uk
e-mail: info@reynoldsgroup.co.uk
Fax: 01634 329079   Tel: 01322 277200

RIDGEWAY STUDIOS SCHOOL OF PERFORMING ARTS
Fairley House, Andrews Lane
Cheshunt, Herts EN7 6LB
Website: www.ridgewaystudios.co.uk
e-mail: info@ridgewaystudios.co.uk
Fax: 01992 633844   Tel: 01992 633775

S.A.M. YOUTH AGENCY
London Road Business Centre
Suite 3:2, 106 London Road
Liverpool L3 5JY   Tel/Fax: 0151-608 9655

SBZ AGENCY
PO Box 350, Ashford, Kent TN24 9ZE
e-mail: sbzagency@aol.com   Tel/Fax: 01233 650045

SCALLYWAGS AGENCY Ltd
90-94 Ley Street, Ilford, Essex IG1 4BX
Website: www.scallywags.co.uk
e-mail: kids@scallywags.co.uk
Fax: 020-8553 4849   Tel: 020-8553 9999

SCHER ANNA THEATRE The
Anna Scher Theatre
70-72 Barnsbury Road, London N1 0ES
e-mail: abby@astm.co.uk
Fax: 020-7833 9467   Tel: 020-7278 2101

SCREAM MANAGEMENT
32 Clifton Street, Blackpool, Lancs FY1 1JP
Website: www.screammanagement.com
e-mail: info@screammanagement.com
Fax: 01253 750829   Tel: 01253 750820

SEQUINS THEATRICAL AGENCY
Winsome, 8 Summerhill Grove
Enfield EN1 2HY   Tel: 020-8360 4015

SHARONA STAGE SCHOOL AGENCY & MANAGEMENT
82 Grennell Road, Sutton, Surrey SM1 3DN
Fax: 020-8642 2364   Tel: 020-8642 9396

SINGER Sandra ASSOCIATES
21 Cotswold Road
Westcliff on Sea, Essex SS0 8AA
Website: www.sandrasinger.com
e-mail: sandrasingeruk@aol.com
Fax: 01702 339393   Tel: 01702 331616

SMITH Elisabeth Ltd
81 Headstone Road, Harrow, Middlesex HA1 1PQ
Website: www.elisabethsmith.com
e-mail: models@elisabethsmith.com
Fax: 020-8861 1880   Tel: 020-8863 2331

SOUTH WEST CASTINGS Ltd
The Courtyard
Whitchurch, Ross-on-Wye HR9 6DA
Website: www.southwestcasting.co.uk
e-mail: agent@southwestcasting.co.uk
Fax: 01600 891099   Tel: 01600 891160

SPEAKE Barbara AGENCY
East Acton Lane, London W3 7EG
e-mail: speakekids@aol.com
Fax: 020-8740 6542   Tel: 020-8743 6096

SPORTS ENTERTAINMENT & MEDIA GROUP
98 Cockfosters Road
Barnet, Herts EN4 0DP
Fax: 020-8447 4251   Tel: 020-8447 4250

STAGE 01 THEATRE SCHOOL & AGENCY
32 Westbury Lane, Buckhurst Hill, Essex IG9 5PL
Website: www.stage01.com
e-mail: stage01@lineone.net
Mobile: 07939 121154   Tel/Fax: 020-8506 0949

STAGE 84 YORKSHIRE SCHOOL OF PERFORMING ARTS
Old Bell Chapel, Town Lane
Bradford, West Yorks BD10 8PR
e-mail: valeriejackson@stage84.com
Mobile: 07785 244984   Tel/Fax: 01274 569197

STAGE KIDS DRAMA SCHOOL & AGENCY
1 Greenfield
Welwyn Garden City
Herts AL8 7HW
Website: www.stagekids.co.uk   Tel: 01707 328359

STAGE PLUS AGENCY
Park Meadow House, 28 Wycombe Road
Princes Risborough
Bucks HP27 0DH   Tel: 01844 342137

STAGECOACH AGENCY
The Courthouse, Elm Grove
Walton-on-Thames, Surrey KT12 1LZ
Website: www.stagecoach.co.uk
e-mail: vmoore@stagecoach.co.uk
Fax: 01932 222894   Tel: 01932 254333

STARLINGS THEATRICAL AGENCY
45 Viola Close, South Ockendon, Essex RM15 6JF
Website: www.webspawner.com/users/starlings
e-mail: starlings@blueyonder.co.uk
Mobile: 07941 653463   Tel: 01708 859109

STARSHINE CHILDREN'S THEATRE WORKSHOP & AGENCY
St Helier Congregational Church
Green Lane, Morden, Surrey SM4
e-mail: starshinectw@aol.com   Mobile: 07939 398630

STONELANDS SCHOOL OF BALLET & THEATRE ARTS
170A Church Road
Hove, East Sussex BN3 2DJ
Website: www.stonelandsschool.co.uk
e-mail: www@stonelandsschool.co.uk
Fax: 01273 770444   Tel: 01273 770445

SUMMERS Mark MANAGEMENT & AGENCY
9 Hansard Mews
Kensington, London W14 8BJ
Website: www.marksummers.com
e-mail: mark@marksummers.com
Fax: 0870 4435623   Tel: 0870 4435621

SUPERARTS AGENCY
26-28 Ambergate Street
London SE17 3RX   Tel/Fax: 020-7735 4975

T.A.A.
(See ARTS ACADEMY The)

TANWOOD
46 Bath Road, Swindon, Wilts SN1 4AY
Fax: 01793 643219   Tel: 01793 523895

THAMES VALLEY THEATRICAL AGENCY
PO Box 233, Wallingford, Oxfordshire OX10 9ZN
Website: www.thamesvalleytheatricalagency.co.uk
e-mail: donna@thamesvalleytheatricalagency.co.uk
                         Tel/Fax: 01491 659009

THEATRE ARTS (WEST LONDON)
18 Kingsdale Gardens
Notting Hill, London W11 4TZ
e-mail: theatreartswestlondon@hotmail.com
                         Tel/Fax: 020-7603 3471

THEATRE EXPRESS
PO Box 97, Cleveleys FY5 5XA   Tel: 0870 2430462

THOMPSON Jim CHILDREN'S SECTION
(Jenny Donnison)
Herricks, School Lane
Arundel, West Sussex BN18 9DR
Fax: 01903 885887   Tel: 01903 885757

TOP-SPOTS AGENCY
(Commercials, Films, Babies to Adults)
314 Haydons Road
Wimbledon, London SW19 8JZ
Website: www.topspots.co.uk   Tel: 020-8543 7766

TOTS 2 TEENS Ltd
6 Fulham Park Studios
Fulham Park Road
London SW6 4LW
Website: www.tots2teens.ltd.uk
e-mail: natalie@tots2teens.ltd.uk
Fax: 020-7371 9953   Tel: 020-7610 9529

TOTS 2 TEENS

**Representing
children and teenagers for Film,
Television, Theatre, Commercials
and Modelling**

**Tel: 020 7610 9529 Fax: 020 7371 9953
e-mail: natalie@tots2teens.ltd.uk**

TOTS-TWENTIES AGENCY
Suite 3 Ground Floor, Clements Court
Clements Lane, Ilford, Essex IG1 2QY
Website: www.tots-twenties.co.uk
e-mail: sara@tots-twenties.co.uk
Fax: 020-8553 1880   Tel: 020-8478 1848

TROUPERS.COM
3 Shirragh Way, Port Erin, Isle of Man
Website: www.troupers.com
e-mail: info@troupers.com   Mobile: 07624 470123

TRULY SCRUMPTIOUS Ltd
16-24 Underwood Street, London N1 7JQ
Website: www.trulyscrumptious.co.uk
e-mail: bookings@trulyscrumptious.co.uk
Fax: 020-7251 5767   Tel: 020-7608 3806

TUESDAYS CHILD
Oakfield House, Tytherington Business Park
Springwood Way
Macclesfield, Cheshire SK10 2XA
Website: www.tuesdayschildagency.co.uk
e-mail: bookings@tuesdayschildagency.co.uk
Tel/Fax: 01625 501765   Tel: 01625 612244

TWINS
(see PC THEATRICAL & MODEL AGENCY)

TWINS & TRIPLETS
(Identical Babies, Children, Teenagers & Adults
for Film/Television)
Holmhurst Road
Upper Belvedere, Kent DA17 6HW
Website: www.twins.triplets.freeuk.com
e-mail: twinsontv@aol.com
Fax: 01322 447250   Tel: 01322 440184

URBAN ANGELS MODELLING AGENCY
Unit 310, The Chandlery
50 Westminster Bridge Road, London SE1 7QY
e-mail: intro@urbanangelsagency.com
Fax: 0870 8710046   Tel: 0870 8710045

VALLÉ ACADEMY THEATRICAL AGENCY The
Wilton House, Delamare Road
Cheshunt, Herts EN8 9SG
Website: www.valleacademy.co.uk
e-mail: agency@valleacademy.co.uk
Fax: 01992 622868   Tel: 01992 622861

VISIONS AGENCY
Foxbury Studios, 39A Foxbury Road
Bromley, Kent BR1 4DG
e-mail: frances.cooper@talk21.com
                         Tel/Fax: 020-8466 7782

WHITEHALL PERFORMING ARTS CENTRE
Rayleigh Road, Leigh-on-Sea
Essex SS9 5UU   Tel/Fax: 01702 529290

WHIZZ KIDS STAGE & SCREEN AGENCY
3 Marshall Road, Cambridge CB1 7TY
Website: www.whizzkidsdrama.co.uk
e-mail: goforit@whizzkidsdrama.co.uk
Fax: 01223 512431   Tel: 01223 416474

WINGS AGENCY
(Affiliated to Angels Theatre School)
19 Victoria Road, Godalming, Surrey GU7 1JR
e-mail: wingsagency@hotmail.com
Fax: 01483 429966   Tel: 01483 428844

WYSE AGENCY
1 Hill Farm Road, Whittlesford, Cambs CB2 4NB
e-mail: frances.wyse@btinternet.com
Fax: 01223 839414   Tel: 01223 832288

YOUNG 'UNS AGENCY
Sylvia Young Theatre School
Rossmore Road, Marylebone, London NW1 6NJ
e-mail: enquiries@youngunsagency.co.uk
Fax: 020-7723 1040   Tel: 020-7723 0037

YOUNG ACTORS FILE The
65 Stafford Street, Old Town, Swindon SN1 3PF
e-mail: young.actorsfile@virgin.net
                         Tel/Fax: 01793 423688

YOUNGBLOOD
The Talent Partnership, Riverside Studios
Crisp Road, Hammersmith, London W6 9RL
e-mail: info@thetalentpartnership.co.uk
Fax: 020-8237 1041   Tel: 020-8237 1040

YOUNGSTAR AGENCY
Starlight Television & Theatre School
5 Union Castle House, Canute Road
Southampton SO14 3FJ
e-mail: starlightyt@aol.com
Fax: 023-8045 5816   Tel: 023-8033 9322

2 CASTING AGENCY & MANAGEMENT
Tiptoes House, 2 Collingwood Place, Layton
Blackpool FY3 8HU
Fax: 01253 302610   Tel: 01253 302614

10 TWENTY TWO CASTING
PO Box 1022, Liverpool L69 5WZ
Fax: 0151-207 4230   Tel: 0151-298 1022

2020 CASTING Ltd
2020 Hopgood Street, London W12 7JU
Website: www.2020casting.com
e-mail: info@2020casting.com
Fax: 020-8735 2727   Tel: 020-8746 2020

A LITTLE EXTRA!
67 Stafford Street
Old Town, Swindon, Wiltshire SN1 3PF
Website: www.a-little-extra.co.uk
e-mail: young.actorsfile@virgin.net
                         Tel/Fax: 01793 423688

**ADF MANAGEMENT &
MODEL CASTING AGENCY**
17 Thorley Lane, Timperley, Altrincham WA15
Website: www.adfmanagement.co.uk
e-mail: info@adfmanagement.co.uk
Fax: 0161-282 5083   Tel: 0870 7771360

ALLSORTS
1 Cathedral Street, London SE1 9DE
Website: www.allsortstheagency.co.uk
e-mail: joannaallsorts@aol.com
Fax: 020-7403 1656   Tel: 020-7403 4834

AVENUE ARTISTES Ltd
8 Winn Road, Southampton SO17 1EN
Website: www.avenueartistes.com
e-mail: info@avenueartistes.com
Fax: 023-8090 5703   Tel: 023-8055 1000

AWA - ANDREA WILDER AGENCY
23 Cambrian Drive, Colwyn Bay, Conwy LL28 4SL
Website: www.awagency.co.uk
e-mail: casting@awagency.co.uk
Fax: 07092 249314   Tel: 01492 547542

BALDIES CASTING AGENCY
(The only agency purely for bald people)
6 Marlott Road, Poole, Dorset BH15 3DX
Mobile: 07860 290437   Tel: 01202 666001

BILL & CHRISTIAN @JB AGENCY ONLINE Ltd
7 Stonehills Mansions, 8 Streatham High Road
London SW16 1DD
Website: www.jb-agency.com
e-mail: christian@jb-agency.com
Fax: 020-8769 9567   Tel: 020-8769 0123

BRISTOL EXTRA SERVICE TEAM (B.E.S.T.)
(Ernest Jones)
(Film & TV Actors, Extras, Speciality Artists)
21 Ellesmere, Thornbury, Near Bristol BS35 2ER
e-mail: ernestjones.best@virgin.net
Mobile: 07951 955759   Tel/Fax: 01454 411628

BROADCASTING
Unit 23 Canalot Studios, 222 Kensal Road
London W10 5BN
Fax: 020-7460 5223   Tel: 020-7460 5222

BROMLEY CASTING
(Film & TV)
77 Widmore Road, Bromley, Kent BR1 3AA
Website: www.bromleycasting.tv
e-mail: admin@bromleycasting.tv
                         Tel/Fax: 020-8466 8239

BROOK Dolly CASTING AGENCY
PO Box 5436, Dunmow CM6 1WW
Fax: 01371 875996   Tel: 01371 875767

NEMESIS

www.nemesisagency.co.uk

Extras, Walk-Ons, Crowd Artistes, Fashion and Photographic Models
Largest selection of professional equity and non equity supporting artistes in the North West

Manchester Head Office tel. 0161 237 1515
Leeds tel. 0113 244 4644 **Birmingham** tel. 0121 554 7878
Premier city centre casting studios in all three locations

CAIRNS AGENCY The
(Maureen Cairns)
Forsyth House, 1st Floor
111 Union Street, Glasgow G1 3TA
e-mail: the-cairns-agency@west-end-management.co.uk
Fax: 0141-226 8983   Tel: 0141-226 8941

CAMCAST
Laragain
Upper Banavie, Fort William
Inverness-shire PH33 7PB
Website: www.camcast.co.uk
e-mail: anne@camcast.co.uk
Fax: 01397 772456   Tel: 01397 772523

CASTING COLLECTIVE Ltd The
Olympic House
317-321 Latimer Road, London W10 6RA
e-mail: enquiries@castingcollective.co.uk
Fax: 020-8962 0333   Tel: 020-8962 0099

CASTING FACES UK
Global House
1 Ashley Avenue
Epsom, Surrey KT18 5AD
Website: www.castingfaces.com
e-mail: office@castingfaces.com
Fax: 0871 4337304   Tel: 020-8823 9333

CASTING NETWORK Ltd The
122A The Broadway
Tolworth, Surbiton, Surrey KT6 7HT
Website: www.thecastingnetwork.co.uk
e-mail: casting-network@talk21.com
Fax: 020-8390 0605   Tel: 020-8339 9090

CELEX CASTING & MANAGEMENT
(Children available)
11 Glencroft Drive, Stenson Fields, Derby DE24 3LS
Website: www.celex.co.uk
e-mail: anne@celex.co.uk
Fax: 01332 232115   Tel: 01332 232445

CENTRAL CASTING Ltd
(See also KNIGHT Ray CASTING)
21A Lambolle Place
Belsize Park, London NW3 4PG
Website: www.rayknight.co.uk
e-mail: casting@rayknight.co.uk
Fax: 020-7722 2322   Tel: 020-7722 4111

COAST 2 COAST PERSONALITIES
6 Fulham Park Studios, Fulham Park Road
London SW6 4LW
Website: www.coast2coastpersonalities.com
e-mail: natalie@c2cp.co.uk
Fax: 020-7371 9953   Tel: 020-7736 1602

ELLIOTT AGENCY
The Specialists for Professional 1st Class Walk-ons

The Elliott Agency, PO Box 2772, Lewes, Sussex BN8 4DW, UK
Tel: 00 44 (0)1273 401264 Fax: 00 44 (0)1273 400814 Internet: www.elliottagency.co.uk

MAC-10

Casting

Actors
Walk-ons
Presenters
Models
Dancers
Licensed chaperones

Tel: +44 (0) 161 275 9510

Tel / Fax: +44 (0) 161 275 9610

Office 69
2 Hellidon Close
Ardwick
Manchester
M12 4AH

info@MAC-10.co.uk
www.MAC-10.co.uk

CORNWALL FILM AGENCY
East Trevelmond Farm
Trevelmond, Liskeard, Cornwall PL14 4LY
e-mail: frances@cornwall-film-agency.fsnet.co.uk
Tel/Fax: 01579 321858

CYBER-ARTISTS
In The Can Ltd, The Studio, Kingsway Court
Queen's Gardens, Hove BN3 2LP
Website: www.cyberartists.co.uk
e-mail: cyber.1@btclick.com
Fax: 01273 739984   Tel: 01273 821821

DAVID AGENCY The
153 Battersea Rise, London SW11 1HP
Website: www.davidagency.net
e-mail: casting@davidagency.net
Fax: 020-7924 2334   Tel: 020-7223 7720

DRAG QUEEN AGENCY The
(David Gordon)
58 Newland Road
Worthing, West Sussex BN11 1JX
e-mail: lavendersub@hotmail.com
Tel: 01903 202895

ELLIOTT AGENCY The
PO Box 2772, Lewes, Sussex BN8 4DW
Website: www.elliottagency.co.uk
e-mail: info@elliottagency.co.uk
Fax: 01273 400814   Tel: 01273 401264

EUROKIDS & ADULTS INTERNATIONAL CASTING & MODEL AGENCY
The Warehouse Studios, Glaziers Lane, Culcheth
Warrington, Cheshire WA3 4AQ
Website: www.eka-agency.com
e-mail: info@eka-agency.com
Fax: 01925 767563   Tel: 0871 7501575

EXTRAS UNLIMITED.COM
9 Hansard Mews, Kensington, London W14 8BJ
Website: www.extrasunlimited.com
e-mail: info@extrasunlimited.com
Fax: 0870 4435621   Tel: 0870 4435622

EXTRASPECIAL Ltd
38 Commercial Street, London E1 6LP
Website: www.extraspecial2000.com
e-mail: info@skybluecasting.com
Fax: 020-7375 1466   Tel: 020-7375 1400

FACES CASTING AGENCY
95 Ditchling Road, Brighton, East Sussex BN1 4ST
Fax: 01273 719165   Tel: 01273 571989

FACT PRESENTATIONS
Unit 123, Aberdeen House, The Aberdeen Centre
22-24 Highbury Grove, London N1 2EA
e-mail: factartists@onetel.net.uk
Fax: 020-7359 2581   Tel: 020-7359 4289

FBI AGENCY Ltd The
PO Box 250, Leeds LS1 2AZ
e-mail: casting@fbi-agency.ltd.uk Tel/Fax: 07050 222747

FBI Ltd
4th Floor, 21-24 Kirby Street, London EC1N 8TS
Website: www.fullybooked-inc.com
e-mail: fbi@dircon.co.uk
Fax: 020-7242 8125   Tel: 020-7242 5542

FLOSS EXTRAS
14 Ritz Buildings
Church Road, Tunbridge Wells, Kent TN1 1HP
Website: www.newmangroup.co.uk
e-mail: floss.extras@newmangroup.co.uk
Fax: 01892 514173   Tel: 01892 524122

FRESH AGENTS
Whitepoint Studios
Unit 2, Hove Business Centre Fonthill Road
Hove, East Sussex BN3 6HA
Website: www.freshagents.com
e-mail: info@freshagents.com
Fax: 01273 711778   Tel: 01273 711777

G2
15 Lexham Mews. London W8 6JW
Website: www.g2casting.com
e-mail: g2@galloways.ltd.uk
Fax: 020-7376 2416   Tel: 020-7376 2133

GETTINON.TV
8 Hop Gardens, London WC2N 4EH
Website: www.gettinon.tv
e-mail: info@gettinon.tv
Fax: 020-7240 5599   Tel: 020-7240 9966

GUYS & DOLLS CASTING
Trafalgar House
Grenville Place, Mill Hill, London NW7 3SA
Fax: 020-8381 0080   Tel: 020-8906 4144

HOWE Janet CASTING AGENCY
Studio 1, Whitebridge Estate
Whitebridge Lane Stone, Staffs ST15 8LQ
e-mail: janet@jhowecasting.fsbusiness.co.uk
Tel/Fax: 01785 818480   Tel/Fax: 01785 816888

40 Princess Street, Manchester M1 6DE
e-mail: janet@jhowecasting.fsbusiness.co.uk
Mobile: 07801 942178   Tel/Fax: 0161-233 0700

J B AGENCY Ltd
7 Stonehill Mansions, 8 Streatham High Road
London SW16 1DD
Fax: 020-8769 9567   Tel: 020-8769 0123

JACLYN 2000
52 Bessember Road, Norwich, Norfok NR4 6DQ
Website: www.jaclyn2000.co.uk
Fax: 01603 612532   Tel: 01603 622027

KNIGHT Ray CASTING
(See also CENTRAL CASTING Ltd)
21A Lambolle Place, Belsize Park, London NW3 4PG
Website: www.rayknight.co.uk
e-mail: casting@rayknight.co.uk
Fax: 020-7722 2322   Tel: 020-7722 4111

KREATE Productions
Unit 210, 30 Great Guildford Street, London SE1 0HS
e-mail: kreate@btconnect.com
Fax: 020-7401 3003   Tel: 020-7401 9007

LEE'S PEOPLE
60 Poland Street, London W1F 7NT
Website: www.lees-people.co.uk
e-mail: lee@lees-people.co.uk
Fax: 020-7734 3033   Tel: 020-7734 5775

LEGENDS CASTING AGENCY
Jubilee Business Centre, Suite 16, Exeter Road
London NW2 2UF
e-mail: castingextras@yahoo.co.uk
Fax: 020-8453 7533   Tel: 020-8453 7536

LEMON CASTING & MANAGEMENT
23 Lucas Road, Farnworth, Bolton BL4 9RP
e-mail: andreaking.tv@ntlworld.com
Mobile: 07752 455510   Tel/Fax: 01204 456253

LINTON MANAGEMENT
3 The Rock, Bury BL9 0JP
Fax: 0161-761 1999   Tel: 0161-761 2020

MAC-10 CASTING AGENCY
Office 69, 2 Hellidon Close, Ardwick
Manchester M12 4AH
Website: www.mac-10.co.uk
e-mail: info@mac-10.co.uk
Fax: 0161-275 9610   Tel: 0161-275 9510

MAD DOG CASTING Ltd
Top Floor, 10 Warwick Street, London W1B 5LZ
e-mail: info@maddogcasting.com
Fax: 020-7287 5983   Tel: 020-7434 1211

M.E.P. MANAGEMENT
1 Malvern Avenue, Highams Park, London E4 9NP
Website: www.global-theatre-company.net
e-mail: mep@btclick.com   Tel/Fax: 020-8523 3540

NEMESIS AGENCY
54 Princess Street, Manchester M1 6HS
Website: www.nemesisagency.co.uk
Fax: 0161-236 1771   Tel: 0161-237 1515

NIDGES CASTING AGENCY
Half Moon Chambers, Chapel Walks
Manchester M2 1HN
e-mail: moneypenny@nidgescasting.co.uk
Fax: 0161-832 5219   Tel: 0161-832 8259

NORTHERN PROFESSIONALS CASTING COMPANY
21 Cresswell Avenue, North Shields
Tyne & Wear NE29 9BQ
e-mail: bill.gerard@northpro83.freeserve.co.uk
Fax: 0191-296 3243   Tel: 0191-257 8635

ORIENTAL AFRO ASIAN ARTISTS
(FBI Ltd) 4th Floor, 20-24 Kirby St, London EC1N 8TS
Website: www.fullybooked-inc.com
e-mail: fbi@dircon.co.uk
Fax: 020-7242 8125   Tel: 020-7242 5542

ORIENTAL CASTING AGENCY Ltd (Peggy Sirr)
(Afro/Asian Artists)
1 Wyatt Park Road, Streatham Hill, London SW2 3TN
Website: www.orientalcasting.com
e-mail: peggy.sirr@btconnect.com
Fax: 020-8674 9303   Tel: 020-8671 8538

PC THEATRICAL & MODEL AGENCY
10 Strathmore Gdns, Edgware, Middlesex HA8 5HJ
Website: www.twinagency.com
e-mail: twinagy@aol.com
Fax: 020-8933 3418   Tel: 020-8381 2229

PHA CASTING
Tanzaro House, Ardwick Green North
Manchester M12 6FZ
Website: www.pha-agency.co.uk
e-mail: info@pha-agency.co.uk
Fax: 0161-273 4567   Tel: 0161-273 4444

PHOENIX AGENCY
PO Box 387, Bristol BS99 3JZ
Fax: 0117-973 4160   Tel: 0117-973 1100

POWER MODEL MANAGEMENT CASTING AGENCY
Capitol Hse, 2-4 Heigham St, Norwich NR2 4TE
Website: www.powermodelmanagement.co.uk
e-mail: powermodelmanagement@btinternet.com
Fax: 01603 621101   Tel: 01603 621100

PRAETORIAN ASSOCIATES
(Specialist Action Extras)
Pierie Lodge, 61 Spruce Hills, London E17 4LB
Website: www.praetorianasc.com
e-mail: info@praetorianasc.com
Fax: 020-8923 7177   Tel: 020-8923 9075

PRIDE ARTIST MANAGEMENT
The Burnside Centre, Burnside Crescent
Middleton
Manchester M24 5NN
Website: www.pride-artist-management.co.uk
e-mail: extras@pride-artist-management.co.uk
                                Tel/Fax: 0161-643 6266

REYNOLDS Sandra MODEL & CASTING AGENTS
62 Bell Street
London NW1 6SP
Website: www.sandrareynolds.co.uk
e-mail: tessa@sandrareynolds.co.uk
Fax: 020-7387 5848   Tel: 020-7387 5858

35 St Georges Street, Norwich NR3 1DA
Fax: 01603 219825   Tel: 01603 623842

RUBICON ARTISTS AGENCY
27 Inderwick Road, Crouch End
London N8 9LB   Tel/Fax: 020-8374 1836

SKYBLUE CASTING Ltd
38 Commercial Street, London E1 6LP
e-mail: info@skyblue-extraspecial.com
Fax: 020-7375 1466   Tel: 020-7375 1400

SO DAM TUFF Ltd
(Men Only)
The Coach House, Battersea Square
136 West Bridge Road
London SW11 3PF
Website: www.sodamtuff.com
e-mail: tiger@sodamtuff.com
Fax: 020-7352 0001   Tel: 020-7223 7377

SOUTH WEST CASTING Ltd
The Courtyard, Whitchurch, Ross-on-Wye HR9 6DA
Website: www.southwestcasting.co.uk
e-mail: agent@southwestcasting.co.uk
Fax: 01600 891099   Tel: 01600 891160

STAV'S CAST
82 Station Crescent, Sth Tottenham N15 5BD
Website: www.stavscasting.co.uk
e-mail: stavscast@yahoo.co.uk
Mobile: 07816 336158   Tel: 020-8802 6341

TONER CASTING Ltd
Unit E6, Brunswick Small Business Centre
Brunswick Dock, Liverpool L3 4BD
Website: www.tonercasting.com
e-mail: tonercasting@btconnect.com
Fax: 0151-707 8414   Tel: 0151-708 6400

TROUPERS.COM
3 Shirragh Way, Port Erin, Isle of Man
Website: www.troupers.com
e-mail: info@troupers.com   Mobile: 07624 470123

UGLY ENTERPRISES Ltd
Tigris House, 256 Edgware Road, London W2 1DS
Website: www.ugly.org   e-mail: info@ugly.org
Fax: 020-7402 0507   Tel: 020-7402 5564

UNITED COLOURS OF LONDON Ltd
(FBI) 4th Floor, 20-24 Kirby Street, London EC1N 8TS
Website: www.fullybooked-inc.com
e-mail: fbi@dircon.co.uk
Fax: 020-7242 8125   Tel: 020-7242 5542

VIABLE NETWORKS Ltd
(Trading as Zen Directories)
Suite 21, 571 Finchley Rd, Hampstead, NW3 7BN
Website: www.zendirectories.co.uk
e-mail: zendirectories@talk21.com
Fax: 020-8458 9718   Tel: 020-8458 9671

For information regarding membership of the
Personal Managers' Association please contact:
Personal Managers' Association Ltd
Rivercroft, 1 Summer Road, East Molesey, Surrey KT8 9LX
Tel: 020-8398 9796
* Denotes PMA Membership

A & B PERSONAL MANAGEMENT Ltd*
Paurelle House
91 Regent Street, London W1B 4EL
e-mail: billellis@aandb.co.uk
Fax: 020-7734 6318   Tel: 020-7734 6047

A M HEATH & Co Ltd
(Fiction & Non-Fiction only)
79 St Martin's Lane, London WC2N 4RE
Fax: 020-7497 2561   Tel: 020-7836 4271

ABNER STEIN
10 Roland Gardens
London SW7 3PH
e-mail: abner@abnerstein.co.uk
Fax: 020-7370 6316   Tel: 020-7373 0456

ACTAC
7 Isles Court, Ramsbury
Wiltshire SN8 2QW
Fax: 01672 520166   Tel: 01672 520274

AGENCY (LONDON) Ltd The*
24 Pottery Lane
Holland Park, London W11 4LZ
e-mail: info@theagency.co.uk
Fax: 020-7727 9037   Tel: 020-7727 1346

A.J. ASSOCIATES LITERARY AGENTS Ltd
Scripts Department
Rough Lee Barn
Higher House Lane, White Coppice
Chorley PR6 9BU
e-mail: info@ajassociates.net
Tel/Fax: 01257 273148   Tel: 01257 269788

ASPER Pauline*
Jacobs Cottage, Reservoir Lane
Sedlescombe, East Sussex TN33 0PJ
e-mail: pauline.asper@virgin.net
                              Tel/Fax: 01424 870412

BERLIN ASSOCIATES
14 Floral Street
London WC2E 9DH   Tel: 020-7287 9000

BLAKE FRIEDMANN
(Novels, Non-Fiction & TV/Film Scripts)
122 Arlington Road
London NW1 7HP
Website: www.blakefriedmann.co.uk
e-mail: julian@blakefriedmann.co.uk
Fax: 020-7284 0442   Tel: 020-7284 0408

BRITTEN Nigel MANAGEMENT*
Suite 508, Riverbank House
1 Putney Bridge Approach
London SW6 3JD
e-mail: nbm.office@virgin.net
Fax: 020-7384 3862   Tel: 020-7384 3842

BRODIE Alan REPRESENTATION Ltd*
(Incorporating Michael Imison Playwrights)
211 Piccadilly
London W1J 9HF
Website: www.alanbrodie.com
e-mail: info@alanbrodie.com
Fax: 020-7917 2872   Tel: 020-7917 2871

BRYANT Peter (WRITERS)
3 Jasper Road
London SE19 1SJ
Fax: 020-8670 7310   Tel: 020-8670 7820

BURKEMAN Brie*
14 Neville Court
Abbey Road, London NW8 9DD
e-mail: brie.burkeman@mail.com
Fax: 0709 2239111   Tel: 0709 2239113

CANN Alexandra REPRESENTATION*
12 Abingdon Road, London W8 6AF
e-mail: enquiries@alexandracann.com
Fax: 020-7938 4228   Tel: 020-7938 4002

CASAROTTO RAMSAY & ASSOCIATES Ltd*
National House
60-66 Wardour Street
London W1V 4ND
Website: www.casarotto.uk.com
e-mail: agents@casarotto.uk.com
Fax: 020-7287 9128   Tel: 020-7287 4450

CLOWES Jonathan Ltd*
10 Iron Bridge House
Bridge Approach
London NW1 8BD
Fax: 020-7722 7677   Tel: 020-7722 7674

COCHRANE Elspeth PERSONAL MANAGEMENT*
Suite 7
23 The Coda Centre
189 Munster Road
Fulham, London SW6 6AW
e-mail: info@pji.uk.com
Fax: 020-7381 3301   Tel: 020-7381 5525

CREATIVE MEDIA CONSULTANCY
(No unsolicited scripts, first instance sypnopsis only)
22 Kingsbury Avenue, Dunstable
Bedfordshire LU5 4PU   Tel/Fax: 01582 510869

CURTIS BROWN GROUP Ltd*
Haymarket House
28-29 Haymarket
London SW1Y 4SP
e-mail: cb@curtisbrown.co.uk
Fax: 020-7393 4401   Tel: 020-7396 6600

DAISH Judy ASSOCIATES Ltd*
2 St Charles Place, London W10 6EG
Fax: 020-8964 8966   Tel: 020-8964 8811

DENCH ARNOLD AGENCY The*
10 Newburgh Street
London W1F 7RN
e-mail: contact@dencharnold.com
Fax: 020-7439 1355   Tel: 020-7437 4551

de WOLFE Felix*
Garden Offices
51 Maida Vale, London W9 1SD
e-mail: info@felixdewolfe.com
Fax: 020-7289 5731   Tel: 020-7289 5770

DREW Bryan Ltd
Mezzanine, Quadrant House
80-82 Regent Street, London W1B 5AU
e-mail: bryan@bryandrewltd.com
Fax: 020-7437 0561   Tel: 020-7437 2293

FARNES Norma MANAGEMENT
9 Orme Court, London W2 4RL
Fax: 020-7792 2110   Tel: 020-7727 1544

FILLINGHAM Janet ASSOCIATES
52 Lowther Road, London SW13 9NU
e-mail: janet@jfillassoc.co.uk
Fax: 020-8748 7374   Tel: 020-8748 5594

FILM RIGHTS Ltd
Mezzanine, Quadrant House
80-82 Regent Street, London W1B 5AU
Website: www.filmrights.ltd.uk
e-mail: information@filmrights.ltd.uk
Fax: 020-7734 0044   Tel: 020-7734 9911

FITCH Laurence Ltd
Mezzanine
Quadrant House
80-82 Regent Street, London W1B 5AU
Fax: 020-7734 0044   Tel: 020-7734 9911

FOSTER Jill Ltd*
9 Barb Mews, London W6 7PA
Fax: 020-7602 9336   Tel: 020-7602 1263

FRENCH Samuel Ltd*
52 Fitzroy Street
Fitzrovia, London W1T 5JR
Website: www.samuelfrench-london.co.uk
e-mail: theatre@samuelfrench-london.co.uk
Fax: 020-7387 2161   Tel: 020-7387 9373

FUTERMAN, ROSE & ASSOCIATES
(TV/Film/Stage Play Scripts)
Heston Court Business Park
Camp Road, Wimbledon
London SW19 4UW
Website: www.futermanrose.co.uk
e-mail: guy@futermanrose.co.uk
Fax: 020-8605 2162   Tel: 020-8947 0188

GILLIS Pamela MANAGEMENT
46 Sheldon Avenue
London N6 4JR
Fax: 020-8341 5564   Tel: 020-8340 7868

GLASS Eric Ltd
25 Ladbroke Grove
London W11 1PS
e-mail: eglassltd@aol.com
Fax: 020-7229 6220   Tel: 020-7229 9500

HALL Rod AGENCY Ltd The*
3 Charlotte Mews
London W1T 4DZ
Website: www.rodhallagency.com
e-mail: office@rodhallagency.com
Fax: 020-7637 0807   Tel: 020-7637 0706

HANCOCK Roger Ltd*
4 Water Lane
London NW1 8NZ
e-mail: info@rogerhancock.com
Fax: 020-7267 0705   Tel: 020-7267 4418

HATTON Richard Ltd*
29 Roehampton Gate
London SW15 5JR
Fax: 020-8876 8278   Tel: 020-8876 6699

HIGHAM David ASSOCIATES Ltd*
5-8 Lower John Street
Golden Square
London W1F 9HA
e-mail: dha@davidhigham.co.uk
Fax: 020-7437 1072   Tel: 020-7434 5900

HOSKINS Valerie ASSOCIATES Ltd
20 Charlotte Street, London W1T 2NA
e-mail: vha@vhassociates.co.uk
Fax: 020-7637 4493   Tel: 020-7637 4490

HOWARD Amanda ASSOCIATES Ltd*
21 Berwick Street, London W1F 0PZ
Fax: 020-7287 7785   Tel: 020-7287 9277

HURLEY LOWE MANAGEMENT*
3 Cromwell Place, London SW7 2JE
Fax: 020-7589 9405   Tel: 020-7581 1515

I C M (International Creative Management)*
Oxford House, 76 Oxford Street, London W1D 1BS
Fax: 020-7323 0101   Tel: 020-7636 6565

IMISON Michael PLAYWRIGHTS Ltd
(See BRODIE Alan REPRESENTATION Ltd)

KANAL Roberta
82 Constance Road, Twickenham
Middlesex TW2 7JA
Fax: 020-8894 7952   Tel: 020-8894 2277

KASS Michelle ASSOCIATES*
36-38 Glasshouse Street, London W1B 5DL
Fax: 020-7734 3394   Tel: 020-7439 1624

LE BARS Tessa MANAGEMENT*
(Existing Clients Only)
54 Birchwood Road, Petts Wood, Kent BR5 1NZ
e-mail: tessa.lebars@ntlworld.com
Mobile: 07860 287255   Tel/Fax: 01689 837084

LONDON MANAGEMENT*
14 Floral Street
London WC2E 9DH   Tel: 020-7287 9000

LOWE Ian
Glan Dulas
Cusop, Hay-on-Wye, Hereford HR3 5RQ
e-mail: ianlowe@scripts-uk.demon.co.uk
Tel/Fax: 01497 821780

MACFARLANE CHARD ASSOCIATES Ltd*
33 Percy Street, London W1T 2LN
Website: www.macfarlane-chard.co.uk
e-mail: derick@macfarlane-chard.co.uk
Fax: 020-7636 7751   Tel: 020-7636 7751

MACNAUGHTON LORD 2000 Ltd
19 Margravine Gardens, London W6 8RL
Website: www.ml2000.org.uk
e-mail: info@ml2000.org.uk
Fax: 020-8741 7443   Tel: 020-8741 0606

MANN Andrew Ltd*
1 Old Compton Street
London W1D 5JA
e-mail: manscript@onetel.net.uk
Fax: 020-7287 9264   Tel: 020-7734 4751

MANS Johnny PRODUCTIONS Ltd
PO Box 196, Hoddesdon, Herts EN10 7WQ
Fax: 01992 470516   Tel: 01992 470907

MARJACQ SCRIPTS Ltd
34 Devonshire Place
London W1G 6JW
Website: www.marjacq.com
e-mail: enquiries@marjacq.com
Fax: 020-7935 9115   Tel: 020-7935 9499

MARVIN Blanche*
21A St Johns Wood High Street
London NW8 7NG
e-mail: blanchemarvin17@hotmail.com
Tel/Fax: 020-7722 2313

M.B.A. LITERARY AGENTS Ltd*
62 Grafton Way, London W1T 5DW
e-mail: agent@mbalit.co.uk
Fax: 020-7387 2042   Tel: 020-7387 2076

McLEAN Bill PERSONAL MANAGEMENT Ltd
23B Deodar Road
London SW15 2NP   Tel: 020-8789 8191

ML 2000 Ltd
(See MACNAUGHTON LORD 2000 Ltd)

MORRIS William AGENCY (UK) Ltd*
52-53 Poland Street
London W1F 7LX
Fax: 020-7534 6900   Tel: 020-7534 6800

NARROW ROAD COMPANY The*
182 Brighton Road
Coulsdon, Surrey CR5 2NF
e-mail: richardireson@narrowroad.co.uk
Fax: 020-8763 2558   Tel: 020-8763 9895

P F D*
Drury House
34-43 Russell Street, London WC2B 5HA
Fax: 020-7836 9539   Tel: 020-7344 1000

PLAYS AND MUSICALS GROUP The
Lantern House, 84 Littlehaven Lane
Horsham, West Sussex RH12 4JB
Website: www.playsandmusicals.co.uk
e-mail: sales@playsandmusicals.co.uk
Fax: 0700 5938843   Tel: 0700 5938842

POLLINGER Ltd
9 Staple Inn
Holborn, London WC1V 7QH
Website: www.pollingerltd.com
e-mail: info@pollingerltd.com
Fax: 020-7242 5737   Tel: 020-7404 0342

ROSICA COLIN Ltd
1 Clareville Grove Mews
London SW7 5AH
Fax: 020-7244 6441   Tel: 020-7370 1080

RUPERT CREW Ltd
(No Plays, Films or TV scripts)
1A King's Mews, London WC1N 2JA
e-mail: rupertcrew@compuserve.com
Fax: 020-7831 7914   Tel: 020-7242 8586

SAYLE SCREEN Ltd*
(Writers, Screenwriters & Directors for Film & TV)
11 Jubilee Place, London SW3 3TD
Fax: 020-7823 3363   Tel: 020-7823 3883

SEIFERT Linda MANAGEMENT
91 Berwick Street, London W1F 0NE
e-mail: contact@lindaseifert.com
Fax: 020-7292 7391   Tel: 020-7292 7390

SHARLAND ORGANISATION Ltd*
The Manor House, Manor Street
Raunds, Northants NN9 6JW
e-mail: tsoshar@aol.com
Fax: 01933 624860   Tel: 01933 626600

SHEIL LAND ASSOCIATES Ltd*
(Literary, Theatre & Film)
43 Doughty Street, London WC1N 2LH
e-mail: info@sheilland.co.uk
Fax: 020-7831 2127   Tel: 020-7405 9351

STEEL Elaine*
(Writers' Agent)
110 Gloucester Avenue, London NW1 8HX
e-mail: ecmsteel@aol.com
Fax: 020-8341 9807   Tel: 020-8348 0918

STEINBERG Micheline ASSOCIATES*
4th Floor
104 Great Portland Street, London W1W 6PE
e-mail: info@steinplays.com   Tel: 020-7631 1310

STEVENS Rochelle & Co*
2 Terretts Place, Upper Street, London N1 1QZ
Fax: 020-7354 5729   Tel: 020-7359 3900

TENNYSON AGENCY The
10 Cleveland Avenue, Merton Park
London SW20 9EW
e-mail: enquiries@tenagy.co.uk
Tel/Fax: 020-8543 5939

THEATRE OF LITERATURE
(c/o Calder Publications)
51 The Cut, London SE1 8LF
Fax: 020-7928 5930   Tel: 020-7633 0599

THURLEY J M MANAGEMENT
Archery House, 33 Archery Square
Walmer, Deal CT14 7AY
e-mail: jmthurley@aol.com
Fax: 01304 371416   Tel: 01304 371721

TYRELL Julia MANAGEMENT*
55 Fairbridge Road
London N19 3EW
e-mail: julia@jtmanagement.co.uk
Fax: 020-7272 2400   Tel: 020-7272 4000

WARE Cecily LITERARY AGENTS*
19C John Spencer Square
London N1 2LZ
e-mail: info@cecilyware.com
Fax: 020-7226 9828   Tel: 020-7359 3787

WEINBERGER Josef Ltd*
12-14 Mortimer Street, London W1T 3JJ
Website: www.josef-weinberger.com
e-mail: general.info@jwmail.co.uk
Fax: 020-7436 9616   Tel: 020-7580 2827

ALEXANDER PERSONAL MANAGEMENT Ltd
PO Box 834
Hemel Hempstead, Hertfordshire HP3 9ZP
Website: www.apmassociates.net
e-mail: apm@apmassociates.net
Fax: 01442 241099   Tel: 01442 252907

A.P.M. (Linda French)
(See ALEXANDER PERSONAL MANAGEMENT Ltd)

ARLINGTON ENTERPRISES Ltd
1-3 Charlotte Street
London W1T 1RD
Website: www.arlingtonenterprises.co.uk
e-mail: info@arlington.enterprises.co.uk
Fax: 020-7580 4994   Tel: 020-7580 0702

BLACKBURN SACHS ASSOCIATES
2-4 Noel Street
London W1F 8GB
Website: www.blackburnsachsassociates.com
e-mail: presenters@blackburnsachsassociates.com
Fax: 020-7292 7576   Tel: 020-7292 7555

BURNETT GRANGER ASSOCIATES Ltd
3 Clifford Street
London W1S 2LF
Fax: 020-7287 3239   Tel: 020-7437 8008

CAMERON Sara MANAGEMENT
(See TAKE THREE MANAGEMENT)

CANTOR WISE REPRESENTATION
(See TAKE THREE MANAGEMENT)

CHASE PERSONAL MANAGEMENT
Celebrity Division of Modelplan
4th Floor, 4 Golden Square
London W1F 9HT
e-mail: sue@sammon.fsnet.co.uk
Mobile: 07775 683955   Tel: 020-7287 8444

COMEDY CLUB
165 Peckham Rye
London SE15 3HZ
Website: www.comedyclub.org.uk
e-mail: comedyclub@cwcom.net
Fax: 020-7732 9292   Tel: 020-7732 3434

CRAWFORDS
6 Brook Street, London W1S 1BB
Website: www.crawfords.tv
e-mail: cr@wfords.com
Fax: 020-7355 1084   Tel: 020-7629 6464

CURTIS BROWN GROUP Ltd
Haymarket House
28-29 Haymarket
London SW1Y 4SP
e-mail: presenters@curtisbrown.co.uk
Fax: 020-7393 4401   Tel: 020-7393 4400

CYBER-ARTISTS
In The Can Ltd, The Studio
Kingsway Court, Queen's Gardens, Hove BN3 2LP
Website: www.cyberartists.co.uk
e-mail: cyber.1@btclick.com
Fax: 01273 739984   Tel: 01273 821821

DAVID ANTHONY PROMOTIONS
PO Box 286
Warrington, Cheshire WA2 8GA
Website: www.davewarwick.co.uk
e-mail: dave@davewarwick.co.uk
Fax: 01925 416589   Tel: 01925 632496

DOWNES PRESENTERS AGENCY
96 Broadway, Bexleyheath, Kent DA6 7DE
e-mail: downes@presentersagency.com
Fax: 020-8301 5591   Tel: 020-8304 0541

EVANS Jacque MANAGEMENT Ltd
Top Floor Suite
14 Holmesley Road, London SE23 1PJ
e-mail: jacque@jemltd.demon.co.uk
Fax: 020-8699 5192   Tel: 020-8699 1202

EXCELLENT TALENT COMPANY The
53 Goodge Street
London W1T 1TG
Website: www.excellentvoice.co.uk
e-mail: ruth@excellentvoice.co.uk
Fax: 020-7636 1631   Tel: 020-7636 1636

FBI AGENCY Ltd The
PO Box 250, Leeds LS1 2AZ
e-mail: j.spencer@fbi-agency.ltd.uk
                         Tel/Fax: 07050 222747

FLETCHER ASSOCIATES
(Broadcast & Media)
25 Parkway, London N20 0XN
Fax: 020-8361 8866   Tel: 020-8361 8061

FOX ARTIST MANAGEMENT Ltd
Concorde House
101 Shepherds Bush Road
London W6 7LP
e-mail: fox.artist@btinternet.com
Fax: 020-7603 2352   Tel: 020-7602 8822

GAY Noel ARTISTS
19 Denmark Street
London WC2H 8NA
Website: www.noelgay.com
Fax: 020-7287 1816   Tel: 020-7836 3941

GRANT James MANAGEMENT
Syon Lodge
201 London Road
Isleworth, Middlesex TW7 5BH
Website: www.jamesgrant.co.uk
e-mail: darren@jamesgrant.co.uk
Fax: 020-8232 4101   Tel: 020-8232 4100

GURNETT J. PERSONAL MANAGEMENT Ltd
2 New Kings Road, London SW6 4SA
Website: www.jgpm.co.uk
e-mail: mail@jgpm.co.uk
Fax: 020-7736 5455   Tel: 020-7736 7828

HICKS Jeremy ASSOCIATES
11-12 Tottenham Mews
London W1T 4AG
Website: www.jeremyhicks.com
e-mail: hicksworld@aol.com
Fax: 020-7636 8880   Tel: 020-7636 8008

HOBBS Liz GROUP Ltd
First Floor
65 London Road
Newark, Notts NG24 1RZ
Website: www.lizhobbsgroup.com
e-mail: casting@lizhobbsgroup.com
Fax: 0870 3337009   Tel: 08700 702702

HUGHES Jane MANAGEMENT
The Coach House
PO Box 123
Knutsford, Cheshire WA16 9HX   Tel: 01565 650040

INTERNATIONAL ARTISTES Ltd
4th Floor
Holborn Hall
193-197 High Holborn
London WC1V 7BD
e-mail: (name)@intart.co.uk
Fax: 020-7404 9865   Tel: 020-7025 0600

IVELAW-CHAPMAN Julie
The Chase
Chaseside Close
Cheddington
Beds LU7 0SA
e-mail: jic@collectorsworldwide.co.uk
Fax: 01296 662451   Tel: 01296 662441

JAYMEDIA
(Nigel Jay)
171 Sandbach Road
Lawton Heath End
Church Lawton, Cheshire ST7 3RA
e-mail: media@jaymedia.co.uk
Fax: 0870 1209079   Tel: 01270 884453

JLA (Jeremy Lee Associates Ltd)
4 Stratford Place
London W1C 1AT
e-mail: talk@jla.co.uk
Fax: 020-7907 2801   Tel: 020-7907 2800

JOHN David ASSOCIATES
6 Victoria Crescent Road
Glasgow G12 9DB
Website: www.davidjohnassociates.co.uk
e-mail: info@davidjohnassociates.co.uk
Fax: 0141-357 1300   Tel: 0141-357 0532

KBJ MANAGEMENT Ltd
(TV Presenters)
7 Soho Street
London W1D 3DQ
e-mail: candida@kbjmgt.co.uk
Fax: 020-7287 1191   Tel: 020-7434 6767

KNIGHT AYTON MANAGEMENT
114 St Martin's Lane
London WC2N 4BE
Website: www.knightayton.co.uk
e-mail: info@knightayton.co.uk
Fax: 020-7836 8333   Tel: 020-7836 5333

LADKIN Michael PERSONAL MANAGEMENT
Suite 1, Ground Floor
1 Duchess Street
London W1W 6AN
e-mail: ladkinm@aol.com
Fax: 020-7436 4627   Tel: 020-7436 4626

MARKS PRODUCTIONS Ltd
2 Gloucester Gate Mews
London NW1 4AD
Fax: 020-7486 2165   Tel: 020-7486 2001

MARSH Billy ASSOCIATES Ltd
174-178 North Gower Street
London NW1 2NB
e-mail: talent@billymarsh.co.uk
Fax: 020-7388 6848   Tel: 020-7388 6858

McLEAN-WILLIAMS
212 Piccadilly
London W1J 9HG
e-mail: alex@mclean-williams.com
Fax: 020-7917 2805   Tel: 020-7917 2806

MEDIA PEOPLE
12 Nottingham Place
London W1M 3FA
Website: www.celebrity.co.uk
e-mail: info@celebrity.co.uk
Fax: 020-7224 6060   Tel: 020-7224 5050

MILES John ORGANISATION
Cadbury Camp Lane
Clapton-in-Gordano
Bristol BS20 7SB
e-mail: john@johnmiles.org.uk
Fax: 01275 810186   Tel: 01275 854675

MPC ENTERTAINMENT
MPC House
15-16 Maple Mews, London NW6 5UZ
e-mail: mpc@mpce.com
Fax: 020-7624 4220   Tel: 020-7624 1184

MTC (UK) Ltd
20 York Street, London W1U 6PU
Website: www.mtc-uk.com
e-mail: enquiries@mtc-uk.com
Fax: 020-7935 8066   Tel: 020-7935 8000

NCI MANAGEMENT Ltd
51 Queen Anne Street, London W1G 9HS
Website: www.nci-management.com
e-mail: info@nci-management.com
Fax: 020-7487 4258   Tel: 020-7224 3960

NOEL John MANAGEMENT
2nd Floor
10A Belmont Street
London NW1 8HH
e-mail: john@johnnoel.com
Fax: 020-7428 8401   Tel: 020-7428 8400

OFF THE KERB PRODUCTIONS
3rd Floor
Hammer House
113-117 Wardour Street
London W1F 0UN
Website: www.offthekerb.co.uk
e-mail: offthekerb@aol.com
Fax: 020-7437 0647   Tel: 020-7437 0607

22 Thornhill Crescent
London N1 1BJ
e-mail: info@offthekerb.co.uk
Fax: 020-7700 4646   Tel: 020-7700 4477

PHA CASTING
Tanzaro House
Ardwick Green North
Manchester M12 6FZ
Website: www.pha-agency.co.uk
e-mail: info@pha-agency.co.uk
Fax: 0161-273 4567   Tel: 0161-273 4444

PRINCESS TALENT MANAGEMENT
Newcombe House
45 Notting Hill Gate
London W11 3LQ
Website: www.princess.uk.com
e-mail: talent@princess.uk.com
Fax: 020-7908 1934   Tel: 020-7243 5100

PVA MANAGEMENT Ltd
Hallow Park
Hallow, Worcester WR2 6PG
e-mail: clients@pva.co.uk
Fax: 01905 641842　　　　Tel: 01905 640663

QDOS Ltd
8 King Street
Covent Garden
London WC2E 8HN
e-mail: info@qdosentertainment.plc.uk
Fax: 020-7240 4956　　　　Tel: 020-7240 5052

QUADRAPHOLD MANAGEMENT
Queens Chambers
Queen Street
Blackpool, Lancashire FY1 1PD
Website: www.quadraphold.com
e-mail: info@quadraphold.com
Fax: 0870 7708814　　　　Tel: 0870 7708818

RAZZAMATAZZ MANAGEMENT
Mulberry Cottage
Park Farm
Haxted Road
Lingfield RH7 6DE
e-mail: mcgrogan@tinyworld.co.uk
Fax: 01342 835433　　　　Tel: 01342 835359

RDF MANAGEMENT
The Gloucester Building
Kensington Village
Avonmore Road
London W14 8RF
e-mail: debi.allen@rdfmanagement.com
Fax: 020-7013 4101　　　　Tel: 020-7013 4103

RHINO MANAGEMENT
Oak Porch House
5 Western Road
Nazeing, Essex EN9 2QN
Website: www.rhino-management.com
e-mail: info@rhino-management.co.uk
Mobile: 07901 528988　　　　Tel/Fax: 01992 893259

RK COMMERCIALS
205 Chudleigh Road
London SE4 1EG
Website: www.rkcommercials.com
e-mail: mail@rkcommercials.com
Fax: 020-8690 7999　　　　Tel: 020-8690 6542

ROSEMAN ORGANISATION The
51 Queen Anne Street
London W1G 9HS
Website: www.theromanorganisation.co.uk
e-mail: info@theromanorganisation.co.uk
Fax: 020-7486 4600　　　　Tel: 020-7486 4500

RUBY TALENT
Apartment 8
Goldcrest Building
1 Lexington Street
London W1F 9TA
e-mail: tara@ruby-talent.co.uk
Fax: 020-7439 1649　　　　Tel: 020-7439 4554

SILVER FOX ARTIST MANAGEMENT
8-18 Rampart Street
London E1 2LA
Website: www.silverfoxartist.co.uk
e-mail: enquiries@silverfoxartist.co.uk
Fax: 020-7791 2842　　　　Tel: 020-7791 2952

SINGER Sandra ASSOCIATES
21 Cotswold Road
Westcliff on Sea
Essex SS0 8AA
Website: www.sandrasinger.com
e-mail: sandrasingeruk@aol.com
Fax: 01702 339393   Tel: 01702 331616

SOMETHIN' ELSE
(Grant Michaels)
Units 1-4
1A Old Nichol Street
London E2 7HR
e-mail: grant.michaels@somethin-else.com
Fax: 020-7739 9799   Tel: 020-7204 1969

SOUTHWEST MANAGEMENT AND CASTING Ltd
The Courtyard
Whitchurch
Ross-on-Wye HR9 6DA
Website: www.southwestcasting.co.uk
e-mail: agent@southwestcasting.co.uk
Fax: 01600 891099   Tel: 01600 892005

SPEAK-EASY Ltd
1 Dairy Yard
High Street
Market Harborough
Leics LE16 7NL
Website: www.speak-easy.co.uk
e-mail: enquiries@speak-easy.co.uk
Fax: 01858 461994   Tel: 0870 0135126

STORM ARTISTS MANAGEMENT
4th Floor
6-10 Lexington Street
London W1F 0LB
e-mail: info@stormartists.co.uk
Fax: 020-7437 4314   Tel: 020-7437 4313

TAKE THREE MANAGEMENT
110 Gloucester Avenue
Primrose Hill
London NW1 8HX
e-mail: info@take3management.co.uk
Fax: 020-7209 3770   Tel: 020-7209 3777

TALKBACK MANAGEMENT
20-21 Newman Street
London W1T 1PG
Fax: 020-7861 8061   Tel: 020-7861 8060

TF ASSOCIATES
(Tony Fitzpatrick)
Suite 104, 137-149 Godwell Road
Davina House, London EC1V 7ET
Website: www.tf-associates.com
e-mail: tony.fitzpatrick@tf-associates.com
Fax: 07000 400707   Tel: 07000 300707

UNIQUE MANAGEMENT GROUP
Beaumont House
Kensington Village, Avonmore Road
London W14 8TS
e-mail: celebrities@uniquegroup.co.uk
Fax: 020-7605 1101   Tel: 020-7605 1100

V R M
Laser House
Waterfront Quay, Salford Quays
Manchester M5 2XW
Fax: 0161-888 2242   Tel: 0161-874 5741

VAGABOND HEART
2 Grassmere Road
Hornchurch, Essex RM11 3DP
e-mail: vagabond@virgin.net   Tel: 01708 781994

VENTURE ARTISTES
(In Association with George Heathcote
Management)
38 Great Queen Street
London WC2B 5AA
e-mail: seamuslyte@freeuk.com
Fax: 020-7404 8681   Tel: 020-7404 8680

WILLCOCKS John MEDIA AGENCY Ltd
34 Carisbrook Close
Enfield, Middlesex EN1 3NB
Fax: 020-8292 5060   Tel: 020-8364 4556

AD VOICE
Oxford House
76 Oxford Street, London W1D 1BS
Fax: 020-7323 0101   Tel: 020-7323 2345

ANOTHER TONGUE VOICES Ltd
The Basement
10 D'Arblay Street, London W1F 8DS
Website: www.anothertongue.com
e-mail: info@anothertongue.com
Fax: 020-7494 7080   Tel: 020-7494 0300

ASQUITH & HORNER
Write with SAE
The Studio
14 College Road
Bromley, Kent BR1 3NS
Fax: 020-8313 0443   Tel: 020-8466 5580

BURNETT GRANGER ASSOCIATES Ltd
3 Clifford Street
London W1S 2LF
e-mail: raphael@burnettgranger.co.uk
Fax: 020-7287 3239   Tel: 020-7437 8029

CALYPSO VOICES
25-26 Poland Street
London W1F 8QN
e-mail: calypso@calypsovoices.com
Fax: 020-7437 0410   Tel: 020-7734 6415

CAMPBELL ASSOCIATES
2 Chelsea Cloisters
Sloane Avenue, Chelsea
London SW3 3DW
e-mail: campbell.associates@btopenworld.com
Fax: 020-7584 8799   Tel: 020-7584 5586

CASTAWAY
7 Garrick Street
London WC2E 9AR
Website: www.castaway.org.uk
e-mail: sheila@castaway.org.uk
Fax: 020-7240 2772   Tel: 020-7240 2345

CONWAY VAN GELDER Ltd
(Kate Plumpton)
3rd Floor
18-21 Jermyn Street
London SW1Y 6HP
e-mail: kate@conwayvg.co.uk
Fax: 020-7494 3324   Tel: 020-7287 1070

CYBER-ARTISTS
In The Can Ltd
The Studio
Kingsway Court
Queen's Gardens, Hove BN3 2LP
Website: www.cyberartists.co.uk
e-mail: cyber.1@btclick.com
Fax: 01273 739984   Tel: 01273 821821

DIAMOND MANAGEMENT
31 Percy Street
London W1T 2DD
e-mail: agents@diman.co.uk
Fax: 020-7631 0500   Tel: 020-7631 0400

DOUBLEFVOICES
(Singers Agency)
1 Hunters Lodge
Bodiam
East Sussex TN32 2UE
e-mail: rob@doublefvoices.com
Mobile: 07976 927764   Tel: 01580 830071

DREW Bryan Ltd
Mezzanine
Quadrant House
80-82 Regent Street
London W1B 5AU
e-mail: bryan@bryandrewltd.com
Fax: 020-7437 0561   Tel: 020-7437 2293

EVANS O'BRIEN
115 Humber Road
London SE3 7LW
Website: www.evansobrien.co.uk
e-mail: eobvoice@dircon.co.uk
Fax: 020-8293 7066   Tel: 020-8293 7077

EXCELLENT VOICE COMPANY
53 Goodge Street
London W1T 1TG
Website: www.excellentvoice.co.uk
e-mail: info@excellentvoice.co.uk
Fax: 020-7636 1631   Tel: 020-7636 1636

FOREIGN VERSIONS Ltd
(Translation)
Bakerloo Chambers
304 Edgware Road
London W2 1DY
Website: www.foreignversions.com
e-mail: info@foreignversions.co.uk
Fax: 020-7723 5018   Tel: 020-7723 5744

GAY Noel VOICES
19 Denmark Street
London WC2H 8NA
Website: www.noelgay.com
Fax: 020-7287 1816   Tel: 020-7836 3941

GORDON & FRENCH
12-13 Poland Street
London W1F 8QB
e-mail: mail@gordonandfrench.net
Fax: 020-7734 4832   Tel: 020-7734 4818

HOBSON'S SINGERS
62 Chiswick High Road
London W4 1SY
Website: www.hobsons-international.com
e-mail: singers@hobsons-international.com
Fax: 020-8996 5350   Tel: 020-8995 3628

HOBSON'S VOICES
62 Chiswick High Road
London W4 1SY
Website: www.hobsons-international.com
e-mail: voices@hobsons-international.com
Fax: 020-8996 5350   Tel: 020-8995 3628

HOPE Sally ASSOCIATES
108 Leonard Street
London EC2A 4XS
e-mail: casting@sallyhope.biz
Fax: 020-7613 4848   Tel: 020-7613 5353

HOWARD Amanda ASSOCIATES
21 Berwick Street
London W1F 0PZ
Website: www.amandahowardassociates.co.uk
e-mail: mail@amandahowardassociates.co.uk
Fax: 020-7287 7785   Tel: 020-7287 9277

INTERNATIONAL ARTISTES VOICE OVERS
(Nicola Sandon)
4th Floor, Holborn Hall
193-197 High Holborn
London WC1V 7BD
Website: www.intart.co.uk
e-mail: nikki@intart.co.uk
Fax: 020-7404 9865   Tel: 020-7025 0609

KIDZTALK Ltd
(Children's Voices aged 4-24)
Website: www.kidztalk.com
e-mail: studio@kidztalk.com
Fax: 01737 352456   Tel: 01737 350808

LIP SERVICE
60-66 Wardour Street
London W1F 0TA
Website: www.lipservice.co.uk
e-mail: bookings@lipservice.co.uk
Fax: 020-7734 3373   Tel: 020-7734 3393

MANSON Andrew
(Genuine Americans only)
288 Munster Road
London SW6 6BQ
Website: www.andrewmanson.com
e-mail: post@andrewmanson.com
Fax: 020-7381 8874   Tel: 020-7386 9158

MARKHAM & FROGGATT Ltd
4 Windmill Street, London W1T 2HZ
e-mail: fiona@markhamfroggatt.co.uk
Fax: 020-7637 5233   Tel: 020-7636 4412

MBA
3rd Floor Suite
10-11 Lower John Street
London W1F 9EB
e-mail: info@braidman.com
Fax: 020-7439 3600   Tel: 020-7437 0817

McREDDIE Ken Ltd
91 Regent Street
London W1B 4EL
Fax: 020-7734 6530   Tel: 020-7439 1456

NOEL John MANAGEMENT
2nd Floor
10A Belmont Street
London NW1 8HH
e-mail: john@johnnoel.com
Fax: 020-7428 8401   Tel: 020-7428 8400

NUTOPIA VOICES
Number 8
132 Charing Cross Road
London WC2H 0LA
Website: www.nutopia.co.uk
Fax: 029-2070 9440   Mobile: 07801 493133

P F D
Drury House
34-43 Russell Street
London WC2B 5HA
Fax: 020-7836 9544   Tel: 020-7344 1010

QVOICE
8 King Street
Covent Garden
London WC2E 8HN
Website: www.qvoice.co.uk
e-mail: info@qvoice.co.uk
Fax: 020-7240 4956   Tel: 020-7420 6825

RABBIT VOCAL MANAGEMENT
2nd Floor
18 Broadwick Street
London W1F 8HS
Website: www.rabbit.uk.net
e-mail: info@rabbit.uk.net
Fax: 020-7287 6566   Tel: 020-7287 6466

RHINO MANAGEMENT
Oak Porch House
5 Western Road
Nazeing, Essex EN9 2QN
Website: www.rhino-management.com
e-mail: info@rhino-management.co.uk
Mobile: 07901 528988   Tel/Fax: 01992 893259

RHUBARB
Bakerloo Chambers
304 Edgware Road, London W2 1DY
Website: www.rhubarb.co.uk
e-mail: enquiries@rhubarb.co.uk
Fax: 020-7724 1030   Tel: 020-7724 1300

SHINING MANAGEMENT Ltd
82C Shirland Road, London W9 2EQ
Website: www.shiningvoices.com
e-mail: info@shiningvoices.com
Fax: 020-7286 6123   Tel: 020-7286 6092

SOUTHWEST MANAGEMENT & CASTING Ltd
The Courtyard
Whitchurch, Ross-on-Wye HR9 6DA
Website: www.southwestcasting.co.uk
e-mail: agent@southwestcasting.co.uk
Fax: 01600 891099   Tel: 01600 892005

SPEAK Ltd
140 Devonshire Road
Chiswick, London W4 2AW
Website: www.speak.ltd.uk
e-mail: info@speak.ltd.uk
Fax: 020-8742 1333   Tel: 020-8742 1001

SPEAKERS CORNER AT CRAWFORDS
6 Brook Street
London W1S 1BB
e-mail: vo@crawfords.tv
Fax: 020-7355 1084   Tel: 020-7629 6464

SPEAK-EASY Ltd
1 Dairy Yard
High Street, Market Harborough
Leicestershire LE16 7NL
Website: www.speak-easy.co.uk
e-mail: enquiries@speak-easy.co.uk
Fax: 01858 461994   Tel: 0870 0135126

STONE Richard PARTNERSHIP The
2 Henrietta Street
London WC2E 8PS
e-mail: all@richstonepart.co.uk
Fax: 020-7497 0869   Tel: 020-7497 0849

do you know how to judge a quality voice-over showreel?

Consistently produce Showreels of the highest Standard.
David Hodge - Hobson's Voices

Very high quality. I've always been impressed
Sheila - Castaway Voice Agency

Definitely the best Showreels
Penny Warnes - Earache Voice Agency

A professional and high quality Showreel
Penny Brown - Voicecall

the voice agencies do.

Register now for your FREE introductory workshop

A quality voice Showreel should not only demonstrate your vocal range, age and abilities, it should only contain material you are vocally suited to and are able to reproduce in any studio session.
By focusing your efforts on training, you will become more experienced and professional, taking less time to produce your final Showreel. Being able to accurately reproduce what's on your Showreel will greatly increase your ability to get work.

Our FREE voice-over workshop is the ideal introduction to the voice industry.
It covers everything you need to know, from finding your unique vocal style to discovering what type of scripts to include on your Voice Showreel. You will learn how the industry works and how to get work from the industry. This interactive workshop will allow you to successfully plan your next steps towards a career in voice-over.

Topics covered include: understanding your role as a voice-over artist, basic vocal skills and techniques, how to correctly identify your vocal strengths and abilities, understanding the different types of vocal delivery, mic technique, studio etiquette and helping you to plan your next move.

Our more intensive voice-over workshop gives you the experience your need.
Voice agencies and clients prefer artists who've had experience, but getting experience is difficult. This voice-over workshop focuses on practical exercises that allow you to learn the skills and techniques to come across as confident and professional.

Learn to communicate effectively.
Like any job, being a voice-over requires training and practice. As a voice artist, your job isn't about how you sound, but how you make the listener feel. It involves using your voice to accurately interpret the script so that it successfully sells, teaches, persuades, explains or enlightens the listener, and satisfies your client.

The Intensive Voice-Over Workshop.
This course covers a large range of skills and techniques. Topics include: understanding your role as a voice-over artist, types of voice work available, discovering different vocal styles, the importance of correctly identifying your vocal strengths and abilities, exploring your creative vocal range, vocal techniques and exercises, script interpretation, mic technique, understanding commercial scripts, working with documentary narration and corporate scripts, studio protocol, self-marketing techniques and how to get a voice agent.

The Voice Showreel.
The Voice Showreel is designed to represent your voice, range and abilities. It is an effective tool in auditioning your voice and gives both agents and professional clients a good idea of your place within the voice-over market.

We produce your showreel in exactly the same way as the industry would produce commercial work.
We don't produce demos we produce the real thing; real commercials, real documentaries and real talking books. We place your voice with the right script and the right music to create a totally authentic package. The listener believes they are hearing your voice doing real work because in essenceÉ they are.

We never re-cycle a script.
Because your Voice Showreel is the first thing an agent or client hears it is essential that they hear a fresh script and not one they have heard over and over again. For this reason we never re-cycle a script ensuring the Showreel is as individual as you are.

Free colour on-body printed CD's.
We never put a sticky label on your duplicated CD's and lower the presentation of your final Showreel. Best of all we include duplicated CD's in each of our Showreel packages for FREE.

Your duplicated Showreel in your hand at the end of the session.
Because we produce our CD's in-house, you can have your Showreel duplications in your hand at the end of the session. So you don't have to wait for a delivery to move your career forward.

Comfortable, soundproofed, air-conditioned studios.
Our two studios and vocal booths are fully soundproofed and air-conditioned with ample room to relax and focus on your training or your Showreel.

Top of the range Pro Tools Digital recording environment .
The audio quality of the Showreel is essential in professionally presenting your voice to agencies and clients. Because of this we have invested heavily in the best equipment creating a totally silent Digital environment where the only thing on the Showreel is what we put there.

Industry Contacts provided for FREE.
Our website provides instant access to industry contacts along with a wealth of related information to help you succeed.

Still not convinced? Then the Audition Package is the best way to find out if voice-over is for you.
You're given several types of scripts to record to establish where your 'natural' read and style lies. Once your performance level and abilities have been evaluated, together, we decide if you should take the next step and invest in training or a full Voice Showreel package. This session is designed to clarify for you as well as for us, the direction in which you need to focus. If you decide to record a full Showreel package, we will refund 50% towards the cost.

Call (020) 8995 3232 to register for your free introductory Workshop or visit our website at http://www.theshowreel.com

the**Showreel**.com
trust us to get it right

Knightsbridge House, 229 Acton Lane, Chiswick, London W4 5DD   tel (020) 8995 3232   email info@theshowreel.com

SUMMERS Mark MANAGEMENT & AGENCY
9 Hansard Mews
Kensington, London W14 8BJ
Website: www.marksummers.com
e-mail: mark@marksummers.com
Fax: 0870 4435623   Tel: 0870 4435621

TALKING HEADS
2-4 Noel Street
London W1F 8GB
Website: www.talkingheadsvoices.com
e-mail: voices@talkingheadsvoices.com
Fax: 020-7292 7576   Tel: 020-7292 7575

TERRY Sue VOICES Ltd
18 Broadwick Street
London W1F 8HS
Website: www.sueterryvoices.co.uk
Fax: 020-7434 2042   Tel: 020-7434 2040

TONGUE & GROOVE
3 Stevenson Square
Manchester M1 1DN
Website: www.tongueandgroove.co.uk
e-mail: info@tongueandgroove.co.uk
Fax: 0161-237 1809   Tel: 0161-228 2469

VACCA Roxane VOICES
73 Beak Street, London W1F 9SR
Website: www.voiceover.org.uk
e-mail: mail@roxanevaccavoices.com
Fax: 020-7734 8086   Tel: 020-7734 8085

VOCAL POINT
25 Denmark Street, London WC2H 8NJ
Website: www.vocalpoint.net
e-mail: enquiries@vocalpoint.net
Fax: 020-7419 0699   Tel: 020-7419 0700

VOICE & SCRIPT INTERNATIONAL
Aradco House
132 Cleveland Street
London W1T 6AB
Website: www.vsi.tv
e-mail: info@vsi.tv
Fax: 020-7692 7711   Tel: 020-7692 7700

VOICE BOX
Laser House
Waterfront Quay
Salford Quays
Manchester M5 2XW
Website: www.thevoicebox.co.uk
Fax: 0161-888 2242   Tel: 0161-874 5741

VOICE SHOP
Bakerloo Chambers
304 Edgware Road
London W2 1DY
Website: www.voice-shop.co.uk
e-mail: info@voice-shop.co.uk
Fax: 020-7706 1002   Tel: 020-7402 3966

VOICE SQUAD
62 Blenheim Gardens
London NW2 4NT
Website: www.voicesquad.com
e-mail: bookem@voicesquad.com
Fax: 020-8452 7944   Tel: 020-8450 4451

VOICEBANK, THE IRISH VOICE-OVER AGENCY
The Barracks
76 Irishtown Road
Dublin 4, Eire
Website: www.voicebank.ie
e-mail: voicebank@voicebank.ie
Fax: 00 353 1 6607850   Tel: 00 353 1 6687234

VOICECALL
67A Gondar Gardens
London NW6 1EP
e-mail: voicecall@blueyonder.co.uk   Tel: 020-7209 1064

WOOTTON Suzy VOICES
75 Shelley Street
Kingsley
Northampton NN2 7HZ
e-mail: suzy@suzywoottonvoices.com
Fax: 0870 7659668   Tel: 0870 7659660

YAKETY YAK
8 Bloomsbury Square
London WC1A 2NE
Website: www.yaketyyak.co.uk
e-mail: info@yaketyyak.co.uk
Fax: 020-7404 6109   Tel: 020-7430 2600

Animals

A1 ANIMALS
(Farm, Domestic & Exotic Animals)
Folly Farm
Folly Lane, Bramley
Hants RG26 5BD
Website: www.a1animals.co.uk
e-mail: info@a1animals.freeserve.co.uk
Fax: 01256 880653   Tel: 01256 880993

ABNALLS HORSES
Abnalls Farm
Cross in Hand Lane
Lichfield, Staffs WS13 8DZ
e-mail: carolynsj@dial.pipex.com
Fax: 01543 417226   Tel: 01543 417075

ALTERNATIVE ANIMALS
(Animatronics/Taxidermy)
28 Greaves Road
High Wycombe, Bucks HP13 7JU
Website: www.animalworld.org.uk
e-mail: animalworld@bushinternet.com
Fax: 01494 441385   Tel: 01494 448710

AMAZING STUNT DOGS
18 Rosewood Avenue
Kingsway, Rugby
Warwickshire CV22 5PJ
Website: www.amazingstuntdogs.co.uk
Mobile: 07759 804813   Tel: 01788 812703

ANIMAL ACTING
(Stunts, Prop, Horse-Drawn Vehicles)
15 Wolstenvale Close, Middleton
Manchester M24 2HP
Website: www.animalacting.com
e-mail: information@animalacting.com
Fax: 0161-655 3700   Tel: 0800 387755

ANIMAL ACTORS
95 Ditching Road, Brighton
Sussex BN1 4ST   Tel: 020-8654 0450

ANIMAL AMBASSADORS
Old Forest
Hampstead Norreys Road
Hermitage, Berks RG18 9SA
e-mail: kayweston@tiscali.co.uk
Mobile: 07831 558594   Tel/Fax: 01635 200900

ANIMAL ARK
(Animals & Animal Prop Shop)
Studio
29 Somerset Road, Brentford
Middlesex TW8 8BT
Website: www.animal-ark.co.uk
e-mail: info@animal-ark.co.uk
Fax: 020-8560 5762   Tel: 020-8560 3029

ANIMAL ARRANGERS
(Animal Suppliers & Co-ordinators)
28 Greaves Road
High Wycombe, Bucks HP13 7JU
Fax: 07930 439895   Tel: 01494 448710

ANIMAL CASTING
89 Tilehurst Road, Earlsfield,
London SW1B 3EX
e-mail: silcresta@aol.com
Mobile: 07956 246450   Tel: 020-8874 9530

ANIMAL WELFARE FILMING FEDERATION
28 Greaves Road, High Wycombe, Bucks HP13 7JU
Fax: 07930 439895   Mobile: 07770 666088

ANIMAL WELFARE INSPECTION SERVICES
(Independent Consultancy of All Aspects of Use of
Animals in Media Productions)
15B St Anne's Road, Eastbourne BN21 2AJ
e-mail: animal.insp.svcs@amserve.net
          Tel/Fax: 01323 726105

ANIMAL WORLD
(Trevor Smith)
19 Greaves Road
High Wycombe, Bucks HP13 7JU
Website: www.animalworld.org.uk
e-mail: animalworld@bushinternet.com
Fax: 01494 441385   Tel: 01494 442750

ANIMALATION
16 Wiltshire Avenue
Crowthorne
Berks RG45 6NG
Fax: 01344 779437   Tel: 01344 775244

ANIMALS GALORE
208 Smallfield Road
Horley, Surrey RH6 9LS
Fax: 01342 841546   Tel: 01342 842400

ANIMALS O KAY
3 Queen Street
Chipperfield
Kings Langley, Herts WD4 9BT
Website: www.animalsokay.com
e-mail: kay@animalsokay.com
Fax: 01923 269076   Tel: 01923 291277

A-Z ANIMALS Ltd
The Bell House
Bell Lane, Fetcham, Surrey KT22 9ND
e-mail: xlence@a-zanimals.com
Fax: 01372 377666   Tel: 01372 377111

A-Z DOGS
The Bell House
Bell Lane, Fetcham, Surrey KT22 9ND
e-mail: dogs@a-zanimals.com
Fax: 01372 377666   Tel: 020-7248 6222

BOORMAN-WOODS Sue
(Specializing in Domestic Cats, Rodents,
Poultry & Farm Stock)
White Rocks Farm
Underriver
Sevenoaks, Kent TN15 0SL
Website: www.animalspromotions.co.uk
e-mail: happyhounds@yahoo.co.uk
Fax: 01732 763767   Tel: 01732 762913

BUGS & THINGS
28 Greaves Road
High Wycombe
Bucks HP13 7JU
Website: www.animalworld.org.uk
e-mail: 07956564715@one2one.net
Fax: 01494 441385   Tel: 01494 448710

CANINE FILM ACADEMY The
57C Cheapside Road, Ascot, Berks SL5 7QR
Website: www.thecaninefilmacademy.com
e-mail: katie.cfa@virgin.net
Mobile: 07767 341424   Tel: 01344 291465

CHEESEMAN Virginia
21 Willow Close, Flackwell Heath
High Wycombe, Bucks HP10 9LH
Website: www.virginiacheeseman.co.uk
e-mail: virginia@virginiacheeseman.co.uk
                                        Tel: 01628 522632

CLIFT Pauline
15 Gwendale
Pinkneys Green
Maidenhead, Berks SL6 6SH
e-mail: paulineclift@btclick.com
                              Tel/Fax: 01628 788564

COTSWOLD FARM PARK
(Rare Breeds Survival Centre)
Guiting Power, Cheltenham
Gloucestershire GL54 5UG
Fax: 01451 850423   Tel: 01451 850307

CREATURE FEATURE
(Animal Agent)
Gubhill Farm
Ae, Dumfries, Scotland DG1 1RL
Website: www.creaturefeature.co.uk
e-mail: david@creaturefeature.co.uk
Mobile: 07770 774866   Tel/Fax: 01387 860648

DOLBADARN FILM HORSES
Dolbadarn Hotel, High Street
Llanberis, Gwynedd, North Wales
Website: www.filmhorses.co.uk
e-mail: info@filmhorses.co.uk Tel/Fax: 01286 870277

DUDLEY Yvonne
(Glamour Dog)
55 Cambridge Park, Wanstead
London E11 2PR   Tel: 020-8989 1528

EAST NOLTON RIDING STABLES
Nolton, Nr Newgale, Haverfordwest
Pembrokeshire SA62 3NW
Website: www.noltonstables.com
e-mail: noltonstables@aol.com
Fax: 01437 710967   Tel: 01437 710360

FILM HORSES
(Horses, Saddlery, Equestrian Centre)
The Shire Horse Centre
Bath Road, Littlewick Green
Maidenhead, Berks SL6 3QA
Website: www.filmhorses.com
Mobile: 07831 629662   Tel/Fax: 01628 822770

FREE ANIMAL CONSULTANT SERVICES
28 Greaves Road
High Wycombe, Bucks HP13 7JU
Fax: 01494 441385   Tel: 08000 749383

GET STUFFED
(Taxidermy)
105 Essex Road, London N1 2SL
Website: www.thegetstuffed.co.uk
e-mail: taxidermy@thegetstuffed.co.uk
Fax: 020-7359 8253   Tel: 020-7226 1364

GRAY Robin COMMENTARIES
(Equestrian Equipment)
Comptons
Isington, Alton
Hants GU34 4PL
e-mail: gray@isington.fsnet.co.uk   Tel: 01420 23347

HORSES - JAMES MACKIE - CAVALRY AND OTHER
Cownham Farm
Broadwell, Moreton in Marsh
Gloucestershire GL56 0TT
e-mail: jo@eventing.net
Fax: 01451 832442   Tel: 01451 870157

JANIMALS Ltd
(Specialists in Training, Handling & Supplying all Species for Film, Television etc)
25 Strathcona Avenue
Bookham, Surrey KT23 4HW
Fax: 01372 456232   Tel: 01372 456969

KNIGHTS OF ARKLEY The
Glyn Sylen Farm
Five Roads, Llanelli SA15 5BJ
Website: www.knightsofarkley.com
e-mail: penny@knightsofarkley.fsnet.co.uk
                              Tel/Fax: 01269 861001

McLEOD Janis
(Trick Performing Dogs for Stage & TV)
10 Edinburgh Road
Wallasey, Merseyside CH45 4LR
e-mail: janswonderdogs@myway.com
Mobile: 07818 263147   Tel/Fax: 0151-200 7174

MILLENNIUM BUGS
(Live Insects)
28 Greaves Road
High Wycombe, Bucks HP13 7JU
e-mail: animalworld@bushinternet.com
Fax: 01494 441385   Tel: 01494 448710

MORTON Geoff
(Shire Horse & Equipment)
Hasholme Carr Farm
Holme on Spalding Moor
York YO43 4BD   Tel: 01430 860393

OTTERS
(Tame Otters) (Daphne & Martin Neville)
Baker's Mill
Frampton Mansell, Stroud, Glos GL6 8JH
e-mail: martin.neville@ukgateway.net
                              Tel: 01285 760234

PATCHETTS EQUESTRIAN CENTRE
Hillfield Lane
Aldenham, Watford, Herts WD25 8PE
Website: www.patchetts.co.uk
Fax: 01923 859289   Tel: 01923 855776

PROP FARM Ltd
(Pat Ward)
Grange Farm
Elmton, Nr Creswell
North Derbyshire S80 4LX
e-mail: pat/les@propfarm.free-online.co.uk
Fax: 01909 721465   Tel: 01909 723100

RATS!
(Trained Fancy Rats and Handler)
e-mail: esbat@blueyonder.co.uk Tel: 020-8683 2173

ROCKWOOD ANIMALS ON FILM
Lewis Terrace, Llanbradach, Caerphilly CF83 3JZ
Website: www.rockwoodanimals.com
e-mail: rockwood@gxn.co.uk
Mobile: 07973 930983   Tel: 029-2088 5420

SCHOOL OF NATIONAL EQUITATION Ltd
(Sam Humphrey)
Bunny Hill Top, Costock, Loughborough
Leicestershire LE12 6XE
Website: www.bunny-hill.co.uk
e-mail: sam@bunny-hill.co.uk
Fax: 01509 856067   Tel: 01509 852366

STUDIO & TV HIRE
(Stuffed Animal Specialists)
3 Ariel Way
Wood Lane, White City
London W12 7SL
Website: www.stvhire.com
e-mail: enquiries@stvhire.com
Fax: 020-8740 9662   Tel: 020-8749 3445

STUNT DOGS
3 The Chestnuts
Clifton, Deddington, Oxon OX15 0PE
e-mail: gill@euro-stuntdogs.co.uk
                              Tel/Fax: 01869 338546

STUNTS APOCALYPSE
(Ian Van Temperley)
PO Box 11
Frodsham, Cheshire WA6 8GZ
Website: www.horsemen-of-the-apocalypse.co.uk
e-mail: Ian@stuntsapocalypse.co.uk
Mobile: 07887 602749   Tel: 01928 788040

SUZANNE'S RIDING SCHOOL
(Rural Surroundings)
Copse & Brookshill Farms
Brookshill Drive
Harrow Weald, Middlesex HA3 6SB
Fax: 020-8420 6461   Tel: 020-8954 3618

TATE Olive
(Trained Dogs & Cats)
49 Upton Road, Bexleyheath
Kent DA6 8LW
Mobile: 07710 933163   Tel/Fax: 020-8303 0683

TATE'S Nigel DOGSTARS
4 Hoads Wood Gardens
Ashford, Kent TN25 4QB
Website: www.dogstars.co.uk
e-mail: animals@dogstars.co.uk
Fax: 07092 031929   Tel: 01233 635439

THORNE'S OF WINDSOR
(Beekeeping & Other Insect Suppliers)
Oakley Green Farm, Oakley Green
Windsor, Berks SL4 4PZ
e-mail: mattallan@aol.com
Fax: 01753 830605   Tel: 01753 830256

VET FOR PERFORMING ANIMALS
(Dr L. Black, Veterinary Surgeon)
Hamshere Cottage
The Street, Wonersh, Guildford GU5 0PF
e-mail: lenblack@spekvet.freeserve.co.uk
                              Tel/Fax: 01483 898561

WELLINGTON RIDING
Basingstoke Road
Heckfield RG27 0LJ
Fax: 0118-932 6661   Tel: 0118-932 6308

WHITE DOVE COMPANY Ltd The
(Provision of up to 100 Doves for Release)
The Dovecote
9-11 High Beech Road
Loughton, Essex IG10 4BN
Website: www.thewhitedovecompany.co.uk
e-mail: thewhitedovecompany@lineone.net
Fax: 020-8502 2461   Tel: 020-8508 1414

WOLF AND HOUND SPECIALISTS The
(Tame Wolves and Hounds)
The UK Wolf Conservation Trust
UK Wolf Centre, Butlers Farm
Beenham, Berks RG7 5NT
Website: www.ukwolf.org
e-mail: ukwct@ukwolf.org   Tel: 0118-971 3330

ARTS COUNCIL ENGLAND, EAST
Norfolk, Suffolk, Bedfordshire, Cambridgeshire
Essex, Hertfordshire, and the unitary authorities of
Luton, Peterborough, Southend-on-Sea and Thurrock
Eden House
48-49 Bateman Street
Cambridge CB2 1LR
Website: www.artscouncil.org.uk
e-mail: east@artscouncil.org.uk
Fax: 0870 2421271   Tel: 01223 454400

ARTS COUNCIL ENGLAND, EAST MIDLANDS
Derbyshire, Leicestershire, Lincolnshire excluding
North and North East Lincolnshire, Northamptonshire,
Nottinghamshire and the Unitary Authorities of Derby
and Rutland
St Nicholas Court, 25-27 Castle Gate
Nottingham NG1 7AR
Website: www.artscouncil.org.uk
e-mail: eastmidlands@artscouncil.org.uk
Fax: 0115-950 2467   Tel: 0115-989 7520

ARTS COUNCIL ENGLAND, LONDON
The arts funding and development agency for the
32 London boroughs and the Corporation of London
2 Pear Tree Court, London EC1R 0DS
Website: www.artscouncil.org.uk
e-mail: london@artscouncil.org.uk
Fax: 020-7608 4100   Tel: 020-7608 6100

ARTS COUNCIL ENGLAND, NORTH EAST
Teeside, Durham, Northumberland, Tyne and Wear
Central Square, Forth Street
Newcastle upon Tyne NE1 3PJ
Website: www.artscouncil.org.uk
e-mail: northeast@artscouncil.org.uk
Fax: 0191-230 1020   Tel: 0191-255 8500

ARTS COUNCIL ENGLAND, NORTH WEST
Greater Manchester, Merseyside, Lancashire
Cheshire & Cumbria
Manchester House, 22 Bridge Street
Manchester M3 3AB
Website: www.artscouncil.org.uk
e-mail: northwest@artscouncil.org.uk
Fax: 0161-834 6969   Tel: 0161-834 6644

ARTS COUNCIL ENGLAND, SOUTH EAST
Sovereign House
Church Street
Brighton BN1 1RA
Website: www.artscouncil.org.uk
e-mail: southeast@artscouncil.org.uk
Fax: 0870 2421257   Tel: 01273 763000

ARTS COUNCIL ENGLAND, SOUTH WEST
Cornwall, Devon, Dorset, Gloucestershire, Somerset
and Wiltshire and the Unitary Authorities of Bristol
Bath, Torbay and Swindon
Bradninch Place, Gandy Street, Exeter
Devon EX4 3LS
Website: www.artscouncil.org.uk
e-mail: southwest@artscouncil.org.uk
Fax: 01392 229229   Tel: 01392 218188

ARTS COUNCIL ENGLAND, WEST MIDLANDS
Herefordshire, Worcestershire, Staffordshire,
Warwickshire and Shropshire, Stoke-on-Trent, Telford
and Wrekin and districts of Birmingham, Coventry,
Dudley, Sandwell, Solihull, Walsall &
Wolverhampton
82 Granville Street, Birmingham B1 2LH
Website: www.artscouncil.org.uk
e-mail: westmidlands@artscouncil.org.uk
Fax: 0121-643 7239   Tel: 0121-631 3121

ARTS COUNCIL ENGLAND, YORKSHIRE
21 Bond Street
Dewsbury
West Yorkshire WF13 1AX
Website: www.artscouncil.org.uk
e-mail: yorkshire@artscouncil.org.uk
Fax: 01924 466522   Tel: 01924 455555

ARTS COUNCIL OF WALES,
MID & WEST WALES OFFICE
Ceredigion, Camarthenshire
Pembrokeshire, Powys, Swansea
Neath, Port Talbot
6 Gardd Llydaw, Jackson's Lane
Carmarthen, Carmarthenshire SA31 1QD
Website: www.artswales.org
Fax: 01267 233084   Tel: 01267 234248

ARTS COUNCIL OF WALES,
NORTH WALES OFFICE
Anglesey
Gwynedd, Conwy
Denbighshire, Flintshire, Wrexham
36 Prince's Drive, Colwyn Bay
Conwy LL29 8LA
Website: www.artswales.org
Fax: 01492 533677   Tel: 01492 533440

ARTS COUNCIL OF WALES,
SOUTH WALES OFFICE
9 Museum Place
Cardiff CF10 3NX
Website: www.artswales.org
Fax: 029-2022 1447   Tel: 029-2037 6500

ALDERSHOT
West End Centre, Queens Road
Aldershot, Hants GU11 3JD
BO: 01252 330040   Admin: 01252 408040

ANDOVER
Cricklade Theatre, Charlton Road
Andover, Hants SP10 1EJ
e-mail: ssharp@cricklade.ac.uk
Fax: 01264 360066   Tel: 01264 360063

BAMPTON
West Ox Arts
WOA Gallery, Market Square, Bampton
Oxfordshire OX18 2JH
Administrator: Abigail Ballinger
e-mail: www.westoxarts@yahoo.co.uk
                              Tel: 01993 850137

BANGOR
Theatr Gwynedd, Ffordd Deiniol, Bangor
Gwynedd LL57 2TL
Website: www.theatrgwynedd.co.uk
e-mail: theatr@theatrgwynedd.co.uk
BO: 01248 351708   Admin: 01248 351707

BEDHAMPTON
(See HAVANT)

BILLERICAY
Billericay Arts Association
The Fold
72 Laindon Road, Billericay
Essex CM12 9LD
Secretary: Edmond Philpott   Tel: 01277 659286

BINGLEY
Bingley Arts Centre
Main Street, Bingley
West Yorkshire BD16 2LZ
Head of Halls: Mark Davies   Tel: 01274 431576

BIRMINGHAM
The Custard Factory
Gibb Street, Digbeth
Birmingham B9 4AA
Website: www.custardfactory.com
e-mail: post@custardfactory.com
Fax: 0121-604 8888   Tel: 0121-693 7777

BIRMINGHAM
Midlands Arts Centre
Cannon Hill Park, Birmingham B12 9QH
Director: Dorothy Wilson
BO: 0121-440 3838   Admin: 0121-440 4221

BOSTON
Blackfriars Arts Centre
Spain Lane, Boston
Lincolnshire PE21 6HP
Website: www.blackfriars.uk.com
e-mail: marketing@blackfriars.uk.com
Fax: 01205 358855   Tel: 01205 363108

BRACKNELL
South Hill Park Arts Centre, Bracknell
Ringmead, Berkshire RG12 7PA
Chief Executive: Ron McAllister
Fax: 01344 411427   Tel: 01344 484858

BRADFORD
Theatre in the Mill
University of Bradford
Shearbridge Road, Bradford
West Yorkshire BD7 1DP
e-mail: theatre-manager@brad.ac.uk
                              Tel: 01274 233188

BRAINTREE
The Town Hall Centre
Market Square
Braintree, Essex CM7 3YG
General Manager: Jean Grice   Tel: 01376 557776

BRENTFORD
Watermans
40 High Street
Brentford TW8 0DS
Fax: 020-8232 1030
BO: 020-8232 1010   Admin: 020-8232 1020

BRIDGWATER
Bridgwater Arts Centre
11-13 Castle Street
Bridgwater, Somerset TA6 3DD
Website: www.bridgwaterartscentre.co.uk
e-mail: info@bridgwaterartscentre.co.uk
                              Tel: 01278 422700

BRIGHTON
Gardner Arts Centre
University of Sussex
Falmer, Brighton BN1 9RA
Director: Sue Webster
Website: www.gardnerarts.co.uk
e-mail: info@gardnerarts.co.uk
Fax: 01273 678551
BO: 01273 685861   Admin: 01273 685447

BRISTOL
Arnolfini, 16 Narrow Quay, Bristol BS1 4QA
Operations Manager: Polly Cole
Director: Caroline Collier
e-mail: arnolfini@arnolfini.demon.co.uk
Fax: 0117-925 3876   Tel: 0117-929 9191

BUILTH WELLS
Wyeside Arts Centre
Castle Street, Builth Wells, Powys LD2 3BN
Fax: 01982 553995   Tel: 01982 553668

BURTON UPON TRENT
The Brewhouse
Union Street, Burton upon Trent, Staffs DE14 1EB
Arts Manager: Rachel Walker
Administrator: Mike Mear
Website: www.brewhouse.co.uk
e-mail: info@brewhouse.co.uk
Fax: 01283 515106
BO: 01283 516030   Admin: 01283 567720

BURY
The Met Arts Centre
Market Street, Bury, Lancs BL9 0BW
Director: Ged Kelly
e-mail: mail@themet.biz
Fax: 0161-763 5056
BO: 0161-761 2216   Admin: 0161-761 7107

CANNOCK
Prince of Wales Centre
Church Sreet, Cannock, Staffs WS11 1DE
General Manager:
Richard Kay   Tel: 01543 466453

CARDIFF
Chapter Arts Centre
Market Road, Canton, Cardiff CF5 1QE
Theatre Programmer: James Tyson
BO: 029-2030 4400   Admin: 029-2031 1050

CHESTERFIELD
The Arts Centre
Chesterfield College, Sheffield Road
Chesterfield, Derbyshire S41 7LL
Co-ordinator: Joe Littlewood
                              Tel/Fax: 01246 500578

CHIPPING NORTON
The Theatre, 2 Spring Street
Chipping Norton
Oxfordshire OX7 5NL
Website: www.chippingnortontheatre.co.uk
e-mail: admin@chippingnortontheatre.co.uk
Fax: 01608 642324
Box Office: 01608 642350   Admin: 01608 642349

CHRISTCHURCH
The Regent Centre
51 High Street, Christchurch, Dorset BH23 1AS
General Manager: David Hopkins
Website: www.regentcentre.co.uk
e-mail: info@regentcentre.co.uk
Fax: 01202 479952
BO: 01202 499148   Admin: 01202 479819

CIRENCESTER
Brewery Arts
Brewery Court, Cirencester, Glos GL7 1JH
Artistic Director: Dan Scrivener
e-mail: admin@breweryarts.freeserve.co.uk
Fax: 01285 644060
BO: 01285 655522   Admin: 01285 657181

COLCHESTER
Colchester Arts Centre
Church Street, Colchester, Essex CO1 1NF
Director: Anthony Roberts
Website: www.colchesterartscentre.com
e-mail: info@colchesterartscentre.co.uk
Tel: 01206 500900

CORNWALL
Sterts Theatre & Arts Centre, Upton Cross
Liskeard, Cornwall PL14 5AZ
Tel/Fax: 01579 362962   Tel/Fax: 01579 362382

COVENTRY
Warwick Arts Centre
University of Warwick, Coventry CV4 7AL
Director: Alan Rivett
Website: www.warwickartscentre.co.uk
e-mail: arts.centre@warwick.ac.uk
BO: 024-7652 4524   Admin: 024-7652 3734

CUMBERNAULD
Cumbernauld Theatre, Kildrum
Cumbernauld G67 2BN
Administrator: Debra Jaffrey
Artistic Director: Simon Sharkey
Fax: 01236 738408
BO: 01236 732887   Admin: 01236 737235

DARLINGTON
Darlington Arts Centre
Vane Terrace, Darlington
County Durham DL3 7AX
BO: 01325 486555   Admin: 01325 483271

DORSET
Bryanston Arts Centre
Blandford Forum, Dorset DT11 0PX
Administrator: Sarah Bachra
Artistic Director: Jane Quan
e-mail: bac@bryanston.co.uk
Fax: 01258 484506   Tel: 01258 456533

EDINBURGH
Netherbow: Scottish Storytelling Centre
The Netherbow, 43-45 High Street
Edinburgh EH1 1SR
Director: Dr Donald Smith
Website: www.storytellingcentre.org.uk
e-mail: netherbow-storytelling@dial.pipex.com
Tel: 0131-556 9579

EDINBURGH
Theatre Workshop
34 Hamilton Place
Edinburgh EH3 5AX
Director: Robert Rae
Fax: 0131-220 0112   Tel: 0131-225 7942

EPSOM
Playhouse, Ashley Avenue
Epsom, Surrey KT18 5AL
Venues Manager: Trevor Mitchell
Website: www.epsomplayhouse.co.uk
e-mail: tmitchell@epsom-ewell.gov.uk
Fax: 01372 726228
BO: 01372 742555   Admin: 01372 742226

EVESHAM
Evesham Arts Centre
Victoria Avenue, Evesham
Worcestershire WR11 4QH
Director: Lauri Griffith-Jones   Tel: 01386 446067
BO: 01386 45567   Theatre: 01386 48883

EXETER
Exeter Phoenix
Bradninch Place, Gandy Street
Exeter, Devon EX4 3LS
Business Manager: Patrick Cunningham
e-mail: admin@exeterphoenix.org.uk
Fax: 01392 667599
BO: 01392 667080   Admin: 01392 667060

FAREHAM
Ashcroft Arts Centre
Osborn Road, Fareham
Hants PO16 7DX
Director/Programmer: Annabel Cook
Website: www.hants.org.uk/ashcroft
e-mail: ashcroft@hants.gov.uk
Fax: 01329 825661
BO: 01329 310600   Tel: 01329 235161

FROME
Merlin Theatre
Bath Road, Frome
Somerset BA11 2HG
Website: www.merlintheatre.co.uk
BO: 01373 465949   Admin: 01373 461360

GAINSBOROUGH
Trinity Arts Centre
Trinity Street, Gainsborough
Lincolnshire DN21 2AL
e-mail: info@trinityarts.demon.co.uk
Fax: 01427 811198
BO: 01427 676655   Admin: 01427 810298

GREAT TORRINGTON
The Plough Arts Centre
9-11 Fore Street
Great Torrington, Devon EX38 8HQ
Website: www.plough-arts.org
BO: 01805 624624   Admin: 01805 622552

HARLECH
Theatr Ardudwy
Harlech
Gwynedd LL46 2PU
Theatre Director: Mickey Plum   BO: 01766 780667

HAVANT
Havant Arts Centre
East Street, Havant, Hants PO9 1BS
Director: Amanda Eels
Website: www.havantartsactive.org
e-mail: info@havantartsactive.org
Fax: 023-9249 8577
BO: 023-9247 2700   Admin: 023-9248 0113

HEMEL HEMPSTEAD
Old Town Hall Arts Centre
High Street, Hemel Hempstead, Herts HP1 3AE
General Manager: Alison Young
Website: www.oldtownhall.co.uk
e-mail: othadmin@dacorum.gov.uk
BO: 01442 228091   Admin: 01442 228095

HEXHAM
Queens Hall Arts, Beaumont Street
Hexham, Northumberland NE46 3LS
Artistic Director: Geof Keys
Website: www.queenshall.co.uk
e-mail: boxoffice@queenshall.co.uk
Fax: 01434 652478   Tel: 01434 652476

HORSHAM
The Capitol
North Street, Horsham, West Sussex RH12 1RL
General Manager: Michael Gattrell
Fax: 01403 215268   Tel: 01403 215100

HUDDERSFIELD
Kirklees (various venues)
Kirklees Cultural Services, Red Doles Lane
Huddersfield HD2 1YF
Head of Performing Arts: Glenis Burgess
BO: 01484 223200   Admin: 01484 226300

INVERNESS
Eden Court Theatre, Bishop's Road
Inverness IV3 5SA
Director: Colin Marr
e-mail: admin@eden-court.co.uk
BO: 01463 234234   Admin: 01463 239841

JERSEY
Jersey Arts Centre
Phillips Street, St Helier, Jersey JE2 4SW
Director: Daniel Austin
Administrator: Graeme Humphries
Fax: 01534 726788
BO: 01534 700444   Admin: 01534 700400

KENDAL
Brewery Arts Centre
Highgate, Kendal, Cumbria LA9 4HE
Chief Executive: Sam Mason
BO: 01539 725133   Admin: 01539 722833

KING'S LYNN
Corn Exchange
Tuesday Market Place, King's Lynn
Norfolk PE30 1JW
Marketing Manager: Suzanne Hopp
e-mail: suzanne.hopp@west-norfolk.gov.uk
Fax: 01553 762141
Tel: 01553 765565   BO: 01553 764864

KING'S LYNN
King's Lynn Arts Centre
27-29 King's Street
King's Lynn, Norfolk PE30 1HA
Fax: 01553 762141
Tel: 01553 765565   BO: 01553 764864

LEICESTER
Phoenix Arts Centre
21 Upper Brown Street
Leicester LE1 5TE
e-mail: jeanne@phoenix.org.uk
BO: 0116-255 4854   Admin: 0116-224 7700

LICHFIELD
Lichfield District Arts Association
Donegal House, Bore Street, Lichfield WS13 6NE
Director: Brian Pretty
Website: www.lichfieldarts.org.uk
e-mail: theinfo@lichfieldarts.org.uk
Fax: 01543 308211   Tel: 01543 262223

LIVERPOOL
Bluecoat Arts Centre
School Lane, Liverpool L1 3BX
Director: Bryan Biggs
e-mail: admin@bluecoatartscentre.com
                                        Tel: 0151-709 5297

LONDON
Artsdepot (Opens May 2004)
5 Nether Street, North Finchley, London N12
Website: www.artsdepot.co.uk
e-mail: info@artsdepot.co.uk
Fax: 020-8364 9037
BO: 020-8449 0048   Admin: 020-8449 5189

LONDON
BAC
Lavender Hill, Battersea, London SW11 5TN
Website: www.bac.org.uk
e-mail: mailbox@bac.org.uk
Fax: 020-7978 5207
BO: 020-7223 2223   Admin: 020-7223 6557

LONDON
Chats Palace
42-44 Brooksby's Walk
Hackney, London E9 6DF
Administrator: Mick Reed
                              BO/Admin: 020-8533 0227

LONDON
Cockpit Theatre
Gateforth Street, London NW8 8EH
e-mail: dave.wybrow@cwc.ac.uk
Fax: 020-7258 2921
BO: 020-7258 2925   Admin: 020-7258 2920

LONDON
The Drill Hall
16 Chenies Street, London WC1E 7EX
Website: www.drillhall.co.uk
e-mail: admin@drillhall.co.uk
Fax: 020-7307 5062   Tel: 020-7307 5061

LONDON
Hoxton Hall Arts Centre
130 Hoxton Street, London N1 6SH
Venue Manager: Jonathan Salisbury
Website: www.hoxtonhall.co.uk
e-mail: office@hoxtonhall.co.uk
Fax: 020-7729 3815
BO: 020-7739 5431   Admin: 020-7684 0060

LONDON
Institute of Contemporary Arts
The Mall, London SW1Y 5AH
Director, Performing Arts and International Projects:
Vivienne Gaskin
Website: www.ica.org.uk
e-mail: vivienneg@ica.org.uk
Fax: 020-7306 0122
Admin: 020-7930 0493   BO: 020-7930 3647

LONDON
Islington Arts Factory
2 Parkhurst Road, London N7 0SF
e-mail: islington@artsfactory.fsnet.co.uk
Fax: 020-7700 7229   Tel: 020-7607 0561

LONDON
Jacksons Lane
269A Archway Road
London N6 5AA
Fax: 020-8348 2424
BO: 020-8341 4421   Admin: 020-8340 5226

LONDON
The Nettlefold
West Norwood Library Centre
1 Norwood High Street, London SE27 9JX
Centre Development Officers: Joanne Johnson
Mark Sheehan
Fax: 020-7926 8071   Admin/BO: 020-7926 8070

LONDON
October Gallery
24 Old Gloucester Street
London WC1N 3AL
Contact: Chili Hawes
Website: www.theoctobergallery.com
e-mail: octobergallery@compuserve.com
Fax: 020-7405 1851   Tel: 020-7242 7367

LONDON
Oval House Theatre
52-54 Kennington Oval
London SE11 5SW
Programmer: Karena Johnson
Director: Deborah Bestwick
Website: www.ovalhouse.com
e-mail: info@ovalhouse.com   Tel: 020-7582 0080

LONDON
Polish Social & Cultural Association
238-246 King Street
London W6 0RF   Tel: 020-8741 1940

LONDON
Riverside Studios
Crisp Road
Hammersmith
London W6 9RL
Website: www.riversidestudios.co.uk
e-mail: online@riversidestudios.co.uk
Fax: 020-8237 1001
BO: 020-8237 1111   Tel: 020-8237 1000

LOWESTOFT
Seagull Theatre, Morton Road
Lowestoft, Suffolk NR33 0JH
Advisory Drama Teacher: Sandra Redsell
Fax: 01502 515338   Tel: 01502 562863

MAIDENHEAD
Norden Farm Centre For The Arts
Altwood Road, Maidenhead SL6 4PF
Director: Annabel Turpin
Website: www.nordenfarm.org
e-mail: admin@nordenfarm.org
Fax: 01628 682525
BO: 01628 788997   Admin: 01628 682555

MAIDSTONE
Corn Exchange Complex, Earl Street
Maidstone, Kent ME14 1PL
Commercial Manager: Mandy Hare
Fax: 01622 602194
BO: 01622 758611   Admin: 01622 753922

MANCHESTER
Green Room
54-56 Whitworth Street West
Manchester M1 5WW
Artistic Director: Garfield Allen
Website: www.greenroomarts.org
e-mail: info@greenroomarts.org
Fax: 0161-615 0516
BO: 0161-615 0500   Admin: 0161-615 0515

MANCHESTER
The Lowry
Pier 8, Salford Quays M50 3AZ
Theatre Production Bookings: Louise Ormerod
Website: www.thelowry.com
e-mail: info@thelowry.com
Fax: 0161-876 2021
BO: 0870 1112000   Admin: 0161-876 2020

MANSFIELD
New Perspectives Theatre Company
The Old Library, Leeming Street
Mansfield, Notts NG18 1NG
Website: www.newperspectives.co.uk
e-mail: info@newperspectives.co.uk
Tel: 01623 635225

MILFORD HAVEN
Torch Theatre, St Peter's Road
Milford Haven, Pembrokeshire SA73 2BU
Artistic Director: Peter Doran
Website: www.torchtheatre.org
e-mail: info@torchtheatre.co.uk
Fax: 01646 698919
BO: 01646 695267   Admin: 01646 694192

NEWPORT (Isle of Wight)
Quay Arts
Sea Street, Newport Harbour
Isle of Wight PO30 5BD
Fax: 01983 526606
BO: 01983 528825   Tel: 01983 822490

NORWICH
Norwich Arts Centre
St Benedicts Street, Norwich, Norfolk NR2 4PG
Website: www.norwichartscentre.co.uk
e-mail: iancallell@norwichartscentre.co.uk
BO: 01603 660352   Admin: 01603 660387

NUNEATON
Abbey Theatre & Arts Centre
Pool Bank Street, Nuneaton, Warks CV11 5DB
Chairman: Tony Deeming
Website: www.abbeytheatre.co.uk
e-mail: admin@abbeytheatre.co.uk
Tel: 024-7632 7359   BO: 024-7635 4090

PLYMOUTH
Plymouth Arts Centre
38 Looe Street, Plymouth, Devon PL4 0EB
Director: Ian Hutchinson
Website: www.plymouthac.org.uk
e-mail: arts@plymouthac.org.uk
Fax: 01752 206118   Tel: 01752 206114

POOLE
Poole Centre for The Arts
Kingland Road, Poole, Dorset BH15 1UG
Website: www.lighthousepoole.co.uk
BO: 01202 685222   Admin: 01202 665334

RADLETT
The Radlett Centre
1 Aldenham Avenue, Radlett, Herts WD7 8HL
Website: www.radlettcentre.co.uk
Fax: 01923 857592   Tel: 01923 857546

ROTHERHAM
Rotherham Theatres
Walker Place, Rotherham
South Yorkshire S65 1JH
Strategic Leader Culture/Leisure/Lifelong Learning:
Phil Rodgers
Website: www.rotherham.gov.uk
BO: 01709 823621   Admin: 01709 823641

SALISBURY
Salisbury Arts Centre
Bedwin Street, Salisbury, Wiltshire SP1 3UT
e-mail: info@salisburyarts.co.uk
Fax: 01722 331742
BO: 01722 321744   Admin: 01722 430700

SHREWSBURY
Shrewsbury & District Arts Association
The Gateway, Chester Street, Shrewsbury
Shropshire SY1 1NB
e-mail: gateway.centre@shropshire-cc.gov.uk
                              Tel: 01743 355159

SOUTHPORT
Southport Arts Centre
Lord Street, Southport, Merseyside PR8 1DB
Website: www.seftonarts.co.uk
e-mail: artsops@seftonarts.co.uk
BO: 01704 540011   Admin: 01704 540004

STAMFORD
Stamford Arts Centre
27 St Mary's Street, Stamford, Lincolnshire PE9 2DL
General Manager: David Popple
Fax: 01780 766690
BO: 01780 763203   Admin: 01780 480846

STIRLING
MacRobert
University of Stirling, Stirling FK9 4LA
Director: Liz Moran
Website: www.macrobert.org
BO: 01786 466666   Admin: 01786 467155

SWANSEA
Taliesin Arts Centre
University of Wales Swansea, Singleton Park
Swansea SA2 8PZ
General Manager: Sybil Crouch
Website: www.taliesinartscentre.co.uk
e-mail: s.e.crouch@swansea.ac.uk
                              Tel: 01792 295438

SWINDON
Wyvern Theatre, Theatre Square
Swindon, Wiltshire SN1 1QN
BO: 01793 524481   Admin: 01793 535534

TAUNTON
Brewhouse
Coal Orchard, Taunton, Somerset TA1 1JL
Artistic Director: Glenys Gill
Website: www.brewhouse-theatre.co.uk
e-mail: brewhouse@btconnect.co.uk
Fax: 01823 323116
BO: 01823 283244   Admin: 01823 274608

TOTNES
Dartington Arts
The Barn, Dartington Hall
Totnes, Devon TQ9 6DE
e-mail: admin@dartingtonarts.co.uk
BO: 01803 847070   Admin: 01803 847074

TUNBRIDGE WELLS
Trinity Theatre & Arts Centre
Church Road, Tunbridge Wells, Kent TN1 1JP
Director: Adrian Berry
BO: 01892 678678   Admin: 01892 678670

ULEY
Prema
South Street
Uley, Nr Dursley, Glos GL11 5SS
Director: Gordon Scott
Website: www.prema.demon.co.uk
e-mail: info@prema.demon.co.uk
Fax: 01453 860123   Tel: 01453 860703

VALE OF GLAMORGAN
St Donats Arts Centre
St Donats Castle
The Vale of Glamorgan CF61 1WF
Artistic Director: David Ambrose
Fax: 01446 799101   Tel: 01446 799099

WAKEFIELD
Wakefield Arts Centre
Wakefield College
Thornes Park Centre
Thornes Park, Horbury Road Wakefield WF2 8QZ
Facilities Officer: Carole Clark
e-mail: c-clark@wakcoll.ac.uk   Tel: 01924 789824

WALLSEND
Buddle Arts Centre
258B Station Road
Wallsend, Tyne & Wear NE28 8RG
Contact: Geoffrey A Perkins
Fax: 0191-200 7142   Tel: 0191-200 7132

WASHINGTON
The Arts Centre Washington
Biddick Lane, Fatfield, District 7, Washington
Tyne & Wear NE38 8AB
Fax: 0191-219 3466   Tel: 0191-219 3455

WELLINGBOROUGH
The Castle, Castle Way, Wellingborough
Northants NN8 1XA
Executive Director: Graham Brown
Artistic Director: David Bown
Website: www.thecastle.org.uk
e-mail: info@thecastle.org.uk
Fax: 01933 229888   Tel: 01933 229022

WIMBORNE
Layard Theatre
Canford School, Canford Magna
Wimborne, Dorset BH21 3AD
Director of Drama: Stephen Hattersley
Administrator: Christine Haynes
e-mail: layardtheatre@canford.com
Fax: 01202 847525
BO: 01202 847525   Admin: 01202 847529

WINCHESTER
Tower Arts Centre
Romsey Road
Winchester, Hampshire SO22 5PW
Director: John Tellett
Website: www.towerarts.co.uk   Tel: 01962 867986

WINDSOR
Windsor Arts Centre
St Leonard's Road
Windsor, Berks SL4 3BL
Director: Debbie Stubbs
Website: www.windsorartscentre.org
e-mail: admin@windsorartscentre.org
Fax: 01753 621527
BO: 01753 859336   Admin: 01753 859421

WOLVERHAMPTON
Afro-Caribbean Cultural Centre
2 Clarence Street
Wolverhampton WV1 4JH
Arts Co-ordinator: CJ Antonio   Tel: 01902 420109

WREXHAM
Wrexham Arts Centre
Rhosddu Road
Wrexham LL11 1AU
e-mail: arts.centre@wrexham.gov.uk
Fax: 01978 292611   Tel: 01978 292093

A C A CASTING
(Catherine Arton)
4 Aldridge Road Villas, London W11 1BP
e-mail: casting@acacasting.com
Tel/Fax: 020-7792 8497

ADAMSON Joanne CASTING
4 Hillthorpe Square
Leeds LS28 8NQ
e-mail: watts07@hotmail.com   Mobile: 07787 311270

AILION Pippa
3 Towton Road, London SE27 9EE
Tel/Fax: 020-8670 4816   Tel: 020-8761 7095

ALEXANDER Pam CDG
49 Stanley Road, Heaton Moor, Stockport SK4 4HW
e-mail: pam.alexander@virgin.net
Mobile: 07715 119158   Tel: 0161-431 6529

ALL DIRECTIONS OF LONDON
7 Rupert Court, Off Wardour Street
London W1D 6EB   Tel: 020-7437 5879

ALL KIDS CASTING
(Children & Young Performers)
PO Box 3242, Barnet, Hertfordshire EN5 2XR
Website: www.allkidscasting.com
e-mail: jenny@allkidscasting.com
Tel: 020-8364 9220

ANDREW Dorothy CASTING
Campus Manor, Childwall Abbey Road
Childwall, Liverpool L16 0JP
Fax: 0151-722 9079   Tel: 0151-722 9122

ARNELL Jane
Flat 2, 39 St Peter's Square
London W6 9NN

BAIG Shaheen
11 Deane House
27 Greenwood Place, London NW5 1LB
Fax: 020-7482 5565   Tel: 020-7482 6070

BALDIES CASTING AGENCY
(The only agency purely for bald people)
6 Marlott Road, Poole, Dorset BH15 3DX
Mobile: 07860 290437   Tel: 01202 666001

BARBOUR Penny
Rosemary Cottage, Fontridge Lane
Etchingham, East Sussex TN19 7DD

BARNES Michael CDG
25 Old Oak Road
London W3 7HN
Fax: 020-8742 9385   Tel: 020-8749 1354

BARTLETT Carolyn CDG
22 Barton Road, London W14 9HD

**BBC DRAMA SERIES CASTING -
BBC CENTRE HOUSE**
Room DG03
56 Wood Lane, London W12 7SB
Fax: 020-8576 4947   Tel: 020-8225 6475

BBC DRAMA SERIES CASTING - BBC ELSTREE
Neptune House, Room N412
Clarendon Road, Borehamwood
Herts WD6 1JF
Fax: 020-8228 8311   Tel: 020-8228 8620

BEARDSALL Sarah CDG
73 Wells Street
London W1T 3QG
e-mail: casting@beardsall.com
Fax: 020-7436 8859   Tel: 020-7323 4040

BEATTIE Victoria
Unit 19, The John Cotton Building
Sunnyside, Edinburgh EH7 5RA
e-mail: victoria@victoriabeattie.com
Fax: 0131-652 4001   Tel: 0131-652 4002

BERTRAND Leila CASTING
53 Hormead Road
London W9 3NQ
e-mail: leilabcasting@aol.com
Tel/Fax: 020-8964 0683

BEVAN Lucy
c/o Twickenham Studios
St Margaret's
Twickenham TW1 2AW   Tel: 020-8607 8888

BEWICK Maureen CASTING
104A Dartmouth Road
London NW2 4HB

BEXFIELD Glenn
(See BBC DRAMA SERIES CASTING - BBC CENTRE HOUSE)

BIG FISH CASTING Ltd
(Des Hamilton & Kahleen Crawford)
The Pearce Institute
840 Govan Road, Glasgow G51 3UU
Website: www.sigmafilms.com
Fax: 0141-445 6900   Tel: 0141-425 1725

BILL The
Thames Television Ltd
Talkback Thames Studios
1 Deer Park Road
Merton, London SW19 3TL   Tel: 020-8540 0600

BIRD Sarah CDG
PO Box 32658, London W14 0XA
Fax: 020-7602 8601   Tel: 020-7371 3248

BOULTING Lucy CDG
7 Gravel Road, Twickenham Green
Middlesex TW2 6RH
e-mail: hill@boulting.freeserve.co.uk

BRACKE Siobhan CDG
Basement Flat, 22A The Barons
St Margaret's TW1 2AP   Tel: 020-8891 5686

BROADCASTING
(Lesley Beastall, Sophie North & Jon Levene)
23 Canalot Studios, 222 Kensal Road
London W10 5BN
e-mail: broadcasting@btclick.com
Fax: 020-7460 5223   Tel: 020-7460 5220

BRUFFIN Susie CDG
133 Hartswood Road
London W12 9NG   Tel: 020-8740 9895

BRUSCHELLE Barbara
(See CASTING UNLIMITED LONDON & LOS ANGELES)

CAIRD LITTLEWOOD CASTING
(Angela Caird)
PO Box MT 86, Leeds LS17 8YQ
e-mail: cairdlitt@aol.com
Fax: 0113-266 6068   Tel: 0113-288 8014

CALEDONIA CASTING
(Scottish Actors)
70 Weinwood Avenue, Glasgow G69 6HS
e-mail: liz@caledoniacasting.co.uk
                           Mobile: 07776 183583

CAMERON Polly
(See BBC DRAMA SERIES CASTING - BBC CENTRE HOUSE)

CANDID CASTING
2nd Floor
111-113 Great Titchfield Street
London W1W 6RY
e-mail: mail@candidcasting.co.uk
Fax: 020-7636 5522   Tel: 020-7636 6644

CANNON DUDLEY & ASSOCIATES
43A Belsize Square, London NW3 4HN
e-mail: cdacasting@blueyonder.co.uk
Fax: 020-7433 3599   Tel: 020-7433 3393

CANNON John CDG
(See ROYAL SHAKESPEARE COMPANY)

CARLING Di CASTING CDG
1st Floor, 49 Frith Street
London W1D 4SG
Fax: 020-7287 6844   Tel: 020-7287 6446

CARLTON TELEVISION
35-38 Portman Square, London W1H 0NU
Fax: 020-7612 7528   Tel: 020-7486 6688

CARROLL Anji CDG
4 Nesfield Drive
Winterley, Cheshire CW11 4NT
e-mail: anjicarrollcdg@yahoo.co.uk
                           Tel/Fax: 01270 588803

CASTING ANGELS The
(London & Paris)
Suite 4, 14 College Road, Bromley
Kent BR1 3NS   Tel/Fax: 020-8313 0443

CASTING COMPANY (UK) The
(Michelle Guish CDG, Associate Gaby Kester)
3rd Floor Rear
112-114 Wardour Street, London W1F 0TS
Fax: 020-7434 2346   Tel: 020-7734 4954

CASTING CONNECTION The
(Michael Syers)
Dalrossie House, 16 Victoria Grove
Stockport, Cheshire SK4 5BU
Fax: 0161-442 7280   Tel: 0161-432 4122

CASTING COUCH PRODUCTIONS Ltd
(Moira Townsend)
97 Riffel Road, London NW2 4PG
e-mail: moiratownsend@yahoo.co.uk
Fax: 020-8208 2373   Tel: 020-8438 9679

CASTING DIRECTORS The
(Gillian Hawser & Caroline Hutchings)
24 Cloncurry Street, London SW6 6DS
Fax: Gillian: 020-7731 0738
e-mail: gillian.hawser@virgin.net
e-mail: carohutchings@hotmail.com
Fax: Caroline: 020-8336 1067   Tel: 020-7731 5988

CASTING UK
(Andrew Mann)
88-90 Gray's Inn Road, London WC1X 8AA
Website: www.castinguk.com
e-mail: info@castinguk.com
Fax: 020-7430 1155   Tel: 020-7430 1122

CASTING UNLIMITED (LONDON)
9 Hansard Mews, Kensington, London W14 8BJ
e-mail: info@castingdirector.co.uk
Fax: 0870 4435623   Tel: 0870 4435621

CASTING UNLIMITED (LOS ANGELES)
e-mail: info@castingdirector.co.uk

CATLIFF Suzy CDG
PO Box 32658, London W14 0XA
e-mail: suzy_catliff@hotmail.com
Fax: 020-7602 8601   Tel: 020-7371 3248

CELEBRITY MANAGEMENT Ltd
12 Nottingham Place, London W1U 5NE
Website: www.celebrity.co.uk
e-mail: info@celebrity.co.uk
Fax: 020-7224 6060   Tel: 020-7224 5050

CHADBON Millie
26 Clevedon Close
London N16 7LD   Mobile: 07810 430308

CHARD Alison CDG
23 Groveside Court, Lombard Road
Battersea, London SW11 3RQ
e-mail: alisonchard@castingdirector.freeserve.co.uk
                Tel/Fax: 020-7223 9125

CHARKHAM CASTING
(Beth Charkham)
Suite 5.1, Moray House
23-31 Great Titchfield Street
London W1W 7PA
e-mail: charkhamcasting@btconnect.com
Fax: 020-7436 4943   Tel: 020-7436 4842

CLARK Andrea
(See ZIMMERMANN Jeremy CASTING)

COGAN Ben
(See BBC DRAMA SERIES CASTING - BBC CENTRE HOUSE)

COHEN Abi CASTING
11 Deane House, 27 Greenwood Place
London NW5 1LB
Fax: 020-7482 5565   Tel: 020-7485 5445

COLLINS Jayne CASTING
38 Commercial Street, London E1 6LP
Website: www.jaynecollinscasting.com
e-mail: info@jaynecollinscasting.com
Fax: 020-7422 0015   Tel: 020-7422 0014

COLLINS Katrina
(See BBC DRAMA SERIES CASTING - BBC ELSTREE)

MICHELLE LIVINGSTONE

KEVIN WHATELY

JOHN FLETCHER

PHOTOGRAPHER

020-8203-4816

COMMERCIALS CASTING UK
220 Church Lane
Woodford, Stockport SK7 1PQ
Fax: 0161-439 0622   Tel: 0161-439 6825

CORDORAY Lin
66 Cardross Street, London W6 0DR

COTTON Irene CDG
25 Druce Road
Dulwich Village
London SE21 7DW
e-mail: oliver36@btopenworld.com
Tel/Fax: 020-8299 2787   Tel: 020-8299 1595

CRAMPSIE Julia
(See BBC DRAMA SERIES CASTING - BBC CENTRE HOUSE)

CRANE Carole CASTING
63 Clockhouse Road
Beckenham, Kent BR3 4JO
Website: www.carolecranecasting.com
e-mail: crane.shot@virgin.net

9 Oakbrook Court, Sheffield S10 3HR
Mobile: 07976 869442   Tel/Fax: 0114-230 8801

CRAWFORD Margaret
92 Castelnau, London SW13 9EU

CROCODILE CASTING COMPANY The
(C. Gibbs & T. Saban)
9 Ashley Close
Hendon, London NW4 1PH
Website: www.crocodilecasting.com
e-mail: croccast@aol.com
Fax: 020-8203 7711   Tel: 020-8203 7009

CROWE Sarah CASTING
24 Poland Street
London W1F 8QL
e-mail: sarah@sarahcrowecasting.co.uk
Fax: 020-7287 2147   Tel: 020-7734 5464

CROWLEY POOLE CASTING
11 Goodwins Court
London WC2N 4LL
Fax: 020-7379 5971   Tel: 020-7379 5965

CROWLEY Suzanne CDG
(See CROWLEY POOLE CASTING)

CYBER-ARTISTS
In The Can Ltd
The Studio, Kingsway Court
Queen's Gardens, Hove BN3 2LP
Website: www.cyberartists.co.uk
e-mail: cyber.1@btclick.com
Fax: 01273 739984   Tel/Fax: 01273 821821

DAVIES Jane CASTING Ltd
(Jane Davies CDG & John Connor CDG)
PO Box 680, Sutton, Surrey SM1 3ZG
e-mail: info@janedaviescasting.co.uk
Fax: 020-8644 9746   Tel: 020-8715 1036

DAVIS Leo (Miss)
(JUST CASTING)
128 Talbot Road, London W11 1JA
Fax: 020-7792 3043   Tel: 020-7229 3471

DAVY Gary CDG
33 Fitzroy Street, London W1T 6DU
Fax: 020-7636 0881   Tel: 020-7636 0880

DAY Kate CDG
Pound Cottage
27 The Green South
Warborough
Oxon OX10 7DR   Tel/Fax: 01865 858709

DE FREITAS Paul CDG
6 Brook Street, Mayfair, London W1S 1BB

DEITCH Jane
(See BBC DRAMA SERIES CASTING - BBC CENTRE HOUSE)

DENMAN Jack CASTING
Burgess House, Main Street, Farnsfield
Notts NG22 8EF   Tel/Fax: 01623 882272

DENNISON Lee ASSOCIATES
Fushion, 27 Old Gloucester Street
London WC1N 3XX
e-mail: castings@fushion-uk.com
Fax: 08700 111020   Tel: 08700 111100

DICKENS Laura CDG
11 Egerton Court, Paradise Road
Richmond, Surrey TW9 1LN
e-mail: lauraadickens@aol.com
          Mobile: 07958 665468

Cora Bissett

Roger Allam

Jane Kahler

DOWD Kate
64 Knightsbridge, London SW1X 7JF
Fax: 020-7590 9636   Tel: 020-7590 9635

DRURY Malcolm CDG
34 Tabor Road
London W6 0BW   Tel: 020-8748 9232

DUDLEY Carol CDG
(See CANNON DUDLEY & ASSOCIATES)

DUFF Julia CDG
73 Wells Street, London W1T 3QG
Fax: 020-7436 8859   Tel: 020-7436 8860

DUFF Maureen CDG
(See STEVENS Gail CASTING)

DUFFY Jennifer CDG
42 Old Compton Street, London W1D 4TX
Fax: 020-7287 7752   Tel: 020-7287 7751

EAST Irene CASTING CDG
40 Brookwood Ave, Barnes, London SW13 0LR
e-mail: irneast@aol.com   Tel: 020-8876 5686

EJ CASTING
Lower Ground Floor, 86 Vassall Road
London SW9 6JA
e-mail: info@ejcasting.com
Mobile: 07976 726869   Tel: 020-7564 2688

EMMERSON Chloe
110 Goldhawk Road
London W12 8HD   Tel/Fax: 020-8749 0439

ET-NIK-A PRIME MANAGEMENT & CASTINGS Ltd
Balfour House, 46-54 Great Titchfield Street
London W1W 7QA
Website: www.et-nik-a.co.uk
e-mail: info@et-nik-a.co.uk
Fax: 020-7299 3558   Tel: 020-7299 3555

EVANS Karen
Carlton Television, 35-38 Portman Square
London W1H 6NU

EVANS Kate
(See KATE & ALI CASTING)

EVANS Richard CDG
10 Shirley Road, London W4 1DD
Website: www.evanscasting.co.uk
e-mail: contact@revanscasting.co.uk
Fax: 020-8742 1010   Tel: 020-8994 6304

FEARNLEY Ali
(See KATE & ALI CASTING)

FIELDEN Ann
5 Rectory Lane, London SW17 9PZ
Fax: 020-8672 4803   Tel: 020-8767 3939

FIELDEN Cornelia
Waterside, 99 Rotherhithe Street, London SE16 4NF
Fax: 020-7394 0016   Tel: 020-7394 1444

FIGGIS Susie
19 Spencer Rise
London NW5 1AR   Tel: 020-7482 2200

FILDES Bunny CASTING CDG
56 Wigmore Street
London W1   Tel: 020-7935 1254

FINCHER Sally CDG
Carlton Television, 35-38 Portman Square
London W1H 6NU

FOTHERGILL Janey CASTING
3rd Floor Suite, 10-11 Lower John Street
London WIF 9EB   Tel/Fax: 020-7287 2304

FOX Celestia
5 Clapham Common Northside, London SW4 0QW
e-mail: celestia.fox@virgin.net

FRAZER Janie CDG
London Weekend TV, Television Centre
South Bank, London SE1 9LT
e-mail: janie.frazer@granadamedia.com
        Tel: 020-7261 3848

FRECK Rachel
e-mail: rachelfreck@btopenworld.com
        Tel: 020-8673 2455

FRISBY Jane CASTING CDG
51 Ridge Road, London N8 9LJ
e-mail: jane.frisby@tiscali.co.uk

FUNNELL Caroline CDG
25 Rattray Road, London SW2 1AZ
Fax: 020-7326 1713   Tel: 020-7326 4417

GALLIE Joyce
37 Westcroft Square, London W6 0TA

GANE CASTING
(Natasha Gane)
1 The Willows, 1025 High Road, London N20 0QE
e-mail: natasha@ganecasting.com
Fax: 020-8446 2508   Tel: 020-8446 2551

GB CASTING UK Ltd (Karin Grainger)
1 Charlotte Street, London W1T 1RD
e-mail: kggbuk@lineone.net
Fax: 020-7255 1899   Tel: 020-7636 2437

GILLHAM Tracey CDG
(Entertainment - Comedy)
BBC Television Centre, Wood Lane
London W12 7RJ
Fax: 020-8576 4414   Tel: 020-8225 8488

GOLD Nina CDG
10 Kempe Road, London NW6 6SJ
e-mail: nina@ninagold.co.uk
Fax: 020-8968 6777   Tel: 020-8960 6099

GOLDWYN Lauren CASTING INC
14 Dean Street, London W1D 3RS
e-mail: realcreate@aol.com
Fax: 020-7437 4221   Tel: 020-7437 4188

GOOCH Miranda CASTING
102 Leighton Gardens, London NW10 3PR
e-mail: mirandagooch@hotmail.com
Fax: 020-8962 9579   Tel: 020-8962 9578

GRAYBURN Lesley
74 Leigh Gardens, London NW10 5HP
Fax: 020-8969 2846   Tel: 020-8969 6112

GREEN Jill CASTING CDG
52 Tottenham Street, London W1T 4RN
Fax: 020-7580 6048   Tel: 020-7580 6037

GREENE Francesca CASTING
79 Ashworth Mansions, London W9 1LN
Fax: 020-7266 9001   Tel: 020-7286 5957

GRESHAM Marcia CDG
3 Langthorne Street
London SW6 6JT   Tel: 020-7381 2876

GROSVENOR CASTING
(Angela Grosvenor CDG)
27 Rowena Crescent, London SW11 2PT
Fax: 020-7652 6256   Tel: 020-7738 0449

GUISH Michelle CDG
(See CASTING COMPANY (UK) The)

HALL David CDG
85 Shorrolds Road, London SW6 7TU
e-mail: justdavidhall@hotmail.com
Fax: 020-7381 3288   Tel: 020-7381 0066

Adrian and Neil Rayment

Anne Reid

Photography by
ANGUS DEUCHAR
t. 020 8286 3303 m. 07973 600728
www.ActorsPhotos.co.uk

HALL Janet
1 Shore Avenue, Shaw, Oldham OL2 8DA
e-mail: hall@stage257.fsbusiness.co.uk
Mobile: 07780 783489   Tel: 01706 291459

HALL Pippa
(Children & Teenagers only)
128 Talbot Road, London W11 1JA
e-mail: pippahall.casting@virgin.net
                              Tel/Fax: 020-8785 7184

HAMMOND Louis
c/o The Casting Company (UK)
3rd Floor, 112-114 Wardour Street, London W1F 0TS
Fax: 020-7434 2346   Tel: 020-7734 4954

HANCOCK Gemma CDG
The Rosary
Broad Street, Cuckfield
West Sussex RH17 5DL
e-mail: gemma.hancock@virgin.net
                              Tel/Fax: 01444 441398

HARE Jackie
3 Billington Place, Milford Road
Lymington, Hampshire SO41 8JQ
e-mail: jackiehare@cast73.fsnet.co.uk
                              Tel/Fax: 01590 688664

HARKIN Julie
135 Old Ford Road, London E2 9QD
e-mail: harkin_julie@hotmail.com
                              Mobile: 07989 578820

HARRIS Lisa
290 Coulsdon Road, Old Coulsdon
Surrey CR5 1EB   Mobile: 07956 561247

HAWSER Gillian CASTING
24 Cloncurry Street, London SW6 6DS
e-mail: gillian.hawser@virgin.net
Fax: 020-7731 0738   Tel: 020-7731 5988

HAYFIELD Judi CDG
Granada Television, Quay Street
Manchester M60 9EA
Fax: 0161-827 2853   Tel: 0161-832 7211

HICKLING Matthew
(See BBC DRAMA SERIES CASTING - BBC ELSTREE)

HILL Serena
Sydney Theatre Company, Pier 4
Hickson Road, Walsh Bay, NSW 2000, Australia
e-mail: shill@sydneytheatre.com.au
                              Tel: 00 612 925 01700

HILTON Carrie
HG14, Aberdeen Centre
22-24 Highbury Grove, London N5 2EA
Fax: 020-7359 5378   Tel: 020-7226 8897

HOOTKINS Polly CDG
PO Box 25191, London SW1V 2WN
e-mail: phootkins@clara.net
Fax: 020-7828 5051   Tel: 020-7233 8724

HORAN Julia
26 Falkland Road
London NW5 2PX   Tel: 020-7267 5261

HOWE Gary
34 Orbit Street, Roath
Cardiff CF24 0JX
Tel/Fax: 029-2025 0181   Tel: 029-2033 1341

HUBBARD CASTING
(Ros Hubbard, John Hubbard, Dan Hubbard CDG)
2nd Floor, 19 Charlotte Street, London W1T 1RL
e-mail: email@hubbardcasting.com
Fax: 020-7636 7117   Tel: 020-7636 9991

HUBBARD CASTING (DUBLIN)
(Mary Maguire)
15 The Stiles Road, Clontarf, Dublin 3, Eire

HUGHES Sarah
Stephen Joseph Theatre, Westborough
Scarborough
North Yorkshire YO11 1JW   Tel: 01723 370540

HUGHES Sylvia
Casting Suite, The Deanwater
Wilmslow Road, Woodford, Cheshire SK7 1RJ
Fax: 01565 723707   Tel: 01565 722707

HUTCHINGS Caroline
PO Box 1119, Kingston & Surbiton KT2 7WY
e-mail: carohutchings@hotmail.com
Fax: 020-8336 1067   Mobile: 07768 615343

INTERNATIONAL CASTING
(Elaine Grainger)
Flint Cottage, Duncton, Petworth
West Sussex GU28 0LT
e-mail: e.grainger@virgin.net
Mobile: 07932 741794   Tel: 01798 343556

JACKSON Sue
Yorkshire Television, The TV Centre, Leeds LS3 1JS

JAFFA SILLS CASTING
(Craig Sills CDG & Janis Jaffa)
67 Starfield Road, London W12 9SN
e-mail: jaffasills@supaworld.com
Fax: 020-8743 9561   Tel: 020-7565 2877

JAFFREY Jennifer
136 Hicks Avenue, Greenford, Middlesex UB6 8HB
e-mail: jaffreymag@aol.com
Fax: 020-8575 0369   Tel: 020-8578 2899

JAY Jina CASTING CDG
1st & 2nd Floors, 50 Chiswick High Road
London W4 1SZ
Fax: 020-8994 8654   Tel: 020-8995 9090

JELOWICKI Ilenka
(Mad Dog Casting Ltd)
Top Floor, 10 Warwick Street, London W1B 5LZ
e-mail: ilenka@maddogcasting.com
Fax: 020-7287 5983   Tel: 020-7434 1211

JENKINS Lucy CDG
74 High Street, Hampton Wick
Kingston-upon-Thames KT1 4DQ
e-mail: lucy@littlejenkins.freeserve.co.uk
Fax: 020-8977 0466   Tel: 020-8943 5328

JN CASTING & PRODUCTION
The Worx, 16-24 Underwood Street, London N1 7JQ
e-mail: james@jncasting.com
Fax: 020-7684 8587   Tel: 020-7684 8586

JOHN Priscilla CDG
PO Box 22477, London W6 0GT
Fax: 020-8741 4005   Tel: 020-8741 4212

JOHNSON Alex CASTING
15 McGregor Road, London W11 1DE
e-mail: alex@alexjon.demon.co.uk
Fax: 020-7229 1665   Tel: 020-7229 8779

JOHNSON Marilyn CDG
1st Floor, 11 Goodwins Court, London WC2N 4LL
e-mail: marilynjohnson@lineone.net
Fax: 020-7497 5530   Tel: 020-7497 5552

JONES Doreen CDG
PO Box 22478, London W6 0WJ
Fax: 020-8748 8533   Tel: 020-8746 3782

JONES Sam CDG
6th Floor, International House
223 Regent Street, London W1R 7DB
e-mail: get@samjones.fsnet.co.uk
Fax: 020-7493 7890   Tel: 020-7493 5456

JONES Sue CDG
24 Nicoll Road, London NW10 9AB
Fax: 020-8838 1130   Tel: 020-8838 5153

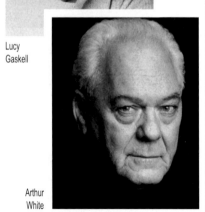

Brenda
Fricker

Lucy
Gaskell

Arthur
White

KATE & ALI CASTING
1st Floor, 26 Goodge Street, London W1T 2QG
e-mail: katealicasting@btclick.com
Fax: 020-7636 8080   Tel: 020-7636 4040

KEENAN Philip
33 Mary Ann Gardens, London SE8 3DP
e-mail: casting@philipkeenan.com
                                        Tel: 020-8469 0300

KEOGH Beverley
40 Princess Street
Manchester M1 6DE
e-mail: beverley@beverleykeogh.tv
Fax: 0161-920 9715   Tel: 0161-920 9714

KESTER Gaby
(See CASTING COMPANY (UK) The)

KESTON Sam
(Children, Young People, Families)
Fax: 01628 822461   Tel: 01628 822982 Ext 4

KING Andrea
e-mail: andreaking.tv@ntlworld.com
Mobile: 07752 455510   Tel: 01204 456253

KNIGHT-SMITH Jerry CDG
c/o Royal Exchange Theatre
St Ann's Square, Manchester M2 7DH
Fax: 0161-615 6691   Tel: 0161-615 6761

KOREL Suzy CDG
20 Blenheim Road, London NW8 0LX
e-mail: suzy@korel.org
Fax: 020-7372 3964   Tel: 020-7624 6435

KYLE CASTING
The Summerhouse, Thames House
54 Thames Street, Hampton TW12 2DX
Fax: 020-8274 8423   Tel: 020-8274 8096

LAYTON & NORCLIFFE CASTING
(Belinda Norcliffe, Claudie Layton &
Alix Charpentier)
Unit 308, Canalot Studios
222 Kensal Road, London W10 5BN
e-mail: casting@laytonnorcliffe.com
Fax: 020-8968 1330   Tel: 020-8964 2055

LESSALL Matthew
Unit 5, Gun Wharf
241 Old Ford Road, London E3 5QB
e-mail: lessallcasting@hotmail.com
Fax: 020-8980 2211   Tel: 020-8980 0117

LEVINSON Sharon
30 Stratford Villas, London NW1 9SG
e-mail: sharonlev@aol.com
Fax: 020-7916 5872   Tel: 020-7485 2057

LINDSAY-STEWART Karen CDG
PO Box 2301, London W1A 1PT
Fax: 020-7439 0548   Tel: 020-7439 0544

LIP SERVICE CASTING
(Voice-Overs only)
60-66 Wardour Street, London W1F 0TA
Website: www.lipservice.co.uk
e-mail: castings@lipservice.co.uk
Fax: 020-7734 3373   Tel: 020-7734 3393

LODESTONE CASTING
(Matt Colbeck & Paul J Hare)
Henlly's House, 59 Caverswall Road
Blythe Bridge, Staffordshire ST11 9BG
e-mail: lodestone@onetel.net.uk
                                        Mobile: 07967 354395

MacGABHANN Dorothy
15 Sandycove Avenue East, Sandycove
Co. Dublin, Eire
Fax: 00 353 1 2846865   Tel: 00 353 1 2807242

MARSHALL Sophie
Royal Exchange Theatre Company
St Ann's Square, Manchester M2 7DH
Website: www.royalexchange.co.uk
Fax: 0161-832 0881   Tel: 0161-833 9333

McCANN Joan CDG
26 Hereford Road, London W3 9JW
Fax: 020-8992 8715   Tel: 020-8993 1747

McLEOD Carolyn
PO Box 26495, London SE10 0WO
e-mail: carolynmcleodcasting@hotmail.com
          Tel/Fax: 0704 4001720

McMANUS BAYLEY Ltd
(Sarah McManus & Justine Bayley)
111 Westbourne Studios, 242 Acklam Road
London W1D 5JJ
e-mail: justine@mcmanusbayley.com
Fax: 020-7524 7733   Tel: 020-7524 7722

McMURRICH Chrissie
16 Spring Vale Avenue, Brentford
Middlesex TW8 9QH   Tel: 020-8568 0137

McSHANE Sooki CDG
8A Piermont Road, East Dulwich
London SE22 0LN   Tel/Fax: 020-8693 7411

McWILLIAMS Debbie
e-mail: debbiemcwilliams@hotmail.com
          Mobile: 07785 575805

MOISELLE Frank
7 Corrig Avenue, Dun Laoghaire, Co. Dublin, Eire
Fax: 00 353 1 2803277   Tel: 00 353 1 2802857

MOISELLE Nuala
7 Corrig Avenue, Dun Laoghaire, Co. Dublin, Eire
Fax: 00 353 1 2803277   Tel: 00 353 1 2802857

MORRISON Melika
12A Rosebank, Holyport Road
London SW6 6LG   Tel/Fax: 020-7381 1571

MUGSHOTS
(Jacqui Morris)
50 Frith Street, London W1D 4SQ
Fax: 020-7437 0308   Tel: 020-7292 0555

NEEDLEMAN Sue
19 Stanhope Gardens, London NW7 2JD
Fax: 020-8959 0225   Tel: 020-8959 1550

NOEL CASTING
(Specializing in Character Actors, Ethnic & Asian
Actors)
Suite 501, International House
223 Regent Street, London W1B 2QD
e-mail: noelcasting@yahoo.com
Fax: 020-7544 1090   Tel: 020-7544 1010

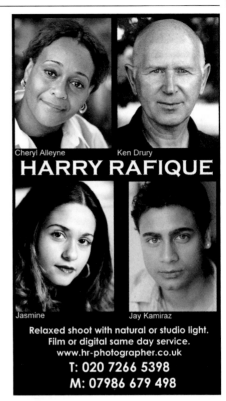

Cheryl Alleyne   Ken Drury

HARRY RAFIQUE

Jasmine   Jay Kamiraz

Relaxed shoot with natural or studio light.
Film or digital same day service.
www.hr-photographer.co.uk
T: 020 7266 5398
M: 07986 679 498

O'BRIEN Debbie
72 High Street, Ashwell, Nr Baldock, Herts SG7 5NS
Fax: 01462 743110   Tel: 01462 742919

PAGE Jamie CASTING
PO Box 2944, London W1A 6ET

PAIN David
(See BBC DRAMA SERIES CASTING - BBC ELSTREE)

PALMER Helena
(See CANNON DUDLEY & ASSOCIATES)

PARRISS Susie CASTING CDG
PO Box 40, Morden SM4 4WJ
Fax: 020-8543 3327   Tel: 020-8543 3326

PEARCE WOOLGAR CASTING
(Prop. Francesca Woolgar CDG)
Mayfair Hse, 14-16 Headon St, London W1B 4DA
Website: www.pearcewoolgar.com
          Tel/Fax: 020-8667 0527

DAN RABIN
PHOTOGRAPHER

07940 519 331
020 7739 7568

Ben Price 2003

PERRYMENT Mandy CASTING
e-mail: mandy@perryment-cast.demon.co.uk
Fax: 01372 472795   Tel: 01372 472794

PETTS Tree CASTING
125 Hendon Way, London NW2 2NA
e-mail: casting@treepetts.co.uk
Fax: 020-8905 5968   Tel: 020-8458 8898

PLANTIN Kate
37 Albany Mews, Kingston-upon-Thames
Surrey KT2 5SL
e-mail: kateplantin@hotmail.com
Fax: 020-8549 7299   Tel: 020-8546 4577

POLENTARUTTI Tania CASTING CDG
Top Floor, 37 Berwick Street, London W1F 8RS
Fax: 020-7734 3549   Tel: 020-7734 1819

POOLE Gilly CDG
(See CROWLEY POOLE CASTING)

PROCTOR Carl CDG
15B Bury Place, London WC1A 2JB
e-mail: carlproctor@blueyonder.co.uk
Fax: 020-7916 2533   Tel: 020-7681 0034

PRYOR Andy CDG
7 Garrick Street, London WC2E 9AR
Fax: 020-7836 8299   Tel: 020-7836 8298

REICH Liora
25 Manor Park Road
London N2 0SN   Tel: 020-8444 1686

REYNOLDS Simone CDG
60 Hebdon Road, London SW17 7NN

RHODES JAMES Kate CDG
HG14, The Aberdeen Centre
22-24 Highbury Grove, London N5 2EA
e-mail: katekrj@aol.com
Fax: 020-7359 5378   Tel: 020-7704 8186

ROBERTSON Sasha CASTING CDG
19 Wendell Road, London W12 9RS
e-mail: casting@sasharobertson.com
Fax: 020-8740 1396   Tel: 020-8740 0817

RODRIGUEZ Corinne
11 Lytton Avenue, London N13 4EH
Fax: 020-8886 5564

ROFFE Danielle CDG
33 Fitroy Street, London W1T 6DU
Fax: 020-7636 0881   Tel: 020-7636 0880

**ROYAL NATIONAL THEATRE
CASTING DEPARTMENT**
(Casting Director: Toby Whale CDG
Deputy Casting Director: Gabrielle Dawes
Casting Assistant: Alastair Coomer)
Upper Ground, South Bank, London SE1 9PX
Fax: 020-7452 3340   Tel: 020-7452 3336

ROYAL SHAKESPEARE COMPANY
(Casting Director: John Cannon CDG
Casting Co-ordinator: Hannah Miller)
1 Earlham Street, London WC2H 9LL
e-mail: john.cannon@rsc.org.uk
                         Tel: 020-7845 0505/0500

SBS Ltd
(The Casting Information Service)
Suite 1, 16 Sidmouth Road, London NW2 5JX
e-mail: casting@sbsltd.demon.co.uk
Fax: 020-8459 7442   Tel: 020-8451 2852

SCHILLER Ginny
180A Graham Road, London E8 1BS
e-mail: ginny.schiller@virgin.net
Fax: 020-8525 1049   Tel: 020-8525 1637

SCOTT Laura CDG
56 Rowena Crescent, London SW11 2PT
Website: www.castingdirectorsguild.co.uk
e-mail: laurascottcasting@mac.com
Fax: 020-7924 1907   Tel: 020-7978 6336

Louise Scodie

GREG WOODWARD
Photographer
020 8455 5321
07855 434 869

SEARCHERS The
70 Sylvia Court, Cavendish Street, London N1 7PG
e-mail: waynerw.searchers@blueyonder.co.uk
Fax: 07958 922829   Tel: 020-7684 5763

SEECOOMAR Nadira
PO Box 167, Twickenham TW1 2UP
Fax: 020-8744 1274   Tel: 020-8892 8478

SELWAY Mary CDG
c/o Twickenham Studios, St Margaret's
Twickenham TW1 2AW   Tel: 020-8607 8888

SHAW Philip
Suite 476, 2 Old Brompton Road
South Kensington, London SW7 3DQ
e-mail: shawcastlond@aol.com
Fax: 020-8408 1193   Tel: 020-8715 8943

SHEPHERD Debbie CASTING
Suite 16, 63 St Martin's Lane, London WC2N 4JS
e-mail: info@debbieshepherd.com
Fax: 020-7240 4640   Tel: 020-7240 0400

SINGER Sandra ASSOCIATES
21 Cotswold Road, Westcliff on Sea, Essex SS0 8AA
Website: www.sandrasinger.com
e-mail: sandra.singeruk@aol.com
Fax: 01702 339393   Tel: 01702 331616

SMITH Michelle CDG
220 Church Lane, Woodford, Stockport SK7 1PQ
Fax: 0161-439 0622   Tel: 0161-439 6825

SMITH Suzanne CDG
33 Fitzroy Street, London W1T 6DU
e-mail: zan@dircon.co.uk
Fax: 020-7436 9690   Tel: 020-7436 9255

SPON Wendy CDG
c/o ACT Productions, 20-22 Stukeley Street
London WC2B 5LR   Tel: 020-7438 9599

STAFFORD Emma
33 Stopes Road, Radcliffe
Manchester M25 6TL   Tel: 0161-748 7940

STARK CASTING
e-mail: stark.casting@virgin.net
Mobile: 07956 150689   Tel: 020-8800 0060

STEELE Mandy
89 Mayfield Road
London N8 9LN
e-mail: mandy@mandysteele.com
Fax: 0870 1329017   Tel: 020-8341 1918

STEVENS Gail CASTING CDG
2 Sutton Lane
54A Clerkenwell Road
London EC1M 5PS
Fax: 020-7253 6574   Tel: 020-7253 6532

STEVENSON Sam
103 Whitecross Street, London EC1Y 8JD
e-mail: samstevenson@blueyonder.co.uk

STEWART Amanda CASTING
Apartment 1, 35 Fortess Road
London NW5 1AD   Tel: 020-7485 7973

STOLL Liz
(See BBC DRAMA SERIES CASTING - BBC CENTRE HOUSE)

STYLE Emma CDG
97 Third Avenue, London W10 4HS
Fax: 020-8960 8323   Tel: 020-8969 5099

SUMMERS Mark (LONDON)
See CASTING UNLIMITED (LONDON)

SUMMERS Mark (LOS ANGELES)
See CASTING UNLIMITED (LOS ANGELES)

SYERS Michael
(See CASTING CONNECTION The)

SYSON Lucinda CDG
11 Goodwins Court
London WC2N 4LL
e-mail: lscasting@yahoo.co.uk
Fax: 020-7240 7710   Tel: 020-7379 4868

TABAK Amanda CDG
(See CANDID CASTING)

TEECE Shirley
106 North View Road
London N8 7LP   Tel: 020-8347 9241

TOBIAS SHAW Rose
219 Liverpool Road
London N1 1LX   Fax: 020-7609 9028

TOPOLSKI Tessa
25 Clifton Hill
London NW8 0QE   Tel: 020-7328 6393

TOPPS CASTING
(Nicola Topping)
The Media Centre
7 Northumberland Street
Huddersfield HD1 1RL
e-mail: topps.casting@btopenworld.com
Fax: 01484 320787   Tel: 01484 511988

TREVELLICK Jill CDG
123 Rathcoole Gardens
London N8 9PH
e-mail: jill@trevellick.force9.co.uk
Fax: 020-8348 7400   Tel: 020-8340 2734

TREVIS Sarah CDG
c/o Twickenham Studios
St Margaret's
Twickenham TW1 2AW   Tel: 020-8607 8888

VAN OST & MILLINGTON CASTING
(Valerie Van Ost & Andrew Millington)
PO Box 115
Petersfield GU31 5BB
Fax: 020-7436 9858   Tel: 020-7436 9838

VAUGHAN Sally
2 Kennington Park Place
London SE11 4AS   Tel: 020-7735 6539

VITAL PRODUCTIONS
PO Box 26441
London SE10 9GZ
e-mail: mail@vital-productions.co.uk
          Tel/Fax: 020-8316 4497

VOSSER Anne CASTING CDG
PO Box 203
Aldershot GU12 4YB
e-mail: vossercasting@ntlworld.com
Fax: 01252 404716   Tel: 01252 404715

WEIR Fiona
c/o Twickenham Studios
St Margaret's
Twickenham TW1 2AW   Tel: 020-8607 8888

WEST June
Granada Television
Quay Street, Manchester M60 9EA
Fax: 0161-827 2004   Tel: 0161-832 7211

WESTERN Matt CASTING CDG
4th Floor
193 Wardour Street
London W1V 3FA
e-mail: matt@mattwestern.co.uk
Fax: 020-7439 1941   Tel: 020-7434 1230

WHALE Toby CDG
80 Shakespeare Road
London W3 6SN
Website: www.whalecasting.com
e-mail: toby@whalecasting.com
Fax: 020-8993 8096   Tel: 020-8993 2821

WHITALL Keith
(Theatre Only)
10 Woodlands Avenue
West Byfleet, Surrey KT14 6AT   Tel: 01932 343655

WILLIS Catherine
(See BBC DRAMA SERIES CASTING - BBC CENTRE HOUSE)

WOODHAMS Keith CASTING
20 Lowther Hill
London SE23 1PY
e-mail: kwoodhams@mcmail.com
Fax: 020-8314 1950   Tel: 020-8314 1677

WOODWARD Tara CASTING
Top Flat
93 Gloucester Avenue
Primrose Hill, London NW1 8LB
e-mail: tara_woodward@yahoo.com
Fax: 020-7681 8574   Tel: 020-7586 3487

WOOLGAR Francesca CDG
(See PEARCE WOOLGAR CASTING)

ZIMMERMANN Jeremy CASTING
Clareville House
26-27 Oxendon Street
London SW1Y 4EL
Fax: 020-7925 0708   Tel: 020-7925 0707

Concert & Exhibition Halls

AMADEUS CENTRE The
50 Shirland Road, London W9 2JA
e-mail: amadeus@amadeuscentre.co.uk
Fax: 020-7266 1225   Tel: 020-7286 1686

BARBICAN EXHIBITION CENTRE
Barbican, Silk Street, London EC2Y 8DS
Fax: 020-7382 7263   Tel: 020-7382 7053

BIRMINGHAM SYMPHONY HALL
Broad Street, Birmingham B1 2EA
Website: www.symphonyhall.co.uk
e-mail: symphonyhall@necgroup.co.uk   BO: 0121-780 3333

BLACKHEATH HALLS
23 Lee Road, Blackheath, London SE3 9RQ
Website: www.blackheathhalls.com
e-mail: mail@blackheathhalls.com
Fax: 020-8852 5154   BO: 020-8463 0100

CENTRAL HALL - WESTMINSTER
Storey's Gate, Westminster, London SW1H 9NH
Website: www.c-h-w.com
e-mail: events@c-h-w.co.uk   Tel: 020-7222 8010

EARL'S COURT & OLYMPIA EXHIBITION CENTRES
Warwick Road, London SW5 9TA
Website: www.eco.co.uk
e-mail: marketing@eco.co.uk   Tel: 020-7385 1200

FAIRFIELD HALLS
Park Lane, Croydon CR9 1DG   BO: 020-8681 0821

FERNEHAM HALL
Osborn Road, Fareham, Hants PO16 7DB
e-mail: boxoffice@fareham.gov.uk   Tel: 01329 824864

GORDON CRAIG THEATRE
Stevenage Arts & Leisure Centre
Lytton Way, Stevenage, Herts SG1 1LZ
Website: www.stevenage-leisure.co.uk
e-mail: gordoncraig@stevenage-leisure.co.uk
BO: 08700 131030   Tel: 01483 242642

HEXAGON The
Queen's Walk, Reading RG1 7UA
Website: www.readingarts.com
e-mail: boxoffice@readingarts.com
Fax: 0118-939 0028   Admin: 0118-939 0390

MARMALADE
Studio B5R, Metropolitan Wharf, London E1W 3SS
Website: www.marmaladegallery.com
e-mail: info@marmaladegallery.com   Tel: 020-7702 2193

MINERVA STUDIO THEATRE
Oaklands Park, Chichester, West Sussex PO19 6AP
Website: www.cft.org.uk
Fax: 01243 787288   Tel: 01243 784437

NATIONAL CONCERT HALL OF WALES The
St David's Hall, The Hayes, Cardiff CF10 1SH
Website: www.stdavidshallcardiff.co.uk
Fax: 029-2087 8599   Tel: 029-2087 8500

OLYMPIA EXHIBITION CENTRES
Hammersmith Road, Kensington, London W14 8UX
Fax: 020-7598 2500   Tel: 020-7385 1200

RIVERSIDE STUDIOS
Crisp Road, London W6 9RL
Website: www.riversidestudios.co.uk
e-mail: online@riversidestudios.co.uk
BO: 020-8237 1111   Tel: 020-8237 1000

ROYAL ALBERT HALL
Kensington Gore, London SW7 2AP
Website: www.royalalberthall.com
e-mail: admin@royalalberthall.com
Fax: 020-7823 7725   Tel: 020-7589 3203

SOUTH BANK CENTRE
(Including The Royal Festival Hall, Queen Elizabeth Hall,
Purcell, Room & Hayward Gallery, London SE1 8XX
Website: www.rfh.org.uk   BO: 020-7921 0601

ST JOHN'S
Smith Square, London SW1P 3HA
Website: www.sjss.org.uk
Fax: 020-7233 1618   Tel: 020-7222 1061

VENUES @ BAC
Battersea Arts Centre, Lavender Hill
Battersea, London SW11 5TN   Tel: 020-7326 8211

WEMBLEY CONFERENCE & EXHIBITION CENTRE &
WEMBLEY ARENA Wembley HA9 0DW
Website: www.whatsonwembley.com
BO: 0870 7390739   Admin: 020-8902 8833

WIGMORE HALL
36 Wigmore Street, London W1U 2BP
e-mail: info@wigmore-hall.org.uk   BO: 020-7935 2141

Concert Promoters & Agents

ARTISTE MANAGEMENT PRODUCTIONS Ltd (Promotion)
65 Newman Street, London W1T 6EG
Website: www.harveygoldsmith.com
e-mail: mail@harveygoldsmith.com
Fax: 020-7224 0111   Tel: 020-7224 1992

ASKONAS HOLT Ltd (Classical Music)
Lonsdale Chambers
27 Chancery Lane, London WC2A 1PF
Website: www.askonasholt.co.uk
e-mail: info@askonasholt.co.uk
Fax: 020-7400 1799   Tel: 020-7400 1700

AVALON PROMOTIONS Ltd
4A Exmoor Street, London W10 6BD
Fax: 020-7598 7334   Tel: 020-7598 7333

BARRUCCI LEISURE ENTERPRISES Ltd (Promoters)
45-47 Cheval Place, London SW7 1EW
e-mail: barrucci@barrucci.co.uk
Fax: 020-7581 2509   Tel: 020-7225 2255

BLOCK Derek ARTISTES AGENCY
70-76 Bell Street, Marylebone, London NW1 6SP
e-mail: dbaa@derekblock.demon.co.uk
Fax: 020-7724 2102   Tel: 020-7724 2101

CITY CONCERT ORGANISATION Ltd The
PO Box 3145, Lichfield WS13 6YN
Website: www.cityconcert.com
e-mail: admin@cityconcert.com   Tel/Fax: 01543 262286

FLYING MUSIC
110 Clarendon Road, London W11 2HR
Website: www.flyingmusic.com
e-mail: info@flyingmusic.com
Fax: 020-7221 5016   Tel: 020-7221 7799

GUBBAY Raymond Ltd
Knight House, 29-31 East Barnet Road
New Barnet, Hertfordshire EN4 8RN
Website: www.raymondgubbay.co.uk
e-mail: info@raymondgubbay.co.uk
Fax: 020-8216 3001   Tel: 020-8216 3000

HOBBS Liz EVENTS
First Floor, 65 London Road, Newark
Nottinghamshire NG24 1RZ
Website: www.lizhobbsgroup.com
e-mail: events@lizhobbsgroup.com
Fax: 0870 3337009   Tel: 08700 702702

HOCHHAUSER Victor
4 Oak Hill Way, London NW3 7LR
Fax: 020-7431 2531   Tel: 020-7794 0987

IMG ARTS & ENTERTAINMENT
Pier House, Strand on the Green
London W4 3NN
Fax: 020-8233 5001   Tel: 020-8233 5000

KARUSHI PROMOTIONS
Golden Cross House
8 Duncannon Str, London WC2N 4JF
Website: www.karushi.com   e-mail: ed@karushi.com
Fax: 020-7484 5151   Tel: 020-7484 5040

McINTYRE Phil PROMOTIONS Ltd
2nd Floor, 35 Soho Square, London W1D 3QX
e-mail: reception@pmcintyre.co.uk
Fax: 020-7439 2280   Tel: 020-7439 2270

RBM (Comedy)
3rd Floor, 18 Broadwick Street, London W1V 1FG
Website: www.rbmcomedy.com
e-mail: info@rbmcomedy.com
Fax: 020-7287 5020   Tel: 020-7287 5010

S.F.X.
35-36 Grosvenor Street, London W1K 4QX
Website: www.sfxsports.co.uk
Fax: 0870 7490517   Tel: 020-7529 4300

ZANDER Peter CONCERT MANAGEMENT
22 Romilly Street, London W1D 5AG
e-mail: peterzan.berlin@virgin.net   Tel: 020-7437 4767

ABLE SECURITY
117 Waverley Road, Plumstead
London SE18 7TH   Tel/Fax: 020-8317 6899

ACE ARRANGEMENTS Ltd
(Entertainment Providers, Parties/Corporate Events)
7 Berghem Mews, Blythe Road, London W14 0HN
e-mail: sally.allen@ace-uk.biz
Fax: 020-7751 1275   Tel: 020-7603 3444

ACTOR'S 'ONE-STOP' SHOP The
(Showreels, Photographs, CV's)
54 Belsize Avenue, London N13 4TJ
Website: www.actorsone-stopshop.com
e-mail: info@actorsone-stopshop.com
                          Tel/Fax: 020-8888 9666

AGENT FILE
(Software for Agents)
Website: www.agentfile.com
e-mail: info@agentfile.com   Mobile: 07956 544764

AON Ltd (Trading as AON/ALBERT G. RUBEN)
(Insurance Brokers)
Pinewood Studios, Pinewood Road
Iver, Bucks SL0 0NH
Website: www.aon.co.uk
Fax: 01753 653152   Tel: 01753 658200

ARTON Michael PhD
(Historical Research, Technical Advisor)
122 Sunningfields Road, London NW4 4RE
e-mail: michael@arton.freeserve.co.uk
                          Tel/Fax: 020-8203 2733

ARTS VA The
(Bronwyn Robertson) (Administrative Support for
Individuals & Organisations)
PO Box 2911, Stratford-upon-Avon CV37 9WU
Website: www.thartsva.com
e-mail: bronwyn@theartsva.com
Fax: 01789 552818   Tel: 01789 552559

ATKINS Chris & COMPANY
(Accountants & Business Consultants)
Astra House, Arklow Rd, London SE14 6EB
e-mail: jerry@chrisatkins.co.uk   Tel: 020-8691 4100

BERGER Harvey FCA
(Chartered Accountant)
18 Chalk Lane, Cockfosters
Barnet, Herts EN4 9HJ
e-mail: harvey.berger@tesco.net
                          Tel/Fax: 020-8449 9328

BIG PICTURE
(Part-time Work in Computer Retail Industry)
13 Netherwood Road, London W14 0BL
e-mail: info@abigpicture.co.uk   Tel: 020-7371 4455

BLACKMORE Lawrence
(Production Accountant)
Suite 5, 26 Charing Cross Rd, London WC2H 0DG
Fax: 020-7836 3156   Tel: 020-7240 1817

BOWKER ORFORD
(Chartered Accountants)
15-19 Cavendish Place, London W1G 0DD
e-mail: morford@bowkerorford.com
Fax: 020-7580 3909   Tel: 020-7636 6391

BREBNER ALLEN TRAPP
(Chartered Accountants)
180 Wardour Street, London W1F 8LB
Website: www.brebner.co.uk
e-mail: partners@brebner.co.uk
Fax: 020-7287 5315   Tel: 020-7734 2244

BRECKMAN & COMPANY
(Chartered Accountants)
49 South Molton Street
London W1K 5LH   Tel: 020-7499 2292

BRITISH ASSOCIATION FOR DRAMA THERAPISTS The
41 Broomhouse Lane, London SW6 3DP
e-mail: gillian@badth.demon.co.uk
                          Tel/Fax: 020-7731 0160

BROOK-REYNOLDS Natalie
(Freelance Stage Manager/Floor Manager TV &
Theatre. Member of SMA, Equity & BECTU)
Website: www.nataliebrookreynoldsuk.pwp.blueyonder.co.uk
e-mail: nataliebrookreynolds@blueyonder.co.uk
Fax: 0871 2429919   Tel: 020-8350 0877

CARTER Robert (Solicitor)
8 West Street, London WC2H 9NG
Fax: 020-7836 2786   Tel: 020-7836 2785

CASTLE MAGICAL SERVICES
(Magical Consultants) (Michael Shepherd)
Broompark, 131 Tadcaster Road
Dringhouses, York YO24 1QJ
e-mail: michael@castle.evesham.net
                          Tel/Fax: 01904 709500

CAULKETT Robin DipSM, MIIRSM
(Abseiling, Rope Work)
3 Churchill Way, Mitchell Dean, Glos GL17 0AZ
Mobile: 07970 442003   Tel: 01594 825865

COBO
(Performing Arts, Entertainment & Leisure
Marketing)
43A Garthorne Road
London SE23 1EP
Website: www.theatrenet.com
e-mail: admin@cobomedia.com
Fax: 020-8291 4969   Tel: 020-8291 7079

COMPAGNIE LIAN
(Artist Promotion, Image Consultancy, Business
Seminars, Copy Writing, Translation Services)
2 Ravenscourt Park, London W6 0TH
e-mail: lian@noraarmani.com
Mobile: 07766 706415   Tel: 020-8563 0220

COOPER Margaret (Art Director)
c/o 75/1 Old College Street, Sleima, Malta
e-mail: mediacorp1@yahoo.com
Mobile: 00 356 9925 2925   Tel: 00 356 21 342338

CREATIVE INDUSTRIES DEVELOPMENT AGENCY (CIDA)
(Professional Development & Business Support for
Artists & Creative Businesses)
Media Centre, Northumberland Street
Huddersfield, West Yorkshire HD1 1RL
Website: www.cida.org   e-mail: info@cida.org
Fax: 01484 483150   Tel: 01484 483140

DOWLING Fabiela (IT Applications)
(One to One Computer Training)
66 Berkeley Close, Ruislip HA4 6LF
Website: www.computertraining121.co.uk
e-mail: fabiela@tiscali.co.uk   Tel/Fax: 01895 673691

DYNAMIC FX Ltd
(Magical Entertainment Company)
Regent House, 291 Kirkdale, London SE26 4QD
e-mail: mail@dynamicfx.co.uk
Fax: 020-8659 8118   Tel: 020-8659 8130

EAGLES Steve
(International Sharpshooter & Firearms Lecturer)
Wivenhoe, 46 Hartwood Road
Southport, Merseyside PR9 9AW
e-mail: sn03@dial.pipex.com
Mobile: 07721 464611   Tel/Fax: 01704 547884

EARLE Kenneth PERSONAL MANAGEMENT
214 Brixton Road, London SW9 6AP
Fax: 020-7274 9529   Tel: 020-7274 1219

ENTERTRAIN UK Ltd
(Entertainment Consultants)
14 Hawthorne Court, Rickmansworth Road
Pinner, Middlesex HA5 3UN
Website: www.entertrainltd.com   Tel: 020-8429 2171

EQUITY INSURANCE SERVICES
131-133 New London Road
Chelmsford, Essex CM2 0QZ
Website: www.equity-ins-services.com
e-mail: enquiries@equity-ins-services.com
Fax: 01245 491641   Tel: 01245 357854

EXECUTIVE AUDIO VISUAL
(Showreels for Actors & Presenters)
80 York Street
London W1H 1QW   Tel/Fax: 020-7723 4488

FACADE
(Creation and Production of Musicals)
43A Garthorne Road, London SE23 1EP
e-mail: facade@cobomedia.com   Tel: 020-8291 7079

FILMANGEL
(Film Finance & Script Services)
110 Trafalgar Road, Portslade
East Sussex BN41 1GS
Website: www.filmangel.co.uk
e-mail: filmangels@freenetname.co.uk
Fax: 01277 05451   Tel: 01273 27733

FORD Jonathan & Co
(Chartered Accountants)
The Coach House, 31 View Road
Rainhill, Merseyside L35 0LF
Website: www.jonathanford.co.uk
e-mail: info@jonathanford.co.uk   Tel: 0151-426 4512

FREE ELECTRON
(Website Design)
45 Alpha Street, Slough, Berks SL1 1RA
Website: www.free-electron.co.uk
e-mail: info@free-electron.co.uk
                              Tel/Fax: 01753 693074

FUNKTIONZ Ltd
(Specialist Casting Agents & Security)
399 Hackney Road, London E2 8PP
e-mail: funktionze9@hotmail.com
Fax: 020-7729 4736   Tel: 020-7729 9962

GORDON LEIGHTON
(Chartered Accountants, Business Advisors)
50 Queen Anne Street, London W1G 9HQ
Website: www.gordonl.co.uk   e-mail: gl@gordonl.com
Fax: 020-7487 2566   Tel: 020-7935 5737

HARVEY MONTGOMERY Ltd
(Chartered Accountants)
3 The Fairfield, Farnham, Surrey GU9 8AH
Website: www.harveymontgomery.co.uk
e-mail: harveyca@btconnect.com
Fax: 01252 734394   Tel: 01252 734388

HASLAM Dominic
(Arranger & Composer)
c/o Sandra Singer Associates
21 Cotswold Road, Westcliff-on-Sea, Essex SS0 8AA
Website: www.sandrasinger.com
e-mail: sandrasingeruk@aol.com
Fax: 01702 339393   Tel: 01702 331616

HATSTAND Helena
(Special Skills Performer, Circus, Whip Cracking,
Fire-eating, Juggling. Solo/Double/Triple Group Acts)
39 Old Church Road, Stepney, London E1 0QB
Website: www.hatstandcircus.co.uk
e-mail: helenahatstand@btopenworld.com
                              Tel/Fax: 020-7791 2541

HAYES Susan
(Choreographer)
84A Shaftesbury Road, London N19 4QN
e-mail: susan.hayes@blueyonder.co.uk
Mobile: 07721 927714   Tel/Fax: 020-7686 0306

HERITAGE RAILWAY ASSOCIATION
7 Robert Close, Potters Bar, Herts EN6 2DH
Website: www.ukhrail.uel.ac.uk   Tel: 01707 643568

HOMEMATCH PROPERTY FINANCE
(Mortgages for Entertainers)
6 Shaw Street, Worcester WR1 3QQ
e-mail: chrisjcatchpole@aol.com
Fax: 01905 22121   Tel: 01905 22007

HONRI Peter
(Music Hall Consultant)
1 Evingar Road, Whitchurch
Hants RG28 7EY   Tel: 01256 892162

HUSSEY Daniel
(International Paranormal Occult Investigator &
Consultant)
PO Box 24250, London SE9 3ZH
Website: www.lifeafterdeath.net
e-mail: enquiries@paranormaloccultinvestigator.com
Mobile: 07764 428318   Tel: 020-8378 6844

C

I R A - INDEPENDENT REVIEWS ARTS SERVICES
(Stories from World of Film/Art/Showbiz))
12 Hemingford Close, London N12 9HF
e-mail: e.lovatt@btinternet.com
Mobile: 07956 212916   Tel/Fax: 020-8343 7437

IMAGE DIGGERS
(Slide/Stills/Audio/Video Library & Theme Research)
618B Finchley Road, London NW11 7RR
Website: http://imagediggers.netfilms.com
e-mail: ziph@macunlimited.net
                          Tel/Fax: 020-8455 4564

IMPACT AGENCY
(Public Relations)
3 Bloomsbury Place, London WC1A 2QL
Fax: 020-7580 7200   Tel: 020-7580 1770

JACKSON Kim
(Arts Education Consultancy)
1 Mellor Road, Leicester LE3 6HN
e-mail: jacksongillespie@hotmail.com
                          Tel: 0116-233 8432

JFL
(Recruitment Consultants)
47 New Bond Street, London W1S 1DJ
Fax: 020-7493 7161   Tel: 020-7493 8824

JOSHI CLINIC The
57 Wimpole Street, London W1G 8YW
Fax: 020-7486 9622   Tel: 020-7487 5456

KEAN LANYON
(Graphic Designers & Marketing Consultants)
Rose Cottage, Aberdeen Centre
22 Highbury Grove, London N5 2EA
Website: www.keanlanyon.com
e-mail: sharon@keanlanyon.com
Fax: 020-7359 0199   Tel: 020-7354 3574

KELLER Don
(Marketing Consultancy & Project Management)
65 Glenwood Road, Harringay, London N15 3JS
e-mail: donkeller@waitrose.com
Fax: 020-8809 6825   Tel: 020-8800 4882

KERR John CHARTERED ACCOUNTANTS
369-375 Eaton Road
West Derby, Liverpool L12 2AH
e-mail: advice@jkca.co.uk
Fax: 0151-228 3792   Tel: 0151-228 8977

KIEVE Paul
(Magical Effects for Theatre & Film)
23 Terrace Road, South Hackney
London E9 7ES
Website: www.stageillusion.com
e-mail: mail@stageillusion.com   Tel/Fax: 020-8985 6188

LAMBOLLE Robert
(Script Evaluation/Editing)
618B Finchley Road, London NW11 7RR
Website: http://readingandrighting.netfirms.com
e-mail: ziph@macunlimited.net Tel/Fax: 020-8455 4564

LARK INSURANCE BROKING GROUP
(Insurance Brokers)
Wigham House, Wakering Road, Barking
Essex IG11 8PJ
Fax: 020-8557 2430   Tel: 020-8557 2300

LEEP MARKETING & PR
(Marketing, Press and Publicity)
Top Floor, 21 Denmark Street
London WC2H 8NA
e-mail: philip@leep.biz
Fax: 020-7916 0031   Tel: 020-7916 0030

LINGUA FRANCA
(French Dialogue & Script Translators/Subtitlers)
12 Ack Lane West, Cheadle Hulme
Cheshire SK8 7EL   Tel: 0161-485 3357

LOCATION TUTORS NATIONWIDE
(Fully Qualified/ Experienced Support Teachers,
Covering all Key Stages in National Curriculum)
16 Poplar Walk, Herne Hill
London SE24 0BU
Fax: 020-7207 8794   Tel: 020-7978 8898

LOVE Billie HISTORICAL PHOTOGRAPHS
(Picture Research. Formerly 'Amanda' Theatrical
Portraiture)
3 Winton Street, Ryde
Isle of Wight PO33 2BX   Tel: 01983 812572

McKENNA Deborah Ltd
(Celebrity Chefs & Lifestyle Presenters)
Claridge House, 29 Barnes High Street
London SW13 9LW
e-mail: info@deborahmckenna.com
Fax: 020-8392 2462   Tel: 020-8876 7566

MEDIA LEGAL
(Education Services)
83 Clarendon Road
Sevenoaks
Kent TN13 1ET   Tel: 01732 460592

MILDENBERG Vanessa
(Choreographer of Theatre)
30 Mount Ephraim Road
London SW16 1LW
Mobile: 07796 264828   Tel: 020-8769 6099

MILITARY ADVISORY & INSTRUCTION SPECIALISTS
(John Sessions) (Advice on Weapons, Drill
Period to Present. Ex-Army Instructors)
e-mail: johnmusic1@ntlworld.com   Tel: 01904 491198

MILLER ALLAN Ann
(Private Lessons, Consultancy, Choreography)
The Belly Dance Centre, Mayfield
5 Rother Road, Seaford
East Sussex BN25 4HT   Tel: 01323 899083

MORGAN Jane ASSOCIATES
(Marketing & Media)
8 Heathville Road, London N19 3AJ
e-mail: morgans@dircon.co.uk
Fax: 020-7263 9877   Tel: 020-7263 9867

MULLEN Julie
(Improvisors/Comedy Consultancy)
The Impro Lab, 34 Watts Lane
Teddington Lock TW11 8HQ   Mobile: 07956 877839

NEATE Rodger PRODUCTION MANAGEMENT
15 Southcote Road, London N19 5BJ
e-mail: rneate@dircon.co.uk
Fax: 020-7697 8237   Tel: 020-7609 9538

NEOVISION
(Location & Production Services)
46 rue de Berne, 1201 Geneva, Switzerland
Website: www.neovisionprod.com
e-mail: info@neovisionprod.com
Fax: (41 22) 741 1208   Tel: (41 79) 357 5417

NETWORK The
(Security & Investigation Services.
Contact: Ross Barker-Chesterton)
29 Queensdown Road
London E5 8NN
e-mail: network.sis@btinternet.com   Tel: 07951 147268

NUTOPIA MUSIC
(Music for Film & Television)
Number 8, 132 Charing Cross Road
London WC2H 0LA
Website: www.nutopia.co.uk
Fax: 029-2070 9440   Tel/Fax: 07801 493133

NWA-UK HAMMERLOCK
(Wrestling Events, Training & Promotion)
PO Box 282, Ashford, Kent TN23 7ZZ
e-mail: nwauk@hammerlockwrestling.com
Fax: 01233 336757   Tel: 01233 663828

NYMAN LIBSON PAUL
(Chartered Accountants)
Regina House, 124 Finchley Road, London NW3 5JS
Website: www.nymanlibsonpaul.co.uk
e-mail: entertainment@nymanlibsonpaul.co.uk
Fax: 020-7433 2401   Tel: 020-7433 2400

ORANGE TREE STUDIO & MUSIC SERVICES
(Original Music/Composition & Production)
Po Box 99, Kings Langley WD4 8FB
Website: www.orangetreestudio.com
e-mail: richard@orangetreestudio.com
Mobile: 07768 146200   Tel: 01923 440550

PARKER John
(Ghostwriter)
21 Hindsleys Place, London SE23 2NF
e-mail: parkerwrite@yahoo   Tel: 020-8244 5816

RETROGRAPH NOSTALGIA ARCHIVE
(Nostalgia Picture Consultants 1880-1970)
10 Hanover Crescent, Brighton BN2 9SB
Website: www.retrograph.com
e-mail: retropix1@aol.com   Tel: 01273 687554

RIPLEY-DUGGAN PARTNERSHIP The
(Tour Booking)
52 Tottenham Street, London W1T 4RN
e-mail: info@ripleyduggan.com   Tel: 020-7436 1392

SEAGER Martin
(Composer/Lyricist for Film/TV/Theatre)
14 Neal's Yard, Covent Garden WC2H 9DP
e-mail: martinseager@onetel.net.uk Tel: 020-8943 4145

SHAW Bernard
(Specialist in Recording and Directing
Voice Tapes)
Horton Manor, Canterbury CT4 7LG
Website: www.bernardshaw.co.uk
e-mail: bernard@bernardshaw.co.uk
          Tel/Fax: 01227-730843

SINGER Sandra PUBLIC RELATIONS
(Entertainers, Promotions Staff & Events)
21 Cotswold Road
Westcliff-on-Sea, Essex SS0 8AA
e-mail: sandrasingeruk@aol.com
Fax: 01702 339393   Tel: 01702 331616

SPEAKERPOWER.CO.UK
48 Fellows Road, London NW3 3LH
Website: www.speakerpower.co.uk
e-mail: barbara@speakerpower.co.uk
Fax: 020-7722 5255   Tel: 020-7586 4361

SPENCER Ivor
(Professional Toastmaster, Events Organiser
& Head Butler)
12 Little Bornes
Dulwich, London SE21 8SE
Website: www.ivorspencer.com
e-mail: ivor@ivorspencer.com
Fax: 020-8670 0055   Tel: 020-8670 5585

SPORTS WORKSHOP PROMOTIONS Ltd
(Production Advisors, Sport, Stunts, Safety)
PO Box 878
Crystal Palace National Sports Centre
London SE19 2BH
e-mail: info@sportspromotions.co.uk
Fax: 020-8776 7772   Tel: 020-8659 4561

STUNT ACTION SPECIALISTS
110 Trafalgar Road
Portslade
East Sussex BN41 1GS
Website: www.stuntactionspecialists.com
e-mail: wayne@stuntactionspecialists.co.uk
Fax: 01273 708699   Tel: 01273 230214

SUMMERS David & COMPANY
(Chartered Accountants)
Argo House
Kilburn Park Road
London NW6 5LF
e-mail: dsummersfca@hotmail.com
Fax: 020-7644 0678   Tel: 020-7644 0478

TAKE FIVE CASTING STUDIO
(Showreels)
25 Ganton Street
London W1F 9BP
Website: www.takefivestudio.co.uk
e-mail: info@takefivestudio.co.uk
Fax: 020-7287 3035   Tel: 020-7287 2120

**TANI MORENA, SPANISH CHOREOGRAPHY
FOR PROFESSIONALS**
(Theatre, Opera, Ballet)   Tel: 020-8452 0407

TARLO LYONS
(Solicitors)
Watchmaker Court,
33 St John's Lane
London EC1M 4DB
Website: www.tarlolyons.com
e-mail: info@tarlolyons.com
Fax: 020-7814 9421   Tel: 020-7405 2000

TAYLOR Chris
(Arts Administration)
1 Chichester Terrace
Brighton BN2 1FG
e-mail: chris.taylor@clara.co.uk
Fax: 01273 675922   Tel: 01273 625132

TELESCRIPT Ltd
The Barn
Handpost Farmhouse
Maidens Green, Berkshire RG42 6LD
Fax: 01344 890655   Tel: 01344 890470

THEATRE PROJECTS CONSULTANTS
4 Apollo Studios
Charlton Kings Road
London NW5 2SW
Website: www.tpcworld.com
Fax: 020-7284 0636   Tel: 020-7482 4224

THORNTON W. M. Lt Cdr MBE RD RNR
(Military Adviser & Researcher)
37 Wolsey Close
Southall, Middlesex UB2 4NQ
e-mail: maitland@thornton44.fsnet.co.uk
                              Tel: 020-8574 4425

TODD Carole
(Director/Choreographer)
c/o Chris Davis - International Artistes
4th Floor, Holborn Hall
193-195 High Holborn
London WC1V 7BD
Website: www.caroletodd.me.uk
e-mail: chris@intart.co.uk
Fax: 020-7404 9865   Tel: 020-7025 0600

TODS MURRAY WS
(Richard Findlay Entertainment Lawyer)
66 Queen Street
Edinburgh EH2 4NE
e-mail: richard.findlay@todsmurray.com
Fax: 0131-300 2202   Tel: 0131-226 4771

TOUCHWOOD PRODUCTION STUDIO
(Voice-Over Showreels, Digital Editing etc)
Knightsbridge House
229 Acton Lane
Chiswick, London W4 5DD
Fax: 020-8995 2144   Tel: 020-8995 3232

TV UK Ltd/LATITUDE MEDIA COURSES
(Voice-Over Courses, Alan Meyer)
PO Box 2183
London W1A 1UB
Website: www.tvuk.net
e-mail: alanmeyer@tvuk.net   Tel: 020-7727 7447

UC PRODUCTIONS
(Production & Event Management)
22 Freshfield Place
Brighton, East Sussex BN2 0BN
e-mail: byford@ucproductions.co.uk
Fax: 01273 606402   Tel: 01273 623972

UNITED KINGfDOM COPYRIGHT BUREAU
(Script Services)
110 Trafalgar Road
Portslade
East Sussex BN41 1GS
Website: www.copyrightbureau.co.uk
e-mail: info@copyrightbureau.co.uk
Fax: 01273 705451   Tel: 01273 277333

UPFRONT TELEVISION Ltd
(Celebrity)
39-41 New Oxford Street
London WC1A 1BN
e-mail: upfront@btinternet.com
Fax: 020-7836 7701   Tel: 020-7836 7702

VANTIS MORTON THORNTON
(Accountants/Business Advisers)
Torrington House
47 Holywell Hill
St Albans
Hertfordshire AL1 1HD
e-mail: ian.skelton@vantisplc.com
Fax: 01727 861052   Tel: 01727 838255

VENTURINO Antonio
(Commedia dell'arte, Mask Specialist &
Movement Director)
Coup de Masque
97 Moore Road
Mapperley, Nottingham NG3 6EJ
e-mail: a-and-t@coup-de-masque.fsnet.co.uk
                              Tel/Fax: 0115-985 8409

VERNON Doremy
(Author 'Tiller Girls'/Archivist/Dance Routines
Tiller Girl Style)
16 Ouseley Road
London SW12 8EF   Tel/Fax: 020-8767 6944

VSI
132 Cleveland Street
London W1T 6AB
Website: www.vsi.tv   e-mail: info@vsi.tv
Fax: 020-7692 7711   Tel: 020-7692 7700

WEB CREATIONS
(Tim Groves)
31A Cobden Road
South Norwood, London SE25 5NY
Website: www.tgwc.co.uk
e-mail: info@tgwc.co.uk   Mobile: 07764 740182

WELBOURNE Jacqueline
(Circus Trainer, Choreographer, Consultant)
43 Kingsway Avenue
Kingswood, Bristol BS15 8AN
e-mail: jackie@welbourne.co.uk
Mobile: 07977 247287   Tel/Fax: 0117-947 7042

WHITE Leonard
(Production & Script Consultant)
Highlands
40 Hill Crest Road
Newhaven, Brighton
East Sussex BN9 9EG
e-mail: leoguy.white@virgin.net
                              Tel/Fax: 01273 514473

WITCH FINDER GENERAL
(Occult Consultants)
BCM Akademia
London WC1N 3XX
e-mail: esbat@blueyonder.co.uk   Tel: 020-8683 2173

WWW.PUPPETSPRESENT.COM
c/o Peter Charlesworth & Associates
68 Old Brompton Road
London SW7 3LD
Website: www.puppetspresent.com
e-mail: puppetspresent@btinternet.com
                              Tel: 020-7581 2478

YOUNGBLOOD Ltd
(Dramatic Action Specialists)
20 Aintree Street
Fulham, London SW6 7QU
Website: www.youngblood.org.uk
e-mail: info@youngblood.org.uk
Mobile: 07813 463102   Tel: 0845 6449418

ACADEMY COSTUMES
50 Rushworth Street, London SE1 0RB
Website: www.academycostumes.com
e-mail: academyco@aol.com
Fax: 020-7928 6287   Tel: 020-7620 0771

ANELLO & DAVIDE Ltd
(Bespoke, Bridal, Dance & Theatrical Footwear)
26-28 Standard Road, Park Royal, London NW10 6EU
Fax: 020-8965 4111   Tel: 020-8963 1220

ANGELS
(Fancy Dress & Revue)
119 Shaftesbury Avenue, London WC2H 8AE
Website: www.fancydress.com
e-mail: party@fancydress.com
Fax: 020-7240 9527   Tel: 020-7836 5678

ANGELS PARIS
(Costume and Uniform Hire)
Cap 18, 189 rue d'Aubervilles, 75018 Paris, France
Website: www.angels.fr
e-mail: angels@angels.fr
Fax: 00 33 1 44 729060   Tel: 00 33 1 44 728282

ANGELS THE COSTUMIERS
1 Garrick Road, London NW9 6AA
Website: www.angels.uk.com
e-mail: angels@angels.uk.com
Fax: 020-8202 1820   Tel: 020-8202 2244

ANGELS WIGS
(Wig Hire/Makers, Facial Hair Suppliers)
1 Garrick Road, London NW9 6AA
Website: www.angels.uk.com
e-mail: wigs@angels.uk.com
Fax: 020-8202 1820   Tel: 020-8202 2244

ANICHINI Carlo
(Hairdresser)
14 Piccadilly Arcade
London SW1Y 6NH   Tel: 020-7493 5692

ARMS & ARCHERY
(Armour, Weaponry, Chain Mail, Warrior Costumes)
The Coach House
London Road
Ware, Herts SG12 9QU
e-mail: tgou104885@aol.com
Fax: 01920 461044   Tel: 01920 460335

BABOO William
(Theatrical Tailor)
46 Berwick Street
London W1F 8SG   Tel: 020-7434 1680

BAHADLY R
(Hair & Make-Up Specialist, incl. Bald Caps,
Ageing & Casualty)
48 Ivy Meade Road, Macclesfield, Cheshire
Mobile: 07973 553073   Tel: 01625 615878

BBC COSTUME & WIGS
172-178 Victoria Road, North Acton, London W3 6UL
Fax: 020-8993 7040   Tel: 020-8576 1761

BERTRAND Henry
(London Stockhouse for Silk)
52 Holmes Road, London NW5 3AB
Website: www.henrybertrand.co.uk
e-mail: sales@henrybertrand.co.uk
Fax: 020-7424 7001   Tel: 020-7424 7000

BIRMINGHAM COSTUME HIRE
Suites 209-210, Jubilee Centre
130 Pershore Street, Birmingham B5 6ND
e-mail: info@birminghamcostumehire.co.uk
Fax: 0121-622 2758   Tel: 0121-622 3158

BOSANQUET Pamela COSTUME SERVICES
2 Lebanon Park, Twickenham TW1 3DG
e-mail: lily.jones@virgin.net
Fax: 020-8891 6259   Tel: 020-8891 4346

BRYAN PHILIP DAVIES COSTUMES
(Lavish Pantomime/Revue Costumes)
68 Court Road, Lewes, East Sussex BN7 2SA
Website: www.bpdcostumes.co.uk
e-mail: bryan@bpdcostumes.force9.co.uk
Mobile: 07931 249097   Tel/Fax: 01273 481004

BURLINGTONS
(Hairdressers)
14 John Princes Street, London W1G 0JS
Website: www.burlingtonsuk.com
                              Tel: 0870 8701299

CALICO
(Suppliers of Unbleached Calico for
Stage Costumes, Backdrops etc)
3 Ram Passage, High Street
Kingston-upon-Thames KT1 1HH
Website: www.calicofabrics.co.uk
e-mail: sales@calicofabrics.co.uk
Fax: 020-8546 7755   Tel: 020-8541 5274

CATCO MILLINERY
134 Mercers Road
London N19 4PV   Tel: 020-7272 4833

CAVALCADE COSTUMES
(Period & Light Entertainment Costumes
Single Outfits to Full Productions)
57 Pelham Road, London SW19 1NW
Fax: 020-8540 2243   Tel: 020-8540 3513

CHRISANNE Ltd
(Specialist Fabrics & Accessories)
Chrisanne House, 14 Locks Lane
Mitcham, Surrey CR4 2JX
Website: www.chrisanne.co.uk
e-mail: sales@chrisanne.co.uk
Fax: 020-8640 2106   Tel: 020-8640 5921

COLTMAN Mike
(See COSTUME CONSTRUCTION)

COOK Sheila TEXTILES
(Vintage Textiles, Costumes & Accessories
for Sale)
14 Addison Avenue
Holland Park, London W11 4QR
Website: www.sheilacook@sheilacook.co.uk
e-mail: sheilacook@sheilacook.co.uk
Fax: 020-7603 4202   Tel: 020-7603 3003

COOPER Margaret
(Period Costumes)
75/1 Old College Street, Sleima, Malta
e-mail: g1greatdane@yahoo.com
Mobile: 00 356 9925 2925   Tel: 00 356 21 342338

COSPROP Ltd
(Costumes & Accessories)
26-28 Rochester Place, London NW1 9JR
Website: www.cosprop.com
e-mail: enquiries@cosprop.com
Fax: 020-7485 5942   Tel: 020-7485 6731

COSTUME COLLECTION
(Entire Costuming Service)
60 Viola Avenue, Stanwell, Middlesex TW19 7SB
e-mail: costumes4all@hotmail.com
                              Mobile: 07787 974857

COSTUME CONSTRUCTION
(Costumes, Masks, Props, Puppets)
21A Silchester Road, London W10 6SF
Website: www.costumeconstruction.co.uk
                              Tel/Fax: 020-8968 9136

COSTUME REPRODUCTIONS
(Costumiers)
200 Main Road, Goostrey, Cheshire CW4 8PD
Website: www.replicawarehouse.co.uk
e-mail: lesleyedwards@replicawarehouse.co.uk
                              Tel/Fax: 01477 534075

COSTUME STORE The Ltd
16 Station Street, Lewes, East Sussex BN7 2DB
Website: www.thecostumestore.co.uk
Fax: 01273 477191   Tel: 01273 479727

COSTUME STUDIO Ltd
(Costumes & Wigs)
Montgomery House
159-161 Balls Pond Road, London N1 4BG
Website: www.costumestudio.co.uk
e-mail: costume.studio@easynet.co.uk
                              Tel/Fax: 020-7837 6576

COUNTY DRAMA WARDROBE
(Costume Hire only)
25 Gwydir Street
Cambridge CB1 2LG   Tel: 01223 313423

CRAZY CLOTHES CONNECTION
(1920's-1970's for Sale or Hire)
134 Lancaster Road, Ladbroke Grove
London W11 1QU   Tel: 020-7221 3989

ROSEMARIE SWINFIELD
make-up designer

Rosie's Make-up Box
6 Brewer Street, Soho, London W1R 3FS

Author of:
* ✶ Stage Make-Up Step By Step
* ✶ Period Make-Up For The Stage
* ✶ Hair And Wigs For The Stage

Also

Courses, Workshops & Seminars Worldwide

Tel: 07976-965520   e-mail: rosemarie@rosiesmake-up.co.uk   www.rosiesmake-up.co.uk

---

DESIGNER ALTERATIONS
(Restyling & Remodelling of Clothes & Costumes)
220A Queenstown Road
Battersea, London SW8 4LP
Website: www.designeralterations.com
Fax: 020-7622 4148   Tel: 020-7498 4360

EASTON Derek
(Wigs For Theatre, Film & TV)
1 Dorothy Avenue
Peacehaven, East Sussex BN10 8LP
Website: www.derekeastonwigs.co.uk
Mobile: 07768 166733   Tel: 020-7498 4360

EDA ROSE MILLINERY
(Ladies' Model Hat Design & Manufacture)
Lalique, Mongewell, Wallingford
Oxon OX10 8BP   Tel/Fax: 01491 837174

FOSTER Pam ASSOCIATES
(Wig Makers)
Unit 009, The Chandlery
50 Westminster Bridge Road, London SE1 7QY
e-mail: pam@pfosterassoc.demon.co.uk
Fax: 020-7721 7409   Tel: 020-7721 7641

FOX Charles H. Ltd
(Professional Make-Up & Wigs)
22 Tavistock Street, London WC2E 7PY
Website: www.charlesfox.co.uk
Fax: 0870 2001369   Tel: 0870 2000369

FREED OF LONDON
(Dancewear & Danceshoes)
94 St Martin's Lane, London WC2N 4AT
Website: www.freedoflondon.com
e-mail: shop@freed.co.uk
Fax: 020-7240 3061   Tel: 020-7240 0432

Dr. Richard Casson
D E N T A L   C A R E

I provide a complete range of cosmetic and stage dentistry effects for those wishing to add a bit more bite to their big performance.

Free consultation for:

* fangs
* witches teeth
* goofy teeth
* crooked teeth
* replacement of children's missing teeth for stage, television & films

For further information phone or write to
Dr. Richard Casson BDS (GLAS)
on 020 7935 6511/020 7935 8854

6 Milford House, 7 Queen Anne Street,
London W1G 9HN
Website: www.richardcasson.com

COSTUME COLLECTION

Theatre/Period	**Entire Costuming Service**	Ballroom/Ballet
Ice Skating	Accessories Props Footwear	National/Ethnic
Revue/Circus	Finest Fabrics Exquisite Jewelling/Production & Individual	Tribute

Telephone Monica 07787 974 857 or email costmes4all@hotmail.com

---

FUNN Ltd
(Silk, Cotton Wool Stockings, Opaque Opera Tights
& 40's Rayon Stockings)
PO Box 102, Steyning, West Sussex BN44 3DS
e-mail: funn.biz@lycos.com
Fax: 0870 1361780   Tel: 0870 7484081

GAMBA THEATRICAL
(See THEATRICAL FOOTWEAR COMPANY Ltd)

GAV NICOLA THEATRICAL SHOES
1A Suttons Lane, Hornchurch, Essex RM12 6RD
e-mail: sales@gavnicola.freeserve.co.uk
Mobile: 07961 974278   Tel/Fax: 01708 438584

GILLHAM Felicite
(Wig Makers for Theatre, Opera & Film)
15 Newland, Sherborne, Dorset DT9 3JG
e-mail: f.gillham.wigs@gmx.net   Tel: 01935 814328

HAIRAISERS
(Wigs)
9-11 Sunbeam Road, Park Royal, London NW10 6JP
Fax: 020-8963 1600   Tel: 020-8965 2500

HARVEYS OF HOVE
(Theatrical Costumes & Military Specialists)
110 Trafalgar Road, Portslade, Sussex BN41 1GS
e-mail: harveys.costume@ntlworld.com
Fax: 01273 708699   Tel: 01273 430323

HERALD & HEART HATTERS
(Men's & Women's Hats & Headdresses
- Period & Modern)
Church Farm House, East Guldeford, Rye
East Sussex TN31 7PA
Website: www.heraldandheart.com
e-mail: enquiries@heraldandheart.com
                              Tel: 01797 226798

HIREARCHY
(Classic & Contemporary Costume)
45-47 Palmerston Road, Boscombe
Bournemouth, Dorset BH1 4HW
Website: www.hirearchy.co.uk
e-mail: hirearchy1@aol.com   Tel: 01202 394465

HIYA COSTUME
(Hire of Theatre Costumes for Adults & Children)
1-3 Ham Road, Shoreham-by-Sea
Sussex BN43 6PA   Tel: 01273 453421

HODIN Annabel
(Costume Designer/Stylist)
12 Eton Avenue, London NW3 3EH
e-mail: annabelhodin@aol.com
Mobile: 07836 754079   Tel: 020-7431 8761

JULIETTE DESIGNS
(Diamante Jewellery Manufacturers)
90 Yerbury Road, London N19 4RS
Website: stagejewellery.com
Fax: 020-7281 7326   Tel: 020-7263 7878

K & D Ltd
(Footwear)
Unit 7A, Thames Road Industrial Estate,
Thames Road, Silvertown, London E16 2EZ
Website: www.shoemaking.co.uk
e-mail: k&d@shoemaking.co.uk
Fax: 020-7476 5220   Tel: 020-7474 0500

KING Shelley J
(Make-up Artist/Wigdresser)
Vine Bank Cottage, High Street
Limpsfield, Surrey RH8 0DR
Mobile: 07973 249998   Tel: 01883 715095

LANDSFIELD Warren
(Period Legal Wigs)
47 Glenmore Road
London NW3 4DA   Tel: 020-7722 4581

LAURENCE CORNER THEATRICALS
(Theatrical Costumiers - Militaria, Uniforms -
Hire & Sale)
62-64 Hampstead Road
London NW1 2NU
Website: www.laurencecorner.com
Fax: 020-7813 1413   Tel: 020-7813 1010

LEWIS HENRY Ltd
(Dress Makers)
3rd Floor, 42 Great Titchfield Street
London W1P 7AE   Tel: 020-7636 6683

LONDON HAT HOUSE The
(Hatmakers, Masks, Headdresses & Specialist
Dyers)
Unit 006, The Chandlery
50 Westminster Bridge Road
London SE1 7QY   Tel: 020-7721 8771

LUISETTI Martina
(Professional Freelance Make-Up Artist for Film, TV,
Theatre, Fashion)
9 Birchfield House, Birchfield Street, Westferry
London E1G 8EY
e-mail: martola@virgilio.it   Mobile: 07919 652089

MADDERMARKET THEATRE COSTUME HIRE
(Period Clothing, Costume Hire & Wig Hire)
St John's Alley, Norwich NR2 1DR
Website: www.maddermarket.co.uk
e-mail: theatre@maddermarket.co.uk
Fax: 01603 661357   Tel: 01603 626292

MAKEUP CENTRE The
(Make-Up Lessons & Supplies)
52A Walham Grove, London SW6 1QR
Website: www.themake-upcentre.co.uk
e-mail: info@themake-upcentre.co.uk
                              Tel: 020-7381 0213

MANNEE Nichola
(Make-Up Artist)
264A Chapter Road
Dollis Hill
London NW2 5NE
e-mail: nicola_mannee@yahoo.com
Mobile: 07984 644288

MASTER CLEANERS The
(Theatrical Costumes & Antique Garments)
189 Haverstock Hill
London NW3 4QG   Tel: 020-7431 3725

MBA COSTUMES
Goodyear House
52-56 Osnaburgh Street
London NW1 3ND
e-mail: nhowarduk@aol.com
Fax: 020-7383 2038   Tel: 020-7388 4994

McKAY Glynn MASKS
(Specialists in Special Effect Make-Up)
11 Mount Pleasant, Framlingham
Suffolk IP13 9HQ
Mobile: 07780 865073   Tel/Fax: 01728 723865

MIDNIGHT
Costume Design & Wardrobe
e-mail: midnight_wardrobe@hotmail.com
Mobile: 07941 313223

MUMFORD Jean
(Costume Maker)
92B Fortess Road
London NW5 2HJ   Tel: 020-7267 5829

NEW ID
(Makeover & Photographic Studios)
14 John Princes Street, London W1G 0JS
Website: www.newidstudios.com   Tel: 0870 8701299

C

NICOLERENEE
(Wedding & Evening Dresses/Ball Gowns)
4 Puma Court, Spitalfields, City, London E1 6QG
e-mail: info@nicolerenee.co.uk
Fax: 020-7247 9276   Mobile: 07961 180949

ORIGINAL KNITWEAR
(Inc. Fake Fur)
Waterside, 99 Rotherhithe Street, London SE16 4NF
Fax: 020-7231 9051   Mobile: 07957 376855

PATEY (LONDON) Ltd
Unit 1, 9 Gowlett Road, London SE15 4HX
Website: www.pateyhats.com
e-mail: pateyhats@aol.com
Fax: 020-7732 9538   Tel: 020-7635 0030

PERMODE
(Costume)
46 Berwick Street
London W1F 8SG   Tel: 020-7434 1680

PINK POINTES DANCEWEAR
1A Suttons Lane, Hornchurch, Essex RM12 6RD
e-mail: sales@gavnicola.freeserve.co.uk
                              Tel/Fax: 01708 438584

POLAND DENTAL STUDIO
(Film/Stage Dentistry)
1 Devonshire Place, London W1N 1PA
e-mail: polandslab@aol.com
Fax: 020-7486 3952   Tel: 020-7935 6919

PROBLOOD
11 Mount Pleasant, Framlingham
Suffolk IP13 9HQ   Tel/Fax: 01728 723865

PULLON PRODUCTIONS
(Costumiers)
St George's Studio, Wood End Lane, Fillongley
Coventry CV7 8DF
Website: www.pm-productions.co.uk
                              Tel/Fax: 01676 541390

RAINBOW PRODUCTIONS Ltd
(Manufacture & Handling of Costume Characters)
Rainbow House, 56 Windsor Avenue
London SW19 2RR
Website: www.rainbowproductions.co.uk
e-mail: info@rainbowproductions.co.uk
Fax: 020-8545 0777   Tel: 020-8545 0700

ROBBINS Sheila
(Costumes & Wigs)
Broombarn, 7 Ivy Cottages, Hinksey Hill
Oxford OX1 5BQ   Tel/Fax: 01865 735524

ROYAL EXCHANGE THEATRE COSTUME HIRE
(Period Costumes, Wigs & Accessories)
47-53 Swan Street, Manchester M4 4JY
e-mail: costume.hire@royalexchange.co.uk
                              Tel/Fax: 0161-615 6800

ROYAL LYCEUM THEATRE COMPANY
(Theatrical Costume Hire)
29 Roseburn Street, Edinburgh EH12 5PE
Fax: 0131-346 8072   Tel: 0131-337 1997

ROYAL NATIONAL THEATRE
(Costume & Furniture Hire)
Chichester House, Kennington Park Estate
1-3 Brixton Road, London SW9 6DE
e-mail: costume_hire@nationaltheatre.org.uk
Tel: 020-7735 4774 (Costume)   Tel: 020-7820 1358 (Props)

RUMBLE Jane
(Masks, Millinery, Helmets Made to Order)
121 Elmstead Avenue, Wembley
Middlesex HA9 8NT   Tel: 020-8904 6462

RUSSELL HOWARTH Ltd
35 Hoxton Square, London N1 6MM
Fax: 020-7729 0107   Tel: 020-7739 6960

SCOTT Allan COSTUMES
(Costume Hire, Stage, Film & TV)
Offley Works, Unit F, Prima Road
London SW9 0NA   Tel: 020-7793 1197

SEXTON Sally Ann
(Hair & Make-Up Stylist)
31 Sylvester Road, East Finchley, London N2 8HN
Mobile: 07973 802842   Tel: 020-8346 2745

SHOWBIZWIGS Ltd
(Theatrical Wigmakers & Hire)
7 Tumulus Close, Southampton SO19 6RL
Website: www.showbizwigs.co.uk
                              Tel/Fax: 023-8040 6699

SIDE EFFECTS
(Custom-made Character/FX Costumes)
Unit 4, Camberwell Trading Estate, 117 Denmark Rd
London SE5 9LB   e-mail: sfx@lineone.net
Fax: 020-7738 5198   Tel: 020-7738 5199

SINGER Sandra ASSOCIATES
21 Cotswold Road, Westcliff on Sea, Essex SS0 8AA
Website: www.sandrasinger.com
e-mail: sandrasingeruk@aol.com
Fax: 01702 339393   Tel: 01702 331616

SKINNER Rachel MILLINERY
13 Princess Road, London NW1 8JR
Website: www.rachelskinner.co.uk
e-mail: rachel@rachelskinner.co.uk
                              Tel/Fax: 020-7209 0066

SLEIMAN Hilary
(Specialist & Period Knitwear)
72 Godwin Road, London E7 0LG
e-mail: hilary.sleiman@ntlworld.com
Mobile: 07940 555663   Tel: 020-8555 6176

SOFT PROPS
(Costume & Modelmakers)
Unit 4, Camberwell Trading Estate
117-119 Denmark Road, London SE5 9LB
e-mail: jackie@softprops.co.uk
Fax: 020-7738 5198   Tel: 020-7738 6324

STUDIO FOUR COSTUMES
(Childrenswear for Hire to Film & TV)
4 Warple Mews, Warple Way, Acton
London W3 0RF   Tel/Fax: 020-8749 6569

SUMMERS Jane
(Make-Up and Hair Artist)
Bucks Green Cottage, Bucks Green
Bedingfield Eye, Suffolk IP23 7LL
e-mail: janelouisemakeup@aol.com
Mobile: 07836 729800   Tel: 01728 628234

SWINFIELD Rosemarie
(Make-Up Design & Training)
Rosie's Make-Up Box
6 Brewer Street, Soho W1R 3FS
Website: www.rosiesmake-up.co.uk
e-mail: rosemarie@rosiesmake-up.co.uk
                              Mobile: 07976 965520

THEATREKNITS
102C Belgravia Workshops
157-163 Marlborough Road, London N19 4NF
e-mail: trevorcollins@blueyonder.co.uk
Tel/Fax: 020-7561 0044

THEATRICAL FOOTWEAR COMPANY The Ltd
(Trading as GAMBA Theatrical)
Unit 14, Chingford Industrial Centre, Hall Lane
Chingford, London E4 8DJ
e-mail: gambatheatrical@yahoo.com
Fax: 020-8529 7995   Tel: 020-8529 9195

THREE KINGS THEATRICAL SUPPPLY CO The
(Make-Up and Other Theatrical Services)
30 Whites Road, Farnborough, Hampshire GU14 6PD
Website: www.threekingstheatrical.com
e-mail: info@threekingstheatrical.com
Fax: 01252 515516   Tel: 01252 515505

TRENDS PRODUCTIONS Ltd
(Theatrical Costume Hire, Design & Making)
54 Lisson Street, London NW1 5DF
Website: www.trendsgroup.co.uk
e-mail: info@trendsgroup.co.uk
Fax: 020-7258 3591   Tel: 020-7723 8001

TRYFONOS Mary MASKS
(Designer and Maker of Masks and Headdresses)
59 Shaftesbury Road, London N19 4QW
Website: www.marysmasks.com
e-mail: marytryfonos@aol.com
Mobile: 07764 587433   Tel: 020-7561 9880

VICKERS Jean
(Modern & Period Costumes Made)
40 Abingdon Road
London W8 6AR   Tel: 020-7937 2870

WAIN SHIELL & SON Ltd
(High Quality Cloth Merchants)
12 Savile Row, London W1S 3PQ
e-mail: wainshiell@compuserve.com
Fax: 020-7437 0093   Tel: 020-7734 1464
Savile House, 7 Sheffield Road
New Mill, Huddersfield HD7 7EL
Fax: 01484 688796   Tel: 01484 688818

WEST YORKSHIRE FABRICS Ltd
(All Wool Venetian Crepe, Suiting, Barathea,
Cut Lengths)
20 High Ash Drive, Leeds LS17 8RA
e-mail: info@stroud-brothers.demon.co.uk
Tel/Fax: 0870 4439842

WIG ROOM The
22 Coronation Road, Basingstoke, Hants RG21 4HA
e-mail: wigroom@fsbdial.co.uk   Tel/Fax: 01256 415737

WIG SPECIALITIES Ltd
(Wigs & Facial Hair, Hair Extensions etc)
First Floor, 173 Seymour Place, London W1H 4PW
Website: www.wigspecialites.co.uk
e-mail: wigspecialities@btconnect.com
Fax: 020-7723 1566   Tel: 020-7262 6565

WILLIAMS Emma
(Costume Designer & Stylist - Film, TV & Theatre)
e-mail: emmaw@costume.fsnet.co.uk
Mobile: 07710 130345   Tel/Fax: 01225 447169

WILSON Marian WIGS
(Theatrical & Film Wigmaker)
59 Gloucester Street, Faringdon, Oxon SN7 7JA
e-mail: wigmaker@wigmaker.screaming.net
Fax: 01367 242438   Tel: 01367 241696

WORLD OF FANTASY
(Costumes & Props)
Swansnest, Rear of 2 Windmill Road, Hampton Hill
Middlesex TW12 1RH
Fax: 020-8783 1366   Tel: 020-8941 1595

C

DAILY EXPRESS   Tel: 020-7928 8000
Theatre: Robert Gore-Langton
Films: Ryan Gilbey, Alan Hunter
Television: Tim Hulse, Jeremy Novick
Saturday Magazine/Programmes: Pat Stoddart

DAILY MAIL   Tel: 020-7938 6000
Theatre: Michael Coveney
Films: Chris Tookey
Television: Peter Paterson, Christopher Matthew

DAILY STAR   Tel: 020-7928 8000
Show Business & Television: Laura Benjamin
    Julia Etherington, Sean Hamilton, Nigel Pauley
    Debbie Pogue, Gareth Morgan, Ben Todd
    Amy Watts
Films & Video: Alan Frank

DAILY TELEGRAPH   Tel: 020-7538 5000
Theatre: Charles Spencer
Films: Sukhdev Sandhu
Radio: Gillian Reynolds
Dance: Ismene Brown
Art: Richard Dorment
Music: Geoffrey Norris

FINANCIAL TIMES   Tel: 020-7873 3000
Theatre: Alastair MacAulay
Films: Nigel Andrews
Television: Graham McCann

GUARDIAN   Tel: 020-7278 2332
Theatre: Michael Billington
Films: Peter Bradshaw
Television: Nancy Banks-Smith
Radio: Elisabeth Mahoney

INDEPENDENT   Tel: 020-7005 2000
Television: Tom Sutcliffe

LONDON EVENING STANDARD   Tel: 020-7938 6000
Theatre: Nicholas de Jongh
    Rachel Halliburton, Fiona Mount
Films: Alexander Walker
Opera: Fiona Maddocks
Television: Victor Lewis-Smith, Terry Ramsay
Classical Music: Brian Hunt
Radio: Terry Ramsay

MAIL ON SUNDAY   Tel: 020-7938 6000
Theatre: Georgina Brown
Films: Jason Solomons
Television: Jaci Stephen
Radio: Simon Garfield
Features: Nikki Murfitt

MIRROR   Tel: 020-7510 3000
Films: Kevin O'Sullivan
Television: Nicola Methuen

MORNING STAR   Tel: 020-8510 0815
Theatre & Films: Katie Gilmore
Television: Kevin Russell, Alex Reid, Richard Bagley

NEWS OF THE WORLD   Tel: 020-7782 4000
Show Business/Films: Rav Singh, Paul Ross
    Shebah Ronay

OBSERVER   Tel: 020-7278 2332
Theatre: Susanna Clapp
Films: Philip French, Akin Ojumu
Radio: Sue Arnold

SPORT   Tel: 0161-238 8151
Showbusiness/Features: Nick Appleyard

SUN   Tel: 020-7782 4000
Television: Ally Ross

SUNDAY EXPRESS   Tel: 020-7928 8000
Theatre: Robert Gore-Langton
Films: Henry Fitzherbert
Television: David Stephenson
Radio & Arts: Rachel Jane

SUNDAY MIRROR   Tel: 020-7510 3000
Theatre & Television: Ian Hyland
Films: Quentin Falk

SUNDAY PEOPLE   Tel: 020-7510 3000
Television & Radio: Sarah Moolla
Films: Jane Simon
Show Business: Sean O'Brien
Features: Dawn Alford

SUNDAY TELEGRAPH   Tel: 020-7538 5000
Theatre: John Gross
Films: Jenny McCartney
Television: John Preston
Radio: David Sexton

SUNDAY TIMES   Tel: 020-7782 5000
Theatre: John Peter
Films: Cosmo Landesman
Television: A. A. Gill
Radio: Paul Donovan

TIMES   Tel: 020-7782 5000
Theatre: Benedict Nightingale
Films: Barbara Ellen
Television: Joe Joseph
Video: Geoff Brown
Radio: Peter Barnard

THE SPOTLIGHT ®

The most celebrated
casting directory in the world

ADZIDO
Canonbury Business Centre
202 New North Road
London N1 7BJ
e-mail: info@adzido.co.uk
Fax: 020-7704 0300   Tel: 020-7359 7453

AKADEMI
(South Asian Dance in the UK)
Hampstead Town Hall, Haverstock Hill
London NW3 4QP
Website: www.akademi.co.uk
e-mail: info@akademi.co.uk
Fax: 020-7691 3211   Tel: 020-7691 3210

ALSTON Richard DANCE COMPANY
The Place, 17 Duke's Road
London WC1H 9PY
e-mail: radc@theplace.org.uk
Fax: 020-7383 5700   Tel: 020-7387 0324

BALLET CREATIONS
3 Blackbird Way, Bransgore
Nr Christchurch
Hampshire BH23 8LG
Website: www.ballet-creations.co.uk
e-mail: info@ballet-creations.co.uk
                              Tel/Fax: 01425 674163

BALLROOM - LONDON THEATRE OF
(Artistic Director - Paul Harris)
24 Ovett Close
Upper Norwood, London SE19 3RX
e-mail: paulharrisdance@hotmail.com
Mobile: 07958 784462   Tel/Fax: 020-8771 4274

BIRMINGHAM ROYAL BALLET
Thorp Street, Birmingham B5 4AU
Website: www.brb.org.uk
e-mail: administrator@brb.org.uk
Fax: 0121-245 3570   Tel: 0121-245 3500

B.O.P. PRODUCTIONS Ltd
(Jazz Theatre Company)
10 Stayton Road, Sutton
Surrey SM1 1RB
e-mail: info@bop.demon.co.uk   Tel: 020-8641 6959

BRITISH BALLET ORGANIZATION
(Dance Examining Society & Teacher Training)
Woolborough House
39 Lonsdale Road
Barnes SW13 9JP
Website: www.bbo.org.uk
e-mail: bbohq@aol.com   Tel: 020-8748 1241

CAPITAL ARTS THEATRE SCHOOL
(Kathleen Shanks)
Wyllyotts Centre, Darkes Lane
Potters Bar
Hertfordshire EN6 2HN
e-mail: capitalartstheatre@o2.co.uk
Mobile: 07885 232414   Tel/Fax: 020-8449 2342

CHOLMONDELEYS The
LF1.1
Lafone House
The Leathermarket
11-13 Leathermarket Street
London SE1 3HN
e-mail: admin.cholmondeleys@btclick.com
                              Tel: 020-7378 8800

COMPANY OF CRANKS
1st Floor
62 Northfield House
Frensham Street
London SE15 6TN
Website: www.brendanmime.freeuk.com
e-mail: mimetic@freeuk.com   Tel: 020-7358 0571

COUNCIL FOR DANCE EDUCATION & TRAINING
Toynbee Hall
28 Commercial Street, London E1 6LS
Website: www.cdet.org.uk
e-mail: info@cdet.org.uk
Fax: 020-7247 3404   Tel: 09018 800014

DANCE FOR EVERYONE Ltd
30 Sevington Road, London NW4 3RX
e-mail: orders@dfe.org.uk   Tel: 020-8202 7863

DANCE UK
(Including the Healthier Dancer Programme)
Battersea Arts Centre, Lavender Hill
London SW11 5TN
Website: www.danceuk.org
e-mail: info@danceuk.org
Fax: 020-7223 0074   Tel: 020-7228 4990

DANCE UMBRELLA
20 Chancellors Street, London W6 9RN
Website: www.danceumbrella.co.uk
e-mail: mail@danceumbrella.co.uk
Fax: 020-8741 7902   Tel: 020-8741 4040

ENGLISH NATIONAL BALLET Ltd
Markova House
39 Jay Mews, London SW7 2ES
Website: www.ballet.org.uk
e-mail: info@ballet.org.uk
Fax: 020-7225 0827   Tel: 020-7581 1245

FEATHERSTONEHAUGHS The
LF1 .1, Lafone House
The Leathermarket, 11-13 Leathermarket Street
London SE1 3HN
Website: www.thecholmondeleys.org
e-mail: admin@thecholmondeleys.org
                              Tel: 020-7378 8800

GIELGUD BALLET The
Wimbledon Theatre, The Broadway
London SW19 1QG
Website: www.gielgud.com
e-mail: ballet@gielgud.com
Fax: 020-8542 8081   Tel: 020-8542 9712

IDTA (INTERNATIONAL DANCE TEACHERS' ASSOCIATION)
International House
76 Bennett Road, Brighton
East Sussex BN2 5JL
Website: www.idta.co.uk
e-mail: info@idta.co.uk
Fax: 01273 674388   Tel: 01273 685652

KOSH The
(Physical Theatre)
59 Stapleton Hall Road
London N4 3QF
e-mail: info@thekosh.com
Fax: 020-8374 5661   Tel: 020-8374 0407

LONDON CONTEMPORARY DANCE SCHOOL
The Place, 17 Duke's Road
London WC1H 9PY
Website: www.theplace.org.uk
e-mail: lcds@theplace.org.uk
Fax: 020-7387 3976   Tel: 020-7387 0152

LUDUS DANCE AGENCY
Assembly Rooms
King Street, Lancaster LA1 1RE
e-mail: info@ludus.org
Fax: 01524 847744   Tel: 01524 35936

MUDRALAYA DANCE THEATRE
Formerly Pushkala Gopal Unnikrishnan & Co
(Classical Indian Dance-Theatre)
20 Brisbane Road
Ilford, Essex IG1 4SR   Tel/Fax: 020-8554 4054

NATIONAL RESOURCE CENTRE FOR DANCE
University of Surrey
Guildford GU2 7XH
e-mail: nrcd@surrey.ac.uk   Tel: 01483 689316

NORTHERN BALLET THEATRE
West Park Centre
Spen Lane, Leeds LS16 5BE
e-mail: directors@nbtdance.demon.co.uk
Fax: 0113-274 5381   Tel: 0113-274 5355

PHOENIX DANCE THEATRE
3 St Peter's Building
St Peter's Square, Leeds LS9 8AH
Website: www.phoenixdancetheatre.co.uk
e-mail: info@phoenixdancetheatre.co.uk
Fax: 0113-244 4736   Tel: 0113-242 3486

RAMBERT DANCE COMPANY
94 Chiswick High Road
London W4 1SH
Website: www.rambert.org.uk
e-mail: rdc@rambert.org.uk
Fax: 020-8747 8323   Tel: 020-8630 0600

ROYAL BALLET The
Royal Opera House
Covent Garden
London WC2E 9DD
Fax: 020-7212 9502   Tel: 020-7240 1200

RUSS Claire ENSEMBLE
(Choreography, Movement Direction)
74A Queens Road, Twickenham TW1 4ET
Mobile: 07932 680224   Tel/Fax: 020-8892 9281

SCOTTISH BALLET
261 West Princes Street
Glasgow G4 9EE
Website: www.scottishballet.co.uk
e-mail: sb@scottishballet.co.uk
Fax: 0141-331 2629   Tel: 0141-331 2931

SCOTTISH DANCE THEATRE
Dundee Repertory Theatre
Tay Square, Dundee DD1 1PB
Website: www.scottishdancetheatre.com
e-mail: achinn@dundeereptheatre.co.uk
Fax: 01382 228609   Tel: 01382 342600

SOUTH-EAST DANCE - NATIONAL DANCE AGENCY
5 Palace Place
Castle Square, Brighton
East Sussex BN1 1EF
e-mail: southeast.dance@virgin.net
Fax: 01273 205540   Tel: 01273 202032

UNION DANCE COMPANY
c/o Marylebone Dance Studio
12 Lisson Grove
London NW1 6TS
e-mail: union.danceco@virgin.net
Fax: 020-7224 8911   Tel: 020-7724 5765

YORKSHIRE DANCE CENTRE NATIONAL DANCE AGENCY
3 St Peter's Buildings
St Peter's Square, Leeds LS9 8AH
Website: www.everybodydances.com
e-mail: admin@yorkshiredance.org.uk
Tel: 0113-243 9867

Founded in 1979, CDET promotes excellence in dance education and training. It accredits courses at vocational dance schools, advocates on behalf of the private dance teaching communities and provides an information service. CDET is a membership organisation, which includes vocational dance training institutions, teacher organisations, industry bodies and individuals.

The Conference of Professional Dance Schools (CPDS) exists to provide a forum in which representatives from vocational dance training institutions may discuss policy and recommend action in relation to vocational dance training.

- Arts Educational School, Tring Park
- ArtsEd London
- Bird College
- Central School of Ballet
- Hammond School
- Italia Conti Academy of Theatre Arts Ltd
- Laban
- Laine Theatre Arts
- London Contemporary Dance School
- London Studio Centre
- Merseyside Dance and Drama Centre
- Midlands Academy of Dance and Drama
- Performers College
- SLP College
- Stella Mann College
- Urdang Academy

For more info on the CPDS and CDET:

Contact:

Council for Dance Education and Training
Toynbee Hall
28 Commercial StreetLondon E1 6LS
Tel: 020 7247 4030
Fax: 020 7247 3404
Email: info@cdet.org.uk
Website: www.cdet.org.uk

ASH SCHOOL OF THEATRE ARTS
157 Burtons Road, Hampton Hill, Middx TW12 1DX
e-mail: ashschool@hotmail.com   Tel: 020-8979 7038

BALLROOM - LONDON THEATRE OF
(Artistic Director - Paul Harris)
24 Ovett Close, Upper Norwood, London SE19 3RX
e-mail: paulharrisdance@hotmail.com
Mobile: 07958 784462   Tel/Fax: 020-8771 4274

BELLYDANCE CENTRE The
(Private Lessons, Consultancy, Choreography)
Mayfield, 5 Rother Road, Seaford
East Sussex BN25 4HT   Tel: 01323 899083

BIRD COLLEGE OF PERFORMING ARTS
(Dance & Theatre Performance Diploma/BA (Hons)
Degree Course)
Birkbeck Centre, Birkbeck Road
Sidcup, Kent DA14 4DE
Fax: 020-8308 1370   Tel: 020-8300 6004

BODENS STUDIOS
(Performing Arts Classes)
99 East Barnet Road, New Barnet, Herts EN4 8RF
Website: www.bodenstudios.com
e-mail: bodens2692@aol.com
Fax: 020-8449 5212   Tel: 020-8449 0982

CAPITAL ARTS THEATRE SCHOOL
Wyllyotts Centre, Darkes Lane, Potters Bar
Hertfordshire EN6 2HN
e-mail: capitalartstheatre@o2.co.uk
Mobile: 07885 232414   Tel/Fax: 020-8449 2342

CENTRAL SCHOOL OF BALLET
(Dance Classes & Professional Training)
10 Herbal Hill, Clerkenwell Road, London EC1R 5EG
Website: www.centralschoolofballet.co.uk
e-mail: info@csbschool.co.uk
Fax: 020-7833 5571   Tel: 020-7837 6332

CENTRE - PERFORMING ARTS COLLEGE The
Building 62, Level 4, 37 Bowater Road
Charlton, London SE8 5TF
e-mail: dance@thecentrepac.com
                            Tel/Fax: 020-8855 6661

COLIN'S PERFORMING ARTS Ltd
The Studios, 219B North Street, Romford RM1 4QA
Website: www.colinsperformingarts.co.uk
e-mail: admin@colinsperformingarts.co.uk
Fax: 01708 766077   Tel: 01708 766007

COLLECTIVE DANCE & DRAMA
The Studio, Rectory Lane, Rickmansworth
Herts WD3 2AD   Tel/Fax: 020-8428 0037

CONTI Italia ACADEMY
(Full-time 3 year Musical Theatre Course)
Italia Conti House, 23 Goswell Road
London EC1M 7AJ
e-mail: sca@italiaconti36.freeserve.co.uk
Fax: 020-7253 1430   Tel: 020-7608 0047

CUSTARD FACTORY
(Professional Dance Classes and Dance Studio Hire)
Gibb Street, Digbeth, Birmingham B9 4AA
e-mail: custardfactory@clara.net
Fax: 0121-604 8888   Tel: 0121-693 7777

D & B SCHOOL OF PERFORMING ARTS
(3 Year Musical Theatre Course)
Central Studios, 470 Bromley Road
Bromley, Kent BR1 4PN
Website: www.dandbperformingarts.co.uk
e-mail: bonnie@dandbperformingarts.co.uk
Fax: 020-8697 8100   Tel: 020-8698 8880

DANCEWORKS
(Also Fitness, Yoga & Martial Arts Classes,
Studio/Rehearsal Rooms for Hire)
16 Balderton Street
London W1K 6TN   Tel: 020-7629 6183

DUFFILL Drusilla THEATRE SCHOOL
Grove Lodge, Oakwood Road, Burgess Hill
West Sussex RH15 0HZ
e-mail: drusillaschool@btclick.com Tel/Fax: 01444 232672

ELMHURST - SCHOOL FOR DANCE
Heathcote Road, Camberley, Surrey GU15 2EU
Website: www.elmhurstdance.co.uk
e-mail: elmhurst@cableol.co.uk
Fax: 01276 670320 Tel: 01276 65301

EXPRESSIONS ACADEMY OF PERFORMING ARTS
3 Newgate Lane, Mansfield, Nottingham NG18 2LB
e-mail: expressions@route56.co.uk
Fax: 01623 474820 Tel: 01623 424334

GREASEPAINT ANONYMOUS
4 Gallus Close, Winchmore Hill, London N21 1JR
e-mail: info@greasepaintanonymous.co.uk
Fax: 020-8882 9189 Tel: 020-8886 2263

HARRIS Paul (Paul Harris Dance Co)
(Movement for Actors, Choreography, Coaching
in Traditional & Contemporary Social Dance)
24 Ovett Close, Upper Norwood, London SE19 3RX
e-mail: paulharrisdance@hotmail.com
Mobile: 07958 784462 Tel: 020-8771 4274

ISLINGTON ARTS FACTORY
2 Parkhurst Road, London N7 0SF
e-mail: islington@artsfactory.fsnet.co.uk
Fax: 020-7700 7229 Tel: 020-7607 0561

KIDZ IN THE BIZ
61 Stamford Street, Blackfriars, London SE1 9NA
Website: www.kidzinthebiz.co.uk
e-mail: nicky@kidzinthebiz.co.uk
Mobile: 07710 352889 Tel: 01959 542552

LEE Lynn THEATRE SCHOOL The
(Office)
126 Church Road, Benfleet, Essex SS7 4EP
e-mail: lynn@leetheatre.fsnet.co.uk Tel: 01268 795863

LONDON CONTEMPORARY DANCE SCHOOL
(Full-time Contemporary Training at Degree,
Certificate & Postgraduate Level)
The Place, 17 Duke's Road, London WC1H 9PY
Website: www.theplace.org.uk
e-mail: lcds@theplace.org.uk
Fax: 020-7387 3976 Tel: 020-7387 0152

LONDON STUDIO CENTRE
42-50 York Way, London N1 9AB
Website: www.london-studio-centre.co.uk
e-mail: enquire@london-studio-centre.co.uk
Fax: 020-7837 3248 Tel: 020-7837 7741

MANN Stella COLLEGE
(Professional Dance Course for Performers & Teachers)
10 Linden Road, Bedford, Beds MK40 2DA
Website: www.stellamanncollege.co.uk
e-mail: info@stellamanncollege.co.uk
Fax: 01234 217284 Tel: 01234 213331

NORTH LONDON PERFORMING ARTS CENTRE
(Performing Arts Classes 3-19 yrs/All Dance Forms)
76 St James Lane, Muswell Hill, London N10 3DF
e-mail: nlpac@aol.com
Fax: 020-8444 4040 Tel: 020-8444 4544

PAUL'S THEATRE SCHOOL
Fairkytes Arts Centre, 51 Billet Lane
Hornchurch, Essex RM11 1AX
e-mail: paul@the-theatreschool.fsnet.co.uk
Fax: 01708 475286 Tel: 01708 447123

PERFORMERS COLLEGE
Southend Road, Corringham, Essex SS17 8JT
Website: www.performerscollege.co.uk
e-mail: pdc@dircon.co.uk
Fax: 01375 672353 Tel: 01375 672053

PINEAPPLE DANCE STUDIOS
7 Langley Street
London WC2H 9JA Tel: 020-7836 4004

PULLEY Rosina SCHOOL OF STAGE DANCING
5 Lancaster Road
London E11 3EH Tel: 020-8539 7740

RIDGEWAY STUDIOS PERFORMING ARTS COLLEGE
Fairley House, Andrews Lane, Cheshunt
Hertfordshire EN7 6LB
Website: www.ridgewaystudios.co.uk
e-mail: info@ridgewaystudios.co.uk
Fax: 01992 633844 Tel: 01992 633775

ROEBUCK Gavin
(Classical Ballet)
51 Earls Court Square
London SW5 9DG Tel: 020-7370 7324

STEP ONE DANCE AND DRAMA SCHOOL
Rear of 24 Penrhyn Road, Colwyn Bay
Conwy LL29 8LG Tel: 01492 534424

URDANG ACADEMY The
20-22 Shelton Street, Covent Garden
London WC2H 9JJ
Website: www.theurdangacademy.com
e-mail: info@theurdangacademy.com
Fax: 020-7836 7010 Tel: 020-7836 5709

VALLÉ ACADEMY OF PERFORMING ARTS Ltd The
Wilton House, Delamare Road, Cheshunt
Hertfordshire EN8 9SG
Website: www.valleacademy.co.uk
e-mail: enquiries@valleacademy.co.uk
Fax: 01992 622868 Tel: 01992 622862

WHITEHALL PERFORMING ARTS CENTRE
Rayleigh Road, Leigh-on-Sea
Essex SS9 5UU Tel/Fax: 01702 529290

YOUNG Sylvia THEATRE SCHOOL
Rossmore Road, London NW1 6NJ
e-mail: sylvia@sylviayoungtheatreschool.co.uk
Fax: 020-7723 1040 Tel: 020-7402 0673

THE CONFERENCE OF DRAMA SCHOOLS

The Conference of Drama Schools comprises Britain's leading Drama Schools. Founded in 1969, CDS exists in order to strengthen the voice of the member schools, to set and maintain the highest standards of training within the vocational drama sector, and to make it easier for prospective students to understand the range of courses on offer and the application process. The 21 member schools listed offer courses in Acting, Musical Theatre, Directing and Technical Theatre training. A recent survey showed that 86% of British actors working in the profession had relevant professional training. Graduates of CDS courses are currently working on stage, in front of the camera and behind the scenes in theatres and studios across Britain.

CDS MEMBERS OFFER COURSES WHICH ARE:

PROFESSIONAL – you will be trained to work in the theatre by staff with professional experience and by visiting professionals. Students have the opportunity to work in professional theatres and studios.

INTENSIVE – courses are full-time.

WORK ORIENTATED – you are being trained to do a job – although courses lead to an academic qualification, including degrees and masters degrees – these courses are practical training for work.

The best testimony to the success of CDS schools are the actors who have trained at our member schools.

The Conference of Drama Schools publishes The Official Guide to Vocational Courses for Drama and Technical Theatre 2004. For a free copy of this Guide and links to CDS schools please visit our website at
www.drama.ac.uk

To contact CDS E-mail: info@cds.drama.ac.uk or write to:
The Executive Secretary,
CDS Ltd,
PO Box 34252,
London NW5 1XJ

ALRA (ACADEMY OF LIVE AND RECORDED ARTS)
The Royal Victoria Building
Fitzhugh Grove
Trinity Road
London SW18 3SX
Website: www.alra.demon.co.uk
e-mail: acting@alra.demon.co.uk
Fax: 020-8875 0789   Tel: 020-8870 6475

ARTS EDUCATIONAL SCHOOLS LONDON
14 Bath Road, London W4 1LY
Website: www.artsed.co.uk
e-mail: drama@artsed.co.uk
Fax: 020-8987 6699   Tel: 020-8987 6666

BIRMINGHAM SCHOOL OF SPEECH & DRAMA
The Link Building
Paradise Place
Birmingham B3 3HJ
Website: www.bssd.ac.uk
e-mail: bssd@bssd.ac.uk
Fax: 0121-262 6801   Tel: 0121-262 6800

BRISTOL OLD VIC THEATRE SCHOOL
2 Downside Road
Clifton, Bristol BS8 2XF
Website: www.oldvic.ac.uk
e-mail: enquiries@oldvic.ac.uk
Fax: 0117-923 9371   Tel: 0117-973 3535

CENTRAL SCHOOL OF SPEECH & DRAMA
Embassy Theatre, 64 Eton Avenue
Swiss Cottage
London NW3 3HY   Tel: 020-7722 8183

**CONSERVATOIRE FOR ACTING &
MUSICAL THEATRE**
(Incorporating GUILDFORD SCHOOL OF ACTING)
Millmead Terrace
Guildford
Surrey GU2 4YT
Website: www.conservatoire.org
e-mail: enquiries@conservatoire.org
                                     Tel: 01483 560701

CONTI Italia ACADEMY OF THEATRE ARTS
Avondale Road
72 Landor Road
London SW9 9PH
e-mail: acting@sbu.ac.uk
Fax: 020-7737 2728   Tel: 020-7733 3210

CYGNET TRAINING THEATRE
New Theatre
Friars Gate, Exeter
Devon EX2 4AZ
e-mail: cygnetarts@btinternet.com
                                     Tel/Fax: 01392 277189

DRAMA CENTRE LONDON
176 Prince of Wales Road
London NW5 3PT
Website: www.csm.linst.ac.uk/drama
e-mail: drama@linst.ac.uk
Fax: 020-7428 2071   Tel: 020-7428 2070

EAST 15 ACTING SCHOOL
The University of Essex
Hatfields & Corbett Theatre
Rectory Lane
Loughton, Essex IG10 3RY
Website: www.east15.ac.uk
e-mail: east15@essex.ac.uk
Fax: 020-8508 7521   Tel: 020-8508 5983

GUILDFORD SCHOOL OF ACTING
(See CONSERVATOIRE FOR ACTING & MUSICAL THEATRE)

GUILDHALL SCHOOL OF MUSIC & DRAMA
Silk Street
Barbican, London EC2Y 8DT
Website: www.gsmd.ac.uk
e-mail: info@gsmd.ac.uk
Fax: 020-7256 9438   Tel: 020-7382 7149

LAMDA
Colet Hall
155 Talgarth Road, London W14 9DA
Website: www.lamda.org.uk
e-mail: enquiries@lamda.org.uk
Fax: 020-8834 0501   Tel: 020-8834 0500

**MANCHESTER METROPOLITAN UNIVERSITY
SCHOOL OF THEATRE**
The Mabel Tylecote Building
Cavendish Street
Manchester M15 6BG
Website: www.capitoltheatre.co.uk
                                     Tel: 0161-247 1305

MOUNTVIEW
Academy of Theatre Arts
Ralph Richardson Memorial Studios
Kingfisher Place, Clarendon Road
London N22 6XF
Website: www.mountview.ac.uk
e-mail: acting@mountview.ac.uk
Fax: 020-8829 0034   Tel: 020-8881 2201

OXFORD SCHOOL OF DRAMA The
Sansomes Farm Studios
Woodstock, Oxford OX20 1ER
Website: www.oxforddrama.ac.uk
e-mail: info@oxforddrama.ac.uk
Fax: 01993 811220   Tel: 01993 812883

QUEEN MARGARET UNIVERSITY COLLEGE
The Gateway Theatre
Elm Row, Edinburgh EH7 4AH
Website: www.qmuc.ac.uk
e-mail: admissions@qmuc.ac.uk
Fax: 0131-317 3902   Tel: 0131-317 3900

ROSE BRUFORD COLLEGE
Lamorbey Park
Burnt Oak Lane, Sidcup
Kent DA15 9DF
Website: www.bruford.ac.uk
Fax: 020-8308 0542   Tel: 020-8308 2600

ROYAL ACADEMY OF DRAMATIC ART
62-64 Gower Street
London WC1E 6ED
Website: www.rada.org
e-mail: enquiries@rada.ac.uk
Fax: 020-7323 3865   Tel: 020-7636 7076

**ROYAL SCOTTISH ACADEMY OF MUSIC
& DRAMA**
100 Renfrew Street
Glasgow G2 3DB
Website: www.rsamd.ac.uk
e-mail: registry@rsamd.ac.uk   Tel: 0141-332 4101

ROYAL WELSH COLLEGE OF MUSIC & DRAMA
Drama Department
Castle Grounds
Cathays Park, Cardiff CF10 3ER
Website: www.rwcmd.ac.uk
e-mail: drama.admissions@rwcmd.ac.uk
Fax: 029-2039 1302   Tel: 029-2039 1327

**WEBBER DOUGLAS ACADEMY OF
DRAMATIC ART**
30 Clareville Street
London SW7 5AP
e-mail: webberdouglas@btclick.com
Fax: 020-7373 5639   Tel: 020-7370 4154

Abbreviations: SS Stage School for Children **D** Dramatic Art (incl Coaching. Audition Technique etc) **DS** Full time Drama Training **E** Elocution Coaching (incl Correction of Accents. Speech Therapy, Dialects etc) **S** Singing **Md** Modelling **Sp** Specialised Training

A B CENTRE OF PERFORMING ARTS
22 Greek Street, Stockport, Cheshire SK3 8AB
e-mail: ab22@supanet.com   Tel/Fax: 0161-429 7413

ACADEMY DRAMA SCHOOL The
DS (Day, Evening, Full-time 1 or 2 yr Courses,
Preparatory to Post-graduate)
189 Whitechapel Road, London E1 1DN
Website: www.the-acdemy.info
e-mail: ask@the-academy.info   Tel: 020-7377 8735

ACADEMY OF CHILDREN'S THEATRE
(Part-time Children's Theatre School)
373 Lower Addiscombe Road
Croydon CR0 6RJ   Tel: 020-8655 3438

ACE ACCOMPANIST
S (Accompanist and Bands for Rehearsal &
Recordings)
165 Gunnersbury Lane
London W3 8LJ   Tel: 020-8993 2111

ACKERLEY STUDIOS OF SPEECH, DRAMA & PUBLIC SPEAKING
Sp D Margaret Christina Parsons (Principal)
5th Floor, Hanover House, Hanover Street
Liverpool L1 3DZ   Tel: 0151-709 5995

ACT @ SCHOOL
(Drama for Children & Young People)
Part of APM Training Group
PO Box 834, Hemel Hempstead HP3 9ZP
Website: www.apmtraining.co.uk
e-mail: info@apmtraining.co.uk
Fax: 01442 241099   Tel: 01442 252907

ACT ONE DRAMA STUDIO & AGENCY
31 Dobbin Hill, Sheffield S11 7JA
Website: www.actonedrama.co.uk
e-mail: casting@actonedrama.co.uk
Fax: 07971 112153   Tel: 0114-266 7209

ACT UP
(Acting Classes for Everyone)
Unit 88, Battersea Business Centre
99-109 Lavender Hill, London SW11 5QL
Website: www.act-up.co.uk
e-mail: info@act-up.co.uk
Fax: 020-7924 6606   Tel: 020-7924 7701

ACTING & AUDITION SUCCESS
(Philip Rosch LALAM, FVCM, ANEA, BA
Adv. Dip Acting) (Associate Guildhall Teacher)
52 West Heath Court, North End Road
London NW11 7RG   Tel: 020-8731 6686

ACTION LAB
(Part-time Acting Courses, Miranda French)
18 Lansdowne Road, London W11 3LL
Mobile: 07979 623987   Tel: 020-7727 3473

ACTORCLUB
17 Inkerman Road, London NW5 3BT
Website: www.actorclub.co.uk
e-mail: johncunningham@actorclub.fsnet.co.uk
    Mobile: 07956 940453

ACTORS SPACE The
D E Sp (Auditions, Improvisation, Voice and Text)
83 Palmerston Road
Bounds Green, London N22 8QS
Website: www.actorspace.co.uk
e-mail: drama@london.com   Tel: 020-8881 1455

ACTORS' THEATRE SCHOOL
DS
32 Exeter Road, London NW2 4SB
Website: www.mywebaddress.net
e-mail: ats@mywebaddress.net
Fax: 020-8450 1057   Tel: 020-8450 0371

ACTS
(Ayres-Clark Theatre School)
12 Gatward Close, Winchmore Hill
London N21   Tel: 020-8884 4749

A & J THEATRE WORKSHOP
The Open Door Community Centre
Beaumont Road, London SW19
Website: www.ajmanagement.co.uk
Fax: 020-8882 5983   Tel: 020-8882 7716

ALEXANDER Helen
(Audition Technique/Drama School Entry)
14 Chestnut Road, Raynes Park
London SW20 8EB   Tel: 020-8543 4085

ALL EXPRESSIONS
(Children & Teenagers)
42 Myrtle Road, Hounslow, Middlesex TW3 1QD
e-mail: allexpressions386@hotmail.com
                                Tel: 020-85560 8857

ALLSORTS - DRAMA FOR CHILDREN
2 Pember Road, London NW10 5LP
Website: www.allsorts.ltd.uk
e-mail: enquiries@allsorts.ltd.uk
                                Tel/Fax: 020-8969 3249

ALRA (ACADEMY OF LIVE & RECORDED ARTS)
See DRAMA SCHOOLS (Conference of)

AND ALL THAT JAZZ
(Eileen Hughes - Accompanist & Vocal Coaching)
165 Gunnersbury Lane, Acton Town
London W3 8LJ   Tel: 020-8993 2111

ARDEN SCHOOL OF THEATRE The
Sale Road, Northenden, Manchester M23 0DD
e-mail: ast@ccm.ac.uk   Tel/Fax: 0161-957 1715

ARTEMIS FOUNDATION The
25 Athelstan Road, Tuckton, Bournemouth BH6 5LY
Website: www.doorways2power.co.uk
e-mail: artemis@doorways2power.co.uk
                                Tel: 01202 418880

ARTS EDUCATIONAL SCHOOL
(Performing Arts School)
Tring Park, Tring, Hertfordshire HP23 5LX
Website: www.aestring.com
e-mail: info@aestring.com   Tel: 01442 824255

ARTS EDUCATIONAL SCHOOLS LONDON
See DRAMA SCHOOLS (Conference of)

ARTTS INTERNATIONAL
Highfield Grange, Bubwith, North Yorks YO8 6DP
Website: www.artts.co.uk
e-mail: admin@artts.co.uk
Fax: 01757 288253   Tel: 01757 288088

ASH SCHOOL OF THEATRE ARTS
157 Burtons Road
Hampton Hill, Middlesex TW12 1DX
e-mail: ashschool@hotmail.com   Tel: 020-8979 7038

ASHCROFT ACADEMY OF DRAMATIC ART The
(Drama LAMDA, Dance ISTD, Singing, Age 4-18 yrs)
The Studio, 28 Beckenham Road
Beckenham, Kent BR3 4LS
Website: www.ashcroftacademy.co.uk
                                Tel/Fax: 020-8693 8088

ASHFORD Clare BSc, PGCE, LLAM,
ALAM (Recital), ALAM (Acting)
D E
20 The Chase, Coulsdon, Surrey CR5 2EG
e-mail: clareashford@handbag.com
                                Tel: 020-8660 9609

BAC
(Drama Classes, Age 3-12 yrs, YPT Age 13-25 Yrs)
Lavender Hill, London SW11 5TN
e-mail: mailbox@bac.org.uk
Fax: 020-7978 5207   Tel: 020-7223 6557

BARNES Bi Bi
(Feldenkrais Practitioner & Voice Coach)
Rose Cottage, Church Road, Ashmanhaugh
Norwich NR12 8YL
e-mail: bibibarnes@aol.com
Mobile: 07770 375339   Tel: 01603 781281

SCHOOL OF MUSICAL THEATRE
Director: Ian Watt-Smith

Tel: 020 8987 6677   **Fax:** 020 8987 6680
e-mail: mts@artsed.co.uk   **web:** www.artsed.co.uk

SCHOOL OF ACTING
Director: Jane Harrison
Associate Director: Adrian James

Tel: 020 8987 6655   **Fax:** 020 8987 6656
e-mail: drama@artsed.co.uk   **web:** www.artsed.co.uk

BA (Hons) Acting
3 Year Acting Course
An NCDT Accredited Course
Validated by City University

A 3-year course offering the full range of acting skills to Adult students aged 18 or over. The emphasis is on the actor in performance and the relationship with an audience. Classes and tutorial work include: a range of textual, psychological and physical acting techniques, screen acting and broadcasting, voice and speech, movement and dance, mask and theatre history.

MA Acting
The Acting Company - 1 Year Course
An NCDT Accredited Course
Validated by City University
An intensive one year post-graduate acting course offering a fully integrated ensemble training for mature students with a degree or equivalent professional experience. Emphasis is on the pro-active contemporary performer.

Post Diploma BA (Hons) Acting
Validated by City University
1 Year part time degree conversion course for anyone who has graduated since 1995 from a NCDT accredited 3 year acting course: or for those who can offer appropriate professional experience.

BA(Hons) Musical Theatre
Validated by City University
A full time course (18+). A flexible approach providing outstanding training in dance, acting and singing by leading professionals. Training the Complete Performer with excellent employment opportunities for graduates.

Latest Government Inspection praised excellent teaching, high standard of performance skills, well-qualified staff with extensive professional experience, good pastoral and learning support for students.

The Arts Educational Schools
14 Bath Rd, Chiswick, London W4 1LY

BARNES Joan THEATRE SCHOOL
SS D E
20 Green Street, Hazlemere, High Wycombe
Bucks HP15 7RB   Tel: 01494 523193

BATE Richard MA (Theatre) LGSM (TD) PGCE (FE)
Equity
D E
31 Trafalgar Square, Scarborough, YO12 7PZ
Mobile: 07956 172409   Tel: 01723 365654

BECK Eirene
D E
23 Rayne House, 170 Delaware Road
London W9 2LW   Tel: 020-7286 0588

BECKMANN Jane MA
(Spoken Voice Coaching & Accents)
80 Hawkesfield Road, London SE23
e-mail: beckmann@ukgateway.net
                                Mobile: 07957 283370

BELCANTO LONDON ACADEMY Ltd
(Stage School & Agency)
Performance House, 20 Passey Place
Eltham, London SE9 5DQ
e-mail: enquiries@theatretraining.com
Fax: 020-8850 9944   Tel: 020-8850 9888

BENCH Paul MEd, LGSM, ALAM, FRSA, LJBA,
PGCE, ACP (Lings) (Hons), MASC, MIFA (Reg)
D E
1 Whitehall Terrace, Shrewsbury, Shropshire SY2 5AA
e-mail: paulbench@aol.com   Tel/Fax: 01743 233164

BENSKIN Eileen
(Dialect Coach)   Tel: 020-8455 9750

BERKERY Barbara
(Dialogue/Dialect Coach for Film & Television)
ICM, Oxford House, 76 Oxford St, London W1D 1BS
Fax: 020-7323 0101   Tel: 020-7636 6565

BEST SHOT YOUTH THEATRE COMPANY
(Weekly Drama Classes & Theatre Based Holiday
Courses)
1 Queensland Avenue, Wimbledon SW19 3AD
Website: www.bestshot.org.uk
e-mail: enquiries@bestshot.org.uk
                                Tel/Fax: 020-8540 1238

BEST THEATRE ARTS
61 Marshalswick Lane, St Albans, Herts AL1 4UT
Website: www.besttheatrearts.com
e-mail: bestarts@aol.com   Tel: 01727 759634

BILLINGS Una
(Dance Training)
Methodist Church, Askew Road
London W12 9RN   Tel: 020-7603 8156

BIRD COLLEGE
(Drama/Musical Theatre College)
Birkbeck Centre, Birkbeck Road, Sidcup
Kent DA14 4DE
Website: www.birdcollege.co.uk
e-mail: admin@birdcollege.co.uk
Fax: 020-8308 1370   Tel: 020-8300 6004

BIRMINGHAM SCHOOL OF SPEECH & DRAMA
See DRAMA SCHOOLS (Conference of)

BIRMINGHAM THEATRE SCHOOL
The Old Rep Theatre
Station Street, Birmingham B5 4DY
Website: www.thebirminghamtheatreschool.com
e-mail: info@birminghamts.demon.co.uk
                                Tel/Fax: 0121-643 3300

BODENS STUDIOS
D S E SS DS
99 East Barnet Road, New Barnet, Herts EN4 8RF
Website: www.bodenstudios.com
e-mail: bodens2692@aol.com
Fax: 020-8449 5212   Tel: 020-8449 0982

Bodens
Studio & Agency

99 East Barnet Road, New Barnet, Herts EN4 8RF

PERFORMING ARTS CLASSES
Evenings & Weekends

FULLY EQUIPPED

Studios & Theatre Available for Rehearsals & Auditions
(Close to main bus and train routes)

EXAMINATIONS

Acting, Speech & Drama: GUILDHALL, Dance: ISTD
Singing: ASSOCIATED BOARD of THE ROYAL SCHOOLS OF MUSIC

PROFESSIONAL REPRESENTATION

For Children, Teenagers & Adults
A Copy Of The Current 'Boden Agency Casting Book' Of Children
& Young Adults, Is Available On Request.
HOLIDAY COURSES
We Offer A Variety Of Courses And Workshops Throughout The
School Holiday Periods For Children Aged 4 - 17 Years

NEW FROM SEPTEMBER 2004
2 Year Full Time Musical Theatre Course

This course is designed to train ALL ROUND performers in ACTING,
DANCE & SINGING. Students aged 16 & over work towards
attaining a high level of skill in all three disciplines - and towards
examinations in their strongest discipline.

For Classes Contact 020 8449 0982   For Representation Contact 020 8447 0909
www.bodenstudios.com   www.bodensagency.com

**BORLAND Denise MA Voice (Perf), LRAM,
PG Dip RAM, Perf Dip GSMD**
(Singing, Acting & Voice Coach)
25 Frogston Road West, Edinburgh EH10 7AB
e-mail: info@dbsvoicedevelopment.com
Tel: 0131-445 7491

BOURNEMOUTH YOUTH THEATRE The (BYT)
(Klair/Lucinda Spencer)
14 Cooper Dean Drive, Bournemouth BH8 9LN
Website: www.thebyt.come-mail: klair@thebyt.com
Fax: 01202 393290   Tel: 01202 854116

BOYD Beth
D S
10 Prospect Road, Long Ditton
Surbiton, Surrey KT6 5PY   Tel: 020-8398 6768

BRADSHAW Irene
(Private Coach. Voice & Audition Preparation)
Flat F, Welbeck Mansions, Inglewood Road
West Hampstead, London NW6 1QX
Website: www.voicepowerworks.com
Tel: 020-7794 5721

BRAITHWAITE'S ACROBATIC SCHOOL
8 Brookshill Avenue, Harrow Weald
Middlesex   Tel: 020-8954 5638

BRIDGE THEATRE TRAINING CO The
Cecil Sharp House, 2 Regent's Park Road
London NW1 7AY
Website: www.thebridge-tcc.org
Fax: 020-7424 9118   Tel: 020-7424 0860

BRIGHTON SCHOOL OF MUSIC & DRAMA
96 Claremont Road, Seaford
East Sussex BN25 2QA   Tel: 01323 492918

BRISTOL OLD VIC THEATRE SCHOOL
See DRAMA SCHOOLS (Conference of)

**B.R.I.T. SCHOOL FOR PERFORMING ARTS &
TECHNOLOGY The**
60 The Crescent, Croydon CR0 2HN
Fax: 020-8665 8676   Tel: 020-8665 5242

BRITISH AMERICAN DRAMA ACADEMY
14 Gloucester Gate
Regent's Park, London NW1 4HG
Website: www.badaonline.com
Fax: 020-7487 0731   Tel: 020-7487 0730

**BURTON Gwendolen MA, PG Dip
(Performance)**
(Singing Teacher)
70 Barnsbury Road, London N1
e-mail: singing@symbolic.net Mobile: 07771 657261

CAMERON BROWN Jo PGDVS
(Dialect and Voice)
6 The Bow Brook, Gathorne Street
London, E2 0PW. Agent: Representation
Joyce Edwards 020-7735 5736
e-mail: jocameronbrown@hotmail.com
Mobile: 07970 026621   Tel: 020-8981 1005

CAMPBELL Kenneth
S E D
Parkhills, 6 Clevelands Park, Northam
Bideford, North Devon EX39 3QH
e-mail: kencam@tinyworld.co.uk Tel: 01237 425217

CAMPBELL Ross ARCM, Dip RCM (Perf)
(Singing Coach, Accompanist & Music Director)
17 Oldwood Chase
Farnborough, Hants GU14 0QS
e-mail: rosscampbell@ntlworld.com
Tel: 01252 510228

CAPITAL ARTS THEATRE SCHOOL
(Kathleen Shanks)
Wyllyotts Centre, Darkes Lane, Potters Bar
Hertfordshire EN6 2HN
e-mail: capitalartstheatre@o2.co.uk
Mobile: 07885 232414   Tel: 020-8449 2342

CARSHALTON COLLEGE
DS
39 High Street, Carshalton, Surrey SM5 3BB
Website: www.charlescryer.org.uk
e-mail: info@charlescryer.org.uk
Fax: 020-8770 4969   Tel: 020-8770 4950

CARTEURS THEATRICAL AGENCY
170A Church Road, Hove, East Sussex BN3 2DJ
Website: www.stonelandsschool.co.uk
e-mail: dianacarteur@stonelandsschool.co.uk
Fax: 01273 770444   Tel: 01273 770445

CASE Sarah BA Hons, PGDVS
D E (Voice, Text, Auditions)
14 Northern Heights, Crescent Rd, Crouch End
London N8 8AS   Tel: 020-8347 6784

**CELEBRATION THEATRE COMPANY FOR
THE YOUNG**
SS D E S Sp
48 Chiswick Staithe
London W4 3TP   Tel: 020-8994 8886

CENTRAL SCHOOL OF SPEECH & DRAMA
See DRAMA SCHOOLS (Conference of)

CENTRE STAGE SCHOOL OF PERFORMING ARTS
(Students 4-18 years) (Southgate & Chelmsford)
The Croft, 7 Cannon Rd, Southgate N14 7HJ
Website: www.centrestageuk.com
Fax: 020-8886 7555   Tel: 020-8886 4264

CENTRESTAGE SCHOOL OF PERFORMING ARTS
(All Day Saturday Classes, Summer Courses)
7 Cavendish Square, London W1G 0PE
Website: www.centrestageschool.co.uk
e-mail: centrest@dircon.co.uk
Fax: 020-7372 2728   Tel: 020-7328 0788

www.harrispearson.co.uk

64-66 Millman St	T:	020 7430 9890
London	F:	020 7430 9229
WC1N 3EF	E:	agent@harrispearson.co.uk

Personal Representation   Film   Television   Theatre   Commercials

The Spotlight Studio

A dedicated video casting facility

- Fully-equipped studio with advanced video technology

- Studio team including Camera Operator and Assistant

- Cast live to Europe, USA and the rest of the world

- In the heart of London's West End

Contact Amanda Swanne

@ The Spotlight 020 7440 5041

amanda.swanne@spotlightcd.com

The ⬤ Studio

WE CAN
HELP ACTORS'
CHILDREN

Are you:
- a professional actor?
- the parent of a child under 21?
- having trouble with finances?

Please get in touch for a confidential chat.

The Actors' Charitable Trust
020 7242 0111
admin@tactactors.org

TACT can help in many ways: with regular monthly payments, one-off grants, and long-term support and advice.
We help with clothing, childcare, music and drama lessons, school trips, special equipment and adaptations, and in many other ways.

Our website has a link to a list of all the theatrical and entertainment charities which might be able to help you if you do not have children: **www.tactactors.org**

TACT, Africa House, 64 Kingsway, London WC2B 6BD.
Registered charity number 206809.

ACT

HERTFORDSHIRE THEATRE SCHOOL LIMITED

THREE YEAR ACTING & MUSICAL THEATRE COURSE & ONE YEAR COURSE FOR POSTGRADUATES & TEACHERS

Applications now being accepted for the academic year commencing Sept. 2004 from the U.K. and abroad. Please apply for prospectus and audition details from The Registrar, Hertfordshire Theatre School, 40 Queen Street, Hitchin, Herts SG4 9TS or phone 01462 421416. Email: info@htstheatreschool.co.uk Website: www.htstheatreschool.co.uk

CHARD Verona L.RAM, Dip RAM (Musical Theatre)
(Singing Tutor)
Ealing House, 33 Hanger Lane, London W5 3HJ
e-mail: veronachard@aol.com   Tel: 020-8992 1571

CHARLTON Catherine
8 Tudor Gates, Highfield Avenue, London NW9 0QE
e-mail: charlton@zoo.co.uk
Mobile: 07711 079292   Tel: + 36 204 118227

CHARRINGTON Tim
E D
54 Topmast Point, Strafford Street, London E14 8SN
e-mail: tim.charrington@lycos.co.uk
Mobile: 07967 418236   Tel: 020-7987 3028

CHRISKA STAGE SCHOOL
37-39 Whitby Road
Ellesmere Port, Cheshire L64 8AA   Tel: 01928 739166

CHRYSTEL ARTS AGENCY & THEATRE SCHOOL
15 Churchill Road, Edgware, Middlesex HA8 6NX
e-mail: chrystelarts@talk21.com   Tel: 020-8952 1281

CHURCHER Mel MA
(Acting & Vocal Coach)
32 Denman Road, London SE15 5NP
e-mail: melchurcher@hotmail.com   Tel: 020-7701 4593

CIRCUS MANIACS
(Part-time Day & Evenings, Act Preparation, Private Tuition)
Office 8A, The Kingswood Foundation
Britannia Road, Kingswood, Bristol BS15 8DB
e-mail: info@circusmaniacs.com
Mobile: 07977 247287   Tel/Fax: 0117-947 7042

CITY LIT The
(Part-time Day & Evening)
16 Stukeley Street, Off Drury Lane
London WC2B 5LJ   Tel: 020-7430 0544

CLASS ACT THEATRE SCHOOL
(Part-time weekend 5-16yrs) (Principal: Alice Hyde)
(Singing, Musical Theatre & Drama Training)
47 St Margaret's Road
Twickenham, Middlesex TW1 2LL
Fax: 020-8395 2808   Tel: 020-8891 6663

CLEMENTS Anne MA, LGSM
(Drama/Speech/Auditions/Coaching)
293 Shakespeare Tower, Barbican
London EC2Y 8DR   Tel: 020-7374 2748

COLDIRON M J
(Private Coaching, Audition Preparation & Presentation Skills)
21 Chippendale Street, London E5 0BB
e-mail: jiggs@blueyonder.co.uk
Fax: 020-8525 0687   Tel: 020-8533 1506

COLGAN Valerie
The Green, 17 Herbert Street
London NW5 4HA   Tel: 020-7267 2153

COLIN'S PERFORMING ARTS Ltd
(Full-time 3 yr Performing Arts College)
The Studios
219B North Street
Romford, Essex RM1 4QA
Website: www.colinsperformingarts.co.uk
e-mail: admin@colinsperformingarts.co.uk
Fax: 01708 766077   Tel: 01708 766007

COMPAGNIE LIAN
(Voice, Acting, Audition Preparation, Accent, Diction, Speech & Language Coaching)
2 Ravenscourt Park, London W6 0TH
Website: www.noraarmani.com
e-mail: info@noraarmani.com
Mobile: 07766 706415   Tel: 020-8563 0220

Dramascene Drama & Speech Classes

Ages 5-8, 9-11, 12-16
Contact Lynda Gregory LTCL on Leeds **0113-2684519**

**CONSERVATOIRE FOR ACTING & MUSICAL THEATRE
(Incorporating GUILDFORD SCHOOL OF ACTING)**
See DRAMA SCHOOLS (Conference of)

CONTI Dizi
D Sp E
4 Brentmead Place
London NW11 9LH   Tel: 020-8458 5535

CONTI Italia ACADEMY OF THEATRE ARTS
See DRAMA SCHOOLS (Conference of)

CONTI Italia ACADEMY OF THEATRE ARTS Ltd
SS
Italia Conti House, 23 Goswell Road
London EC1M 7AJ
e-mail: sca@italiaconti36.freeserve.co.uk
Fax: 020-7253 1430   Tel: 020-7608 0047

CORNER Clive AGSM, LRAM
(Qualified Teacher, Private Coaching & Audition
Training)
73 Gloucester Road
Hampton, Middlesex TW12 2UQ
e-mail: cornerclive@aol.com   Tel: 020-8287 2726

COURT THEATRE TRAINING COMPANY
The Courtyard Theatre
10 York Way
King's Cross, London N1 9AA
Website: www.thecourtyard.org.uk
e-mail: info@thecourtyard.org.uk
                             Tel/Fax: 020-7833 0870

CREATIVE PERFORMANCE
(Circus Skills, TIE/Workshops, Children 5-11 yrs
Part-time)
20 Pembroke Road, North Wembley
Middlesex HA9 7PD
Website: www.jennymayers.co.uk
e-mail: mjennymayers@aol.com
                             Tel/Fax: 020-8908 0502

CYGNET TRAINING THEATRE
See DRAMA SCHOOLS (Conference of)

DALLA VECCHIA Sara
(Italian Teacher)
549A Chiswick High Road
London W4 3AY   Mobile: 07774 703686

DAVIDSON Clare
D E
30 Highgate West Hill
London N6 6NP
Website: www.csf.edu
e-mail: cdavidson@csf.edu   Tel: 020-8348 0132

D & B SCHOOL OF PERFORMING ARTS
Central Studios
470 Bromley Road, Bromley BR1 4PN
Website: www.dandbperformingarts.co.uk
e-mail: bonnie@dandbperformingarts.co.uk
Fax: 020-8697 8100   Tel: 020-8698 8880

DE COURCY Bridget
S (Singing Teacher)
19 Muswell Road, London N10   Tel: 020-8883 8397

De FLOREZ Jane LGSM
(Singing Teacher - Musical Theatre, Jazz, Classical)
70 Ipsden Buildings
Windmill Walk, Waterloo
London SE1 8LT   Tel: 020-7803 0835

DIGNAN Tess PDVS
(Audition, Text & Voice Coach)
60 Mereton Mansions, Brookmill Road
London SE8 4HS   Tel: 020-8691 4275

DONNELLY Elaine
(Children's Acting Coach)
The Talent Partnership, Riverside Studios
Crisp Road, London W6 9RL   Tel: 020-8237 1040

DRAGON DRAMA
(Drama for Children)
1B Station Road, Hampton Wick, Kingston KT1 4HG
Website: www.dragondrama.co.uk
e-mail: info@dragondrama.co.uk
                             Tel/Fax: 020-8943 1504

DRAMA ASSOCIATION OF WALES
(Summer Courses for Amateur Actors & Directors)
The Old Library, Singleton Road, Splott
Cardiff CF24 2ET
e-mail: aled.daw@virgin.net
Fax: 029-2045 2277   Tel: 029-2045 2200

DRAMA CENTRE LONDON
See DRAMA SCHOOLS (Conference of)

DRAMA STUDIO EDINBURGH The
(Children's weekly drama workshops)
19 Belmont Road, Edinburgh EH14 5DZ
Website: www.thedramastudio.co.uk
e-mail: thedra@thedramastudio.co.uk
Fax: 0131-453 3108   Tel: 0131-453 3284

DRAMA STUDIO LONDON
DS
Grange Court, Grange Road, London W5 5QN
Website: www.dramastudiolondon.co.uk
e-mail: admin@dramastudiolondon.co.uk
Fax: 020-8566 2035   Tel: 020-8579 3897

DRAMASCENE
(Speech and drama classes, 6 - late teens,
Lynda Gregory LTCL)
23 High Ash Avenue, Leeds LS17 8RS
Fax: 0113-268 1162   Tel: 0113-268 4519

D S T M PRODUCTIONS Ltd
(Drama Academy, Children, Teenagers, Adults)
26 Hope Street
Liverpool L1 9BX
Website: www.dstmproductions.co.uk
e-mail: info@dstmproductions.co.uk
Mobile: 07792 071843   Tel/Fax: 0151-709 1709

DUNMORE Simon
(Acting & Audition Tuition)
Website: www.simon.dunmore.btinternet.co.uk
e-mail: simon.dunmore@btinternet.com

DURRENT Peter
(Audition & Rehearsal Pianist & Vocal Coach)
Blacksmiths Cottage
Bures Road, Little Cornard
Sudbury, Suffolk CO10 0NR   Tel: 01787 373483

HOLLY WILSON

LLAM. Actor. Teacher-London Drama Schools.
Voice, Speech & Drama, Audition coaching. Private tuition.
Tel: 020-8878 0015

DYSON Kate LRAM
(Audition Coaching - Drama)
28 Victoria Street
Brighton BN1 3FQ   Tel: 01273 746505

EARNSHAW Susi THEATRE SCHOOL
SS
5 Brook Place, Barnet EN5 2DL
Website: www.susiearnshaw.co.uk
e-mail: casting@susiearnshaw.co.uk
Fax: 020-8364 9618   Tel: 020-8441 6005

EAST 15 ACTING SCHOOL
See DRAMA SCHOOLS (Conference of)

ECOLE INTERNATIONALE DE THEATRE JACQUES LECOQ
57 rue du Faubourg Saint-Denis, 75010 Paris
Website: www.ecole-jacqueslecoq.com
e-mail: ecole-jacqueslecoq@wanadoo.fr
Fax: 00 331 45 234014   Tel: 00 331 47 704478

ELLIOTT CLARKE SCHOOL
(Saturday & Evening Classes in Dance & Drama)
75A Bold Street
Liverpool L1 4EZ   Tel: 0151-709 3323

ENTERTRAIN UK Ltd
(TV Presenter Training)
14 Hawthorne Court, Rickmansworth Road
Pinner, Middlesex HA5 3UN
Website: www.entertrainltd.com
    Tel: 020-8429 2171

EXPRESSIONS ACDEMY OF PERFORMING ARTS
3 Newgate Lane, Mansfield, Notts NG18 2LB
Website: www.expressions-uk.com
e-mail: expressions@route56.co.uk
Fax: 01623 474820   Tel: 01623 424334

FAIRBROTHER Victoria MA, CSSD, LAMDA Dip
15A Davenport Road, Shepherd's Bush
London W12 8NZ
e-mail: victoriafairbrother1@hotmail.com
Mobile: 07789 430535   Tel: 020-8743 6449

FAITH Gordon BA, IPA Dip, REM Sp, MCHC (UK), LRAM
Sp
1 Wavel Mews, Priory Road,
London NW6 3AB   Tel: 020-7328 0446

FAME FACTORY
4 Dawes Lane, The Meads, Wheathampstead
Hertfordshire AL4 8FF   Tel: 01582 831020

FBI AGENCY Ltd
(Acting Classes for Everyone)
PO Box 250, Leeds LS1 2AZ
e-mail: j.spencer@fbi-agency.ltd.uk
    Tel/Fax: 07050 222747

FERRIS Anna MA (Voice Studies, CSSD)
D E
Gil'cup Leaze, Hilton, Blandford Forum DT11 0DB
e-mail: atcferris@aol.com
Mobile: 07905 656661   Tel: 01258 881098

FINBURGH Nina
D Sp
1 Buckingham Mansions, West End Lane
London NW6 1LR   Tel/Fax: 020-7435 9484

FOOTSTEPS THEATRE SCHOOL
145 Bolton Lane, Bradford BD2 4AA
e-mail: helen@footsteps.fslife.co.uk
    Tel/Fax: 020-01274 626353

FORD Carole Ann ADVS
E D Sp
The Ridge, Hendon Wood Lane, London NW7 4HR
Fax: 020-8906 4669   Tel: 020-8959 8159

FORD Robert L
(Drama LAMDA & Audition Coaching)
1st Floor Offices, 35 High Street, Welshpool
Powys SY21 7JP   Tel: 01952 618569

FORREST Dee
(Voice/Dialects, Film & TV)
602A High Road, Leytonstone, London E11 3DA
e-mail: dee_forrest@yahoo.com
Mobile: 01273 204779   Tel: 020-8556 3828

FOX Betty STAGE SCHOOL
The Friends Institute, 220 Moseley Road
Birmingham B12 0DG
e-mail: bettyfox.school@virgin.net
    Tel/Fax: 0121-440 1635

FRANKLIN Michael
(Meisner Technique)
Correspondence: c/o The Spotlight
7 Leicester Place
London WC2H 7RJ   Tel/Fax: 020-8979 9185

FRIEZE Sandra
D E Sp (English & Foreign Actors)
30 Canfield Gardens
London NW6 3LA   Mobile: 07802 865305

FURNESS Simon
(Actor Training/Audition Coaching)
203A Waller Rd, New Cross Gate, London SE14 5LX
e-mail: sfurness@tiscali.co.uk
Mobile: 07931 681173   Tel: 020-7640 9968

GEORGESON Rosalind BA Hons
(Drama for Children) (See DRAGON DRAMA)

GLYNNE Frances THEATRE STUDENTS
SS
12 Stoneleigh Close, Leeds LS17 8FH
e-mail: franandmo@yahoo.co.uk
Fax: 0113-237 1038   Tel: 0113-266 4286

GO FOR IT THEATRE SCHOOL
47 North Lane
Teddington, Middlesex TW11 0HU
Website: www.goforitts.com
e-mail: agency@goforitts.com
Fax: 020-8287 9405
Tel: 020-8943 1120

GRAYSON John
(Vocal Tuition)
14 Lile Crescent, Hanwell, London W7 1AH
e-mail: john@bizzybee.freeserve.co.uk
Mobile: 07702 188031
Tel: 020-8578 3384

GREASEPAINT ANONYMOUS
Youth Theatre & Training Company
4 Gallus Close, Winchmore Hill, London N21 1JR
e-mail: info@greasepaintanonymous.co.uk
Fax: 020-8882 9189
Tel: 020-8886 2263

GREGORY Paul
(Drama Coach)
133 Kenilworth Court
Lower Richmond Road
Putney, London SW15 1HB
Tel: 020-8789 5726

GREVILLE Jeannine THEATRE SCHOOL
Melody House, Gillott's Corner
Henley-on-Thames
Oxon RG9 1QU
Tel: 01491 572000

GROUT Philip
81Clarence Road
London N22 8PG
e-mail: philipgrout@hotmail.com Tel: 020-8881 1800

GUILDFORD SCHOOL OF ACTING
(See CONSERVATOIRE FOR ACTING & MUSICAL
THEATRE in DRAMA SCHOOLS Conference of)

GUILDHALL SCHOOL OF MUSIC & DRAMA
See DRAMA SCHOOLS (Conference of)

HALEY Jennifer STAGE SCHOOL
(Dance RAD, ISTD, Drama LAMDA)
Toad Hall
67 Poppleton Road
London E11 1LP — Tel: 020-8989 8364

HANCOCK Allison LLAM
D E (Dramatic Art, Acting, Voice, Audition
Coaching, Elocution, Speech Correction etc)
38 Eve Road, Isleworth
Middlesex TW7 7HS — Tel/Fax: 020-8891 1073

**HARLEQUIN STUDIOS PERFORMING
ARTS SCHOOL**
(Drama & Dance Training)
223 Southcoast Road, Peacehaven
East Sussex BN10 8LB — Tel: 01273 581742

HARRINGTON Alex
(Audition Coach, Voice Consultant)
42 Petherton Road, London N5 2RG
e-mail: alexhvoice@aol.com
Mobile: 07979 963410 — Tel: 020-7226 2136

**HARRIS Sharon NCSD, LRAM, IPA Dip DA
(London Univ)**
The Harris Drama School
52 Forty Avenue
Wembley, Middlesex HA9 8LQ
e-mail: sharrisltd@aol.com
Fax: 020-8908 4455 — Tel: 020-8908 4451

HARRISON Joy
(Coaching in Audition Technique, Confidence
Building, Text Work & Drama School Entry)
e-mail: joyh@london.com — Tel: 020-7226 8377

HERTFORDSHIRE THEATRE SCHOOL
40 Queen Street
Hitchin, Herts SG4 9TS
Website: www.htstheatreschool.co.uk
e-mail: info@htstheatreschool.co.uk — Tel: 01462 421416

HESTER John LLCM (TD)
D E (Member of The Society of Teachers
of Speech & Drama)
105 Stoneleigh Park Road
Epsom, Surrey KT19 0RF
e-mail: hjohnhester@aol.com — Tel: 020-8393 5705

HEWITT PERFORMING ARTS
160 London Road
Romford, Essex RM7 9QL
e-mail: hewittcontrol@aol.com — Tel: 01708 727784

HIGGS Jessica
(Voice)
41A Barnsbury Street
London N1 1PW — Tel/Fax: 020-7359 7848

HONEYBORNE Jack
S (Accompanist & Coach)
The Studio
165 Gunnersbury Lane
London W3 8LJ — Tel: 020-8993 2111

HOPE STREET Ltd
DS Sp (Physical Theatre Programme, University
Certificate/Workshop Leaders Programme)
13A Hope Street
Liverpool L1 9BQ
Website: www.hope-street.org
e-mail: arts@hope.u-net.com
Fax: 0151-709 3242 — Tel: 0151-708 8007

Drama Studio London

* One year full time ACTING Course
Established 1966 (Accredited by NCDT)

* One year full time DIRECTING Course
Established 1978

* Excellent graduate employment record

* For postgraduate and mature students

* Comprehensive training includes regular productions of classical and modern texts, TV acting and employment classes

Drama Studio London,
Grange Court, Grange Road, London W5 5QN
Tel: 020 8579 3897 Fax: 020 8566 2035
e-mail: Admin@dramastudiolondon.co.uk
www.dramastudiolondon.co.uk

DSL is supported by Friends of Drama Studio London
a registered charity: no 1051375 - President Dame Judi Dench

PHILIP ROSCH
ACTOR & COACH
LALAM; FVCM; ANEA; B.A; Assoc. Guildhall Teachers.
Credits include: Shakespeare's Globe; Young Vic; Human Traffic.

Powerful audition technique
Effective sight-reading / impro.
Career guidance

Recent successful entries include:
Central, LAMDA, Webber Douglas, Rose Bruford, GSA
E15, Mountview, ALRA

020 8731 6686
www.actingandauditionsuccess.com

HOPNER Ernest LLAM
E D Public Speaking
70 Banks Road
West Kirby CH48 0RD   Tel: 0151-625 5641

HOUSEMAN Barbara
(Ex-RSC Voice Dept,
Voice/Text/Acting/Posture/Relaxation)
e-mail: barbarahouseman@hotmail.com
                                   Tel/Fax: 020-8693 9898

HUGHES Elianne
S (Accompanist & Coach for Rehearsal & Auditions)
165 Gunnersbury Lane
London W3 8LJ   Tel: 020-8993 2111

IMAGE MAKERS
(TV Presenters Specialist Coaching
& Showreel Digital Filming)
12 Dain Court
114 Lexham Gardens
London W8 6JF
Fax: 020-7916 7470   Tel: 020-7209 1213

IMPULSE COMPANY The
e-mail: scott@impulsecompany.co.uk
                              Tel/Fax: 020-8892 7292

INDEPENDENT THEATRE WORKSHOP The
2 Mornington Road
Ranelagh, Dublin 6, Eire
Website: www.independent-theatre-workshop.com
e-mail: itw@esatclear.ie   Tel/Fax: 00 353 1 4968808

IVES-CAMERON Elaine BA, MA
(Private Coaching, Dialect (USA, European & RP)
Drama School Entrance/Auditions)
29 King Edward Walk, London SE1 7PR
Mobile: 07980 434513   Tel: 020-7928 3814

JACK Andrew
Vrouwe Johanna
PO Box 412
Weybridge
Surrey KT13 8WL
Website: www.andrewjack.com
                               Mobile: 07836 615839

JAMES Linda RAM Dip Ed, IPD, LRAM
(Dialect Coach)
25 Clifden Road
Brentford
Middlesex TW8 0PB   Tel: 020-8568 2390

JIGSAW PERFORMING ARTS SCHOOL
64-66 High Street
Barnet
Hertforshire EN5 5QR
e-mail: admin@jigsaw-arts.co.uk   Tel: 020-8447 4530

JONES Desmond SCHOOL OF MIME & PHYSICAL THEATRE The
20 Thornton Avenue
London W4 1QG
Website: www.desmondjones.co.uk
e-mail: enquiries@desmondjones.co.uk
                                   Tel: 020-8747 3537

JORDAN Elizabeth MANAGEMENT Ltd
Choroeographers & Fashion Show Co-ordinators,
Model Grooming School)
14 Silver Birch Gardens
London E6 3SX
Website: www.elizabethjordan.co.uk
e-mail: info@elizabethjordan.co.uk
Mobile: 07931 164271   Tel/Fax: 020-7511 6746

JUSTICE Herbert ACADEMY Ltd
SS
PO Box 253, Beckenham
Kent BR3 3WH   Tel: 020-8650 8878

KENT YOUTH THEATRE & AGENCY
Pinks Hill House
Briton Road, Faversham
Kent ME13 8QH
e-mail: richard@kyt.org.uk   Tel/Fax: 01795 534395

KIDS AHEAD STAGE SCHOOL OF TOTTENHAM
Johnston & Mathers Associates Ltd
PO Box 3167, Barnet EN5 2WA
e-mail: joinkidsahead@aol.com
                              Tel/Fax: 020-8449 4968

KIDZ IN THE BIZ
61 Stamford Street, Blackfriars
London SE1 9NA
Website: www.kidzinthebiz.co.uk
e-mail: nicky@kidzinthebiz.co.uk
Mobile: 07710 352889   Tel: 01959 542552

MICHAEL McCALLION
VOICE AND ACTING
AUTHOR OF **THE VOICE BOOK** FABER & FABER
(NEW AND ENLARGED EDITION 1998)
VOICE AND ACTING TUTOR - RADA 1968 - 1980

020-7602 5599
ALEXANDER TECHNIQUE
ANNA McCALLION
MEMBER OF THE SOCIETY OF TEACHERS OF THE ALEXANDER TECHNIQUE

K-BIS THEATRE SCHOOL
Clermont Hall, Cumberland Road, Brighton BN1 6SL
e-mail: k-bis@zoom.co.uk
Mobile: 07798 610010   Tel/Fax: 01273 564366

LAINE THEATRE ARTS (Betty Laine)
The Studios, East Street, Epsom, Surrey KT17 1HH
Website: www.laine-theatre-arts.co.uk
e-mail: info@laine-theatre-arts.co.uk
Fax: 01372 723775   Tel: 01372 724648

LAMDA
See DRAMA SCHOOLS (Conference of)

LAMONT DRAMA SCHOOL & CASTING AGENCY
94 Harington Road, Formby, Liverpool L37 1PQ
Website: www.lamontcasting.co.uk
e-mail: diane@lamontcasting.co.uk
Fax: 01704 872422   Tel: 01704 877024

LANG Margaret
18 Dalkeith Court, 45 Vincent Street
London SW1P 4HH   Tel: 020-7828 4297

LAURIE Rona
(Coach for Auditions & Voice & Speech Technique)
Flat 1, 21 New Quebec Street
London W1H 7SA   Tel: 020-7262 4909

LEAN David Lawson BA Hons, PGCE
(Acting Tuition, LAMDA Exams, Licensed Chaperone)
72 Shaw Drive, Walton-on-Thames
Surrey KT12 2LS   Tel: 01932 230273

LEE STAGE SCHOOL The
(office)
38 The Chase, Rayleigh, Essex SS6 8QN
e-mail: lynn@leetheatre.fsnet.co.uk
          Tel: 01268 773204

66 **E15 Acting School** evolved from Joan Littlewood's
famed Theatre Workshop, which combined classical skills
with improvisational brilliance and a sense of purpose.
For 40 years the school has produced actors, directors
and theatre professionals of the highest calibre. **99**

THREE YEAR BA IN ACTING (NCDT Accredited)

THREE YEAR BA IN CONTEMPORARY THEATRE

THREE YEAR BA IN THEATRE TECHNICAL STUDIES

ONE YEAR DIPLOMA/MA IN ACTING (NCDT Accredited)

ONE YEAR DIPLOMA/MA IN ACTING FOR TV, FILM & RADIO

ONE YEAR FOUNDATION COURSE

SUMMER COURSES

East 15 Acting School
Hatfields, Rectory Lane, Loughton, Essex IG10 3RY
Telephone: 020 8508 5983   Fax: 020 8508 7521
Email: east15@essex.ac.uk   Website: www.east15.ac.uk

University of Essex

2002 Laurence Olivier Award winner
Jodie Osterland in 'The Rivals'

LESLIE Maeve
(Singing, Voice Production, Presentation)
60 Warwick Square
London SW1V 2AL   Tel: 020-7834 4912

LEVENTON Patricia BA Hons
D E Sp
113 Broadhurst Gardens
West Hampstead
London NW6 3BJ
e-mail: patricia@lites2000.com
Mobile: 07703 341062   Tel: 020-7624 5661

LINTON MANAGEMENT
Carol Godby Theatre Workshop
The Studios
Back Broad Street
Bury, Lancs BL9 0DA
Fax: 0161-761 1999   Tel: 0161-763 6420

LIVE & LOUD
(Children & Teenage Drama Coaching)
The S.P.A.C.E.
2nd Floor
188 St Vincent's Street
Glasgow G2 5SP
e-mail: info@west-end-management.co.uk
Fax: 0141-226 8983   Tel: 0141-222 2942

LIVERPOOL INSTITUTE FOR PERFORMING ARTS The
Mount Street
Liverpool L1 9HF
e-mail: reception@lipa.ac.uk
Fax: 0151-330 3131   Tel: 0151-330 3000

LIVINGSTON Dione LRAM, FETC
Sp E D
7 St Luke's Street
Cambridge CB4 3DA   Tel: 01223 365970

LOCATION TUTORS NATIONWIDE
(Fully Qualified/Experienced Support Teachers
Covering all Key Stages of National Curriculum)
16 Poplar Walk
Herne Hill SE24 0BU
Fax: 020-7207 8794   Tel: 020-7978 8898

LONDON ACADEMY OF PERFORMING ARTS (LAPA)
St Matthew's Church
St Petersburgh Place
London W2 4LA
Website: www.lapadrama.com
e-mail: admin@lapadrama.com
Fax: 020-7727 0330   Tel: 020-7727 0220

LONDON DRAMA SCHOOL
(Acting, Speech Training, Singing)
30 Brondesbury Park, London NW6 7DN
Website: www.startek-uk.com
e-mail: enquiries@startek-uk.com
Fax: 020-8830 4992   Tel: 020-8830 0074

LONDON FILMMAKERS STUDIO The
10 Brunswick Centre, off Bernard Street
London WC1N 1AE
e-mail: business@skoob.com
Mobile: 07712 880909   Tel: 020-7278 8760

LONDON SCHOOL OF MUSICAL THEATRE
83 Borough Road
London SE1 1DN
e-mail: enquiries@lsmt.co.uk   Tel/Fax: 020-7407 4455

LONDON STUDIO CENTRE
42-50 York Way
London N1 9AB
Website: www.london-studio-centre.co.uk
e-mail: enquire@london-studio-centre.co.uk
Fax: 020-7837 3248   Tel: 020-7837 7741

LYTTON Gloria
E D
22 Green Road
Oakwood, Southgate
London N14 4AU   Tel: 020-8441 3118

MACKEY Beatrix LGSM
E D (Coaching For Drama, Speech & Communication)
3 The Valley
Stanmore, Winchester
Hants SO22 4DG   Tel: 01962 855533

MADDERMARKET THEATRE
Peter Beck (Education Officer)
Education and Training Department
St John's Alley
Norwich NR2 1DR
Website: www.maddermarket.freeserve.co.uk
e-mail: trainingandeducation@maddermarket.fsnet.co.uk
Fax: 01603 661357   Tel: 01603 628600

**MANCHESTER METROPOLITAN UNIVERSITY
SCHOOL OF THEATRE**
See DRAMA SCHOOLS (Conference of)

MANCHESTER SCHOOL OF ACTING
29 Ardwick Green North
Manchester M12 6DL
e-mail: actorclass@aol.com   Tel/Fax: 0161-877 0250

MARLOW Jean LGSM
D E
32 Exeter Road
London NW2 4SB   Tel: 020-8450 0371

**MARSHALL Elizabeth Tracey LGSM, GSMD,
LGSMD**
(Dialects, Speech Faults, Drama for Stage, Film &
Modelling, Training for Corporates eg.
Presentation Skills)
5 Mount Street, Cromer, Norfolk NR27 9DB
e-mail: marshall@grenedan.demon.co.uk
                         Tel: 01263 515769

**MARTIN Liza GRSM ARMCM (Singing), ARMCM
(Piano)**
(Singing Tuition
Sounds Sensational)   Tel: 020-8348 0346

MASTERS PERFORMING ARTS COLLEGE Ltd
(Musical Theatre/Dance Course)
Arterial Road, Rayleigh
Essex SS6 7UQ   Tel: 01268 777351

McCALLION Michael
D E
Flat 2, 11 Sinclair Gardens
London W14 0AU   Tel: 020-7602 5599

McCRACKEN Jenny
2 Stamford Court, Goldhawk Road
London W6 0XB   Tel: 020-8748 7638

McDAID Marj
1 Chesholm Road
Stoke Newington
London N16 0DP
e-mail: marjmcdaid@hotmail.com
Fax: 020-7502 0412   Tel: 020-7923 4929

MELLECK Lydia
S (Accompnaist & Coach for Auditions &
Repertoire - RADA)
10 Burgess Park Mansions,
London NW6 1DP   Tel: 020-7794 8845

METHOD STUDIO, LONDON The
Conway Hall
25 Red Lion Square
London WC1R 4RL
Website: www.themethodstudio.com
e-mail: info@themethodstudio.com
Fax: 020-7831 8319   Tel: 020-7831 7335

MICHEL Hilary ARCM
(Singing Teacher, Vocal Coaching, Accompanist,
Auditions, Technique)
82 Greenway, Totteridge, London N20 8EJ
Mobile: 07775 780182   Tel: 020-8343 7243

MIDDLESEX UNIVERSITY
(Singing Teaching, Vocal Coaching, Accompanist,
Audition Technique)
Bramley Road
Oakwood, Trent Park, London N14 4YZ
Fax: 020-8441 4672   Tel: 020-8362 5000

MILNER Jack COMEDY WORKSHOPS
88 Pearcroft Road, London E11 4DR
Website: www.jackmilner.com
e-mail: jack@jackmilner.com   Tel: 020-8556 9768

MONTAGE THEATRE
(Dance, Drama, Singing - Children & Adults)
(Director Judy Gordon)
59 Embleton Road, London SE13 7DQ
Website: www.montagetheatre.com
e-mail: info@montagetheatre.com
                                        Tel: 020-8314 5036

MONTFORD DANCE & STAGE ACADEMY
96 Surbiton Court
St Andrews Square
Surbiton, Surrey KT6 4EE
Fax: 020-8287 6015   Tel: 020-8399 9065

MORLEY COLLEGE THEATRE SCHOOL
(LOCN Accredited Evening Theatre School, Daytime
Performing Arts Programme)
61 Westminster Bridge Road
London SE1 7HT
e-mail: keith.brazil@morleycollege.ac.uk
Fax: 020-7928 4074   Tel: 020-7450 1885

MORRIS David SCHOOL FOR
PERFORMING ARTS The
6 Sussex Close, Redbridge, Essex IG4 5DP
Mobile: 07973 129130   Tel: 020-8924 0197

MOUNTVIEW
See DRAMA SCHOOLS (Conference of)

MRS WORTHINGTON'S WORKSHOPS
SS S Md (Part-time Performing Arts
for Children 7-16 Yrs)
16 Ouseley Road
London SW12 8EF   Tel: 020-8767 6944

MURRAY Barbara LGSM, LALAM
129 Northwood Way
Northwood, Middlesex HA6 1RF   Tel: 01923 823182

NATHENSON Zoe
(Film Acting, Audition Technique & Sight Reading)
66E Priory Road
London N8 7EX
e-mail: zoe.nathenson@which.net
Mobile: 07956 833850   Tel: 020-8347 7799

NATIONAL PERFORMING ARTS SCHOOL &
AGENCY The
The Factory Rehearsal Studios
35A Barrow Street
Dublin 4, Eire
e-mail: info@npas.ie   Tel/Fax: 00 353 1 6684035

NEIL Andrew
2 Howley Place, London W2 1XA
e-mail: andrewneil@surf3.net   Tel/Fax: 020-7262 9521

NEW ERA ACADEMY
E D Examination Board (Speech & Drama)
137B Streatham High Road
London SW16 1HJ
e-mail: neweraacademy@aol.com
                                        Tel: 01905 830915

NEWNHAM Caryll
(Singing Teacher)
35 Selwyn Crescent
Hatfield, Hertfordshire AL10 9NL
e-mail: caryll@ntlworld.com
Mobile: 07976 635745   Tel: 01707 267700

NORTH LONDON PERFORMING ARTS CENTRE
(Performing Arts Classes 3-19 yrs, GCSE Drama &
LAMDA Exams)
76 St James Lane
Muswell Hill, London N10 3DF
e-mail: nlpac@aol.com
Fax: 020-8444 4040   Tel: 020-8444 4544

NORTHERN ACADEMY TELEVISION & THEATRE
WORKSHOPS The
24-25 Booth House
Featherstall Road
Oldham OL9 7QT   Tel/Fax: 0161-652 2651

NORTHERN FILM & DRAMA
PO Box 27
Tadcaster, North Yorks LS24 9XS
Website: www.connew.com/nfd
e-mail: alyson@connew.com   Tel/Fax: 01977 681949

NORTHERN THEATRE SCHOOL OF
PERFORMING ARTS
The Studios
Madeley Street, Hull
East Yorkshire HU3 2AH
e-mail: northco75@aol.com
Fax: 01482 212280   Tel: 01482 328627

NUTOPIA ACTORS STUDIO LONDON
(Camera Acting & Presenting Courses)
Number 8, 132 Charing Cross Road
London WC2H 0LA
Website: www.nutopia.co.uk
Fax: 029-2070 9440   Mobile: 07801 493133

CHARLES VERRALL
Formerly Co-Director of Anna Scher Theatre
IMPROVISATION
Saturday morning workshops for renewal, confidence building and enjoyment
1:1 sessions on voice work, auditions and preparation for drama school entrance
Leo Information Limited 19 Matilda Street N1 0LA Tel: 020 7833 1971 e-mail: charles.verrall@virgin.net

O'FARRELL STAGE & THEATRE SCHOOL
(Dance, Drama, Singing)
36 Shirley Street, Canning Town, London E16 1HU
Fax: 020-7476 0010   Tel: 020-7511 9444

OLLERENSHAW Maggie BA (Hons), Dip Ed
D Sp (TV & Theatre Coaching, Career Guidance)
151D Shirland Road, London W9 2EP
e-mail: maggieoll@aol.com   Tel: 020-7286 1126

OLSON Lise
(American Accents, Voice & Text)
17A Park Road, West Kirby, Wirral CH48 4DN
e-mail: l.olson@lipa.ac.uk
Mobile: 07790 877145   Tel: 0151-330 3032

OMOBONI Lino
Sp
2nd Floor, 12 Weltje Road, London W6 9TG
Website: www.bluewand.co.uk
e-mail: lino@bluewand.co.uk
Mobile: 07885 528743   Tel/Fax: 020-8741 2038

OPEN VOICE
(Consultancy, Auditions, Personal Presentation -
Catherine Owen)
9 Bellsmains, Gorebridge
Near Edinburgh EH23 4QD   Tel: 01875 820175

ORTON Leslie LRAM, ALAM, ANEA
E D Sp
141 Ladybrook Lane
Mansfield, Notts NG18 5JH   Tel: 01623 626082

OSBORNE HUGHES John
(Art & Craft of Acting)
Venus Productions Training Department
51 Church Road, London SE19 2TE
e-mail: johughes@loveray.demon.co.uk
Mobile: 07801 950916   Tel: 020-8653 7735

OSCARS COLLEGE OF PERFORMING ARTS Ltd
103 Fitzwilliam Street, Huddersfield HD1 5PS
e-mail: oscarscollege@freeserve.net
Fax: 01484 545036   Tel: 01484 545519

OVERSBY William
(Singing & Vocal Projection) Streatham
e-mail: bill@ward-thomas.co.uk Mobile: 07811 946663

OXFORD SCHOOL OF DRAMA
See DRAMA SCHOOLS (Conference of)

PALMER Jackie STAGE SCHOOL
30 Daws Hill Lane
High Wycombe, Bucks HP11 1PW
Website: www.jackiepalmer.co.uk
e-mail: jackie.palmer@btinternet.com
Fax: 01494 510479   Tel: 01494 510597

PARKES Frances MA, AGSM
(Voice & Acting Coach)
451A Kingston Road,
London SW20 8JP
Agent: Representation
Joyce Edwards 020-7735 5736
e-mail: frances@frances25.demon.co.uk
                    Tel/Fax: 020-8542 2777

PAUL'S THEATRE SCHOOL
Fairkytes Arts Centre
51 Billet Lane, Hornchurch
Essex RM11 1AX
e-mail: paul@the-theatreschool.fsnet.co.uk
Fax: 01708 475286   Tel: 01708 447123

PERFORM
SS
66 Churchway, London NW1 1LT
Fax: 020-7691 4822   Tel: 020-7209 3805

PERFORMANCE LABORATORY
(Workshops & Performance)
24 Lowerwood Court
351 Westbourne Park Road
London W11 1EU
Website: http://performancelab.tripod.com/home.htm
e-mail: performancelaboratory@hotmail.com
                    Tel: 020-7792 0942

PERFORMERS COLLEGE
(Brian Rogers - Susan Stephens)
Southend Road
Corringham, Essex SS17 8JT
Website: www.performerscollege.co.uk
e-mail: pdc@dircon.co.uk
Fax: 01375 672353   Tel: 01375 672053

**PETHICK Fiona & Claire BA Hons
ADB LRAM LGSM**
D Sp (Audition Technique & Musical Theatre)
31 Grove Road, Chertsey, Surrey
e-mail: ata-productions@hotmail.com
                    Tel: 01932 702174

PHELPS Neil
D Sp (Musical Theatre, Private Coaching for
Auditions, Schools, Showbiz, etc)
61 Parkview Court
London SW6 3LL
e-mail: nphelps@freeuk.com   Tel: 020-7731 3419

PILATES INTERNATIONAL
(Physical Coaching, Stage, Film & Dance)
Unit 1
Broadbent Close, 20-22 Highgate High Street
London N6 5JG   Tel/Fax: 020-8348 1442

TIM CHARRINGTON
Dip. C.S.S.D., A.D.V.S., ACTOR & TEACHER
THEATRE, TV & FILM
Accents, Dialects & Standard English
020 7987 3028   mobile 07967 418 236

STAGECOACH

The nationwide group of part-time stage schools

Over 25,000 young people enjoy professional training with us for 3 hours each week alongside the normal academic year. The skills they learn as they act, sing and dance are not just for the stage, they are skills for life.

STAGECOACH THEATRE ARTS SCHOOLS

ENGLAND · SCOTLAND · WALES · IRELAND

The Courthouse, Elm Grove, Walton-on-Thames, Surrey KT12 1LZ   www.stagecoach.co.uk

Tel 01932 254333 Fax 01932 222894

Rose **Bruford College**
Apply now for entry

Providing training and education in theatre and related arts to the highest level through the following range of programmes

Production:
Theatre Design BA (Hons)
Stage Management BA (Hons)
Lighting Design BA (Hons)
Multimedia Design BA (Hons)
Costume Production BA (Hons)
Scenic Arts BA (Hons)
Music Technology BA (Hons)

All degrees are validated by the University of Manchester

For information about students and their public performances please contact:

The Marketing Office, Rose Bruford College Lamorbey Park, Sidcup, Kent DA15 9DF

Tel: 020 8308 2616
Fax 020 8300 2863
E-mail: jackie.winmill@bruford.ac.uk

A University Sector Institution
Principal: Professor Alastair Pearce

Theatre:
Acting BA (Hons)
Directing BA (Hons)
Actor Musicianship BA (Hons)
European Theatre Arts BA (Hons)
American Theatre Arts BA (Hons)
Theatre Arts part time
Theatre Practices MA (Hons)

by Distance Learning:

Theatre Studies BA (Hons)
Opera Studies BA (Hons)
Theatre and Performance Studies MA
Dramatic Writing MA

Places are limited and entry is based on audition or interview which take place throughout the year.

The College is committed to equality of opportunity.

CDS

Rose Bruford College is a registered charity No. 307907 which exists to provide training and education in the theatre and related arts.

THE TELEVISION TRAINING ACADEMY
Screen Acting & TV Presenting courses
One, Two & Five day courses from the people who specialize in television performance. Bespoke training programmes available for Drama schools, colleges & entertainment establishments.
INFO PACK: 01883 346945   **www.televisiontrainingacademy.co.uk**

POLLYANNA CHILDREN'S TRAINING THEATRE
PO Box 30661
London E1W 3GG
Website: www.eada.demon.co.uk/pollyanna
e-mail: pollyanna-mgmt@yahoo.co.uk
Fax: 020-7480 6761   Tel: 020-7702 1937

POLYDOROU Anna MA Voice Studies (CSSD)
(Accents, Voice & Text)
147C Fernhead Road, London W9 3ED
e-mail: annahebe@yahoo.com
Mobile: 07947 071714   Tel: 020-8969 8881

POOR SCHOOL
242 Pentonville Road, London N1 9JY
Website: www.thepoorschool.com
e-mail: acting@thepoorschool.com
Fax: 020-7837 5330   Tel: 020-7837 6030

QUEEN MARGARET UNIVERSITY COLLEGE
See DRAMA SCHOOLS (Conference of)

QUESTORS THEATRE EALING The
12 Mattock Lane, London W5 5BQ
Website: www.questors.org.uk
e-mail: admin@questors.org.uk
Fax: 020-8567 8736   Admin: 020-8567 0011

RADCLIFFE Tom
(Actor Training/Audition Coaching)
203A Waller Road, New Cross Gate
London SE14 5LX   Tel: 020-7207 0499

RAVENSCOURT THEATRE SCHOOL Ltd
Tandy House, 30-40 Dalling Road, London W6 0JB
Website: www.ravenscourttheatreschool.co.uk
e-mail: ravenscourt@hotmail.com
Fax: 020-8741 1786   Tel: 020-8741 0707

RE:ACTORS
15 Montrose Walk, Weybridge, Surrey KT13 8JN
Website: www.reactors.co.uk
e-mail: michael@reactors.co.uk
Fax: 01932 830248   Tel: 01932 888885

RED ONION PERFORMING ARTS CENTRE
(Drama, Dance & Vocal Training,
Age 8 Yrs to Adult)
25 Hilton Grove
Hatherley Mews, London E17 4QP
Website: www.redonion-uk.com
e-mail: info@redonion-uk.com
Fax: 020-8521 6646   Tel: 020-8520 3975

REDROOFS THEATRE SCHOOL
DS SS D E S Sp
Littlewick Green,
Maidenhead, Berks SL6 3QY
Website: www.redroofs.co.uk   Tel: 01628 822982

REP COLLEGE The
17 St Mary's Avenue
Purley on Thames, Berks RG8 8BJ
Website: www.repcollege.com
e-mail: tudor@repcollege.co.uk
          Tel/Fax: 0118-942 1144

REYNOLDS PERFORMING ARTS
(Children/Teenagers)
The Chapel, Old Bexley Ln, Bexley, Kent DA5 2BW
Website: www.reynoldsgroup.co.uk
e-mail: info@reynoldsgroup.co.uk
Fax: 01634 329079   Tel: 01322 277209

REYNOLDS Sandra COLLEGE
(Modelling & Grooming School)
35 St Georges Street, Norwich NR3 1DA
Website: www.sandrareynolds.co.uk
e-mail: tessa@sandrareynolds.co.uk
Fax: 01603 219825   Tel: 01603 623842

RICHMOND DRAMA SCHOOL
DS (One Year Course)
Parkshot Centre
Parkshot, Richmond, Surrey TW9 2RE
e-mail: david.whitworth@racc.ac.uk
          Tel: 020-8439 8944

RIDGEWAY STUDIOS PERFORMING ARTS COLLEGE
Fairley House, Andrews Lane
Cheshunt, Herts EN7 6LB
Website: www.ridgewaystudios.co.uk
e-mail: info@ridgewaystudios.co.uk
Fax: 01992 633844   Tel: 01992 633775

ROSE BRUFORD COLLEGE
See DRAMA SCHOOLS (Conference of)

ROSSENDALE DANCE & DRAMA CENTRE
52 Bridleway
Waterfoot, Rossendale, Lancs BB4 9DS
e-mail: rddc@btinternet.com   Tel: 01706 211161

ROYAL ACADEMY OF DRAMATIC ART
See DRAMA SCHOOLS (Conference of)

ROYAL ACADEMY OF MUSIC
Marylebone Road
London NW1 5HT   Tel: 020-7873 7373

ROYAL SCOTTISH ACADEMY OF MUSIC & DRAMA
See DRAMA SCHOOLS (Conference of)

ROYAL WELSH COLLEGE OF MUSIC & DRAMA
See DRAMA SCHOOLS (Conference of)

SCHER Anna THEATRE The
70-72 Barnsbury Road, London N1 0ES
e-mail: info@astm.co.uk
Fax: 020-7833 9467   Tel: 020-7278 2101

 Dee Forrest PGDVS Dip.DV. *VOICE & SINGING COACH*
DIALECTS: FILMS & TV
AUDITIONS-PROJECTION-DIALECTS-INTERPRETATION-
VOCAL PROBLEMS-PHONETICS-PRESENTATION SKILLS.
Tel: 01273-204779 Mob: 07957 211065

SCHOOL OF THE SCIENCE OF ACTING The
67-83 Seven Sisters Road
London N7 6BU
Website: www.scienceofacting.org.uk
e-mail: find@scienceofacting.org.uk
Fax: 020-7272 0026   Tel: 020-7272 0027

SCREENWRITERS' WORKSHOP
Screenwriters' Centre, Suffolk House
1-8 Whitfield Place, London W1T 5JU
Website: www.lsw.org.uk
e-mail: screenoffice@tiscali.co.uk
          Tel/Fax: 020-7387 5511

SETTELEN Peter
181 Jersey Road
Osterley, Middlesex TW7 4QJ
Website: www.settelen.com
e-mail: talk@settelen.net
Fax: 020-8737 2987   Tel: 020-8737 1616

SHAND Mary PGDVS
D E (Voice Coach)
16 Lark Hill Rise, Winchester SO22 4LX
e-mail: voicehelp@lineone.net
Mobile: 07802 167342   Tel: 01962 855680

SHARONA STAGE SCHOOL AGENCY & MANAGEMENT
82 Grennell Road, Sutton, Surrey SM1 3DN
Fax: 020-8642 2364   Tel: 020-8642 9396

SHARP Judith
(Career Consultant & Coach)
e-mail: sharpjudith@talk21.com
Mobile: 07941 863499   Tel: 020-7263 1403

SHAW Philip
(Actors Consultancy Service, Acting/Voice Coaching)
Suite 476,
2 Old Brompton Road, South Kensington
London SW7 3DQ
e-mail: shawcastlond@aol.com
Fax: 020-8408 1193   Tel: 020-8715 8943

SHENEL Helena
(Singing Teacher)
80 Falkirk House, 165 Maida Vale
London W9 1QX   Tel: 020-7328 2921

SHERRIFF David
(Vocal Coaching, Accompanist, Act Preparation)
Musical Services
106 Mansfield Drive, Merstham, Surrey RH1 3JN
Fax: 01737 271231   Tel: 01737 642829

SINGER Sandra ASSOCIATES
21 Cotswold Road
Westcliff-on-Sea, Essex SS0 8AA
Website: www.sandrasinger.com
e-mail: sandrasingeruk@aol.com
Fax: 01702 339393   Tel: 01702 331616

SOCIETY OF TEACHERS OF SPEECH & DRAMA The
73 Berry Hill Road, Mansfield, Notts NG18 4RU
Website: www.stsd.org.uk
e-mail: ann.p.jones@btinternet.com
          Tel: 01623 627636

SPEAKE Barbara STAGE SCHOOL
East Acton Lane
London W3 7EG
e-mail: speakekids4@aol.com   Tel/Fax: 020-8743 1306

SPEED Anne-Marie Hon ARAM
MA (Voice Studies), CSSD, ADVS, BA
(Vocal Technique, Coaching, Auditions, Accents)
31 Nether Close, Finchley, London N3 1AA
e-mail: anne-marie.speed@virgin.net
Mobile: 07957 272554   Tel: 020-7644 5947

The Actors Company
Auditioning now for October 2004

Not a drama school…
…but an acclaimed company in training

The Actors Company is a One Year Programme for Mature Graduates. The company offers intensive vocational training (40 hours per week) and professional work experience in the West End of London. The course is forty-six weeks in length – thirty-six of which are arranged so that company members support themselves in employment during training.

The Seagull,
Repertory Season 2002
Jermyn Street Theatre

"blessed with good pacing and simple staging. Director David Harris has gathered a necessarily large, talented cast…The company should be commended…"

Paul Vale, The Stage, October 2002

For a prospectus contact:
The London Centre
for Theatre Studies
12–18 Hoxton Street
London N1 6NG
T/F 020 7739 5866
E ldncts@aol.com
www.thelondoncentre
fortheatrestudies.co.uk

LONDON CENTRE FOR THEATRE STUDIES

Graduate employment

Television includes
USA:
The Sopranos
Nash Bridges
The X Files
Sunset Beach
A+E

UK:
EastEnders
The Bill
Brookside
Taggart
High Road
Casualty
Holby City
Hetty Wainthropp Investigates
Hope and Glory
Life as we know it
Jonathan Creek
Footballers' Wives
In Deep
Heartbeat
Emmerdale
Crossroads
This is Dom Joly
Ultimate Force
Doctors

Theatre includes
RNT
RSC
National Theatre of Greece
Chichester Festival Theatre
Bristol Old Vic
Theatr Clwyd
Theatre Royal, Haymarket
Theatre Royal, Nottingham
Royal Lyceum, Edinburgh
Vancouver Playhouse
British Columbia
Royal Court (Upstairs)
Soho Theatre, London
Swansea Grand
Wolverhampton Grand
Theatre Royal, Portsmouth
Redgrave, Farnham
Pier Theatre, Bournemouth
English Theatre, Vienna
Tara Arts
London Fringe
Bridewell Theatre
Battersea Arts
Arcola

Film includes
Death of Klinghoffer
The Prophecy
East is East
Brothers in Trouble

Commercials
Many and varied

MORAY URQUHART
FULLY QUALIFIED TEACHER OF SPEECH AND DRAMA
020 7731 3419   or c/o The Spotlight

SPENCER Jay
(Acting & Audition Tuition)
e-mail: j.spencer@fbi-agency.ltd.uk
Tel/Fax: 07050 321654

STAGE 84 YORKSHIRE SCHOOL OF PERFORMING ARTS
(Evening & Weekend Classes & Summer Schools)
Old Bell Chapel, Town Lane, Bradford
West Yorks BD10 8PR
e-mail: valeriejackson@stage84.com
Mobile: 07785 244984   Tel: 01274 569197

STAGE ONE THEATRE PRODUCTION SCHOOL
32 Westbury Lane, Buckhurst Hill, Essex IG9 5PL
Website: www.stage01.com
e-mail: stage01@lineone.net
Mobile: 07939 121154   Tel: 020-8506 0949

STAGECOACH TRAINING CENTRES FOR THE PERFORMING ARTS
The Courthouse, Elm Grove
Walton-on-Thames, Surrey KT12 1LZ
Website: www.stagecoach.co.uk
e-mail: mail@stagecoach.co.uk
Fax: 01932 222894   Tel: 01932 254333

STARLIGHT TELEVISION & THEATRE SCHOOL
(Evening & Saturday Classes, Drama, Dance, Singing
etc 8 -18 years)
5 Union Castle House,
Canute Road, Southampton SO14 3FJ
e-mail: starlightyt@aol.com
Fax: 023-8045 5816   Tel: 023-8033 9322

STEP ONE DANCE AND DRAMA SCHOOL
Rear of 24 Penrhyn Road, Colwyn Bay
Conwy LL29 8LG   Tel: 01492 534424

STOCKTON RIVERSIDE COLLEGE
(Education & Training)
Harvard Avenue, Thornaby
Stockton TS17 6FB   Tel: 01642 865566

STONELANDS SCHOOL
(Full-time Training in Ballet & Theatre Arts)
170A Church Road
Hove BN3 2DJ
e-mail: dianacarteur@stonelandsschool.co.uk
Fax: 01273 770444   Tel: 01273 770445

STREETON Jane
(Singing Teacher - RADA)
24 Richmond Road, Leytonstone
London E11 4BA   Tel: 020-8556 9297

SWAIN Neil BA (Hons), PGDVS, CSSD
34 Saltash Road
Welling, Kent DA16 1HB
Fax: 020-8306 2934   Tel: 020-8306 2936

SWINDON YOUNG ACTORS
65 Stafford Street, Old Town, Swindon
Wiltshire SN1 3PF
e-mail: young.actorsfile@virgin.net Tel: 01793 423688

SWINFIELD Rosemarie
(Make-Up Design & Training)
Rosie's Make-Up Box
6 Brewer Street, Soho, London W1R 3FS
Website: www.rosiesmake-up.co.uk
e-mail: rosemarie@rosiesmake-up.co.uk
Mobile: 07976 965520

TALENTED KIDS PERFORMING ARTS SCHOOL
(Drama, Musical Theatre Dance Classes 3-23 Yrs)
17 Monastery Gate Villas, Monastery Road
Clondalkin, Dublin 22, Eire
e-mail: talentedkids@hotmail.com
Tel/Fax: 00 353 1 4642160

TELEVISION TRAINING ACADEMY The
16A Campbell Road, Caterham, Surrey CR3 5JL
Website: www.televisiontrainingacademy.co.uk
e-mail: brian@ttta.fsbusiness.co.uk   Tel: 01883 346945

THEATRE ARTS (WEST LONDON)
(Agency & Part-time Classes in Drama,
Dance & Singing)
18 Kingsdale Gardens
Notting Hill, London W11 4TZ
e-mail: theatreartswestlondon@hotmail.com
Tel/Fax: 020-7603 3471

THEATRETRAIN
(6 -18 Yrs, Annual West End Productions
involving all Pupils)
PO Box 117, Ilford, Essex IG3 8PN
Website: www.theatretrain.co.uk
e-mail: info@theatretrain.co.uk   Tel: 01992 560000

THORN Barbara
D Sp (TV & Theatre Coaching, Career Guidance)
51 Parkside, Vanbrugh Park, Blackheath
London SE3 7QF   Tel: 020-8305 0094

TIP TOE STAGE SCHOOL
45 Viola Close, South Ockendon, Essex RM15 6JF
Website: www.tiptoestageschool.com
e-mail: julieecarter@blueyonder.co.uk
Mobile: 07941 653463   Tel: 01708 859109

TO BE OR NOT TO BE
(TV/Film Acting Techniques
Showreels, Theatre/Audition pieces. Lamda Exams)
(Anthony Barnett)
48 Northampton Road,
Kettering, Northants NN15 7JU
Website: www.tobeornottobe.tv
e-mail: tobeornottobe@ntlworld.com
Mobile: 07958 996227

ANNE-MARIE SPEED Hon ARAM MA (Voice Studies) CSSD ADVS BA
Licensed Estill Voice Craft Practioner (Vanguard) Voice & Speech Consultant/Accent & Dialect Coach
🎭 FILM~THEATRE~TV 🎭
ESTILL VOICE TRAINING SYSTEMS
Vocal Technique ~ Speaking & Singing, Estill Voice Craft, Accents, RP, Audition Coaching, Text-Classical and Modern
020 7644 5947   mobile 07957 272 554   e-mail anne-marie.speed@virgin.net

TROTTER William BA, MA, PGDVS
D E Sp
25 Thanet Lodge
Mapesbury Road, London NW2 4JA
Website: www.ukspeech.co.uk
e-mail: william.trotter@ukspeech.co.uk
Tel/Fax: 020-8459 7594

TV ACTING CLASSES
(Elisabeth Charbonneau)
9 Alderton Road, Herne Hill, London SE24 0HS
e-mail: ejcharbonneau@aol.com
Mobile: 07885 621061   Tel: 020-7326 3967

TWICKENHAM THEATRE WORKSHOP FOR CHILDREN
22 Butts Crescent, Hanworth
Middlesex TW13 6HQ   Tel: 020-8898 5882

URQUHART Moray
Write
61 Parkview Court, London SW6 3LL
e-mail: nphelps@freeuk.com

VALLÉ ACADEMY OF PERFORMING ARTS Ltd The
Wilton House
Delamare Road
Cheshunt, Herts EN8 9SG
Website: www.valleacademy.co.uk
e-mail: enquiries@valleacademy.co.uk
Fax: 01992 622868   Tel: 01992 622862

VERRALL Charles
D
19 Matilda Street, London N1 0LA
e-mail: charles.verrall@virgin.net   Tel: 020-7833 1971

ALAN WOODHOUSE Voice Teacher   Acting Coach

clients include: Guildhall School of Music & Drama, BBC Radio, Talkback TV,
R.N.T., Shakespeare's Globe, Royal Opera House, Scuola di Cinema Rome

speech training; voice & text work; preparation for auditions and business presentations

phone/fax 020 8549 1374   e-mail: *alanwoodhouse50@hotmail.com*

VOICE AND THE ALEXANDER TECHNIQUE
(Robert Macdonald)
Flat 5, 17 Hatton Street
London NW8 8PL   Mobile: 07956 852303

VOICE BODY COMMUNICATION
(Patricia Perry)
65 Castelnau, Barnes SW13 9RT
e-mail: ppvoice@blueyonder.co.uk
                               Tel/Fax: 020-8748 9699

VOICE CASTER
(Specialized Training for Voice-Overs & TV Presenters)
Website: www.voicecaster.net
e-mail: info@voicecaster.net
Fax: 020-8455 2344   Tel: 020-8455 2211

VOICE TAPE SERVICES INTERNATIONAL Ltd
(Professional Voice Over Direction & CDs)
80 Netherlands Road, New Barnet, Herts EN5 1BS
e-mail: info@vtsint.co.uk
Fax: 020-8441 4828   Tel: 020-8440 4848

VOXTRAINING Ltd
(Voice-Over Training and Demo CDs)
20 Old Compton Street, London W1D 4TW
Website: www.voxtraining.com
e-mail: info@voxtraining.com
Fax: 020-7434 4414   Tel: 020-7434 4404

WALLACE Elaine BA
D Sp Voice
249 Goldhurst Terrace, London NW6 3EP
e-mail: im@voicebiz.biz   Tel: 020-7625 4049

WALTZER Jack
(Professional Voice-Over Direction & CDs)
5 Minetta Street Apt 2B, New York NY 10012
Website: www.jackwaltzer.com
Tel: 001 (212) 840-1234   Tel: 020-8347 6598

WEBB Bruce
S
Abbots Manor, Kirby Cane, Bungay
Suffolk NR35 2HP   Tel: 01508 518703

WEBBER DOUGLAS ACADEMY OF DRAMATIC ART
See DRAMA SCHOOLS (Conference of)

WELBOUNRE Jackie
(Circus Trainer, Choroegrapher, Consultant)
43 Kingsway Avenue, Kingswood, Bristol BS15 8AN
e-mail: jackie@welbourne.co.uk
Mobile: 07977 247287   Tel/Fax: 0117-947 7042

WESTMINSTER KINGSWAY COLLEGE
(Performing Arts)
Regent's Park Centre, Longford Street
London NW1 3HB
Website: www.westking.ac.uk
e-mail: courseinfo@westking.ac.uk
Fax: 020-7391 6400   Tel: 020-7306 5954

WHITEHALL PERFORMING ARTS CENTRE
Rayleigh Road, Leigh-on-Sea
Essex SS9 5UU   Tel: 01702 529290

WHITWORTH Geoffrey LRAM, MA
S (Piano Accompanist)
789 Finchley Road,
London NW11 8DP   Tel: 020-8458 4281

WILD CREATIVE ARTS THEATRE SCHOOL
(& Private Coaching)
PO Box 222, Rainham, Essex RM13 7WQ
e-mail: wildtm@lineone.net   Tel 01708 505543

WILDER Andrea
D E
23 Cambrian Drive, Colwyn Bay, Conwy LL28 4SL
Website: www.awagency.co.uk
e-mail: andrea@awagency.co.uk
Fax: 07092 249314   Tel: 01492 547542

WILMER Elizabeth J
E D
34 Campden Street
London W8 7ET   Tel: 020-7727 6624

WILSON Holly
3 Worple Street, Mortlake
London SW14 8HE   Tel: 020-8878 0015

WIMBUSH Martin Dip GSMD
D E Sp (Audition Coaching)
Flat 4, 289 Trinity Road
Wandsworth Common
London SW18 3SN   Tel: 020-8877 0086

WINDSOR Judith MA
(American Accents/Dialects)
Woodbine, Victoria Road, Deal, Kent CT14 7AS
e-mail: joyce.edwards@virgin.net
Fax: 020-7820 1845   Tel: 020-7735 5736

WOOD Tessa Teach Cert AGSM, CSSD, PGVDS
(Voice Coach)
11 Chaucer Road, Poets' Corner, London W3 6DR
e-mail: tessaroswood@aol.com   Tel: 020-8896 2659

WOODHOUSE Alan AGSM ADVS
(Voice & Acting Coach)
33 Burton Road, Kingston, Surrey KT2 5TG
e-mail: alanwoodhouse50@hotmail.com
                             Tel/Fax: 020-8549 1374

WOODHOUSE Nan
(Playwright & LAMDA Examiner)
LGSM (Hons Medal) LLAM, LLCM (TD), ALCM
Write
2 New Street
Morecambe, Lancashire LA4 4BW
e-mail: nan.woodhouse@amserve.com

WORTMAN Neville
(Voice Training & Speech Coach)
48 Chiswick Staithe
London W4 3TP
e-mail: nevillewortman@beeb.net
Mobile: 07976 805976   Tel: 020-8994 8886

WRIGG Ann ALAM
E D
The Little House
6 Frith Lane
London NW7 1JA   Tel: 020-8346 6745

WYNN Madeleine
(Director & Acting Coach)
40 Barrie House
Hawksley Court
Albion Road, London N16 0TX
e-mail: madeleine@onetel.net.uk
Tel: 01394 450265   Tel: 020-7249 4487

YOUNG BLOOD Ltd
20 Aintree Street
Fulham
London SW6 7QU
Website: www.youngblood.org.uk
e-mail: info@youngblood.org.uk
Mobile: 07813 463102   Tel: 0845 6449418

YOUNG PERFORMERS THEATRE & POP SCHOOL
SS
Unit 3
Ground Floor, Clements Court
Clements Lane
Ilford, Essex IG1 2QY
e-mail: sara@tots-twenties.co.uk
Fax: 020-8553 1880   Tel: 020-8478 1848

YOUNG STARS
(Part-time Children's Theatre School, Age 8-16 yrs,
Drama, Singing, Dancing)
Allum Hall, Elstree, Hertfordshire
e-mail: youngstars@bigfoot.com
Fax: 020-8950 5701   Tel: 020-8950 5782

YOUNG Sylvia THEATRE SCHOOL
SS
Rossmore Road, London NW1 6NJ
e-mail: sylvia@sylviayoungtheatreschool.co.uk
Fax: 020-7723 1040   Tel: 020-7402 0673

ZANDER Peter
D E SP (German)
22 Romilly Street, London W1D 5AG
Website: freespace.virgin.net/peterzan.berlin
e-mail: peterzan.berlin@virgin.net
Tel: 020-7437 4767

For information on the FIA please contact
International Federation of Actors
Guild House, Upper St Martin's Lane
London WC2H GEG
Fax: 020-7379 8260   Tel: 020-7379 0900
e-mail: office@fia-actors.com

■ **BELGIUM**
ACV - TransCom
Galerie Agora, Rue du Marche aux Herbes 105
Bte 38-40, B-1000 Brussels
e-mail: mhendrickx.transcom@acv-csc.be
Fax: 00 32 2 512 8591   Tel: 00 32 2 549 0769

■ **BELGIUM**
CGSP
Confederation Generale des Services Publics
Place Fontainas 9-11, B-1000 Brussels
Fax: 00 32 2 508 59 02   Tel: 00 32 2 508 58 11

■ **DENMARK**
DANSK ARTIST FORBUND
Vendersgade 24, DK-1363 Copenhagen K
Website: www.artisen.dk
e-mail: artisten@artisten.dk
Fax: 00 45 33 33 73 30   Tel: 00 45 33 32 66 77

■ **DENMARK**
DANSK SKUESPILLERFORBUND
Sankt Knuds Vej 26, DK-1903 Frederiksberg C
Website: www.skuespillerforbundet.dk
e-mail: dsf@skuespillerforbundet.dk
Fax: 00 45 33 24 81 59   Tel: 00 45 33 24 22 00

■ **FINLAND**
SNL - SUOMEN NAYTTELIJALIITTO
Temppelikatu 3-5 A 11, SF-00100 Helsinki
e-mail: suomen.nayttelijaliitto@co.inet.fi
Fax: 00 358 9 4342 7350   Tel: 00 353 9 4342 7311

■ **FRANCE**
SFA
Syndicat Francais des Artistes-Interpretes
21 bis, rue Victor Masse, F-75009 Paris
Website: www.sfa-cgt.fr
e-mail: contact@sfa-cgt.fr
Fax: 00 33 1 53 25 09 01   Tel: 00 33 1 53 25 09 09

■ **GERMANY**
GDBA
Genossenschaft Deutscher Buhnen-Angehoriger
Feldbrunnenstrasse 74, D-20148 Hamburg
Website: www.buehnengenossenschaft.de
e-mail: gdba@buehnengenossenschaft.de
Fax: 00 49 40 45 93 52   Tel: 00 49 40 44 51 85

■ **GREECE**
HAU - HELLENIC ACTORS' UNION
33 Kaniggos Street, GR-106 82 Athens
Website: www.sei.gr
e-mail: sei@greektour.com
Fax: 00 30 10 380 8651   Tel: 00 30 10 383 3742

■ **GREECE**
UGS - UNION OF GREEK SINGERS
130 Patission Street, GR-112 57 Athens
Fax: 00 30 10 823 8321   Tel: 00 30 10 823 8335/6

■ **IRELAND**
SIPTU - IRISH ACTORS' EQUITY GROUP
Liberty Hall, Dublin 1
Website: www.siptu.ie
e-mail: equity@siptu.ie
Fax: 00 353 1 874 3691   Tel: 00 353 1 858 6403

■ **ITALY**
SAI
Sindacato Attori Italiani
Via Ofanto 18, I-00198 Rome
Website: www.cgil.it/sai-slc
e-mail: sai-slc@cgil.it
Fax: 00 39 06 854 6780   Tel: 00 39 06 841 7303/1288

■ **LUXEMBOURG**
OGB-L
Onofhangege Gewerkschaftsbond Letzebuerg
19 rue d'Epernay, B.P. 2031, L-1020 Luxembourg
Website: www.ogb-l.lu
e-mail: joel.jung@ogb-l.lu
Fax: 00 352 486 949   Tel: 00 352 496 005 Ext 213

■ **NETHERLANDS**
FNV KIEM
Kunsten Informatie en Media, Postbus 9354
NL-1006 AJ Amsterdam
Website: www.fnv-kiem.nl
e-mail: fnvkiem@worldonline.nl
Fax: 00 31 20 355 3737   Tel: 00 31 20 355 3636

■ **NORWAY**
NSF
Norsk Skuespillerforbund, Welhavensgate 3
N-0166 Oslo
Website: www.skuespillerforbund.no
e-mail: nsf@skuespillerforbund.no
Fax: 00 47 21 02 71 91   Tel: 00 47 21 02 71 90

■ **PORTUGAL**
STE
Sindicato dos Trabalhadores de Espectaculos
Rua Da Fe 23, 2 do Piso, P-1050 Lisbon
e-mail: sind.trab.espect@mail.telepac.pt
Fax: 00 351 21 885 3787   Tel: 00 351 21 885 2728

■ **SPAIN**
CC.OO.
Plaza Cristino Martos 4, 6a Planta, E-28015 Madrid
e-mail: internacional.fct@fct.ccoo.es
Fax: 00 34 91 548 1613   Tel: 00 34 91 540 9295/37

■ **SPAIN**
FAEE
Federacion de Actores del Estado Espanol
C/Montera 34, 1º Piso, E-28013 Madrid
e-mail: fedactors@retemail.es
Fax: 00 34 91 522 6055   Tel: 00 34 91 522 2804

■ **SWEDEN**
TF TEATERFORBUNDET
Box 12 710, S-112 94 Stockholm
Website: www.teaterforbundet.se
e-mail: info@teaterforbundet.se
Fax: 00 46 8 653 9507   Tel: 00 46 8 441 1300

■ **UK**
EQUITY
Guild House, Upper St Martin's Lane
London WC2H 9EG
Website: www.equity.org.uk
e-mail: info@equity.org.uk
Fax: 020-7379 7001   Tel: 020-7379 6000

ALDEBURGH FESTIVAL OF MUSIC AND THE ARTS
(4 - 20 June 2004)
Aldeburgh Productions
Snape Maltings Concert Hall
Snape Bridge, Nr Saxmundham, Suffolk IP17 1SP
Website: www.aldeburgh.co.uk
e-mail: enquiries@aldeburgh.co.uk
Fax: 01728 687120   BO: 01728 687110

ALMEIDA OPERA
(Late June - Early July 2004)
Almeida Street, Islington, London N1 1TA
Website: www.almeida.co.uk
e-mail: pdickie@almeidatheatre.demon.co.uk
Fax: 020-7288 4901   Admin: 020-7288 4900

BARBICAN INTERNATIONAL THEATRE EVENT (BITE)
(Year Round)
Barbican Theatre, Silk Street, London EC2Y 8DS
Website: www.barbican.org.uk
e-mail: lclark@barbican.org.uk
Fax: 020-7382 7377   Tel: 020-7382 7372

BATH INTERNATIONAL MUSIC FESTIVAL
(21 May - 6 June 2004)
Bath Festivals Trust, 5 Broad Street, Bath BA1 5LJ
Website: www.bathfestivals.org.uk
e-mail: info@bathfestivals.org.uk
Fax: 01225 445551   Tel: 01225 462231

BATH LITERATURE FESTIVAL
(28 Feb - 7 March 2004)
Bath Festivals Trust, 5 Broad Street, Bath BA1 5LJ
Website: www.bathfestivals.org.uk
e-mail: info@bathfestivals.org.uk
Fax: 01225 445551   Tel: 01225 462231

BELFAST FESTIVAL AT QUEEN'S
(24 October - 9 November 2003)
25 College Gardens, Belfast BT9 6BS
Website: www.belfastfestival.com
e-mail: festival@qub.ac.uk
Fax: 028-9066 3733   Tel: 028-9066 7687

BRIGHTON FESTIVAL
(1 - 23 May 2004)
12A Pavilion Buildings, Castle Sq, Brighton BN1 1EE
General Manager: Jane McMorrow
BO: 01273 709709   Admin: 01273 70047

BUXTON FESTIVAL
(10 - 25 July 2004)
5 The Square, Buxton, Derbyshire SK17 6AZ
Website: www.buxtonfestival.co.uk
e-mail: info@buxtonfestival.co.uk
BO: 0845 1272190   Admin: 01298 70395

CHESTER FESTIVALS
(Events: July - October 2004)
8 Abbey Square, Chester CH1 2HU
Contact: Patti Dawson
Website: www.chesterfestivals.co.uk   BO: 01244 320700

CHICHESTER FESTIVITIES
(Not Chichester Festival Theatre)
(28 June - 10 July 2004)
Canon Gate House, South Street
Chichester, West Sussex PO19 1PU
Website: www.chifest.org.uk
Fax: 01243 528356   Tel: 01243 785718

DANCE UMBRELLA
(September - November 2004)
Annual Contemporary Dance Festival
20 Chancellor's Street, London W6 9RN
Website: www.danceumbrella.co.uk
e-mail: mail@danceumbrella.co.uk
Fax: 020-8741 7902   Tel: 020-8741 4040

DUBLIN THEATRE FESTIVAL
(27 September - 9 October 2004)
44 East Essex Street
Temple Bar, Dublin 2, Eire
Website: www.dublintheatrefestival.com
e-mail: info@dublintheatrefestival.com
Fax: 00 353 1 6797709   Tel: 00 353 1 6778439

EDINBURGH FESTIVAL FRINGE
(8 - 30 August 2004)
Festival Fringe Society Ltd
180 High Street
Edinburgh EH1 1QS
Website: www.edfringe.com
e-mail: admin@edfringe.com
Fax: 0131-226 0016   Tel: 0131-226 0026

EDINBURGH INTERNATIONAL FESTIVAL
(15 August - 4 September 2004)
The Hub, Castlehill
Edinburgh EH1 2NE
Website: www.eif.co.uk
e-mail: eif@eif.co.uk   BO: 0131-473 2000

GREENWICH - DOCKLANDS FESTIVALS
(2 - 25 July 2004)
Festival Office
6 College Approach
Greenwich, London SE10 9HY
Website: www.festival.org.uk
e-mail: info@festival.org.uk
Fax: 020-8305 1188   Tel: 020-8305 1818

HARROGATE INTERNATIONAL FESTIVAL
(22 July - 7 August 2004)
1 Victoria Avenue
Harrogate
North Yorkshire HG1 1EQ
Website: www.harrogate-festival.org.uk
e-mail: info@harrogate-festival.org.uk
Fax: 01423 521264   Tel: 01423 562303

INTERNATIONAL FESTIVAL OF MUSICAL THEATRE IN CARDIFF The
(10 - 31 October 2004)
St David's House
Wood Street, Cardiff CF10 1ES
Website: www.cardiffmusicals.com
e-mail: enquiries@cardiffmusicals.com
Fax: 029-2040 4216   Tel: 029-2090 1111

KING'S LYNN FESTIVAL
(18 -31 July 2004)
5 Thoresby College
Queen Street, King's Lynn
Norfolk PE30 1HX
Website: www.kl-festival.freeserve.co.uk
Fax: 01553 767688   Tel: 01553 767557

LIFT - LONDON INTERNATIONAL FESTIVAL OF THEATRE
(Events Throughout 2004)
19-20 Great Sutton Street, London EC1V 0DR
Website: www.liftfest.org
e-mail: info@liftfest.org.uk
Fax: 020-7490 3976   Tel: 020-7490 3964

LLANDOVERY THEATRE ARTS FESTIVAL
(July 2004)
Llandovery Theatre
Stone Street, Llandovery
Carmarthenshire SA20 0DQ
Artistic Directors: Simon Barnes,
Jaqueline Harrison   Tel: 01550 720113

LUDLOW FESTIVAL SOCIETY Ltd
(Summer 2004)
Festival Office, Castle Square, Ludlow
Shropshire SY8 1AY
Fax: 01584 877673   BO: 01584 872150

NORWICH FORUM/VAMP STREET THEATRE FESTIVAL
(Weekends July/August - Norwich, Norfolk)
Vamp Street Theatre Productions, Ealing House
33 Hanger Lane, London W5 3HJ
e-mail: info@vampevents.com
Fax: 020-8932 6169   Tel: 020-8997 3355

Festivals

THE 49th SUNDAY TIMES NATIONAL STUDENT DRAMA FESTIVAL
(31 March - 7 April 2004) Information Office
University of Hull, Scarborough Campus
Filey Road, Scarborough YO11 3AZ
Director: Andrew Loretto
Website: www.nsdf.org.uk   e-mail: info@nsdf.org.uk
Fax: 01723 370815   Tel: 01723 501106

VISIONS - FESTIVAL OF VISUAL PERFORMANCE
(21- 30 October 2004)
University of Brighton Gallery
& Sallis Benney Theatre
University of Brighton, Grand Parade
Brighton BN2 2JY
Director: Linda Lewis   e-mail: visions.fest@bton.ac.uk
Fax: 01273 643038   Tel: 01273 643194

Film & Television Distributors

ASIAN PICTURES INTERNATIONAL
1st Floor, 787 High Road
London E11 4QS
e-mail: asianpictures@bizmane.com
Fax: 020-8558 9891   Tel: 020-8539 6529

BLUE DOLPHIN FILM AND VIDEO
(Film Production/Video Distribution)
40 Langham Street, London W1W 7AS
Website: www.bluedolphinfilms.com
e-mail: info@bluedolphinfilms.com
Fax: 020-7580 7670   Tel: 020-7255 2494

CONTEMPORARY FILMS
24 Southwood Lawn Road, London N6 5SF
Website: www.contemporaryfilms.com
e-mail: inquiries@contemporaryfilms.com
Fax: 020-8348 1238   Tel: 020-8340 5715

GUERILLA FILMS Ltd
35 Thornbury Rd, Isleworth, Middlesex TW7 4LQ
Website: www.guerilla-films.com
e-mail: david@guerilla-films.com
Fax: 020-8758 9364   Tel: 020-8758 1716

HIGH POINT FILMS & TV
(International Sales)
25 Elizabeth Mews NW3 4UH
Website: www.highpointfilms.co.uk
e-mail: sales@highpointfilms.co.uk
Fax: 020-7586 3117   Tel: 020-7586 3686

JACKSON Brian FILMS Ltd
39 Hanover Steps
St George's Fields, Albion St, W2 2YG
e-mail: brianjfilm@aol.com
Fax: 020-7262 5736   Tel: 020-7402 7543

PAN EUROPEAN FILMS
110 Trafalgar Road, Portslade, Sussex BN41 1GS
Website: www.filmangel.co.uk
e-mail: filmangels@freenetname.co.uk
Fax: 01273 705451   Tel: 01273 277333

PATHE DISTRIBUTION Ltd
Kent House
14-17 Market Place
Great Titchfield Street, London W1W 8AR
Website: www.pathe.co.uk
Fax: 020-7631 3568   Tel: 020-7323 5151

SONY PICTURES EUROPE HOUSE
25 Golden Square
London W1F 9LU
Fax: 020-7533 1015   Tel: 020-7533 1000

SOUTHERN STAR SALES
45-49 Mortimer Street
London W1W 8HX
Fax: 020-7436 7426   Tel: 020-7636 9421

SQUIRREL FILMS DISTRIBUTION Ltd
Grice's Wharf
119 Rotherhithe Street
London SE16 4NF
Website: www.sandsfilms.co.uk
Fax: 020-7231 2119   Tel: 020-7231 2209

UIP (UK)
12 Golden Square, London W1A 2JL
Website: www.uip.co.uk
Fax: 020-7534 5202   Tel: 020-7534 5200

UNIVERSAL INTERNATIONAL TELEVISION SERVICES Ltd
5-7 Mandeville Place
London W1U 3AR   Tel: 020-7535 3500

UNIVERSAL PICTURES INTERNATIONAL
Oxford House
76 Oxford Street, London W1D 1BS
Fax: 020-7307 1301   Tel: 020-7307 1300

WARNER BROS PICTURES
Warner House, 98 Theobald's Road
London WC1X 8WB
Fax: 020-7984 5001   Tel: 020-7984 5000

Film Preview Theatres

BRITISH ACADEMY OF FILM & TELEVISION ARTS The
195 Piccadilly, London W1J 9LN
Fax: 020-7734 1792   Tel: 020-7734 0022

BRITISH FILM INSTITUTE
21 Stephen Street, London W1P 1LM
e-mail: roger.young@bfi.org.uk
Fax: 020-7436 7950   Tel: 020-7957 8976

CENTURY THEATRE
(Twentieth Century Fox)
31 Soho Square, London W1D 3AP
e-mail: projection@foxinc.com   Tel: 020-7437 7766

COLUMBIA TRI STAR FILMS (UK)
25 Golden Square, London W1F 9LU
Fax: 020-7533 1015   Tel: 020-7533 1111

DE LANE LEA
75 Dean Street, London W1D 3PU
Website: www.delanelea.com
e-mail: dll@delanelea.com
Fax: 020-7432 3838   Tel: 020-7432 3800

EXECUTIVE THEATRE
(Twentieth Century Fox)
31 Soho Square, London W1D 3AP
e-mail: projection@foxinc.com   Tel: 020-7437 7766

MR YOUNG'S PREVIEW THEATRE
14 D'Arblay Street, London W1F 8DY
Fax: 020-7734 4520   Tel: 020-7437 1771

RSA
(Royal Society of Arts)
8 John Adam Street
London WC2N 6EZ
Website: www.theplacetomeet.org.uk
e-mail: conference@rsa.org.uk
Fax: 020-7321 0271   Tel: 020-7839 5049

TRICYCLE CINEMA
269 Kilburn High Road
London NW6 7JR
Website: www.tricycle.co.uk
e-mail: cinema@tricycle.co.uk   Tel: 020-7328 1000

AC ARTS VIDEO PRODUCTION &
EQUIPMENT HIRE
(Showreels, CV-CD Roms & Websites)
57 East Dulwich Road, London SE22 9AP
Website: www.ac-arts.co.uk
e-mail: admin@ac-arts.co.uk   Mobile: 07957 750246

ACTOR'S 'ONE-STOP' SHOP The
(Showreels, Photographs, CVs)
54 Belsize Avenue
London N13 4TJ
Website: www.actorsone-stopshop.com
e-mail: info@actorsone-stopshop.com
Tel/Fax: 020-8888 9666   Tel: 020-8888 7006

ANVIL POST PRODUCTION
(Studio Manager - Mike Anscombe)
Denham Studios
North Orbital Road
Uxbridge, Middlesex UB9 5HL
Fax: 01895 835006   Tel: 01895 833522

ARK STUDIO Ltd
(Stills - Studio & Location)
Unit 5, 9 Park Hill
London SW4 9NS
e-mail: info@arkstudio.co.uk
Fax: 020-7498 9497   Tel: 020-7622 4000

ARRI MEDIA
3 Highbridge
Oxford Road, Uxbridge
Middlesex UB8 1LX
Website: www.arri.com
e-mail: clientcontacts@arrimedia.com
Fax: 01895 457101   Tel: 01895 457100

ASCENT MEDIA Ltd
(Post-Production Facilities)
Film House, 142 Wardour Street
London W1F 8DD
Website: www.ascentmedia.co.uk
Fax: 020-7878 7870   Tel: 020-7878 0000

ASCENT - MEDIA CAMDEN Ltd
(Post Production Film Facilities)
13 Hawley Crescent
London NW1 8NP
Fax: 020-7485 3667   Tel: 020-7284 7900

ASCENT - MEDIA Ltd
(Video & Satellite, Music & Agency)
Video House
48 Charlotte Street,
London W1T 2NS
Fax: 020-7208 2227   Tel: 020-7208 2200

AUTOMOTIVE ACTION STUNTS
Stunt Rigging & Supplies/Camera Tracking Vehicles)
2 Sheffield House
Park Road, Hampton Hill, Middlesex TW12 1HA
Website: www.carstunts.co.uk
Mobile: 07974 919589   Tel: 020-8977 6186

AXIS FILMS
(Film Equipment Rental)
Shepperton Studios, Studios Rd, Middx TW17 0QD
Website: www.axisfilms.co.uk
e-mail: info@axisfilms.co.uk
Fax: 01932 592246   Tel: 01932 592244

BEWILDERING PICTURES
(Showreel Service) (Graeme Kennedy)
110 - 116 Elmore Street, London N1 3AH
e-mail: gk@bewildering.co.uk
Mobile: 07974 916258   Tel: 020-7354 9101

BRIGHTON FILM FACILITIES
(Complete pre to post service for companies filming
within radius of Brighton)
Contact: Franz von Habsburg MBKS
e-mail: brightonfilmfacilities@btopenworld.com
Fax: 01273 302163   Tel: 01273 302166

CENTRAL FILM FACILITIES
(Camera Tracking Specialists)
Marshbrook Business Park, Church Stretton
Shropshire SY6 6QE
Website: www.centralfilmfacilities.com
Fax: 01694 781468   Tel: 01694 781418

CHANNEL 20 - 20 Ltd
Flint House
91-93 Gray's Inn Road, London WC1X 8TX
Website: www.channel2020.co.uk
e-mail: info@channel2020.co.uk
Fax: 020-7242 4386   Tel: 020-7242 4328

CINE TO VIDEO & FOREIGN TAPE
CONVERSION & DUPLICATING
(Peter J Snell Enterprises)
Amp House, Grove Road, Rochester, Kent ME2 4BX
e-mail: pjstv@blueyonder.co.uk
Fax: 01634 726000   Tel: 01634 723838

CLEAR CUT VIDEO EDITING & FILMING
(Peter J Snell Enterprises)
Amp House, Grove Road
Rochester, Kent ME2 4BX
e-mail: pjstv@blueyonder.co.uk
Fax: 01634 726000   Tel: 01634 723838

CONTACT GROUP Ltd
(Conference, Multimedia & Video Production)
Oakridge, Weston Road, Staffordshire ST16 3RS
e-mail: mail@contactgroup.co.uk
Fax: 01785 610955   Tel: 01785 610966

CRYSTAL MEDIA
28 Castle Street, Edinburgh EH2 3HT
Website: www.crystal.tv
e-mail: info@crystal-media.co.uk
Fax: 0131-240 0989   Tel: 0131-240 0988

CURIOUS YELLOW Ltd
33-37 Hatherley Mews, London E17 4QP
e-mail: info@curiousyellow.co.uk
Fax: 020-8521 6363   Tel: 020-8521 9595

DE LANE LEA
(Film & TV Sound Dubbing & Editing Suite)
75 Dean Street, London W1D 3PU
Website: www.delanelea.com
e-mail: dll@delanelea.com
Fax: 020-7432 3838   Tel: 020-7432 3800

DENMAN PRODUCTIONS
(3D Computer Animation, Film/Video CD Business
Card Showreels)
5 Holly Road, Twickenham, Middlesex TW1 4EA
Website: www.denman.co.uk
e-mail: info@denman.co.uk   Tel: 020-8891 3461

DIVERSE PRODUCTIONS
(Pre and Post-Production)
6 Gorleston Street, London W14 8XS
Fax: 020-7603 2148   Tel: 020-7603 4567

EXECUTIVE AUDIO VISUAL
(Showreels for Actors & TV Presenters)
80 York Street
London W1H 1QW   Tel: 020-7723 4488

FARM DIGITAL POST PRODUCTION The
27 Upper Mount Street, Dublin 2, Eire
Website: www.thefarm.ie
e-mail: info@thefarm.ie
Fax: 353 1 676 8816   Tel: 353 1 676 8812

FOUR WHEEL FILMS
(Crews & Equipment, Full Beta SP Kit)
PO Box 1054, Kingston-upon-Thames, Surrey KT2 5YR
e-mail: david@fwfilms.freeserve.co.uk
Fax: 020-8715 5014   Tel: 020-8715 4861

GREENPARK PRODUCTIONS Ltd
(Film Archives)
Illand, Launceston, Cornwall PL15 7LS
Website: www.greenparkimages.co.uk
e-mail: archives@clips.net
Fax: 01566 782127   Tel: 01566 782107

HULK PRODUCTIONS
(TV Showreels)
PO Box 35762, London E14 8EG
Website: www.hulkproductions.com
e-mail: hulkproductions@aol.com
Tel: 07870 650320

HUNKY DORY PRODUCTIONS Ltd
(Facilities & Crew)
Cambridge House, 135 High Street
Teddington, Middlesex TW11 8HH
Fax: 020-8977 4464   Tel: 020-8943 3006

INTERACTIVE SHOWREELS
(Showreels & Production)
e-mail: interactiveshowreels@btinternet.com
Mobile: 07736 872380   Tel: 020-8575 6005

KINGSTON INMEDIA
Studio K, PO Box 2287
Gerrards Cross, Bucks SL9 8BF
Fax: 01494 876006   Tel: 01494 878297

LENIHAN Sean ASSOCIATES
The Old Chapel
Abbey Hill, Lelant, St Ives
Cornwall TR26 3EB   Tel/Fax: 01736 757557

MAGPIE FILM PRODUCTIONS
31-32 Cheapside
Birmingham B5 6AY
Fax: 0121-666 6077   Tel: 0121-622 5884

MINAMON PRODUCTIONS
(Specialist in Showreels)
117 Downton Avenue
London SW2 3TX
e-mail: info@minamonfilm.co.uk
Fax: 020-8674 1779   Tel: 020-8674 3957

MOVING PICTURE COMPANY The
(Post-Production)
127-133 Wardour Street
London W1F 0NL
Website: www.moving-picture.com
e-mail: mailbox@moving-picture.com
Fax: 020-7287 5187   Tel: 020-7434 3100

PANAVISION UK
Bristol Road
Greenford, Middlesex UB6 8GD
Website: www.panavision.co.uk
Fax: 020-8839 7300   Tel: 020-8839 7333

PANTECHNICON
(Audio Visual, Video, Conference Production,
Design for Print)
90 Lots Road, London SW10 0QD
Website: www.pantechnicon.co.uk
e-mail: info@pantechnicon.co.uk
Fax: 020-7351 0667   Tel: 020-7351 7579

PEAK WHITE VIDEO
1 Latimer Road, Teddington, Middlesex TW11 8QA
Website: www.peakwhite.tv
Fax: 020-8977 8357   Tel: 0870 7405625

PEDIGREE PUNKS
(Interactive CD-Rom & DVD Showreels)
49 Woolstone Road, Forest Hill, London SE23 2TR
Website: www.pedigree-punks.com
e-mail: info@pedigree-punks.com
Tel/Fax: 020-8291 5801

PHA CASTING STUDIO
Tanzaro House, Ardwick Green North
Manchester M12 6FZ
Website: www.pha-agency.co.uk
e-mail: studio@pha-agency.co.uk
Fax: 0161-273 4567   Tel: 0161-273 4444

PRO-LINK RADIO SYSTEMS Ltd
(Radio Microphones and Communications)
4 Woden Court, Saxon Business Park
Hanbury Road, Bromsgrove, Worcestershire B60 4AD
Website: http://prolink-radio.com
e-mail: service@prolink-radio.com
Fax: 01527 577757   Tel: 01527 577788

Q SOUND
(Voice Recording Studio)
Queen's Studios, 121 Salusbury Road
London NW6 6RG
Website: www.qsound.uk.com
e-mail: queries@qsound.uk.com
Fax: 020-7625 5355   Tel: 020-7625 5359

REPLAY Ltd
(Showreels & Performance Recording)
199 Piccadilly, London W1J 9HA
Website: www.replayfilms.co.uk
e-mail: sales@replayfilms.co.uk
Fax: 020-7287 5348   Tel: 020-7287 5334

REYNOLDS George F
(Videographer & Editor, Video Production)
12 Mead Close, Grays
Essex RM16 2TR
e-mail: g.f.reynolds@talk21.com   Tel: 01375 373886

SALON Ltd
(Post Production)
12 Swainson Road, London W3 7XB
Website: www.salonrentals.com
e-mail: hire@salonrentals.com   Tel: 020-8746 7611

SHOWREEL SERVICES
35 Bedfordbury, Covent Garden, London WC2N 4DU
Fax: 020-7379 5210   Tel: 020-7379 6082

STAR PRODUCTIONS
(Facilities)
Star Studios, 36 Lea Bridge Road
London E5 9QD   Tel: 020-8986 4470

TAKE FIVE
(Showreels)
25 Ganton Street, London W1F 9BP
Website: www.takefivestudio.co.uk
e-mail: info@takefivestudio.co.uk
Fax: 020-7287 3035   Tel: 020-7287 2120

TANGAMAX Ltd
(Showreels, DVD, Photography)
28A Harberton Road, London N19 3JR
Website: www.tangamax.pwp.blueyonder.co.uk
e-mail: tangamax@blueyonder.co.uk
Tel/Fax: 020-7281 5908

TO BE OR NOT TO BE
(Showreels/Corporate Films) (Anthony Barnett)
48 Northampton Road
Kettering, Northants NN15 7JU
Website: www.tobeornottobe.tv
e-mail: tobeornottobe@ntlworld.com
Mobile: 07958 996227   Tel/Fax: 01536 359631

TV MEDIA SERVICES Ltd
(Video and Broadcast Facilities)
3rd Floor, 420 Sauchiehall Street
Glasgow G2 3JD
e-mail: tvmsmail@aol.com
Fax: 0141-332 9040   Tel: 0141-331 1993

VFG HIRE Ltd
(Film & TV Equipment Hire)
8 Beresford Avenue
Wembley, Middlesex HA0 1LA
e-mail: info@vfg.co.uk
Fax: 020-8795 3366   Tel: 020-8795 7000

VIDEO CASTING DIRECTORY Ltd
(Production of Performers' Showreels)
1 Triangle House
2 Broomhill Road, London SW18 4HX
e-mail: simon@fightingfilms.com
Fax: 020-8874 8590   Tel: 020-8874 3314

VIDEO INN PRODUCTION
(AV Equipment Hire)
Glebe Farm, Wooton Road, Quinton
Northampton NN7 2EE
Website: www.videoinn.co.uk
e-mail: andy@videoinn.co.uk   Tel: 01604 864868

VIDEOSONICS CINEMA SOUND
(Film & Television Dubbing Facilities)
68A Delancey Street
London NW1 7RY
e-mail: info@videosonics.com
Fax: 020-7419 4470   Tel: 020-7209 0209

VOICE CASTER
(Digital Studio & Video Editing)
Website: www.voicecaster.net
e-mail: info@voicecaster.net   Tel: 020-8455 2211

VOICE CLINIC The
(Demo's)
99 Cobold Road
London NW10 9SL
e-mail: ptmellor@yahoo.co.uk   Tel: 020-8451 7003

VOICE TAPE SERVICES INTERNATIONAL Ltd
(Professional Voice-Over Direction & CDs)
80 Netherlands Road
New Barnet, Herts EN5 1BS
Website: www.vtsint.co.uk
e-mail: info@vtsint.co.uk
Fax: 020-8441 4828   Tel: 020-8440 4848

VSI
132 Cleveland Street
London W1T 6AB
Website: www.vsi.tv
e-mail: info@vsi.tv
Fax: 020-7692 7711   Tel: 020-7692 7700

W6 STUDIO
(Video Production & Editing Facilities)
359 Lillie Road
Fulham, London SW6 7PA
Website: www.w6studio.co.uk
Fax: 020-7381 5252   Tel: 020-7385 2272

WILD IRIS FILMS
59 Brewer Street,
London W1R 3FB
e-mail: joe@wildiris.co.uk
Fax: 020-7494 1764   Tel: 020-8374 4536

PATCHOULi films

Patchouli Films is the all-new division of
Patchouli Entertainment, Manchester's only
one-stop company publishing books, music and
producing theatrical motion pictures

www.patchoulifilms.net   info@patchoulifilms.net

the PLaYgROUND

Der Antrag   Kings Town

Key to areas of specialization:
F Films **FF** Feature Films **CV** Corporate Video **D** Drama
Ch Children's Entertainment
Co Comedy & Light Entertainment
Docs Documentaries

30 BIRD PRODUCTIONS
138A Kingswood Road, Brixton, London SW2 4JL
e-mail: thirtybird.productions@ntlworld.com
Tel/Fax: 020-8678 7034

303 PRODUCTIONS
11 D'Arblay Street, London W1F 8DT
e-mail: philburgess@mac.com
Fax: 020-7494 0956   Tel: 020-7494 0955

ACADEMY COMMERCIALS Ltd
16 West Central Street, London WC1A 1JJ
Fax: 020-7240 0355   Tel: 020-7395 4155

ACTION TIME
35-38 Portman Square, London W1H 6NU
Website: www.action-time.com
e-mail: info@actiontime.co.uk
Fax: 020-7612 7524   Tel: 020-7486 6688

AGE FILM & VIDEO
F CV
Fyletts Barn, The Green, Hawstead, Bury St Edmunds
Suffolk INP 5NP   Tel: 01284 386629

AGRAN BARTON TV Ltd
(See HARBOUR PICTURES)

ALGERNON Ltd
15 Cleveland Mansions
Widley Road, London W9 2LA
e-mail: algernon@breadpudding.co.uk
Fax: 0870 1388516   Tel: 020-7266 1582

ALIBI PRODUCTIONS Plc
35 Long Acre, London WC2E 9JT
Fax: 020-7379 7039   Tel: 020-7845 0420

ALIVE EVENTS
Fulton House, Fulton Road, Wembley Park
Middlesex HA9 0TF
Website: www.aliveevents.co.uk
e-mail: simon@aliveevents.co.uk
Fax: 020-8584 0443   Tel: 020-8584 0444

AN ACQUIRED TASTE TV CORP
F TV D
51 Croham Road, South Croydon CR2 7HD
Fax: 020-8686 5928   Tel: 020-8686 1188

APT FILMS
225A Brecknock Road, London N19 5AA
Website: www.aptfilms.com
e-mail: admin@aptfilms.com
Fax: 020-7482 1587   Tel: 020-7284 1695

APTN
The Interchange
Oval Road
Camden Lock, London NW1 7DZ
Fax: 020-7413 8312   Tel: 020-7482 7400

ARENA FILMS Ltd
TV D
2 Pelham Road, London SW19 1SX
Fax: 020-8540 3992   Tel: 020-8543 3990

ARLINGTON PRODUCTIONS Ltd
TV D Co
Cippenham Court
Cippenham Lane
Cippenham, Nr Slough, Berkshire SL1 5AU
Fax: 01753 691785   Tel: 01753 516767

ART BOX PRODUCTIONS
10 Heatherway
Crowthorne, Berkshire RG45 6HG
Website: www.tonyhart.nildram.co.uk
e-mail: artbox@nildram.co.uk
Tel/Fax: 01344 773638

ASCENT MEDIA Ltd
Film House, 142 Wardour Street, London W1F 8DD
Website: www.ascentmedia.co.uk
e-mail: sally.hart.ivs@ascentmedia.co.uk
Fax: 020-7878 7870   Tel: 020-7878 0000

ASF PRODUCTIONS Ltd
2 Teal Drive, Ducks Hill Road
Northwood, Middlesex HA6 2PT
e-mail: asfc@genmail.net
Fax: 01923 823310   Tel: 01923 829410

**ASHFORD ENTERTAINMENT
CORPORATION Ltd The**
20 The Chase, Coulsdon, Surrey CR5 2EG
Website: www.ashford-entertainment.co.uk
e-mail: info@ashford-entertainment.co.uk
Tel: 020-8645 0667

ASSASSIN FILMS Ltd
74 Holland Park, London W11 3SL
e-mail: info@assassinfilms.co.uk
Fax: 0870 167 2981   Tel: 020-7706 8332

ATLANTIC SEVEN PRODUCTIONS Ltd
52 Lancaster Road
London N4 4PR
Fax: 020-7436 9233   Tel: 020-7263 4435

ATP Ltd
TV Ch D
PO Box 24182, London SW18 2WY
e-mail: atpmedia@ukonline.co.uk
Tel/Fax: 020-7738 9886

ATTICUS TELEVISION Ltd
5 Clare Lawn, London SW14 8BH
e-mail: attwiz@aol.com
Fax: 020-8878 3821   Tel: 020-8487 1173

AVALON TELEVISION Ltd
4A Exmoor Street, London W10 6BD
Fax: 020-7598 7281   Tel: 020-7598 7280

BAILEY Catherine Ltd
110 Gloucester Avenue, Primrose Hill
London NW1 8JA
Fax: 020-7483 4541   Tel: 020-7483 2681

BANANA PARK Ltd
(Animation Production Company)
Banana Park, 6 Cranleigh Mews, London SW11 2QL
Fax: 020-7738 1887   Tel: 020-7228 7136

BARFORD FILM COMPANY The
35 Bedfordbury, London WC2N 4DU
Website: www.barford.co.uk
e-mail: info@barford.co.uk
Fax: 020-7379 5210   Tel: 020-7836 1365

BARRATT Michael
Field Hse, Ascot Rd, Maidenhead, Berkshire SL6 3LD
e-mail: mbarratt@compuserve
Fax: 01628 627737   Tel: 01628 770800

BBC WORLDWIDE Ltd
Woodlands, 80 Wood Lane, London W12 0TT
Fax: 020-8749 0538   Tel: 020-8433 2000

BETTAVISION TV
1 Mount Parade, Cockfosters, Herts EN4 9DD
Fax: 020-8449 8259   Tel: 020-8449 4898

BIRD Martin PRODUCTIONS
TV
Saucelands Barn, Coolham, Horsham
West Sussex RH13 8QG
Website: www.mbptv.com
e-mail: info@mbptv.com
Fax: 01403 741647   Tel: 01403 741620

BIZMANE ENTERTAINMENT Ltd
1st Floor, 787 High Road, London E11 4QS
e-mail: enquiries@bizmane.com
Fax: 020-8558 9891   Tel: 020-8558 4488

BLACK CAT FILMS Ltd
(Write)
10-12 High Street, Great Wakering, Essex SS9 1BG
e-mail: mail@blackcatfilms.co.uk

BLACKBIRD PRODUCTIONS
6 Molasses Row, Plantation Wharf, Battersea
London SW11 3TW
e-mail: enquiries@blackbirdproductions.co.uk
                                     Tel: 020-7924 6440

BLUE FISH MEDIA
39 Ratby Close, Lower Earley, Reading RG6 4ER
Website: www.bfmedia.co.uk
e-mail: ideas@bfmedia.co.uk
Fax: 0118-962 0748   Tel: 0118-975 0272

BLUE WAND PRODUCTIONS Ltd
2nd Floor, 12 Weltje Road, London W6 9TG
Website: www.bluewand.co.uk
e-mail: lino@bluewand.co.uk
Mobile: 07885 528743   Tel/Fax: 020-8741 2038

BLUELINE PRODUCTIONS Ltd
28B Victoria Road, Ruislip, Middlesex HA4 0AB
e-mail: david@blue-line.tv
Fax: 01895 635060   Tel: 01895 635100

BOWE TENNANT PRODUCTIONS
(Specialists Animal Pet Productions)
Applewood House Studio, Ringshall Road
Dagnall, Berkhamsted, Hertfordshire HP4 1RN
Fax: 01442 842453   Tel: 01923 213008

BRIDGE LANE THEATRE COMPANY Ltd
(Film Production & Script Development)
The Studio, 49 Ossulton Way
London N2 0JY   Tel/Fax: 020-8444 0505

BRONCO FILMS
F TV D
The Producers' Centre, 61 Holland Street
Glasgow G2 4NJ
Website: www.broncofilms.co.uk
e-mail: broncofilm@btinternet.com
Fax: 0141-287 6815   Tel: 0141-287 6817

BROOKSIDE PRODUCTIONS Ltd
TV
Campus Manor, Childwall, Abbey Road
Liverpool L16 0JP
Fax: 0151-722 6839   Tel: 0151-722 9122

BRUNSWICK FILMS Ltd
(Formula One Grand Prix Film Library)
26 Macroom Road, Maida Vale, London W9 3HY
e-mail: brunswick.films@virgin.net
Fax: 020-8960 4997   Tel: 020-8960 0066

BUCKMARK PRODUCTIONS
Commer House, Station Road, Tadcaster
North Yorkshire LS24 9JF
Website: www.buckmark.co.uk
e-mail: ed@buckmark.co.uk
Fax: 01937 835901   Tel: 01937 835900

BUENA VISTA PRODUCTIONS
3 Queen Caroline Street, Hammersmith, W6 9PE
Fax: 020-8222 2795   Tel: 020-8222 1000

BURDER FILMS
37 Braidley Road, Meyrick Park
Bournemouth BH2 6JY
Website: www.johnburder.co.uk
e-mail: burderfilms@aol.com   Tel: 01202 295395

CALDERDALE TELEVISION
Dean Clough, Halifax HX3 5AX
e-mail: ctv@calderdaletv.co.uk
Fax: 01422 384532   Tel: 01422 253100

CAMBRIDGE FILM & TELEVISION PRODUCTIONS
Middlewhite Barn, St Georges Way
Impington, Cambridge CB4 9AF
Website: www.cftp.co.uk
e-mail: contact@cftp.co.uk
Fax: 01223 237555   Tel: 01223 236007

CARAVEL FILM TECHNIQUES Ltd
The Great Barn Studios, Cippenham Lane
Slough, Berkshire SL1 5AU
e-mail: ajjcaraveltv@aol.com
Fax: 01494 446662   Tel: 01753 534828

CARDINAL BROADCAST
Hawes Hill Court, Drift Road, Windsor
Berkshire SL4 4QQ
Fax: 01344 891333   Tel: 01344 890099

CARLTON TELEVISION Ltd
35-38 Portman Square, London W1H 6NU
Fax: 020-7486 1132   Tel: 020-7486 6688

CARNIVAL (FILMS & THEATRE) Ltd
12 Raddington Road, London W10 5TG
Website: www.carnival-films.co.uk
Fax: 020-8968 0177   Tel: 020-8968 0968

CARRINGTON Michael TELEVISION & FILM
(See CREATE TV & FILMS Ltd)

CASE TV.COM
204 Mare Street Studios
203-213 Mare Street, London E8 3QE
e-mail: case@casetv.com
Fax: 020-7296 0011   Tel: 020-7296 0010

CASPIAN PRODUCTIONS
15 Ogilvie Terrace, Edinburgh EH11 1NS
e-mail: nigel.h@blueyonder.co.uk
                                Tel/Fax: 0131-346 0283

CELADOR PRODUCTIONS Ltd
39 Long Acre, London WC2E 9LG
Fax: 020-7845 9541   Tel: 020-7240 8101

CELANDINE PRODUCTIONS
39 Pemberton Road
Molesey KT8 9LG
e-mail: producers@celandine.tv Tel: 020-8941 9991

CELTIC FILMS Ltd
21 Grafton Street, London W1S 4EU
e-mail: info@celticfilms.co.uk
Fax: 020-7409 2383   Tel: 020-7409 2080

CENTRE SCREEN PRODUCTIONS
Eastgate, Castle Street, Castlefield
Manchester M3 4LZ
Website: www.centrescreen.co.uk
e-mail: info@centrescreen.co.uk
Fax: 0161-832 8934   Tel: 0161-832 7151

CENTRELINE VIDEO PRODUCTIONS
138 Westwood Road
Tilehurst, Reading RG31 6LL
Website: www.centrelinevideo.com
Tel: 0118-941 0033

CHAKRA PRODUCTIONS
181 Jersey Road, Osterley, Middlesex TW7 4QJ
Website: www.chakra.co.uk
e-mail: talk@chakra.co.uk
Fax: 020-8737 2987   Tel: 020-8737 1616

CHANNEL 20/20 Ltd
20/20 House, 26-28 Talbot Lane, Leicester LE1 4LR
Fax: 0116-222 1113   Tel: 0116-233 2220

CHATSWORTH TELEVISION Ltd
D Co
97-99 Dean Street, London W1D 3TE
Website: www.chatsworth-tv.co.uk
e-mail: television@chatsworth-tv.co.uk
Fax: 020-7437 3301   Tel: 020-7734 4302

CHILDREN'S FILM & TELEVISION FOUNDATION Ltd
Elstree Film & TV Studios, Borehamwood
Hertfordshire WD6 1JG
e-mail: annahome@cftf.onyxnet.co.uk
Fax: 020-8207 0860   Tel: 020-8953 0844

CHX PRODUCTIONS Ltd
2nd Floor, Highgate Business Centre
33 Greenwood Place, London NW5 1LB
e-mail: firstname.surname@chxp.co.uk
Fax: 020-7428 3998   Tel: 020-7428 3999

CINEMA VERITY PRODUCTIONS Ltd
F TV D Co
11 Addison Avenue, London W11 4QS
Fax: 020-7371 3329   Tel: 020-7460 2777

CLARION TELEVISION
The 1929 Building, Merton Abbey Mills
Watermill Way, London SW19 2RD
Website: www.clariontv.com
e-mail: info@clariontv.com
Fax: 07092 9030160   Tel: 020-8540 0110

CLASSIC PICTURES ENTERTAINMENT Ltd
Shepperton Studios, Studios Road
Shepperton, Middlesex TW17 0QD
e-mail: lyn.beardsall@classicpictures.co.uk
Fax: 01932 592046   Tel: 01932 592016

COLLINGWOOD O'HARE ENTERTAINMENT Ltd
10-14 Crown Street, Acton, London W3 8SB
e-mail: info@crownstreet.co.uk
Fax: 020-8993 9595   Tel: 020-8993 3666

COMMERCIAL BREAKS
Anglia Television
Anglia House, Norwich NR1 3JG
Website: www.commercialbreaks.co.uk
e-mail: commercialbreaks@granadamedia.com
Fax: 01603 752610   Tel: 01603 752600

COMMUNICATOR Ltd
199 Upper Street, London N1 1RQ
e-mail: info@communicator.ltd.uk
Fax: 020-7704 8444   Tel: 020-7704 8333

COMTEC Ltd
Unit 19, Tait Road, Croydon, Surrey CR0 2DP
Website: www.comtecav.co.uk
e-mail: info@comtecav.co.uk
Fax: 020-8684 6947   Tel: 020-8684 6615

CONTACT GROUP Ltd
(Conference Production)
Oakridge, Weston Road, Staffordshire ST16 3RS
Website: www.contactgroup.co.uk
e-mail: mail@contactgroup.co.uk
Fax: 01785 610955   Tel: 01785 610966

CONVERGENCE PRODUCTIONS Ltd
10-14 Crown Street, Acton, London W3 8SB
e-mail: info@crownstreet.co.uk
Fax: 020-8993 9595   Tel: 020-8993 3666

COURTYARD PRODUCTIONS
TV Ch Co
Little Postlings Farmhouse, Four Elms, Kent TN8 6NA
Fax: 01732 700534   Tel: 01732 700324

COWBOY FILMS
11-29 Smiths Court, London W1D 7DP
Website: www.cowboyfilms.co.uk
e-mail: info@cowboyfilms.co.uk
Fax: 020-7287 3785   Tel: 020-7287 3808

CREATE TV & FILMS
33 Bath Road, Slough, Berkshire SL1 3UF
Website: www.createtvandfilm.com
e-mail: info@createtvandfilm.com
Fax: 01753 495225   Tel: 08700 949400

CREATIVE CHANNEL Ltd
The Television Centre, La Pouquelaye
St Helier, Jersey JE1 3ZD
e-mail: creative@channeltv.co.uk
Fax: 01534 816889   Tel: 01534 816888

CREATIVE FILM MAKERS Ltd
Pottery Lane Hse, 34A Pottery Lane W11 4LZ
Fax: 020-7229 4999   Tel: 020-7229 5131

CREATIVE FILM PRODUCTIONS
68 Conway Road
London N14 7BE   Tel: 020-8447 8187

CREATIVE MEDIA
(Part of the ITM Group)
Latimer Sq, White Lion Rd, Amersham
Buckinghamshire HP7 9JQ   Tel: 0870 8712233

CREATIVE PARTNERSHIP The
13 Bateman Street, London W1D 3AF
Website: www.creativepartnership.co.uk
Fax: 020-7437 1467   Tel: 020-7439 7762

CROFT TELEVISION & GRAPHICS
Croft House, Progress Business Centre,
Whittle Parkway, Slough, Berkshire SL1 6DQ
Fax: 01628 668791   Tel: 01628 668735

CTVC
Hillside, Merry Hill Road, Bushey
Hertfordshire WD23 1DR
Website: www.ctcv.co.uk
e-mail: ctvc@ctvc.co.uk
Fax: 020-8950 1437   Tel: 020-8950 7919

CUTHBERT Tony PRODUCTIONS
7A Langley Street, London WC2H 9JA
Website: www.tonycuthbert.com
e-mail: info@tonycuthbert.com
Fax: 020-7734 6579   Tel: 020-7437 8884

DALTON FILMS Ltd
127 Hamilton Terrace, London NW8 9QR
Fax: 020-7624 4420   Tel: 020-7328 6169

DAMAGED STOCK PRODUCTIONS
19 Pound Drive, Fishponds, Bristol BS16 2EG
e-mail: andrew.boswell@damagedstock.co.uk
Tel/Fax: 0117-9029527

DARLOW SMITHSON PRODUCTIONS Ltd
4th Floor, Highgate Business Centre
33 Greenwood Place, London NW5 1LB
e-mail: mail@darlowsmithson.com
Fax: 020-7482 7039   Tel: 020-7482 7027

DAWKINS ASSOCIATES Ltd
PO Box 615, Boughton Monchelsea, Kent ME17 4RN
e-mail: da@ccland.demon.co.uk
Fax: 01622 741731   Tel: 01622 741900

DAWSON FILMS
67 Hillfield Park, London N10 3QU
Fax: 020-8352 4708   Tel: 020-8444 6854

DIFFERENT FILMS
PO Box 564, London WC2H 5WA
Website: www.differentfilms.co.uk
e-mail: info@differentfilms.co.uk
Fax: 0845 4585791   Tel: 0845 4585790

DLT ENTERTAINMENT UK Ltd
10 Bedford Square, London WC1B 3RA
Fax: 020-7636 4571   Tel: 020-7631 1184

DON PRODUCTIONS Ltd
26 Shacklewell Lane, London E8 2EZ
Website: www.donproductions.com
e-mail: info@donproductions.com
Fax: 020-7690 4333   Tel: 020-7690 0108

DRAGONFLY FILMS Ltd
King's Head Theatre, 115 Upper St, London N1 1QN
e-mail: brian@dragonflyfilms.co.uk
                            Tel: 020-7354 9259

DRAMA HOUSE The
Coach Road Cottages, Little Saxham
Bury St Edmunds, Suffolk IP29 5LE
Website: www.dramahouse.co.uk
e-mail: jack@dramahouse.co.uk
Fax: 01284 811425   Tel: 01284 810521

DRAMATIS PERSONAE Ltd
(Nathan Silver, Nicolas Kent)
19 Regency Street, London SW1P 4BY
e-mail: nathan.silver@ntlworld.com
                            Tel: 020-7834 9300

DRUMBEAT PRODUCTIONS Ltd
17A Mercer Street, London WC2H 9QT
e-mail: tudorgates@compuserve.com
                            Tel: 020-7836 3710

DUCK LANE FILM COMPANY The
5 Carlisle Street, London W1D 3BL
Fax: 020-7437 2260   Tel: 020-7439 3912

DVA
8 Campbell Court, Bramley, Hampshire RG26 5EG
Website: www.dvafacilities.co.uk
e-mail: barrieg@dva.co.uk
Fax: 01256 882024   Tel: 01256 882032

ECLIPSE PRESENTATIONS Ltd
3 Croydon Road, Beckenham, Kent BR3 4AA
e-mail: info@eclipse-presentations.co.uk
Fax: 020-8650 4635   Tel: 020-8249 6473

ECOSSE FILMS Ltd
Brigade House, 8 Parsons Green, London SW6 4TN
Website: www.ecossefilms.com
e-mail: info@ecossefilms.com
Fax: 020-7736 3436   Tel: 020-7371 0290

EDGE PICTURE COMPANY Ltd The
7 Langley Street, London WC2H 9JA
Website: www.edgepicture.com
e-mail: ask.us@edgepicture.com
Fax: 020-7836 6949   Tel: 020-7836 6262

EDINBURGH FILM PRODUCTIONS
Keeper's House, Traquair, Innerleithen EH44 6PP
Fax: 01896 831199   Tel: 01896 831188

EDUCATIONAL TRAINING FILMS
17 West Hill SW18 1RB   Tel: 020-8870 9933

ELEPHANT PRODUCTIONS
The Studio, 2 Rothamsted Avenue
Harpenden, Hertfordshire AL5 2DB
Fax: 01582 767532   Tel: 01582 621425

ELMGATE PRODUCTIONS
F TV D
Shepperton Studios, Studios Road
Shepperton, Middlesex
e-mail: elmgate@dial.pipex.com
Fax: 01932 569918   Tel: 01932 562611

ENDEMOL PRODUCTIONS Ltd
(Formerly BAZAL PRODUCTIONS Ltd)
Shepherds Building Central, Charecroft
Shepherds Bush, London W14 0EE
Fax: 0870 3331800   Tel: 0870 3331700

ENLIGHTENMENT PRODUCTIONS
CV
East End House
24 Ennerdale, Skelmersdale WN8 6AJ
Website: www.trainingmultimedia.co.uk
                            Tel: 01695 727555

EON PRODUCTIONS Ltd
Eon House, 138 Piccadilly, London W1J 7NR
Fax: 020-7408 1236   Tel: 020-7493 7953

EPA INTERNATIONAL MULTIMEDIA Ltd
31A Regent's Park Road, London NW1 7TL
Fax: 020-7267 8852   Tel: 020-7267 9198

EXCELSIOR GROUP PRODUCTIONS
Dorking Road, Tadworth, Surrey KT20 7TJ
Fax: 01737 813163   Tel: 01737 812673

EYE FILM & TELEVISION
9/11A Dove Street
Norwich, Norfolk NR2 1DE
Website: www.eyefilmandtv.co.uk
e-mail: production@eyefilmandtv.co.uk
Fax: 01603 762420   Tel: 01603 762551

FANTASY FILM COMPANY
74 Vivian Avenue
London NW4 3XG   Tel: 020-8202 4935

FARNHAM FILM COMPANY The
34 Burnt Hill Road, Lower Bourne
Farnham GU10 3LZ
Website: www.farnfilm.com
e-mail: info@farnfilm.com
Fax: 01252 725855   Tel: 01252 710313

FEELGOOD FICTION Ltd
49 Goldhawk Road, London W12 8QP
e-mail: feelgood@feelgoodfiction.co.uk
Fax: 020-8740 6177   Tel: 020-8746 2535

FESTIVAL FILM AND TELEVISION Ltd
Festival House, Tranquil Passage
Blackheath Village, London SE3 0BJ
Website: www.festivalfilm.com
e-mail: info@festivalfilm.com
Fax: 020-8297 1155   Tel: 020-8297 9999

FILM & GENERAL PRODUCTIONS Ltd
4 Bradbrook House, Studio Place, London SW1X 8EL
Fax: 020-7245 9853   Tel: 020-7235 4495

FILMS OF RECORD Ltd
2 Elgin Avenue, London W9 3QP
e-mail: films@filmsofrecord.com
Fax: 020-7286 0444   Tel: 020-7286 0333

FIREDOG MOTION PICTURE
CORPORATION Ltd The
20 The Chase, Coulsdon, Surrey CR5 2EG
Website: www.firedogfilms.co.uk
e-mail: info@firedogfilms.co.uk   Tel: 020-8693 3477

FIRST WRITES RADIO COMPANY
(Radio Drama Company)
Lime Kiln Cottage, High Starlings, Banham
Norfolk NR16 2BS
Website: www.first-writes.co.uk
e-mail: ellen-don@first-writes.co.uk
Fax: 01953 888874   Tel: 01953 888525

FLASHBACK TELEVISION Ltd
11 Bowling Green Lane, London EC1R 0BG
Website: www.flashbacktv.co.uk
e-mail: mailbox@flashbacktv.co.uk
Fax: 020-7490 5610   Tel: 020-7490 8996

Film, Radio, Television & Video Production Companies

FLICK FEATURES Ltd
179 Wardour Street, London W1F 8WY
Fax: 020-7855 3697   Tel: 020-7855 3636

FLYING COLOURS FILM COMPANY The
11 Charlotte Mews, London W1T 4EQ
e-mail: fc@flyingc.co.uk
Fax: 020-7436 3055   Tel: 020-7436 2121

FLYNN PRODUCTIONS Ltd
64 Charlotte Road, London EC2A 3PE
Website: www.flynnproductions.com
e-mail: bryony@flynnproductions.com
Fax: 020-7729 7279   Tel: 020-7729 7291

FOCUS PRODUCTIONS Ltd
PO Box 173, Stratford-upon-Avon
Warwickshire CV37 7ZA
e-mail: maddern@focusproductions.co.uk
Fax: 01789 294845   Tel: 01789 298948

FORSTATER Mark PRODUCTIONS
27 Lonsdale Road, London NW6 6RA
Fax: 020-7624 1124   Tel: 020-7624 1123

FREEHAND PRODUCTIONS Ltd
97 Clacton Road, London E17 8AP
Website: www.freehanduk.com
e-mail: freehanduk@yahoo.com
                              Tel/Fax: 020-8520 7777

FRONT PAGE & CHARISMA FILMS Ltd
Riverbank Hse, 1 Putney Bridge, London SW6 3JD
Fax: 020-7610 6836   Tel: 020-7610 6830

FULL WORKS The
Mill Studio, Crane Mead, Ware
Hertfordshire SG12 9PY   Tel: 01920 444399

FULMAR TELEVISION & FILM Ltd
Pascoe House, 54 Bute Street
Cardiff Bay, Cardiff CF10 5AF
Fax: 029-2045 5111   Tel: 029-2045 5000

GALA PRODUCTIONS Ltd
25 Stamford Brook Road, London W6 0XJ
e-mail: info@galaproductions.co.uk
Fax: 020-8741 2323   Tel: 020-8741 4200

GAMMOND Stephen ASSOCIATES
24 Telegraph Lane
Claygate, Surrey KT10 0DU
e-mail: stephengammond@hotmail.com
                              Tel: 01372 460674

GARRETTS
F TV Commercials
21 Little Portland Street, London W1W 8BT
e-mail: commercials@garretts.co.uk
Fax: 020-7580 6453   Tel: 020-7580 6452

GATES Martin PRODUCTIONS Ltd
Chertsey Chambers, 12 Mercer Street
Covent Garden, London WC2H 9QD
Fax: 020-7836 9712   Tel: 020-7836 9674

GATEWAY TELEVISION PRODUCTIONS
Gemini House,10 Bradgate, Cuffley
Hertfordshire EN6 4RL   Tel: 01707 872054

GAY Noel TELEVISION Ltd
TV D Ch Co
Shepperton Studios, Studios Road
Shepperton, Middlesex TW17 0QD
e-mail: charles.armitage@virgin.net
Fax: 01932 592172   Tel: 01932 592569

GHA GROUP
1 Great Chapel Street, London W1F 8FA
Website: www.ghagroup.co.uk
e-mail: sales@ghagroup.co.uk
Fax: 020-7437 5880   Tel: 020-7439 8705

GLASS PAGE Ltd The
15 De Montfort Street, Leicester LE1 7GE
Fax: 0116-249 2188   Tel: 0116-249 2199

GODMAN Colin PRODUCTIONS
TV D
41 Trelawney Road
Cotham, Bristol BS6 6DY   Tel: 0117-974 1058

GRADE COMPANY The
17 Albermarle Street, Mayfair, London W1S 4HP
Fax: 020-7408 2042   Tel: 020-7409 1925

GRANT NAYLOR PRODUCTIONS Ltd
Rooms 950-951, The David Lean Building
Shepperton Studios, Studios Road
Shepperton, Middlesex TW17 0QD
Fax: 01932 592484   Tel: 01932 592175

GREAT GUNS Ltd
43-45 Camden Road, London NW1 9LR
e-mail: greatguns@greatguns.com
Fax: 020-7692 4422   Tel: 020-7692 4444

GREENPOINT FILMS
F TV D
7 Denmark Street, London WC2H 8LZ
e-mail: info@greenpointfilms.co.uk
Fax: 020-7240 7088   Tel: 020-7240 7066

GUERILLA FILMS Ltd
35 Thornbury Road, Isleworth, Middlesex TW7 4LQ
Website: www.guerilla-films.com
e-mail: david@guerilla-films.com
Fax: 020-8758 9364   Tel: 020-8758 1716

**HAMMERWOOD FILM PRODUCERS
& DISTRIBUTORS**
110 Trafalgar Road, Portslade, Sussex BN41 1GS
Website: www.filmangel.co.uk
e-mail: filmangels@freenetname.co.uk
Fax: 01273 705451   Tel: 01273 277333

HARBOUR PICTURES
11 Langton Street, London SW10 0JL
Website: www.harbourpictures.com
e-mail: info@harbourpictures.com
Fax: 020-7352 3528   Tel: 020-7351 7070

HARTSWOOD FILMS
Twickenham Studios, The Barons
St Margaret's, Twickenham, Middlesex TW1 2AW
Fax: 020-8607 8744   Tel: 020-8607 8736

HASAN SHAH FILMS Ltd
153 Burnham Towers, Adelaide Rd, NW3 3JN
Fax: 020-7483 0662   Tel: 020-7722 2419

HAT TRICK PRODUCTIONS Ltd
TV Co
10 Livonia Street, London W1F 8AF
Fax: 020-7287 9791   Tel: 020-7434 2451

HAWK EYE FILMS
Twickenham Film Studios
The Barons, St Margarets
Twickenham, Middlesex TW1 2AW
Fax: 020-8241 1907   Tel: 020-8607 8873

HEAD Sally PRODUCTIONS
Twickenham Film Studios, The Barons
St Margaret's, Twickenham, Middlesex TW1 2AW
e-mail: admin@shpl.demon.co.uk
Fax: 020-8607 8964   Tel: 020-8607 8730

HEAVY ENTERTAINMENT Ltd
222 Kensal Road, London W10 5BN
Website: www.heavy-entertainment.com
e-mail: info@heavy-entertainment.com
Fax: 020-8960 9003   Tel: 020-8960 9001

HENSON Jim COMPANY
30 Oval Road, Camden, London NW1 7DE
Website: www.henson.com
Fax: 020-7428 4001   Tel: 020-7428 4000

HEWETT Yvonne
Optimum Productions, 32 Thames Eyot, Cross Deep
Twickenham TW1 4QL   Tel: 020-8892 1403

HINCHLIFFE Barrie PRODUCTIONS Ltd
Unit 2A, Utopia Village, 7 Chalcot Road
London NW1 8LH
Fax: 020-7722 6229   Tel: 020-7722 2261

HIT ENTERTAINMENT Plc
5th Floor, Maple Hse, 149 Tottenham Crt Rd W1T 7NF
Website: www.hitentertainment.com
e-mail: creative@hitentertainment.com
Fax: 020-7388 9321   Tel: 020-7554 2500

HOLMES ASSOCIATES & OPEN ROAD FILMS
F TV D
The Studio, 37 Redington Road, London NW3 7QY
e-mail: holmesassociates@blueyonder.co.uk
Fax: 020-7916 9172   Tel: 020-7813 4333

HUDSON FILM Ltd
24 St Leonard's Terrace
London SW3 4QG   Tel/Fax: 020-7730 0002

HUNGRY MAN Ltd
19 Grafton Mews, London W1T 5JB
Website: www.hungryman.com
e-mail: receptionuk@hungryman.com
Fax: 020-7380 8299   Tel: 020-7380 8280

HUNKY DORY PRODUCTIONS Ltd
TV D Co
Cambridge House
135 High Street, Teddington, Middlesex TW11 8HH
Fax: 020-8977 4464   Tel: 020-8943 3006

HURLL Michael TELEVISION Ltd
3rd Floor, Beaumont House, Kensington Village
Avonmore Road, London W14 8TS
e-mail: sgraff@uniquegroup.co.uk
Fax: 020-7605 1201   Tel: 020-7605 1200

HURRICANE FILMS Ltd
19 Hope Street, Liverpool L1 9BQ
Website: www.hurricanefilms.net
e-mail: sol@hurricanefilms.co.uk
Fax: 0151-707 9149   Tel: 0151-707 9700

IAMBIC PRODUCTIONS Ltd
1st Floor, 31 Eastcastle Street, London W1W 8DL
e-mail: team@iambicproductions.com
Fax: 020-7637 7084   Tel: 020-7436 1400

ICON FILMS Ltd
4 West End
Somerset Street, Bristol BS2 8NE
Fax: 0117-942 0386   Tel: 0117-924 8535

IMMEDIA TELEVISION COMMUNICATIONS Ltd
Carlton Studios,
Lenton Lane, Nottingham NG7 2NA
Website: www.immediagroup.co.uk
e-mail: info@immediagroup.co.uk
Fax: 0115-964 5502   Tel: 0115-964 5505

IMP/LONDON
1st Floor, 7-11 French Pl, Shoreditch EC1 6JB
Website: www.imp/london.com
                          Tel/Fax: 020-7729 1736

INFORMATION TRANSFER Ltd
CV (Training Video Packages)
Burleigh House, 15 Newmarket Road
Cambridge CB5 8EG
Fax: 01223 310200   Tel: 01223 312227

INTERESTING TELEVISION Ltd
Oakslade Studios, Station Road, Hatton
Warwick CV35 7LH
Fax: 01926 844045   Tel: 01926 844044

ISIS PRODUCTIONS Ltd
106 Hammersmith Grove, London W6 7HB
Website: www.isis-productions.co.uk
e-mail: isis@isis-productions.com
Fax: 020-8748 3046   Tel: 020-8748 3042

JACKSON Brian FILMS Ltd
F TV Ch
39-41 Hanover Steps, St George's Fields
Albion Street, London W2 2YG
e-mail: brianjfilm@aol.com
Fax: 020-7262 5736   Tel: 020-7402 7543

JMS GROUP Ltd
Hethersett, Norwich, Norfolk NR9 3DL
Website: www.jms-group.com
e-mail: info@jmsradio.co.uk
Fax: 01603 812255   Tel: 01603 811855

JOLL Barrie ASSOCIATES Ltd
58 Frith Street
London W1V 5TA   Tel: 020-7437 9965

JTA CREATIVE COMMUNICATIONS
The Old Rectory, Ombersley, Worcester
Worcestershire WR9 0EW
Website: www.jta.co.uk
e-mail: suzanne@jta.co.uk
Fax: 01905 823401   Tel: 01905 823400

JUSTABOUT PRODUCTIONS
4 Northington Street, London WC1N 2JG
Website: www.justabout.tv
Fax: 020-7692 9080   Tel: 020-7916 6200

KAYE Tony & PARTNERS
27-29 Beak Street, London W1F 9RU
Fax: 020-7025 7501   Tel: 020-7025 7542

KCD FILMS Ltd
6 Eglon Mews, Primrose Hill, London NW1 8YS
e-mail: bill@eglon.freeserve.co.uk
                          Tel: 020-7586 4813

KELPIE FILMS
227 St Andrews Road, Glasgow G41 1PD
Website: www.kelpiefilms.com
e-mail: info@kelpiefilms.com
Fax: 0141-429 8438   Tel: 0141-429 3565

KICK PRODUCTION Ltd
50 Greek Street, Soho, London W1D 4EQ
e-mail: admin@kickproduction.co.uk
Fax: 020-7437 0125   Tel: 020-7287 3757

KINGFISHER TELEVISION
Carlton Studios, Lenton Lane, Nottingham NG7 2NA
Fax: 0115-964 5263   Tel: 0115-964 5262

KNOWLES Dave FILMS
(Also Multimedia Interactive CD-Roms)
34 Ashleigh Close, Hythe SO45 3QP
Website: www.dkfilms.co.uk
e-mail: mail@dkfilms.co.uk
Fax: 023-8084 1600   Tel: 023-8084 2190

LANDSEER PRODUCTIONS Ltd
140 Royal College Street, London NW1 0TA
Website: www.landseerfilms.com
e-mail: mail@landseerfilms.com
Fax: 020-7485 7573   Tel: 020-7485 7333

LARGE BEAST PRODUCTIONS Ltd
38 Rowallan Road, London SW6 6AG
Website: www.largebeastproductions.com
e-mail: e-mail@largebeastproductions.com
                          Tel/Fax: 020-7381 8228

LE PARK TV Ltd
Windmill Studios, 49-51 York Road, Brentford
Middlesex TW8 0QP
Website: www.leparktv.com   e-mail: ian@leparktv.com
Fax: 020-8568 4151   Tel: 020-8568 5855

LENIHAN Sean ASSOCIATES
The Old Chapel, Abbey Hill, Lerant, St Ives
Cornwall TR26 3EB   Tel/Fax: 01736 757557

LIGHT DIVISION
11 Christchurch Gardens, Reading
Berkshire RG2 7AH   Tel: 0118-931 3859

LINK ENTERTAINMENT Ltd
Colet Court
100 Hammersmith Road, London W6 7JP
Fax: 020-8762 6299   Tel: 020-8762 6200

LITTLE BIRD COMPANY Ltd
9 Grafton Mews, London W1T 5HZ
e-mail: info@littlebird.co.uk
Fax: 020-7380 3981   Tel: 020-7380 3980

LITTLE KING COMMUNICATIONS
The Studio, 2 Newport Road, Barnes
London SW13 9PE
Fax: 020-8653 2742   Tel: 020-8741 7658

LITTLE WING FILMS Ltd
The Old Laundry, Ossington Buildings
London W1V 4JZ
Website: www.lwf.info   e-mail: lwf@info
Fax: 020-7935 1970   Tel: 020-7486 6550

LIVE IN FIVE PRODUCTIONS
14 Kingsmead Road, London SW2 3JB
Website: www.liveinfive.co.uk
e-mail: enquiries@liveinfive.co.uk
Fax: 020-8674 5964   Tel: 020-8674 5964

LONDON COLLEGE OF PRINTING SCHOOL OF MEDIA
(Film & Video Division)
Elephant & Castle, London SE1 6SB
Fax: 020-7514 6848   Tel: 020-7514 6500

LONDON FILMS
71 South Audley Street, London W1K 1JA
Website: www.londonfilms.com
Fax: 020-7499 7994   Tel: 020-7499 7800

LONDON SCIENTIFIC FILMS
Mill Studio, Crane Mead, Ware
Hertfordshire SG12 9PY   Tel: 01920 444399

LOOKING GLASS FILMS Ltd
103 Brittany Point, Ethelred Estate
Kennington, London SE11 6UH
e-mail: lookingglassfilm@aol.com
                              Tel/Fax: 020-7735 1363

LOOP COMMUNICATION AGENCY The
Hanover House
Queen Charlotte Street, Bristol BS1 4EX
e-mail: stephen.williams@theloopagency.com
Fax: 0117-311 2041   Tel: 0117-311 2040

MAGICIAN PICTURES Ltd
Suite 2E, Horseshoe Business Park, Upper Lye Lane
Bricket Wood, Hertfordshire AL2 3TA
Website: www.magician-pictures.co.uk
e-mail: admin@magician-pictures.co.uk
Fax: 01923 673808   Tel: 01923 661499

MAGPIE FILM PRODUCTIONS Ltd
31-32 Cheapside, Birmingham B5 6AY
Fax: 0121-666 6077   Tel: 0121-622 5884

MALLINSON TELEVISION PRODUCTIONS
(TV Commercials)
29 Lynedoch Street, Glasgow G3 6EF
e-mail: shoot@mtp.co.uk
Fax: 0141-332 6190   Tel: 0141-332 0589

MALONE GILL PRODUCTIONS Ltd
27 Campden Hill Road, London W8 7DX
e-mail: malonegill@aol.com
Fax: 020-7376 1727   Tel: 020-7937 0557

MANIC TELEVISION & FILM
101 Skyline Plaza, 80 Commercial Rd, E1 1NY
Website: www.themanicgroup.com
e-mail: info@themanicgroup.com
Fax: 020-7709 7867   Tel: 020-7709 0637

MANS Johnny PRODUCTIONS Ltd
PO Box 196, Hoddesdon, Hertfordshire EN10 7WG
Fax: 01992 470516   Tel: 01992 470907

MANSFIELD Mike TELEVISION Ltd
5th Floor, 41-42 Berners Street, London W1T 3NB
e-mail: mikemantv@aol.com
Fax: 020-7580 2582   Tel: 020-7580 2581

MANUEL Jo PRODUCTIONS Ltd
11 Keslake Road, London NW6 6DJ
e-mail: jomanuel@cwcom.net
Fax: 020-8933 5475   Tel: 020-8930 0777

MAP FILMS
3 Bourlet Close, London W1W 7BQ
e-mail: mail@mapfilms.com
Fax: 020-7291 7841   Tel: 020-7291 7840

MARTIN William PRODUCTIONS
The Studio, Tubney Warren Barns, Tubney
Oxfordshire OX13 5QJ
Website: www.wmproductions.co.uk
e-mail: info@wmproductions.co.uk
Fax: 01865 390234   Tel: 01865 390258

MAVERICK MEDIA Ltd
5th Floor, 74 Newman Street, London W1T 3EL
Website: www.maverickmedia.co.uk
e-mail: info@maverickmedia.co.uk
Fax: 020-7323 4143   Tel: 020-7291 3450

MAVERICK TELEVISION
The Custard Factory, Gibb Street
Birmingham B9 4AA
e-mail: mail@mavericktv.co.uk
Fax: 0121-771 1550   Tel: 0121-771 1812

MAX MEDIA
The Lilacs, West End, Woodhurst, Huntingdon
Cambridge PE28 3BH
Website: www.therealmaxmedia.com
e-mail: therealmaxmedia@aol.com
Fax: 01487 823468   Tel: 01487 823608

MAYA VISION INTERNATIONAL
43 New Oxford Street
London WC1A 1BH   Tel: 020-7836 1113

MEANPEACH
11 Coniston Court
Hanger Hill, Weybridge, Surrey KT13 9YR
Website: www.meanpeach.com
e-mail: info@meanpeach.com
Fax: 01932 855598   Tel: 01932 858724

MENTORN
43 Whitfield Street, London W1T 4HA
Fax: 020-7258 6888   Tel: 020-7258 6800

MERCHANT IVORY PRODUCTIONS
46 Lexington Street, London W1F 0LP
Website: www.merchantivory.com
e-mail: miplondon@merchantivory.demon.co.uk
Fax: 020-7734 1579   Tel: 020-7437 1200

MERSEY TELEVISION COMPANY Ltd The
TV
Campus Manor, Childwall, Abbey Road
Liverpool L16 0JP
Fax: 0151-722 6839   Tel: 0151-722 9122

MIGHTY MEDIA
Long Boyds House, PO Box 73, Bourne End
Buckinghamshire SL8 5FJ
Fax: 01628 526530   Tel: 01628 522002

MINAMON PRODUCTIONS
117 Downton Avenue, London SW2 3TX
Website: www.minamonfilm.co.uk
e-mail: info@minamonfilm.co.uk
Fax: 020-8674 1779   Tel: 020-8674 3957

MISTRAL FILM LONDON
31 Oval Road, London NW1 7EA
e-mail: info@mistralfilm.co.uk
Fax: 020-7284 0547   Tel: 020-7284 2300

MODUS OPERANDI FILMS
10 Soho Square, London W1V 6NT
Fax: 020-7287 6852   Tel: 020-7434 1440

MOGUL CORPORATION The
60 Aubert Park, London N5 1TS
Fax: 020-7242 2860   Tel: 020-7242 2850

MOONLIGHT COMMUNICATIONS Ltd
48 Vyse Street, Hockley, Birmingham B18 6HF
e-mail: norman.moonlight@btclick.com
Fax: 0121-551 6455   Tel: 0121-523 6221

MORE Alan FILMS
Pinewood Studios, Pinewood Road
Iver, Bucks SL0 0NH
e-mail: almorefilm@aol.com
Fax: 01753 650988   Tel: 01753 656789

MORNINGSIDE PRODUCTIONS INC
8 Ilchester Place, London W14 8AA
Fax: 020-7602 1047   Tel: 020-7602 2382

MORRISON COMPANY The
302 Clive Court, Maida Vale, London W9 1SF
e-mail: don@morrisonco.com
Fax: 0870 1275065   Tel/Fax: 020-7289 7976

MOSAIC FILMS
The Old Butcher's Shop, St Briavels
Gloucestershire GL15 6TA
e-mail: info@mosaicfilms.com
Fax: 01594 530094   Tel: 01594 530708

MOVE A MOUNTAIN PRODUCTIONS
5 Ashchurch Park Villas, London W12 9SP
Website: www.moveamountain.com
e-mail: mail@moveamountain.com
Fax: 020-8743 3095   Tel: 020-8743 3017

MURPHY Patricia FILMS Ltd
14 Lawford's Wharf, Lyme Street, London NW1 0SF
e-mail: info@patriciamurphy.co.uk
Fax: 020-7485 0555   Tel: 020-7267 0007

NEBRASKA PRODUCTIONS
12 Grove Avenue, London N10 2AR
e-mail: nebraskaprods@aol.com
Fax: 020-8444 2113   Tel: 020-8444 5317

NEW MOON PRODUCTIONS
5 Newburgh Street, London W1F 7RG
Website: www.new-moon.co.uk
e-mail: production@new-moon.co.uk
Fax: 020-7479 7011   Tel: 020-7479 7010

NEWGATE COMPANY
(Radio)
13 Dafford Street, Larkhall, Bath
Somerset BA1 6SW   Tel: 01225 318335

NEXUS PRODUCTIONS Ltd
(Animation for Commercials & Pop Promos)
113-114 Shoreditch High Street, London E1 6JN
Website: www.nexusproductions.com
e-mail: info@nexusproductions.com
Fax: 020-7749 7501   Tel: 020-7749 7500

NUTOPIA FILMS
Number 8, 132 Charing Cross Road
London WC2H 0LA
Website: www.nutopia.co.uk
Fax: 029-2070 9440   Mobile: 07801 493133

OMNI PRODUCTIONS Ltd
Studio 44, Easton Business Centre, Felix Road
Bristol BS5 0HE
Website: www.omniproductions.co.uk
e-mail: creation@omniproductions.co.uk
                                  Tel: 0117-941 5820

ON COMMUNICATION/ON TV
(Work across all Media in Business Communications,
Museum Prods & Broadcast Docs)
5 East St Helen Street, Abingdon, Oxford OX14 5EG
Website: www.oncomms-tv.co.uk
e-mail: on@oncomms-tv.co.uk
Fax: 01235 530581   Tel: 01235 537400

ON SCREEN PRODUCTIONS Ltd
39 Cardiff Road, Llandaff, Cardiff CF5 2DP
Website: www.onscreenproductions.co.uk
e-mail: action@onscreenproductions.co.uk
Fax: 029-2057 8496   Tel: 029-2056 7593

**OPEN DOORS TELEVSION PRODUCTIONS
COMPANY Ltd**
Les Plames, No 6, 2 Rathmore Road
Torquay, Devon TQ2 6NY
e-mail: barrygout@hotmail.com
Mobile: 07899 965420   Tel: 01803 200558

OPEN MIND PRODUCTIONS
6 Newburgh Street, London W1F 7RQ
e-mail: imogen.robertson@openmind.co.uk
Fax: 020-7434 9256   Tel: 020-7437 0624

OPEN SHUTTER PRODUCTIONS Ltd
100 Kings Road, Windsor
Berkshire SL4 2AP   Tel/Fax: 01753 841309

**ORCHARD COMMUNICATIONS
DESIGN GROUP Ltd The**
(Interactive Multimedia Production)
Langler House, Market Place, Somerton
Somerset TA11 7LZ
e-mail: lesley@orchardcdg.co.uk
Fax: 01458 274590   Tel: 01458 274589

ORIGINAL FILM & VIDEO PRODUCTIONS Ltd
84 St Dionis Road, London SW6 4TU
e-mail: original.films@btinternet.com
Fax: 020-7731 0027   Tel: 020-7731 0012

OSBORN Peter PRODUCTION Ltd
Square Red Studio, 249-251 Kensal Road
London W10 5DB
e-mail: peter@peterosborn.net
Fax: 020-8968 1517   Tel: 020-8960 6069

OVC MEDIA Ltd
88 Berkeley Court
Baker Street, London NW1 5ND
Website: www.ovcmedia.com
e-mail: eliot@ovcmedia.co.uk
Fax: 020-7723 3064   Tel: 020-7402 9111

PALADIN INVISION
8 Barb Mews, London W6 7PA
Fax: 020-7371 2160   Tel: 020-7371 2123

PALIN Barry ASSOCIATES
Unit 10, Princeton Court, 55 Felsham Road
London SW15 1AZ
e-mail: mail@barrypalinassociates.com
Fax: 020-8785 0440   Tel: 020-8394 5660

PANTECHNICON
90 Lots Road, London SW10 0QD
e-mail: info@pantechnicon.co.uk
Fax: 020-7351 0667   Tel: 020-7351 7579

PAPER MOON PRODUCTIONS
Wychwood House
Burchetts Green Lane
Littlewick Green, Maidenhead, Berkshire SL6 3QW
e-mail: david@paper-moon.co.uk
Fax: 01628 825949   Tel: 01628 829819

PARADINE David PRODUCTIONS Ltd
1st Floor, 5 St Mary Abbot's Place
Kensington, London W8 6LS
Fax: 020-7602 0411   Tel: 020-7371 3111

PARALLAX INDEPENDENT Ltd
7 Denmark Street, London WC2H 8LZ
Fax: 020-7497 8062   Tel: 020-7836 1478

PARAMOUNT FILM SERVICES Ltd
UIP House, 45 Beadon Road, London W6 0EG
Fax: 020-8563 4266   Tel: 020-8563 4158

PARK VILLAGE Ltd
1 Park Village East, London NW1 7PX
e-mail: reception@parkvillage.co.uk
Fax: 020-7388 3051   Tel: 020-7387 8077

PARLIAMENTARY FILMS Ltd
11A Enterprise House
59-65 Upper Ground, London SE1 9PQ
Fax: 020-7827 9511   Tel: 020-7827 9514

PARTNERS IN PRODUCTION Ltd
Hillview, Hinders Lane
Huntley, Gloucestershire GL19 3EZ
Fax: 01452 830500   Mobile: 07802 967369

PASSION PICTURES Ltd
Animation
3rd Floor, 33-34 Rathbone Place, London W1T 1TN
e-mail: info@passion-pictures.com
Fax: 020-7323 9030   Tel: 020-7323 9933

PATCHOULI FILMS
40 Princess Street, Manchester M1 6DE
Website: www.patchoulifilms.net
e-mail: info@patchoulifilms.net
Fax: 0161-234 0001   Tel: 0161-234 0135

PATHE PICTURES Ltd
Kent House, 14-17 Market Place
Great Titchfield Street, London W1W 8AR
Website: www.pathe.co.uk
Fax: 020-7631 3568   Tel: 020-7323 5151

PCI LIVE DESIGN
(Live Events, Live Design Exhibitions,
Film & Video, 2D & 3D Design)
G4 Harbour Yard
Chelsea Harbour, London SW10 0XD
Fax: 020-7352 7906   Tel: 020-7544 7500

PEARSON TELEVISION
1 Stephen Street, London W1T 1AL
Fax: 020-7691 6100   Tel: 020-7691 6000

PICTURE PALACE FILMS Ltd
13 Egbert Street, London NW1 8LJ
Website: www.picturepalace.com
e-mail: info@picturepalace.com
Fax: 020-7586 9048   Tel: 020-7586 8763

PIE FILMS
Write: PO Box 42301, London N12 9YR
Website: www.pie.uk.net   e-mail: film@pie.uk.net

PIER PRODUCTIONS Ltd
Lower Ground Floor
1 Marlborough Place, Brighton BN1 1TU
e-mail: pieradmin@mistral.co.uk
Fax: 01273 693658   Tel: 01273 691401

PIEREND PRODUCTIONS
34 Fortis Green, London N2 9EL
e-mail: russell@pierend.fsnet.co.uk
Tel: 020-8444 0138

POKER Ltd
143B Whitehall Court
London SW1A 2EL   Tel/Fax: 020-7839 6070

POSITIVE IMAGE Ltd
25 Victoria Street, Windsor, Berkshire SL4 1HE
Fax: 01753 830878   Tel: 01753 842248

POZZITIVE TELEVISION Ltd
Paramount House
162-170 Wardour Street, London W1F 8AB
e-mail: pozzitive@pozzitive.demon.co.uk
Fax: 020-7437 3130   Tel: 020-7734 3258

PRETTY CLEVER PICTURES
Post 59, Shepperton Studios, Studios Road
Shepperton, Middlesex TW17 0QD
e-mail: pcpics@globalnet.co.uk
Fax: 01932 592454   Tel: 01932 592047

PRINCIPAL PICTURES Ltd
Picture House
65 Hopton Street, London SE1 9LR
e-mail: pictures@principalmedia.com
Fax: 020-7928 9886   Tel: 020-7928 9287

PRISM ENTERTAINMENT
1-2 Grand Union Centre
West Row Courtyard, London W10 5AS
Website: www.prismentertainment.co.uk
e-mail: info@prism-e.com
Fax: 020-8969 1012   Tel: 020-8969 1212

PRODUCERS The
8 Berners Mews, London W1T 3AW
Website: www.theproducersfilms.co.uk
Fax: 020-7636 4099   Tel: 020-7636 4226

PRODUCTION LINKS
59 Cotham Hill, Bristol BS6 6JR
Website: www.productionlinks.tv
e-mail: info@productionlinks.tv
Fax: 0117-923 7003   Tel: 0117-906 4344

**PROFESSIONAL MEDICAL
COMMUNICATIONS Ltd**
Grosvenor House, 1 High Street, Edgware
Middlesex HA8 7TA   Tel: 020-8381 1819

PROMENADE ENTERPRISES Ltd
6 Russell Grove, London SW9 6HS
e-mail: promenadeproductions@msn.com
Fax: 020-7564 3026   Tel: 020-7582 9354

PSA Ltd
52 The Downs, Altrincham WA14 2QJ
Fax: 0161-924 0022   Tel: 0161-924 0011

PURPLE FROG MEDIA Ltd
19 Westbourne Gardens, Hove BN3 5PL
e-mail: julie@purplefrogmedia.com
Fax: 01273 775787   Tel: 01273 735475

PVA MANAGEMENT Ltd
Hallow Park, Hallow, Worcs WR2 6PG
e-mail: films@pva.co.uk
Fax: 01905 641842   Tel: 01905 640663

QUADRANT TELEVISION Ltd
17 West Hill
London SW18 1RB
Website: www.quadrant-tv.com
e-mail: quadranttv@aol.com   Tel: 020-8870 9933

QUADRILLION
The Old Barn, Kings Lane, Cookham Dean
Berkshire SL6 9AY
Website: www.quadrillion.tv
e-mail: enq@quadrillion.net
Fax: 01628 487523   Tel: 01628 487522

QUARK TV Ltd
5 Broadway Market Mews
Benjamin Close, London E8 4TS
Website: www.quarktv.co.uk
e-mail: quarktv@btclick.com
Fax: 020-7241 1451   Tel: 020-7254 5049

RAW CHARM Ltd
Ty Cefn, Rectory Road, Cardiff CF5 1QL
Website: www.rawcharm.tv
e-mail: pam@rawcharm.co.uk
Fax: 029-2066 8220   Tel: 029-2064 1511

READ Rodney
45 Richmond Rd, Twickenham, Middx TW1 3AW
e-mail: rodney_read@hotmail.com
Fax: 020-8744 9603   Tel: 020-8891 2875

RECORDED PICTURE COMPANY Ltd
24-26 Hanway Street, London W1T 1UH
Fax: 020-7636 2261   Tel: 020-7636 2251

RED BARN PRODUCTIONS Ltd
118 Clonmore Street, London SW18 5HB
e-mail: film@creativewizard.com
Fax: 020-8516 5948   Tel: 020-8637 0955

RED KITE PRODUCTIONS
89 Giles Street, Edinburgh EH6 6BZ
Website: www.redkite-animation.com
e-mail: info@redkite-animation.com
Fax: 0131-554 6007   Tel: 0131-554 0060

Film, Radio, Television & Video Production Companies

RED ROSE CHAIN
1 Fore Hamlet, Ipswich IP3 8AA
Website: www.redrosechain.co.uk
e-mail: info@redrosechain.co.uk Tel: 01473 288886

REDWEATHER PRODUCTIONS
Easton Business Centre, Felix Road, Bristol BS5 0HE
Website: www.redweather.co.uk
e-mail: info@redweather.co.uk
Fax: 0117-941 5851 Tel: 0117-941 5854

REEL EDITING COMPANY The
65 Goldhawk Road, London W12 8EH
Fax: 020-8743 2345 Tel: 020-8743 5100

REEL THING Ltd The
20 The Chase, Coulsdon, Surrey CR5 2EG
Website: www.reelthing.tv
e-mail: info@reelthing.tv Tel: 020-8668 8188

REPLAY Ltd
199 Piccadilly, London W1J 9HA
Website: www.replayfilms.co.uk
e-mail: sales@replayfilms.co.uk
Fax: 020-7287 5348 Tel: 020-7287 5334

RESOURCE BASE
Television Centre, Southampton SO14 0PZ
Website: www.resource-base.co.uk
e-mail: post@resource-base.co.uk
Fax: 023-8023 6816 Tel: 023-8023 6806

REUTERS TELEVISION
85 Fleet Street, London EC4P 4AJ
Fax: 020-7542 5401 Tel: 020-7250 1122

REVERE ENTERTAINMENT
91 Berwick Street, London W1F 0NE
Fax: 020-7292 8372 Tel: 020-7292 8370

RIVERSIDE TV STUDIOS
Riverside Studios, Crisp Road, London W6 9RL
e-mail: info@riversidetv.co.uk
Fax: 020-8237 1121 Tel: 020-8237 1123

RM ASSOCIATES
Shepherds West, Rockley Road
London W14 0DA Tel: 020-7605 6600

ROCLIFFE
PO Box 37344, London N1 8YB
Website: www.rocliffe.com
e-mail: info@rocliffe.com Tel/Fax: 020-7688 0749

ROGERS Peter PRODUCTIONS Ltd
Pinewood Studios, Iver Heath
Buckinghamshire SL0 0NH Tel: 01753 651700

ROGUE VIDEO
(Video Production)
297 Glyn Road, London E5 0JP
Website: www.roguevideo.com
e-mail: genevieve@roguevideo.com
Mobile: 07711 863573 Tel/Fax: 020-8533 3877

ROOKE Laurence PRODUCTIONS
14 Aspinall House, 155 New Park Road
London SW2 4EY
Mobile: 07765 652058 Tel: 020-8674 3128

ROSE HACKNEY BARBER Ltd
5-6 Kingly Street, London W1B 5PF
Fax: 020-7434 4102 Tel: 020-7439 6697

RSA FILMS
42-44 Beak Street, London W1F 9RH
Fax: 020-7734 4978 Tel: 020-7437 7426

RUSSO Denis ASSOCIATES
F TV Animation
161 Clapham Road, London SW9 0PU
Fax: 020-7582 2725 Tel: 020-7582 9664

SAMUELSON PRODUCTIONS Ltd
13 Manette Street, London W1D 4AW
e-mail: samuelsonp@aol.com
Fax: 020-7439 4901 Tel: 020-7439 4900

SANDS FILMS
Grice's Wharf, 119 Rotherhithe Street
London SE16 4NF
Website: www.sandsfilms.co.uk
Fax: 020-7231 2119 Tel: 020-7231 2209

SCALA PRODUCTIONS Ltd
15 Frith Street, London W1D 4RE
e-mail: scalaprods@aol.com
Fax: 020-7437 3248 Tel: 020-7734 7060

SCIMITAR FILMS Ltd
219 Kensington High Street, London W8 6BD
e-mail: winner@ftech.co.uk
Fax: 020-7602 9217 Tel: 020-7734 8385

SCREEN FIRST Ltd
The Studios
Funnells Farm, Down Street
Nutley, East Sussex TN22 3LF
e-mail: paul.madden@virgin.net
Fax: 01825 713511 Tel: 01825 712034

SCREEN VENTURES
49 Goodge Street
London W1T 1TE Tel: 020-7580 7448

SEDDON Julian FILMS Ltd
(Commercials)
51-53 Mount Pleasant, London WC1X 0AE
e-mail: julian@julianseddonfilms.com
Fax: 020-7405 3721 Tel: 020-7831 3033

SEPTEMBER FILMS Ltd
Glen House, 22 Glenthorne Road
Hammersmith, London W6 0NG
Fax: 020-8741 7214 Tel: 020-8563 9393

SEVENTH ART PRODUCTIONS
63 Ship Street, Brighton BN1 1AE
Website: www.seventh-art.com
e-mail: info@seventh-art.com
Fax: 01273 323777 Tel: 01273 777678

SHART BROS Ltd
52 Lancaster Road, London N4 4PR
Fax: 020-7436 9233 Tel: 020-7263 4435

SHELL FILM & VIDEO UNIT
F CV Docs
Shell Centre, York Road, London SE1 7NA
Fax: 020-7934 7490 Tel: 020-7934 3318

SHELL LIKE
Whitfield House
81 Whitfield Street, London W1T 4HG
Website: www.shelllike.com
e-mail: lucy@shelllike.com
Fax: 020-7255 5255 Tel: 020-7255 5201

SIGHTLINE
(Videos, Commercials, CD-Rom, DVD, Websites)
Dylan House, Town End Road, Godalming
Surrey GU7 1BQ
Website: www.sightline.co.uk
e-mail: admin@sightline.co.uk
Fax: 01483 861516 Tel: 01483 861555

SILK PRODUCTION
13 Berwick Street, London W1F 0PW
Website: www.silkproduction.com
e-mail: production@silkproduction.com
Fax: 020-7494 1748 Tel: 020-7434 3461

SILVER CLOUD TELEVISION
Ivy Cottage
Main Street, Elvington, York YO41 4AA
e-mail: info@silvercloudltd.com
Tel/Fax: 01904 607625

SILVER PRODUCTIONS Ltd
Bridge Farm, Lower Road, Britford
Salisbury, Wiltshire SP5 4DY
Fax: 01722 336227 Tel: 01722 336221

SINDIBAD FILMS Ltd
5th Floor
5 Princes Gate, London SW7 1QJ
Website: www.sindibad.co.uk
e-mail: sindibad@lineone.net
Fax: 020-7823 9137   Tel: 020-7823 7488

SKREBA
Write
17 Gladstone Street, London SE1 6EY

SMITH & WATSON PRODUCTIONS
The Gothic House
Fore Street, Totnes, Devon TQ9 5EH
Website: www.smithandwatson.com
e-mail: info@smithandwatson.com
Fax: 01803 864219   Tel: 01803 863033

SNEEZING TREE FILMS
C
1-2 Bromley Place, London W1T 6DA
e-mail: sneezingtree@compuserve.com
Fax: 020-7927 9909   Tel: 020-7927 9900

SOMERFILM Ltd
20 Stirling Street
Dundee DD3 6PH
e-mail: somerfilm@aol.com
Fax: 0800 4581901   Tel/Fax: 0800 4581900

SONY PICTURES EUROPE HOUSE
25 Golden Square, London W1F 9LU
Fax: 020-7533 1015   Tel: 020-7533 1000

SOREL STUDIOS
10 Palace Court
Palace Road, London SW2 3ED
e-mail: info@sorelstudios.co.uk   Tel/Fax: 020-8671 2168

SOUTHERN STAR
45-49 Mortimer Street
London W1W 8HX   Tel: 020-7636 9421

SPACE CITY PRODUCTIONS
77 Blythe Road, London W14 0HP
Website: www.spacecity.co.uk
e-mail: info@spacecity.co.uk
Fax: 020-7371 4001   Tel: 020-7371 4000

SPEAKEASY PRODUCTIONS Ltd
Wildwood House, Stanley, Perth PH1 4PX
Website: www.speak.co.uk
e-mail: info@speak.co.uk
Fax: 01738 828419   Tel: 01738 828524

SPECIFIC FILMS Ltd
25 Rathbone Street, London W1T 1NQ
e-mail: info@specificfilms.com
Fax: 020-7494 2676   Tel: 020-7580 7476

SPELLBOUND PRODUCTIONS Ltd
90 Cowdenbeath Path
Islington, London N1 0LG
e-mail: phspellbound@hotmail.com
                         Tel/Fax: 020-7713 8066

SPINSTER Ltd
71 Whinney Hill, Holywood, County Down
Northern Ireland BT18 0HG
Website: www.spinster-associates.com
e-mail: info@spinster-associates.com
Fax: 028-9042 2888   Tel: 028-9042 2088

SPIRAL PRODUCTIONS Ltd
Aberdeen Studios, 22 Highbury Grove
London N5 2EA
Fax: 020-7359 6123   Tel: 020-7354 5492

SPIRIT FILMS Ltd
1 Wedgwood Mews, 12-13 Greek Street
London W1D 4BA
e-mail: producer@spiritfilms.co.uk
Fax: 020-7734 9850   Tel: 020-7734 6642

STANDFAST FILMS
F TV D
The Studio, 14 College Rd, Bromley, Kent BR1 3NS
Fax: 020-8313 0443   Tel: 020-8466 5580

STAR PRODUCTIONS
F CV D
Star Studios, 36 Lea Bridge Road
London E5 9QD   Tel: 020-8986 4470

STEEL SPYDA Ltd
96-98 Undley, Lakenheath, Suffolk IP27 9BY
Website: www.steelspyda.com
e-mail: kay.hill@steelspyda.com
Fax: 01842 862880   Tel: 01842 862875

STONE PRODUCTIONS
Lakeside Studio, 62 Mill Street, St Osyth
Essex CO16 8EW
Fax: 01255 822160   Tel: 01255 822172

STRAWBERRY PRODUCTIONS Ltd
36 Priory Avenue, London W4 1TY
e-mail: strawprod1@aol.com
Fax: 020-8742 7675   Tel: 020-8994 4494

STREETWISE TV
11-15 Betterton Street, Covent Garden
London WC2H 9BP
e-mail: streetwisetv@hotmail.com
Fax: 020-7379 0801   Tel: 020-7470 8825

STUDIO AKA
(Animation)
30 Berwick Street, London W1F 8RH
Website: www.studioaka.co.uk
e-mail: info@studioaka.co.uk
Fax: 020-7437 2309   Tel: 020-7434 3581

SUN DANCE FILMS Ltd
6 Glamorgan Road, Hampton Wick, Kingston
Surrey KT1 4HP
Fax: 020-8977 9441   Tel: 020-8977 1791

SUNFLOWER PRODUCTIONS
(Docs TV)
106 Mansfield Drive, Merstham, Surrey RH1 3JN
Fax: 01737 271231   Tel: 01737 642829

SWIVEL FILMS
4th Floor, 23 Denmark Street, London WC2H 8NA
Fax: 020-7240 4486   Tel: 020-7240 4485

TABARD PRODUCTIONS
Adam House, 7-10 Adam Street
London WC2N 6AA
e-mail: info@tabard.co.uk
Fax: 020-7497 0830   Tel: 020-7497 0850

TABLE TOP PRODUCTIONS
1 The Orchard,
Bedford Park, Chiswick, London W4 1JZ
e-mail: berry@tabletopproductions.com
                         Tel/Fax: 020-8742 0507

TAILOR-MADE FILMS
Units 16 & 17, Waterside, 44-48 Wharf Road
London N1 7UX
Website: www.tailormadefilm.net
e-mail: info@tailormadefilms.net
Fax: 020-7253 1117   Tel: 020-7566 0280

TAKE 3 PRODUCTIONS Ltd
72 Margaret Street, London W1W 8ST
Website: www.take3.co.uk
e-mail: mail@take3.co.uk
Fax: 020-7637 4678   Tel: 020-7637 2694

TAKE FIVE PRODUCTIONS
CV Docs
25 Ganton Street, London W1F 9BP
Website: www.takefivestudio.co.uk
Fax: 020-7287 3035   Tel: 020-7287 2120

TALISMAN FILMS Ltd
5 Addison Place, London W11 4RJ
e-mail: email@talismanfilms.com
Fax: 020-7602 7422   Tel: 020-7603 7474

TALKBACK PRODUCTIONS Ltd
20-21 Newman Street, London W1T 1PG
Fax: 020-7861 8001   Tel: 020-7861 8000

TALKING PICTURES
Swallowtiles, High Street, Drayton
St Leonard, Wallingford OX10 7BQ
Website: www.talkingpictures.co.uk
e-mail: info@talkingpictures.co.uk
Fax: 01865 890504   Tel: 01865 890851

TANDEM TV & FILM Ltd
10 Bargrove Avenue
Hemel Hempstead, Herts HP1 1QP
Website: www.tandemtv.com
e-mail: ttv@tandemtv.com
Fax: 01442 219250   Tel: 01442 261576

TAYLOR David ASSOCIATES Ltd
F CV D Ch
25 Wensley Drive, Hazel Grove
Stockport SK7 6EW   Tel/Fax: 01625 850887

TB TV - TONY BASTABLE TELEVISION
The White Hse, Church Rd, Lingfield, Surrey RH7 6AH
e-mail: tbtv@msn.com
Fax: 01342 834600   Tel: 01342 834588

TELEVIRTUAL Ltd
Thorpe House, 7G Thorpe Road, Norwich NR1 1UA
Website: www.televirtual.com
e-mail: sue@televirtual.com
Fax: 01603 764946   Tel: 01603 767493

TELEVISION BUSINESS The
The Old Vicarage, Church Road, Emneth
Norfolk PE14 8AF
Mobile: 07970 088040   Tel: 01945 467157

THIN MAN FILMS
9 Greek Street, London W1D 4DQ
e-mail: info@thinman.co.uk
Fax: 020-7287 5228   Tel: 020-7734 7372

TKO COMMUNICATIONS Ltd
PO Box 130, Hove, Sussex BN3 6QU
e-mail: jskruger@tkogroup.com
Fax: 01273 540969   Tel: 01273 550088

TMB MARKETING COMMUNICATIONS
Milton Heath Hse, Westcott Rd, Dorking RH4 3NB
Website: www.tmbmmarcom.com
e-mail: www.mail@motivation.co.uk
Fax: 01306 877777   Tel: 01306 877000

TOP BANANA
Wassell Grove Business Centre, Wassell Grove Lane
Stourbridge, West Midlands DY9 9JH
Website: www.top-b.com
e-mail: talk@top-b.com
Fax: 01562 881011   Tel: 01562 881010

TOPICAL TELEVISION
Topical Television,
TV Centre, Southampton SO14 0PZ
Fax: 023-8033 9835   Tel: 023-8071 2233

TV MEDIA SERVICES Ltd/TVMS
3rd Floor, 420 Sauchiehall Street, Glasgow G2 3JD
e-mail: mail@tvms.fsnet.co.uk
Fax: 0141-332 9040   Tel: 0141-331 1993

TV PRODUCTION PARTNERSHIP Ltd
4 Fullerton Manor, Fullerton, Hants SP11 7LA
e-mail: dbj@tvpp.tv   Tel: 01264 861440

TVE Ltd
(Broadcast Facilities, Non-Linear Editing)
TVE House, Wick Drive, New Milton
Hampshire BH25 6RH
e-mail: avid@tvehire.com
Fax: 01425 625021   Tel: 01425 625020

TVF
375 City Road, London EC1V 1NB
Fax: 020-7833 2185   Tel: 020-7837 3000

TWENTIETH CENTURY FOX TELEVISION Ltd
Twentieth Century Hse, 31-32 Soho Sq W1D 3AP
Fax: 020-7434 2170   Tel: 020-7437 7766

TWO SIDES TV Ltd
53A Brewer Street, London W1F 9UH
e-mail: info@2sidestv.co.uk
Fax: 020-7287 2289   Tel: 020-7439 9882

TWOFOUR PRODUCTIONS Ltd
Quay West Studios, Old Newnham
Plymouth PL7 5BH
e-mail: enq@twofour.co.uk
Fax: 01752 344224   Tel: 01752 333900

TWOTHREEFIVE Ltd
107-109 Temple Chambers
3-7 Temple Avenue, London EC4Y 0HP
Website: www.twothreefivepictures.com
e-mail: info@twothreefivepictures.com
                                      Tel: 020-7936 3888

TYBURN FILM PRODUCTIONS Ltd
F
Cippenham Court, Cippenham Lane, Cippenham
Nr Slough, Berkshire SL1 5AU
Fax: 01753 691785   Tel: 01753 516767

TYRO PRODUCTIONS
The Coach House, 20A Park Road, Teddington
Middlesex TW11 0AQ
Fax: 020-8943 4901   Tel: 020-8943 4697

UMTV Ltd
4-8 Rodney Street, London N1 9JH
Website: www.umtv.tv   e-mail: production@umtv.tv
Fax: 020-7713 9551   Tel: 020-7278 3021

UNGER Kurt
112 Portsea Hall, Portsea Place, London W2 2BZ
Fax: 020-7706 4818   Tel: 020-7262 9013

UNIQUE TELEVISION
3rd Floor, Beaumont House, Kensington Village
Avonmore Road, London W14 8TS
e-mail: london@uniquegroup.co.uk
Fax: 020-7605 1101   Tel: 020-7605 1100

UNITED PRODUCTIONS & LWT PRODUCTIONS
Drama Department, The London Television Centre
London SE1 9LT   Tel: 020-7620 1620

UNIVERSAL PICTURES/UNIVERSAL STUDIOS Ltd
UIP House, 45 Beadon Road, London W6 0EG
Fax: 020-8563 4331   Tel: 020-8563 4329

VERA
3rd Floor, 66-68 Margaret Street, London W1W 8SR
e-mail: rachael@vera.co.uk
Fax: 020-7436 6117   Tel: 020-7436 6116

VERA MEDIA
(Video Production & Training Company)
30-38 Dock Street, Leeds LS10 1JF
e-mail: vera@vera-media.co.uk
Fax: 0113-242 8739   Tel: 0113-242 8646

VIDEO & FILM PRODUCTION
Robin Hill, The Ridge, Lower Basildon, Reading, Berks
Website: www.videoandfilm.co.uk
e-mail: david.fisher@videoandfilm.co.uk
Mobile: 07836 544955   Tel: 0118-984 2488

VIDEO ARTS
6-7 St Cross Street, London EC1N 8UA
e-mail: sales@videoarts.co.uk
Fax: 020-7400 4900   Tel: 020-7400 4800

VIDEO ENTERPRISES
12 Barbers Wood Road, High Wycombe
Buckinghamshire HP12 4EP
Website: www.videoenterprises-uk.co.uk
e-mail: videoenterprises@btconnect.com
Fax: 01494 534145   Tel: 01494 534144

VIDEOTEL PRODUCTIONS
84 Newman Street, London W1T 3EU
Fax: 020-7299 1818   Tel: 020-7299 1800

VILLAGE PRODUCTIONS
4 Midas Business Centre, Wantz Road, Dagenham
Essex RM10 8PS
e-mail: village000@btclick.com
Fax: 020-8593 0198   Tel: 020-8984 0322

VISAGE TELEVISION Ltd
c/o Instrumental Media, 40 New Bond Street
London W1S 2RX
e-mail: television@visagegroup.com
Fax: 020-7629 8785   Tel: 020-7659 1140

W3KTS Ltd
10 Portland Street, York YO31 7EH
e-mail: chris@w3kts.demon.co.uk   Tel: 01904 647822

W6 STUDIO
(The Complete Video Service)
359 Lillie Road, Fulham, London SW6 7PA
Website: www.w6studio.co.uk
Fax: 020-7381 5252   Tel: 020-7385 2272

WALKOVERS VIDEO PRODUCTION
Brook Cottage, Silver Street, Kington Langley
Nr Chippenham, Wiltshire SN15 5NU
e-mail: walkoversvideo@btinternet.com
Fax: 01249 750155   Tel: 01249 750428

WALNUT MEDIA COMMUNICATIONS Ltd
Crown House, Armley Road, Leeds LS12 2EJ
Website: www.walnutmedia.com
e-mail: mail@walnutmedia.com
Fax: 08707 427080   Tel: 08707 427070

WALSH BROS Ltd
24 Redding House, Harlinger Street
King Henry's Wharf, London SE18 5SR
e-mail: walshbros@mail.com   Tel/Fax: 020-8854 5557

WALSH Steve PRODUCTIONS Ltd
78 Fieldview, London SW18 3HF
Website: www.steve-walsh.com
e-mail: steve@steve-walsh.com
Fax: 020-7924 7461   Tel: 020-7223 6070

WARK CLEMENTS & Co Ltd
Studio 7, The Tollgate, Marine Crescent
Glasgow G51 1HD
Website: www.warkclements.com
e-mail: info@warkclements.co.uk
Fax: 0141-429 1751   Tel: 0141-429 1750

WARNER BROS PRODUCTIONS Ltd
FF
Warner Suite, Pinewood Studios, Iver Heath
Buckinghamshire SL0 0NH
Fax: 01753 655703   Tel: 01753 654545

WARNER SISTERS FILM AND TELEVISION Ltd
The Cottage, Pall Mall Deposit, 124 Barlby Road
London W10 6BL
e-mail: sisters@warnercine.com
Fax: 020-8960 3880   Tel: 020-8876 6911

WEST ONE FILM PRODUCERS Ltd
c/o Richard Hatton Ltd
29 Roehampton Gate
London SW15 5JR
Fax: 020-8876 8278   Tel: 020-8876 6699

WHITE Michael
48 Dean Street, London W1D 5BF
e-mail: contact@michaelwhite.co.uk
Fax: 020-7734 7727   Tel: 020-7734 7707

WHITEHALL FILMS Ltd
10 Lower Common South, London SW15 1BP
e-mail: mwhitehall@email.msn.com
Fax: 020-8788 2340   Tel: 020-8785 3737

WICKES COMPANY The
F TV D
10 Abbey Orchard Street
London SW1P 2LD
e-mail: wickesco@aol.com
Fax: 020-7222 0822   Tel: 020-7222 0820

WILD IRIS FILMS
59 Brewer Street, London W1R 3FB
e-mail: joe@wildiris.co.uk
Fax: 020-7494 1764   Tel: 020-8374 4536

WILD WEST PRODUCTIONS
4 Greenacre Close
Walderslade
Chatham, Kent ME5 7JJ
Website: www.wildwestproductions.com
e-mail: philip@wildwestproductions.com
Mobile: 07904 177937   Tel: 01634 201865

WINNER Michael Ltd
219 Kensington High Street
London W8 6BD
e-mail: winner@ftech.co.uk
Fax: 020-7602 9217   Tel: 020-7734 8385

WORKING TITLE FILMS Ltd
Oxford House
76 Oxford Street
London W1D 1BS
Fax: 020-7307 3001   Tel: 020-7307 3000

WORLD PRODUCTIONS &
WORLD FILM SERVICES Ltd
Eagle House
50 Marshall Street, London W1F 9BQ
Website: www.world-productions.com
Fax: 020-7758 7000   Tel: 020-7734 3536

WORLD WIDE PICTURES Ltd
21-25 St Anne's Court
London W1F 0BJ
Website: www.worldwidegroup.ltd.uk
e-mail: info@worldwidegroup.ltd.uk
Fax: 020-7734 0619   Tel: 020-7434 1121

WORLD'S END
35 Hanvood Road
London SW6 4QP
Website: www.worldsendproductions.com
e-mail: info@worldsendproductions.com
Fax: 020-7731 0406   Tel: 020-7751 9880

WORTHWHILE MOVIE Ltd
(Providing the services of Bruce Pittman as Film
Director)
25 Tolverne Road, London SW20 8RA
Fax: 00 1 (416) 4695894   Tel: 00 1 (416) 4690459

XINGU FILMS
12 Cleveland Row
London SW1A 1DH
Fax: 020-7451 0601   Tel: 020-7451 0600

YOUNGER Greg ASSOCIATES
Baron's Croft
Hare Lane, Blindley Heath
Surrey RH7 6JA
Fax: 01342 833768   Tel: 01342 832515

ZAHRA & REMICK
186 Albert Road,
London N22 7AH   Tel/Fax: 020-8889 6225

ZENITH ENTERTAINMENT Plc
43-45 Dorset Street, London W1U 7NA
Fax: 020-7224 3194   Tel: 020-7224 2440

ZEPHYR FILMS Ltd
48A Goodge Street, London W1T 4LX
e-mail: info@zephyrfilms.co.uk
Fax: 020-7255 3777   Tel: 020-7255 3555

Brighton Film School
Film Director's Courses in Cinematography and Screenwriting
Franz von Habsburg MBKS (BAFTA Member)   01273 302166   www.brightonfilmschool.org.uk
Be in Brighton - where film was pioneered in 1896!

ARTTS SKILLCENTRE
Highfield Grange, Bubwith, North Yorks YO8 6DP
Website: www.artts.co.uk
e-mail: admin@artts.co.uk
Fax: 01757 288253   Tel: 01757 288088

BLAZE THE TRAIL FILM & TELEVISION TRAINING
2nd Floor, 241 High Street, London E17 7BH
Website: www.blaze-the-trail.com
Fax: 020-8520 2358   Tel: 020-8520 4569

BRIGHTON FILM SCHOOL
(Member of the National Association for Higher
Education in the Moving Image (NAHEMI) and the
University Film and Video Association (UFVA).
Part-time Day or Evening Film Directors' Course
includes Screenwriting, 16mm & 35mm
Cinematography and Avid Editing. 3 week full-time
Summer School in August.
Admin & Reg Office: 13 Tudor Close
Dean Court Road, Rottingdean, East Sussex BN2 7DF
Senior Lecturer: Franz von Habsburg MBKS (BAFTA)
Admissions: Meryl von Habsburg BSc MSc Cert Ed
Website: www.brightonfilmschool.org.uk
e-mail: info@brightonfilmschool.org.uk
Fax: 01273 302163   Tel: 01273 302166

LEEDS METROPOLITAN UNIVERSITY
(PG Dip/MA's in Film & Moving Image Production
or Fiction Screenwriting, HND in Moving Image
Production)
The Leeds School of Art, Architecture and Design
H505, Calverley Street, Leeds LS1 3HE
Website: www.lmu.ac.uk
Fax: 0113-283 3139   Tel: 0113-283 2600

LONDON ACADEMY OF RADIO, FILM & TV
American Building
79A Tottenham Court Road, London W1T 4TD
Website: www.media-courses.com
e-mail: help@radio321.com   Tel: 0870 7276677

LONDON FILM ACADEMY
The Old Church, 52A Walham Grove
London SW6 1QR
Website: www.londonfilmacademy.com
e-mail: info@londonfilmacademy.com
Fax: 020-7381 6116   Tel: 020-7386 7711

LONDON FILM SCHOOL The
(2-year MA Course in Film Making)
24 Shelton Street, London WC2H 9UB
e-mail: film.school@lfs.org.uk
Fax: 020-7497 3718   Tel: 020-7836 9642

MIDDLESEX UNIVERSITY
(School of Arts)
Cat Hill, Barnet, Hertfordshire EN4 8HT
Website: www.mdx.ac.uk
Fax: 020-8440 9541   Tel: 020-8411 5000

NATIONAL FILM & TELEVISION SCHOOL
(2-Year MA courses in Direting (Animation, Fiction
or Documentary), Cinematography,
Composing for Film & TV, Editing,
Producing, Production Design,
Post-Production Sound and Screenwriting
Also short courses and project development
programme.
Beaconsfield Studios, Station Road
Beaconsfield, Bucks HP9 1LG
Website: www.nfts-tv.ac.uk
e-mail: admin@nftsfilm-tv.ac.uk
Fax: 01494 674042   Tel: 01494 671234

RE:ACTORS
15 Montrose Walk
Weybridge, Surrey KT13 8JN
Website: www.reactors.co.uk
e-mail: michael@reactors.co.uk
Fax: 01932 830248   Tel: 01932 888885

**SURREY INSTITUTE OF ART & DESIGN UNIVERSITY
COLLEGE**
(3-year BA (Hons) Photography, Film & Video,
Digital Screen Arts, Television Drama,
Arts & Media, Animation)
Falkner Road, Farnham, Surrey GU9 7DS
Website: www.surrart.ac.uk   Tel: 01252 722441

**UNIVERSITY OF WESTMINSTER SCHOOL OF
MEDIA ARTS & DESIGN**
(Degree courses in Film and
Television/Contemporary Media Practice)
Watford Road
Northwick Park, Harrow
Middlesex HA1 3TP   Tel: 020-7911 5000

ARDMORE STUDIOS Ltd
Herbert Road
Bray, Co. Wicklow, Eire
e-mail: film@ardmore.ie
Fax: 00 353 1 2861894   Tel: 00 353 1 2862971

BBC SOUTH (Elstree)
BBC Elstree Centre
Clarendon Road, Borehamwood
Hertfordshire WD6 1JF   Tel: 020-8953 6100

BBC TELEVISION
Television Centre
Wood Lane, Shepherds Bush
London W12 7RJ   Tel: 020-8743 8000

BRAY STUDIOS
Down Place
Water Oakley, Windsor Road
Windsor, Berkshire SL4 5UG
Fax: 01628 770381   Tel: 01628 622111

CAPITAL STUDIOS
Wandsworth Plain
London SW18 1ET
e-mail: info@capitalstudios.com
Fax: 020-8877 0234   Tel: 020-8877 1234

CHELTENHAM FILM STUDIOS Ltd
Arle Court
Hatherley Lane, Cheltenham
Gloucestershire GL51 6PN
Website: www.cheltstudio.com
e-mail: info@cheltstudio.com
Fax: 01242 542 701   Tel: 01242 542 700

CORINTHIAN TELEVISION FACILITIES
(TV Post Production, Studios, Transmission)
87 St John's Wood Terrace, London NW8 6PY
Fax: 020-7483 4264   Tel: 020-7483 6000

EALING STUDIOS
Ealing Green, London W5 5EP
Website: www.ealingstudios.com
e-mail: info@ealingstudios.com
Fax: 020-8758 8658   Tel: 020-8567 6655

ELSTREE FILM & TELEVISION STUDIOS
Shenley Road, Borehamwood
Hertfordshire WD6 1JG
e-mail: info@elstreefilmtv.com
Fax: 020-8905 1135   Tel: 020-8953 1600

FILMLAB UK Ltd The
Unit 415 Pilot Close, Fulmar Way, Wickford
Essex SS11 8YW
Website: www.thefilmlab.com
e-mail: janice@trickylight.com
Fax: 01268 571221   Tel: 01268 571408

HILLSIDE
Merry Hill Road
Bushey, Hertfordshire WD23 1DR
Website: www.hillside-studios.co.uk
e-mail: enquiries@hillside-studios.co.uk
Fax: 020-8421 8085   Tel: 020-8950 7919

LONDON STUDIOS The
London Television Centre
Upper Ground
London SE1 9LT
Fax: 020-7928 8405   Tel: 020-7620 1620

PINEWOOD STUDIOS
Pinewood Road, Iver Heath
Buckinghamshire SL0 0NH
Website: www.pinewood-studios.co.uk
Fax: 01753 656844   Tel: 01753 651700

REUTERS TELEVISION
85 Fleet Street
London EC4P 4AJ   Tel: 020-7250 1122

RIVERSIDE STUDIOS
Crisp Road, London W6 9RL
Website: www.riversidestudios.co.uk
e-mail: online@riversidestudios.co.uk
Fax: 020-8237 1001   Tel: 020-8237 1000

SANDS FILMS/ROTHERHITHE STUDIOS
119 Rotherhithe Street
London SE16 4NF
Fax: 020-7231 2119   Tel: 020-7231 2209

SAVOY HILL STUDIO
Adam House
7-10 Adam Street
London WC2N 6AA
e-mail: savoyhillstudio@tabard.u-net.com
Fax: 020-7520 9023   Tel: 020-7497 0830

SHEPPERTON STUDIOS
Studios Road
Shepperton
Middlesex TW17 0QD
Fax: 01932 568989   Tel: 01932 562611

TEDDINGTON STUDIOS Ltd
Broom Road
Teddington
Middlesex TW11 9NT
Website: www.teddington.tv
e-mail: sales@teddington.tv   Tel: 020-8977 3252

TWICKENHAM FILM STUDIOS Ltd
The Barons
St Margaret's, Twickenham
Middlesex TW1 2AW
Fax: 020-8607 8701   Tel: 020-8607 8888

M.V. DIXIE QUEEN

London's largest cruising/static Mississippi-style paddleboat. High 10' ceilings. 2500 sq. ft. of interior space. 2000 ft. exterior space. Additional restaurant deck. Available for Film/TV location work. Experienced personnel on board can assist with all aspects of waterside filming, permissions etc. Call Nigel Scandrett for a good deal and to discuss the potential of using a river venue.
Thames Luxury Charters 020 8780 1562   Website: www.thamesluxurycharters.co.uk

Compiled By JANICE CRAMER & DAVID BANKS
This is a list of digs recommended by those who have used them.
To keep the list accurate please send recommendations for inclusion to GOOD DIGS GUIDE at The Spotlight.
Thanks to all who did so over the last year.
Entries in Bold have been paid for by the Digs concerned.

ABERDEEN

Milne, Mrs A	5 Sunnyside Walk, Aberdeen AB2 3NZ	01224 638951
Woods, Pat	62 Union Grove, Aberdeen AB10 6RX	01224 586324

AYR

Dunn, Sheila	The Dunn-Thing Guest House, 13 Park Circus, Ayr KA7 2DJ	01292 284531/07987 928685

BATH

Hutton, Cecilia Mrs	**25 Claude Avenue, Bath BA2 1AE**	**01225 332221**
	Website: www.bathholidayhomes.co.uk	
	e-mail: bhh@virgin.net	
Porter, Mrs G	95 Shakespeare Avenue, Bath, Avon BA2 4RQ	01225 420166
Tapley, Jane	Camden Lodgings, 3 Upper Camden Place, Bath BA1 5HX	01225 446561

BELFAST

Cargill, Mrs	Eglantine Guest House, 21 Eglantine Avenue, Belfast BT9 6DW	028-9066 7585
Greer, Nora	59 Rugby Road, Belfast BT7 1PT	028-9032 2120
McCully, Mrs S	28 Eglantine Avenue, Belfast BT9 6DX	028-9068 2031

BILLINGHAM

Bell, Audrey & Reg	14 The Crescent, Linthorpe, Middlesbrough TS5 6SQ	01642 822483
Farminer, Anna	168 Kennedy Gardens, Billingham, Cleveland TS23 3RJ	01642 530205/07946 237381
Gibson, Mrs S	Northwood, 61 Tunstall Avenue, Billingham TS23 3QB	01642 561071/07813 407674
Newton, Mrs Edna	97 Brendon Crescent, Billingham, Cleveland TS23 2QU	01642 647958

BIRMINGHAM

Baker, Mr N K	41 King Edward Road, Mosley, Birmingham B13 8EL	0121-449 8220
Eccles, John	18 Holly Road, Edgbaston, Birmingham B16 9NH	0121-454 4853
Matusiak-Varley, Ms B T	**Red Gables, 69 Handsworth Wood Rd, Handsworth Wood**	
	Birmingham B20 2DH	**Tel/Fax: 0121-686 5942/07711 751105**
Mountain, Marlene P	**268 Monument Road, Edgbaston, Birmingham B16 8XF**	**0121-454 5900**
Wilson, Mrs	17 Yew Tree Road, Edgbaston, Birmingham B15 2LX	0121-440 5182

BLACKPOOL

Chapman, Brian & Liz	Hollywood Apartments, 2-4 Wellington Road, Blackpool FY1 6AR	01253 341633
Lees, Jean	Ascot Flats, 6 Hull Road, Central Blackpool FY1 4QB	01253 621059
The Proprietor	The Brooklyn Hotel, 7 Wilton Parade, Blackpool FY1 2HE	01253 627003
The Proprietor	**The Somerset & Dorset Apartments**	
	22 Barton Avenue, Blackpool FY1 6AP	**01253 346743**

BOLTON

Duckworth, Paul	19 Burnham Avenue, Bolton BL1 6DB	01204 495732/07762 545129

BOURNEMOUTH

Sitton, Martin	Flat 2, 9 St Winifreds Road, Meyrick Park, Bournemouth BH2 6NX	01202 293318

BRADFORD

Calver, Michael	**14 Binyon Gardens, Taverham, Norwich NR8 6SS**	**01603 869260**
Smith, Theresa	8 Moorhead Terrace, Shipley, Bradfford BD18 4LA	01274 778568

BRIGHTON

Benedict, Peter	19 Madeira Place, Brighton BN2 1TN	020-7703 4104
Cleveland, Carol	13 Belgrave Street, Brighton BN2 9NS	01273 602607
Dyson, Kate	28 Victoria Street, Brighton BN1 3FQ	01273 746505
Hamlin, Corinne	Flat 6, Preston Lodge, Little Preston Street, Brighton BN1 2HQ	01273 321346
Merrin, Kate	2a Exton House, 4 Second Avenue, Hove BN3 2LG	07714 672233

BLACKPOOL

Somerset Apartments

VERY HIGH STANDARD - en suite studios & apartments
• Central Heating • Cooker • Fridge • Microwave & TV - **all new**
Beds • Linen provided • 'Highly recommended' by members of the profession
• 10 minutes walk to the Theatre
Irene Chadderton, 22 Barton Avenue, Blackpool FY1 6AP • Tel/Fax: 01253 346743

BRISTOL
Rozario, Jean	Manor Lodge, 21 Station Road, Keynsham, N Somerset BS31 2BH	0117-986 2191
	e-mail: stay@manorlodge.co.uk	

BURY ST EDMUNDS
Bird, Mrs S	30 Crown Street, Bury St Edmunds, Suffolk IP33 1QU	01284 754492
Harrington-Spie, Sue	39 Well Street, Bury St Edmunds, Suffolk IP33 1EQ	01284 768986

BUXTON
Kitchen, Mrs M	Flat 1, 17 Silverlands, Buxton, Derbyshire SK17 6QH	01298 78898
Scruton, Anne & Colin	Griff Guest House, 2 Compton Road, Buxton SK17 9DN	01298 23628

CAMBRIDGE
Hones, Roger	25 Magrath Avenue, Cambridge CB4 3AH	01223 315503

CANTERBURY
Butcher, Jennifer J	5 Vernon Place, Canterbury, Kent CT1 3HG	01227 470712
Dolan, Mrs A	12 Leycroft Close, Canterbury, Kent CT2 7LD	01227 450064
Ellen, Nikki	Crockshard Farmhouse, Wingham, Canterbury CT3 1NY	01227 720464
	Website: www.crockshard.com e-mail: crockshard_bnb@yahoo.com	
Stockbridge, Doris	Tudor House, 6 Best Lane, Canterbury, Kent CT1 2JB	01227 765650

CARDIFF
Blade, Mrs Anne	25 Romilly Road, Canton, Cardiff CF5 1FH	029-2022 5860
Lewis, Nigel	66 Donald Street, Roath, Cardiff CF24 4TR	029-2049 4008
Nelmes, Michael	**12 Darran Street, Cathays, Cardiff, South Glamorgan CF24 4JF**	**029-2034 2166**
Taylor, T & Chichester, P	32 Kincraig Street, Roath, Cardiff, South Glamorgan CF24 3HW	029-2048 6785

CHESTERFIELD
Cook, Linda & Chris	27 Tennyson Avenue, Chesterfield, Derbyshire	01246 202631
Forsyth, Mr & Mrs	Anis Louise Guest House, 34 Clarence Road, Chesterfield S40 1LN	01246 235412
Popplewell, Mr & Mrs	23 Tennyson Avenue, Chesterfield, Derbyshire S40 4SN	01246 201738

CHICHESTER
Beeny, Tricia & Richard	Hunston Mill Holiday Homes, Hunston, Nr Chichester PO20 6AU	01243 783375

COVENTRY
Snelson, Paddy & Bob	**Banner Hill Farmhouse, Rouncil Lane, Kenilworth CV8 1NN**	**01926 852850**

DARLINGTON
Bird, Mrs	Gilling Old Mill, Gilling West, Richmond, N Yorks DL10 5JD	01748 822771
Evans, Jean	26a Pierremont Crescent, Darlington DL3 9PB	01325 252032
Graham, Anne	Holme House, Piercebridge, Darlington DL2 3SY	01325 374280
Kernon, Mr G	George Hotel, Piercebridge, Darlington DL2 3SW	01325 374576

DERBY
Boddy, Susan	St Wilfrid's, Barrow-upon-Trent, Derbyshire DE73 1HB	01332 701384

DUNDEE
Hill, Mrs J	Ash Villa, 216 Arbroath Road, Dundee DD4 7RZ	01382 450831

EASTBOURNE
Allen, Peter	Flat 1, 16 Enys Road, Eastbourne BN21 2DN	01323 730235
Awdry, S	31 Enys Road, Eastbourne BN21 2DH	01323 416147
Chant, David E J	Hamdon, 49 King's Drive, Eastbourne BN21 2NY	01323 722544
Dawson, Jacqui	Lavender House, 14 New Upperton Road, Eastbourne	01323 729988
Weaver, Mr & Mrs	Meads Lodge Holiday Flats, 1 Jevington Gardens	
	Eastbourne BN21 4HR	01323 724362

EDINBURGH

Balnaves, Victoria	17/7 Newhaven Place, Edinburgh EH6 4TW	07729 013841
	e-mail: vickibalnaves@hotmail.com	
Glen Miller, Edna	25 Bellevue Road, Edinburgh EH7 4DL	0131-556 4131
Russell, Helen	**9 Lonsdale Terrace, Edinburgh EH3 9HN**	**0131-229 7219**
	e-mail: helen.tyrrell@vhscotland.org.uk	
Stobbart, Joyce	84 Bellevue Road, Edinburgh EH7 4DE	0131-228 2400/07740 503951

GLASGOW

Baird, David W	6 Beaton Road, Maxwell Park, Glasgow G41 4LA	0141-423 1340/570 5420
Leslie-Carter, Simon	52 Charlotte Street, Glasgow G1 5DW	01436 810264
	Website: www.52charlottestreet.co.uk e-mail: slc@52charlottestreet.co.uk	
Lloyd Jones, David	3 Whittinghame Drive, Kelvinside, Glasgow G12 0XS	0141-339 3331
Robinson, Lesley	28 Marywood Square, Glasgow G41 2BJ	0141-423 6920

GRAVESEND

Greenwood, Mrs S	8 Sutherland Close, Chalk, Gravesend, Kent DA12 4XJ	01474 350819

HULL

	The Arches Guesthouse, 38 Saner Street, Hull HU3 2TR	01482 211558

INVERNESS

Blair, Mrs	McDonald House Hotel, 1 Ardross Terrace, Inverness IV3 5NQ	01463 232878
Kerr-Smith, Jennifer	Ardkeen Tower, 5 Culduthel Road, Inverness	01463 233131
Swart, Mrs	Abermar Guest House, 25 Fairfield Road, Inverness IV3 5QD	01463 239019

IPSWICH

Ball, Bunty	56 Henley Road, Ipswich IP1 3SA	01473 256653
Bennett, Liz	Gayfers, Playford, Ipswich IP6 9DR	01473 623343
Hyde-Johnson, Anne	64 Benton Street, Hadleigh, Ipswich, Suffolk IP7 5AT	01473 823110

ISLE OF WIGHT

Ogston, Sue	'Winward House', 69 Mill Hill Road, Cowes, Isle of Wight PO31 7EQ	01983 280940

KIRKCALDY

Nicol, Mrs	44 Glebe Park, Kirkcaldy, Fife KY1 1BL	01592 264531

LEEDS

Baker, Mrs M	**2 Ridge Mount, (off Cliff Road), Leeds LS6 2HD**	**0113-275 8735**
Kavanagh, Mrs	Novello House, 2 Ladywood Road, Roundhay, Leeds LS8 2QF	0113-265 8330
Littlewood, Bryan		
& Linda	4 Oatland Green, Leeds LS7 1SN	0113-225 3281

LINCOLN

Carnell, Andrew	Tennyson Court Cottages, 3 Tennyson Street, Lincoln LN1 1LZ	01522 533044
Sharpe, Mavis S	Bight House, 17 East Bight, Lincoln LN2 1QH	01522 534477
Ye Old Crowne Inn	(Theatre Pub), Clasketgate, Lincoln LN2 1JS	01522 542896

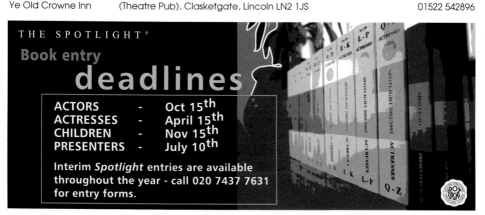

Quinton Hotel
AA B&B
★★★

Comfortable warm rooms, most en-suite with TV, radio, direct dial phones, tea/coffee facilities. Flexible breakfasts, late bar, pool table, darts, piano and karaoke. Free light suppers. Mini-bus service to and from Theatre. Railway and Bus.

36 Church Walks, Llandudno. Tel/Fax: 01492-876879   Email: susanmarybell@yahoo.co.uk

LIVERPOOL

Cowie, Kate	Flat 5, 2 Fulwood Road, Liverpool L17 5AG	0151-726 0061/709 9434
Double, Ross	5 Percy Street, Liverpool L8 7LT	0151-708 8821
Maloney, Anne	16 Sandown Lane, Wavertree, Liverpool L15 8HY	0151-734 4839
McGuinness, Damian	Seapark Apartments, (office) 51 Alexandra Road, Southport, Merseyside PR9 9HD	01704 500444

LLANDUDNO

Bell, Alan	Quinton Hotel, 36 Church Walks, Llandudno LL30 2HN	01492 876879

LONDON

Allen, Mrs I	Flat 2, 9 Dorset Square, London NW1 6QB	020-7723 3979
Broughton, Mrs P A	31 Ringstead Road, Catford, London SE6 2BU	020-8461 0146
Cardinal, Maggie	17a Gaisford Street, London NW5	020-7681 7376
Cobban, Carole	138 Tottenham Road, London N1 4DY	020-7249 4627
Guess, Maggie	36 Federal Road, Perivale, Middlesex UB6 7AW	020-8991 0918
Mesure, Nicholas	16 St Alfege Passage, Greenwich, London SE10 9JS	020-8853 4337
Rothner, Stephanie	44 Grove Road, North Finchley, London N12 0AP	020-8446 1604
Rothner, Dora	23 The Ridgeway, London N3 2PG	020-8346 0246
Shaw, Lindy	11 Baronsmede, Acton, London W5 4LS	020-8567 0877
Walsh, Genevieve	37 Kelvedon House, Guildford Road, Stockwell, London SW8 2DN	020-7627 0024

MALVERN

Emuss, Mrs	Priory Holme, 18 Avenue Road, Malvern WR14 3AR	01684 568455
McLeod, Mr & Mrs	Sidney House, 40 Worcester Road, Malvern WR14 4AA	01684 574994

MANCHESTER

Dyson, Mrs E	33 Danesmoor Road, West Didsbury, Manchester M20 3JT	0161-434 5410
Heaton, Miriam	58 Tamworth Avenue, Whitefield, Manchester M45 6UA	0161-773 4490
Jones, P M	375 Bury New Road, Whitefield, Manchester M45 7SU	0161-766 9243
Martin, David & Dolan, Jez	86 Stanley Road, Old Trafford, Manchester M16 9DH	0161-848 9231
Prichard, Fiona & John	45 Bamford Road, Didsbury, Manchester M20 2QP	0161-434 4877
Robinson, Rachael	4 Park View, Ladybarn, Manchester M14 6SY	07810 566524
Twist, Susan	45 Osborne Road, Levenshulme, Manchester M19 2DU	0161-225 1591

MILFORD HAVEN

Henricksen, Bruce & Diana	**Belhaven Hse Hotel Ltd, 29 Hamilton Terrace, Milford Haven SA73 3JJ** Website: www.westwaleshotels.com e-mail: hbruceh@businessunmetered.com	**01646 695983/Fax: 01646 690787**

MOLD

Major, Mr & Mrs	The Mount, Higher Kinnerton, Chester CH4 9BQ	01244 660275

NEWARK-ON-TRENT

Burns, Anne	69 Harcourt Street, Newark-on-Trent, Notts NG24 1RG	01636 702801

NEWCASTLE UPON TYNE

Charlton, Tot	Ryton Grange, Ryton, Tyne and Wear NE40 3UN	0191-413 3878
Guy, Thomas	11 Rokeby Drive, Gosforth, Newcastle upon Tyne NE3 4JY e-mail: thomas-guy@freeuk.com	0191-285 7057
Kalaugher, Mary & Cross, Dave	4 Tankerville Terrace, Jesmond, Newcastle upon Tyne NE2 3AH	0191-281 0475
Moffatt, Madaleine	**9 Curtis Road, Fenham NE4 9BH**	**0191-272 5318**
Stansfield, Mrs P	Rosebury Hotel, 2 Rosebury Crescent Jesmond, Newcastle upon Tyne NE2 1ET,	0191-281 3363
Steele, Miss M E	7 Stoneyhurst Road, South Gosforth Newcastle upon Tyne NE3 1PR	0191-285 7771

NEWPORT

Price, Dinah	'Great House', Isca Road, Old Village, Caerleon, Gwent NP18 1QG	
	Website: www.visitgreathouse.net	
	e-mail: dinah.price@amserve.net	01633 420216

NORWICH

Calver, Michael	14 Binyon Gardens, Taverham, Norwich NR8 6SS	01603 869260
Edgeley, Julia	8 Chester Street, Norwich NR2 2AY	01603 612833
Moore, Maureen	63 Surrey Street, Norwich NR1 3PG	01603 621979
Much, Cathy	128 Southwell Road, Norwich NR1 3RS	01603 632787
Yord, Cherry	Whitegates, 181 Norwich Road, Wroxham NR12 8RZ	01603 781037

NOTTINGHAM

Davis, Barbara	3 Tattershall Drive, The Park, Nottingham NG7 1BX	0115-947 4179
Offord, Mrs	5 Tattershall Drive, The Park, Nottingham NG7 1BX	0115-947 6924
Santos, Mrs S	Eastwood Farm, Hagg Lane, Epperstone, Nottingham NG14 6AX	0115-966 3018
Walker, Christine	18a Cavendish Cresent North, The Park, Nottingham NG7 1BA	0115-947 2485

OLDHAM

Wardle, Kate	292 Turf Lane, Royton, Oldham	0161-624 4191

OXFORD

Petty, Susan	74 Corn Street, Witney, Oxford OX28 6BS	01993 703035

PLYMOUTH

Carson, Mr & Mrs	6 Beech Cottages, Parsonage Rd, Newton Ferrers, Nr Plymouth PL8 1AX	01752 872124
Humphreys, John	Lyttleton Guest House (Self-Catering)	
& Sandra	4 Cresent Avenue, Plymouth PL1 3AN	01752 220176
Noble, Julia	Ashgrove Hotel, 218 Citadel Road, The Hoe, Plymouth PL1 3BB	01752 664046
Spencer, Hugh & Eloise	10 Grand Parade, Plymouth PL1 3DF	01752 664066

POOLE
Burnett, Mrs	63 Orchard Avenue, Parkstone, Poole, Dorset BH14 8AH	01202 743877
Moore, Sarah	Harbour View, 11 Harbour View Road, Poole BH14 0PD	01202 734763
Saunders, Mrs	1 Harbour Shallows, 15 Whitecliff Road, Poole BH14 8DU	01202 741637

READING
Estate Office	Mapledurham House and Watermill	
	Mapledurham Estate, Reading RG4 7TR	0118-972 3350

SHEFFIELD
Craig, J & Rosen, B	**59 Nether Edge Road, Sheffield S7 1RW**	**0114-258 1337**
Gillespie, Carole	251 Western Road, Crookes, Sheffield S10 1LE	0114-266 2666
Godfrey, Liz	12 Victoria Road, Sheffield S10 2DL	0114-266 9389
Horton, Jane &		
Cullumbine, Lynn	223 Cemetery Road, Sheffield S11 8FQ	0114-255 6092
Slack, Penny	Rivelin Glen Quarry, Rivelin Valley Road, Sheffield S6 5SE	0114-234 0382
	Website: www.quarryhouse.org.uk e-mail: pennyslack@aol.com	

SOUTHAMPTON
Cuzzolin, Sandrea	15 Methuen Street, Inner Avenue, Southampton SO14 6FL	023-8063 7345

SOUTHSEA & PORTSMOUTH
Tyrell, Wendy	Douglas Cottage, 27 Somerset Road, Southsea PO5 2NL	023-9282 1453

STOKE-ON-TRENT
Griffiths, Dorothy	40 Princes Road, Hartshill, Stoke-on-Trent	01782 416198
Hindmoor, Mrs	Verdon Guest House, 44 Charles Street, Hanley,	
	Stoke-on-Trent ST1 3JY	01782 264244
Meredith, Mr & Mrs K	**Bank End Farm Cottages, Hammond Avenue,**	
	Brown Edge, Stoke-on-Trent, Staffs ST6 8QU	**01782 502160**

STRATFORD-UPON-AVON
Caterham House Hotlel	58-59 Rother Street, Stratford-upon-Avon CV37 6LT	01789 267309

SUNDERLAND
Clifford, Hazel	Ravensbourne Guest House, 106 Beach Road,	
	South Shields, Tyne and Wear NE33 2NE	0191-456 5849
Henderson, Mrs	22 Park Parade, Roker, Sunderland SR6 9LU	0191-565 6511

TORQUAY
Lovsey, Frank & Irena	Silverton Holiday Apts, 217 St Marychurch Road, Torquay TQ1 3JT	01803 327147

WESTCLIFF
Hussey, Joy	42a Ceylon Road, Westcliff-on-Sea SS0 7HP	07946 413496
Moulding, Mark	24a Elderton Road, Westcliff-on-Sea, Essex	01702 344965
Swan, Nicola	7 Old Leigh Road, Leigh, Essex	01702 471600

WINCHESTER
Fetherston-Dilke, Mrs	85 Christchurch Road, Winchester SO23 9QY	01962 868661

WOKING
Goodson, Peter	1a Horsell Moor, Woking	01483 760208

WOLVERHAMPTON
Bell, Julia	Treetops, The Hem, Shifnal, Shropshire TF11 9PS	01952 460566
Nixon, Sonia	39 Stubbs Road, Pennfields, Wolverhampton WV3 7DJ	01902 339744
Riggs, Peter A	'Bethesda', 56 Chapel Lane, Codsall, Nr Wolverhampton WV8 2EJ	01902 844068

WORCESTER
Crossland, Chris	Greenlands, Uphampton, Ombersley, Worcester WR9 0JP	01905 620873

WORTHING
Stewart, Mollie	School House, 11 Ambrose Place, Worthing BN11 1PZ	01903 206823

YORK
Abbey Apts	7 St Marys, Bootham, York YO30 7DD	01904 636154
Blacklock, Tom	155 Lowther Street, York YO3 7LZ	01904 620487
Blower, Iris & Dennis	Dalescroft Guest House, 10 Southlands Road, York YO23 1NP	01904 626801
Harrand, Greg	Hedley House Hotel & Apts, 3 Bootham Terrace, York YO3 7DH	01904 637404

Healing With Hypnosis

Performance & Audition Anxiety
Confidence, Stage Fright etc

Harness your Inner Power to
Release Creative Blocks

Deborah J Monshin MNSPH GHR

01752 880880

Plymouth • Totnes • Tavistock

www.devon-hypnosis.co.uk

ALEXANDER ALLIANCE
(Alexander Technique, Voice and Audition Coaching)
3 Hazelwood Drive
St Albans, Herts   Tel: 01727 843633

ALEXANDER CENTRE The Bloomsbury
(Alexander Technique)
Bristol House, 80A Southampton Row
London WC1B 4BB
Website: www.alexcentre.com
e-mail: bloomsbury.alexandercentre@btinternet.com
                                         Tel: 020-7404 5348

ALEXANDER TECHNIQUE
(Jackie Coote MSTAT)
27 Britannia Road SW6 2HJ   Tel: 020-7731 1061

ALEXANDER TECHNIQUE & VOICE
(Robert Macdonald)
Flat 5, 17 Hatton Street
London NW8 8PL   Mobile: 07956 852303

ARTS CLINIC The
(Psychological Counselling, Personal & Professional Development)
14 Devonshire Place, London W1G 6HX
e-mail: mail@artsclinic.co.uk
Fax: 020-7224 6256   Tel: 020-7935 1242

ASPEY ASSOCIATES
(Management & Team Training, Counselling,
Human Resources)
8 Bloomsbury Square
London WC1A 2LQ
Website: www.aspey.com
e-mail: hr@aspey.com
Fax: 020-7405 5541   Tel: 020-7405 0500

BODYWISE
(Alexander Technique)
119 Roman Road
London E2 0QN
e-mail: inf@bodywisehealth.org   Tel: 020-8981 6938

BUPA
(Private Medical Insurance)
Website: www.bupa.com
e-mail: affnitysales@bupa.com
                    Tel: 0800 600500 (ref 8740)

BURGESS Chris
(Counselling for Performing Artists)
81 Arne House
Tyers Street
London SE11 5EZ   Tel: 020-7582 8229

CONSTRUCTIVE TEACHING CENTRE Ltd
(Alexander Technique Teacher Training)
18 Lansdowne Road
London W11 3LL
Website: www.alexandertek.com
e-mail: info@alexandertek.com   Tel: 020-7727 7222

CORTEEN Paola MSTAT
(Alexander Technique)
10A Eversley Park Road
London N21 1JU
e-mail: pmcorteen@yahoo.co.uk
                    Tel: 020-8882 7898

COURTENAY Julian
(NLP Master Practitioner)
42 Langdon Park Road
London N6 5QG
e-mail: julian@mentalfitness.uk.com
                    Tel: 020-8348 9033

CREATINGPLENTY COACHING
(Building Self-Esteem, Enhancing Confidence)
Website: www.kick-start-your-self-esteem.com
                    Tel: 0845 1220491

CUSSONS Nicola Dip ITEC
(Holistic Massage Therapist, Qualified & Insured)
The Factory Fitness & Dance Centre
407 Hornsey Road
London N19 4DX
Mobile: 07713 629952   Tel/Fax: 020-7272 6262

DAVENPORT Dr Charlotte
(Psycotherapy, Hypnotherapy & Reiki Services)
106 Glenthorne Road
Truro, Cornwall TR3 6UA
e-mail: charlotte@blackshawl.freeserve.co.uk
Mobile: 07814 593260   Tel: 01872 273119

DREAM
(Reflexology, Head, Neck & Shoulder Massage in
the Workplace)
117B Gaisford Street
London NW5 2EG
Website: www.dreamtherapies.co.uk
e-mail: dreamtherapies@hotmail.com
                    Mobile: 07973 731026

EDWARDS Simon MCA Hyp
(Hypnotherapy for Professionals in Film,
TV & Theatre)
15 Station Road
Quainton, Nr Aylesbury
Buckinghamshire HP22 4BW
e-mail: hypnotherapisttothestars@o2.co.uk
Mobile: 07889 333680   Tel: 01296 651259

EVOLUTION HEALTHCARE
(Health & Weight Management)
3 Brunel Close
Romford, Essex RM1 4GR
Website: www.4u2diet.net
e-mail: evoloution-health@supanet.com
Fax: 07092 393594   Tel: 01708 724029

FAITH Gordon BA DHC MCHC (UK)
(Hypnotherapy, Obstacles to Performing,
Positive Affirmation, Focusing)
1 Wavel Mews
Priory Road
London NW6 3AB   Tel: 020-7328 0446

FITNESS 4U PERSONAL TRAINING
(Leigh Jones)
e-mail: fitness4upersonaltraining@hotmail.com
                    Mobile: 07957 333921

FITNESS COACH The
(Jamie Baird)
Agua at The Sanderson
50 Berners Street, London W1T 4AT
e-mail: jamie@thefitnesscoach.co.uk
                    Tel: 07970 782476

**GILMOUR (HEALING) CENTRE
INTERNATIONAL The**
(Dr Glenn J Gilmour DD, MSc D)
(Clairvoyant, Healer, Personal Consultant
Investigator of Psychic Phenomena)
Website: www.sandrasinger.com   Tel: 01702 331616

GIRAUDON Olivier
(Alexander Technique Teacher)
22 Lake Road, Verwood
Dorset BH31 6BX   Tel: 01202 813636

HAMMOND John B. Ed (Hons) ICHFST
(Fitness Consultancy, Sports & Relaxation Massage)
4 Glencree, Billericay
Essex CM11 1EB
Mobile: 07703 185198   Tel/Fax: 01277 632830

HEIDELBACH Sabine MSTAT
(Alexander Technique)
50 Hillside Grove
London N14 6HE   Tel: 020-8882 8562

PROACTIVE BODY MANAGEMENT

Looking to get in shape and improve your fitness levels for that critical role or audition?

PBM can help you prepare by providing the expertise on a one to one basis to help you meet your true potential. We will work together to improve your posture, flexibility, fitness, confidence and leave you looking and feeling great.

PBM specialise in providing unique personalised fitness programmes, as well as advice on nutrition to suit your needs. So whether you are a resting actor or currently in a production, PBM has the know how to help you succeed.

For more information contact Mark: -
Tel No 020 8429 2342   **Mobile Tel No** 07985 695 327
E-mail markevanssmith@msn.com.

HYPNOTHERAPY & PSYCHOTHERAPY
(Including Performance Improvement,
Karen Mann DCH DHP)
9 Spencer House
Vale of Health
Hampstead
London NW3 1AS
Website: www.karenmann.co.uk   Tel: 020-7794 5843

MAGIC KEY PARTNERSHIP The
(Lyn Burgess - Life Coach)
4 Bewley Street
London SW19 1XB
Website: www.magickey.biz
e-mail: lyn@magickey.co.uk   Tel: 0845 1297401

MATRIX ENERGY FIELD THERAPY
121 Church Road
Wimbledon
London SW19 5AH
e-mail: donnie@lovingorganization.org
Mobile: 07762 821828

McCALLION Anna
(Alexander Technique)
Flat 2, 11 Sinclair Gardens
London W14 0AU   Tel: 020-7602 5599

MESURE Steve
(Science Theatre Practitioners)
10 Warren Drive, Chelsfield, Kent BR6 6EX
e-mail: steve.mesure@ntlworld.com
Tel: 01689 812200

Dr. Richard Casson
DENTAL CARE

Confidence comes from looking good and feeling great. Boost your confidence with a winning smile.

Free consultation for:

* cosmetic fillings
* orthodontics (teeth straightening)
* bleaching
* veneers
* crowns & bridges
* implants
* hygienist

For further information phone or write to
Dr. Richard Casson BDS (Glas)
on 020 7935 6511/020 7935 8854

6 Milford House, 7 Queen Anne Street,
London W1G 9HN
Website: www.richardcasson.com

"RAINBOWS END" Solutions for Actors' Professional and Personal Problems.
Established Director/Hypnotherapist helps you Banish: Stress, Panic Attacks, Phobias.
Maximise your Potential and Confidence in Auditions, Performance, Creativity & Life.
020 8549 4691   07903 261 214   e-mail: genefoad@hotmail.com

MINDSCI CLINIC
(Clinical Hypnotism)
34 Willow Bank
Ham, Richmond
Surrey TW10 7QX
Website: http://mindsci-clinic.com
e-mail: info@mindsci-clinic.com
Tel/Fax: 020-8948 2439

MONSHIN Deborah J MNSPH
(Healing with Hypnosis)
Plymouth
Totnes, Tavistock
e-mail: deborahmonshin@hotmail.com
Tel: 01752 880880

NORTON Michael R
(Implant/Reconstructive Dentistry)
98 Harley Street
London W1G 7HZ
Website: www.nortonimplants.com
e-mail: drnorton@nortonimplants.com
Fax: 020-7486 9119   Tel: 020-7486 9229

PEAK PERFORMANCE TRAINING
(Tina Reibl, Hypnotherapy, NLP
Success Strategies)
42 The Broadway
Maidenhead
Berkshire SL6 1LU
e-mail: tina.reibl@tesco.net   Tel: 01628 633509

PERSONAL EVOLUTION
49 Babbacombe Gardens
Redbridge, Ilford
Essex IG4 5LZ
Website: www.personal-evolution.com
e-mail: infoevolution@aol.com
Mobile: 07905 893204   Tel/Fax: 020-8550 6348

POLAND DENTAL STUDIOS
(Film/Stage Dentistry)
1 Devonshire Place
London W1N 1PA
Fax: 020-7486 3952   Tel: 020-7935 6919

PRIDE MEDIA ASSOCIATION Ltd
(Alternative Therapies, Psychic & Paranormal
Phenomena)
The Burnside Centre
38 Burnside Crescent
Middleton, Manchester M24 5NN
Website: www.prideradio.co.uk
e-mail: pma@prideradio.co.uk
Tel/Fax: 0161-643 6266

PROACTIVE BODY MANAGEMENT
e-mail: markevansmith@msn.com   Tel: 020-8429 2342

PRYCE Jacqui-Lee BFKA ABA BAWLA
(Personal Trainer, Qualified Aerobics, Weight-Lifting
Instructor, Kick/Muay Thai Boxing & Boxing)
e-mail: getfitquick@hotmail.com
Mobile: 07930 304809

RAINBOW'S END
(Hypno-Relaxation™. Clinical Hypnotherapy,
Creativity & Performance Enhancement for Media
Professionals)
23 Windsor Road, Kingston-upon-Thames
Surrey KT2 5EY
Website: www.rainbows-end.freeservers.com
e-mail: rainbows_end_hypnotherapy@hotmail.com
Mobile: 07903 261214   Tel: 020-8549 4691

**STAT (The Society of Teachers
of the Alexander Technique)**
1st Floor, Linton House
39-51 Highgate Road, London NW5 1RS
e-mail: enquiries@stat.org.uk
Fax: 020-7482 5435   Tel: 020-7284 3338

THEATRICAL DENTISTRY
(Richard D Casson)
6 Milford House, 7 Queen Anne Street
London W1G 9HN
Website: www.richardcasson.com
Tel/Fax: 020-7935 8854

TRUEWAYS
(Tasha Sangster, Holistic Practitioner in Indian
Head Massage, Facelift Massage & Feng Shui)
8 Brangton Road
London SE11 5PY   Tel: 020-7403 6564

TURNER Jeff
(Psychotherapy, Counselling & Performance
Coaching)
Life Management Systems
14 Randell's Road, London N1 0DH
Website: www.lifemanagement.co.uk
e-mail: info@lifemanagement.co.uk
Tel: 020-7837 9871

VITAL TOUCH The
(On-Site Massage Company)
11 Evering Road
London N16 7PX
Website: www.thevitaltouch.com
e-mail: suzi@thevitaltouch.com
Mobile: 07976 263691   Tel: 020-7249 4209

WILD DREAM CONSULTANCY
(Achievement Training, Confidence Class,
Personal Development)   Tel: 020-8374 3924

HYPNOTHERAPY, PSYCHOTHERAPY, REIKI HEALING
DR. CHARLOTTE DAVENPORT BSc (Hons)., Cert.Health.Psy., D.Clin.Psy., Dip.Hyp C.Psychol., BSCH (Assoc)

• Self Esteem/Confidence • Stress Management • Phobias • Performance Anxiety
• Panic Attacks • Depression • Weight Control • Smoking Cessation • Post Traumatic Stress

Harley Street, London Telephone: 020 7467 8380   Truro, Cornwall Telephone: 01872 273119 Mobile: 07814593260
e-mail: charlotte@blackshawl.freeserve.co.uk

BROOMHILL OPERA
Wiltons Music Hall, Graces Alley
Ensign Street, London E1 8JB
e-mail: opera@broomhill.demon.co.uk
Fax: 020-7702 1414   Tel: 020-7702 9555

CARL ROSA OPERA
359 Hackney Road, London E2 8PR
e-mail: mail@carlrosaopera.co.uk
Fax: 020-7613 0859   Tel: 020-7613 0777

DUAL CONTROL INTERNATIONAL THEATRE
Admiral Offices, Historic Dockyard
Chatham, Kent ME4 4TZ
e-mail: info@ellenkentinternational.co.uk
Fax: 01634 819149   Tel: 01634 819141

ENGLISH NATIONAL OPERA
London Coliseum
St Martin's Lane, London WC2N 4ES
Website: www.eno.org
Fax: 020-7845 9277   Tel: 020-7836 0111

ENGLISH TOURING OPERA
(James Conway)
1st Floor, 52-54 Rosebery Avenue
London EC1R 4RP
Website: www.englishtouringopera.org.uk
e-mail: admin@englishtouringopera.org.uk
Fax: 020-7713 8686   Tel: 020-7833 2555

GLYNDEBOURNE FESTIVAL OPERA
Glyndebourne, Lewes
East Sussex BN8 5UU   Tel: 01273 812321

GRANGE PARK OPERA
5 Chancery Lane, London EC4 1BU
Website: www.grangeparkopera.co.uk
e-mail: info@grangeparkopera.co.uk
Fax: 020-7320 5429   Tel: 020-7320 5586

GUBBAY Raymond Ltd
Knight House, 29-31 East Barnet Road, New Barnet
Hertfordshire EN4 8RN
Website: www.raymondgubbay.co.uk
e-mail: info@raymondgubbay.co.uk
Fax: 020-8216 3001   Tel: 020-8216 3000

KENTISH OPERA
Watermede, Wickhurst Road
Sevenoaks, Weald, Kent TN14 6LX
Website: www.kentishopera.fsnet.co.uk
    Tel: 01732 463284

LONDON OPERA PLAYERS
32 Trinity Court, 170A Gloucester Terrace
London W2 6HN
Website: www.operaplayers.co.uk
e-mail: info@operaplayers.co.uk
Fax: 0700 5802121   Mobile: 07779 225921

MUSIC THEATRE LONDON
Chertsey Chambers, 12 Mercer Street
London WC2H 9QD
Website: www.mtl.org.uk
e-mail: musictheatre.london@virgin.net
Fax: 020-7240 0805   Tel: 020-7240 0919

OPERA DELLA LUNA
7 Cotmore House
Fringford, Bicester
Oxfordshire OX27 8RQ
Website: www.operadellaluna.org
e-mail: operadellaluna@aol.com
Fax: 01869 323533   Tel: 01869 325131

OPERA NORTH
Grand Theatre, 46 New Briggate, Leeds LS1 6NU
Website: www.operanorth.co.uk
Fax: 0113-244 0418   Tel: 0113-243 9999

PEGASUS OPERA COMPANY Ltd
The Brix, St Matthew's
Brixton Hill, London SW2 1JF
Website: www.pegopera.org   Tel/Fax: 020-7501 9501

PIMLICO OPERA
5 Chancery Lane, London EC4A 1BU
e-mail: pimlico@grangeparkopera.co.uk
Fax: 020-7320 5429   Tel: 020-7320 5586

ROYAL OPERA The
Royal Opera House
Covent Garden, London WC2E 9DD
Website: www.royaloperahouse.org.uk
    Tel: 020-7240 1200

SCOTTISH OPERA
39 Elmbank Crescent, Glasgow G2 4PT
Website: www.scottishopera.org.uk
    Tel: 0141-248 4567

WELSH NATIONAL OPERA
John Street, Cardiff CF10 5SP
Website: www.wno.org.uk
e-mail: marketing@wno.org.uk
Fax: 029-2048 3050   Tel: 029-2046 4666

ACTING POSITIVE
22 Chaldon Road, London SW6 7NJ
e-mail: ianflintoff@aol.com   Tel: 020-7385 3800

ACTORCLUB Ltd
17 Inkerman Road, London NW5 3BT
Website: www.actorclub.co.uk
e-mail: johncunningham@actorclub.fsnet.co.uk
                                     Tel: 020-7267 2759

ACTORS CENTRE (NORTHERN)
(See NORTHERN ACTORS CENTRE)

ACTORS CENTRE The (LONDON)
1A Tower Street, London WC2H 9NP
Website: www.actorscentre.co.uk
e-mail: act@actorscentre.co.uk
Fax: 020-7240 3896   Tel: 020-7240 3940

ACTORS CENTRE The NORTH-EAST
2nd Floor, 1 Black Swan Court, Westgate Road
Newcastle upon Tyne NE1 1SG
Website: www.actorscentrene.co.uk
e-mail: actorscentrene@yahoo.com
                                     Tel: 0191-221 0158

ACTORS' ADVISORY SERVICE
29 Talbot Road, Twickenham
Middlesex TW2 6SJ   Tel: 020-8287 2839

ACTORS' BENEVOLENT FUND
6 Adam Street, London WC2N 6AD
Website: www.actorsbenevolentfund.co.uk
e-mail: office@abf.org.uk
Fax: 020-7836 8978   Tel: 020-7836 6378

ACTORS' CHARITABLE TRUST
Africa House, 64-78 Kingsway, London WC2B 6BD
e-mail: admin@tactactors.org
Fax: 020-7242 0234   Tel: 020-7242 0111

ACTORS' CHURCH UNION
St Paul's Church, Bedford Street, London WC2E 9ED
e-mail: actors_church_union@yahoo.co.uk
                                     Tel: 020-7240 0344

ADVERTISING ASSOCIATION
Abford House, 15 Wilton Road, London SW1V 1NJ
e-mail: aa@adassoc.org.uk
Fax: 020-7931 0376   Tel: 020-7828 2771

**AFTRA (American Federation of Television &
Radio Artists)**
5757 Wilshire Boulevard, 9th Floor
Los Angeles CA 90036   Tel: (323) 634-8100

**AFTRA (American Federation of Television &
Radio Artists)**
260 Madison Avenue, New York NY 10016
Fax: (212) 545-1238   Tel: (212) 532-0800

AGENTS' ASSOCIATION (Great Britain)
54 Keyes House
Dolphin Square, London SW1V 3NA
Website: www.agents-uk.com
e-mail: association@agents-uk.com
Fax: 020-7821 0261   Tel: 020-7834 0515

AMATEUR DRAMATICS & OPERATICS DOTCOM
(Worldwide Directory of Amateur Theatre -
Jill Eccleston)
Website: www.amateurdramatics.com
e-mail: editor@amateurdramatics.com
Fax: 0870 1694836   Tel: 01257 450386

ARTS & BUSINESS
Nutmeg House
60 Gainsford St, Butlers Wharf, London SE1 2NY
e-mail: head.office@aandb.org.uk
Fax: 020-7407 7527   Tel: 020-7378 8143

**ARTS & ENTERTAINMENT TECHNICAL TRAINING
INITIATIVE (AETTI)**
Lower Ground
14 Blenheim Terrace, London NW8 0EB
e-mail: aetti@sumack.freeserve.co.uk
Fax: 020-7328 5035   Tel: 01332 751740

ARTS CENTRE GROUP The
ACG@Intermission, St Saviours, Walton Place
London SW3 1SA
Website: www.artscentregroup.org.uk
e-mail: info@artscentregroup.org.uk
Fax: 0870 7060964   Tel: 020-7581 2777

ARTS COUNCIL ENGLAND
14 Great Peter Street, London SW1P 3NQ
Website: www.artscouncil.org.uk
e-mail: enquiries@artscouncil.org.uk
Fax: 020-7973 6590   Tel: 0845 300 6200

ARTS COUNCIL NORTHERN IRELAND
MacNeice House
77 Malone Road, Belfast BT9 6AQ
Fax: 028-9066 1715   Tel: 028-9038 5200

ARTS COUNCIL WALES
9 Museum Place, Cardiff CF10 3NX
Website: www.artswales.org.uk
e-mail: info@artswales.org.uk
Fax: 029-2022 1447   Tel: 029-2037 6500

ARTSLINE
(Disability Access Information Service)
54 Chalton Street, London NW1 1HS
e-mail: access@artsline.org.uk
Fax: 020-7383 2653   Tel: 020-7388 2227

**ASSOCIATION OF BRITISH THEATRE
TECHNICIANS**
47 Bermondsey Street, London SE1 3XT
Website: www.abtt.org.uk
Fax: 020-7378 6170   Tel: 020-7403 3778

ASSOCIATION OF LIGHTING DESIGNERS
PO Box 89, Welwyn Garden City AL7 1ZW
Website: www.ald.org.uk
e-mail: office@ald.org.uk
Fax: 020-7622 4148   Tel/Fax: 01707 891848

ASSOCIATION OF MODEL AGENTS
122 Brompton Road
London SW3 1JE   Info. Line: 09068 517644

**ASSOCIATION OF PROFESSIONAL THEATRE FOR
CHILDREN & YOUNG PEOPLE (APT)**
c/o Brian Bishop, Warwick Arts Centre
University of Warwick, Coventry CV4 7AL
e-mail: b.c.bishop@warwick.ac.uk
Fax: 024-7652 3883   Tel: 024-7652 4252

BECTU
(See BROADCASTING ENTERTAINMENT
CINEMATOGRAPH & THEATRE UNION)

**BRITISH ACADEMY OF COMPOSERS
& SONGWRITERS The**
2nd Floor, British Music House, 26 Berners Street
London W1T 3LR
Website: www.britishacademy.com
e-mail: info@britishacademy.com
Fax: 020-7636 2212   Tel: 020-7636 2929

**BRITISH ACADEMY OF FILM &
TELEVISION ARTS The**
195 Piccadilly, London W1J 9LN
Website: www.bafta.org
e-mail: membership@bafta.org
Fax: 020-7437 0473   Tel: 020-7734 0022

**BRITISH ACADEMY OF FILM & TELEVISION
ARTS/LOS ANGELES The**
8533 Melrose Avenue, Suite D
West Hollywood, CA 90069
e-mail: info@baftala.org
Fax: (310) 854-6002   Tel: (310) 652-4121

**BRITISH ACADEMY OF STAGE &
SCREEN COMBAT**
Suite 280, 37 Store Street, London WC1E 7QF
Website: www.bassc.org
e-mail: info@bassc.org   Tel: 020-8352 0605

BRITISH ASSOCIATION FOR PERFORMING ARTS MEDICINE
196 Shaftesbury Avenue
London WC2H 8JF   Tel: 020-7240 3331

BRITISH ASSOCIATION OF DRAMA THERAPISTS The
41 Broomhouse Lane, London SW6 3DP
Website: www.badth.co.uk
e-mail: gillian@badth.demon.co.uk
                    Tel/Fax: 020-7731 0160

BRITISH BOARD OF FILM CLASSIFICATION
3 Soho Square, London W1D 3HD
Website: www.bbfc.co.uk
Fax: 020-7287 0141   Tel: 020-7440 1570

BRITISH COUNCIL The
(Drama & Dance Unit)
10 Spring Gardens, London SW1A 2BN
Website: www.britishcouncil.org/arts
e-mail: theatredance@britishcouncil.org
                    Tel: 020-7389 3010

BRITISH FILM INSTITUTE
21 Stephen Street, London W1T 1LN
e-mail: library@bfi.org.uk
Fax: 020-7436 2338   Tel: 020-7255 1444

BRITISH LIBRARY SOUND ARCHIVE
96 Euston Road, London NW1 2DB
Website: www.bl.uk/nsa
e-mail: sound-archive@bl.uk
Fax: 020-7412 7441   Tel: 020-7412 7440

BRITISH MUSIC HALL SOCIETY
(Secretary: Daphne Masterton)
82 Fernlea Road
London SW12 9RW   Tel: 020-8673 2175

BROADCASTING ENTERTAINMENT CINEMATOGRAPH & THEATRE UNION (BECTU) (Formerly BETA & ACTT)
375-377 Clapham Road, London SW9 9BT
e-mail: smacdonald@bectu.org.uk
Fax: 020-7346 0901   Tel: 020-7346 0900

CASTING DIRECTORS' GUILD
PO Box 34403, London W6 0YG
Website: www.castingdirectorsguild.co.uk
                    Tel/Fax: 020-8741 1951

CATHOLIC STAGE GUILD
(Write SAE)
Ms Molly Steele (Hon Secretary), 1 Maiden Lane
London WC2E 7NB   Tel: 020-7240 1221

CELEBRATE
(Creative Events Development)
1 Hill Street, Jackson Bridge, Holmfirth
West Yorkshire HD9 1LZ
e-mail: info@celebrateprojects.co.uk
                    Tel: 01484 688219

CELEBRITY SERVICE Ltd
Room 203-209, 93-97 Regent Street
London W1B 4ES
e-mail: celebritylondon@aol.com
Fax: 020-7494 3500   Tel: 020-7439 9840

CHILDREN'S FILM & TELEVISION FOUNDATION Ltd
Elstree Film & Television Studios
Borehamwood, Hertfordshire WD6 1JG
e-mail: annahome@cftf.onyxnet.co.uk
Fax: 020-8207 0860   Tel: 020-8953 0844

CINEMA & TELEVISION BENEVOLENT FUND (CTBF)
22 Golden Square, London W1F 9AD
Website: www.ctbf.co.uk
e-mail: charity@ctbf.co.uk
Fax: 020-7437 7186   Tel: 020-7437 6567

CINEMA EXHIBITORS' ASSOCIATION
22 Golden Square, London W1F 9JW
e-mail: cea@cinemauk.ftech.co.uk
Fax: 020-7734 6147   Tel: 020-7734 9551

CLUB FOR ACTS & ACTORS
(Incorporating Concert Artistes Association)
20 Bedford Street
London WC2E 9HP   Office: 020-7836 3172

COI COMMUNICATIONS
(Television)
Hercules Road
London SE1 7DU
e-mail: eileen.newton@coi.gsi.gov.uk
Fax: 020-7261 8776   Tel: 020-7261 8220

COMPANY OF CRANKS
1st Floor, 62 Northfield House
Frensham Street, London SE15 6TN
e-mail: mimetic@freeuk.com   Tel: 020-7358 0571

CONCERT ARTISTES ASSOCIATION
(See CLUB FOR ACTS & ACTORS)

CONFERENCE OF DRAMA SCHOOLS
(Saul Hyman, Executive Secretary)
PO Box 34252
London NW5 1XJ
Website: www.drama.ac.uk
e-mail: enquiries@cds.drama.ac.uk

COUNCIL FOR DANCE EDUCATION & TRAINING (CDET) The
Toynbee Hall, 28 Commercial Street
London E1 6LS
Website: www.cdet.org.uk
e-mail: info@cdet.org.uk
Fax: 020-7247 3404   Tel: 0901 8800014

CPMA
(Co-operative Personal Management Association)
The Secretary, c/o 1 Mellor Road
Leicester LE3 6HN
e-mail: cpmauk@yahoo.co.uk
Fax: 0116-223 5537   Tel: 0116-233 8432

CREATIVE INDUSTRIES DEVELOPMENT AGENCY (CIDA)
(Professional development & business support for artists & creative businesses)
Media Centre, Northumberland Street
Huddersfield, West Yorkshire HD1 1RL
Website: www.cida.org
e-mail: info@cida.org
Fax: 01484 483150   Tel: 01484 483140

CRITICS' CIRCLE The
c/o 69 Marylebone Lane, London W1U 2PH
Website: www.criticscircle.org.uk
                                     Tel: 020-7224 1410

DANCE UK
(Including the Healthier Dancer Programme & 'The UK Choreographers' Directory')
Battersea Arts Centre, Lavender Hill
London SW11 5TN
Website: www.danceuk.org
e-mail: info@danceuk.org
Fax: 020-7223 0074   Tel: 020-7228 4990

D'OYLY CARTE OPERA COMPANY
The Powerhouse
6 Sancroft Street, London SE11 5UD
Website: www.doylycarte.org.uk
e-mail: mail@doylycarte.org.uk
Fax: 020-7793 7300   Tel: 020-7793 7100

DENVILLE HALL
(Nursing Home)
62 Ducks Hill Road, Northwood, Middlesex HA6 2SB
Website: www.denvillehall.org
e-mail: denvillehall@yahoo.com
Fax: 01923 841855   Residents: 01923 820805

DEVOTEES of HAMMER FILMS PRESERVATION SOCIETY The
(Fan Club)
14 Kingsdale Road, London SE18 2DG
e-mail: 07960969318@one2one.net
                                     Tel: 020-8244 8640

DIRECTORS GUILD OF GREAT BRITAIN
Acorn House, 314-320 Gray's Inn Road
London WC1X 8DP
Website: www.dggb.org
e-mail: info@dggb.org
Fax: 020-7278 4742   Tel: 020-7278 4343

DIRECTORS' & PRODUCERS' RIGHTS SOCIETY
Victoria Chambers, 16-18 Strutton Ground
London SW1P 2HP
e-mail: info@dprs.org.uk
Fax: 020-7227 4755   Tel: 020-7227 4757

DRAMA ASSOCIATION OF WALES
(Specialist Drama Lending Library)
The Old Library, Singleton Road, Splott
Cardiff CF24 2ET
Fax: 029-2045 2277   Tel: 029-2045 2200

DRAMATURGS' NETWORK
(Network of Professional Dramaturgs)
139B Tooting Bec Road
London SW17 8BW
Website: www.dramaturgy.co.uk
e-mail: info@dramaturgy.co.uk   Tel: 020-8767 6004

EDINBURGHREVIEW.COM
The Bull Theatre, 68 The High Street, Barnet
Hertfordshire EN5 5SJ
Website: www.edinburghreview.com
e-mail: mail@edinburghreview.com
Fax: 020-8449 5252   Tel: 020-8449 7800

ENGLISH FOLK DANCE & SONG SOCIETY
Cecil Sharp House, 2 Regent's Park Road
London NW1 7AY
Website: www.efdss.org.info
e-mail: info@efdss.org
Fax: 020-7284 0534   Tel: 020-7485 2206

EQUITY inc Variety Artistes' Federation
Guild House, Upper St Martin's Lane
London WC2H 9EG
Website: www.equity.org.uk
e-mail: info@equity.org.uk
Fax: 020-7379 7001   Tel: 020-7379 6000

(North West)
Conavon Court
12 Blackfriars Street, Salford M3 5BQ
e-mail: info@manchester-equity.org.uk
Fax: 0161-839 3133   Tel: 0161-832 3183

(Scotland & Northern Ireland)
114 Union Street, Glasgow G1 3QQ
e-mail: igilchrist@glasgow.equity.org.uk
Fax: 0141-248 2473   Tel: 0141-248 2472

(Wales & South West)
Transport House
1 Cathedral Road, Cardiff CF1 9SD
e-mail: info@cardiff-equity.co.uk
Fax: 029-2023 0754   Tel: 029-2039 7971

ETF (Equity Trust Fund)
Suite 222, Africa House, 64 Kingsway
London WC2B 6BD
Fax: 020-7831 4953   Tel: 020-7404 6041

FAA (See FILM ARTISTS ASSOCIATION)

FILM ARTISTS ASSOCIATION
(Amalgamated with BECTU)
373-377 Clapham Road, London SW9
Fax: 020-7437 8268   Tel: 020-7437 8506

FILM LONDON
20 Euston Centre, Regent's Place, London NW1 3JH
Website: www.filmlondon.org.uk
e-mail: info@filmlondon.org.uk
Fax: 020-7387 8788   Tel: 020-7387 8787

GLASGOW FILM FINANCE
(Production Finance for Feature Films)
City Chambers, Glasgow G2 1DU
Fax: 0141-287 0311   Tel: 0141-287 0424

GRAND ORDER OF WATER RATS
328 Gray's Inn Road, London WC1X 8BZ
Website: www.gowr.net
e-mail: water.rats@virgin.net
Fax: 020-7278 1765   Tel: 020-7278 3248

GROUP LINE
(Group Bookings for London Theatre)
22-24 Torrington Place, London WC1E 7HJ
Fax: 020-7436 6287   Tel: 020-7580 6793

GUILD OF BRITISH CAMERA TECHNICIANS The
Metropolitan Centre, Bristol Road
Greenford, Middlesex UB6 8GD
Fax: 020-8813 2111   Tel: 020-8813 1999

GUY Gillian ASSOCIATES
84A Tachbrook Street, London SW1V 2NB
Website: www.show-pairs.co.uk
Fax: 020-7976 5885   Tel: 020-7976 5888

INDEPENDENT THEATRE COUNCIL (ITC)
12 The Leathermarket, Weston Street SE1 3ER
e-mail: admin@itc-arts.org
Fax: 020-7403 1745   Tel: 020-7403 1727

INSIGHT ARTS TRUST
7-15 Greatorex Street, London E1 5NF
e-mail: iat@insightartstrust.demon.co.uk
Fax: 020-7247 8077   Tel: 020-7247 0778

the actors centre

A space of energy and inspiration where professional actors can experiment, share creativity, meet new challenges and pursue excellence.

A meeting place where professional actors can develop ideas, exchange information and support one another.

Subsidised Classes

- audition technique
- dialect
- sight reading
- singing
- voice

- film
- musical theatre
- poetry reading
- radio
- television
- writing

- Alexander technique
- fencing/stage combat
- movement
- dance

- career advice
- casting sessions
- financial advice

Tristan Bates Theatre

A vibrant and varied programme of new and developing work

The Green Room Bar and Restaurant

Drinks & Snacks

Audition Rooms

Available for hire - ranging from 10 x 15 ft to 22 x 29 ft
Line-Learning service available

If you would like a copy of our current programme please telephone:

020 7240 3940

1A Tower Street Covent Garden WC2H 9NP

or

admin@actorscentre.co.uk

Founding Patron: Lord Olivier
Patron: 1983-94: Sir Alec Guinness

Patron: Sir Alan Bates
Artistic Director: Matthew Lloyd

INTERNATIONAL FEDERATION OF ACTORS (FIA)
Guild House, Upper St Martin's Lane
London WC2H 9EG
Website: www.fia-actors.com
e-mail: office@fia-actors.com
Fax: 020-7379 8260   Tel: 020-7379 0900

INTERNATIONAL THEATRE INSTITUTE
Goldsmiths College, University of London
Lewisham Way, New Cross, London SE14 6NW
Website: http://iti.gold.ac.uk
e-mail: iti@gold.ac.uk
Fax: 020-7919 7277   Tel: 020-7919 7276

**INTERNATIONAL VISUAL COMMUNICATION
ASSOCIATION (IVCA)**
19 Pepper Street, Glengall Bridge, London E14 9RP
e-mail: info@ivca.org
Fax: 020-7512 0591   Tel: 020-7512 0571

IRISH ACTORS' EQUITY GROUP (SIPTU)
9th Floor, Liberty Hall, Dublin 1, Eire
Fax: 00 353 1 8743691   Tel: 00 353 1 8586403

IRVING SOCIETY The
(Michael Kilgarriff, Chairman)
10 Kings Avenue, London W5 2SH
e-mail: chairman@theirvingsociety.org.uk
                           Tel: 020-8566 8301

ITC
(Formerly INDEPENDENT TELEVISION COMMISSION -
See OFCOM)

ITC
(See INDEPENDENT THEATRE COUNCIL)

ITV - NETWORK Ltd
200 Gray's Inn Road, London WC1X 8HF
Fax: 020-7843 8158   Tel: 020-7843 8000

**LIAISON OF ACTORS, MANAGEMENTS &
PLAYWRIGHTS (LAMP)**
(W Robi)
86A Elgin Avenue
London W9   Tel: 020-7289 3031

LONDON SCHOOL OF CAPOEIRA The
Units 1 & 2 Leeds Place
Tollington Park, London N4 3RQ
Website: www.londonschoolofcapoeira.co.uk
                           Tel: 020-7281 2020

LONDON SHAKESPEARE WORKOUT The
181A Faunce House
Doddington Grove, Kennington, London SE17 3TB
Website: www.londonshakespeare.org.uk
e-mail: londonswo@hotmail.com
Fax: 020-7735 5911   Tel: 020-7793 9755

**MANDER & MITCHENSON THEATRE
COLLECTION**
Jerwood Library of the Performing Arts
King Charles Building, Old Royal Naval College
Greenwich, London SE10 9JF
e-mail: rmangan@tcm.ac.uk
Fax: 020-8305 3993   Tel: 020-8305 4426

**MECHANICAL-COPYRIGHT PROTECTION
SOCIETY Ltd (MCPS)**
Elgar House, 41 Streatham High Road
London SW16 1ER   Tel: 020-8664 4400

MUSICIANS' UNION
60-64 Clapham Road, London SW9 0JJ
Fax: 020-7582 9805   Tel: 020-7582 5566

**NATIONAL ASSOCIATION OF YOUTH THEATRES
(NAYT)**
Arts Centre, Vane Terrace, Darlington DL3 7AX
Website: www.nayt.org.uk
e-mail: naytuk@aol.com
Fax: 01325 363313   Tel: 01325 363330

NATIONAL CAMPAIGN FOR THE ARTS
Pegasus House, 37-43 Sackville Street
London W1S 3EH
Website: www.artscampaign.org.uk
e-mail: nca@artscampaign.org.uk
Fax: 020-7333 0660   Tel: 020-7333 0375

NATIONAL COUNCIL FOR DRAMA TRAINING
1-7 Woburn Walk, Bloomsbury, London WC1H 0JJ
Website: www.ncdt.co.uk
e-mail: info@ncdt.co.uk
Fax: 020-7387 3860   Tel: 020-7387 3650

NATIONAL ENTERTAINMENT AGENTS COUNCIL
PO Box 112, Seaford, East Sussex BN25 2DQ
Website: www.wfo@neac.org
e-mail: wfo@neac.org
Fax: 0870 7557613   Tel: 0870 7557612

NATIONAL FILM THEATRE
South Bank, Waterloo, London SE1 8XT
Website: www.bfi.org.uk   Tel: 020-7928 3535

NATIONAL RESOURCE CENTRE FOR DANCE
University of Surrey, Guildford, Surrey GU2 7XH
Website: www.surrey.ac.uk/nrcd
e-mail: nrcd@surrey.ac.uk   Tel: 01483 259316

NATIONAL YOUTH MUSIC THEATRE
5th Floor, The Palace Theatre
Shaftesbury Avenue, London W1D 5AY
Website: www.nymt.org.uk
e-mail: enquiries@nymt.org.uk
Fax: 020-7734 7515   Tel: 020-7734 7478

**NODA
(National Operatic & Dramatic Association)**
Noda House, 58-60 Lincoln Road
Peterborough PE1 2RZ
Website: www.noda.org.uk
e-mail: everyone@noda.org.uk
Fax: 0870 7702490   Tel: 0870 7702480

NORTH AMERICAN ACTORS' ASSOCIATION
1 De Vere Cottages
Canning Place, London W8 5AA
Website: www.naaa.org.uk
e-mail: americanactors@aol.com
                           Tel/Fax: 020-7938 4722

NORTH WEST PLAYWRIGHTS
18 St Margaret's Chambers, 5 Newton Street
Manchester M1 1HL
Website: www.newplaysnw.com
e-mail: newplaysnw@hotmail.com
                           Tel/Fax: 0161-237 1978

NORTHERN ACTORS CENTRE
21-23 Oldham Street, Manchester M1 1JG
Website: www.northernactorscentre.co.uk
e-mail: info@northernactorscentre.co.uk
                           Tel/Fax: 0161-819 2513

OFCOM
Office of Communications, Riverside House
2A Southwark Bridge Road, London SE1 9HA
e-mail: webmaster@ofcom.org.uk
Fax: 020-7981 3333   Tel: 020-7297 2076

**PACT (PRODUCERS ALLIANCE FOR CINEMA &
TELEVISION)**
(Trade Association for Independent Television,
Feature Film & New Media Production Companies)
45 Mortimer Street, London W1W 8HJ
Website: www.pact.co.uk
e-mail: enquiries@pact.co.uk
Fax: 020-7331 6700   Tel: 020-7331 6000

PERFORMING RIGHT SOCIETY Ltd
29-33 Berners Street, London W1T 3AB
Fax: 020-7306 4455   Tel: 020-7580 5544

PERSONAL MANAGERS' ASSOCIATION Ltd
Rivercroft, 1 Summer Road
East Molesey
Surrey KT8 9LX
e-mail: info@thepma.com   Tel/Fax: 020-8398 9796

RADIO AUTHORITY The
Holbrook House, 14 Great Queen Street
Holborn, London WC2B 5DG
Fax: 020-7405 7062   Tel: 020-7430 2724

ROYAL TELEVISION SOCIETY
Holborn Hall, 100 Gray's Inn Rd, London WC1X 8AL
Website: www.rts.org.uk
e-mail: info@rts.org.uk
Fax: 020-7430 0924   Tel: 020-7430 1000

ROYAL THEATRICAL FUND
11 Garrick Street, London WC2E 9AR
e-mail: admin@trtf.com
Fax: 020-7379 8273   Tel: 020-7836 3322

S A G
(Screen Actors Guild)
1515 Broadway, 44th Floor
New York NY 10036   Tel: (212) 944-1030

S A G
(Screen Actors Guild)
5757 Wilshire Boulevard
Los Angeles, CA 90036-3600
Fax: (323) 549-6656   Tel: (323) 954-1600

SAMPAD SOUTH ASIAN ARTS DEVELOPMENT
(Promotes the appreciation & practice of South
Asian Arts)
c/o Mac Cannon Hill Park, Birmingham B12 9QH
Website: www.sampad.org.uk
e-mail: info@sampad.org.uk
Fax: 0121-440 8667   Tel: 0121-446 4312

SAVE LONDON'S THEATRES CAMPAIGN
Guild House, Upper St Martin's Lane
London WC2H 9EG
Fax: 020-7379 7001   Tel: 020-7670 0270

SCOTTISH ARTS COUNCIL
12 Manor Place, Edinburgh EH3 7DD
Fax: 0131-225 9833   Tel: 0131-226 6051

SCOTTISH SCREEN PRODUCTION & DEVELOPMENT
249 West George Street, Glasgow G2 4QE
Website: www.scottishscreen.com
e-mail: info@scottishscreen.com
Fax: 0141-302 1711   Tel: 0141-302 1700

SCREENWRITER'S WORKSHOP The
Screenwriters' Centre, Suffolk House
1-8 Whitfield Place, London W1T 5JU
Website: www.lsw.org.uk
e-mail: screenoffice@tiscali.co.uk
Tel: 020-7387 5511

SCRIPT
(West Midlands Playwrights, Scriptwriters - Training
& Support)
Unit 107 The Greenhouse, The Custard Factory
Gibb Street,
Birmingham B9 4AA   Tel/Fax: 0121-224 7415

SOCIETY FOR THEATRE RESEARCH
c/o The Theatre Museum, 1E Tavistock Street
London WC2E 7PR
Website: www.blot.co.uk/str
e-mail: e.cottis@btinternet.com

SOCIETY OF AUTHORS
84 Drayton Gardens, London SW10 9SB
e-mail: info@societyofauthors.org
Tel: 020-7373 6642

SOCIETY OF BRITISH THEATRE DESIGNERS
47 Bermondsey Street, London SE1 3XT
Website: www.theatredesign.org.uk
Fax: 020-7378 6170   Tel: 020-7403 3778

SOCIETY OF LONDON THEATRE (SOLT)
32 Rose Street, London WC2E 9ET
e-mail: enquiries@solttma.co.uk
Fax: 020-7557 6799   Tel: 020-7557 6700

SOCIETY OF TEACHERS OF SPEECH & DRAMA The
Registered Office:
73 Berry Hill Road, Mansfield
Nottinghamshire NG18 4RU
Website: www.stsd.org.uk
e-mail: ann.p.jones@btinternet.com
                                Tel: 01623 627636

SOCIETY OF THEATRE CONSULTANTS
47 Bermondsey Street
London SE1 3XT
Fax: 020-7378 6170   Tel: 020-7403 3778

STAGE CRICKET CLUB
39-41 Hanover Steps
St George's Fields
Albion Street, London W2 2YG
e-mail: brianjfilm@aol.com
Fax: 020-7262 5736   Tel: 020-7402 7543

STAGE GOLFING SOCIETY
Sudbrook Park
Sudbrook Lane
Richmond
Surrey TW10 7AS   Tel: 020-8940 8861

STAGE MANAGEMENT ASSOCIATION
47 Bermondsey Street
London SE1 3XT
Website: www.stagemanagementassociation.co.uk
e-mail: admin@stagemanagementassociation.co.uk
Fax: 020-7378 6170   Tel: 020-7403 6655

STANDING CONFERENCE OF YOUNG PEOPLES THEATRE (SCYPT)
(Office Manager: Ray Beaumont)
Valleys Kids, Penygraig Community Project
1 Cross Street, Penygraig, Tonypandy
Rhonda Cynon Taff CF40 1LD
Fax: 01443 420877   Tel: 01443 438770

THEATRE INVESTMENT FUND Ltd
32 Rose Street
London WC2E 9ET
Fax: 020-7557 6799   Tel: 020-7557 6737

THEATRE MUSEUM The
1E Tavistock Street
London WC2E 7PR
Website: www.theatremuseum.org
Fax: 020-7943 4777   Tel: 020-7943 4700

THEATRES TRUST The
22 Charing Cross Road
London WC2H 0QL
Website: www.theatrestrust.org.uk
e-mail: info@theatrestrust.org.uk
Fax: 020-7836 3302   Tel: 020-7836 8591

THEATRICAL GUILD The
PO Box 22712
London N22 5AG
Website: www.the-theatrical-guild-org-uk
e-mail: admin@the-theatrical-guild.org.uk
                                Tel: 020-8889 7570

THEATRICAL MANAGEMENT ASSOCIATION
(See TMA)

TMA
(Theatrical Management Association)
32 Rose Street, London WC2E 9ET
Website: www.tmauk.org
e-mail: enquiries@solttma.co.uk
Fax: 020-7557 6799   Tel: 020-7557 6700

UK CHOREOGRAPHERS' DIRECTORY The
(See DANCE UK)

UK FILM COUNCIL INTERNATIONAL
10 Little Portland Street, London W1W 7JG
Website: www.filmcouncil.org.uk
e-mail: internationalinfo@ukfilmcouncil.org.uk
Fax: 020-7861 7864   Tel: 020-7861 7860

UK THEATRE CLUBS
54 Swallow Drive
London NW10 8TG
e-mail: uktheatreclubs@aol.com
                                Tel/Fax: 020-8459 3972

UNITED KINGDOM COPYRIGHT BUREAU
110 Trafalgar Road
Portslade, East Sussex BN41 1GS
Website: www.copyrightbureau.co.uk
e-mail: info@copyrightbureau.co.uk
Fax: 01273 705451   Tel: 01273 277333

VARIETY & LIGHT ENTERTAINMENT COUNCIL
54 Keyes House
Dolphin Square, London SW1V 3NA
Fax: 020-7821 0261   Tel: 020-7798 5622

VARIETY CLUB OF GREAT BRITAIN
Variety Club House, 93 Bayham Street
London NW1 0AG
Website: www.varietyclub.org.uk
e-mail: info@varietyclub.org.uk
Fax: 020-7428 8111   Tel: 020-7428 8100

VOICE GUILD OF GREAT BRITAIN The
c/o 275 Kennington Road
London SE11 6BY
Fax: 020-7820 1845   Tel: 020-7735 5736

WOLFF Peter THEATRE TRUST The
(Peter Wolff)
Flat 22, 7 Princess Gate
London SW7 1QL
Website: www.peterwolfftheatretrust.org
e-mail: pmwolff@msn.com
Fax: 020-7581 1917   Mobile: 07767 242552

WOMEN IN FILM AND TELEVISION
6 Langley Street
London WC2H 9JA
e-mail: info@wftv.org.uk
Fax: 020-7379 1625   Tel: 020-7240 4875

WRITERNET
Cabin V, Clarendon Buildings
25 Horsell Road London N5 1XL
Website: www.writernet.org.uk
e-mail: writernet@btinternet.com
Fax: 020-7609 7557   Tel: 020-7609 7474

WRITERS' GUILD OF GREAT BRITAIN The
15 Britannia Street
London WC1X 9JN
Website: www.writersguild.org.uk
e-mail: admin@writersguild.org.uk
Fax: 020-7833 4777   Tel: 020-7833 0777 ext 203

Photographers

Each photographer listed in this section has taken an advertisement in this edition.
Also see Index to Advertisers pages 325-326.

- **1st CLASS PHOTOGRAPHY** — M 07813 282391 F 0121-624 2405
- **ACTIVE PHOTOGRAPHY** — www.chrishallphotography.co.uk info@chrishallphotography.co.uk T 0800 7812412 M 07831 541342
- **ACTOR'S ONE STOP SHOP** — www.actorsone-stopshop.com T 020-8888 7006
- **ALLEN Stuart** — www.stuartallenphotos.com M 07776 258829
- **ANNAND Simon** — simonannand@blueyonder.co.uk T 020-7241 6725 M 07884 446776
- **BACON Ric** — www.ricbacon.co.uk M 07970 970799
- **BAKER Chris** — T 020-8441 3851
- **BAKER Sophie** — T 020-8340 3850
- **BARKANY Bob** — www.barkany.com/casting bob@barkany.com M 07973 666243
- **BRACEY Louise** — T 020-8993 0175
- **BRIERLEY Marcus** — M 07930 937641
- **BURNETT Sheila** — www.sheilaburnett-photography.com T 020-7289 3058
- **CARPENTER TURNER Robert** — www.carpenterturner.co.uk T 020-7624 2225 F 020-7624 7731
- **CARTER Charlie** — T 020-7751 0575
- **CLARK John** — www.johnclarkphotography.com clarkdigital@btopenworld.com T 020-8854 4069 M 07702 627237
- **COOK Mark** — www.markcookphotography.com T 0121-240 8950
- **CURTIS Michael** — www.michaelcurtis-photographer.com T 01923 897285
- **DANCESCENE PHOTOGRAPHIC** — T 01737 552874 M 07702 747123
- **DAVID Grant** — gdman@gdman.fsnet.co.uk M 07930 331373
- **DEBAL** — debal@abeautifulimage.com T 020-8568 2122
- **DELANY Louise** — T 020-8451 6239 M 07802 418592
- **DE LENG Stephanie** — www.stephaniedelengphotos.co.uk T 0151-476 1563 M 07740 927765
- **DEUCHAR Angus** — www.actorsphotos.co.uk T 020-8286 3303 M 07973 600728
- **DOCKAR-DRYSDALE Jonathan** — j.d-d@lineone.net T 020-8560 1077 M 07711 006191
- **DOYLE Paul** — info@pauldoylefoto.co.uk T/F 020-8577 3967 M 07939 097121
- **DYE Debbie** — www.debbiedye.com M 07957 653913
- **EDDOWES Mike** — www.theatre.photography.co.uk mike@photo-publicity.co.uk T 01903 882525 M 07970 141005
- **EVANS Owen** — M 07940 700294
- **EYRE Anne** — www.eyrephoto.co.uk T 020-7638 1289
- **FERNANDES David** — www.image2film.com T 01273 549967 M 07958 272333
- **FLETCHER John** — T 020-8203 4816
- **FONTAINE Desi** — www.desifontaine.co.uk T 020-8878 4348
- **GERRISH Darren** — gerrishdarren@hotmail.com M 07770 815753
- **GILL James** — T 020-7735 5632
- **GREENBERG Natasha** — T 020-8677 8753 M 07932 618111
- **GREGAN Nick** — www.nickgregan.com nick@nickgreganphotos.demon.co.uk T 020-7538 1249 M 07774 421878 F 020-7538 8778
- **GROGAN Claire** — www.clairegrogan.co.uk T 020-7272 1845 M 07932 635381
- **HALL Peter** — www.peterhall-photo.co.uk T 020-8981 2822 M 07803 345495
- **HARPER Fran** — M 07765 954326
- **HART Zara** — sara.g@freezone.co.uk T 020-7722 5606 M 07889 172962
- **HARWOOD-STAMPER Daniel** — T 020-7930 1372
- **HASTINGS Magnus** — T 020-7700 6475 M 07905 304705
- **HELSEL Brent** — www.first-look.com/headshots M 07949 194406
- **HUNTER Remy** — www.remyhunter.co.uk T 020-7431 8055 M 07766 760724
- **IMAGE 2** — www.image2photography.co.uk T 01923 775098
- **JAM PHOTOGRAPHIC** — www.jamphotographic.co.uk M 07791 360068
- **JEFFERSON Paris** — T 020-7404 3219 M 07876 586601
- **JOHNSON Olyden** — www.olyden.com freeheadshots@olyden.com T 020-7837 0994
- **KELLY Luke** — T 020-8878 2823
- **LATIMER Carole** — T 020-7727 9371 F 020-7229 9306
- **LAWTON Steve** — stevelawton@clara.co.uk M 07973 307487
- **LB PHOTOGRAPHY** — T 01737 224578 M 07885 966192

Photographers

• LENTON Murray	www.theatrephotogrpahy.co.uk murray@theatrephotography.co.uk T 020-7733 6769 M 07941 427458
• LINDSAY Sophie	M 07850 576325
• MAD PHOTOGRAPHY	www.mad-photography.co.uk T 020-8363 4182
• MOORE Casey	www.caseymoore.com casey@caseymoore.com M 07974 188105
• NAMDAR Fatimah	T 020-8341 1332
• NEMAR Ken	www.nemarphotography.co.uk M 07958 511001
• NEW ID	www.newidstudios.com T 0870 8701299
• ORION PHOTOGRAPHY	www.orionphotography.co.uk info@orionphotography.co.uk M 07789 404225
• PASSMORE George	georgepassmore@mac.com M 07775 658515
• PASSPORT PHOTO SERVICE	T 020-7629 8540
• PIKE James	www.jimpix.com/headshots T 01273 731745 M 07905 945995
• POLLARD Michael	www.michaelpollard.co.uk T 0161-456 7470
• RABIN Dan	T 020-7739 7568 M 07940 519331
• RAFIQUE Harry	www.hr-photographer.co.uk T 020-7266 5398 M 07986 679498
• RENDELL Jeremy	www.jeremyrendell.com jeremy.rendell@btconnect.com T 020-7732 1122 M 07860 277411
• RIEDEL Katrin	riedelkatrin@hotmail.com M 07957 790876
• STJOHN Amanda	T 01892 521282 M 07732 771384
• SAYER Howard	www.howardsayer.co.uk howardsayer@btconnect.com M 07860 559891
• SCHNEITER Peter	T 020-8764 1181 M 07929 710483
• SHAKESPEARE LANE Catherine	T 020-7226 7694
• SHERWIN Tony	www.tonysherwinphotography.com T 01782 848499 M 07776 157016
• SIMPKIN Peter	www.petersimpkin.co.uk petersimpkin@aol.com T 020-8883 2727
• SINGH Shangara	www.shanagarsingh.com email@shangarasingh.com T 020-8801 3051 M 07860 465857
• SMITH Lucy	www.thatlucy.co.uk T 020-8521 1347
• SPENCER Cameron	M 07787 950244
• STILL Rosie	www.rosiestillphotography.com T 020-8857 6920 M 07957 318919
• STRAEGER Anthony	www.straegerphoto.co.uk T 020-8769 7031 M 07961 184888
• SUMMERS Caroline	T 020-7223 7669
• TEN 8 - PHOTO	M 07734 032635 M 07958 750886
• TM PHOTOGRAPHY	www.tmphotography.co.uk tm.photography@ntlworld.com T 020-8924 4694 M 07931 755252
• ULLATHORNE Steve	www.ullapix.com steve@ullapix.com M 07961 380969
• VANDYCK Katie	www.iphotou.co.uk T 01273 475218
• WAITE Charlie	landscape@charliewaite.com M 07831 364764
• WALTON John	www.casting-image.com T 020-8533 3126 M 07905 311408
• WATSON Robin	www.robinwatson.biz robin@robinwatson.biz T 020-7833 1982 M 07956 416943
• WHITE Sharon	www.whitephotography.co.uk egwhite@tiscali.co.uk T 020-8241 8508 M 07941 144782
• WILL C	www.london-photographer.com billy_snapper@hotmail.com T/F 020-8438 0202 M 07712 669953
• WOODWARD Greg	T 020-8455 5321 M 07855 434869
• WOOLNOUGH Laura	T 020-8693 9596 M 07941 018957
• WORKMAN Robert	www.robertworkman.demon.co.uk T 020-7385 5442
• XFOLIO	www.xfolio.co.uk M 07952 944048

Press Cutting Agencies

DURRANTS
(Media Monitoring Agency), Discovery House
28-42 Banner Street, London EC1Y 8QE
Website: www.durrants.co.uk e-mail: sales@durrants.co.uk
Fax: 020-7674 0222   Tel: 020-7674 0200

INFORMATION BUREAU The
51 The Business Centre, 103 Lavender Hill SW11 5QL
Website: www.informationbureau.co.uk
e-mail: info@informationbureau.co.uk
Fax: 020-7738 2513   Tel: 020-7924 4414

INTERNATIONAL PRESS-CUTTING BUREAU
224-236 Walworth Road, London SE17 1JE
e-mail: ipcb2000@aol.com
Fax: 020-7701 4489   Tel: 020-7708 2113

McCALLUM MEDIA MONITOR
Tower House, 10 Possil Road, Glasgow G4 9SY
Website: www.press-cuttings.com
Fax: 0141-333 1811   Tel: 0141-333 1822

TNS MEDIA INTELLIGENCE
6th Floor
292 Vauxhall Bridge Road
London SW1V 1AE
Fax: 020-7963 7609   Tel: 020-7963 7605

XTREME INFORMATION
891/2 Worship Street, London EC2A 2BF
Website: www.xtremeinformation.com
Fax: 020-7377 6103   Tel: 020-7377 1742

07000 BIG TOP
(Big Top, Seating, Circus)
The Arts Exchange, Congleton, Cheshire CW12 1JG
Website: www.arts-exchange.com
e-mail: phillipgandey@netcentral.co.uk
Fax: 01260 270777   Tel: 01260 276627

10 OUT OF 10 PRODUCTIONS Ltd
(Lighting, Sound, AV Hire, Sales & Installation)
Unit 14, Forest Hill Business Centre
Clyde Vale, London SE23 3JF
Website: www.10outof10.co.uk
e-mail: sales@10outof10.co.uk
Fax: 020-8699 8968   Tel: 0845 1235664

20TH CENTURY FUNFAIR FACTORY
(Fun Fair Locations, Equipment and Prop Hire)
5 Bonds Drive, Pennypot Lane, Chobham
Surrey GU24 8DJ
Mobile: 07976 297735   Tel: 01276 485893

3D CREATIONS
(Production Design, Scenery Contractors,
Prop Makers & Scenic Artists)
9A Bells Road, Gorleston-on-Sea
Great Yarmouth, Norfolk NR31 6BB
Website: www.3d-creations.co.uk
e-mail: 3dcreations@rjt.co.uk
Fax: 01493 443124   Tel: 01493 652055

ACROBAT PRODUCTIONS
(Artistes & Advisors)
The Circus Space, Coronet Street
Hackney, London N1 6HD
Website: www.acrobatproductions.co.uk
e-mail: info@acrobatproductions.co.uk
Tel/Fax: 020-7613 5259

ADAMS ENGRAVING
Unit G1A
The Mayford Centre
Mayford Green, Woking GU22 0PP
Website: www.adamsengraving@pncl.co.uk
Fax: 01483 751787   Tel: 01483 725792

AERONAUTIC
(Function Balloons)
46 Burrage Place
Plumstead, London SE18 7BE
Website: www.aeronautic.org.uk
e-mail: sales@aeronautic.org.uk
Fax: 01322 448272   Mobile: 07956 369890

AFX (UK) Ltd
(incorporating Kirby's Flying Ballets)
8 Greenford Avenue, Hanwell, London W7 3QP
Website: www.kirbysflying.co.uk
e-mail: andy@afxuk.com
Mobile: 07958 285608   Tel/Fax: 020-8723 8552

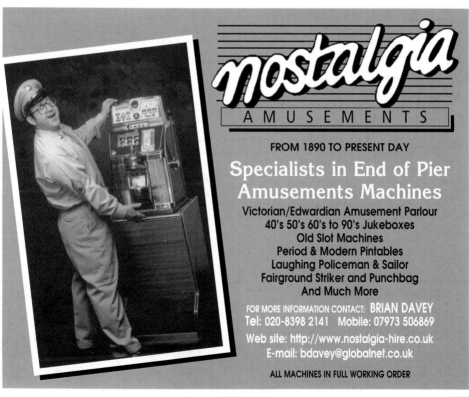

AIRBOURNE SYSTEMS INTERNATIONAL
(All Skydiving Requirements Arranged. Parachute
Hire - Period & Modern)
8 Burns Crescent, Chelmsford
Essex CM2 0TS   Tel: 01245 268772

ALCHEMICAL LABORATORIES ETC
(Medieval Science & Technology Recreated for
Museums & Films)
2 Stapleford Lane, Coddington, Newark
Nottinghamshire NG24 2QZ
Website: www.jackgreene.co.uk   Tel: 01636 707836

ALL SCENE ALL PROPS
(Props, Masks, Painting & Scenery Makers)
443-445 Holloway Road, London N7 6LW
Website: www.allscene.net
e-mail: info@allscene.net   Tel/Fax: 020-7561 9231

ANCHOR MARINE FILM & TELEVISION
(Boat Location, Charter, Maritime Co-ordinators)
Spikemead Farm, Poles Lane, Lowfield Heath
West Sussex RH11 0PX
e-mail: amsfilm@aol.com
Fax: 01293 551558   Tel: 01293 538188

ANELLO & DAVIDE
(Theatrical Footwear)
Shop: 47 Beauchamp Place, Chelsea
London SW3 1NX
Website: www.handmadeshoes.co.uk
Fax: 020-7225 3375   Tel: 020-7225 2468

ANGLO PACIFIC INTERNATIONAL Plc
(Freight Forwarders & Removal Services)
Unit 1, Bush Industrial Estate, Standard Road
North Acton, London NW10 6DF
Website: www.anglopacific.co.uk
Fax: 020-8965 4954   Tel: 020-8965 1234

ANIMAL ARK
(Animals & Natural History Props)
The Studio, 29 Somerset Road
Brentford
Middlesex TW8 8BT
Website: www.animal-ark.co.uk
e-mail: info@animal-ark.co.uk
Fax: 020-8560 5762   Tel: 020-8560 3029

AQUARIUS
(Film & TV Stills Library)
PO Box 5, Hastings TN34 1HR
Website: www.aquariuscollection.com
e-mail: aquarius.lib@clara.net
Fax: 01424 717704   Tel: 01424 721196

AQUATECH
(Camera Boats)
Epney, Gloucestershire GL2 7LN
Website: www.aquatech-uk.com
e-mail: office@aquatech-uk.com
Fax: 01452 741958   Tel: 01452 740559

ARCHERY CENTRE The
(Archery Tuition)
PO Box 39, Battle
East Sussex TN33 0ZT   Tel: 01424 777183

ARMS & ARCHERY
(Armour, Weaponry, Chainmail, X-bows,
Longbows)
The Coach House, London Road, Ware
Hertfordshire SG12 9QU
e-mail: tgou104885@aol.com
Fax: 01920 461044   Tel: 01920 460335

ART
(Art Consultant, Supplier of Paintings & Sculpture)
66 Josephine Avenue, London SW2 2LA
Website: www.artstar.clara.net
e-mail: h_artstar@hotmail.com
Fax: 07970 455956   Tel: 07967 294985

ART DIRECTORS & TRIP PHOTO LIBRARY
(Colour Slides - All Subjects)
57 Burdon Lane, Cheam, Surrey SM2 7BY
Website: www.artdirectors.co.uk
e-mail: images@artdirectors.co.uk
Fax: 020-8395 7230   Tel: 020-8642 3593

A. S. DESIGNS
(Theatrical Designer, Sets, Costumes, Heads
Masks, Puppets etc)
Website: www.astheatricaldesign.co.uk
e-mail: maryannscadding@btinternet.com
Fax: 01279 435642   Tel: 01279 722416

ASH Riky
(Equity Registered Stunt Performer/Co-ordinator)
c/o 65 Britania Avenue, Nottingham NG6 0EA
Website: www.fallingforyou.tv
Mobile: 07850 471227   Tel: 0115-849 3470

ATP EUROPE Ltd
(Design, Print & Repro)
ATP House, 12 Sovereign Park
London NW10 7QP
e-mail: info@atpeurope.com
Fax: 020-8961 7743   Tel: 020-8961 0001

BAD DOG DESIGN/3-D PRODUCTIONS
(3D Productions, 3D Models, Props, Sets)
Fir Tree Cottage, Fish Pool Hill
Brentry, Bristol BS10 6SW
e-mail: info@baddogdesign.co.uk
Fax: 0117-959 1245   Tel: 0117-959 2011

BAPTY 2000 Ltd
(Weapons, Dressing, Props etc)
Witley Works, Witley Gardens
Norwood Green
Middlesex UB2 4ES
e-mail: hire@bapty.demon.co.uk
Fax: 020-8571 5700   Tel: 020-8574 7700

BARHAM ASSOCIATES
(65-foot Classic Motor Yacht available for
Water-based Events, Cowes Week etc)
6 Liberty Row, The Square, Hamble
Southampton SO31 4RR
Website: www.classicyachtcharter.co.uk
e-mail: info@classicyachtcharter.co.uk
                             Tel/Fax: 023-8045 8778

BARNES CATERERS Ltd
8 Ripley Drive, Normanton, Wakefield
West Yorkshire WF6 1QT   Tel/Fax: 01924 892332

BARTON Joe
(Puppeteer, Model & Prop Maker)
7 Brands Hill Avenue, High Wycombe
Buckinghamshire   Tel: 01494 439056

BASINGSTOKE PRESS The
Digital House, The Loddon Centre
Wade Road, Basingstoke, Hampshire RG24 8QW
Website: www.basingstokepress.co.uk
e-mail: sales@baspress.co.uk
Fax: 01256 840383   Tel: 01256 467771

BEAT ABOUT THE BUSH
(Musical Instruments)
Unit 23, Enterprise Way, Triangle Business Centre
Salter Street, London NW10 6UG
Fax: 020-8969 2281   Tel: 020-8960 2087

BENSON'S JUMPAROUND ACTIVITY CENTRES
(Chester Benson Inflatables & Soft Play Equipment,
Bouncy Castles)
PO Box 4227, Worthing BN11 5ST
Website: www.davebensonphillips.co.uk
e-mail: davebensonphillips@yahoo.com
Fax: 01903 700389   Tel: 01903 248258

BIANCHERI The
(The Lampie's Coolest Tool)
T & D House, 7 Woodville Road, London E17 7ER
Mobile: 07973 663154   Tel: 020-8521 6408

BIANCHI AVIATION FILM SERVICES
(Historic & other Aircraft)
Wycombe Air Park, Booker, Marlow
Buckinghamshire SL7 3DP
e-mail: info@bianchiaviation.com
Fax: 01494 461236   Tel: 01494 449810

BIDDLES Ltd
(Quality Book Binders & Printers)
Unit 26, Rollesby Road
Hardwick Industrial Estate
King's Lynn, Norfolk PE30 4LS
Website: www.biddles.co.uk
e-mail: enquiries@biddles.co.uk
Fax: 01553 764633   Tel: 01553 764728

BLACKOUT Ltd
280 Weston Road, London SW19 2QA
Website: www.blackout-ltd.com
e-mail: info@blackout-tabtrack.com
Fax: 020-8687 8500   Tel: 020-8687 8400

BLUEBELL RAILWAY Plc
(Steam Locomotives, Pullman Coaches
Period Stations, Much Film Experience)
Sheffield Park Station, East Sussex TN22 3QL
Website: www.bluebell-railway.co.uk
Fax: 01825 720804   Tel: 01825 720800

P

BOSCO LIGHTING
(Design/Technical Consultancy)
63 Nimrod Road, London SW16 6SZ
e-mail: boscolx@lineone.net   Tel: 020-8769 3470

BRISTOL (UK) Ltd
(Scenic Paint & StageFloor Duo Suppliers)
12 The Arches, Maygrove Road, London NW6 2DS
Website: www.bristolpaint.com
Fax: 020-7372 5242   Tel: 020-7624 4370

BRITISH-FOOD-GROCERIES
(British Food Export Service for British People
Working Overseas)
46 Burrage Place, Plumstead, London SE18 7BE
Website: www.british-food-groceries.co.uk
e-mail: sales@directfoods.uk.com
                              Tel/Fax: 01322 448272

BRODIE & MIDDLETON Ltd
(Theatrical Suppliers, Paints, Powders, Glitter etc)
68 Drury Lane, London WC2B 5SP
Website: www.brodies.net
e-mail: info@brodies.net
Fax: 020-7497 8425   Tel: 020-7836 3289

BROOK-REYNOLDS Natalie
(Freelance Stage Manager/Floor Manager.
Member of SMA, Equity & BECTU)
Website: www.nataliebrookreynoldsuk.pwp.blueyonder.co.uk
e-mail: nataliebrookreynolds@blueyonder.co.uk
Fax: 0871 2429919   Tel: 020-8350 0877

CANDLE MAKERS SUPPLIES
The Wax & Dyecraft Centre
28 Blythe Road, London W14 0HA
Website: www.candlemakers.co.uk
e-mail: candles@candlemakers.co.uk
Fax: 020-7602 2796   Tel: 020-7602 4031

CAPITAL ORGANISATION Ltd The
Capital House, 804 Oxford Avenue
Slough, Berkshire SL1 4LN
Fax: 01753 696401   Tel: 01753 696410

CHALFONT CLEANERS & DYERS Ltd
(Dry Cleaners, Launderers & Dyers, Stage Curtains
& Costumes)
222 Baker Street
London NW1 5RT   Tel: 020-7935 7316

CHEVALIER EVENT DESIGN
(Corporate Hospitality Caterers)
Studio 4-5, Garnett Close
Watford
Hertfordshire WD24 7GN
Website: www.chevalier.co.uk
e-mail: enquiries@chevalier.co.uk
Fax: 01923 211704   Tel: 01923 211703

CHRISANNE Ltd
(Specialist Fabrics & Accessories for
Theatre & Dance)
Chrisanne House, 14 Locks Lane, Mitcham CR4 2JX
Website: www.chrisanne.co.uk
e-mail: sales@chrisanne.co.uk
Fax: 020-8640 2106   Tel: 020-8640 5921

CIRCUS MANIACS
(Circus Equipment, Rigging & Training)
Office 8A, The Kingswood Foundation
Britannia Road, Kingswood, Bristol BS15 8DB
e-mail: info@circusmaniacs.com
Mobile: 07977 247287   Tel/Fax: 0117-947 7042

CIRCUS PROMOTIONS
(Entertainers)
36 St Lukes Road, Tunbridge Wells
Kent TN4 9JH   Tel: 01892 537964

CLARK DAVIS
(Stationery & Office Equipment)
Units 5 & 6, Meridian Trading Estate
20 Bugsbys Way, Charlton, London SE7 7SJ
e-mail: s.fenn@clarkdavis.co.uk
Fax: 020-7240 2106   Tel: 020-7836 5703

CLARKE Donald
(Historical Interpreter, Role Playing)
80 Warden Avenue, Rayners Lane, Harrow
Middlesex HA2 9LW
Mobile: 07811 606285   Tel: 020-8866 2997

CLEANING & FLAME RETARDING SERVICE The
Unit 3, Grange Farm Industrial Units, Grange Road
Tiptree, Essex CO5 0QQ
Website: www.flameretarding.co.uk
e-mail: email@flameretarding.co.uk
Fax: 01621 819803   Tel: 01621 818477

CLEVELAND COLLEGE OF ART & DESIGN
Green Lane, Linthorpe, Middlesbrough TS5 7RJ
Website: www.ccad.ac.uk
Fax: 01642 288828   Tel: 01642 288000

COMPTON Mike & Rosi
(Costumes, Props & Models)
11 Woodstock Road, Croydon, Surrey CR0 1JS
e-mail: mikeandrosicompton@btopenworld.com
Fax: 020-8681 3126   Tel: 020-8680 4364

CONCEPT ENGINEERING Ltd
(Smoke, Fog, Snow etc)
7 Woodlands Business Pk, Woodlands Park Avenue
Maidenhead, Berkshire SL6 3UA
Website: www.concept-smoke.co.uk
Fax: 01628 826261   Tel: 01628 825555

COOK Sheila
(Textiles, Costumes & Accessories for Hire/Sale)
283 Westbourne Grove, London W11 2QA
e-mail: sheilacook@sheilacook.co.uk
Fax: 020-7229 3855   Tel: 020-7792 8001

CRESTA BLINDS Ltd
(Supplier of Vertical Blinds)
Crown Works, Tetnall Street, Dudley DY2 8SA
Website: www.crestablindsltd.co.uk
e-mail: info@crestablindsltd.co.uk
Fax: 01384 457675   Tel: 01384 255523

CROCKSHARD FARMHOUSE
(Bed & Breakfast, Contact: Nicola Ellen)
Wingham, Canterbury, Kent CT3 1NY
e-mail: crockshard_bnb@yahoo.com
Tel: 01227 720464

CROFTS Andrew
(Book Writing Services)
Westlands Grange, West Grinstead
Horsham, West Sussex RH13 8LZ
Website: www.andrewcrofts.com
Tel/Fax: 01403 864518

CUE ACTION POOL PROMOTIONS
(Advice for UK & US Pool, Snooker, Trick Shots)
PO Box 3941, Colchester, Essex CO2 8HN
Website: www.cueaction.com
e-mail: sales@cueaction.com
Fax: 01206 729480   Tel: 07000 868689

DARK SIDE
(Photographic Repro Service)
4 Helmet Row, London EC1V 3QJ
Website: www.darksidephoto.co.uk
e-mail: info@darksidephoto.co.uk
Fax: 020-7250 1771   Tel: 020-7250 1200

DAVEY Brian
(See NOSTALGIA AMUSEMENTS)

DEAN Audrey Vincente
(Soft Dolls, Toys & Figures to Order, No Hire)
76 Burlington Avenue, Kew, Surrey TW9 4DH
e-mail: audreymiller@waitrose.com
Tel: 020-8876 6441

DESIGN ASYLUM
(Design, Web & Print)
Crown House, North Circular Road
Park Royal, London NW10 7PN
Website: www.2dwp.net
e-mail: info@2dwp.net   Tel/Fax: 020-8838 3555

DESIGN PROJECTS
Perrysfield Farm, Broadham Green
Old Oxted, Surrey RH8 9PG
Fax: 01883 723707   Tel: 01883 730262

DEVEREUX K W & Sons
(Removals)
Daimler Drive, Cowpen Industrial Estate, Billingham
Cleveland TS23 4JD
Fax: 01642 566664   Tel: 01642 560854

DONOGHUE Phil PRODUCTIONS
6 Harbour House, Harbour Way, Shoreham Beach
West Sussex BN43 5HZ
Mobile: 07802 179801   Tel/Fax: 01273 465165

DORANS PROPMAKERS/SET BUILDERS
53 Derby Road, Ashbourne, Derbyshire DE6 1BH
Website: www.doarnsprops.com
e-mail: props@dorans.demon.co.uk   Tel/Fax: 01335 300064

DRIVING CENTRE The
(Expert Driving Instructors - All Vehicles)
6 Marlott Road, Poole, Dorset BH15 3DX
Mobile: 07860 290437   Tel: 01202 666001

DURRENT Peter
(Audition & Rehearsal Pianist, Cocktail Pianist,
Composer, Vocal Coach)
Blacksmiths Cottage, Bures Road
Little Cornard, Sudbury
Suffolk CO10 0NR   Tel: 01787 373483

EAT TO THE BEAT
(Production Location Caterers)
Studio 4-5, Garnett Close, Watford
Hertfordshire WD24 7GN
Website: www.eattothebeat.com
e-mail: enquiries@eattothebeat.com
Fax: 01923 211704   Tel: 01923 211702

EATON'S SEASHELLS
Website: www.eatonsseashells.co.uk
e-mail: eatonsseashells@freenet.co.uk
                         Tel/Fax: 020-8539 5288

ECCENTRIC TRADING COMPANY Ltd
(Antique Furniture & Props) incorporating
COMPUHIRE (Computer Hire)
Unit 2, Frogmore Estate, Acton Lane
London NW10 7NQ
Website: www.compuhire.com
e-mail: info@compuhire.com   Tel: 020-8453 1125

ELECTRO SIGNS Ltd
97 Vallentin Road, London E17 3JJ
Fax: 020-8520 8127   Tel: 020-8521 8066

ELMS LESTERS PAINTING ROOMS
(Scenic Painting)
1-3-5 Flitcroft Street, London WC2H 8DH
e-mail: office@elmslesters.co.uk
Fax: 020-7379 0789   Tel: 020-7836 6747

ENCHANTING FOREST
(Bespoke Props)
Unit 6, Machin Industrial Estate, Gotham
Nottingham NG11 0HH   Tel/Fax: 0115-983 0777

ESCORT GUNLEATHER
(Custom Leathercraft)
602 High Road, Benfleet, Essex SS7 5RW
Website: www.escortgunleather.com
e-mail: info@escortgunleather.com
Fax: 01268 566775   Tel: 01268 792769

EVANS Peter STUDIOS Ltd
(Scenic Embellishment, Vacuum Forming)
(Catalogue Available)
1 Frederick Street, Luton, Bedfordshire LU2 7QW
e-mail: peter@peterevansstudios.co.uk
Fax: 01582 481329   Tel: 01582 725730

FAB 'N' FUNKY
(Prop Hire Specialist 50's - 70's)
18-20 Brunel Road, London W3 7XR
Website: www.fabnfunky.co.uk
Fax: 020-8743 2662   Tel: 020-8746 7746

FACADE
(Musical Production Services)
43A Garthorne Road, London SE23 1EP
e-mail: facade@cobomedia.com
                         Tel: 020-8291 7079

FAIRGROUNDS TRADITIONAL
Halstead, Fovant, Salisbury, Wiltshire SP3 5NL
Website: www.pozzy.co.uk
e-mail: s-vpostlethwaite@fovant.fsnet.co.uk
Mobile: 07710 287251   Tel: 01722 714786

**FALCONS STUNT DISPLAY TEAM COMBAT
THROUGH THE AGES**
(Medieval Displays, Combat Display Team,
Stunt Action Specialists)
110 Trafalgar Road, Portslade
East Sussex BN41 1GS
Fax: 01273 708699   Tel: 01273 411862

FILM MEDICAL SERVICES
Units 5 & 7, Commercial Way
Park Royal, London NW10 7XF
Website: www.filmmedical.co.uk
e-mail: filmmed@aol.com
Fax: 020-8961 7427   Tel: 020-8961 3222

FIND ME ANOTHER
(Theatrical Prop Hire & Services. Gardenalia,
Kitchen, Dairy & Farming Bygones)
Mills Barnes, c/o Tenzing Grove, Luton
Bedfordshire LU1 5JJ
Website: www.findmeanother.co.uk
e-mail: info@findmeanother.co.uk
Mobile: 07885 777751   Tel/Fax: 01582 415834

FIREBRAND
(Flambeaux Hire & Sales)
Leac na ban, By Lochgilphead, Argyll PA31 8PF
e-mail: alex@firebrand.fsnet.co.uk
                         Tel/Fax: 01546 870310

FLAMENCO PRODUCTIONS
(Entertainers)
Sevilla 4 Cormorant Rise, Lower Wick
Worcester WR2 4BA   Tel: 01905 424083

FLINT HIRE & SUPPLY Ltd
Queen's Row, London SE17 2PX
Website: www.flints.co.uk
e-mail: sales@flints.co.uk
Fax: 020-7708 4189   Tel: 020-7703 9786

FLYING BY FOY
(Flying Effects for Theatre, TV, Corporate
Events etc)
Unit 4, Borehamwood Enterprise Centre
Theobald Street, Borehamwood
Hertfordshire WD6 4RQ
Website: www.flyingbyfoy.co.uk
e-mail: mail@flyingbyfoy.co.uk
Fax: 020-8236 0235   Tel: 020-8236 0234

FOXTROT PRODUCTIONS Ltd
(Armoury Services, Firearms, Weapons &
Costume Hire)
Unit 46 Canalot Production Studios
222 Kensal Road
London W10 5BN   Tel: 020-8964 3555

FREEDALE PRESS
(Printing)
36 Hedley Street, Maidstone, Kent ME14 5AD
e-mail: freedalepress@blueyonder.co.uk
Fax: 01622 200131   Tel: 01622 200123

FROST John NEWSPAPERS
(Historical Newspaper Service)
22B Rosemary Avenue, Enfield, Middlesex EN2 0SS
Website: www.johnfrostnewspapers.com
e-mail: andrew@johnfrostnewspapers.com
                         Tel: 020-8366 1392

FULL EFFECT The
(Event Suppliers)
4 Arkwright Industrial Estate
Arkwright Road, Bedford MK42 0LQ
Website: www.thefulleffect.co.uk
e-mail: mark.harrison@tfe.co.uk
Fax: 01234 214445   Tel: 01234 269099

GAMBA
(Theatrical Shoes and Wholesale Danceware)
1 Northfield Industrial Estate
Beresford Avenue, Wembley HA0 1XS
Fax: 020-8903 6669   Tel: 020-8810 7667

GAMBA
(Dancewear & Ballet Shoes)
3 Garrick Street, Covent Garden
London WC2E 9BF
Fax: 020-7497 0754   Tel: 020-7437 0704

GAV NICOLA THEATRICAL SHOES
1A Suttons Lane, Hornchurch, Essex RM12 6RD
e-mail: sales@gavnicola.freeserve.co.uk
Mobile: 07961 974278   TelFax: 01708 438584

GET STUFFED
(Taxidermy)
105 Essex Road, London N1 2SL
Website: www.thegetstuffed.co.uk
e-mail: taxidermy@thegetstuffed.co.uk
Fax: 020-7359 8253   Tel: 020-7226 1364

GLOBAL CEILINGS & TILES
(Designers, Suppliers, Installers)
1B Argyle Road, Argyle Corner, Ealing
London W13 0LL
Website: www.globalceiling.co.uk
Mobile: 07976 159402   Tel: 020-8810 5914

GORGEOUS GOURMETS
(Caterers & Equipment Hire)
Gresham Way, Wimbledon SW19 8ED
Website: www.gorgeousgourmets.co.uk
e-mail: events@gorgeousgourmets.co.uk
Fax: 020-8946 1639   Tel: 020-8944 7771

GOULD Gillian ANTIQUES
(Scientific & Marine Antiques & Collectables)
18A Belsize Park Gardens, Belsize Park
London NW3 4LH
e-mail: gillgould@dealwith.com
Fax: 020-7419 0400   Tel: 020-7419 0500

GRADAV HIRE & SALES Ltd
(Lighting & Sound Hire/Sales)
Units C6 & C9 Hastingwood Trading Estate
Harbet Road, Edmonton, London N18 3HU
e-mail: office@gradav.co.uk
Fax: 020-8803 5060   Tel: 020-8803 7400

GRAY Robin COMMENTARIES
(Saddles, Bridles, Racing Colours & Hunting Attire)
Comptons, Isington, Alton, Hampshire GU34 4PL
e-mail: gray@isington.fsnet.co.uk
                                Tel/Fax: 01420 23347

GREENPROPS
(Prop Suppliers, Artificial Trees, Plants,
Flowers, Fruit, Grass etc)
West Bovey Farm
Waterrow, Somerset TA4 2BA
Website: www.greenprops.com
e-mail: trevor@greenprops.com
Fax: 01398 361307   Tel: 01398 361531

HAMPTON COURT HOUSE
(1857 Country House & Grounds)
East Molesey KT8 9BS
Website: www.hamptoncourthouse.com
Fax: 020-8977 5357   Tel: 020-8943 0889

HARLEQUIN Plc
(Floors for Stage, Opera, Dance, Concert,
Shows & Events)
Festival House, Chapman Way
Turnbridge Wells, Kent TN2 3EF
Website: www.harlequinfloors.com
e-mail: sales@harlequinfloors.co.uk
Fax: 01892 514222   Tel: 01892 514888

HARLEQUIN PROMOTIONS
(Fun Casinos, Scalextric & Race Nights)
Harlequin House, 13 Gurton Road
Coggleshall, Essex CO6 1QL
Website: www.harlequin-casinos.co.uk
e-mail: john@harlequin-casinos.co.uk
                                Tel: 01376 563385

HAWES Joanne
(Children's Administrator for Theatre, Film & TV)
21 Westfield Road, Maidenhead
Berkshire SL6 5AU
e-mail: jo.hawes@virgin.net
Fax: 01628 672884   Tel: 01628 773048

HERON & DRIVER
(Scenic Furniture & Prop Makers)
Unit 7, Dockley Road Industrial Estate
Rotherhithe, London SE16 3SF
Website: www.herondriver.co.uk
e-mail: mail@herondriver.co.uk
Fax: 020-7394 8680   Tel: 020-7394 8688

HEWER Richard
(Props Maker)
7 Sion Lane, Bristol BS8 4BE   Tel/Fax: 0117-973 8760

HI-FLI (Flying Effects)
2 Boland Drive
Manchester M14 6DS
e-mail: mikefrost@hi-fli.co.uk
                                   Tel/Fax: 0161-224 6082

HOWARD Rex DRAPES Ltd
Acton Park Industrial Estate, Eastman Road
The Vale, London W3 7QS
Fax: 020-8740 5994   Tel: 020-8740 5881

IMAGERY
(Painting & Decoration)
420G, 9 Sims House
Commercial Road
London E1 1LD   Mobile: 07956 512074

IMPACT DISTRIBUTION & MARKETING
(Leaflet & Poster Distribution & Display)
Tuscany Wharf, 4B Orsman Road
London N1 5QJ
Website: www.impact@uk.com
e-mail: admin@impact.uk.com
Fax: 020-7729 5994   Tel: 020-7729 5978

IMPACT PERCUSSION
(Percussion Instruments for Sale)
Unit 7 Goose Green Trading Estate
47 East Dulwich Road, London SE22 9BN
e-mail: sales@impactpercussion.com
Fax: 020-8299 6704   Tel: 020-8299 6700

INTERNATIONAL CLOWNS DIRECTORY The
(Salvo The Clown)
13 Second Avenue, Kingsleigh Park
Thundersley, Essex SS7 3QD   Tel: 01268 745791

JAPAN PROMOTIONS
(Organise Japanese Events)
200 Russell Court, 3 Woburn Place
London WC1H 0ND   Tel/Fax: 020-7278 4099

JESSAMINE Bob
(Scene Painting, Prop Making)
4 Matlock Avenue, Birkdale, Southport
Merseyside PR8 5EZ
Website: www.rscsjessamine.supernet.com
e-mail: rscsjessamine@supanet.com
                                      Tel: 01704 564521

JULIETTE DESIGNS
(Diamante Jewellery Manufacturer, Necklaces,
Crowns etc)
90 Yerbury Road, London N19 4RS
Website: www.stagejewellery.com
Fax: 020-7281 7326   Tel: 020-7263 7878

K & D Ltd
(Footwear)
Unit 7A, Thames Road Industrial Estate
Thames Road, Silvertown, London E16 2EZ
Website: www.shoemaking.co.uk
e-mail: k&d@shoemaking.co.uk
Fax: 020-7476 5220   Tel: 020-7474 0500

KEW BRIDGE STEAM MUSEUM
(Steam Museum)
Green Dragon Lane, Brentford, Middlesex TW8 0EN
Website: www.kbsm.org
e-mail: info@kbsm.org
Fax: 020-8569 9978   Tel: 020-8568 4757

KIRKLAND Cindy at CREATIVE WORKS UK Ltd
(Freelance Floral Designer)
Website: www.ckworks.net
e-mail: info@ckworks.net   Mobile: 07976 449681

KNEBWORTH HOUSE, GARDENS & PARK
(Knebworth)
Hertfordshire SG3 6PY   Tel: 01438 812661

K. W. PROPS
(Propmaking)
Unit J304
Tower Bridge Business Complex
100 Clements Road, London SE16 4DG
e-mail: kwprops@gmx.co.uk   Tel/Fax: 020-8299 6785

LAREDO Alex
(Expert with Ropes, Bullwhips, Shooting, Riding)
29 Lincoln Road, Dorking
Surrey RH4 1TE   Tel: 01306 889423

LAREDO WILD WEST TOWN
(Wild West Entertainments)
19 Surrenden Road, Staplehurst
Tonbridge, Kent TN12 0LY
Website: www.laredo.org.uk
e-mail: enquiries@laredo.org.uk   Tel: 01474 706129

LEES-NEWSOME Ltd
(Manufacturers of Flame Retardant Fabrics)
Ashley Street, Westwood, Oldham
Lancashire OL9 6LS
e-mail: info@leesnewsome.co.uk
Fax: 0161-627 3362   Tel: 0161-652 1321

LEIGHTON HALL
(Historic House)
Carnforth, Lancs, Lancashire LA5 9ST
Website: www.leightonhall.co.uk
e-mail: leightonhall@yahoo.co.uk
Fax: 01524 720357   Tel: 01524 734474

**LEVRANT Stephen - HERITAGE
ARCHITECTURE Ltd**
(Historic Buildings & Interiors Consultants)
363 West End Lane
West Hampstead
London NW6 1LP
e-mail: levrant@aol.com
Fax: 020-7794 9712   Tel: 020-7435 7502

LONDON BUSINESS EQUIPMENT
(Authorised Canon Dealer)
527-529 High Road
Leytonstone, London E11 4PB
Website: www.londonbusinessequipment.com
e-mail: sales@londonbusinessequipment.com
Fax: 020-8556 4865   Tel: 020-8558 0024

LONDON UNDERWATER CENTRE
(Pre-holiday Scuba Courses in Victoria)
QMSC 223 Vauxhall Bridge Road
London SW1V 1EL   Tel/Fax: 020-7630 7443

LONG Alan
(Gun Hire & Weapons Armourer)
PO Box 6079, Birmingham B28 0FF
Fax: 0121-624 9060   Mobile: 07976 953375

LONO DRINKS COMPANY The
1 The Paddock, Church Street, Meysey Hampton
Gloucestershire GL7 5JX
Website: www.lono.co.uk
e-mail: info@lono.co.uk   Tel/Fax: 01285 850682

LOS KAOS
(Entertainment & Circus Skills)
Kaos Towers, 346 Tunbridge Road
Maidstone, Kent ME16 8TG
Website: www.loskaos.co.uk   Tel/Fax: 01622 727433

www.ENCHANTINGFOREST.co.uk

Makers of Props & Effects for the Entertainment & Exhibition Industry

TEL/FAX: 0115 9830 777   EMAIL: INFO@ENCHANTINGFOREST.CO.UK
UNIT 6 MACHIN INDUSTRIAL ESTATE, NOTTINGHAM ROAD, GOTHAM, NOTTINGHAM, NG11 0HH

LYON EQUIPMENT
(Petzl & Beal Rope Access Equipment (PPE) for
Industrial & Theatrical Work)
Rise Hill Mill, Dent, Sedbergh
Cumbria LA10 5QL
Website: www.lyon.co.uk
e-mail: info@lyon.co.uk
Fax: 01539 625454   Tel: 01539 625493

M A C
(Sound Hire)
1-2 Attenburys Park
Park Road, Altrincham
Cheshire WA14 5QE
Website: www.macsound.co.uk
e-mail: hire@macsound.co.uk
Fax: 0161-962 9423   Tel: 0161-969 8311

MACKIE Sally LOCATIONS
(Location Finding & Management)
Cownham Farm, Broadwell
Moreton-in-Marsh
Gloucestershire GL56 0TT
Website: www.sallymackie-locations.com
e-mail: sallymackie@lokations.freeserve.co.uk
Fax: 01451 832442   Tel: 01451 830294

MADDERMARKET THEATRE
(Furniture, Props, Costumes & Accessories)
(Contact Rhett Davies, Resident Stage Manager)
St John's Alley, Norwich NR2 1DR
Website: www.maddermarket.co.uk
e-mail: theatre@maddermarket.freeserve.co.uk
Fax: 01603 661357   Tel: 01603 626560

MAGICAL MART
(Magic, Ventriloquists' Dolls, Punch & Judy,
Hire & Advising. Callers by Appointment)
42 Christchurch Road, Sidcup, Kent DA15 7HQ
Website: www.johnstylesentertainer.co.uk
                          Tel/Fax: 020-8300 3579

MANSON TRASH
(Ex-Guards Drill Instructor)
Make your soldiers look and sound real.
                          Tel: 020-8747 3510

MARINE UNDERWATER EQUIPMENT
(Watersports Equipment)
Ocean Leisure (Main Branch)
11-14 Northumberland Avenue
London WC2N 5AQ
e-mail: info@oceanleisure.co.uk
Fax: 020-7930 3032   Tel: 020-7930 5050

Call Benson's
JUMPAROUND ACTIVITY CENTRES
for **INFLATABLE FUN** and **SOFT PLAY EQUIPMENT**
BOUNCY CASTLES * **BALL PONDS** - for children and adults
TODDLERS PARTY HIRE PACKAGES
INDOOR/OUTDOOR EVENTS * **CHILDREN'S PARTIES**
CORPORATE EVENTS

WORTHING **01903 - 248258**

Write to: **BENSON'S**
JUMPAROUND ACTIVITY CENTRES
P.O. BOX 4227 WORTHING BN11 5ST

email: davebensonphillips@yahoo.com
website: www.davebensonphillips.co.uk

MARKSON PIANOS
8 Chester Court, Albany Street, London NW1 4BU
Website: www.pianosuk.co.uk
e-mail: info@pianosuk.co.uk
Fax: 020-7224 0957 　　　　Tel: 020-7935 8682

McDONALD ROWE (SCULPTURE) Ltd
20 Southfield Way, St Albans, Hertfordshire AL4 9JJ
e-mail: mcdonald@stalbans01.freeserve.co.uk
　　　　　　　　　　　　　Tel: 01727 765277

MIDNIGHT ELECTRONICS
(Sound Hire)
Off Quay Building, Foundry Lane
Newcastle upon Tyne NE6 1LH
Website: www.midnightelectronics.co.uk
e-mail: info@midnightelectronics.co.uk
Fax: 0191-224 0080 　　　　Tel: 0191-224 0088

MILITARY, MODELS & MINATURES
(Model Figures)
38A Horsell Road, London N5 1XP
e-mail: figsculpt@aol.com
Fax: 020-7700 4624 　　　　Tel: 020-7700 7036

MODEL BOX Ltd
(Computer Aided Design & Design Services)
20 Merton Industrial Park, Jubilee Way
London SW19 3WL
Website: www.modelbox.co.uk
e-mail: info@modelbox.co.uk
Fax: 020-8254 4721 　　　　Tel: 020-8254 4720

MORTON G & L
(Horses/Farming)
Hashome Carr, Holme-on-Spalding Moor
Yorkshire YO43 4BD 　　　　Tel: 01430 860393

MOULDART
(Mouldmaking, Props, Sculpture)
Nile House Studios, Nile Street
Burslem, Stoke-on-Trent
Website: www.mouldart.co.uk
e-mail: mouldart@aol.com
Mobile: 07786 473443 　　　　Tel: 01782 577727

NEWENS Chas MARINE co Ltd
(Boats for Sale, Marine Props etc)
The Boathouse, Embankment, Putney
London SW15 1LB
Fax: 020-8780 2339 　　　　Tel: 020-8788 4587

NEWMAN HIRE COMPANY
16 The Vale, Acton, London W3 7SB
e-mail: info@newman-hire.co.uk 　Tel: 020-8743 0741

NORTHERN LIGHT
Assembly Street, Leith, Edinburgh EH6 7RG
Website: www.northernlight.co.uk
e-mail: enquiries@northernlight.co.uk
Fax: 0131-553 3296 　　　　Tel: 0131-553 2383

NOSTALGIA AMUSEMENTS
(Brian Davey)
22 Greenwood Close, Thames Ditton KT7 0BG
Mobile: 07973 506869 　　　　Tel: 020-8398 2141

**NOTTINGHAM JOUSTING ASSOCIATION
SCHOOL OF NATIONAL EQUITATION Ltd**
(Jousting & Medieval Tournaments, Horses
& Riders for Films & TV)
Bunny Hill Top, Costock, Loughborough
Leicestershire LE12 6XE
Website: www.bunny-hill.co.uk
e-mail: info@bunny-hill.co.uk
Fax: 01509 856067 　　　　Tel: 01509 852366

OCEAN LEISURE
(Scuba Diving, Watersports)
11-14 Northumberland Avenue
London WC2N 5AQ
Fax: 020-7930 3032 　　　　Tel: 020-7930 5050

OFFSTAGE
(Theatre & Film Bookshop)
37 Chalk Farm Road, London NW1 8AJ
e-mail: offstagebookshop@aol.com
Fax: 020-7916 8046 　　　　Tel: 020-7485 4996

PALAVA ARTS
(Digital Media, Musical Composition &
Production Services)
43 Kingsway Avenue
Kingswood, Bristol BS15 8DB
e-mail: sam@palava-arts.com 　Tel/Fax: 0117-961 6858

PATERSON Helen
(Typing Services)
40 Whitelands House, London SW3 4QY
e-mail: pater@waitrose.com 　　Tel: 020-7730 6428

PENDLEBURYS CANDLE COMPANY
(Church Candles & Requisites)
Church House, Portland Avenue
Stamford Hill, London N16 6HJ
e-mail: books@pendleburys.demon.co.uk
　　　　　　　　　　　Tel/Fax: 020-8809 4922

PERIOD PETROL PUMPS FOR HIRE
Website: www.periodpetrolpump.co.uk
　　　　　　　　　　　　Tel: 01379 643978

PERIOD PROPS AND LIGHTING Ltd
17-23 Stirling Road, London W3 8DJ
Website: www.periodpropsandlighting.co.uk
e-mail: pplprops@supanet.com
Fax: 020-8993 4637 　　　　Tel: 020-8992 6901

PHOSPHENE
(Lighting, Sound & Accessories. Design, Sales, Hire)
Milton Road South, Stowmarket, Suffolk IP14 1EZ
Website: www.phosphene.co.uk
e-mail: cliff@phosphene.freeserve.co.uk
　　　　　　　　　　　　Tel: 01449 770011

PHYSICALITY Ltd
(Physical Skills Specialists)
265-267 Ilford Lane, Ilford, Essex IG1 2SD
Website: www.physicality.co.uk
e-mail: info@physicality.co.uk
Fax: 020-8491 2801 　　　　Tel: 020-8491 2800

PICKFORDS Ltd
Heritage House
345 Southbury Road, Enfield EN1 1UP
Fax: 020-8219 8001 　　　　Tel: 020-8219 8000

PICTURES PROPS CO Ltd
(TV, Film & Stage Hire)
12-16 Brunel Road, London W3 7XR
Fax: 020-8740 5846 　　　　Tel: 020-8749 2433

PINK POINTES DANCEWEAR
1A Suttons Lane
Hornchurch, Essex RM12 6RD
e-mail: sales@gavnicola.freeserve.co.uk
　　　　　　　　　　　Tel/Fax: 01708 438584

PISTOL DESIGN
(Theatre Posters, Design)
45 Thorney Road, Emsworth PO10 8BL
Website: www.pistol-design.co.uk
e-mail: studio@pistol-design.co.uk
　　　　　　　　　　　　Tel: 01243 389758

PLAYBOARD PUPPETS
2 Ockendon Mews
London N1 3JL 　　　　Tel/Fax: 020-7226 5911

POLAND Anna: SCULPTOR AND MODELMAKER
(Sculpture, Models, Puppets, Masks etc)
Salterns, Old Bursledon, Southampton
Hampshire SO31 8DH
e-mail: annapoland@hotmail.com
　　　　　　　　　　　　Tel: 023-8040 5166

POLLEX PROPS / FIREBRAND
(Prop Makers)
Leac na Ban, Tayvallich
Lochgilphead, Argyll PA31 8PF
e-mail: alex@firebrand.fsnet.co.uk
Tel/Fax: 01546 870310

PRAETORIAN ASSOCIATES
(Personal Safety & Anti-Stalking Consultancy)
Suite 501, 2 Old Brompton Road, London SW7 3DG
Website: www.praetorianasc.com
e-mail: info@praetorianasc.com
Fax: 020-8923 7177   Tel: 020-8923 9075

PRAETORIAN PROCUREMENT SERVICES - SA
(Providing Services for the Film/TV Industry within
South Africa)
Suite 501, 2 Old Brompton Road, London SW7 3DG
Website: www.praetorianasc.com
e-mail: info@praetorianasc.com
Fax: 020-8923 7177   Tel: 020-8923 9075

PROBLOOD
11 Mount Pleasant, Framlingham,
Suffolk IP13 9HQ   Tel/Fax: 01728 723865

PROFESSOR PATTEN'S PUNCH & JUDY
(Hire & Performances/Advice on Traditional Show)
14 The Crest, Goffs Oak, Hertfordshire EN7 5NP
Website: www.dennispatten.co.uk
Tel: 01707 873262

PROFILE PRINTS
(Photographic Processing)
Courtwood Film Service Ltd, Freepost TO55
Penzance, Cornwall TR18 2BF
Website: www.courtwood.co.uk
e-mail: people@courtwood.co.uk
Fax: 01736 350203   Tel: 01736 365222

PROP FARM Ltd
(Pat Ward)
Grange Farm, Elmton, Nr Creswell
North Derbyshire S80 4LX
e-mail: pat/les@propfarm.free-online.co.uk
Fax: 01909 721465   Tel: 01909 723100

PROP ROTATION
41 Trelawney Road, Cotham
Bristol BS6 6DY   Tel: 0117-974 1058

PROPS GALORE
(Period Textiles/Jewellery)
15 Brunel Road, London W3 7XR
e-mail: propsgalore@farley.co.uk
Fax: 020-8354 1866   Tel: 020-8746 1222

PUNCH & JUDY PUPPETS & BOOTHS
(Hire & Advisory Service, Callers by Appointment)
42 Christchurch Road, Sidcup, Kent DA15 7HQ
Website: www.johnstylesentertainer.co.uk
Tel/Fax: 020-8300 3579

Q2Q
(Production Solutions)
22-24 Torrington Place
London WC1E 7HJ
Website: www.Q2Q.ltd.uk
e-mail: admin@Q2Q.ltd.uk
Fax: 020-7580 6652   Tel: 020-7907 7042

RAINBOW PRODUCTIONS Ltd
(Manufacture & Handling of Costume Characters)
Rainbow House, 56 Windsor Avenue
London SW19 2RR
Website: www.rainbowproductions.co.uk
e-mail: info@rainbowproductions.co.uk
Fax: 020-8545 0777   Tel: 020-8545 0700

RENT-A-CLOWN
(Mattie Faint)
37 Sekeforde Street, Clerkenwell
London EC1R 0HA   Tel/Fax: 020-7608 0312

RENT-A-SWORD
(Alan M Meek)
180 Frog Grove Lane, Wood Street Village
Guildford, Surrey GU3 3HD
Fax: 01483 236684   Tel: 01483 234084

REPLAY Ltd
(Showreels & TV Facilities Hire)
199 Piccadilly, London W1J 9HA
Website: www.replayfilms.co.uk
e-mail: sales@replayfilms.co.uk
Fax: 020-7287 5348   Tel: 020-7287 5334

RETROGRAPH NOSTALGIA ARCHIVE
(Posters & Packaging 1880-1970, Picture
Library/Photo Stills/Ephemera/Fine Arts 1870-1970)
10 Hanover Crescent, Brighton, East Sussex BN2 9SB
Website: www.retrograph.com
e-mail: retropix1@aol.com   Tel: 01273 687554

RICO THE CIRCUS CLOWN
20 Orchard Road, Sanderstead
South Croydon CR2 9LU   Tel: 01689 846887

ROOTSTEIN Adel Ltd
(Mannequin Hire)
9 Beaumont Avenue
London W14 9LP
Fax: 020-7381 3263   Tel: 020-7381 1447

**ROYAL HORTICULTURAL HALLS & CONFERENCE
CENTRE**
(Film Location: Art Deco & Edwardian Buildings)
80 Vincent Square, London SW1P 2PE
Website: www.horticultural-halls.co.uk
e-mail: maugiel@rhs.org.uk
Fax: 020-7834 2072   Tel: 020-7828 4125

P

ROYAL SHAKESPEARE COMPANY COSTUME HIRE WARDROBE
Timothy's Bridge Road
Stratford-upon-Avon
Warwickshire CV37 9UY   Tel/Fax: 01789 205920

ROYER Hugo INTERNATIONAL Ltd
(Hair & Wig Materials)
10 Lakeside Business Park
Swan Lake, Sandhurst
Berkshire GU47 9DN
Website: www.royer.co.uk
e-mail: enquiries@royer.co.uk
Fax: 01252 878852   Tel: 01252 878811

RUDKIN DESIGN
(Design Consultants, Brochures, Advertising, Corporate etc)
10 Cottesbrooke Park
Heartlands Business Park
Daventry, Northamptonshire NN11 5YL
e-mail: studio@rudkindesign.com
Fax: 01327 872728   Tel: 01327 301770

RUMBLE Jane
(Props to Order, No Hire)
121 Elmstead Avenue, Wembley
Middlesex HA9 8NT   Tel: 020-8904 6462

S + H TECHNICAL SUPPORT GROUP
(Star Cloths, Drapes)
Unit A The Old Laundry, Chambercombe Road
Ilfracombe, Devon EX34 9PH
Website: www.starcloth.co.uk
e-mail: enquiries@starcloth.co.uk
Fax: 01271 865423   Tel: 01271 866832

SABAH
(Stylist, Costumes, Wardrobe, Sets, Props)
6267 Bay Club Drive, Apt 3, Fort Lauderdale
Florida 33308 USA
e-mail: sabah561@aol.com

SAPEX SCRIPTS
Millennium Studios, 5 Elstree Way
Borehamwood, Hertfordshire WD6 1SF
Website: www.sapex.co.uk
e-mail: scripts@sapex.co.uk
Fax: 020-8236 1591   Tel: 020-8236 1600

SCENA PRODUCTIONS Ltd
240 Camberwell Road, London SE5 0DP
e-mail: scena@pro.com
Fax: 020-7703 7012   Tel: 020-7703 4444

SCENE TWO HIRE
(Film & TV Props Hire)
18-20 Brunel Road, Acton, London W3 7XR
Website: www.scene2hire.co.uk
e-mail: sales@scene2hire.co.uk
Fax: 020-8743 2662   Tel: 020-8740 5544

SCENICS
Copse Field Farm, Cawlow Lane, Warslow
Buxton SK17 0HE   Tel: 01298 84762

SCHULTZ & WIREMU FABRIC EFFECTS
(Dyeing/Printing/Distressing)
Unit B202 Faircharm Studios, 8-12 Creekside
London SE8 3DX
Website: www.schultz-wiremufabricfx.co.uk
e-mail: schultz_wiremfx@onetel.net.uk
Tel/Fax: 020-8469 0151

SCRIPTRIGHT
(S.C. Hill - Script/Manuscript Typing Services/Script Reading Services)
6 Valetta Road, London W3 7TN
e-mail: samc.hill@virgin.net
Fax: 020-8740 6486   Tel: 020-8740 7303

SCRIPTS BY ARGYLE
(Play, Film & Book. Word Processing, Copying & Binding)
St John's Buildings, 43 Clerkenwell Road
London EC1M 5RS
Website: www.scriptsbyargyle.co.uk
e-mail: scripts.typing@virgin.net
Fax: 020-7608 1642   Tel: 020-7608 2095

SHAOLIN WAY
(Martial Arts, Lion Dance & Martial Arts Supplies)
10 Little Newport Street, London WC2H 7JJ
e-mail: shaolinway@btclick.com
Fax: 020-7287 6548   Tel: 020-7734 6391

21 Baron Street, Angel
London N1 9EX   Tel: 020-7837 1118

SHER SYSTEM The
(Helping Skin with Acne & Rosacea)
30 New Bond Street, London W1S 2RN
Website: www.sher.co.uk/skincare/
e-mail: skincare@sher.co.uk
Fax: 020-7629 7021   Tel: 020-7499 4022

SHIRLEY LEAF & PETAL COMPANY Ltd
(Flower Makers Museum)
58A High Street, Old Town, Hastings
East Sussex TN34 3EN   Tel/Fax: 01424 427793

SHOP FITTINGS DIRECT
Unit 3, The Interchange, Colonial Way
Watford, Hertfordshire WD24 4PR
Fax: 01923 232326   Tel: 01923 232425

SIDE EFFECTS
(Props, Models & FX)
Unit 4, Camberwell Trading Estate
117 Denmark Road, London SE5 9LB
e-mail: sfx@lineone.net
Fax: 020-7738 5198   Tel: 020-7738 5199

SILVER Sam KENSINGTON Ltd
(Special Eye Effects)
37 Kensington Church Street, London W8 4LL
e-mail: admin@samsilveropticians.com
Fax: 020-7937 8969   Tel: 020-7937 8282

SMITH Tom
(Blacksmith)
Unit 2, Lopen Works, Lopen Road, Edmonton
London N18 1PU   Tel/Fax: 020-8884 2626

SNOW BUSINESS
(Snow/Winter Effects on Any Scale)
The Snow Mill, Bridge Road, Ebley
Gloucestershire, Stroud GL5 4TR
Website: www.snowfx.com
e-mail: snow@snowbusiness.com
Tel/Fax: 01453 840077

SOFT PROPS
(Costume & Modelmakers)
Unit 4, Camberwell Trading Estate
117-119 Denmark Road, London SE5 9LB
e-mail: jackie@softprops.co.uk
Fax: 020-7738 5198   Tel: 020-7738 6324

STEELDECK RENTALS
(Theatre & Staging Equipment)
King's Cross Freight Depot
York Way, London N1 0UZ
e-mail: steeldeck@aol.com
Fax: 020-7278 3403   Tel: 020-7833 2031

STEELDECK SALES Ltd
(Modular Staging)
King's Cross Freight Depot
York Way, London N1 0UZ
e-mail: steeldeck@aol.com
Fax: 020-7278 3403   Tel: 020-7833 2031

STIRLING Rob
(Carpentry & Joinery)
Copse Field Farm, Cawlow Lane, Warslow
Buxton SK17 0HE   Tel: 01298 84762

STUDIO & TV HIRE
3 Ariel Way, Wood Lane
White City, London W12 7SL
Website: www.stvhire.com
e-mail: enquiries@stvhire.com
Fax: 020-8740 9662   Tel: 020-8749 3445

STUDIO FOUR COSTUMES
4 Warple Mews, Warple Way, Acton
London W3 0RF   Tel/Fax: 020-8749 6569

STUNT ACTION SPECIALISTS (S.A.S.)
(Corporate Stunt Work)
110 Trafalgar Road, Portslade, Sussex BN41 1GS
Website: www.stuntactionspecialists.com
e-mail: wayne@stuntactionspecialists.co.uk
Fax: 01273 708699   Tel: 01273 230214

SUPERSCRIPTS
(Audio Typing, Rushes, Post-Prod Scripts)
14 Cambridge Grove Road, Kingston
Surrey KT1 3JJ   Mobile: 07890 972595

56 New Road, Hanworth, Middlesex TW13 6TQ
e-mail: jackie@superscripts.fsnet.co.uk
Mobile: 07971 671011   Tel: 020-8898 7933

TAYLOR Charlotte
(Stylist/Props Buyer)
18 Eleanor Grove, Barnes
London SW13 0JN
e-mail: charlotte-taylor@breathemail.net
Mobile: 07836 708904   Tel/Fax: 020-8876 9085

TECHNIQUES
(Property Makers)
15 Danehurst Avenue
Leicester LE3 6DB   Tel/Fax: 0116-285 7294

TELESCRIPT PROMPTING Ltd
The Barn, Handpost Farmhouse
Maidens Green
Bracknell, Berkshire RG42 6LD
Fax: 01344 890655   Tel: 01344 890470

TESTMAN P.A.T.
(Portable Electrical Appliance Testing,
Specialists in Theatre)
7 Woodville Road, London E17 7ER
Mobile: 07973 663154   Tel: 020-8521 6408

THEATRESEARCH
(Theatre Consultants)
Dacre Hall, Dacre, North Yorkshire HG3 4ET
Website: www.theatresearch.co.uk
e-mail: info@theatresearch.co.uk
Fax: 01423 781957   Tel: 01423 780497

THEME TRADERS Ltd
(Props)
The Stadium, Oaklands Road, London NW2 6DL
Website: www.themetraders.com
e-mail: mailroom@themetraders.com
Fax: 020-8450 7322   Tel: 020-8452 8518

TOP SHOW
(Props & Scenery, Conference Specialists)
North Lane, Huntington
York YO32 9SU   Tel/Fax: 01904 750022

TRANSCRIPTS
(Audio + LTC/Post-prod)
#2, 6 Cornwall Gardens
London SW7 4AL
e-mail: lucy@transcripts.demon.co.uk
Mobile: 07973 200197   Tel: 020-7584 9758

TRAPEZE & AERIAL COACH/CHOREOGRAPHER
(Jacqueline Welbourne)
43 Kingsway Avenue
Kingswood, Bristol BS15 8AN
e-mail: jackie@welbourne.co.uk
Mobile: 07977 247287   Tel/Fax: 0117-947 7042

TROPICAL SURROUNDS Ltd
(Distributors & Installers of Natural Fencing &
Screening Materials)
The Old Grain Store
Redenham Park Farm
Redenham, Nr Andover
Hampshire SP11 9AQ
Fax: 01264 773660   Tel: 01264 773009

TRYFONOS Mary MASKS
(Mask, Headdress & Puppet Specialist)
59 Shaftesbury Road
London N19 4QW
Website: www.marysmasks.com
e-mail: marytryfonos@aol.com
Mobile: 07764 587433   Tel: 020-7561 9880

TURN ON LIGHTING
(Antique Lighting c1840-1940)
116-118 Islington High Street
Camden Passage
London N1 8EG   Tel/Fax: 020-7359 7616

UPSTAGE
(Event Design & Production Management)
Studio A, 14 Ayres Street, Flat Iron Yard
London SE1 1ES
Website: www.upstagelivecom.co.uk
e-mail: post@upstagelivecom.co.uk
Fax: 020-7403 6511   Tel: 020-7403 6510

VENTRILOQUIST DOLLS HOME
(Hire & Helpful Hints, Callers by Appointment)
42 Christchurch Road
Sidcup, Kent DA15 7HQ
Website: www.johnstylesentertainer.co.uk
Tel/Fax: 020-8300 3579

VENTRILOQUIST DUMMY HIRE
(Dennis Patten - Hire & Advice)
14 The Crest, Goffs Oak
Hertfordshire EN7 5NP
Website: www.dennispatten.co.uk
Tel: 01707 873262

VENYFLEX COMPANY
(Drapes, Tabs, Blinds)
1 Holly Road, Hampton Hill
Middlesex TW12 1QF   Tel: 020-8977 3780

VINMAG ARCHIVE Ltd
84-90 Digby Road, London E9 6HX
Website: www.vinmag.com
e-mail: piclib@vinmag.com
Fax: 020-8533 7283   Tel: 020-8533 7588

VIRGIN ATLANTIC AIRWAYS Ltd
(Reservations)
The Office
Crawley Business Quarter
Manor Royal
West Sussex RH10 9NU
Website: www.virgin.com/atlantic
Fax: 01293 444123   Tel: 01293 561721

VISUALEYES IMAGING SERVICES
(Photographic Reproduction)
11 West Street, London WC2H 9NE
Website: www.visphoto.co.uk
e-mail: imaging@visphoto.co.uk
Fax: 020-7240 0050   Tel: 020-7836 3004

VOCALEYES
(Suppliers of Audio Description for Theatrical
Performance)
25 Short Street
London SE1 8LJ
Website: www.vocaleyes.co.uk
e-mail: enquiries@vocaleyes.co.uk
Fax: 020-7928 2225   Tel: 020-7261 9199

WEBBER Peter HIRE/RITZ STUDIOS
(Music Equipment Hire, Rehearsal Studios)
110-112 Disraeli Road
London SW15 2DX
e-mail: lee.webber@virgin.net
Fax: 020-8877 1036   Tel: 020-8870 1335

WESTED LEATHERS COMPANY
(Suede & Leather Suppliers/Manufacturers)
Little Wested House
Wested Lane, Swanley, Kent BR8 8EF
e-mail: wested@wested.com
Fax: 01322 667039   Tel: 01322 660654

WESTWARD Lynn
(Window Blind Specialist)
273 The Vale, Acton, London W3 7QA
Fax: 020-8740 9836   Tel: 020-8740 8756

WHITEHORN Simon
(Sound Design)
57 Acre Lane, London SW2 5TN
Website: www.orbitalsound.co.uk
e-mail: simon.whitehorn@orbitalsound.co.uk
Fax: 020-7501 6869   Tel: 020-7501 6868

WILLIAMS Frank
(Bottles, Jars, Footwarmers & Flagons 1870-1940)
33 Enstone Road
Ickenham, Uxbridge, Middlesex
e-mail: wllmsfrn4@aol.com   Tel: 01895 672495

WILTSHIRE A. F.
(Agricultural Engineers)
The Agricultural Centre
Alfold Road, Dunsfold
Surrey GU8 4NP
e-mail: team@afwiltshire.fsnet.co.uk
Fax: 01483 200491   Tel: 01483 200516

WINSHIP Geoff
The Knights of Merrie England Ltd
153 Salisbury Road
Burton, Christchurch BH23 7JS
Website: www.medievaljousting.com
e-mail: geoff@medievaljousting.com
Fax: 01202 483666   Tel: 01202 483777

WOODEN CANAL BOAT SOCIETY
(Historic Canal Boats)
5 Oaken Clough Terrace, Limehurst
Ashton-under-Lyne, Lancashire OL7 9NY
Website: www.wcbs.org.uk
e-mail: chris-wcbs@people-link.net
Mobile: 07855 601589   Tel: 0161-330 2315

WORBEY Darryl STUDIOS
(Specialist Puppet Design)
Ground Floor
33 York Grove, London SE15 2NY
e-mail: dworbey@freewire.co.uk
Fax: 020-7635 6397   Tel: 020-7639 8090

WORLD OF FANTASY
(Props and Costumes)
Swansnest
Rear of 2 Windmill Road
Hampton Hill
Middlesex TW12 1RH
Website: www.swansflight.com
e-mail: swansflight@aol.com
Fax: 020-8783 1366   Tel: 020-8941 1595

WORLD OF ILLUSION
4 Sunnyside
Wimbledon SW19 4SL
Website: www.parasoltheatre.co.uk
e-mail: parasoltheatre@waitrose.com
Fax: 020-8946 0228   Tel: 020-8946 9478

WWW.PUPPETSPRESENT.COM
c/o Peter Charlesworth & Associates
68 Old Brompton Road
London SW7 3LD
Website: www.puppetspresent.com
e-mail: puppetspresent@btinternet.com
Tel: 020-7581 2478

A & C BLACK (Publicity Dept)
37 Soho Square, London W1D 3QZ
e-mail: publicity@acblack.com
Fax: 020-7758 0222   Tel: 020-7758 0200

ACADEMY PLAYERS DIRECTORY
1313 North Vine Street, Hollywood, CA 90028
Website: www.playersdirectory.com
e-mail: players@oscars.org
Fax: (310) 550-5034   Tel: (310) 247-3000

A C I D PUBLICATIONS
Suite 247, 37 Store Street, London WC1E 7BS
e-mail: acidnews@aol.com   Tel/Fax: 07050 205206

ACTING: A DRAMA STUDIO SOURCE BOOK
(Peter Owen Publishers)
73 Kenway Road, London SW5 0RE
Website: www.peterowen.com
e-mail: admin@peterowen.com   Tel: 020-7373 5628

ACTORS' HANDBOOK
(Bloomsbury Publishing Plc)
38 Soho Square, London W1D 3HB
Website: www.bloomsbury.com
e-mail: webmaster@bloomsbury.com
Fax: 020-7434 0151   Tel: 020-7494 2111

AMATEUR STAGE MAGAZINE & COMMUNITY ARTS DIRECTORY
(Platform Publications Ltd)
Hampden Hse, 2 Weymouth St, London W1W 5BT
e-mail: cvtheatre@aol.com
Fax: 020-7636 2323   Tel: 020-7636 4343

ANNUAIRE DU CINEMA BELLEFAYE
(French Actors' Directory, Production, Technicians & All Technical Industries & Suppliers)
38 rue Etienne Marcel, 75002 Paris
Website: www.bellefaye.com
e-mail: contact@bellefaye.com
Fax: 00 331 42 33 39 00   Tel: 00 331 42 33 52 52

ARTISTES & AGENTS
(Richmond House Publishing Co)
70-76 Bell St, Marylebone, London NW1 6SP
Website: www.rhpco.co.uk
e-mail: sales@rhpco.co.uk
Fax: 020-7224 9688   Tel: 020-7224 9666

AUDITION NOW
(Weekly Casting Publication)
Lifegroup Ltd, Garden Studios
11-15 Betterton Street, Covent Garden
London WC2H 9BP   Tel: 0800 0966144

AURORA METRO PRESS (1979)
(Drama, Fiction, Reference & International Literature in English Translation)
4 Osier Mews, Chiswick, London W4 2NT
Website: www.aurorametro.com
e-mail: ampress@netcomuk.co.uk
Fax: 020-8742 2925   Tel: 020-8747 1953

BIRTH OF THEATRE The - STAGE BY STAGE
(Drama/Theatre Studies/History/Reference)
(Peter Owen Publishers)
73 Kenway Road, London SW5 0RE
e-mail: admin@peterowen.com
Fax: 020-7373 6760   Tel: 020-7373 5628

BRITISH NATIONAL FILM & VIDEO CATALOGUE
(British Film Institute)
21 Stephen Street, London W1T 1LN
Website: www.bfi.org.uk
e-mail: maureen.brown@bfi.org.uk
Fax: 020-7436 7950   Tel: 020-7957 4706

BRITISH PERFORMING ARTS YEARBOOK
(Rhinegold Publishing)
241 Shaftesbury Avenue, London WC2H 8TF
Website: www.rhinegold.co.uk
e-mail: bpay@rhinegold.co.uk Tel: 020-7333 1721

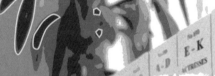

P

BRITISH THEATRE DIRECTORY
(Richmond House Publishing Co)
70 -76 Bell Street, Marylebone, London NW1 6SP
Website: www.rhpco .co.uk
e-mail: sales@rhpco.co.uk
Fax: 020-7224 9688   Tel: 020-7224 9666

BROADCAST
33-39 Bowling Green Lane, London EC1R 0DA
Website: www.broadcastnow.co.uk
Fax: 020-7505 8020   Tel: 020-7505 8014

CALDER PUBLICATIONS
51 The Cut, London SE1 8LF
e-mail: info@calderpublications.com
Fax: 020-7928 5930   Tel: 020-7633 0599

CASTCALL & CASTFAX
(Casting Information Services)
106 Wilsden Avenue, Luton LU1 5HR
Website: www.castcall.co.uk
e-mail: admin@castcall.co.uk
Fax: 01582 480736   Tel: 01582 456213

CASTWEB
7 St Luke's Avenue, London SW4 7LG
Website: www.castweb.co.uk
e-mail: castweb@netcomuk.co.uk
Fax: 020-7720 2879   Tel: 020-7720 9002

CELEBRITY BULLETIN The
Rooms 203-209, 93-97 Regent St, London W1B 4ES
e-mail: celebritylondon@aol.com
Fax: 020-7494 3500   Tel: 020-7439 9840

CELEBRITY SERVICE Ltd
Rooms 203-209, 93-97 Regent St, London W1B 4ES
e-mail: celebritylondon@aol.com
Fax: 020-7494 3500   Tel: 020-7439 9840

CHAPPELL OF BOND STREET
(Sheet Music, Musical Instruments, Pianos
Synthesizers, Keyboards)
50 New Bond Street, London W1S 1RD
Fax: 020-7491 0133   Tel: 020-7491 2777

CONFERENCE & INCENTIVE TRAVEL MAGAZINE
174 Hammersmith Road, London W6 7JP
Website: www.citymagazine.com
e-mail: city@haynet.com
Fax: 020-8267 4192   Tel: 020-8267 4307

CREATIVE HANDBOOK
(Reed Business Information)
Windsor Court, East Grinstead House
East Grinstead, West Sussex RH19 1XA
Website: www.chb.com   e-mail: chb@reedinfo.co.uk
Fax: 01342 332072   Tel: 01342 332034

DANCE EXPRESSION
(A. E. Morgan Publications Ltd)
51 Earl's Court Square, London SW5 9DG
Website: www.danceexpressionsmag.co.uk
                              Tel: 020-7370 7324

DIRECTING DRAMA
(Peter Owen Publishers)
73 Kenway Road, London SW5 0RE
Website: www.peterowen.com
e-mail: admin@peterowen.com   Tel: 020-7373 5628

EQUITY JOURNAL
Guild Hse, Upper St Martin's Lane, WC2H 9EG
Website: www.equity.org.uk   e-mail: info@equity.org.uk
Fax: 020-7379 6074   Tel: 020-7379 5185

FILMLOG
(Subscriptions)
PO Box 100, Broadstairs, Kent CT10 1UJ
Tel: 01843 860885   Tel: 01843 866538

FORESIGHT
(The Profile Group), 6-7 St Cross Street
London EC1N 8UA
Website: www.foresightonline.co.uk
Fax: 020-7430 1089   Tel: 020-7405 4455

HOLLYWOOD REPORTER The
Endeavour House
189 Shaftesbury Avenue, London WC2H 8TJ
Website: www.hollywoodreporter.com
e-mail: london_one@eu.hollywoodreporter.com
Fax: 020-7420 6054   Tel: 020-7420 6003

KAY'S UK & EUROPEAN PRODUCTION MANUALS
Trinity Mews
Cambridge Gardens, London W10 6JH
Website: www.kays.co.uk   e-mail: info@kays.co.uk
Fax: 020-8960 6700   Tel: 020-8960 6900

KEMP'S FILM, TV & VIDEO
(Reed Business Information)
East Grinstead House, East Grinstead
West Sussex RH19 1XA
Website: www.kftv.com
e-mail: phewson@reedinfo.co.uk
Fax: 01342 332072   Tel: 01342 332022

KNOWLEDGE The
Riverbank House
Angel Lane, Tonbridge, Kent TN9 1SE
Website: www.theknowledgeonline.com
e-mail: knowledge@cmpinformation.com
Fax: 01732 368324   Tel: 01732 377591

LIMELIGHT The
(Limelight Publications, Contacts & Casting
Directory)
Postal Address: PO Box 760, Randpark Ridge
2156, Gauteng, South Africa
Website: www.limelight.co.za
e-mail: barbara@limelight.co.za
                              Tel/Fax: 00 27 11 793 7231

MAKING OF THE PROFESSIONAL ACTOR The
(Peter Owen Publishers)
73 Kenway Road, London SW5 0RE
Website: www.peterowen.com
e-mail: admin@peterowen.com
                              Tel: 020-7373 5628

MUSIC WEEK DIRECTORY
CMP Information
Ludgate Hse, 245 Blackfriars Rd, London SE1 9UR
Website: www.musicweek.com   Tel: 01732 364422

MUSICAL STAGES
(Musical Theatre Magazine)
Box 8365, London W14 0GL
Website: www.musicalstage.co.uk
e-mail: editor@musicalstages.co.uk
                              Tel/Fax: 020-7603 2221

OFFICIAL LONDON SEATING PLAN GUIDE The
(Richmond House Publishing Co)
70-76 Bell Street, Marylebone, London NW1 6SP
Website: www.rhpco.co.uk   e-mail: sales@rhpco.co.uk
Fax: 020-7224 9688   Tel: 020-7224 9666

PA LISTINGS Ltd
292 Vauxhall Bridge Rd, London SW1V 1AE
Website: www.pa.press.net
e-mail: arts@listings.press.net
Fax: 020-7963 7800   Tel: 020-7963 7707

PANTOMIME BOOK The
(Peter Owen Publishers)
73 Kenway Road, London SW5 0RE
Website: www.peterowen.com
e-mail: admin@peterowen.com   Tel: 020-7373 5628

PCR
(See PRODUCTION & CASTING REPORT)

**PERFORMING ARTS YEARBOOK FOR EUROPE
(PAYE)**
(Alain Charles Arts Publishing Ltd)
Unit A402A, Tower Bridge Business Complex
100 Clements Road, London SE16 4DG
e-mail: paye@api.com
Fax: 020-7394 8753   Tel: 020-7232 5800

PLAYERS' GUIDE
(In Association with THE SPOTLIGHT & BREAKDOWN SERVICES Ltd USA)
123 West 44th Street, #2J, New York NY 10036
Website: www.playersguideny.com
e-mail: playersguide@breakdownservices.com
Fax: (212) 302-3495   Tel: (212) 302-9474

PLAYS INTERNATIONAL
33A Lurline Gardens
London SW11 4DD   Tel/Fax: 020-7720 1950

**PRESENTER'S CONTACT FILE The/
PRESENTER'S YEAR PLANNER The**
Presenter Promotions
123 Corporation Road
Gillingham, Kent ME7 1RG
Website: www.presenterpromotions.com
e-mail: info@presenterpromotions.com
Fax: 01634 316771   Tel: 01634 851077

PRESENTERS SPOTLIGHT
7 Leicester Place, London WC2H 7RJ
Website: www.spotlightcd.com e-mail: info@spotlightcd.com
Fax: 020-7437 5881   Tel: 020-7437 7631

PRESENTING FOR TV & VIDEO
(Joanne Zorian-Lynn, published by A & C Black)
A & C Black Customer Services
e-mail: sales@acblack.com   Tel: 01480 212666

PRESS PLANNER
(The Profile Group)
6-7 St Cross Street
London EC1N 8UA
Website: www.forwardplanning.co.uk
e-mail: info@pressplanner.co.uk
Fax: 020-7405 4347   Tel: 020-7405 4455

**PRODUCERS ALLIANCE FOR CINEMA
& TELEVISION**
(Pact Directory of Independent Producers/
Art of the Deal/Rights Clearance)
45 Mortimer Street, London W1W 8HJ
Website: www.pact.co.uk   e-mail: enquiries@pact.co.uk
Fax: 020-7331 6700   Tel: 020-7331 6000

PRODUCTION & CASTING REPORT
(Editorial)
PO Box 11, London N1 7JZ
Website: www.pcrnewsletter.com
Fax: 020-7566 8284   Tel: 020-7566 8282

PRODUCTION & CASTING REPORT
(Subscriptions)
PO Box 100, Broadstairs, Kent CT10 1UJ
Website: www.pcrnewsletter.com   Tel: 01843 860860

RADIO TIMES
80 Wood Lane, London W12 0TT
e-mail: radio.times@bbc.co.uk
Fax: 020-8433 3923   Tel: 0870 6084455

RICHMOND HOUSE PUBLISHING COMPANY Ltd
70-76 Bell Street
Marylebone, London NW1 6SP
Website: www.rhpco.co.uk
e-mail: sales@rhpco.co.uk
Fax: 020-7224 9688   Tel: 020-7224 9666

SCREEN INTERNATIONAL
33-39 Bowling Green Lane, London EC1R 0DA
Website: www.screeninternational.com
e-mail: annmarie.oconnor@media.emap.com
Fax: 020-7505 8117   Tel: 020-7505 8080

SCRIPT BREAKDOWN SERVICE Ltd
Suite 1, 16 Sidmouth Road
London NW2 5JX
e-mail: casting@sbsltd.demon.co.uk
Fax: 020-8459 7442   Tel: 020-8451 2852

SHOWCALL
47 Bermondsey Street, London SE1 3XT
Website: www.showcall.co.uk
e-mail: info@thestage.co.uk
Fax: 020-7378 0480   Tel: 020-7403 1818

**SHOWCAST: The AUSTRALASIAN CASTING
DIRECTORY**
PO Box 2001, Leumeah, NSW 2560 Australia
Website: www.showcast.com.au
e-mail: brian@showcast.com.au
Fax: 02 4647 4167   Tel: 02 4647 4166

SIGHT & SOUND
(British Film Institute)
21 Stephen Street, London W1T 1LN
Website: www.bfi.org.uk/sightandsound/
e-mail: s&s@bfi.org.uk
Fax: 020-7436 2327   Tel: 020-7255 1444

SPEECH FOR THE SPEAKER
(Peter Owen Publishers)
73 Kenway Road, London SW5 0RE
Website: www.peterowen.com
e-mail: admin@peterowen.com   Tel: 020-7373 5628

SPOTLIGHT CASTING DIRECTORY The
7 Leicester Place, London WC2H 7RJ
Website: www.spotlightcd.com
e-mail: info@spotlightcd.com
Fax: 020-7437 5881   Tel: 020-7437 7631

STAGE NEWSPAPER Ltd The
47 Bermondsey Street, London SE1 3XT
Website: www.thestage.co.uk
e-mail: editor@thestage.co.uk
Fax: 020-7357 9287   Tel: 020-7403 1818

TELEVISUAL
12-26 Lexington Street, London W1R 4HQ
Website: www.televisual.com
Fax: 020-7970 6733   Tel: 020-7970 6541

THEATRE RECORD
305 Whitton Dene, Isleworth, Middlesex TW7 7NE
Website: www.theatrerecord.com
e-mail: editor@theatrerecord.com
Fax: 020-8893 9677   Tel: 020-8737 8489

THEATRE REPORT
(Subscriptions)
PO Box 100, Broadstairs, Kent CT10 1UJ
Website: www.pcrnewsletter.com
Tel: 01843 860885   Tel: 01843 866538

TIME OUT GROUP Ltd
Universal Hse, 251 Tottenham Crt Rd, W1T 7AB
Website: www.timeout.com
e-mail: net@timeout.co.uk
Fax: 020-7813 6001   Tel: 020-7813 3000

TV TIMES
IPC Magazines
Kings Reach Tower
Stamford Street, London SE1 9LS
Fax: 020-7261 7888   Tel: 020-7261 7000

VARIETY NEWSPAPER
7th Floor, 84 Theobalds Road
London WC1X 8RR
Website: www.variety.com
Fax: 020-7611 4581   Tel: 020-7611 4580

VOICE BOOK The
(Michael McCallion, published by Faber & Faber)
TBS Distribution
e-mail: sales@tbs-ltd.co.uk   Tel: 01206 255678

WHITE BOOK The
Bank House, 23 Warwick Road
Coventry CV1 2EW   Tel: 024-7657 1171

Publicity & Press Representatives

ARTHUR Anna PRESS & PR
52 Tottenham Street, London W1T 4RN
Website: www.aapr.co.uk
e-mail: name@aapr.co.uk
Fax: 020-7637 2984
Tel: 020-7637 2994

ASSOCIATES The
(Film & Video Publicity Specialists)
39-41 North Road, London N7 9DP
Website: www.the-associates.co.uk
e-mail: info@the-associates.co.uk
Fax: 020-7609 2249
Tel: 020-7700 3388

AVALON PUBLIC RELATIONS
(Marketing/Arts)
4A Exmoor Street, London W10 6BD
e-mail: edt@avalonuk.com
Fax: 020-7598 7223
Tel: 020-7598 7222

BARLOW Tony ASSOCIATES
(Press & Marketing for Music, Dance & Theatre)
3 Choumert Square, London SE15 4RE
Website: www.tonybarlowarts.com
e-mail: artspublicity@hotmail.com
Mobile: 07774 407385
Tel/Fax: 020-7358 9291

BETTER ENGLISH PROOF-READING
Apartment 238, Beaux Arts Buildings
10-18 Manor Gardens, Islington, London N7 6JS
Website: www.better-english.net
e-mail: infocom@dial.pipex.com
Tel/Fax: 020-8374 6040

BOLTON Erica & QUINN Jane Ltd
10 Pottery Lane, London W11 4LZ
e-mail: e.mail@boltonquinn.com
Fax: 020-7221 8100
Tel: 020-7221 5000

BORKOWSKI Mark PR & IMPROPERGANDA Ltd
2nd Floor, 12 Oval Road, London NW1 7DH
Website: www.borkowski.co.uk
e-mail: vicki@borkowski.co.uk
Fax: 020-7482 5400
Tel: 020-7482 4000

CAHOOTS PRODUCTION & PR
(Denise Silvey, Martin Rumble)
32 Champion Grove, London SE5 8BW
Website: www.cahootstheatre.co.uk
e-mail: cahootstheatreco@aol.com
Tel/Fax: 020-7738 4250

CELEBRATE
(Creative Events Promotion)
1 Hill Street, Jackson Bridge, Holmfirth HD9 1LZ
e-mail: info@celebrateprojects.co.uk
Tel: 01484 688219

CENTRESTAGE PUBLIC RELATIONS
Yeates Cottage, 27 Wellington Terrace
Knaphill, Woking, Surrey GU21 2AP
e-mail: dellayedwards@hotmail.com
Tel: 01483 487808

CHAPMAN Guy ASSOCIATES
(Marketing & Press Support)
33 Southampton Street, London WC2E 7HE
e-mail: admin@g-c-a.co.uk
Fax: 020-7379 8484
Tel: 020-7379 7474

CHESTON Judith PUBLICITY
30 Telegraph Street, Shipston-on-Stour
Warwickshire CV36 4DA
e-mail: cheston@shipstononstour1.freeserve.co.uk
Fax: 01608 663772
Tel: 01608 661198

COBO
(Performing Arts, Entertainment & Leisure
Marketing)
43A Garthorne Road, London SE23 1EP
Website: www.theatrenet.com
e-mail: admin@cobomedia.com
Fax: 020-8291 4969
Tel: 020-8291 7079

COLE STEVENS
c/o 139 Belmont Rd, Harrow Weald, Middx HA3 7PL
Website: www.colestevens.com
e-mail: email@colestevens.com
Mobile: 07956 511051
Tel: 020-8692 2870

CUE CONSULTANTS
18 Barrington Court, London N10 1QG
e-mail: cueconsultants@hotmail.com
Fax: 020-8883 4197
Mobile: 07974 704909

DAVEY Christine ASSOCIATES
29 Victoria Road, Eton Wick, Windsor
Berkshire SL4 6LY
Fax: 01753 851123
Tel: 01753 852619

DAVIDSON Dennis ASSOCIATES
Royalty House
72-74 Dean Street, London W1D 3SG
e-mail: info@ddapr.com
Fax: 020-7437 6358
Tel: 020-7534 6000

DUNBAR Chloe PREMIER PR
91 Berwick Street, London W1F 0NE
e-mail: chloe@premiermaxworks.co.uk
Fax: 020-7734 2024
Tel: 020-7292 8352

EILENBERG Charlotte ASSOCIATES
6 Balfour Road, London N5 2HB
e-mail: charlotte.eilenberg@dsl.pipex.com
Tel/Fax: 020-7354 2155

ELSON Howard PROMOTIONS
16 Penn Ave, Chesham, Buckinghamshire HP5 2HS
e-mail: helson1029@aol.com
Fax: 01494 784760
Tel: 01494 785873

GADABOUTS Ltd
(Theatre Marketing & Promotions)
54 Friary Road, London N12 9PB
Website: www.gadabouts.co.uk
e-mail: events@gadabouts.fsnet.co.uk
Tel/Fax: 020-8445 5450

GAYNOR Avril ASSOCIATES
76 Probyn House, Page Street, London SW1P 4BQ
e-mail: gaynorama@aol.com
Tel/Fax: 020-7976 6522

GOODMAN Deborah PUBLICITY
25 Glenmere Avenue, London NW7 2LT
e-mail: publicity@dgpr.co.uk
Fax: 020-8959 7875
Tel: 020-8959 9980

HOLMES Robert
5 Launceton Close
Tamworth, Staffordshire B77 2JB
e-mail: robertgholmes@hotmail.com
Tel/Fax: 01827 701188

HYMAN Sue ASSOCIATES Ltd
St Martin's House
59 Martin's Lane, London WC2N 4JS
e-mail: sue.hyman@btinternet.com
Fax: 020-7379 4944
Tel: 020-7379 8420

IMPACT AGENCY
3 Bloomsbury Place, London WC1A 2QL
e-mail: mail@impactagency.co.uk
Fax: 020-7580 7200
Tel: 020-7580 1770

KEAN LANYON
(Sharon Kean)
Rose Cottage, The Aberdeen Centre
22 Highbury Grove, London N5 2EA
Website: www.keanlanyon.com
e-mail: sharon@keanlanyon.com
Fax: 020-7359 0199
Tel: 020-7354 3574

KELLER Don ARTS MARKETING
65 Glenwood Road, Harringay, London N15 3JS
e-mail: donkeller@waitrose.com
Fax: 020-8809 6825
Tel: 020-8800 4882

KWPR
(Kevin Wilson Public Relations)
187 Drury Lane, London WC2B 5QD
Website: www.kwpr.co.uk
e-mail: kwshout@aol.com
Fax: 020-7430 0364
Tel: 020-7430 2060

LAKE-SMITH GRIFFIN ASSOCIATES
15 Maiden Lane, Covent Garden, WC2E 7NG
e-mail: lakesmithgriffin@aol.com
Fax: 020-7836 1040
Tel: 020-7836 1020

LAVER Richard PUBLICITY
3 Troy Court, High Street Kensington, London W8 7RA
e-mail: richardlaver@btconnect.com
Fax: 020-7937 7322   Tel: 020-7937 7322

LEEP MARKEING & PR
(Marketing, Press & Publicity)
Top Floor, 21 Denmark Street, London WC2H 8NA
e-mail: philip@leep.biz
Fax: 020-7916 0031   Tel: 020-7916 0030

MAYER Anne PR
82 Mortimer Road, London N1 4LH
e-mail: annemayer@btopenworld.com
Fax: 020-7254 8227   Tel: 020-7254 7391

McDONALD & RUTTER
34 Bloomsbury Street, London WC1B 3QJ
e-mail: info@mcdonaldrutter.com
Fax: 020-7637 3690   Tel: 020-7637 2600

McDONALD Charles
(See McDONALD & RUTTER)

MITCHELL Jackie
(JM Communications)
4 Sims Cottages, The Green, Claygate
Surrey KT10 0JH
Website: www.jackiem.com
e-mail: pr@jackiem.com
Fax: 01372 471073   Tel: 01372 465041

MITCHELL Sarah PARTNERSHIP The
Third Floor, 87 Wardour Street, London W1F 0UA
Website: www.thesmp.com
e-mail: sarah@thesmp.com
Fax: 020-7434 1954   Tel: 020-7434 1944

MORGAN Jane ASSOCIATES
(Marketing & Media)
8 Heathville Road, London N19 3AJ
e-mail: morgans@dircon.co.uk
Fax: 020-7263 9877   Tel: 020-7263 9867

MORGAN Kim MEDIA & MARKETING
2 Averill Street, Hammersmith, London W6 8EB
e-mail: kim@kimmorgan-pr.com
Mobile: 07939 591403   Tel/Fax: 020-7381 4115

NELSON BOSTOCK COMMUNICATIONS
Compass House
22 Redan Place, London W2 4SA
Website: www.nelsonbostock.com
e-mail: sue.skeats@nelsonbostock.com
Fax: 020-7727 2025   Tel: 020-7229 4400

NEWLEY Patrick ASSOCIATES
45 Kingscourt Road, London SW16 1JA
e-mail: patricknewley@yahoo.com
Tel/Fax: 020-8677 0477

PARKER James ASSOCIATES
67 Richmond Park Road
London SW14 8JY
e-mail: jimparkerjpa@hotmail.com
Tel/Fax: 020-8876 1918

PARKER John PUBLICITY
21 Hindsleys Place, London SE23 2NF
e-mail: parkerwrite@yahoo
Tel: 020-8244 5816

POWELL Martin COMMUNICATIONS
1 Lyons Court, Long Ashton Business Park
Yanley Lane, Bristol BS41 9LB
e-mail: info@martin-powell.com
Fax: 01275 393933   Tel: 01275 394400

PR CONTACT Ltd The
83 Charlotte Street, London W1T 4PR
e-mail: pressoffice@theprcontact.com
Fax: 020-7323 1070   Tel: 020-7323 1200

PR PEOPLE The
1 St James Drive, Sale, Cheshire M33 7QX
e-mail: pr.people@btinternet.com
Fax: 0161-976 2758   Tel: 0161-976 2729

PREMIER PR
91 Berwick Street, London W1F 0NE
Website: www.premierpr.com
Fax: 020-7734 2024   Tel: 020-7292 8330

PUBLIC EYE COMMUNICATIONS Ltd
Suite 318, Plaza, 535 Kings Road, London SW10 0SZ
e-mail: ciara@publiceye.co.uk
Fax: 020-7351 1010   Tel: 020-7351 1555

RKM PUBLIC RELATIONS
(London. Los Angeles)
83 Replingham Road, London SW18 5LU
Website: www.rkmpr.com
e-mail: info@rkmpr.com
Fax: 020-8516 8909   Tel: 020-8516 9669

S & X MEDIA
(Contact: Roulla Xenides)
405F The Big Peg, Vyse Street
Birmingham B18 6NF
e-mail: roulla@sx-media.com
Fax: 0121-694 6494   Tel: 0121-604 6366

SAVIDENT Paul
(Marketing & Press Management)
199 Wardour Street, London W1F 8JN
Website: www.savident.com e-mail: info@savident.com
Fax: 020-7734 3007   Tel: 020-7734 8400

SHIPPEN Martin MARKETING & MEDIA
91 Dyne Road, London NW6 7DR
e-mail: m.shippen@virgin.net
Mobile: 07956 879165   Tel/Fax: 020-7372 3788

SINGER Sandra ASSOCIATES
(Corporate Services)
21 Cotswold Road, Westcliff-on-Sea, Essex SS0 8AA
Website: www.sandrasinger.com
e-mail: sandrasingeruk@aol.com
Fax: 01702 339393   Tel: 01702 331616

TAYLOR HERRING COMMUNICATIONS Ltd
107 Freston Road, London W11 4BD
Website: www.taylorherring.com
e-mail: james@taylorherring.com
Fax: 020-7313 2551   Tel: 020-7313 2550

THOMPSON Peter ASSOCIATES
Flat One, 12 Bourchier Street, London W1V 5HN
Fax: 020-7439 1202   Tel: 020-7439 1210

THORNBORROW Bridget
110 Newark Street, London E1 2ES
e-mail: b.thornborrow@btinternet.com
Fax: 020-7247 4144   Tel: 020-7247 4437

TOWN HOUSE PUBLICITY Ltd
(Theatre & Television PR)
45 Islington Park Street, London N1 1QB
e-mail: thp@townhousepublicity.co.uk
Fax: 020-7359 6026   Tel: 020-7226 7450

TRE-VETT Eddie
Brink House, Avon Castle
Ringwood
Hampshire BH24 2BL   Tel: 01425 475544

WILLIAMS Tei PRESS & ARTS MARKETING
7 Acre End Street, Eynsham, Oxfordshire OX29 4PE
e-mail: tei@artsmarketing.demon.co.uk
Fax: 01865 884240   Tel: 01865 883139

WILSON Stella PUBLICITY
130 Calabria Road, London N5 1HT
e-mail: stella@starmaker.demon.co.uk
Fax: 020-7354 2242   Tel: 020-7354 5672

WINGHAM Maureen
PRESS & PUBLIC RELATIONS
PO Box 125, Stowmarket, Suffolk IP14 1PB
e-mail: mjw.wingham@virgin.net
Fax: 01449 771400   Tel: 01449 771200

WRIGHT Peter
(See CUE CONSULTANTS)

BBC RADIO, Broadcasting House, London W1A 1AA
Tel: 020-7580 4468 (Main Switchboard)

■ DRAMA

BBC Radio Drama
Bush House
The Aldwych, London WC2B 4PH
Tel: 020-7580 4468 (Main Switchboard)

Production
Head	Gordon House
Production Executive	Rebecca Wilmhurst
Co-ordinator Radio	
Drama Company	Cynthia Fagan

Executive Producers
World Service	Marion Nancarrow
London	Sally Avens
	Jeremy Mortimer
Manchester	Sue Roberts
Birmingham	Vanessa Whitburn

Senior Producers
Ned Chaillet	David Hitchinson (Westway)
Cherry Cookson	Keri Davies (Archers)
	James Peries (Asian Soap)

Producers - London
Marc Beeby	Tracey Neale
Pam Fraser Solomon	Jonquil Panting
Claire Grove	Mary Peate
Peter Kavanagh	Janet Whitaker
Duncan Minshull	Rishi Sankar (World Service)

Producers - Manchester
Pauline Harris	Jim Poyseri
Nadia Molinar	Polly Thomas

Producers Birmingham
Julie Beckett (Archers)	Jenny Stephens
Peter Wild	Kate Oates (Archers)

Diversity Development
Director	Shabina Aslam

Development Producers
Naylah Ahmed (Birmingham)	Pam Marshall
Toby Swift	Liz Webb

Writersroom
Director	Kate Rowland
Co-ordinator	Jessica Dromgoole

BROADCAST

Radio Drama - BBC Scotland
Head	Patrick Rayner
Editor, Radio Drama	Bruce Young
Management Assistant	Sue Meek

Producers
Gaynor Macfarlane	David Jackson Young
Lu Kemp	

Radio Drama - BBC Wales
Geri Thomas	Alison Hindell

Radio Drama - BBC Northern Ireland
All enquiries to Anne Simpson

■ LIGHT ENTERTAINMENT/RADIO PRODUCTION

Head, Light Entertainment Radio	
	John Pidgeon
Finance Manager	David Goodfellow

Producers
Adam Bromley	Ed Morrish
Dawn Ellis	Simon Nicholls
Tilusha Ghelami	Will Saunders
Claire Jones	Carol Smith
Katie Mansden	Mario Stylianides
	Katie Tyrrell

Radio Administrator	Sarah Wright
Radio Administrator Asst	Liana Ross

■ NEWS AND CURRENT AFFAIRS

BBC News (Television & Radio)
Television Centre
Wood Lane, London W12 7RJ
Tel: 020-8576 7178   Fax: 020-8576 7120

Director News	Richard Sambrook
Deputy Director News	Mark Damazer
Head of Television News	Roger Mosey
Deputy Head of Television News	Rachel Atwell
Head of Radio News	Stephen Mitchell
Head of Political Programmes	Francesca Unsworth

■ RADIO SPORT

Head of Sport	Gordon Turnbull

■ CONTROLLERS
Director of Radio	Jenny Abramsky

RADIO 1
Controller	Andy Parfitt

RADIO 2
Controller	James Moir

RADIO 3
Controller	Roger Wright

RADIO 4
Controller	Helen Boaden

RADIO 5
Controller	Bob Shennan

■ BBC NEW WRITING

BBC Writersroom
1 Mortimer Street
London W1T 3JA   Tel: 020-7765 2703
e-mail: new.writing@bbc.co.uk
Website: www.bbc.co.uk/writersroom

Creative Director	Kate Rowland
Newwriting Co-ordinator	Jessica Dromgoole

R

BBC RADIO BRISTOL
PO Box 194, Bristol BS99 7QT
Fax: 0117-923 8323   Tel: 0117-974 1111
Managing Editor: Jenny Lacey
News Editor: Dawn Trevett

BBC CAMBRIDGE
Broadcasting House
104 Hills Road, Cambridge CB2 1LD
Fax: 01223 460832   Tel: 01223 259696
Managing Editor: David Martin
Assistant Editor: Patrick Davies

BBC RADIO CLEVELAND
PO Box 95 FM, Middlesbrough TS1 5DG
Website: www.bbc.co.uk/tees
Fax: 01642 211356   Tel: 01642 225211
Managing Editor: Andrew Glover

BBC RADIO CORNWALL
Phoenix Wharf, Truro, Cornwall TR1 1UA
Fax: 01872 275045   Tel: 01872 275421
Managing Editor: Pauline Causey

BBC COVENTRY & WARWICKSHIRE
Holt Court, 1 Greyfriars Road, Coventry CV1 2WR
Fax: 024-7657 0100   Tel: 024-7686 0086
Senior Broadcast Journalist: Sue Curtis

BBC RADIO CUMBRIA
Annetwell Street, Carlisle, Cumbria CA3 8BB
Fax: 01228 511195   Tel: 01228 592444
Managing Editor: Nigel Dyson

BBC RADIO DERBY
PO Box 104.5, Derby DE1 3HL   Tel: 01332 361111
Managing Editor: Simon Cornes

BBC RADIO DEVON
PO Box 1034, Plymouth PL3 5YQ
Fax: 01752 234564   Tel: 01752 260323
Managing Editor: John Lilley

BBC ESSEX
PO Box 765, Chelmsford
Essex CM2 9XB   Tel: 01245 616000
Managing Editor: Margaret Hyde

BBC RADIO GLOUCESTERSHIRE
London Road
Gloucester GL1 1SW   Tel: 01452 308585
Managing Editor: Mark Hurrell

BBC RADIO GUERNSEY
Broadcasting House, Bulwer Avenue
St Sampsons, Channel Islands GY2 4LA
e-mail: radio.guernsey@bbc.co.uk
Fax: 01481 200361   Tel: 01481 200600
Senior Broadcast Journalist: Simon Alexander

BBC HEREFORD & WORCESTER
Hylton Road
Worcester WR2 5WW   Tel: 01905 748485
Managing Editor: James Coghill

BBC RADIO HUMBERSIDE
9 Chapel Street, Hull HU1 3NU
e-mail: radio.humberside@bbc.co.uk
Fax: 01482 226409   Tel: 01482 323232
Executive Managing Editor: Helen Thomas

BBC RADIO JERSEY
18 Parade Road, St Helier, Jersey JE2 3PL
Fax: 01534 732569   Tel: 01534 870000
Senior Broadcast Journalist: Matthew Price
News Editor: Sarah Scriven

BBC RADIO KENT
The Great Hall
Mount Pleasant Road, Tunbridge Wells
Kent TN1 1QQ   Tel: 01892 670000
Managing Editor: Robert Wallis

BBC RADIO LANCASHIRE
20-26 Darwen Street, Blackburn
Lancashire BB2 2EA   Tel: 01254 262411
Editor: John Clayton

BBC RADIO LEEDS
Broadcasting House
Woodhouse Lane
Leeds LS2 9PN
Fax: 0113-242 0652   Tel: 0113-244 2131
Managing Editor: Richard Whitaker

BBC RADIO LEICESTER
Epic House, Charles Street
Leicester LE1 3SH
Fax: 0116-251 1463   Tel: 0116-251 6688
Managing Editor: Liam McCarthy

BBC RADIO LINCOLNSHIRE
PO Box 219, Newport
Lincoln LN1 3XY
Fax: 01522 511058   Tel: 01522 511411
Station Editor: Charlie Partridge

BBC LIVE 94.9
35C Marylebone High Street
London W1U 4QA
Fax: 020-7486 4045   Tel: 020-7208 9200
Managing Editor: David Robey
Assistant News Editor: Wyn Baptist
Assistant Editor General Programmes: Paul Leaper

BBC GMR
PO Box 951, Oxford Road
Manchester M60 1SD   Tel: 0161-200 2000
Editor: Steve Taylor

BBC RADIO MERSEYSIDE
55 Paradise Street
Liverpool L1 3BP
Website: www.bbc.co.uk/liverpool
e-mail: radio.merseyside@bbc.co.uk
Managing Editor: Mick Ord   Tel: 0151-708 5500

BBC RADIO NEWCASTLE
Broadcasting Centre
Barrack Road, Fenham
Newcastle upon Tyne NE99 1RN
Fax: 0191-232 5082   Tel: 0191-232 4141
Editor: Sarah Drummond

BBC RADIO NORFOLK
The Forum, Millennium Plain, Norwich NR2 1BH
Website: www.bbc.co.uk/norfolk
e-mail: david.clayton@bbc.co.uk
Fax: 01603 667949   Tel: 01603 617411
Managing Editor: David Clayton

BBC NORTHAMPTON
Broadcasting House, Abington Street
Northampton NN1 2BH
e-mail: northampton@bbc.co.uk
Fax: 01604 230709   Tel: 01604 239100
Manager: David Clargo
Senior Broadcast Journalists: Mike Day, Jo Griffith

BBC RADIO NOTTINGHAM
London Road, Nottingham NG2 4UU
Fax: 0115-902 1985   Tel: 0115-955 0500
Editor: Mike Bettison
Editor News Gathering: Emma Agnew

BBC RADIO SHEFFIELD
54 Shoreham Street, Sheffield S1 4RS
Fax: 0114-267 5454   Tel: 0114-273 1177
Managing Editor: Gary Keown
Senior Broadcast Journalist News: David Holmes

BBC RADIO SHROPSHIRE
2-4 Boscobel Drive, Shrewsbury, Shropshire SY1 3TT
e-mail: radio.shropshire@bbc.co.uk
Fax: 01743 271702   Tel: 01743 248484
Editor: Tim Pemberton
Senior Broadcast Journalist News: John Shone

Radio (BBC Local)

BBC RADIO SOLENT
Broadcasting House, Havelock Road
Southampton SO14 7PW
e-mail: solent@bbc.co.uk
Fax: 023-8033 9648   Tel: 023-8063 1311
Managing Editor: Mia Costello

BBC SOUTHERN COUNTIES RADIO
Broadcasting Centre, Guildford, Surrey GU2 5AP
e-mail: southern.counties.radio@bbc.co.uk
Fax: 01483 304952   Tel: 01483 306306
Managing Editor: Mike Hapgood
Head of Output: Sara David

BBC RADIO STOKE
Cheapside, Hanley, Stoke-on-Trent
Staffordshire ST1 1JJ
Website: www.bbc.co.uk/stoke
e-mail: radio.stoke@bbc.co.uk
Fax: 01782 289115   Tel: 01782 208080
Managing Editor: Sue Owen

BBC RADIO SUFFOLK
Broadcasting Hse, St Matthews St, Ipswich IP1 3EP
Website: www.bbc.co.uk/suffolk
e-mail: radiosuffolk@bbc.co.uk
Editor: Gerald Main   Tel: 01473 250000

BBC RADIO SWINDON & BBC RADIO WILTSHIRE
Broadcasting House
56-58 Prospect Place
Swindon SN1 3RW
Fax: 01793 513650   Tel: 01793 513626
Manager: Tony Worgan

BBC THREE COUNTIES RADIO
1 Hastings Street, Luton LU1 5XL
e-mail: 3cr@bbc.co.uk
Fax: 01582 401467   Tel: 01582 637400
Managing Editor: Mark Norman

BBC RADIO WM (WEST MIDLANDS)
PO Box 206
Birmingham B5 7SD
Fax: 0121-472 3174   Tel: 0121-432 9000
Editor Local Services: Keith Beech

BBC RADIO YORK
20 Bootham Row
York YO30 7BR
Website: www.bbc.co.uk/radioyork
e-mail: radio.york@bbc.co.uk
Fax: 01904 610937   Tel: 01904 641351
Managing Editor: Matt Youdale

Radio (Independent Local)

ABERDEEN
Northsound Radio
45 Kings Gate, Aberdeen AB15 4EL
e-mail: northsound@srh.co.uk   Tel: 01224 337000

AYR
West Sound & West FM
Radio House
54A Holmston Road, Ayr KA7 3BE
e-mail: westfm@srh.co.uk   Tel: 01292 283662

BELFAST
City Beat 96.7 FM
PO Box 967, Belfast BT9 5DF
Fax: 028-9020 0023   Tel: 028-9020 5967

BELFAST
Downtown Radio
Newtownards, Co Down BT23 4ES
e-mail: alastair.mcdowell@downtown.co.uk
          Tel: 028-9181 5555

BERKSHIRE & NORTH HAMPSHIRE
2-Ten FM
PO Box 2020, Reading
Berkshire RG31 7FG   Tel: 0118-945 4400

BIRMINGHAM
96.4 BRMB & Capital Gold
9 Brindley Place
Birmingham B1 2DJ
Fax: 0121-245 5245   Tel: 0121-245 5000

BORDERS The
Radio Borders Ltd
Tweedside Park, Galashiels TD1 3TD
Fax: 0845 3457080   Tel: 01896 759444

BRADFORD
Sunrise Radio
30 Chapel Street
Little Germany, Bradford BD1 5DN
Fax: 01274 371711   Tel: 01274 735043

**BRADFORD, HUDDERSFIELD, HALIFAX
KEIGHLEY & DEWSBURY**
The Pulse/West Yorkshire's Classic Gold
Forster Square, Bradford BD1 5NE
e-mail: general@pulse.co.uk   Tel: 01274 203040

BRIGHTON, EASTBOURNE & HASTINGS
Southern FM
Radio House, PO Box 2000
Brighton BN41 2SS   Tel: 01273 430111

BRISTOL
GWR FM & Classic Gold 1260
1 Passage Street, PO Box 2000
Bristol BS99 7SN   Tel: 0117-984 3200

CAMBRIDGE & NEWMARKET
Q 103 FM
PO Box 103
The Vision Park, Chivers Way
Histon Cambridge CB4 9WW   Tel: 01223 235255

CARDIFF & NEWPORT
Red Dragon FM & Capital Gold
Atlantic Wharf
Cardiff Bay, Cardiff CF10 4DJ
e-mail: mail@reddragonfm.co.uk
          Tel: 029-2066 2066

CHESTER, NORTH WALES & WIRRAL
Marcher Radio Group Ltd
The Studios, Mold Road
Wrexham LL11 4AF
Website: www.mfmradio.co.uk
e-mail: sarah.smithard@musicradio.com
          Tel: 01978 752202
Managing Director: Sarah Smithard

COVENTRY
KIX 96.2 FM
Watch Close, Spon Street
Coventry CV1 3LN   Tel: 024-7652 5656

COVENTRY
Mercia FM
Hertford Place
Coventry CV1 3TT   Tel: 024-7686 8200

DUMFRIES
West Sound FM
Unit 40
The Loreburn Centre, High Street
Dumfries DG1 2BD   Tel: 01387 250999

DUNDEE & PERTH
Tay FM & Radio Tay AM
PO Box 123
6 North Isla Street, Dundee DD3 7JQ
Website: www.radiotay.co.uk
e-mail: tayfm@radiotay.co.uk   Tel: 01382 200800

EDINBURGH
Radio Forth Ltd
Forth House
Forth Street, Edinburgh EH1 3LE
Website: www.forthonline.co.uk
e-mail: info@radioforth.co.uk   Tel: 0131-556 9255

EXETER & TORBAY
Gemini Radio Ltd
Hawthorn House
Exeter Business Park
Exeter EX1 3QS   Tel: 01392 444444

FALKIRK
Central FM
201-203 High Street
Falkirk FK1 1DU   Tel: 01324 611164

GLASGOW
Radio Clyde FM1 & Clyde 2 AM
3 South Avenue
Clydebank Business Park
Glasgow G81 2RX   Tel: 0141-565 2200

GLOUCESTER & CHELTENHAM
Severn Sound FM & Classic Gold
Bridge Studios, Eastgate Centre
Gloucester GL1 1SS   Tel: 01452 313200

GREAT YARMOUTH & NORWICH
Radio Broadland FM & Classic Gold Digital
St Georges Plain, 47-49 Colegate
Norwich NR3 1DB   Tel: 01603 630621

GUILDFORD
96.4 The Eagle FM & County Sound 1566 MW
County Sound Radio Network Ltd
Dolphin House
3 North Street, Guildford
Surrey GU1 4AA
e-mail: eagle@countysound.co.uk
    Tel: 01483 300964

HEREFORD & WORCESTER
Wyvern FM
5-6 Barbourne Terrace
Worcester WR1 3JZ
Website: www.musicradio.com   Tel: 01905 612212

INVERNESS
Moray Firth Radio
PO Box 271
Scorguie Place, Inverness IV3 8UJ
e-mail: mfr@mfr.co.uk
Fax: 01463 243224   Tel: 01463 224433

IPSWICH
SGR-FM
Radio House
Alpha Business Park
Whitehouse Road
Ipswich IP1 5LT   Tel: 01473 461000

ISLE OF WIGHT
Isle of Wight Radio
Dodnor Park Newport
Isle of Wight PO30 5XE
e-mail: admin@iwradio.co.uk
Fax: 01983 821690   Tel: 01983 822557

KENT
Invicta FM & Capital Gold
Radio House, John Wilson Business Park
Whitstable Kent CT5 3QX
e-mail: info@invictafm.com   Tel: 01227 772004

KETTERING & CORBY
Connect FM 97.2 & 107.4 FM
Centre 2000, Robinson Close
Telford Way Industrial Estate, Kettering
Northamptonshire NN16 8PU   Tel: 01536 412413

LEEDS
96.3 Radio Aire & Magic 828
PO Box 2000, 51 Burley Road
Leeds LS3 1LR   Tel: 0113-283 5500

LEICESTER
Leicester Sound
6 Dominus Way, Meridian Business Park
Leicester LE19 1RP   Tel: 0116-256 1300

LEICESTER, NOTTINGHAM & DERBY
96 Trent FM & Classic Gold GEM
29-31 Castle Gate
Nottingham NG1 7AP   Tel: 0115-952 7000

LIVERPOOL
Radio City
St Johns Beacon
1 Houghton Street
Liverpool L1 1RL
Website: www.radiocity.co.uk   Tel: 0151-472 6800

LONDON
Capital Radio Plc
30 Leicester Square
London WC2H 7LA   Tel: 020-7766 6000

LONDON
Choice FM
291-299 Borough High Street
London SE1 1JG   Tel: 020-7378 3969

LONDON
Classic FM
7 Swallow Place
Oxford Circus
London W1B 2AG   Tel: 020-7343 9000

LONDON
Heart 106.2 FM
The Chrysalis Building
Bramley Road
London W10 6SP   Tel: 020-7468 1062

LONDON
ITN Radio
200 Gray's Inn Road
London WC1X 8XZ   Tel: 020-7430 4814

LONDON
Jazz FM 102.2
26-27 Castlereagh Street
London W1H 5DL
Website: www.jazzfm.com
e-mail: info@jazzfm.com   Tel: 020-7706 4100

LONDON
London Greek Radio
437 High Road, Finchley
London N12 0AF   Tel: 020-8800 8001

LONDON
Magic 105.4 FM
Mappin House
4 Winsley Street
London W1W 8HF   Tel: 020-7436 1515

LONDON
Time 106.8 FM
2 Basildon Road
London SE2 0EW   Tel: 020-8311 3112

LONDON
Virgin Radio
1 Golden Square
London W1F 9DJ   Tel: 020-7434 1215

LUTON & BEDFORD
97.6 Chiltern FM & Classic Gold 792/828
Broadcast Centre
Chiltern Road
Dunstable LU6 1HQ   Tel: 01582 676200

MANCHESTER
Key 103 FM & Magic 1152
Piccadilly Radio Ltd
Castle Quay, Castle Field
Manchester M15 4PR   Tel: 0161-288 5000

MILTON KEYNES
FM 103 Horizon
14 Vincent Avenue
Milton Keynes Broadcast Centre, Crownhill
Milton Keynes MK8 0AB   Tel: 01908 269111

NORTHAMPTON
Northhants 96/Classic Gold 1557
Northamptonshire Digital
19-21 St Edmunds Road, Northampton NN1 5DY
e-mail: reception@northants96.musicradio.com
                        Tel: 01604 795600

NOTTINGHAM & DERBY
96 Trent FM
29-31 Castle Gate, Nottingham NG1 7AP
e-mail: admin@musicradio.com   Tel: 0115-952 7000

OXFORD & BANBURY
Fox FM
Brush House, Pony Road
Oxford OX4 2XR   Tel: 01865 871000

PETERBOROUGH
102.7 Hereward FM & Classic Gold
PO Box 225, Queensgate Centre
Peterborough PE1 1XJ   Tel: 01733 460460

PLYMOUTH
Plymouth Sound Radio
Earl's Acre, Alma Road
Plymouth PL3 4HX   Tel: 01752 275600

PORTSMOUTH & SOUTHAMPTON
Capitol Radio Group South
Radio House, Whittle Avenue
Segensworth West, Fareham
Hampshire PO15 5SH   Tel: 01489 589911

SOMERSET
Orchard FM
Haygrove House, Shoreditch
Taunton TA3 7BT   Tel: 01823 338448

SOUTH MANCHESTER
Imagine FM
Regent House, Heaton Lane, Stockport
Cheshire SK4 1BX
e-mail: reception@imaginefm.net
                        Tel: 0161-609 1400

SOUTHEND
Essex FM & Classic Gold Breeze
(Ten 17, SGR Colchester-all part of
GWR Group PLC)
Radio House, 19-20 Clifftown Road
Southend-on-Sea, Essex SS1 1SX
Fax: 01702 345224   Tel: 01702 333711

STOKE-ON-TRENT & STAFFORD
Signal Radio
Stoke Road, Stoke-on-Trent
Staffordshire ST4 2SR
Website: www.signaonel.co.uk
e-mail: info@signalradio.com   Tel: 01782 441300

SWANSEA
96.4 FM The Wave
Victoria Road, Gowerton
Swansea SA4 3AB   Tel: 01792 511964

TEESSIDE
TFM 96.6 & Magic 1170
Yale Crescent, Thornaby
Stockton on Tees
Cleveland TS17 6AA   Tel: 01642 888222

TYNE & WEAR & NORTHUMBERLAND, DURHAM
Metro Radio
Newcastle upon Tyne NE99 1BB   Tel: 0191-420 0971

WEST SUSSEX & SURREY
102.7 Mercury FM
9 The Stanley Centre, Kelvin Way, Manor Royal
Crawley, West Sussex RH10 9SE
e-mail: name@musicradio.com   Tel: 01293 519161

**WOLVERHAMPTON & BLACK COUNTRY/
SHREWSBURY & TELFORD**
Beacon FM & Classic Gold
267 Tettenhall Road
Wolverhampton WV6 0DE   Tel: 01902 461300

YORKSHIRE
Hallam FM & Magic AM
Radio House, 900 Herries Road, Hillsborough
Sheffield S6 1RH   Tel: 0114-209 1000

YORKSHIRE & LINCOLNSHIRE
96.9 Viking FM & Magic 1161 AM
Commercial Road
Hull HU1 2SG   Tel: 01482 325141

A1 VOX Ltd
(Spoken Word Audio, ISDN Links, Demo CDs &
Audio Clips)
20 Old Compton Street
London W1D 4TW
Website: www.a1vox.com
e-mail: info@a1vox.com
Fax: 020-7434 4414   Tel: 020-7434 4404

ABBEY ROAD STUDIOS
3 Abbey Road
St John's Wood
London NW8 9AY
Website: www.abbeyroad.com
e-mail: info@abbeyroad.com
Fax: 020-7266 7250   Tel: 020-7266 7000

AIR STUDIOS (LYNDHURST) Ltd
Lyndhurst Hall, Lyndhurst Road
London NW3 5NG
Fax: 020-7794 8518   Tel: 020-7794 0660

AIR-EDEL RECORDING STUDIOS Ltd
18 Rodmarton Street
London W1U 8BJ
e-mail: trevorbest@air-edel.co.uk
Fax: 020-7224 0344   Tel: 020-7486 6466

ANGEL RECORDING STUDIOS Ltd
311 Upper Street
London N1 2TU
e-mail: angel@angelstudio.co.uk
Fax: 020-7226 9624   Tel: 020-7354 2525

ASCENT MEDIA Ltd
Film House
142 Wardour Street
London W1F 8DD
Website: www.ascentmedia.co.uk
Fax: 020-7878 7870   Tel: 020-7878 0000

AUDIOLAB WEST STREET
3 West Street
Buckingham MK18 1HL
Website: www.alab.co.uk
e-mail: office@alab.co.uk
Mobile: 07739 807159   Tel/Fax: 01280 822814

BLACKHEATH HALLS
23 Lee Road, Blackheath
London SE3 9RQ
Website: www.blackheathhalls.com
e-mail: mail@blackheathhalls.com
Fax: 020-8852 5154   Tel: 020-8318 9758

CHANNEL 20/20 Ltd
20/20 House
26-28 Talbot Lane
Leicester LE1 4LR
Website: www.channel2020.co.uk
Fax: 0116-222 1113   Tel: 0116-233 2220

CRYING OUT LOUD
(Voice-Over Specialists/Voice-over Demo CDs)
Website: www.cryingoutloud.co.uk
e-mail: simon@cryingoutloud.co.uk
Mobile: 07946 533108   Mobile: 07796 266268

DE LANE LEA SOUND
(Post Production, Re-Recording Studios)
75 Dean Street
London W1D 3PU
Website: www.delanelea.com
e-mail: dll@delanelea.com
Fax: 020-7432 3838   Tel: 020-7432 3800

ELMS STUDIOS DIGITAL
(Mac G4/Logic Platinum/Emu Systems, 02R,
Music Composing/Scoring & VOs)
Addiscombe, 10 Empress Avenue
London E12 5ES
Website: www.impulse-music.co.uk/elms-studio
e-mail: phillawrence@elmsstudios.com
                            Tel: 020-8518 8629

ESSENTIAL MUSIC
20 Great Chapel Street
London W1F 8FW
e-mail: essentialmusic@hotmail.com
Fax: 020-7287 3597   Tel: 020-7439 7113

FARM DIGITAL POST PRODUCTION The
27 Upper Mount Street
Eire, Dublin 2
Website: www.thefarm.ie
e-mail: info@thefarm.ie
Fax: 353 1 676 8816   Tel: 353 1 676 8812

HEAVY ENTERTAINMENT Ltd
222 Kensal Road
London W10 5BN
Website: www.heavy-entertainment.com
e-mail: info@heavy-entertainment.com
Fax: 020-8960 9003   Tel: 020-8960 9001

ISLAND 41
(Voice-over Recording Studio)
29 Ash Grove, London W5 4AX
Website: www.island41.com
e-mail: info@island41.com
Fax: 020-8567 5183   Tel: 020-8567 5140

JMS GROUP Ltd
3 Montagu Row, London W1U 6DY
Website: www.jms-group.com
e-mail: info@jmslondon.co.uk
Fax: 020-7224 4035   Tel: 020-7224 1031

Hethersett, Norwich
Norfolk NR9 3DL
Fax: 01603 812255   Tel: 01603 811855

KONK STUDIOS
84-86 Tottenham Lane
London N8 7EE
e-mail: linda@konkstudios.com
Fax: 020-8348 3952   Tel: 020-8340 7873

LANSDOWNE RECORDING STUDIOS Ltd
Lansdowne House
Lansdowne Road
London W11 3LP
Website: www.cts-lansdowne.co.uk
e-mail: info@cts-lansdowne.co.uk
Fax: 020-7792 8904   Tel: 020-7727 0041

MAKING TRACKS RECORDING STUDIO
(Voice Tapes/Open Reel & Digital Multi-Track
Recording)
52 St Swithins Road
Tankerton, Kent CT5 2HX
Website: www.young-sounds.com/makingtracks.html
e-mail: jfield@young-sounds.com
Fax: 01277 277851   Tel: 01277 275120

MOTIVATION SOUND STUDIOS
35A Broadhurst Gardens
London NW6 3QT
Website: www.motivationsound.co.uk
e-mail: info@motivationsound.co.uk
Fax: 020-7624 4879   Tel: 020-7328 8305

Need a London Studio?

- ISDN Links
- Digital Audio Editing
- Radio Programme Production
- In-house Voice-over team available
- Voice-over Training and Demo CDs
- Audio clips for Spotlight

The friendly alternative in the heart of Soho

A1 VOX - *studios for voice work via ISDN*
RECORDINGS - *DAT, MiniDisc, CD-R, WAV, MP3*
EXPERT - *digital editing and production*
TRAINING - *in the art of Voice-over*
NOBODY - *does tailor-made Voice-over Demos like we do!*

A1 VOX Ltd
20 Old Compton Street
London W1D 4TW
Tel 020 7434 4404
Fax 020 7434 4414
e-mail info@a1vox.com

www.a1vox.com

ORANGE ROOM MUSIC
4 Kendal Court
Railway Road, Newhaven
East Sussex BN9 0AY
Website: www.orangeroommusic.co.uk
e-mail: orangeroommusic@aol.com
Fax: 01273 612811   Tel: 01273 612825

OTHERWISE STUDIOS
61D Gleneldon Road, London SW16 2BH
Website: www.otherwisestudios.com
e-mail: info@otherwisestudios.com
                            Tel: 020-8769 7793

RED FACILITIES
61 Timberbush, Leith, Edinburgh EH6 6QW
Website: www.redfacilities.com
e-mail: doit@redfacilities.com
Fax: 0131-555 0088   Tel: 0131-555 2288

SARM STUDIOS WEST Ltd
8-10 Basing Street, London W11 1ET
Fax: 020-7221 9247   Tel: 020-7229 1229

SHAW Bernard
(Specialist in Recording & Directing Voice Tapes)
Horton Manor, Canterbury CT4 7LG
Website: www.bernardshaw.co.uk
e-mail: bernard@bernardshaw.co.uk
                        Tel/Fax: 01227 730843

SHOWREEL The
(Voice-Over Showreels, Digital Editing etc)
Knightsbridge House, 229 Acton Lane
Chiswick, London W4 5DD
Website: www.theshowreel.com
e-mail: info@theshowreel.com
Fax: 020-8995 2144   Tel: 020-8995 3232

SILVER-TONGUED PRODUCTIONS
(Specialising in Voice Reels)
Website: www.silver-tongued.co.uk
e-mail: contact-us@silver-tongued.co.uk
            Tel/Fax: 0870 2407408 (London)

SONY MUSIC
31-37 Whitfield Street, London W1T 2SS
Fax: 020-7580 0543   Tel: 020-7636 3434

SOUND CONCEPTION
82-84 York Road, Bristol BS3 4AL
e-mail: k-dubb@talk21.com
Fax: 0117-963 5059   Tel: 0117-966 2932

SOUND HOUSE POST PRODUCTION Ltd The
10th Floor, Astley House, Quay Street
Manchester M3 4AE
Website: www.thesoundhouse.tv
e-mail: suekean@thesoundhouse.tv
Fax: 0161-832 7266   Tel: 0161-832 7299

STERLING SOUND
(Voice-over, Demo CDs, Jingles & Commercials)
8A Barry Road
London SE22 0HU
e-mail: bob@mintman.co.uk   Tel: 020-8693 2976

STUDIO AVP
82 Clifton Hill, London NW8 0JT
Fax: 020-7624 9112   Tel: 020-7624 9111

STUDIO-74
(Quality Voice-over Demos & Sound Recording)
74 Laburnum Close
London N11 3PA
Website: www.studio-74.co.uk
e-mail: info@studio-74.co.uk   Tel: 020-8361 1898

TOUCHWOOD AUDIO PRODUCTIONS
6 Hyde Park Terrace
Leeds
West Yorkshire LS6 1BJ
e-mail: bruce.touchwood@hotmail.com
                            Tel: 0113-278 7180

UNIVERSAL SOUND (JUST PLAY) Ltd
Old Farm Lane
London East Road
Amersham, Buckinghamshire HP7 9DH
Website: www.justplay.co.uk
e-mail: foley@justplay.co.uk
Fax: 01494 723500   Tel: 01494 723400

VOICE OVER DEMOS
61 Cropley Street
London N1 7JB
Website: www.voiceoverdemos.co.uk
e-mail: daniel@voiceoverdemos.co.uk
                            Tel: 020-7684 1645

WFS Ltd
(Sound Transfer/Optical & Magnetic)
Warwick Sound
111A Wardour Street
London W1F 0UJ
Website: www.warwicksound.com
e-mail: info@warwicksound.com
Fax: 020-7439 0372   Tel: 020-7437 5532

WORLDWIDE SOUND Ltd
21-25 St Anne's Court
Soho
London W1F 0BJ
Website: www.worldwidegroup.ltd.uk
e-mail: sound@worldwidegroup.ltd.uk
Fax: 020-7734 0619   Tel: 020-7434 1121

ACTORS CENTRE The (LONDON)
(Audition Space Only)
1A Tower Street, London WC2H 9NP
e-mail: admin@actorscentre.co.uk
Fax: 020-7240 3896   Tel: 020-7240 3940

ADI The
218 Lambeth Road, London SE1 7JY
e-mail: info@adiplay.org.uk
Fax: 020-7401 2816   Tel: 020-7928 6160

ALFORD HOUSE
Aveline Street
London SE11 5DQ   Tel: 020-7735 1519

ALRA (Academy of Live and Recorded Arts)
Royal Victoria Patriotic Building, Fitzhugh Grove
Trinity Road, London SW18 3SX
Website: www.alra.demon.co.uk/events
e-mail: acting@alra.demon.co.uk
Fax: 020-8875 0789   Tel: 020-8870 6475

AMADEUS CENTRE The
50 Shirland Road, Little Venice, London W9 2JA
Website: www.amadeuscentre.co.uk
e-mail: amadeus@amadeuscentre.co.uk
Fax: 020-7266 1225   Tel: 020-7286 1686

AMERICAN CHURCH IN LONDON The
Whitefield Memorial Church
79A Tottenham Court Road, London W1T 4TD
Website: www.americanchurchinlondon.org
e-mail: latchcourt@amchurch.fsnet.co.uk
Fax: 020-7580 5013   Tel: 020-7580 2791

ARTSADMIN
(Toynbee Studios)
28 Commercial Street, London E1 6AB
Website: www.artsadmin.co.uk/aaresources
e-mail: admin@artsadmin.co.uk
Fax: 020-7247 5103   Tel: 020-7247 5102

BAC
Lavender Hill, London SW11 5TN
Website: www.bac.org.uk
e-mail: mailbox@bac.org.uk
Fax: 020-7978 5207   Tel: 020-7223 6557

BELSIZE MUSIC ROOMS
(Casting, Auditioning, Filming)
67 Belsize Lane, Hampstead, London NW3 5AX
Website: www.belsize-music-rooms.co.uk
e-mail: info@belsize-music-rooms.co.uk
Fax: 020-7916 0222   Tel: 020-7916 0111

BIG CITY STUDIOS
Montgomery House
159-161 Balls Pond Road
Islington, London N1 4BG
Website: www.pineapple-agency.com
Fax: 020-7241 3006   Tel: 020-7241 6655

BRIXTON ST VINCENTS COMMUNITY CENTRE
Talma Road, London SW2 1AS
Fax: 020-7326 1713   Tel: 020-7326 4417

CASTING CABIN The
19 Denmark Street
London WC2H 8NA
Website: www.castingspace.com
e-mail: thecastingcabin@btconnect.com
Fax: 020-7379 5444   Tel: 020-7379 0444

CASTING STUDIOS INTERNATIONAL Ltd
Ramillies House, 1-2 Ramillies Street
London W1F 7LN
Website: www.castingstudios.com
e-mail: info@castingstudios.co.uk
Fax: 020-7437 2080   Tel: 020-7437 2070

The
Spotlight Rooms

- ☐ Central location

- ☐ Bright, air-conditioned

- ☐ Competitive rates

- ☐ TV/VCR/Video Camera

- ☐ Waiting room with receptionist service

- ☐ Free access to *Spotlight* directories and *Spotlight Interactive*

NEW! THE SPOTLIGHT STUDIO: A DEDICATED VIDEO CASTING FACILITY

www.spotlightcd.com/rooms

For bookings please call

020 7440 5021

or email
casting@spotlightcd.com

The UK's Premier Casting Rooms in the heart of the West End

CASTING SUITE The
10 Warwick Street, London W1R 5RA
Website: www.thecastingsuite.com
e-mail: info@thecastingsuite.com
Fax: 020-7494 0803   Tel: 020-7434 2331

CECIL SHARP HOUSE
(Elinor Pearson)
2 Regent's Park Road, London NW1 7AY
Website: www.efdss.org   e-mail: hire@efdss.org
Fax: 020-7284 0534   Tel: 020-7485 2206

CENTRAL LONDON GOLF CENTRE
Burntwood Lane, London SW17 0AT
Website: www.clgc.co.uk
Fax: 020-8874 7447   Tel: 020-8871 2468

CENTRAL STUDIOS
470 Bromley Road, Bromley, Kent BR1 4PN
Website: www.dandbperformingarts.co.uk
e-mail: bonnie@dandbperformingarts.co.uk
Fax: 020-8697 8100   Tel: 020-8698 8880

CHATS PALACE ARTS CENTRE
42-44 Brooksby's Walk, Hackney, London E9 6DF
Fax: 020-8985 6878   Tel: 020-8533 0227

CHELSEA THEATRE
World's End Place
King's Road, London SW10 0DR
Website: www.chelseatheatre.org.uk
Fax: 020-7352 2024   Tel: 020-7352 1967

CIRCUS MANIACS
(Circus Skills Rehearsal & Casting Facilities)
Office 8A, The Kingswood Foundation
Britannia Road, Kingswood, Bristol BS15 8DB
e-mail: rehearse@circusmaniacs.com
Mobile: 07977 247287   Tel/Fax: 0117-947 7042

CLAPHAM COMMUNITY PROJECT
St Anne's Hall, Venn Street, London SW4 0BN
Website: www.claphamcommunityproject.org.uk
e-mail: admin@claphamcommunityproject.org.uk
Tel/Fax: 020-7720 8731

CLEAN BREAK CENTRE FOR THEATRE & THE ARTS
2 Patshull Road, London NW5 2LB
e-mail: general@cleanbreak.org.uk
Fax: 020-7482 8611   Tel: 020-7482 8600

CLUB FOR ACTS & ACTORS
(Incorporating Concert Artistes Association)
20 Bedford Street
London WC2E 9HP   Tel: 020-7836 3172

COPTIC STREET STUDIO Ltd
9 Coptic Street, London WC1A 1NH
Fax: 020-7636 1414   Tel: 020-7636 2030

COVENT GARDEN
CASTING SUITES & AUDITION ROOMS
29 Maiden Lane, Covent Garden
London WC2E 7JS   Tel: 020-7240 1438

CRAGRATS Ltd
The Mill, Dunford Road, Holmfirth
Huddersfield HD9 2AR
Website: www.cragrats.com
e-mail: lindsay@cragrats.com
Fax: 01484 686212   Tel: 01484 686451

CUSTARD FACTORY The
Gibb Street, Digbeth, Birmingham B9 4AA
e-mail: post@custardfactory.com
Fax: 0121-604 8888   Tel: 0121-693 7777

DANCE ATTIC STUDIOS
368 North End Road
London SW6   Tel: 020-7610 2055

DANCE COMPANY The
(Sue Hann)
76 High Street, Beckenham, Kent BR3 1ED
e-mail: dancecomp@aol.com
Fax: 020-8402 1414   Tel: 020-8402 2424

DANCEWORKS
16 Balderton Street, London W1K 6TN
Fax: 020-7629 2909   Tel: 020-7318 4100

DIAMOND DANCE STUDIO
6-8 Vestry Street, London N1 7RE
Website: www.diamondstudio.co.uk
e-mail: gem@diamonddance.com
Fax: 020-7251 8379   Tel: 020-7251 8858

DIORAMA ARTS
34 Osnaburgh Street, London NW1 3ND
Website: www.diorama-arts.org.uk
e-mail: admin@diorama-arts.org.uk
                                 Tel: 020-7916 5467

DRILL HALL The
16 Chenies Street
London WC1E 7EX
Website: www.drillhall.co.uk
e-mail: admin@drillhall.co.uk
Fax: 020-7307 5062   Tel: 020-7307 5061

EALING STUDIOS
Ealing Green
London W5 5EP
Website: www.ealingstudios.com
e-mail: bookings@ealingstudios.com
Fax: 020-8758 8658   Tel: 020-8567 6655

ELMS LESTERS PAINTING ROOMS
1-3-5 Flitcroft Street
London WC2H 8DH
e-mail: info@elmslester.co.uk
Fax: 020-7379 0789   Tel: 020-7836 6747

ENGLISH FOLK DANCE & SONG SOCIETY
Cecil Sharp House
2 Regent's Park Road, London NW1 7AY
Website: www.efdss.org
e-mail: info@efdss.org
Fax: 020-7284 0534   Tel: 020-7485 2206

ENGLISH NATIONAL OPERA
Lilian Baylis Hse, 165 Broadhurst Gdns, NW6 3AX
Website: www.eno.org   e-mail: receptionlbh@eno.org
Fax: 020-7625 3398   Tel: 020-7624 7711

ESSEX HALL
Unitarian Headquarters
1-6 Essex Street, London WC2R 3HY
Fax: 020-7240 3089   Tel: 020-7240 2384

ETCETERA THEATRE
265 Camden High Street, London NW1 7BU
e-mail: etceteratheatre@hotmail.com
Fax: 020-7482 0378   Tel: 020-7482 4857

EUROKIDS & ADULTS CASTING STUDIOS
The Warehouse Studios
Glaziers Lane, Culcheth
Warrington, Cheshire WA3 4AQ
Website: www.eka-agency.com
e-mail: info@eka-agency.com
Fax: 01925 767563   Tel: 0871 7501575

FACTORY DANCE CENTRE
407 Hornsey Road, London N19 4DX
e-mail: info@tangolondon.com
Fax: 020-7272 1327   Tel: 020-7272 1122

FSU LONDON STUDY CENTRE
98-104 Great Russell Street, London WC1B 3LA
Fax: 020-8202 6797   Tel: 020-7813 3223

HAMILTON ROAD CENTRE
1 Hamilton Road, Stratford, London E15 3AE
Fax: 020-7476 0050   Tel: 020-7473 0395

HAMPSTEAD THEATRE
Eton Avenue, Swiss Cottage, London NW3 3EU
Website: www.hampsteadtheatre.com
e-mail: info@hampsteadtheatre.com
Fax: 020-7449 4201   Tel: 020-7449 4200

HEN & CHICKENS THEATRE
Unrestricted View
Above Hen & Chickens Theatre Bar
109 St Paul's Road, London N1 2NA
Website: www.henandchickens.com
e-mail: james@henandchickens.com
                                   Tel: 020-7704 2001

HER MAJESTY'S THEATRE
(Michael Townsend)
Haymarket, London SW1Y 4QL
Website: www.rutheatres.com
e-mail: mike.townsend@rutheatres.com
                                   Tel: 020-7494 5200

HOLY INNOCENTS CHURCH
Paddenswick Road, London W6 0UB
e-mail: innocent@fish.co.uk
Fax: 020-8563 8735   Tel: 020-8748 2286

HOPE STREET Ltd
13A Hope Street, Liverpool L1 9BQ
Website: www.hope-street.org
e-mail: arts@hopest.u-net.com
Fax: 0151-709 3242   Tel: 0151-708 8007

ISLINGTON ARTS FACTORY
2 Parkhurst Road, London N7 0SF
Website: www.islingtonartsfactory.org.uk
e-mail: iaf@islingtonartsfactory.fsnet.co.uk
Fax: 020-7700 7229   Tel: 020-7607 0561

JACKSONS LANE ARTS CENTRE
(Various Spaces inc. Rehearsal Rooms &
Theatre Hire)
269A Archway Road, London N6 5AA
Website: www.jacksonslane.org.uk
e-mail: mail@jacksonslane.org.uk
                                   Tel: 020-8340 5226

JERWOOD SPACE
171 Union Street, London SE1 0LN
Website: www.jerwoodspace.co.uk
e-mail: space@jerwoodspace.co.uk
Fax: 020-7654 0172   Tel: 020-7654 0171

K M C AGENCIES
PO Box 122, 48 Great Ancoats Street
Manchester M4 5AB
Website: www.kmcagencies.co.uk
e-mail: studios@kmcagencies.co.uk
Fax: 0161-237 9812   Tel: 0161-237 3009

LA MAISON VERTE
31 Avenue Henri Mas
34320 Roujan, France
Website: www.lamaisonverte.co.uk
e-mail: nicole.russell@wanadoo.fr
Fax: 00 334 67246998   Tel: 00 334 67248852

LIVE THEATRE The
27 Broad Chare, Quayside
Newcastle upon Tyne NE1 3DQ
Website: www.live.org.uk
e-mail: info@live.org.uk   Tel: 0191-261 2694

LONDON BUBBLE THEATRE COMPANY Ltd
5 Elephant Lane, London SE16 4JD
Website: www.londonbubble.org.uk
e-mail: admin@londonbubble.org.uk
Fax: 020-7231 2366   Tel: 020-7237 4434

LONDON SCHOOL OF CAPOEIRA
Units 1 & 2 Leeds Place
Tollington Park, London N4 3RQ
Website: www.londonschoolofcapoeira.co.uk
          Tel: 020-7281 2020

LONDON STUDIO CENTRE
42-50 York Way, London N1 9AB
e-mail: enquire@london-studio-centre.co.uk
Fax: 020-7837 3248   Tel: 020-7837 7741

LONDON WELSH TRUST Ltd
157-163 Gray's Inn Road, London WC1X 8UE
Fax: 020-7837 6268   Tel: 020-7837 3722

LOUNGE The
7th Floor, 4 Golden Square, London W1F 9HT
e-mail: info@thelounge.uk.com
Fax: 020-7494 9901   Tel: 020-7494 9933

MACKINTOSH Cameron REHEARSAL STUDIO
The Tricycle, 269 Kilburn High Road
London NW6 7JR
Website: www.tricycle.co.uk
e-mail: admin@tricycle.co.uk
Fax: 020-7328 0795   Tel: 020-7372 6611

MADDERMARKET THEATRE
St John's Alley, Norwich, Norfolk NR2 1DR
Website: www.maddermarket.co.uk
e-mail: theatre@maddermarket.co.uk
Fax: 01603 661357   Tel: 01603 626560

MARMALADE STUDIO
Studio B5R Metropolitan Wharf
Wapping Wall, London E1W 3SS
Website: www.marmaladegallery.com
e-mail: info@marmaladegallery.com
                    Tel/Fax: 020-7702 2193

MARIA ASSUMPTA CENTRE The
23 Kensington Sq, Kensington, London W8 5HN
e-mail: welcome@mariaassumpta-centre.org.uk
Fax: 020-7361 4710   Tel: 020-7361 4700

**MARYMOUNT COLLEGE OF FORDHAM
UNIVERSITY LONDON CENTRE**
22 Brownlow Mews, London WC1N 2LA
Fax: 020-7831 7185   Tel: 020-7242 7004

MOBERLY SPORTS & EDUCATION CENTRE
Kilburn Lane, London W10 4AH
Fax: 020-7641 5878   Tel: 020-7641 4807

MOUNTVIEW
Academy of Theatre Arts
Ralph Richardson Memorial Studios
Kingfisher Place, Clarendon Road, London N22 6XF
Website: www.mountview.ac.uk
e-mail: acting@mountview.ac.uk
Fax: 020-8829 0034   Tel: 020-8881 2201

NATIONAL YOUTH THEATRE OF GREAT BRITAIN
443-445 Holloway Road, London N7 6LW
Website: www.nyt.org.uk   e-mail: info@nyt.org.uk
Fax: 020-7281 8246   Tel: 020-7281 3863

NEAL'S YARD MEETING ROOMS
14 Neal's Yard, Covent Garden
London WC2H 9DP
Website: www.nealsyardmeetingrooms.com
e-mail: info@nealsyardmeetingrooms.com
Fax: 020-7836 6489   Tel: 020-7379 0141

NETTLEFOLD The
West Norwood Library Centre
1 Norwood High Street, London SE27 9JX
e-mail: thenettlefold@lambeth.co.uk
Fax: 020-7926 8071   Tel: 020-7926 8070

NORTH LONDON PERFORMING ARTS CENTRE
(Production & Casting Office Facilities)
76 St James Lane,
Muswell Hill, London N10 3DF
Website: www.nlpac.co.uk
e-mail: nlpac@aol.com
Fax: 020-8444 4040   Tel: 020-8444 4544

OCTOBER GALLERY
24 Old Gloucester Street, London WC1N 3AL
Website: www.theoctobergallery.com
e-mail: rentals@ukgateway.net
Fax: 020-7405 1851   Tel: 020-7831 1618

OLD VIC THEATRE
Waterloo Road
London SE1 8NB   Tel: 020-7928 2651

OPEN DOOR COMMUNITY CENTRE
Beaumont Road
Wimbledon SW19 6TF
Website: www.wandsworth.gov.uk
e-mail: opendoor@wandsworth.gov.uk
                    Tel/Fax: 020-8871 8174

OUT OF JOINT
7 Thane Works, Thane Villas, London N7 7PH
Website: www.outofjoint.co.uk
e-mail: ojo@outofjoint.co.uk
Fax: 020-7609 0203   Tel: 020-7609 0207

OVAL HOUSE
52-54 Kennington Oval, London SE11 5SW
Website: www.ovalhouse.com
e-mail: info@ovalhouse.com   Tel: 020-7582 0080

PAINES PLOUGH AUDITION SPACE
4th Floor, 43 Aldwych, London WC2B 4DN
Website: www.painesplough.com
e-mail: office@painesplough.com
Fax: 020-7240 4534   Tel: 020-7240 4533

PEOPLE SHOW
People Show Studios
Pollard Row, London E2 6NB
Website: www.peopleshow.co.uk
e-mail: people@peopleshow.co.uk
Fax: 020-7739 0203   Tel: 020-7729 1841

PINEAPPLE STUDIOS
7 Langley Street, London WC2H 9JA
Website: www.pineapple.uk.com
e-mail: studios@pineapple.uk.com
Fax: 020-7836 0803   Tel: 020-7836 4004

PLACE The (Contemporary Dance Trust)
17 Duke's Road, London WC1H 9PY
Website: www.theplace.org.uk
Fax: 020-7383 4851   Tel: 020-7387 0161

PLAY Ltd
(See ADI The)

PLAYGROUND PERFORMING ARTS STUDIO The
Unit 8, Latimer Road
London W10 6RQ
Website: www.the-playground.co.uk
e-mail: info@the-playground.co.uk
Tel/Fax: 020-8960 0110

POOR SCHOOL The
242 Pentonville Road
London N1 9JY
Tel: 020-7837 6030

QUESTORS THEATRE EALING The
12 Mattock Lane, London W5 5BQ
Website: www.questors.org.uk
e-mail: paul@questors.org.uk
Fax: 020-8567 8736
Tel: 020-8567 0011

QUICKSILVER THEATRE
The Glass Hse, 4 Enfield Rd, London N1 5AZ
Website: www.quicksilvertheatre.org
e-mail: talktous@quicksilvertheatre.org
Fax: 020-7254 3119
Tel: 020-7241 2942

RAMBERT DANCE COMPANY
(Claire Drakeley)
94 Chiswick High Road, London W4 1SH
Website: www.rambert.org.uk
e-mail: rdc@rambert.org.uk
Fax: 020-8747 8323
Tel: 020-8630 0601

REALLY USEFUL THEATRE
(Michael Townsend)
Manor House, 21 Soho Square, London W1D 3QP
Website: www.rutheatres.com
e-mail: mike.townsend@rutheatres.com
Fax: 020-7434 1217
Tel: 020-7494 5200

R

RED ONION DANCE STUDIO
25 Hilton Grove
Hatherley Mews, London E17 4QP
e-mail: info@redonionstudios.co.uk
Fax: 020-8521 6646   Tel: 020-8520 3975

ROOFTOP STUDIO THEATRE
Rooftop Studio, Somerfield Arcade, Stone
Staffordshire ST15 8AU
Fax: 01785 818176   Tel: 01785 761233

ROTHERHITHE STUDIOS
119 Rotherhithe Street, London SE16 4NF
Website: www.sandsfilms.co.uk
e-mail: o.stockman@sandsfilms.co.uk
Fax: 020-7231 2119   Tel: 020-7231 2209

ROYAL ACADEMY OF DANCE
36 Battersea Square, London SW11 3RA
Website: www.rad.org.uk
e-mail: info@rad.org.uk
Fax: 020-7924 3129   Tel: 020-7326 8000

ROYAL SHAKESPEARE COMPANY
35 Clapham High Street, London SW4 7TW
Fax: 020-7498 0472   Tel: 020-7720 9941

S.P.A.C.E. The
(Studio for Performing Arts & Creative Enterprise)
188 St Vincent Street
2nd Floor, Glasgow G2 5SP
e-mail: info@west-end-management.co.uk
Fax: 0141-226 8983   Tel: 0141-222 2942

SCHER Anna THEATRE
70-72 Barnsbury Road, Islington, London N1 0ES
Website: www.astm.co.uk
e-mail: info@astm.co.uk
Fax: 020-7833 9467   Tel: 020-7278 2101

SCREEN WEST
136-142 Bramley Road, London W10 6SR
e-mail: sarah.alliston@jbcp.co.uk
Fax: 020-7565 3077   Tel: 020-7565 3102

SEA CADET DRILL HALL
Fairways, Off Broom Road
Teddington   Tel: 01784 241020

SEBBON STREET COMMUNITY CENTRE
Sebbon Street, Islington
London N1   Tel: 020-7354 2015

SHARED EXPERIENCE THEATRE
The Soho Laundry, 9 Dufours Place, London W1F 7SJ
Website: www.sharedexperience.org.uk
e-mail: admin@setheatre.co.uk
Fax: 020-7287 8763   Tel: 020 7734 8570

SOHO GYMS
Covent Garden Gym, 12 Macklin Street
London WC2B 5NF
Website: www.sohogyms.com
Fax: 020-7242 0899   Tel: 020-7242 1290

Earl's Court Gym, 254 Earl's Court Road
London SW5 9AD
Fax: 020-7244 6893   Tel: 020-7370 1402

Camden Town Gym, 193 Camden High Street
London NW1 7JY
Fax: 020-7267 0500   Tel: 020-7482 4524

Clapham Common Gym, 95-97 Clapham High St
London SW4 7TB
Fax: 020-7720 6510   Tel: 020-7720 0321

SOHO THEATRE & WRITERS' CENTRE
21 Dean Street, London W1D 3NE
Website: www.sohotheatre.com
e-mail: mail@sohotheatre.com
Fax: 020-7287 5061   Tel: 020-7478 0117

SOUTHALL COMMUNITY CENTRE
(Rehearsal/Location Work)
20 Merrick Road
Southall, London UB2 4AU
Fax: 020-8574 3459   Tel: 020-8574 3458

SPOTLIGHT The
2nd Floor
7 Leicester Place WC2H 7RJ
Website: www.spotlightcd.com/rooms
e-mail: info@spotlightcd.com
Fax: 020-7437 5881   Tel: 020-7437 7631

ST GEORGE'S CHURCH BLOOMSBURY
Vestry Hall
7 Little Russell Street
London WC1E 6DP
Website: www.stgeorgesbloomsbury.org.uk
e-mail: holmado@aol.com   Tel: 020-7405 3044

ST JAMES'S CHURCH PICCADILLY
197 Piccadilly, London W1J 9LL
Website: www.st-james-piccadilly.org
Fax: 020-7734 7449   Tel: 020-7734 4511

ST JOHN'S CHURCH
Waterloo Road, Southbank
London SE1 8TY
Fax: 020-7928 4470   Tel: 020-7633 9819

ST JOHN'S METHODIST CHURCH
9-11 East Hill, Wandsworth, London SW18 2HT
Tel: 020-8874 4780   Tel: 020-8871 9124

ST MARY ABBOTS HALL
Vicarage Gate
Kensington, London W8 4HN
Website: www.stmaryabbots.freeserve.co.uk
e-mail: terry.pritchard@gmx.net
Fax: 020-7368 6505   Tel: 020-7937 8885

ST MARY NEWINGTON CHURCH HALL
The Parish Office
57 Kennington Park Road
London SE11 4JQ   Tel: 020-7735 1894

ST MARY'S CHURCH HALL PADDINGTON
c/o Bill Kenwright Ltd
106 Harrow Road, London W2 1RR
e-mail: info@kenwright.com
Fax: 020-7446 6222   Tel: 020-7446 6200

TAKE FIVE CASTING STUDIO
(Casting Suite)
25 Ganton Street, London W1F 9BP
Website: www.takefivestudio.co.uk
e-mail: info@takefivestudio.co.uk
Fax: 020-7287 3035   Tel: 020-7287 2120

THEATRE ENTERTAINMENTS Ltd
42 Theobalds Road
London WC1X 8NW
e-mail: info@sweet-uk.net
Fax: 020-7404 6412   Tel: 020-7404 6411

THEATRE ROYAL DRURY LANE
(Michael Townsend)
Catherine Street
London WC2B 5JF
Website: www.rutheatres.com
e-mail: mike.townsend@rutheatres.com
          Tel: 020-7494 5200

**THRESH Melody MANAGEMENT
ASSOCIATES Ltd (MTM)**
MTM House
27 Ardwick Green North
Ardwick, Manchester M12 6DL
e-mail: melodythreshmtm@aol.com
Fax: 0161-273 5455   Tel: 0161-273 5445

Rehearsal Rooms & Casting Suites

TRESTLE ARTS BASE
(Home of Trestle Theatre Company)
Russet Drive, St Albans
Hertfordshire AL4 0JQ
Website: www.trestle.org.uk
e-mail: admin@trestle.org.uk
Fax: 01727 855558　　　　　Tel: 01727 850150

TRICYCLE The
269 Kilburn High Road, London NW6 7JR
Website: www.tricycle.co.uk
e-mail: admin@tricycle.co.uk
Fax: 020-7328 0795　　　　　Tel: 020-7372 6611

TWICKENHAM SEA CADETS
Fairways
Off Broom Road, Teddington
Middlesex TW11 9PL　　　　　Tel: 01784 241020

UCL BLOOMSBURY The
15 Gordon Street, London WC1H 0AH
Website: www.thebloomsbury.com
e-mail: blooms.theatre@ucl.ac.uk
　　　　　　　　　　　　　　Tel: 020-7679 2777

UNION CHAPEL PROJECT
Compton Avenue, London N1 2XD
Website: www.unionchapel.org.uk
e-mail: spacehire@unionchapel.org.uk
Fax: 020-7354 8343　　　　　Tel: 020-7226 3750

URDANG ACADEMY The
20-22 Shelton Street
Covent Garden
London WC2H 9JJ
Website: www.urdang-academy.co.uk
e-mail: info@theurdangacademy.com
Fax: 020-7836 7010　　　　　Tel: 020-7836 5709

WATERMANS
40 High Street
Brentford TW8 0DS
Fax: 020-8232 1030　　　　　Tel: 020-8232 1020

WILDITCH COMMUNITY CENTRE
48 Culvert Road
Battersea, London SW11 5BB
Website: www.wandsworth.gov.uk/playservices/community/htm
e-mail: wilditch@wandsworth.gov.uk
　　　　　　　　　　　　Tel/Fax: 020-8871 8172

Y TOURING
10 Lennox Road
Finsbury Park, London N4 3JQ
e-mail: d.jackson@ytouring.org.uk
Fax: 020-7272 8413　　　　　Tel: 020-7272 5755

YOUNG Sylvia THEATRE SCHOOL
Rossmore Road
Marylebone, London NW1 6NJ
e-mail: sylvia@sylviayoungtheatreschool.co.uk
Fax: 020-7723 1040　　　　　Tel: 020-7723 0037

Role Play Companies / Theatre Skills in Business

ACT UP
Unit 88
99-109 Lavender Hill
London SW11 5QL
Website: www.act-up.co.uk
e-mail: info@act-up.co.uk
Fax: 020-7924 6606　　　　　Tel: 020-7924 7701

CRAGRATS Ltd
Cragrats Mill
Dunford Road, Holmfirth
Huddersfield HD9 2AR
Website: www.cragrats.com
e-mail: jill@cragrats.com
Fax: 01484 686212　　　　　Tel: 01484 686451

INTERACT
Southbank House
Black Prince Road
London SE1 7SJ
Website: www.interactrolepay.com
e-mail: info@interactroleplay.com
Fax: 020-7793 4245　　　　　Tel: 020-7793 4145

ROLEPLAY UK
2 St Mary's Hill
Stamford PE9 2DW
Website: www.roleplayuk.com
Fax: 01780 764436　　　　　Tel: 01780 761960

STEPS DRAMA LEARNING DEVELOPMENT
Unit 13.2.2
The Leathermarket
Weston Street
London SE1 3ER
Website: www.stepsdrama.com
e-mail: mail@stepsdrama.com
Fax: 020-7403 0909　　　　　Tel: 020-7403 9000

TURNING POINT THEATRE COMPANY
20 Couper Meadows
Digby
Exeter, Devon EX2 7TF
Website: www.eclipse.co.uk/ turningpointtheatre.co.uk
e-mail: turningpoint@eclipse.co.uk
Fax: 01392 446279　　　　　Tel: 01392 446818

It is essential that anyone undertaking a journey to the studios below, double checks these routes. Owing to constant changes of rail/bus companies/operators routes may change.

BBC TELEVISION

UNDERGROUND — CENTRAL LINE to WHITE CITY. Turn left from tube, cross zebra crossing. Studios outside station.

BBC South (Elstree) — BOREHAMWOOD

Trains from KING'S CROSS - Thames Link. Take stopping train to Elstree then walk (7/8 mins) down Shenley High St.
UNDERGROUND — NORTHERN LINE to EDGWARE or HIGH BARNET. 107 & 292 BUSES FROM EDGWARE VIA HIGH BARNET TO BOREHAMWOOD.

BRAY STUDIOS (BRAYSWICK)

BR Train from PADDINGTON to MAIDENHEAD, then take taxi to studios.
BR WATERLOO - WINDSOR RIVERSIDE, then take taxi. Coach from VICTORIA to WINDSOR, then take taxi.

HILLSIDE STUDIOS

Train from EUSTON (Network SE) to WATFORD JUNCTION, then taxi. UNDERGROUND — METROPOLITAN LINE to WATFORD, then taxi. Fast Trains from the Midlands & the North also stop at Watford Junction. If catching slow train get off at Bushey/Oxhey then catch taxi from rank outside. UNDERGROUND JUBILEE LINE to STANMORE then take taxi, or METROPOLITAN LINE & change at Baker Street or Wembley Park.

THE LONDON STUDIOS
(LONDON TELEVISION CENTRE)

UNDERGROUND (Bakerloo, Jubilee and Northern Lines) to WATERLOO then follow signs to Royal National Theatre then two buildings along.

PINEWOOD

UNDERGROUND — METROPOLITAN or PICCADILLY LINE to UXBRIDGE. Taxi rank outside statio, takes about 10 minutes. BRITISH RAIL WESTERN REGION — PADDINGTON to SLOUGH. Taxis from SLOUGH or BUS to IVER HEATH.

RIVERSIDE STUDIOS

UNDERGROUND — HAMMERSMITH and CITY, DISTRICT or PICCADILLY LINE to HAMMERSMITH — then short walk to studios (behind the London Apollo Hammersmith). Numerous BUS ROUTES from the WEST END. 5 minutes from Hammersmith Broadway.

ROTHERHITHE STUDIOS

UNDERGROUND — DISTRICT LINE onto WHITECHAPEL — then change to EAST LONDON LINE to ROTHERHITHE. JUBILEE LINE to CANADA WATER then EAST LONDON LINE to ROTHERHITHE.
BUS — 188 from EUSTON STATION via WATERLOO or 47 from LONDON BRIDGE, or 381 from WATERLOO, (best one to catch - stops outside Studios).

SHEPPERTON STUDIOS

BRITISH RAIL — SOUTHERN REGION WATERLOO to SHEPPERTON then BUS Route 400 to studios.

TEDDINGTON STUDIOS
(THAMES TELEVISION)

BRITISH RAIL — WATERLOO to TEDDINGTON. Cross over footbridge at station. Come out of Station Road entrance, TURN LEFT past Garden Centre. (Nat West on right hand side) TURN RIGHT, walk 10 mins to set of lights, cross over into Ferry Road, follow road to Studios (next to Anglers Pub on river). UNDERGROUND — DISTRICT LINE to RICHMOND — then take taxi or Bus R68 to TEDDINGTON to top of Ferry Road. Ask for Landmark Centre. Then go back to traffic lights, cross, continue past the Tide End Public House to Anglers Pub etc.

TWICKENHAM

BRITISH RAIL — SOUTHERN REGION — WATERLOO to ST MARGARET'S. UNDERGROUND — DISTRICT LINE to RICHMOND then SOUTHERN REGION or BUS 37 to ST MARGARET'S.

3D SET COMPANY
(Sets & Scenery Design & Construction)
106 Temperance Street
Manchester M12 6HR
Fax: 0161-273 6786   Tel: 0161-273 8831

ALBEMARLE OF LONDON
(Suppliers of Scenery & Costumes Construction/Hire)
74 Mortimer Street
London W1N 7DF
Website: www.freespace.virgin.net/albemarle.productions
e-mail: albemarle.productions@virgin.net
Fax: 020-7323 3074   Tel: 020-7631 0135

ALL SCENE ALL PROPS
(Scenery, Props, Painting Contractors)
443-445 Holloway Road
London N7 6LW
e-mail: info@allscene.net   Tel/Fax: 020-7561 9231

BLACKOUT Ltd
(Unitrack Track Systems, Automation, Drape & Rigging)
280 Weston Road, London SW19 2QA
Website: www.blackout-ltd.com
e-mail: info@blackout-tabtrack.com
Fax: 020-8687 8500   Tel: 020-8687 8400

BRISTOL (UK) Ltd
(Scenic Paint & StageFloor Duo Suppliers)
12 The Arches, Maygrove Road
London NW6 2DS
Website: www.bristolpaint.com
e-mail: tech.sales@bristolpaint.com
Fax: 020-7372 5242   Tel: 020-7624 4370

CCT LIGHTING Ltd
(Lighting, Dimmers, Sound & Stage Machinery)
Hindle House, Traffic Street
Nottingham NG2 1NE
Website: www.cctlighting.com
e-mail: office@cctlighting.co.uk
Fax: 0115-986 2546   Tel: 0115-986 2722

DISCO ENTERTAINMENTS
(Disc Jockeys/Mobile Discos)
12 Mead Close, Grays, Essex RM16 2TR
e-mail: disco-entertainments@talk21.com
Tel: 01375 373886

DOBSON SOUND PRODUCTION Ltd
(Sound Hire, Design & Installation)
66 Windsor Avenue, Merton, London SW19 2RR
e-mail: enquiries@dobsonsound.co.uk
Fax: 020-8543 3636   Tel: 020-8545 0202

DOVETAIL SPECIALIST SCENERY
(Scenery, Prop & Furniture Builders)
42-50 York Way, London N1 9AB
e-mail: daria@ntlworld.com   Tel/Fax: 020-7278 7379

FISHER Charles STAGING Ltd
Unit 4 Redhouse Farm, Bridgehewick
Ripon, North Yorkshire HG4 5AY
Website: www.charlesfisher.co.uk
e-mail: info@charlesfisher.co.uk   Tel: 01765 601604

FUTURIST PROJECTS Ltd
136 Thornes Lane
Wakefield, West Yorkshire WF2 7RE
Fax: 01924 298700   Tel: 01924 298900

HARLEQUIN (British Harlequin Plc)
Festival House
4 Chapman Way
Tunbridge Wells
Kent TN2 3EF
Website: www.harlequinfloors.com
e-mail: sales@harlequinfloors.co.uk
Fax: 01892 514222   Tel: 01892 514888

HENSHALL John
(Director of Lighting & Photography)
68 The High Street
Stanford in the Vale, Oxfordshire SN7 8NL
e-mail: john@epi-centre.com   Tel: 01367 710191

HERON & DRIVER
(Scenic Furniture & Structural Prop Makers)
Unit 7, Dockley Road Industrial Estate
Rotherhithe
London SE16 3SF
Website: www.herondriver.co.uk
e-mail: mail@herondriver.co.uk
Fax: 020-7394 8680   Tel: 020-7394 8688

KNIGHT Robert/TOP OF THE BILL
1-2 Wyvern Way, Henwood
Ashford, Kent TN24 8DW
Fax: 01233 634999   Tel: 01233 634777

LEE LIGHTING Ltd
Wycombe Road, Wembley
Middlesex HA0 1QD
e-mail: info@lee.co.uk
Fax: 020-8902 5500   Tel: 020-8900 2900

LEL HIRE
(Set Construction)
Unit 28C Nuralite Centre
Canal Road, Higham, Kent ME3 7JA
Website: www.lelhires.com
e-mail: info@lelhires.com
Fax: 01474 824790   Tel: 0845 130882

LIGHT WORKS Ltd
2A Greenwood Road
London E8 1AB
Fax: 020-7254 0306   Tel: 020-7249 3627

MALTBURY Ltd
(Portable Staging Sales & Consultancy)
11 Hollingbury Terrace, Brighton BN1 7JE
Website: www.maltbury.com
e-mail: info@maltbury.com
Fax: 01273 504748   Tel/Fax: 0845 1308881

MARPLES Ken CONSTRUCTION
Honeybee Cottage
Millens Lane, Hornton, Banbury
Oxfordshire OX15 6BS
e-mail: ken@marplesk.freeserve.co.uk
Mobile: 07831 281574   Tel/Fax: 01295 670302

MASSEY Bob ASSOCIATES
(Electrical & Mechanical Stage Consultants)
9 Worrall Avenue, Arnold
Nottinghamshire NG5 7GN
Website: www.bobmasseyassociates.co.uk
e-mail: bm.associates@virgin.net
Tel/Fax: 0115-967 3969

MODELBOX
(Computer Aided Design & Design Services)
20 Merton Industrial Park, Jubilee Way
London SW19 3WL
Website: www.modelbox.co.uk
e-mail: info@modelbox.co.uk
Fax: 020-8254 4721   Tel: 020-8254 4720

NEED Paul J
(Lighting Designer)
Unit 14, Forest Hill Business Centre
Clyde Vale
London SE23 3JF
Website: www.10outof10.co.uk
e-mail: paul@10outof10.co.uk
Fax: 020-8699 8968   Tel: 020-8291 6885

NORTHERN LIGHT
(Lighting, Sound, Communications & Stage
Equipment)
Assembly Street
Leith, Edinburgh EH6 7RG
Website: www.northernlight.co.uk
e-mail: enquiries@northernlight.co.uk
Fax: 0131-553 3296   Tel: 0131-553 2383

ORBITAL
(Sound Hire & Design)
57 Acre Lane, Brixton
London SW2 5TN
e-mail: hire@orbitalsound.co.uk
Fax: 020-7501 6869   Tel: 020-7501 6868

P.L. PARSONS SCENERY MAKERS
King's Cross Freight Depot
York Way, London N1 0UZ
Fax: 020-7278 3403   Tel: 020-7833 2031

RED SHIFT LIGHTING
(Lighting Design & Hire Services)
South-east London
Website: www.redshiftlighting.co.uk
e-mail: ben@redshiftlighting.co.uk
                         Mobile: 07816 879561

RETROGRAPH NOSTALGIA ARCHIVE
(Posters/Prints/Ephemera for Interiors/Exteriors
1880-1970)
10 Hanover Cresent, Brighton BN2 9SB
Website: www.retrograph.com
e-mail: retropix1@aol.com   Tel: 01273 687554

RWS ELECTRICAL & AUDIO CONTRACTORS
(Lighting & Sound, All Apsects of Electrical Services,
Design & Consultancy)
1 Spinners Close
Biddenden
Kent TN27 8AY
Website: www.rwselectrical.com   Tel: 01580 291764

SCENERY JESSEL
(Scenery Builders/Stage Supplies)
Unit B, New Baltic Wharf
Oxestalls Road, Deptford
London SE8 5RJ
e-mail: sceneryjessel@ntlworld.com
Fax: 020-8694 2430   Tel: 020-8469 2777

SCOTT FLEARY Ltd
(Creative Construction Company)
Unit 2, Southside Industrial Estate
Havelock Terrace
London SW8 4AS
e-mail: scenery@scottflearyltd.com
Fax: 020-7622 0322   Tel: 020-7978 1787

LEL Hire Ltd
Staging & Platform Specialist
Unit 28c Nuralite Ind, Centre, Canal Rd, Higham, Rochester, Kent ME3 7JA
Tel: 01474 824 267 Fax: 01474 824790
E-mail: info@lelhires.com

STAGE SYSTEMS
(Designers & Suppliers of Modular Staging, Tiering &
Auditorium Seating)
Stage House
Prince William Road
Loughborough LE11 5GU
Website: www.stagesystems.co.uk
e-mail: info@stagesystems.co.uk
Fax: 01509 233146   Tel: 01509 611021

STAGECRAFT Ltd
(Hire & Sales of Lighting, Sound, Audio Visual for
Conference & Live Events)
Ashfield Trading Estate
Salisbury, Wiltshire SP2 7HL
Website: www.stagecraft.co.uk
e-mail: hire@stagecraft.co.uk
Fax: 01722 414076   Tel: 01722 326055

STORM LIGHTING Ltd
Unit 6, Wintonlea Industrial Estate
Monument Way West
Woking, Surrey GU21 5EN
e-mail: info@stormlighting.co.uk
Fax: 01483 757710   Tel: 01483 757211

STRAND LIGHTING Ltd
(Lighting Equipment for Stage, Studio, Film & TV)
Unit 3, Hammersmith Studios
Yeldham Road
London W6 8JF
e-mail: sales@stranduk.com
Fax: 020-8735 9799   Tel: 020-8735 9790

SUFFOLK SCENERY
28 The Street, Brettenham
Ipswich, Suffolk IP7 7QP
Website: www.suffolkscenery.co.uk
e-mail: piehatch@aol.com
Fax: 01449 737620   Tel: 01449 736679

SUPOTCO GROUP
(Production - Lighting, Set Construction & Scenery)
3-5 Valentine Place
London SE1 8QH
Fax: 020-7928 6082   Tel: 020-7928 5474

THEME PARTY COMPANY The
(Set Design Backdrops & Props)
21-37 Third Avenue
London E13 8AW
Fax: 020-8471 2111   Tel: 020-8471 3111

TMS INTERNATIONAL Ltd
Western Wharf
Livesey Place,
Peckham Park Road
London SE15 6SL
Fax: 020-7277 5147   Tel: 020-7277 5156

TOBEM SERVICES
(Theatrical Lighting)
Glen Orrin
Felcourt, East Grinstead
West Sussex RH19 2LE
e-mail: valerieandterry@btclick.com
                         Tel: 01342 870438

TOP SHOW
(Props, Scenery, Conference Specialists)
North Lane, Huntington
York YO32 9SU   Tel: 01904 750022

VAMPEVENTS
Ealing House
33 Hanger Lane
London W5 3HJ
e-mail: info@vampevents.com
Fax: 020-8932 6169   Tel: 020-8997 3355

WEST John ASSOCIATES
(Designers & Scenic Artists - Film, TV & Display)
103 Abbotswood Close
Winyates Green, Redditch
Worcestershire B98 0QF
e-mail: johnwest@blueyonder.co.uk
Mobile: 07753 637451   Tel/Fax: 01527 516771

WHITE LIGHT (Electrics) Ltd
(Stage & TV Lighting)
20 Merton Industrial Park
Jubilee Way
London SW19 3WL
Website: www.whitelight.ltd.uk
e-mail: info@whitelight.ltd.uk
Fax: 020-8254 4601   Tel: 020-8254 4600

WHITEHORN Simon
(Sound Design)
57 Acre Lane
London SW2 5TN
e-mail: simon@orbitalsound.co.uk
Fax: 020-7501 6869   Tel: 020-7501 6868

WOOD Rod
(Scenic Artist, Backdrops, Scenery, Props & Design)
41 Montserrat Road, London SW15 2LD
Mobile: 07887 697646   Tel: 020-8788 1941

BBC Television, Wood Lane, London W12 7RJ
Tel: 020-8743 8000

■ **TALENT RIGHTS GROUP**

BBC Production
172 - 178 Victoria Road, W3 6UL

Head of Talent Rights Group   Simon Hayward-Tapp

LITERARY COPYRIGHT
Rights Manager   Neil Hunt
Rights Executives   Sharon Cowley
                                     Sue Dickson
                                  Andrew Downey
                                   James Dundas
                                       Gail Finn
                                  Julie Gallagher
                                    David Knight
                                   Sally Millwood
                                    Hilary Sagar

FACTUAL, ARTS & CLASSICAL MUSIC
Rights Manager   Simon Brown
Rights Executives   Lorraine Clark
                                 Penelope Davies
                                    Hilary Dodds
                                 Caroline Edwards
                                     John Hunter
                                  Alison Johnston
                                    Ken McHale
                                    Shirley Noel
                                 Shelagh Morrison
                                   Annie Pollard
                                    Pamela Wise

MUSICAL COPYRIGHT
Senior Rights Manager, Music   Nicky Bignell
Rights Executives   Peter Bradbury
                                 Sally Dunsford
                                      Liz Evans
                                 Catherine Grimes
                                 Debbie Rogerson

DRAMA ENTERTAINMENT & CHILDRENS
Rights Manager Performance   John Holland
Rights Executives   Maggie Anson
                                 Stephanie Beynon
                                  Mike Bickerdike
                                     Sally Dean
                                 Marie-Louise Hagan
                                 Amanda Kimpton
                                 Lesley Longhurst
                                    David Marum
                                  Thalia Reynolds
                                  Lloyd Shepherd

ENGLISH REGIONS:

BIRMINGHAM - Pebble Mill
Contracts Manager   Andrea Coles

BRISTOL
Contracts Manager   Annie Thomas

MANCHESTER
Contracts Executive   Shirley Chadwick

■ **DRAMA**

Controller, Continuing Drama Series   Mal Young
Head of Films &
  Single Drama   David Thompson
Head of Drama Serials   Laura Mackie
Head of Development,
  Drama Serials   Sarah Brown

Executive Producers, Drama Series
Serena Cullen   Simon Lewis
Alexei de Keyser   Tracey Scoffield
Sue Hogg   Mervyn Watson
Kathleen Hutchison

Producers, Drama Series
Chris Ballentyne   Victoria Fea
Beverley Dartnall   Deborah Jones

Executive Producers, Drama Serials
Ruth Caleb (Single Films)   Phillippa Giles
Hilary Salmon   Jessica Pope
Sally Haynes   Simon Curtis
Kate Harwood   Mervyn Watson

Producers, Drama Serials
Kate Bartlett   Diederick Santer
Kate Lewis   David Snodin
Liza Marshall   Pier Wilkie
Paul Rutman

■ **COMMISSIONING**

Controller Factual Commissioning   Nicola Moody
Controller Entertainment Commissioning Jane Lush
Controller Drama Commissioning   Jane Tranter
Head of Drama Commissioning,
  Genre Executive TV Management
  & Support Services   Sarah Brandeist
Head of Drama Commissioning, Independents
                                   Gareth Neame

■ **NEWS AND CURRENT AFFAIRS**

BBC News (Television & Radio)
Television Centre
Wood Lane, London W12 7RJ
Tel: 020-8576 7178   Fax: 020-8576 7120

Director News   Richard Sambrook
Deputy Director News   Mark Damazer
Head of Television News   Roger Mosey
Deputy Head of Television News   Rachel Atwell
Head of Radio News   Stephen Mitchell
Head of Political Programmes Francesca Unsworth

■ DOCUMENTARIES & CONTEMPORARY FACTUAL GROUP

Controller of DCFG	Anne Morrison
Deputy Controller	Donna Taberer
Head of Production	Steve Wallis
Head of Programmes, Birmingham	Tessa Finch
Acting Head of Programmes, Bristol	Mark Hill

■ FACTUAL & LEARNING

Creative Directors	Vicki Barrass
	Nick Vaughan-Barratt
	Andy Batten-Foster
	Owen Gay
Head of Development	Rachel Innes-Lursden

■ ARTS

BBC Television (Arts)
201 Wood Lane
London W12 7TS   Tel: 020-8752 5490

Creative Director	Mark Harrison
Editor, Arena	Antony Wall
Editor, Arts Series	Kim Thomas
Editor, Arts Features	Basil Comely
Editor, Imagine	Claire Lewis
Editor, Talk & Events	David Okuefuna

■ MUSIC

Head of Classical Music	Peter Maniura

■ CHILDREN'S PROGRAMMES

Head of CBBC	Elaine Sperber
Head of Entertainment, CBBC	Anne Gilchrist

Head of CBBC News & Factual programmes	Roy Milani
Head of Pre-School, CBBC	Clare Elstow
Head of Acquisitions & Co-Productions, CBBC	Theresa Plummer Andrews
Head of CBBC, Scotland	Claire Mundell

■ SPORT

Director of Sport	Peter Salmon
Director, Sports Rights & Finance	Dominic Coles
Controller Radio Five Live	Bob Shennan
Head of Major Events	Dave Gordon
Head of Football & Boxing	Niall Sloane
Head of Programmes & Planning	Pat Younge
Head of General Sports	Barbara Slater
Head of Radio Sport	Gordon Turnbull
Head of New Media, Sports News & Development	Andrew Thompson

■ SCIENCE

Creative Director for Science	John Lynch
Director of Development, Specialist Factual	Michael Mosley
Series Producer	Cameron Balbirnie
Development Executive	Sacha Baveystock
Series Producer, Specialist Factual	Mathew Barrett
Series Producer, Specialist Factual	Tina Fletcher

■ NEW WRITING

BBC Writersroom
1 Mortimer Street
London W1T 3JA   Tel: 020-7765 2703
e-mail: new.writing@bbc.co.uk
Website: www.bbc.co.uk/writersroom

Creative Director	Kate Rowland
New Writing Co-ordinator	Jessica Dromgoole

■ BBC BRISTOL

Broadcasting House
Whiteladies Road
Bristol BS8 2LR   Tel: 0117-973 2211

NETWORK TELEVISION AND RADIO
FEATURES

Creative Directors	Andy Batten-Foster
	Mark Hill
Executive Producers	Dick Colthurst
	Michael Poole
	Julia Simmons

TELEVISION
Producers

Lyn Barlow	Kim Littlemore
Robert Bayley	Jane Lomas
Mark Bristow	Susan McDermott
Kathryn Broome	Julian Mercer
Michelle Burgess	Kathryn Moore
Roy Chapman	Helen Nabarro
Linda Cleeve	Martin Paithorpe
Hannah Corneck	Ian Pye
Peter Firstbrook	Amanda Reilly
Steve Greenwood	Kelly Richardson
Trevor Hill	Peter Smith
Jeremy Howe	Ben Southwell
Chris Hutchins	Miranda Steed
David Hutt	Jonny Young
Sarah Johnson	Jo Vale
Peter Lawrence	Tom Ware
Christopher Lewis	

RADIO

Unit Manager, Radio	Kate Chaney
Editors	Elizabeth Burke
	Fiona Cooper

Producers

Viv Beeby	Jane Greenwood
John Byrne	Jeremy Howe
Frances Byrnes	Kate McCall
Sara Davies	David Olusoga
Tim Dee	Lucy Willmore
Paul Dodgson	

NATURAL HISTORY UNIT

Head of Natural History Unit	Neil Nightingale
Editor The Natural World	Tim Martin

Television Producers

Paul Appleby	Liz Green
Melinda Barker	Martin Hughes-Games
Miles Barton	Mark Jacobs
Karen Bass	Hilary Jeffkins
Vanessa Belowitz	Mark Linfield
Mike Beynon	Neil Lucas
Lucy Bowden	Patrick Morris
Andrew Byatt	Stephen Moss
Paul Chapman	Mike Salisbury
Mary Colwell	Jo Sarsby
Huw Cordey	Tim Scoones
Yvonne Ellis	Mary Summerhill
Mark Flowers	James Walton
Sara Ford	

Managing Editor NHU Radio	Julian Hector
Director of Development	Martin Hughes-Games

■ BBC WEST

Whiteladies Road
Bristol BS8 2LR   Tel: 0117-973 2211

Head of Regional & Local Programmes,
including BBC West, Radio Bristol & Somerset Sound,
Radio Gloucestershire
& BBC Wiltshire Sound   Andrew Wilson
Series Producer, Current Affairs Documentaries
                                        James MacAlpine

Editor, Political Unit	Paul Bartrop
Editors, Output	Jane Kinghorn
	Stephanie Marshall

■ BBC SOUTH WEST

Seymour Road
Mannamead
Plymouth PL3 5BD   Tel: 01752 229201

Head of Local & Regional Programmes	Leo Devine
Editor TV Current Affairs	Simon Willis
News Editor	Simon Read

■ BBC SOUTH

Havelock Road
Southampton SO14 7PU   Tel: 023-8022 6201

Head of Regional & Local Programmes	Eve Turner
Managing Editor, BBC Oxford	Phil Ashworth
Managing Editor, Radio Solent	Mia Costello
Managing Editor, Radio Berkshire	Marianne Bell

■ BBC LONDON

PO Box 94.9
London W1A 6FL   Tel: 020-7208 9200

BBC London News:
TV: The Politics Show
Radio: BBC London Radio 94.9FM
Online: BBC London online

Executive Editor	Michael MacFarlane
News/Output Editor	tba
Executive Producer, First Sight	Dippy Chaudhray
Managing Editor BBC Radio London 94.9FM	
	David Robey
Political Editor	Tim Donovan
Editor, BBC London Online	Claire Timms

■ BBC SOUTH EAST

c/o BBC Radio Kent
The Great Hall, Mount Pleasant Road
Tunbridge Wells
Kent TN1 1QQ   Tel: 01892 670000

Head of Regional & Local Programmes BBC South East	Laura Ellis
Managing Editor BBC Radio Kent	Robert Wallace
Managing Editor BBC Southern Counties	Mike Hapgood
News Gathering Editor BBC South East Today	Quentin Smith

Advanced casting information. Breakdowns covering theatre, television, films and commercials. Early leads and unique free telephone information service for subscribers. Who's Where indices including casting directors. Over 35 years PCR has built up an unbeatable network of leads and information. Subscribing costs only £27.50 for 5 weekly issues. Every Monday direct to you by post.

Editorial Office:
PCR P.O. Box 11, London N1 7JZ
020-7566 8282
Subscription Office:
PCR P.O. Box 100, Broadstairs, Kent CT10 1UJ
01843 860885
www.pcrnewsletter.com

■ BBC NORTH WEST

New Broadcasting House
Oxford Road
Manchester M60 1SJ   Tel: 0161-200 2020
Website: www.bbc.co.uk/manchester

Entertainment & Features

Head of Entertainment Group   Wayne Garvie

Religion & Ethics

Head of Religion & Ethics   Alan Bookbinder

Network News & Current Affairs

Editor   Dave Stanford

Regional & Local Programmes

Head of Regional & Local
   Programmes North West   Martin Brooks
Head of Regional & Local
   Programmes Yorks & Incs: Colin Philpott
Head of Regional & Local Programmes
   North East & Cumbria   Wendy Pilmer

■ BBC BIRMINGHAM

BBC Birmingham
Pebble Mill Road
Birmingham B5 7QQ
Fax: 0121-432 8634   Tel: 0121-432 8888

English Regions

Controller, English Regions. Head of Centre
   (Birmingham)   Andy Griffee
Head of New Services, English Regions   John Allen
Head of Finance, English Regions   Julie Bertolini
Senior Manager, Press & PR   Andy Pike
Secretary, English Regions   Louise Hall

Head of Regional & Local
   Programmes West Midlands   David Holdsworth
Director, Mailbox Project   Paresh Solanki

Factual & Learning
BBC Birmingham

Head of Programmes   Tessa Finch
Managing Editor   Jane Booth

Network Radio

Editor, Factual Radio & Rural Affairs
   Andrew Thorman
Editor, Specialist Programmes, Radio 2
   David Barber

Drama

Head of Production BBC
   Birmingham   Trevor West
Editor Radio Drama
   & The Archers   Vanessa Whitburn

■ SCOTLAND

Glasgow
Broadcasting House
Queen Margaret Drive
Glasgow G12 8DG   Tel: 0141-339 8844

SCOTTISH DIRECTION GROUP

Controller Scotland   John McCormick
Head of Network Programmes   Colin Cameron
Head of Comedy & Entertainment   Mike Bolland
Executive Editor New Media   Julie Adair
Commissioning Editor, TV   Ewan Angus

Head of Radio   Maggie Cunningham
Head of Programmes Scotland   Ken MacQuarrie
Head of TV Drama, Scotland   Barbara Mckissack
Head of Gaelic & Children's   Donalda Mackinnon
Head of News and Current Affairs   Blair Jenkins
Head of Factual, Scotland   Andrea Millar
Head of Sport   Neil Fraser
Head of North   Andrew Jones
Head of Finance & Business Affairs   Irene Tweedie
Head of Production   Nancy Braid
Head of Human Resources and Internal
   Communications   Steve Ansell
Head of Marketing and Communications
Mairead Ferguson
Head of Public Policy   Ian Small

Edinburgh
The Tun
Holyrood Road
Edinburgh EH8 8JF   Tel: 0131-557 5677

Aberdeen
Broadcasting House
Beechgrove Terrace
Aberdeen AB15 5ZT   Tel: 01224 625233

Dumfries
BBC Dumfries
Elmbank, Lovers Walk
Dumfries DG1 1NZ   Tel: 01387 268008

Dundee
66 Nethergate
Nethergate Centre
Dundee DD1 4ER   Tel: 01382 202481

Inverness
BBC Inverness
Broadcasting House
7 Culduthel Road
Inverness IV2 4AD   Tel: 01463 720720

Orkney
BBC Radio Orkney
Castle Street
Kirkwall
Orkney KW15 1DF   Tel: 01856 873939

Portree
Clydesdale Bank Buildings
Somerled Square
Portree
Isle of Skye IV51 9BT   Tel: 01478 612005

Selkirk
BBC Selkirk
Old Municipal Buildings
High Street
Selkirk TD7 4JX   Tel: 01750 21884

Shetland
BBC Shetland
Pitt Lane
Lerwick
Shetland ZE1 0DW   Tel: 01595 694747

Stornoway
Radio nan Gaidheal
Rosebank
Church Street
Stornoway
Isle of Lewis HS1 2LS   Tel: 01851 705000

THE SPOTLIGHT ®

The most celebrated casting directory in the world

■ **WALES**
Broadcasting House
Llandaff
Cardiff CF5 2YQ   Tel: 029-2032 2000

Controller	Menna Richards
Head of Programmes (Welsh)	Keith Jones
Head of Programmes (English)	Clare Hudson
Head of Public Affairs	tba
Head of Marketing & Communication	Huw Roberts
Acting Head of News & Current Affairs	Mark O'Callaghan
Head of Personnel	Keith Rawlings
Head of Finance	Gareth Powell
Head of Drama	tba
Head of Sport	Nigel Walker
Head of North Wales	Marian Wyn Jones
Head of Factual	Adrian Davies
Head of Education	Eleri Wyn-Lewis
Editor Radio Wales	Julie Barton
Editor Radio Cymru	Aled Glynne Davies

■ **NORTHERN IRELAND**

Belfast
Ormeau Avenue
Belfast BT2 8HQ   Tel: 028-9033 8000

Controller	Anna Carragher
Head of Broadcasting	Tim Cooke
Head of News & Current Affairs	Andrew Colman
Head of Drama	Robert Cooper
Head of Factual & Learning	Bruce Batten
Head of Entertainment & Events	Mike Edgar
Head of Finance	Crawford MacLean
Head of Personnel	Liz Torrans
Head of Marketing & Development	Peter Johnston
Head of Programme Operations	Stephen Beckett

Londonderry
BBC Radio Foyle   Tel: 028-7126 2244
Editor Foyle   Ana Leddy

ANGLIA TELEVISION LTD

Head Office

Anglia House Norwich NR1 3JG
Fax: 01603 631032   Tel: 01603 615151
East of England: Weekday & Weekend

Regional News Centres

Cambridge

26 Newmarket Road, Cambridge CB5 8DT
Fax: 01223 467106   Tel: 01223 467076
Reporters: Matthew Hudson, Phillipa Heap

Chelmsford

64-68 New London Road, Chelmsford CM1 0YU
Fax: 01245 267228   Tel: 01245 357676
Reporters: Timothy Evans, Diane Stradling

Luton

16 Park Street, Luton LU1 3EP
Fax: 01582 401214   Tel: 01582 729666
Reporter: Charlotte Fisher

Northampton

77B Abington Street, Northampton NN1 2BH
Fax: 01604 629856   Tel: 01604 624343
Reporter: Karl Heidel

Peterborough

6 Bretton Green Village
Rightwell, Bretton, Peterborough PE3 8DY
Fax: 01733 269424   Tel: 01733 269440
Reporter: Piers Hopkirk

Ipswich

Hubbard House, Civic Drive, Ipswich IP1 2QA
Fax: 01473 233279   Tel: 01473 226157
Reporters: Rebecca Atherstone, Simon Newton,
Diane Stradling

BORDER TELEVISION PLC

Head Office & Studios

The Television Centre
Carlisle CA1 3NT   Tel: 01228 525101
Southern Scotland
North-West England,
North Northumberland and the Isle of Man;
Weekday and Weekend

Chairman   Charles Allen
Managing Director   Paddy Merrall
Controller of Programmes   Neil Robinson

CARLTON COMMUNICATIONS

25 Knightsbridge, London SW1X 7RZ
Fax: 020-7663 6300   Tel: 020-7663 6363

Chairman   Michael Green

CARLTON TELEVISION

London

101 St Martin's Lane, London WC2N 4RF
Fax: 020-7240 4171   Tel: 020-7240 4000
Chief Executive of Carlton Channels   Clive Jones
Director of Programmes and
    Managing Director of Carlton Productions
                                        Steve Hewlett
Chief Executive, Carlton Sales   Martin Bowley
Finance Director   Mike Green
Director of Regional & Public Affairs   Hardeep Kalsi

PRODUCTION

London

35-38 Portman Square, London W1H 0NU
Fax: 020-7486 1132   Tel: 020-7486 6688
Director of Programmes and
Managing Director of Carlton Productions
                                        Steve Hewlett
Controller, Business Affairs   Martin Baker
Director of Drama &
    Co-production   Jonathan Powell
Executive Producer, Drama   Sharon Bloom
Controller, Children's & Young
    People's Programmes   David Mercer
Controller of Light Entertainment   Mark Wells
Controller, Factual Entertainment   Nick Bullen
Director of Factual Group   Polly Bide
Director of Factual Programmes Richard Clemmow
Head of Regional Programmes
    (Based at 101 St Martin's Lane, London)
                                        Emma Barker
Head of Regional Programmes
    (Based at Gas Street, Birmingham)
                                        Duncan Rycroft
Director of Programmes, HTV Wales
    (Based at Culverhouse Cross, Cardiff)   Ellis Owen

East Midlands

Carlton Studios, Lenton Lane
Nottingham NG7 2NA
Fax: 0115-964 5552   Tel: 0115-986 3322

Westcountry

Western Wood Way
Langage Science Park, Plymouth PL7 5BQ
Fax: 01752 333444   Tel: 01752 333333
Director of Programmes - Westcountry
& HTV West   Jane McCloskey

BROADCASTING

Carlton Broadcasting

London:
101 St Martin's Lane, London WC2N 4RF
Fax: 020-7240 4171   Tel: 020-7240 4000
London Television Centre
Upper Ground, London SE1 9LT   Tel: 020-7620 1620

Central Broadcasting

West Midlands:
Central Court, Gas Street
Birmingham B1 2JT   Tel: 0121-643 9898

East Midlands:
Carlton Studios, Lenton Lane
Nottingham NG7 2NA
Fax: 0115-964 5552   Tel: 0115-986 3322

South Midlands:
Windrush Court, Abingdon Business Park
Abingdon, Oxford OX1 1SA
Fax: 01235 524024   Tel: 01235 554123

Westcountry Television:

Western Wood Way
Langage Science Park, Plymouth PL7 5BQ
Fax: 01752 333444   Tel: 01752 333333

Chairman   Clive Jones
Managing Director,
  HTV West & Wales   Jeremy Payne
Managing Director,
  Carlton Broadcasting Central Region   Ian Squires
Managing Director, Carlton Broadcasting
  West Country Region   Mark Haskell
Controller of Features &
  Programme Development   Caroline Righton
Controller Broadcasting   Coleena Reid
Head of Regional Acquisitions & Planning
                                      David Joel
Head of Presentation   Wendy Chapman
Head of Presentation & Programme
  Planning (Central)   David Burge
Controller, Sport   Gary Newbon
Controller, News & Operations   Laurie Upshon
Editor, Central News West   Dan Barton
Editor, Central News East   Mike Blair
Editor, Central News South   Ian Rumsey
Controller of News &
  Current Affairs, West Country   Phil Carrodus
Head of News, HTV West   Steve Eggington
Head of News, HTV Wales   John G Williams
Finance Director
  of Carlton Broadcasting   Ian Hughes

FACILITIES AND STUDIOS

Outside Broadcasting
Carlton 021
12-13 Gravelly Hill Industrial Estate
Birmingham B24 8HZ
Fax: 0121-327 7021   Tel: 0121-327 2021
Managing Director   Ed Everest

Carlton Studios
Lenton Lane, Nottingham NG7 2NA
Fax: 0115-964 5552   Tel: 0115-986 3322
Managing Director   Ian Squires

SALES

London
101 St Martin's Lane
London WC2N 4RF
Fax: 020-7240 4171   Tel: 020-7240 4000

Manchester
1st Floor Brazenose House West
Lincoln Square
Manchester M2 5AS
Fax: 0161-835 8001   Tel: 0161-835 8001

Westcountry
Western Wood Way
Langage Science Park
Plymouth PL7 5BQ
Fax: 01752 333444   Tel: 01752 333333

Birmingham
Central Court, Gas Street
Birmingham B1 2JT   Tel: 0121-643 9898

HTV
Culverhouse Cross, Cardiff CF5 6XJ
Fax: 029-2059 7183   Tel: 029-2059 7183
Chief Executive of Carlton Sales   Martin Bowley
Managing Director of Carlton Sales   Steve Platt
Sales Director   Gary Digby
Director of Marketing, Sales   Fran Cassidy

CHANNEL TELEVISION ltd

Registered Office

The Television Centre
La Pouquelaye, St Helier, Jersey JE1 3ZD
Channel Islands
Fax: 01534 816817   Tel: 01534 816816
Channel Islands: Weekday and Weekend

Managing Director   Michael Lucas
Director of Programmes   Karen Rankine
Director of Sales   Gordon de Ste. Croix
Director of Transmission
  & Resources   Kevin Banner
Director of Finance   Amanda Trotman
News Editor   Allan Watts

CHANNEL FOUR TELEVISION CORPORATION

London Office

124 Horseferry Road
London SW1P 2TX
Fax: 020-7306 8116   Tel: 020-7396 4444

Members of the Board

Chairman	Vanni Treves
Deputy Chairman	Barry Cox
Chief Executive	Mark Thompson
Managing Director	David Scott
Director of Programmes	Tim Gardam
Commercial Director	Andy Barnes
Managing Director 4 Ventures Ltd	Rob Woodward

Non-Executive Directors

Millie Banerjee	Robin Miller
Peter Bazalgette	Ian Ritchie
Barry Cox	Joe Sinyor
Andrew Graham	Vanni Treves

Company Secretary: Andrew Brann

Heads of Department

Head of Airtime Management	Merlin Inkley
Head of Commercial & Marketing Strategy	Hugh Johnson
Head of Information Systems	Ian Dobb
Director of Human Resources	Peter Meier
Head of Presentation	Steve White
Head of Business Affairs	Andrew Brann
Head of Legal & Compliance	Jan Tomalin
Group Controller of Finance	Tony Moore
Managing Director of 4Learning	Heather Rabbatts
Managing Editor Commissioning	Janey Walker
Director of Nations and Regions	Stuart Cosgrove
Controller of Programme Acquisitions	June Dromgoole
Acting Head of News and Current Affairs	Dorothy Byrne
Head of Entertainment	Danielle Lux
Head of Drama	John Yorke
Director of Marketing	Polly Cochrane
Head of Corporate Relations	John Newbigin
Controller of Broadcasting	Rosemary Newell
Head of Press and Publicity	Matt Baker
Director of Marketing & Commercial Development	Polly Cochrane
Chief Executive - FilmFour Ltd	Paul Webster
Head of Corporate Relations	John Newbigin
Controller Broadcasting	Rosemary Newell
Head of Press & Publicity	Matt Baker
Deputy Commercial Director & Managing Director of 4 Services	Anmar Kawash
Head of Features & Factual Entertainment	Ben Frow
Head of Marketing	Bill Griffin
Head of Market Planning	Claire Grimmond
Managing Director 4 Channels	Dan Brooke
Head of Sponsorship	David Charlesworth
Head of Specialist Factual	Janice Hadlow
Chief Engineer	Jim Hart
Head of Strategy	Jonathan Thompson

Head of Facilities Management	Julie Bunn
Head of Scheduling	Julie Oldroyd
Head of Client & Strategic Sales	Mike Parker
Managing Director of 4 Rights	Paul Sowerbutts
Finance Director	Sue Ford
Head of Film	Tessa Ross
Head of Documentaries	Peter Dale

Commissioning Editors

Entertainment	Caroline Leddy
Drama	Lucy Richer

CHANNEL 5 BROADCASTING

22 Long Acre, London WC2E 9LY
Fax: 020-7550 5554   Tel: 020-7550 5555
Website: www.five.tv

Chief Executive	Jane Lighting
Director of Programmes	Kevin Lygo
Marketing Director	David Pullan
Deputy Chief Executive	Nick Milligan
Director of Finance	Grant Murray
Director of Legal & Business Affairs Colin Campbell	
Director of Broadcasting	Ashley Hill
Director of Acquisitions	Jeff Ford
Senior Programme Controller News & Current Affairs	Chris Shaw
Controller of Entertainment	Andrew Newman
Controller of Factual	Dan Chambers
Controller of Factual Entertainment	Sue Murphy
Controller of Youth Music & Interactive	Sham Sandhu
Controller of Drama	Corinne Hollingworth
Controller of Sport	Robert Charles
Controller of Children's	Nick Wilson
Controller of Daytime, Arts & Religion	Kim Peat

GMTV

London Television Centre
Upper Ground, London SE1 9TT
Fax: 020-7827 7001   Tel: 020-7827 7000

Chairman	Donald Emslie
Managing Director	Paul Corley
Director of Programmes	Peter McHugh
Finance Director	Rhian Walker
Director of Sales	Clive Crouch
Head of Press	Nikki Johnceline
Managing Editor	John Scammell
Editor	Martin Frizell
Chief Engineer	Geoff Wright

GRAMPIAN TELEVISION LTD

Television Centre
Craigshaw Business Park
West Tullos
Aberseen AB12 3QH
Fax: 01224 848800
Website: www.grampiantv.co.uk
Tel: 01224 848848

Managing Director	Derrick Thomson
Head of News & Current Affairs	Henry Eagles
Production Resources Manager	Iain Macdonald

GRANADA

GRANADA plc

The London Television Centre
Upper Ground
London SE1 9LT
Tel: 020-7620 1620

LWT
London Television Centre
Upper Ground
London SE1 9LT
Tel: 020-7620 1620

Granada Television
Quay Street
Manchester M60 9EA
Tel: 0161-832 7211

Yorkshire Television
Television Centre
Leeds LS3 1JS
Tel: 0113-243 8283

Tyne Tees Television
City Road
Newcastle upon tyne NE1 2AL
Tel: 0191-261 0181

Anglia TV
Anglia House
Norwich NR1 3JG
Tel: 01603 615151

Meridian Broadcasting
Television Centre
Southampton SO14 OPZ
Tel: 02380 222555

Border Television
TV Centre
Carlisle, Cumbria CA1 3NT
Tel: 01228 525101

Granada Animation
2nd Floor, 16 Hatfields
London SE1 8DJ
Tel: 020-7620 1620

Granada Wild
One Whiteladies Road
Bristol BS8 1NU
Tel: 0117-975 4800

Granada Sport
Television Centre
Southampton SO14 OPZ
Tel: 023-8071 2307

Granada Film
48 Leicester Square
London WC2H 7FB
Tel: 020-7491 1441

Granada Learning
Granada Television
Quay Street
Manchester M60 9EA
Tel: 0161-827 2927

Letts Education
Auld Dine House, Auld Dine Place
London W12 8AW
Tel: 020-8740 2266

Granada International
48 Leicester Square
London WC2H 7FB
Tel: 020-7491 1441

Granada Commercial Ventures
200 Grays Inn Road
London WC1X 8X2
Tel: 020-7396 6000

Granada plc - Executive Board

Executive Chairman	Charles Allen CBE
Chief Executive	Steve Morrison
Finance Director & Deputy Chairman, Media Ventures	Henry Staunton
Commercial Director	Graham Parrott
Managing Director Operations	Jules Burns
Cheif Executive, Granada Content	Simon Shaps
Chief Executive, Broadcasting & Enterprises	Mick Desmond

HTV GROUP LTD

Television Centre
Culverhouse Cross
Cardiff CF5 6XJ
Tel: 029-2059 0590

Television Centre, Bath Road
Bristol BS4 3HG
Tel: 0117-972 2722

Wales/West of England: All week

Group Managing Director	Jeremy Payne
Controller, HTV Wales	Elis Owen
Director of Programmes	Jane McCloskey
HTV Wales Head of Drama Development	Peter Edwards
HTV Wales Head of Factual Development	Paul Calverley

INDEPENDENT TELEVISION NEWS

200 Gray's Inn Road
London WC1X 8XZ
Tel: 020-7833 3000

Chief Executive & Editor-in-Chief	Stewart Purvis
Editor, ITV News	David Mannian
Editor, Channel 4 News	Jim Gray
Editor 5 News	Gary Rogers
Director of Public Affairs	Sophie Jones

LWT HOLDINGS PLC

The London Television Centre
Upper Ground
London SE1 9LT   Tel: 020-7620 1620
London 5.10 pm Friday to 6 am Monday

Executives of the LWT Group

Controller of Arts & Features LWT	Melvyn Bragg
Controller of Drama	
LWT & United Productions	Michele Buck
Controller of Factual, LWT	Will Smith

Directors

Executive Chairman, Granada	Charles Allen
Managing Director, LWT	Christy Swords

MERIDIAN

MERIDIAN BROADCASTING LTD

Television Centre
Southampton SO14 0PZ
Fax: 023-8033 5050   Tel: 023-8022 2555
Website: www.meridiantv.com

Board

Chairman	Charles Allen
MD Granada Broadcasting & Enterprises	
	Mick Desmond
Director of Financial Control,	
Granada Broadcasting	Mike Fegan
Director of Regional Sales,	
Granada Enterprises	David Croft
Managing Director, Meridian	Lindsay Charlton
Controller of	
Regional Programmes	Mark Southgate
Head of News	Andy Cooper
Director of Marketing &	
Commercial Affairs	Martin Morrall

Executives

Managing Director	Lindsay Charlton
Controller of Regional Programmes	
Mark Southgate	
Head of News	Andy Cooper
Director of Marketing &	
Commercial Affairs	Martin Morrall
General Manager	Jan Beal
Controller, Personnel	Richard Thurstin
Finance Manager	Sian Harvey
Head of Engineering & Transmission	Jez Bray
Head of Regional Affairs	Alison Pope

S4C

S4C-THE WELSH FOURTH CHANNEL

Parc Tý Glas, Llanisien, Cardiff CF14 5DU
Fax: 029-2075 4444   Tel: 029-2074 7444
e-mail: s4c@s4c.co.uk

The Welsh Fourth Channel Authority

Chair	Elan Closs Stephens
Members:	Dr. Christopher Llewelyn
Cefin Campbell	Nic Parry
Eira Davies	Enid Rowlands
Carys Howell	Huw Wynne-Griffiths

Senior Staff

Chief Executive	Huw Jones
Director of Corporate Affairs	Alun Davies
Director of Programming	Huw Eirug
Director of Engineering & Technology	Arshad Rasul
Head of Marketing	Eleri Twynog Davies
Director of Finance	
& Human Resouces	Kathryn Morris
Managing Director S4C Masnachol	Wyn Innes
Head of Press	Hannah Thomas
Head of Human Resources	Kay Walters

scottish tv

SCOTTISH TELEVISION (Part of SMG Group)

Glasgow Office

200 Renfield Street, Glasgow G2 3PR
Fax: 0141-300 3030   Tel: 0141-300 3000
Website: www.scottishtv.co.uk

Chief Executive (SMG Television)	Donald Emslie
Managing Director	Sandy Ross
Head of News & Current Affairs	Paul McKinney

London Office

1 Golden Square
London W1F 9DJ   Tel: 020-7663 2300

tv productions   Incorporating Ginger Television
                      (Part of SMG)

Glasgow Office

200 Renfield Street
Glasgow G2 3PR
Fax: 0141-300 3030   Tel: 0141-300 3000

Chief Executive	Donald Emslie (SMG Television)
Managing Director	Elizabeth Partyka
Head of Drama	Eric Coulter
Head of Factual	Helen Alexander

London Office

1 Golden Square
London W1F 9DJ   Tel: 020-7663 2300

Tyne Tees Television

TYNE TEES TELEVISION

The Television Centre, City Road
Newcastle upon Tyne NE1 2AL
Fax: 0191-261 2302   Tel: 0191-261 0181

Teeside Studio

Colman's Nook
Belasis Hall Technology Park
Billingham
Cleveland TS23 4EG
Fax: 01642 566560   Tel: 01642 566999

North East and North Yorkshire:
Weekday and Weekend

Chairman	Charles Allen
Managing Director	Margaret Fay
Controller of Programmes	Graeme Thompson
Managing Editor, News	Graham Marples
Head of Network Features	Mark Robinson
Head of Sport	Roger Tames
Head of New Media	Malcolm Wright
Editor, Current Affairs	
& Features	Jane Bolesworth

ULSTER TELEVISION PLC

Havelock House
Ormeau Road
Belfast BT7 1EB
Fax: 028-9024 6695   Tel: 028-9032 8122

Northern Ireland: Weekday and Weekend

Chairman	J B McGuckian BSc (Econ)
Group Chief Executive	J McCann BSc, FCA
Financial Director	Jim Downey
Director of Television	A Bremner
Head of Press & Public Relations	Orla McKibbin
Head of News & Current Affairs	R Morrison
Sales Director	P Hutchinson

Yorkshire Television

YORKSHIRE TELEVISION LTD

The Television Centre
Leeds LS3 1JS
Fax: 0113-244 5107   Tel: 0113-243 8283

London Office

London Television Centre
Uppeground
London SE1 9LT   Tel: 020-7620 1620

Hull Office

23 Brook Street
The Prospect Centre
Hull HU2 8PN   Tel: 01482 24488

Sheffield Office

Charter Square
Sheffield S1 3EJ   Tel: 0114-272 3262

Lincoln Office

88 Bailgate
Lincoln LN1 3AR   Tel: 01522 530738

Grimsby Office

Margaret Street
Immingham
North East Lincs DN40 1LE   Tel: 01469 510661

York Office

8 Coppergate
York YO1 1NR   Tel: 01904 610066

Executives

Managing Director	David M B Croft
Controller of Programmes (YTV)	Clare Morrow
Controller, Features	Sam Anthony
Director of Business Affairs	Filip Cieslik
Head of News	Will Venters
Controller of Drama, YTV	Carolyn Reynolds
Controller of Comedy Drama	
& Drama Features	David Reynolds
Controller of Drama, Yorkshire-Tyne Tees	
Productions	Keith Richardson
Director of Finance, Yorkshire-Tyne Tees	
Productions	Ian Roe
Director of Programmes	John Whiston
Head of Regional Features	Mark Witty

SKY Satellite Television
BRITISH SKY BROADCASTING LIMITED (BSkyB)
6 Centaurs Business Park
Grant Way
Isleworth
Middlesex TW7 5QD
Fax: 020-7705 3030   Tel: 020-7705 3000

Chief Executive	Tony Ball
Chief Operating Officer	Richard Freudenstein
Managing Director, Sky Networks	Dawn Airey
Managing Director, Sky Sports	Vic Wakeling
Director of Broadcasting & Production	
	Mark Sharman
Head of Sky News	Nick Pollard
Director of Public Affairs	Ray Gallagher
Director of Communications	Julian Eccles

30 BIRD PRODUCTIONS
138A Kingswood Road
Brixton, London SW2 4JL
e-mail: thirtybirdproductions@ntlworld.com
Tel: 020-8678 7034

ACORN ENTERTAINMENTS Ltd
PO Box 64, Cirencester, Gloucestershire GL7 5YD
Website: www.huttrussell.org.com
e-mail: acornents@btconnect.com
Fax: 01285 642291   Tel: 01285 644622

ACT OUT THEATRE
36 Lord Street, Radcliffe, Manchester M26 3BA
e-mail: nigeladams@talk21.com
Tel/Fax: 0161-724 6625

ACT PRODUCTIONS Ltd
20-22 Stukeley Street, London WC2B 5LR
Website: www.actproductions.co.uk
e-mail: info@act.tt
Fax: 020-7242 3548   Tel: 020-7438 9500

ACTORS OF DIONYSUS
44-46 Old Steine, Brighton BN1 1NH
Website: www.actorsofdionysus.com
e-mail: info@actorsofdionysus.com
Fax: 01273 220025   Tel: 01273 320396

ACTORS TOURING COMPANY (ATC)
Alford House, Aveline Street, London SE11 5DQ
Website: www.atc-online.com
e-mail: atc@atc-online.com   Tel: 020-7735 8311

AD PRODUCTIONS
(See HILTON Adrian Ltd)

ADMIRATION THEATRE
PO Box 448, London WC2B 5US
Website: www.admirationtheatre.co.uk
e-mail: enquiries@admirationtheatre.co.uk
Tel/Fax: 020-7692 3698

AJTC THEATRE COMPANY
28 Rydes Hill Crescent
Guildford, Surrey GU2 9UH
Website: www.ajtctheatre.co.uk
e-mail: ajtc@ntlworld.com   Tel/Fax: 01483 232795

AKA PRODUCTIONS
First Floor, 115 Shaftesbury Avenue
Cambridge Circus, London WC2H 8AF
Website: www.akauk.com
e-mail: aka@akauk.com
Fax: 020-7836 8787   Tel: 020-7836 4747

AMBASSADOR THEATRE GROUP
Duke of York's Theatre, 104 St Martin's Lane
London WC2N 4BG
e-mail: atglondon@theambassadors.com
Fax: 020-7854 7001   Tel: 020-7854 7000

ARTS MANAGEMENT
Pinewood Studios, Iver Heath
Buckinghamshire SL0 0NH
Fax: 01753 785443   Tel: 01753 785444

ATP Ltd
PO Box 24182, London SW18 2WY
e-mail: atpmedia@ukonline.co.uk
Tel/Fax: 020-7738 9886

ATTIC THEATRE COMPANY (LONDON) Ltd
Wimbledon Theatre, The Broadway
London SW19 1QG
Website: www.attictheatre.com
e-mail: info@attictheatre.com
Tel/Fax: 020-8543 7838

BACCHAI PRODUCTIONS
(Write)
10-12 High Street, Great wakering, Essex SS3 0EQ
e-mail: mail@bacchai.com

BACKGROUND Ltd
49 Tamarind Court
1 Gainsford Street, London SE1 2NE
e-mail: insight@background.co.uk
Fax: 020-7357 9520   Tel: 020-7357 9515

BAMBOO GROVE THEATRE COMPANY
Crogo Mains, Corsock, Castle Douglas
Kirkcudbrightshire DG7 3DR
Website: www.bamboogrovetheatre.co.uk
e-mail: cally@bamboogrovetheatre.co.uk
Tel: 07810 514622

BARKING PRODUCTIONS/INSTANT WIT
(Comedy Improvisation/Corporate Entertainment
& Training)
PO Box 597, Bristol BS99 2BB
Website: www.barkingproductions.co.uk
e-mail: info@barkingproductions.co.uk
Fax: 0117-908 5384   Tel: 0117-939 3171

BEE & BUSTLE ENTERPRISES
32 Exeter Road, London NW2 4SB
Website: www.beeandbustle.co.uk
e-mail: info@beeandbustle.co.uk
Fax: 020-8450 1057   Tel: 020-8450 0371

BHJ Ltd
(Brian Hewitt-Jones)
Curlews House, Crowle DN17 4JS
Fax: 01724 711088   Tel: 01724 712459

BIG DOG PRODUCTIONS Ltd
(Martin Roddy)
16 Kirkwick Avenue, Harpenden
Hertfordshire AL5 2QN
e-mail: bigdog@kirkwick.demon.co.uk
Fax: 01582 467349   Tel: 01582 467344

BIRMINGHAM STAGE COMPANY The
Suite 228 The Linen Hall, 162 Regent Street
London W1B 5TG
Website: www.birminghamstage.net
e-mail: info@birminghamstage.net
Fax: 020-7437 3395   Tel: 020-7437 3391

BLUE BOX ENTERTAINMENT Ltd
The Penthouse
7 Leicester Place, London WC2H 7RJ
Website: www.blue-box.biz
e-mail: info@blue-box.biz
Fax: 020-7734 7185   Tel: 020-7434 4214

BOJANGLES PRODUCTIONS & BYRAM Paul
PO Box 171, Chorley PR7 3GE
Website: www.bojanglesproductions.com
e-mail: info@bojanglesproductions.com
Fax: 0870 4434124   Tel: 0870 2406713

BORDERLINE THEATRE COMPANY
North Harbour Street, Ayr KA8 8AA
e-mail: enquiries@borderlinetheatre.co.uk
Tel: 01292 281010

B & R PRODUCTIONS Ltd
First Floor, 66A Grt Titchfield St, London W1W 7QH
Fax: 020-7436 6603   Tel: 020-7580 5277

BREAKWITH PRODUCTIONS Ltd
7 London Court, Frogmore, London SW18 1HH
e-mail: breakwithprodsltd@supanet.com
Tel/Fax: 020-8871 4999

BRIDGE LANE THEATRE COMPANY Ltd
The Studio, 49 Ossulton Way
London N2 0JY   Tel/Fax: 020-8444 0505

BRIGHTON REVUE COMPANY The
(BRC PRODUCTIONS)
Write: 139 Freshfield Road, Brighton BN2 2YE
Website: www.brightonrevue.fsnet.co.uk
e-mail: enquiries@brightonrevue.fsnet.co.uk
Fax: 01273 672646

BRITISH ACTORS THEATRE COMPANY Ltd The
28 Stanmer Avenue, Saltdean
Brighton BN2 8QL   Tel: 01273 308737

BRITISH STAGE PRODUCTIONS
Victoria Buildings, 1B Sherwood Street
Scarborough, North Yorkshire YO11 1SR
e-mail: office@bstage.giointernet.co.uk
Fax: 01723 501328   Tel: 01723 507186

BRIT-POL THEATRE Ltd
10 Bristol Gardens, London W9 2JG
Website: www.britpol.uktheatre.net
e-mail: admin@britpol.uktheatre.net
                                    Tel: 020-7266 0323

BROADHOUSE PRODUCTIONS Ltd
38 Stourcliffe Close, Stourcliffe Street
London W1H 5AR
e-mail: admin@broadhouse.co.uk
Fax: 020-7402 2173   Tel: 020-7402 0624

BROOKE Nick Ltd
The Penthouse, 7 Leicester Place, London WC2H 7RJ
e-mail: info@nickbrooke.com
Fax: 020-7734 3184   Tel: 020-7851 0393

BROOKS Sacha Ltd
3rd Floor, 55 Greek Street, London W1D 3DT
e-mail: info@sacha.com
Fax: 020-7437 0930   Tel: 020-7437 2900

BUSH THEATRE
Shepherd's Bush Green, London W12 8QD
Website: www.bushtheatre.co.uk
e-mail: info@bushtheatre.co.uk
Fax: 020-7602 7614   Tel: 020-7602 3703

CAPRICORN STAGE (& SCREEN) DIRECTIONS
9 Spencer House, Vale of Health, Hampstead
London NW3 1AS   Tel: 020-7794 5843

CARPENTER Earl CONCERTS Ltd
PO Box 745, Guildford, Surrey GU3 1XJ
e-mail: ecconcerts@dial.pipex.com
                                    Tel/Fax: 01483 810685

CASSANDRA THEATRE COMPANY
(Vanessa Mildenberg, Clare Bloomer)
Flat 3, 30 Ephraim Road, London SW16 1LW
e-mail: vm_cassandratc@yahoo.co.uk
Mobile: 07796 264828   Tel: 020-8769 6099

CAVALCADE THEATRE COMPANY Ltd
(Plays, Musicals & Tribute Shows, Cabaret,
Children's Shows)
57 Pelham Road, London SW19 1NW
Fax: 020-8540 2243   Tel: 020-8540 3513

CELEBRATION
(Theatre Company for the Young)
48 Chiswick Staithe
London W4 3TP   Tel: 020-8994 8886

CENTRELINE PRODUCTIONS
Unit 7, 93 Paul Street, London EC2A 4NY
Website: www.c-line.dircon.co.uk
e-mail: info@centrelinenet.com
Fax: 020-7251 9255   Tel: 020-7251 9251

CHANNEL THEATRE COMPANY
Central Studios, 36 Park Place
Margate, Kent CT9 1LE
Website: www.channel-theatre.co.uk
e-mail: info@channel-theatre.co.uk
Fax: 01843 280088   Tel: 01843 280077

CHAPMAN Duggie ASSOCIATES
(Pantomime, Concerts, Musicals)
The Old Coach House, 202 Common Edge Road
Blackpool FY4 5DG
Website: www.duggiechapman.co.uk
e-mail: duggie@chapmanassociates.fsnet.co.uk
Fax: 0115-946 1831   Tel: 01253 691823

CHAPMAN Guy PRODUCTIONS
33 Southampton Street, London WC2E 7HE
e-mail: guy@g-c.a.co.uk
Fax: 020-7379 8484   Tel: 020-7379 7474

CHICHESTER FESTIVAL THEATRE
Oaklands Park, Chichester, West Sussex PO19 4AP
Website: www.cft.org.uk
e-mail: admin@cft.org.uk
Fax: 01243 787288   Tel: 01243 784437

CHICKEN SHED THEATRE
Chase Side, Southgate, London N14 4PE
Website: www.chickenshed.org.uk
e-mail: info@chickenshed.org.uk
Minicom: 020-8350 0676   Tel: 020-8351 6161

CHRYSALIS THEATRE COMPANY Ltd
Write: 3A Pasley Street, Plymouth, Devon PL1 3JT

CHURCHILL THEATRE BROMLEY Ltd
Churchill Theatre, High Street
Bromley, Kent BR1 1HA
Website: www.churchilltheatre.co.uk
Fax: 020-8290 6968   Tel: 020-8464 7131

CLASSIC REACTION THEATRE COMPANY
Clovelly, Cagefoot Lane, Henfield
West Sussex BN5 9HD
e-mail: crtcproductions@aol.com
                                    Tel/Fax: 01273 492612

CLEAR CHANNEL ENTERTAINMENT (CCE)
35/36 Grosvenor Street, London W1K 4QX
Website: www.cclive.co.uk
e-mail: enquiries@clearchannel.co.uk
Fax: 08707 490517   Tel: 020-7529 4300

CLOSE FOR COMFORT THEATRE COMPANY
34 Boleyn Walk, Leatherhead, Surrey KT22 7HU
Website: www.hometown.aol.com/close4comf
e-mail: close4comf@aol.com   Tel: 01372 378613

CODRON Michael PLAYS Ltd
Aldwych Theatre Offices, London WC2B 4DF
Fax: 020-7240 8467   Tel: 020-7240 8291

COGO-FAWCETT Robert
58 Hythe Road, Brighton BN1 6JS
e-mail: robertcogo_fawcett@hotmail.com
                                    Mobile: 07973 938634

COLE KITCHENN Ltd
Nederlander House
7 Great Russell Street, London WC1B 3NH
Fax: 020-7580 2992   Tel: 020-7580 2772

COMPASS THEATRE COMPANY
Carver Street Institute
24 Rockingham Lane, Sheffield S1 4FW
Website: www.compasstheatrecompany.com
e-mail: info@compasstheatrecompany.com
Fax: 0114-278 6931   Tel: 0114-275 5328

CONCORDANCE
(Neil McPherson)
7 Defoe House, Barbican, London EC2Y 8DN
Website: www.concordance.org.uk
e-mail: admin@concordance.org.uk
Fax: 020-7835 1853   Tel: 020-7638 9073

CONTEMPORARY STAGE COMPANY
3 Etchingham Park Road, Finchley, London N3 2DU
Website: www.contemporarystage.co.uk
e-mail: contemp.stage@britishlibrary.net
Fax: 020-8349 2458   Tel: 020-8349 4402

CONWAY Clive CELEBRITY PRODUCTIONS
32 Grove Street, Oxford OX2 7JT
Website: www.celebrityproductions.info
e-mail: clive.conway@ntlworld.com
Fax: 01865 514409   Tel: 01865 514830

COONEY Ray PLAYS
Everglades, 29 Salmons Road
Chessington, Surrey KT9 2JE
Website: www.raycooneyplays.co.uk
e-mail: alan@raycooneyplays.co.uk
Fax: 020-8397 0070   Tel: 020-8397 0021

CRISP THEATRE
8 Cornwallis Crescent, Clifton, Bristol BS8 4PL
Website: www.crisptheatre.com
e-mail: crisptheatre@hotmail.com
                              Tel/Fax: 0117-973 7106

CTG COTSWOLD THEATRE GROUP
Write
Sandford Cottage, Shipton Road
Milton-under-Wychwood, Oxfordshire OX7 6JT
Fax: 01993 776071

DAVIES Alma
2857 Paradise Road
Las Vegas NV 89109
Fax: (702) 341-5681   Tel: (702) 254-3775

DEAD EARNEST THEATRE
57 Burton Street, Sheffield S6 2HH
Website: www.deadearnest.co.uk
e-mail: info@deadearnest.co.uk   Tel: 0114-233 4579

DEAN Lee
PO Box 10703, London WC2H 9ED
Fax: 020-7836 6968   Tel: 020-7497 5111

DELFONT MACKINTOSH THEATRES Ltd
(Theatre Owners)
Strand Theatre
Aldwych, London WC2B 4LD
e-mail: info@delfont-mackintosh.com
Fax: 020-7240 3831   Tel: 020-7379 4431

DISNEY THEATRICAL PRODUCTIONS (UK) Ltd
Lyceum Theatre, 21 Wellington Street
London WC2E 7RQ
Fax: 020-7845 0999   Tel: 020-7845 0900

DONNA MARIA COMPANY
16 Bell Meadow, Dulwich, London SE19 1HP
Website: www.donna-marias-world.co.uk
e-mail: info@donna-marias-world.co.uk
                              Tel: 020-8670 7814

DOODAH THEATRE
27 St Peter's Way, Ealing
London W5 2QR
e-mail: doodahtc@aol.com   Tel: 020-8991 5903

DORE Katharine MANAGEMENT &
PRODUCTIONS Ltd (KDM)
Horseshoe Wharf, 6A Clink Street, London SE1 9FD
Website: www.kdmanagement.co.uk
e-mail: info@kdmanagement.co.uk
Fax: 020-7357 8002   Tel: 020-7357 6633

DRAMATIS PERSONAE Ltd
(Nathan Silver, Nicolas Kent)
19 Regency Street, London SW1P 4BY
e-mail: nathan.silver@ntlworld.com
                              Tel: 020-7834 9300

DUAL CONTROL OPERA & BALLET
INTERNATIONAL
Admiral's Office
Historic Dockyard, Chatham, Kent ME4 4TZ
e-mail: info@ellenkentinternational.co.uk
Fax: 01634 819149   Tel: 01634 819141

EACH WORLD PRODUCTIONS
43 Moormead Road, St Margaret's
Twickenham TW1 1JS
Fax: 020-8744 0676   Tel: 020-8892 0908

EASTERN ANGLES THEATRE COMPANY
(Touring)
Sir John Mills Theatre
Gatacre Road, Ipswich, Suffolk IP1 2LQ
Website: www.easternangles.co.uk
e-mail: admin@easternangles.co.uk
Fax: 01473 384999   Tel: 01473 218202

ELLIOTT Paul Ltd
(Triumph Entertainment Ltd)
Suite 3, Waldorf Chambers, 11 Aldwych WC2B 4DG
e-mail: pelliott@paulelliott.ltd.uk
Fax: 020-7379 4860   Tel: 020-7379 4870

EMPTY SPACE THEATRE COMPANY
32 Kenbrook House, Leighton Road
Kentish Town, London NW5 2QN
e-mail: estc@dircon.co.uk
Fax: 0870 9090103   Tel: 0870 9090102

ENGLISH CHAMBER THEATRE
18 The Crooked Billet
London SW19 4RQ   Tel: 020-8946 9898

ENGLISH NATIONAL OPERA
London Coliseum
St Martin's Lane, London WC2N 4ES
Fax: 020-7845 9277   Tel: 020-7836 0111

ENGLISH STAGE COMPANY Ltd
Royal Court, Sloane Square, London SW1W 8AS
Website: www.royalcourttheatre.com
e-mail: info@royalcourttheatre.com
Fax: 020-7565 5001   Tel: 020-7565 5050

ENGLISH THEATRE COMPANY Ltd
(TMA Member)
Nybrogatan 35
114 39 Stockholm, Sweden
Website: www.englishtheatre.se
e-mail: etc.ltd@telia.com
Fax: 00 46 8660 1159   Tel: 00 46 8662 4133

ENGLISH TOURING THEATRE
25 Short Street, London SE1 8LJ
Website: www.englishtouringtheatre.co.uk
e-mail: admin@englishtouringtheatre.co.uk
Fax: 020-7450 1991   Tel: 020-7450 1990

ENTERTAINMENT BUSINESS Ltd The
199 Piccadilly, London W1J 9HA
Fax: 020-7287 5144   Tel: 020-7734 8555

EUROPEAN THEATRE COMPANY The
39 Oxford Avenue, London SW20 8LS
Website: www.europeantheatre.co.uk
e-mail: admin@europeantheatre.co.uk
Fax: 020-8544 1999   Tel: 020-8544 1994

FACADE
(Musicals)
43A Garthorne Road, London SE23 1EP
e-mail: facade@cobomedia.com
Tel: 020-8291 7079

FACE TO FACE THEATRE PRODUCTIONS Ltd
(Write)
10 St Fillans Road, Stepps, Glasgow G33 6LW
e-mail: robinfacetoface@hotmail.com

FARRAH Paul PRODUCTIONS
Strand Theatre Offices, London WC2B 4LD
e-mail: pfpltd@aol.com
Fax: 01293 451336
Tel: 01293 442695

FELL Andrew Ltd
4 Ching Court, 49-51 Monmouth Street
London WC2H 9EY
e-mail: hq@andrewfell.co.uk
Fax: 020-7240 2499
Tel: 020-7240 2420

FIELDING Harold
69 Strand on the Green
London W4 3PF
Tel: 020-8673 4323

FIERY ANGEL Ltd
22-24 Torrington Place, London WC1E 7HF
Website: www.fiery-angel.com
e-mail: admin@fiery-angel.com
Fax: 020-7580 6652
Tel: 020-7907 7040

FLEIGHTON PRODUCTIONS Ltd
1-2 Wyrern Way, Henwood, Ashford
Kent TN24 8DW SE1 0RB
Fax: 01233 634999
Tel: 01233 634777

FLUXX
(Improvised Theatre)
Sebbon Street Centre
Sebbon Street, London N1 2DZ
Website: www.fluxx.co.uk
e-mail: admin@fluxx.co.uk
Tel: 020-8348 3658

FORBIDDEN THEATRE COMPANY
Diorama Arts Centre, 34 Osnaburgh Street
London NW1 3ND
Website: www.forbidden.org.uk
e-mail: info@forbidden.org.uk
Tel/Fax: 020-7813 1025

FORD Vanessa PRODUCTIONS Ltd
Upper House Farm, Upper House Lane
Shamley Green, Surrey GU5 0SX
Website: www.vfpltd.com
e-mail: vanessa@vfpltd.fsnet.co.uk
Fax: 01483 271509
Tel: 01483 268530

FOX Robert Ltd
6 Beauchamp Place, London SW3 1NG
e-mail: info@robertfoxltd.com
Fax: 020-7225 1638
Tel: 020-7584 6855

FREEDMAN Bill Ltd
Room 311, Bedford Chambers, The Piazza
Covent Garden, London WC2E 8HA
Fax: 020-7836 9903
Tel: 020-7836 9900

FREEFLOW PRODUCTIONS Ltd
The Wilde Theatre, South Hill Park Arts Centre
Ringmead, Bracknell, Berkshire RG12 7PA
Website: www.freeflowproductions.co.uk
e-mail: info@freeflowproductions.co.uk
Tel: 01344 426464

FRIEDMAN Sonia PRODUCTIONS
New Ambassadors Theatre, West Street
London WC2H 9ND
Website: www.soniafriedman.com
e-mail: admin@soniafriedman.com
Fax: 020-7395 5455
Tel: 020-7395 5454

FUTURA MUSIC (PRODUCTIONS) Ltd
(Write only)
29 Emanuel Hse, Rochester Row, London SW1P 1BS

GALE PRODUCTIONS
24 Wimbledon Park Road, London SW18 1LT
e-mail: gale.prod@which.net
Fax: 020-8875 1582
Tel: 020-8870 1149

GALLEON THEATRE COMPANY Ltd
(Alice De Sousa)
Greenwich Playhouse
Greenwich BR Station Forecourt
189 Greenwich High Road, London SE10 8JA
Website: www.galleontheatre.co.uk
e-mail: boxoffice@galleontheatre.co.uk
Fax: 020-8969 2910
Tel: 020-8858 9256

GLASS David ENSEMBLE
59 Brewer Street, London W1F 9UN
Website: www.davidglassensemble.com
e-mail: dg.ensemble@virgin.net
Fax: 020-7734 0365
Tel: 020-7734 6030

GODOT COMPANY
51 The Cut, London SE1 8LF
Tel: 020-7633 0599

GOOD COMPANY
at St Michaels, Powis Road, Brighton BN1 3HJ
e-mail: admin@goodcompany.idps.co.uk
Fax: 01273 779955
Tel: 01273 771777

GOSS Gerald Ltd
19 Gloucester Street, London SW1V 2DB
Fax: 020-7592 9301
Tel: 020-7592 9202

GOUCHER Mark Ltd
2nd Floor, 20-22 Stukeley Street, London WC2B 5LR
e-mail: info@markgoucher.com
Fax: 020-7488 9577
Tel: 020-7438 9570

GRAEAE THEATRE COMPANY
LVS Resource Centre
356 Holloway Road, London N7 6PA
Website: www.graeae.org
e-mail: info@graeae.org
Fax: 020-7609 7324
Tel: 020-7700 2455

GRAHAM David ENTERTAINMENT Ltd
72 New Bond Street, London W1S 1RR
Website: www.davidgraham.co.uk
e-mail: info@davidgraham.co.uk
Fax: 0870 3211700
Tel: 0870 3211600

GREAT WESTERN STAGE
East Trevelmond Farm, Trevelmond
Liskeard, Cornwall PL14 4LT
e-mail: admin@greatwesternstage.fsnet.co.uk
Tel/Fax: 01579 321858

GREEN & LENAGAN Ltd
140 Buckingham Palace Road, London SW1W 9SA
e-mail: postbox@greenandlenagan.co.uk
Fax: 020-7881 9661
Tel: 020-7881 9660

HALE Ivan Ltd
5 Denmark Street, London WC2H 8LP
e-mail: ivanhaleltd@hotmail.com
Fax: 020-7240 6949
Tel: 020-7240 9800

HAMPSTEAD THEATRE PRODUCTIONS Ltd
Eton Avenue, Swiss Cottage, London NW3 3EU
Website: www.hampsteadtheatre.com
e-mail: info@hampsteadtheatre.com
Fax: 020-7449 4201
Tel: 020-7449 4200

HANDSTAND PRODUCTIONS
13 Hope Street, Liverpool L1 9BH
Website: www.handstand-uk.com
e-mail: info@handstand-uk.com
Fax: 0151-709 3515
Tel: 0151-708 7441

HARLEY CINE LIBRE PRODUCTIONS
68 New Cavendish Street, London W1G 8TE
e-mail: harleyprods@aol.com
Fax: 020-8202 8863   Tel: 020-7580 3247

HAYMARKET THEATRE COMPANY Ltd
Wote Street, Basingstoke, Hampshire RG21 7NW
Website: www.haymarket@org.uk
e-mail: info@haymarket.org.uk
Fax: 01256 357130   Tel: 01256 323073

HENDERSON Glynis PRODUCTIONS
69 Charlotte Street, London W1T 4PJ
e-mail: info@ghmp.co.uk
Fax: 020-7436 1489   Tel: 020-7580 9644

HESTER John PRODUCTIONS
(Intimate Mysteries Theatre Company)
105 Stoneleigh Park Road, Epsom, Surrey KT19 0RF
e-mail: hjohnhester@aol.com
Tel/Fax: 020-8393 5705

HILTON Adrian Ltd
(Write)
Priory House, Amersham Road, Beaconsfield
Buckinghamshire HP9 2HA

HISS & BOO COMPANY Ltd The
(Ian Liston)
Nyes Hill, Wineham Lane, Bolney
West Sussex RH17 5SD
Website: www.hissboo.co.uk
e-mail: ian@hissboo.co.uk
Fax: 01444 882057   Tel: 01444 881707

HISTORIA THEATRE COMPANY
8 Cloudesley Square, London N1 0HT
e-mail: kateprice@lineone.net
Fax: 020-7278 4733   Tel: 020-7837 8008

HOLMAN Paul ASSOCIATES Ltd
20 Deane Avenue
South Ruislip, Middlesex HA4 6SR
Website: www.paulholmanassociates.co.uk
e-mail: paulholmanassociates@blueyonder.co.uk
Fax: 020-8582 2557   Tel: 020-8845 9408

HOLT Thelma Ltd
Waldorf Chambers
11 Aldwych, London WC2B 4DG
Website: www.thelmaholt.co.uk
e-mail: thelma@dircon.co.uk
Fax: 020-7836 9832   Tel: 020-7379 0438

HOUSE OF GULLIVER
(Write)
55 Goldfield Road, Tring, Hertfordshire HP23 4BA

HULL TRUCK THEATRE
Spring Street, Hull HU2 8RW
Website: www.hulltruck.co.uk
e-mail: admin@hulltruck.co.uk
Fax: 01482 581182   Tel: 01482 224800

HUTT RUSSELL PRODUCTIONS Ltd
PO Box 64, Cirencester, Gloucestershire GL7 5YD
Website: www.huttrussellorg.com
e-mail: shows@huttrussellorg.com
Fax: 01285 642291   Tel: 01285 644622

IMAGE MUSICAL THEATRE
23 Sedgeford Road, Shepherd's Bush
London W12 0NA
Website: www.imagemusicaltheatre.co.uk
e-mail: brianthresh@image-theatre-co.demon.uk
Fax: 020-8749 9294   Tel: 020-8743 9380

IMAGINATION ENTERTAINMENTS
25 Store Street, South Crescent, London WC1E 7BL
Website: www.imagination.com
e-mail: entertainments@imagination.com
Fax: 020-7323 5801   Tel: 020-7323 3300

Richard Jordan Productions Ltd

- Producing
- General Management
  UK and International Productions,
  and International Festivals
- Consultancy

Richard Jordan Productions Ltd
Mews Studios, 16 Vernon Yard
London W11 2DX

Tel: 020 7243 9001
Fax: 020 7313 9667
e-mail: richard.jordan@virgin.net

INCISOR
30 Brondesbury Park, London NW6 7DN
Website: www.festival-edinburgh.com
e-mail: sarah.mann4@btopenworld.com
Fax: 020-8830 4992   Tel: 020-8830 0074

INDIGO ENTERTAINMENTS
Tynymynydd, Bryneglwys, Corwen
Denbighshire LL21 9NP
Website: www.indigoentertainments.com
e-mail: info@indigoentertainments.com
Tel: 01978 790211

INSIDE INTELLIGENCE
(Musical & Contemporary Opera Products)
13 Athlone Close, London E5 8HD
Website: www.inside-intelligence.nildram.co.uk
e-mail: admin@inside-intelligence.org.uk
Tel/Fax: 020-8986 8013

INTERNATIONAL THEATRE & MUSIC Ltd
(Piers Chater Robinson)
Shakespeare House, Theatre Street
London SW11 5ND
Website: www.internationaltheatreandmusic.com
e-mail: inttheatre@aol.com
Fax: 020-7801 6317   Tel: 020-7801 6316

ISLEWORTH ACTORS COMPANY
38 Eve Road, Isleworth
Middlesex TW7 7HS   Tel/Fax: 020-8891 1073

JACKSON Richard
48 William Mews,
London SW1X 9HQ   Tel/Fax: 020-7235 3759

JAMES Bruce PRODUCTIONS Ltd
68 St Georges Park Avenue
Westcliff-on-Sea, Essex SS0 9UD
Website: www.brucejamesproductions.co.uk
e-mail: info@brucejamesproductions.co.uk
Tel/Fax: 01702 335970

JOHNSON David
85B Torriano Avenue, London NW5 2RX
e-mail: david@johnsontemple.co.uk
Tel: 020-7284 3733

JOHNSON Gareth Ltd
Plas Hafren, Egwyswrw, Crymych
Pembrokeshire SA41 3UL
e-mail: gjltd@macunlimited.net
Fax: 07779 007845   Tel: 07770 225227

JORDAN Andy PRODUCTIONS Ltd
5 Underwood Cottages, The Coombe
Streatley-on-Thames, Berkshire RG8 9RA
e-mail: ANDYJAndyjordan@aol.com
Mobile: 07775 615205   Tel/Fax: 01491 871297

JORDAN Richard PRODUCTIONS Ltd
Mews Studios, 16 Vernon Yard, London W11 2DX
e-mail: richard.jordan@virgin.net
Fax: 020-7313 9667   Tel: 020-7243 9001

KARUSHI PROMOTIONS
Golden Cross House, 8 Duncannon Street
London WC2N 4JF
Website: www.karushi.com
e-mail: ed@karushi.com
Fax: 020-7484 5151   Tel: 020-7484 5040

KDM
Horseshoe Wharf, 6A Clink Street, London SE1 9FD
Website: www.kdmanagement.co.uk
e-mail: info@kdmanagement.co.uk
Fax: 020-7357 8002   Tel: 020-7357 6633

KELLY Robert C Ltd
The Alhambra Suite
82 Mitchell Street, Glasgow G1 3NA
Website: www.robertckelly.co.uk
e-mail: robert@robertckelly.co.uk
Fax: 0141-229 1441   Tel: 0141-229 1444

KENWRIGHT Bill Ltd
BKL House, 106 Harrow Road, Off Howley Place
London W2 1RR
e-mail: info@kenwright.com
Fax: 020-7446 6222   Tel: 020-7446 6200

KING'S HEAD THEATRE PRODUCTION Ltd
115 Upper Street, London N1 1QN
Fax: 020-7226 8507   Tel: 020-7226 8561

KIRK David PRODUCTIONS
11A Marwick Terrace, St Leonards-on-Sea
East Sussex TN38 0RE   Tel: 01424 445081

LIMELIGHT ENTERTAINMENT PRODUCTIONS Ltd
The Gateway, 2A Rathmore Rd, London SE7 7QW
Fax: 020-8305 2684   Tel: 020-8858 6141

LINNIT PRODUCTIONS Ltd
123A King's Road, London SW3 4PL
Fax: 020-7352 3450   Tel: 020-7352 7722

LIVE THEATRE
7-8 Trinity Chare
Quayside, Newcastle upon Tyne NE1 3DF
Website: www.live.org.uk   Tel: 0191-261 2694

LLOYD-JAMES Adrian
36 Fleece Road, Long Ditton, Surrey KT6 5JN
e-mail: tabsproductions@bushinternet.com
                              Tel: 020-8398 6746

LONDON BUBBLE THEATRE COMPANY Ltd
5 Elephant Lane, London SE16 4JD
Website: www.londonbubble.org.uk
e-mail: admin@londonbubble.org.uk
Fax: 020-7231 2366   Tel: 020-7237 4434

**LONDON COMPANY INTERNATIONAL
PLAYS Ltd The**
(No CV's please)
PO Box 4458, London SW1X 8XP
e-mail: derek@glynnes.co.uk
Fax: 020-7486 2164   Tel: 020-7486 3166

LONDON PRODUCTIONS Ltd
PO Box 10703, London WC2H 9ED
Fax: 020-7836 6968   Tel: 020-7497 5111

LYRIC HAMMERSMITH PRODUCTIONS
58 Hythe Road, Brighton BN1 6JS
e-mail: robertcogo_fawcett@hotmail.com
                    Mobile: 07973 938634

MACKINTOSH Cameron Ltd
1 Bedford Square, London WC1B 3RB
Fax: 020-7436 2683   Tel: 020-7637 8866

MACNAGHTEN PRODUCTIONS Ltd
Dundarave, Bushmills, Co. Antrim
Northern Ireland BT57 8ST
Fax: 028-2073 2575   Tel: 028-2073 1215

MALCOLM Christopher Ltd
1 Calton Road, Bath BA2 4PP
Website: www.rockyhorror.co.uk
e-mail: cmalcolm@btconnect.com
Fax: 01225 427778   Tel: 01225 445459

MANS Johnny PRODUCTIONS Ltd
PO Box 196, Hoddesdon, Hertfordshire EN10 7WG
Fax: 01992 470516   Tel: 01992 470907

MASTERSON Guy PRODUCTIONS
(Write)
The Bull Theatre, 68 High Street, Barnet
Hertfordshire EN5 5SJ
Website: www.guymasterson.com
e-mail: admin@guymasterson.com
Fax: 020-8449 5252   Tel: 020-8449 7800

MDP (Marilyn Davis Productions)
16 Millers Court, Chiswick Mall, London W4 2PF
e-mail: davismarilynproductions@hotmail.com
Fax: 020-8563 2018   Tel: 020-8748 1202

MEADOW Jeremy
(See TEG PRODUCTIONS Ltd)

MENZIES Lee Ltd
118-120 Wardour Street, London W1V 3LA
Website: www.leemenzies.co.uk
e-mail: leemenzies@leemenzies.co.uk
Fax: 020-7734 4224   Tel: 020-7734 9559

MERLIN MUSICALS Ltd/MERLIN PRODUCTIONS
The Swan Theatre, The Moors, Worcester WR1 3EF
e-mail: richard@merlinoffice.fsnet.co.uk
                    Tel/Fax: 01905 731900

METRO ENTERTAINMENT Ltd
Strand Theatre Offices, London WC2B 4LD
e-mail: info@metroentertainmentltd.com
Fax: 01293 451336   Tel: 01293 442695

METRO PRODUCTIONS
11 Keyford Place, Frome
Somerset BA11 1JE   Tel: 01373 462812

MIDDLE GROUND THEATRE COMPANY
3 Gordon Terrace, Malvern Wells, Malvern
Worcestershire WR14 4ER
e-mail: middleground@tinyworld.co.uk
Fax: 01684 574472   Tel: 01684 577231

MITCHELL Matthew Ltd
Flat 5, 65 Cumberland Street, London SW1V 4LY
e-mail: mmitch@dircon.co.uk
Fax: 020-7834 8738   Tel: 020-7630 8881

MONSTER PRODUCTIONS
Buddle Arts Centre, 258B Station Road, Wallsend
Tyne & Wear NE28 8RG
Website: www.monsterproductions.co.uk
e-mail: info@monsterproductions.co.uk
Fax: 0191-240 4016   Tel: 0191-240 4011

MOVING TALENT
Ground Floor, 29 Ardwick Green North
Manchester M12 6DL
e-mail: movingtalent@aol.com   Tel: 0161-877 0250

MOVING THEATRE
16 Laughton Lodge, Laughton, Nr Lewes
East Sussex BN8 6BY
Website: www.movingtheatre.com
e-mail: info@movingtheatre.com
Fax: 01323 815736   Tel: 01323 815726

Stage Presence

PO Box 7579 London NW3 1WA

020-7794-9140

MU-LAN THEATRE COMPANY
The Albany, Douglas Way, London SE8 4AG
Website: www.mu-lan.org
e-mail: mailbox@mu-lan.org
Fax: 020-8694 0618   Tel: 020-8694 0557

MUSIC THEATRE LONDON
Chertsey Chambers, 12 Mercer Street
London WC2H 9QD
Website: www.mtl.org.uk
e-mail: musictheatre.london@virgin.net
Fax: 020-7240 0805   Tel: 020-7240 0919

MUZIKANSKY
The Forum, Fonthill
The Common
Tunbridge Wells TN4 8YU
Website: www.mzky.co.uk
e-mail: admin@mzky.co.uk   Tel/Fax: 01892 542260

NEW END THEATRE
27 New End, Hampstead, London NW3 1JD
Website: www.newendtheatre.co.uk
e-mail: briandaniels@newendtheatre.co.uk
Fax: 020-7472 5808   Tel: 020-7472 5800

NEW SHAKESPEARE COMPANY Ltd The
Open Air Theatre, The Iron Works, Inner Circle
Regent's Park, London NW1 4NR
Website: www.openairtheatre.org
Fax: 020-7487 4562   Tel: 020-7935 5756

NEW VIC THEATRE OF LONDON Inc
Suite 42, 91 St Martin's Lane
London WC2H 0DL   Tel/Fax: 020-7240 2929

NEW VIC WORKSHOP Ltd
15 Bedford Place, Brighton BN1 2PT
e-mail: newvicworkshop@lineone.net
Fax: 01273 776663   Tel: 01273 775126

NEWPALM PRODUCTIONS
26 Cavendish Avenue, London N3 3QN
Fax: 020-8346 8257   Tel: 020-8349 0802

NITRO
(Formerly Black Theatre Co-operative)
6 Brewery Road, London N7 9NH
Website: www.nitro.co.uk
e-mail: btc@dircon.co.uk
Fax: 020-7609 1221   Tel: 020-7609 1331

NORTHERN BROADSIDES THEATRE COMPANY
Dean Clough, Halifax HX3 5AX
e-mail: sue@northern-broadsides.co.uk
Fax: 01422 383175   Tel: 01422 369704

**NORTHERN STAGE
(THEATRICAL PRODUCTIONS) Ltd**
Newcastle Playhouse, Barras Bridge
Newcastle upon Tyne NE1 7RH
Website: www.northernstage.com
e-mail: info@northernstage.com
Fax: 0191-261 8093   Tel: 0191-232 3366

NORWELL LAPLEY ASSOCIATES
Lapley Hall, Lapley, Staffordshire ST19 9JR
Website: www.norwelllapley.co.uk
e-mail: norwelllapley@freeuk.com
Fax: 01785 841992   Tel: 01785 841991

NOT THE NATIONAL THEATRE
(Write) (Small/Mid-Scale Touring - UK & Abroad)
101 Broadhurst Gardens, London NW6 3BJ

NTC TOURING THEATRE COMPANY
The Playhouse, Bondgate Without, Alnwick
Northumberland NE66 1PQ
Website: www.ntc-touringtheatre.co.uk
e-mail: admin@ntc-touringtheatre.co.uk
Fax: 01665 605837   Tel: 01665 602586

O'BRIEN Barry (1968) Ltd
26 Cavendish Avenue, London N3 3QN
Fax: 020-8346 8257   Tel: 020-8346 8011

OFF THE CUFF THEATRE COMPANY
First Floor, 52 Crowndale Road, London NW1 1TP
e-mail: otctheatre@aol.com   Tel: 020-7691 1577

OLD VIC PRODUCTIONS Plc
The Old Vic Theatre, The Cut, Waterloo
London SE1 8NB
e-mail: ovp@oldvictheatre.com
Fax: 020-7261 9161   Tel: 020-7928 2651

OPEN AIR THEATRE
(See NEW SHAKESPEARE COMPANY Ltd The)

OPERA & BALLET INTERNATIONAL Ltd
(International Opera & Ballet Producers)
Admiral's Offices, The Historic Dockyard
Chatham, Kent ME4 4TZ
e-mail: info@ellenkentinternational.co.uk
Fax: 01634 819149   Tel: 01634 819141

OUT OF JOINT
7 Thane Works, Thane Villas, London N7 7PH
Website: www.outofjoint.co.uk
e-mail: ojo@outofjoint.co.uk
Fax: 020-7609 0203   Tel: 020-7609 0207

OUT OF THE BLUE PRODUCTIONS Ltd
48 Conduit Street, London W1S 2YR
Website: www.otbp.com
e-mail: info@otbp.com
Fax: 020-7734 3678   Tel: 020-7734 1345

OVATION
1 Prince of Wales Passage, London NW1 3EF
Website: www.ovationproductions.com
e-mail: events@ovationproductions.com
Fax: 020-7380 0404   Tel: 020-7387 2342

OXFORD STAGE COMPANY
Chertsey Chambers, 12 Mercer Street
London WC2H 9QD
Website: www.oxfordstage.co.uk
e-mail: info@oxfordstage.co.uk
Fax: 020-7438 9941   Tel: 020-7438 9940

PAINES PLOUGH
Fourth Floor, 43 Aldwych, London WC2B 4DN
Website: www.painesplough.com
e-mail: office@painesplough.com
Fax: 020-7240 4534   Tel: 020-7240 4533

PARASOL PRODUCTIONS
Garden House, 4 Sunnyside, Wimbledon SW19 4SL
Website: www.parasoltheatre.co.uk
e-mail: parasoltheatre@waitrose.com
Fax: 020-8946 0228   Tel: 020-8946 9478

T

PENDLE PRODUCTIONS
Bridge Farm, 249 Hawes Side Lane
Blackpool FY4 4AA
Website: www.pendleproductions.co.uk
e-mail: admin@pendleproductions.co.uk
Tel/Fax: 01254 59590

PENTABUS
(National Touring Company for New Writing)
Bromfield, Ludlow, Shropshire SY8 2JU
Website: www.pentabus.co.uk
e-mail: firstname@pentabus.co.uk
Fax: 01584 856254   Tel: 01584 856564

PEOPLE SHOW
People Show Studios, Pollard Row, London E2 6NB
Website: www.peopleshow.co.uk
e-mail: people@peopleshow.co.uk
Fax: 020-7739 0203   Tel: 020-7729 1841

PERFORMANCE BUSINESS
15 Montrose Walk, Weybridge, Surrey KT13 8JN
Website: www.reactors.co.uk
e-mail: michael@theperformancebusiness.com
Fax: 01932 830248   Tel: 01932 888885

PILOT THEATRE COMPANY
(New Writing & Multi Media YPT)
Production Office, c/o York Theatre Royal
St Leonards Place, York YO1 7HD
Website: www.pilot-theatre.com
e-mail: info@pilot-theatre.com
Fax: 01904 656378   Tel: 01904 635755

PLANTAGENET PRODUCTIONS
Westridge (Open Centre), (Drawing Room Recitals),
Star Lane, Andover Road, Highclere
Nr Newbury RG20 9PJ   Tel: 01635 253322

PLUNGE PRODUCTIONS Ltd
9 Whittington Road, London N22 8YS
Website: www.plungeproductions.com
e-mail: info@plungeproductions.com
Tel/Fax: 020-8888 6608

POLKA THEATRE FOR CHILDREN
240 The Broadway, Wimbledon SW19 1SB
Website: www.polkatheatre.com
e-mail: admin@polkatheatre.com
Fax: 020-8545 8365   Tel: 020-8543 4888

POSTER Kim
The Penthouse, Charles House
7 Leicester Place, London WC2H 7RJ
e-mail: office@stanhopeprod.com
Fax: 020-7734 7185   Tel: 020-7734 0710

PROMENADE ENTERPRISES Ltd
6 Russell Grove, London SW9 6HS
e-mail: promenadeproductions@msn.com
Fax: 020-7564 3026   Tel: 020-7582 9354

P&S PRODUCTIONS
Top Flat, 51 Norroy Road, London SW15 1PQ
e-mail: timsawers@msn.com   Tel/Fax: 020-8780 9115

PUGH David Ltd
Canaletto Yard
41 Beak Street, London W1F 9SB
e-mail: dpl@davidpughltd.com
Fax: 020-7287 8856   Tel: 020-7434 9757

PURSUED BY A BEAR PRODUCTIONS
6 Glenluce Road
Blackheath, London SE3 7SB
Website: www.pbab.org
e-mail: pbab@pbab.org   Tel/Fax: 020-8480 9514

PW PRODUCTIONS Ltd
The Penthouse
7 Leicester Place, London WC2H 7RJ
Website: www.pwprods.co.uk
Fax: 020-7734 7185   Tel: 020-7734 7184

QDOS ENTERTAINMENT (THEATRE) Ltd
8 King Street, London WC2E 8HN
Fax: 020-7379 4892   Tel: 020-7836 2795

Qdos House, Queen Margaret's Road,
Scarborough North Yorkshire YO11 2SA
Fax: 01723 361958   Tel: 01723 500038

QUANTUM THEATRE
The Old Button Factory
1-11 Bannockburn Road
Plumstead, London SE18 1ET
Website: www.quantumtheatre.co.uk
e-mail: quantumtheatre@btinternet.com
Tel: 020-8317 9000

RAGGED RAINBOW PRODUCTIONS Ltd
45 Nightingale Lane, Crouch End, London N8 7RA
e-mail: rainbowrp@onetel.net.uk
Tel/Fax: 020-8341 6241

RAGS & FEATHERS THEATRE COMPANY
80 Summer Road
Thames Ditton, Surrey KT7 0QP
e-mail: jill@ragsandfeathers.freeserve.co.uk
Mobile: 07958 724374   Tel: 020-8224 2203

RAIN OR SHINE THEATRE COMPANY
25 Paddock Gardens, Longlevens
Gloucester GL2 0ED
Website: www.rainorshine.co.uk
e-mail: theatre@rainorshine.co.uk
Tel/Fax: 01452 521575

REALLY USEFUL GROUP Ltd The
22 Tower Street, London WC2H 9TW
Fax: 020-7240 1204   Tel: 020-7240 0880

REALLY USEFUL THEATRES
(Theatre Operators)
Manor House
21 Soho Square, London W1D 3QP
Website: www.rutheatres.com
e-mail: info@rutheatres.com
Fax: 020-7434 1217   Tel: 020-7494 5200

RED ROOM The
Cabin Q, Clarendon Buildings, 11 Ronalds Road
London N5 1XJ
Website: www.theredroom.org.uk
e-mail: info@theredroom.org.uk
Fax: 020-7607 8451   Tel: 020-7697 8685

RED ROSE CHAIN
1 Fore Hamlet, Ipswich IP3 8AA
Website: www.redrosechain.co.uk
e-mail: info@redrosechain.co.uk
Tel: 01473 288886

RED SHIFT THEATRE COMPANY
TRG2 Trowbray House, 108 Weston Street
London SE1 3QB
Website: www.redshifttheatreco.co.uk
e-mail: mail@redshifttheatreco.co.uk
Fax: 020-7378 9789   Tel: 020-7378 9787

REDINGTON Michael Ltd
10 Maunsel Street, London SW1P 2QL
Fax: 020-7828 6947   Tel: 020-7834 5119

RELEASE THEATRE COMPANY
(Small Scale, Fringe Venues, TIE Touring)
70 Ivydale Road, London SE15 3BS
Website: www.releasetheatrecompany.co.uk
e-mail: releasetheatreco@yahoo.co.uk
Mobile: 07900 823611

REVEAL THEATRE COMPANY
40 Pirehill Lane, Walton
Stone, Staffordshire ST15 0JN
e-mail: revealtheatre@hotmail.com
Tel: 01785 814052

RHO DELTA Ltd
(Greg Ripley-Duggan)
52 Tottenham Street
London W1T 4RN
e-mail: info@ripleyduggan.com Tel: 020-7436 1392

RICHMOND PRODUCTIONS
47 Moor Mead Road, St Margaret's
Twickenham TW1 1JS
e-mail: alister@richmondproductions.co.uk
Mobile: 07968 026768   Tel/Fax: 020-8891 2280

ROCKET THEATRE COMPANY
245 Broadfield Road, Manchester M14 7JT
Website: www.rockettheatre.co.uk
e-mail: martin@rockettheatre.co.uk
Mobile: 07788 723570   Tel: 0161-226 8788

ROSE Michael Ltd
The Old Dairy, Throop Road, Holdenhurst
Bournemouth, Dorset BH8 0DL
e-mail: mrl@mrltheatre.u-net.com
Fax: 01202 522311   Tel: 01202 522711

ROSENTHAL Suzanna Ltd
PO Box 40001, London N6 4YA
e-mail: admin@suzannarosenthal.com
Tel/Fax: 020-8340 4421

ROYAL COURT THEATRE PRODUCTIONS Ltd
Sloane Square, London SW1W 8AS
Website: www.royalcourttheatre.com
e-mail: info@royalcourttheatre.com
Fax: 020-7565 5001   Tel: 020-7565 5050

ROYAL EXCHANGE THEATRE COMPANY
St Ann's Square, Manchester M2 7DH
Website: www.royalexchange.co.uk
Tel: 0161-833 9333

ROYAL NATIONAL THEATRE
South Bank, London SE1 9PX
Website: www.nt-online.org.uk
e-mail: marketing@nationaltheatre.org.uk
Fax: 020-7452 3344   Tel: 020-7452 3333

ROYAL SHAKESPEARE COMPANY
1 Earlham Street, London WC2H 9LL
Website: www.rsc.org.uk
Fax: 020-7845 0505   Tel: 020-7845 0500

ROYAL SHAKESPEARE THEATRE
Stratford-upon-Avon CV37 6BB
Fax: 01789 294810   Tel: 01789 296655

RUBINSTEIN Mark Ltd
The Old Vic Theatre, The Cut, London SE1 8NB
e-mail: info@mrluk.com
Fax: 020-7261 9161   Tel: 020-7928 2651

SALBERG & STEPHENSON Ltd
18 Soho Square, London W1D 3QL
e-mail: soholondon@aol.com
Fax: 020-7025 8100   Tel: 020-7025 8701

SANDPIPER PRODUCTIONS Ltd
49A Ossington Street, London W2 4LY
e-mail: harold@sanditen.fsworld.co.uk
Fax: 020-7229 6710   Tel: 020-7229 6708

SCAMP
Sutherland Callow Arts Management and
Production
46 Church Lane, Arlesley, Bedfordshire SG15 6UX
Website: www.scamptheatre.com
e-mail: admin@scamptheatre.com
Mobile: 07710 49111   Tel: 01462 734843

SECOND SIGHT PRODUCTIONS
(Second Productions of Plays)
TEG Productions (Second Sight) Ltd
11-15 Betterton Street, London WC2H 9BP
Fax: 020-7836 9454   Tel: 020-7379 1066

SHARED EXPERIENCE THEATRE
(National/International Touring)
The Soho Laundry, 9 Dufour's Pl, London W1F 7SJ
Website: www.setheatre.co.uk
e-mail: admin@setheatre.co.uk
Fax: 020-7287 8763   Tel: 020-7434 9248

SHARLAND Elizabeth
Suite 12, 30 New Compton Street
London WC2H 8DN   Tel: 020-7836 4203

SHOW OF STRENGTH
74 Chessel Street, Bedminster, Bristol BS3 3DN
Fax: 0117-902 0196   Tel: 0117-902 0235

SINDEN Marc PRODUCTIONS
11 Garrick Street, London WC2E 9AR
Website: www.sindenproductions.com
e-mail: mail@sindenproductions.com
Tel/Fax: 020-8455 3278

SOHO THEATRE COMPANY
21 Dean Street, London W1D 3NE
Website: www.sohotheatre.com
e-mail: mail@sohotheatre.com
Fax: 020-7287 5061   Tel: 020-7287 5060

SPHINX THEATRE COMPANY The
25 Short Street, London SE1 8LJ
Website: www.sphinxtheatre.co.uk
Fax: 020-7401 9995   Tel: 020-7401 9993

SPIEGEL Adam PRODUCTIONS
2nd Floor, 20-22 Stukeley Street, London WC2B 5LR
e-mail: claudia@adamspiegel.com
Fax: 020-7438 9577   Tel: 020-7438 9565

SPLATS ENTERTAINMENT
5 Denmark Street, London WC2H 8LP
e-mail: admin@splatsentertainment.com
Fax: 020-7240 8409   Tel: 020-7240 8400

STACEY Barrie UK PRODUCTIONS Ltd
Flat 8, 132 Charing Cross Road, London WC2H 0LA
Website: www.barriestacey.com
e-mail: hopkinstacey@aol.com
Fax: 020-7836 2949   Tel: 020-7836 4128

STAGE FURTHER PRODUCTIONS Ltd
Westgate, Stansted Road, Eastbourne
East Sussex BN22 8LG
e-mail: inferno@stagefurther.co.uk
Fax: 01323 736127   Tel: 01323 739478

STAGE HOLDING UK
Swan House, 52 Poland Street, London W1F 7NH
Fax: 020-7025 6971   Tel: 020-7025 6970

STAGE PRESENCE
(Mark Bentley)
PO Box 7579, London NW3 1WA
e-mail: contact@stage-presence.co.uk
Tel: 020-7794 9140

STANHOPE PRODUCTIONS Ltd
The Penthouse, Charles House
7 Leicester Place, London WC2H 7RJ
e-mail: office@stanhopeprod.com
Fax: 020-7734 7185 ·
Tel: 020-7734 0710

STEAM INDUSTRY The
The Finborough Theatre
118 Finborough Road, London SW10 9ED
Website: www.steamindustry.co.uk
e-mail: admin@steamindustry.co.uk
Fax: 020-7835 1853
Tel: 020-7244 7439

SUSPECT CULTURE
CCA, 350 Sauchiehall Street, Glasgow G2 3JD
Website: www.suspectculture.com
e-mail: julie@suspectculture.co.uk
Fax: 0141-332 8823
Tel: 0141-332 9775

SUTHERLAND Martin
430 Merton Road, London SW18 5AE
Website: www.martinsutherland.co.uk
e-mail: info@martinsutherland.co.uk
Tel: 020-8875 0220

SWALLOW PRODUCTIONS (UK) Ltd
32 Blenheim Gardens
Wembley Park
Middlesex HA9 7NP
e-mail: swproduk@aol.com   Tel/Fax: 020-8904 7024

TABS PRODUCTIONS
36 Fleece Road, Long Ditton, Surrey KT6 5JN
e-mail: tabsproductions@bushinternet.com
Tel: 020-8398 6746

TALAWA THEATRE COMPANY
23-25 Great Sutton Street, London EC1V 0DN
Website: www.talawa.com
e-mail: hq@talawa.com
Fax: 020-7251 5969
Tel: 020-7251 6644

TAMASHA THEATRE COMPANY Ltd
Unit E, 11 Ronalds Road, London N5 1XJ
Website: www.tamasha.org.uk
e-mail: info@tamasha.org.uk
Fax: 020-7609 2722
Tel: 020-7609 2411

TAMBAR Ltd
PO Box LB689
London W1A 9LB
e-mail: tambarltd@hotmail.com   Tel: 020-8342 8882

TBA MUSIC Ltd
24 Clifton Hill, London NW8 0QG
e-mail: mail@tbamusic.freeserve.co.uk
Fax: 020-7372 0802
Tel: 0845 1203722

TEG PRODUCTIONS Ltd
11-15 Betterton Street, London WC2H 9BP
Fax: 020-7836 9454
Tel: 020-7379 1066

Winnington Hall, Winnington, Northwich
Cheshire CW8 4DU
Fax: 01606 872701
Tel: 01606 872700

TEMPLE Richard PRODUCTIONS
Revolver House, 15 Kensington High Street
London W8 5NP
e-mail: richard@richardtempleproductions.com
Fax: 020-7376 0916
Tel: 020-7376 0915

TEN PENCE PRODUCTIONS/RED LEAF
(Simon Fielder)
1 The Cuttings, Banbury Road, Bicester
Oxfordshire OX26 3NJ
e-mail: tenpenceproductions@yahoo.co.uk
Tel/Fax: 01869 327311

TENTH PLANET PRODUCTIONS
75 Woodland Gardens, London N10 3UD
Website: www.tenthplanetproductions.com
e-mail: admin@tenthplanetproductions.com
Fax: 020-8883 1708
Tel: 020-8442 2659

THEATRE ABSOLUTE
57-61 Corporation Street, Coventry CV1 1GQ
Website: www.theatreabsolute.co.uk
e-mail: info@theatreabsolute.co.uk
Tel: 024-7625 7380

THEATRE DE COMPLICITE
14 Angler's Lane, London NW5 3DE
e-mail: email@complicite.org
Fax: 020-7485 7701
Tel: 020-7485 7700

THEATRE OF COMEDY COMPANY Ltd
Shaftesbury Theatre
210 Shaftesbury Avenue, London WC2H 8DP
Fax: 020-7836 8181
Tel: 020-7379 3345

THEATRE ROYAL HAYMARKET PRODUCTIONS
Theatre Royal Haymarket, London SW1Y 4HT
e-mail: amc@trh.co.uk
Fax: 020-7389 9698
Tel: 020-7389 9669

THEATRE ROYAL STRATFORD EAST
Gerry Raffles Square
Stratford, London E15 1BN
Website: www.stratfordeast.com
e-mail: theatreroyal@stratfordeast.com
Tel: 020-8534 7374

THEATRE SANS FRONTIERES
The Queen's Hall Arts Centre
Beaumont Street, Hexham NE46 3LS
Website: www.theatresansfrontieres.co.uk
e-mail: admin@tsfront.co.uk
Fax: 01434 607206
Tel: 01434 652484

THEATRE SET-UP Ltd
(International Touring)
12 Fairlawn Close, Southgate, London N14 4JX
Website: www.ts-u.co.uk   Tel/Fax: 020-8886 9572

THEATRE TOURS INTERNATIONAL
The Bull Theatre, 68 The High Street
Barnet, Hertfordshire EN5 5SJ
Website: www.theatretoursinternational.com
e-mail: mail@theatretoursinternational.com
Fax: 020-8449 5252
Tel: 020-8449 7800

TOWER THEATRE COMPANY
(Full-time non professional)
11 Canonbury Pl, Islington, London N1 2NQ
Website: www.towertheatre.org.uk
e-mail: info@towertheatre.freeserve.co.uk
Tel/Fax: 020-7226 5111

TRADING FACES
(Mask & Physical Theatre)
2 Bridge View
Bridge St, Abingdon OX14 3HN
Website: www.tradingfaces.co.uk
e-mail: office@tradingfaces.demon.co.uk
Fax: 01235 553403
Tel: 01235 550829

TRENDS PRODUCTIONS Ltd
54 Lisson Street, London NW1 5DF
e-mail: info@trendsgroup.co.uk
Fax: 020-7258 3591
Tel: 020-7723 8001

TRESTLE THEATRE COMPANY
(Touring Mask Theatre)
Trestle Arts Base, Russet Drive, Hertfordshire
St Albans AL4 0JQ
Website: www.trestle.org.uk
e-mail: admin@trestle.org.uk
Fax: 01727 855558
Tel: 01727 850950

Theatre Producers

TRIUMPH ENTERTAINMENT Ltd
(DUNCAN C WELDON)
Suite 4, Waldorf Chambers, 11 Aldwych
London WC2B 4DG
e-mail: dcwtpp@aol.com
Fax: 020-7343 8801   Tel: 020-7343 8800

TURTLE KEY ARTS
Ladbroke Hall, 79 Barlby Road, London W10 6AZ
e-mail: admin@turtlekeyarts.org.uk
Fax: 020-8964 4080   Tel: 020-8964 5060

TWIST & CHEETHAM
39 Rosslyn Crescent, Edinburgh EH6 5AT
e-mail: ben.twist@blueyonder.co.uk
                    Tel/Fax: 0131-477 7425

TWO'S COMPANY
244 Upland Road, London SE22 0DN
e-mail: 2scompany@britishlibrary.net
Fax: 020-8299 3714   Tel: 020-8299 4593

UK ARTS INTERNATIONAL
Second Floor
6 Shaw Street, Worcester WR1 3QQ
Website: www.ukarts.com   e-mail: ukarts@ukarts.com
Fax: 01905 22868   Tel: 01905 26424

UK PRODUCTIONS Ltd
Lime House, 78 Meadrow
Godalming, Surrey GU7 3HT
Website: www.ukproductions.co.uk
e-mail: mail@ukproductions.co.uk
Fax: 01483 418486   Tel: 01483 423600

UNRESTRICTED VIEW
Above Hen & Chickens Theatre Bar
109 St Paul's Road, London N1 2NA
Website: www.henandchickens.com
e-mail: james@henandchickens.com
                    Tel: 020-7704 2001

VANCE Charles
CV Productions Ltd
Hampden Hse, 2 Weymouth St, London W1W 5BT
e-mail: cvtheatre@aol.com
Fax: 020-7636 2323   Tel: 020-7636 4343

VANDER ELST Anthony PRODUCTIONS
The Studio, 14 College Road, Bromley, Kent BR1 3NS
Fax: 020-8313 0443   Tel: 020-8466 5580

VOLCANO THEATRE COMPANY Ltd
176 Hanover Street, Swansea SA1 6BP
Website: www.volcanotheatre.co.uk
e-mail: volcano.tc@virgin.net
Fax: 01792 467563   Tel: 01792 472772

WALLBANK John ASSOCIATES
60 Barclay Road, London E11 3DG
Fax: 020-8928 0339   Tel: 020-8530 7386

WAREHOUSE THEATRE COMPANY
Dingwall Road, Croydon CR0 2NF
e-mail: info@warehousetheatre.co.uk
Fax: 020-8688 6699   Tel: 020-8681 1257

WARWICK John EVENTS
37 Great Russell St, Russell Hse, WC1B 3PP
Website: www.jwevents.co.uk
e-mail: info@jweventsltd.co.uk
Fax: 020-7436 3354   Tel: 020-7436 3355

WAVE ENTERTAINMENT Ltd
308 Desborough Avenue, High Wycombe
Buckinghamshire HP11 2TJ
Website: www.wave-entertainment.co.uk
e-mail: paul@wave-entertainment.co.uk
Mobile: 07736 309290   Tel/Fax: 0870 7606263

WAX Kenneth H Ltd
The Penthouse, 7 Leicester Place, London WC2H 7RJ
Fax: 020-7734 7185   Tel: 020-7734 7184

WEAVER-HUGHES ENSEMBLE
12B Carholme Road, London SE23 2HS
Website: www.weaverhughensemble.co.uk
e-mail: ensemble@weaverhughesensemble.co.uk
                    Tel/Fax: 020-8291 0514

WHITALL Keith
10 Woodlands Avenue, West Byfleet
Surrey KT14 6AT   Tel: 01932 343655

WHITE Michael
48 Dean Street, London W1D 5BF
e-mail: contact@michaelwhite.co.uk
Fax: 020-7734 7727   Tel: 020-7734 7707

WILDCARD THEATRE COMPANY
PO Box 267, High Wycombe
Buckinghamshire HP11 2WB
Website: www.wildcardtheatre.org.uk
e-mail: admin@wildcardtheatre.org.uk
Fax: 07092 024967   Tel: 01494 439375

WILLIAMS Anthony PRODUCTIONS Ltd
Unit 4, The Studio, Throstle Mill, Bacup
Lancashire OL13 0AY
Website: www.awproductions.co.uk
e-mail: info@awproductions.co.uk
Fax: 01706 871729   Tel: 01706 871720

WILLIAMSON R J COMPANY Ltd
8 Adelaide Grove, London W12 0JJ
Website: www.openairshakespeare.co.uk
e-mail: robert@openairshakespeare.co.uk
                    Tel/Fax: 020-8749 4427

WILLS Newton MANAGEMENT
The Studio, 29 Springvale Avenue
Brentford, Middx TW8 9QH
e-mail: newtoncttg@aol.com
Fax: 00 33 2418 23108   Mobile: 07989 398381

WINGATE Olivia PRODUCTIONS Ltd
68 Delancey Street, London NW1 7RY
e-mail: info@owproductions.co.uk
                    Tel/Fax: 020-7485 1861

WISHBONE
40 Pilgrims' Cloisters, 116 Sedgmoor Pl, SE5 7RQ
Website: www.wishbonetheatre.org.uk
e-mail: karen@wishbonetheatre.org.uk
                    Tel/Fax: 020-7708 2897

WIZARD PRESENTS
2 Lord Hills Road, London W2 6PD
e-mail: info@wizardpresents.co.uk
Fax: 020-7286 7377   Tel: 020-7286 7277

WOOD Kevin PRODUCTIONS
5 Archery Square, Walmer, Deal, Kent CT14 7JA
e-mail: kevin.wood.organisation@dial.pipex.com
Fax: 01304 381192   Tel: 01304 365515

WRESTLING SCHOOL The
(The Howard Baker Company)
42 Durlston Road London E5 8RR
Website: www.members.aol.com/wrestles
                    Tel/Fax: 020-8442 4229

X-PRODUCTIONS AT THE SHAW THEATRE
Novotel Euston London Hotel
100-110 Euston Road, London NW1 2AJ
Website: www.shawtheatre.com
e-mail: nina@shawhteatre.com
Tel: 020-7383 4887 (Hire)   Tel: 020-7387 6864 (BO)

YELLOW EARTH THEATRE
Diorama Arts Centre, 34 Osnaburgh Street
London NW1 3ND
Website: www.yellowearth.org
e-mail: admin@yellowearth.org
Fax: 020-7209 2327   Tel: 020-7209 2326

YOUNG VIC
66 The Cut, London SE1 8LZ
Website: www.youngvic.org
e-mail: info@youngvic.org
Fax: 020-7922 8401   Tel: 020-7922 8400

291

7:84 THEATRE COMPANY (SCOTLAND) Ltd
333 Woodlands Road, Glasgow G3 6NG
Website: www.784theatre.com
e-mail: admin@784theatre.com
Fax: 0141-334 3369   Tel: 0141-334 6686

ABERYSTWYTH ARTS CENTRE
Penglais, Aberystwyth, Ceredigion SY23 3DE
Website: www.aber.ac.uk/artscentre
e-mail: lla@aber.ac.uk
Fax: 01970 622883   Tel: 01970 622882

ACTORCLUB Ltd
17 Inkerman Road
London NW5 3BT   Tel: 020-7267 2759

AGE EXCHANGE THEATRE TRUST
The Reminiscence Centre, 11 Blackheath Village
London SE3 9LA
Website: www.age-exchange.org.uk
e-mail: administrator@age-exchange.org.uk
Fax: 020-8318 0060   Tel: 020-8318 9105

ALTERNATIVE ARTS
Top Studio, Bethnal Green Training Centre
Deal Street, London E1 5HZ
Website: www.alternative arts.co.uk
e-mail: info@alternativearts.co.uk
Fax: 020-7375 0484   Tel: 020-7375 0441

ANGLES THEATRE The
Alexandra Road
Wisbech, Cambridgeshire PE13 1HQ
Fax: 01945 481768   Tel: 01945 585587

ASHCROFT YOUTH THEATRE
Ashcroft Academy of Dramatic Art, The Studio
28 Beckenham Road, Beckenham, Kent BR3 4LS
Website: www.ashcroftacademy.co.uk
                  Tel/Fax: 020-8693 8088

ASHTON GROUP CONTEMPORARY THEATRE The
Old Fire Station, Abbey Road,
Barrow-in-Furness, Cumbria LA14 1XH
Website: www.ashtongroup.co.uk
e-mail: admin@ashtongroup.co.uk
                  Tel/Fax: 01229 430636

ATTIC THEATRE COMPANY (LONDON) Ltd
Wimbledon Theatre, The Broadway
London SW19 1QG
Website: www.attictheatre.com
e-mail: info@attictheatre.com
                  Tel/Fax: 020-8543 7838

BADAC THEATRE COMPANY
6 Hornbeam House, Hornbeam
Buckhurst Hill, Essex IG9 6JU
Website: www.badactheatre.com
e-mail: steve@badactheatre.com
                  Tel: 020-8505 3775

BANNER THEATRE
Friends Institute, 220 Moseley Road, Highgate
Birmingham B12 0DG
e-mail: voices@btinternet.com
Fax: 0121-440 0459   Tel: 0121-440 0460

BECK THEATRE
Grange Road, Hayes
Middlesex UB3 2UE   Tel: 020-8561 7506

BLUNDERBUS THEATRE COMPANY Ltd
The Mick Jagger Centre, Shepherds Lane
Dartford DA1 2JZ
Website: www.blunderbus.co.uk
e-mail: admin@blunderbus.co.uk
Fax: 01322 286285   Tel: 01322 286284

BORDERLINE THEATRE COMPANY
North Harbour Street, Ayr KA8 8AA
Fax: 01292 263825   Tel: 01292 281010

BRAVE NEW WORLD THEATRE COMPANY
Second Floor, 79 Highbury Hill, London N5 1SX
e-mail: spencer.hinton@virgin.net

BRITISH ASIAN THEATRE COMPANY
Star Studios, 36 Leabridge Road
London E5 9QD   Tel: 020-8986 4470

BRUVVERS THEATRE COMPANY
(Touring on Tyneside)
The Fun Palace, 36 Lime Street
Newcastle upon Tyne NE1 2PQ
Website: www.thefunplace.co.uk
e-mail: mikeofbruvvers@hotmail.com
                  Tel: 0191-261 9230

CAPITAL ARTS YOUTH THEATRE
Wyllyotts Centre, Darkes Lane, Potters Bar
Hertfordshire EN6 2HN
e-mail: capitalartstheatre@o2.co.uk
Mobile: 07885 232414   Tel/Fax: 020-8449 2342

CARIB THEATRE COMPANY
73 Lancelot Road, Wembley, Middlesex HA0 2AN
e-mail: caribtheatre@aol.com
                  Tel/Fax: 020-8795 0576

CAUGHT IN THE ACT
The Brix, Brixton Hill, London SW2 1JF
Website: www.caughtintheact.co.uk
e-mail: cita@caughtintheact.co.uk
                  Tel/Fax: 020-7733 2950

CAVALCADE THEATRE COMPANY
Write: (Touring Shows - Musicals, Pantomimes,
Music Hall Comedy & Rock 'n' Roll)
57 Pelham Road, London SW19 1NW
Fax: 020-8540 3513

CENTRE FOR PERFORMANCE RESEARCH
6 Science Park, Aberystwyth SY23 3AH
Website: www.thecpr.org.uk
e-mail: cprwww@aber.ac.uk
Fax: 01970 622132   Tel: 01970 622133

CHALKFOOT THEATRE ARTS
Central Studios, 36 Park Place
Margate, Kent CT9 1LE
Website: www.chalkfoot.org.uk
e-mail: info@chalkfoot.org.uk
Fax: 01843 280088   Tel: 01843 280077

CHANGELING The
14 The Terrace
Rochester, Kent ME1 1XN
e-mail: mail@thechangeling.com
                  Tel: 01634 831957

CHATS PALACE ARTS CENTRE
42-44 Brooksby's Walk, Hackney, London E9 6DF
Fax: 020-8985 6878   Tel: 020-8533 0227

CHERUB COMPANY LONDON The
81 The Cut, Waterloo, London SE1 8LL
Website: www.cherub.org.uk
e-mail: visnevski@cherub.org.uk
                  Tel/Fax: 020-7928 1033

CHICKEN SHED THEATRE
Chase Side, Southgate, London N14 4PE
Website: www.chickenshed.org.uk
e-mail: info@chickenshed.org.uk
Minicom: 020-8350 0676   Tel: 020-8351 6161

CIRCUS MANIACS YOUTH CIRCUS
(International Award-Winning Youth Circus
Company)
Office 8A, The Kingswood Foundation
Britannia Road, Kingswood, Bristol BS15 8DB
e-mail: youthcircus@circusmaniacs.com
Mobile: 07977 247287   Tel/Fax: 0117-947 7042

CLEAN BREAK THEATRE COMPANY
2 Patshull Road, London NW5 2LB
e-mail: general@cleanbreak.org.uk
Fax: 020-7482 8611   Tel: 020-7482 8600

CLOSE FOR COMFORT THEATRE COMPANY
34 Boleyn Walk, Leatherhead, Surrey KT22 7HU
Website: www.hometown.aol.com/close4comf
e-mail: close4comf@aol.com   Tel: 01372 378613

COLLUSION THEATRE COMPANY
Millworks, Field Road, Busby, Glasgow G76 8SE
Website: www.collusiontheatre.co.uk
e-mail: admin@collusiontheatre.co.uk
Fax: 0141-644 4163   Tel: 0141-644 0163

COMPANY OF CRANKS The
1st Floor, 62 Northfield House
Frensham Street, London SE15 6TN
e-mail: mimetic@freeuk.com   Tel: 020-7358 0571

COMPLETE WORKS THEATRE COMPANY Ltd The
12 Willowford, Bancroft Park, Milton Keynes
Buckinghamshire MK13 0RH
Website: www.tcw.org.uk
e-mail: info@tcw.org.uk
Fax: 01908 320263   Tel: 01908 316256

CORNELIUS & JONES ORIGINAL PRODUCTIONS
49 Carters Close, Sherington, Newport Pagnell
Buckinghamshire MK16 9NW
Website: www.corneliusjones.com
e-mail: admin@corneliusjones.com
Fax: 01908 216400   Tel: 01908 612593

CRAGRATS Ltd
The Mill, Dunford Road, Holmfirth
Huddersfield HD9 2AR
Website: www.cragrats.com
e-mail: alex@cragrats.com
Fax: 01484 686212   Tel: 01484 686451

CTC THEATRE
Arts Centre, Vane Terrace, Darlington
County Durham DL3 7AX
Website: www.ctctheatre.org.uk
e-mail: ctc@ctctheatre.org.uk
Fax: 01325 369404   Tel: 01325 352004

CUT-CLOTH THEATRE
41 Beresford Road
London N5 2HR   Tel: 020-7503 4393

ELAN WALES
(European Live Arts Network)
17 Douglas Buildings, Royal Stuart Lane
Cardiff CF10 5EL
Website: www.elanw.demon.co.uk
e-mail: info@elan-wales.fsnet.co.uk
          Tel/Fax: 029-2019 0077

EMPTY SPACE THEATRE COMPANY
32 Kenbrook House, Leighton Road
London NW5 2QN
e-mail: estc@dircon.co.uk
Fax: 0870 9090103   Tel: 0870 9090102

EUROPEAN THEATRE COMPANY The
39 Oxford Avenue, London SW20 8LS
Website: www.europeantheatre.co.uk
e-mail: admin@europeantheatre.co.uk
Fax: 020-8544 1999   Tel: 020-8544 1994

FAMILY CURIOSO THEATRE COMPANY
100 Shaftesbury Road, London N19 4QR
Website: www.familycurioso.co.uk
e-mail: mail@familycurioso.co.uk
          Tel: 020-7281 5783

FOREST FORGE THEATRE COMPANY
The Theatre Centre, Endeavour Park
Crow Arch Lane, Ringwood, Hampshire BH24 1SF
e-mail: theatre@forestforge.demon.co.uk
Fax: 01425 471158   Tel: 01425 470188

FOURSIGHT THEATRE Ltd
Newhampton Arts Centre, Dunkley Street
Wolverhampton WV1 4AN
Website: www.foursight.theatre.boltblue.net
e-mail: foursight.theatre@boltblue.net
Fax: 01902 428413   Tel: 01902 714257

FRANTIC THEATRE COMPANY
32 Woodlane, Falmouth TR11 4RF
Website: www.frantictheatre.com
e-mail: info@frantictheatre.com
          Tel/Fax: 01326 312985

FUTURES THEATRE COMPANY
Room 10, The Deptford Albany, Douglas Way
London SE8 4AG
e-mail: futures_theatre@btconnect.com
Fax: 020-8694 0289   Tel: 020-8694 8655

GALLEON THEATRE COMPANY Ltd
Greenwich Playhouse, Greenwich BR Station
Forecourt, 189 Greenwich High Road
London SE10 8JA
Website: www.galleontheatre.co.uk
Fax: 020-8969 2910   Tel: 020-8858 9256

GRANGE ARTS CENTRE
Rochdale Road, Oldham
Greater Manchester OL9 6EA
e-mail: joanne.draper@oldham.ac.uk
Fax: 0161-785 4263   Tel: 0161-785 4239

GREASEPAINT ANONYMOUS
4 Gallus Close, Winchmore Hill, London N21 1JR
e-mail: info@greasepaintanonymous.co.uk
Fax: 020-8882 9189   Tel: 020-8886 2263

GREENWICH & LEWISHAM'S YOUNG PEOPLES THEATRE (GYPT)
Burrage Road, London SE18 7JZ
e-mail: postbox@gypt.co.uk
Fax: 020-8317 8595   Tel: 020-8854 1316

HACKNEY YOUNG PEOPLE'S YOUTH THEATRE
Hoxton Hall Theatre & Arts Centre
130 Hoxton Street, London N1 6SH
Website: www.hoxtonhall.co.uk
e-mail: office@hoxtonhall.co.uk
Fax: 020-7729 3815   Tel: 020-7684 0060

HALF MOON YOUNG PEOPLE'S THEATRE
43 White Horse Road, London E1 0ND
Website: www.halfmoon.org.uk
e-mail: admin@halfmoon.org.uk
Fax: 020-7709 8914   Tel: 020-7265 8138

HIJINX THEATRE
(Adults with Learning Disabilities, Community)
Bay Chambers, West Bute Street
Cardiff Bay CF10 5BB
Website: www.hijinx.org.uk
e-mail: info@hijinx.org.uk
Fax: 029-2030 0332   Tel: 029-2030 0331

HISTORIA THEATRE COMPANY
8 Cloudesley Square, London N1 0HT
e-mail: kateprice@lineone.net
Fax: 020-7278 4733   Tel: 020-7837 8008

HORLA
The Rose & Crown Theatre
59-61 High Street, Hampton Wick, Surrey KT1 4DG
Website: www.horla.co.uk
e-mail: info@horla.co.uk   Tel/Fax: 020-8296 0242

ICON THEATRE
66 Borthwick Road, London E15 1UE
e-mail: sally@icontheatre.org.uk   Tel: 020-8534 0618

IMAGE MUSICAL THEATRE
23 Sedgeford Road, Shepherd's Bush
London W12 0NA
Website: www.imagemusicaltheatre.co.uk
e-mail: brian@image-theatre-co.demon.co.uk
Fax: 020-8749 9294   Tel: 020-8743 9380

IMMEDIATE THEATRE
Unit C2/62 Beechwood Road, London E8 3DY
e-mail: immediatejo@aol.com
Fax: 020-7683 0247   Tel: 020-7683 0233

IN TOTO PRODUCTIONS
Basement Flat
7 Montpelier Villas, Brighton BN1 3DH
e-mail: admin@intoto.freeserve.co.uk
Tel/Fax: 01273 205863

INOCENTE ART & FILM Ltd
(Film, Multimedia, Music Videos & two Rock 'n Roll
Musicals)
5 Denmans Lane
Haywards Heath, Sussex RH16 2LA
e-mail: tarascas@btinternet.com
Mobile: 07973 518132

ISOSCELES COMEDY COMPANY
7 Amity Grove, Raynes Park, London SW20 0LQ
Website: www.isosceles.freeserve.co.uk
e-mail: patanddave@isosceles.freeserve.co.uk
Tel: 020-8946 3905

KOMEDIA
44-47 Gardner Street, Brighton BN1 1UN
Website: www.komedia.co.uk
e-mail: info@komedia.co.uk
Fax: 01273 647102   Tel: 01273 647101

LADDER TO THE MOON ENTERTAINMENT
66A St Ann's Hill, London SW18 2SB
e-mail: enquiries@laddertothemoon.co.uk
Mobile: 07711 984378

LATCHMERE THEATRE
(Chris Fisher)
Unit 5A, Imex Business Centre, Ingate Place
London SW8 3NS
e-mail: fisher.falcon@zen.co.uk
Fax: 020-7978 2631   Tel: 020-7978 2620

LEIGHTON BUZZARD YOUTH THEATRE
1 Clifford Avenue, Bletchley
Milton Keynes MK2 2LT
e-mail: andycllr@aol.com
Mobile: 07736 520930   Tel: 01908 3742223

LITTLE ACTORS THEATRE COMPANY
12 Hardy Close, Surrey Quays, London SE16 6RT
e-mail: littleactorstheatrecompany@hotmail.com
Fax: 0870 1645895   Tel: 020-7231 6083

LIVE THEATRE
(New Writing)
7-8 Trinity Chare, Quayside
Newcastle upon Tyne NE1 3DF
Website: www.live.org.uk
e-mail: info@live.org.uk
Fax: 0191-232 2224   Tel: 0191-261 2694

LOGOS THEATRE COMPANY
48 Taybridge Road
London SW11 5PT   Tel: 020-7228 4374

LONDON ACTORS THEATRE COMPANY
Unit 5A, Imex Business Centre
Ingate Place, London SW8 3NS
e-mail: fisher.falcon@zen.co.uk
Fax: 020-7978 2631   Tel: 020-7978 2620

LONDON BUBBLE THEATRE COMPANY Ltd
5 Elephant Lane, London SE16 4JD
Website: www.londonbubble.org.uk
e-mail: admin@londonbubble.org.uk
Fax: 020-7231 2366   Tel: 020-7237 4434

LSW: JUNIOR INTER-ACT
181A Faunce House, Doddington Grove
London SE17 3TB
Website: www.londonshakespeare.org.uk
e-mail: londonswo@hotmail.com
Fax: 020-7735 5911   Tel: 020-7793 9755

LSW: PRISON PROJECT
181A Faunce House
Doddington Grove, Kennington, London SE17 3TB
Website: www.londonshakespeare.org.uk
e-mail: londonswo@hotmail.com
Fax: 020-7735 5911   Tel: 020-7793 9755

LSW: SENIOR RE-ACTION
181A Faunce House, Doddington Grove
London SE17 3TB
Website: www.londonshakespeare.org.uk
e-mail: londonswo@hotmail.com
Fax: 020-7735 5911   Tel: 020-7793 9755

LUNG HAS THEATRE COMPANY
Central Hall, West Tollcross, Edinburgh EH3 9BP
e-mail: info@lunghas.co.uk
Fax: 0131-229 8965   Tel: 0131-228 8998

M6 THEATRE COMPANY
Hamer CP School, Albert Royds Street
Rochdale OL16 2SU
e-mail: info@m6theatre.co.uk
Fax: 01706 711700   Tel: 01706 355898

MADDERMARKET THEATRE
(Resident Community Theatre Company &
Small-Scale Producing & Receiving House)
St John's Alley, Norwich NR2 1DR
Website: www.maddermarket.co.uk
e-mail: theatre@maddermarket.co.uk
Fax: 01603 661357   Tel: 01603 626560

MAN MELA THEATRE COMPANY
(Admin Contact: Caroline Goffin)
PO Box 24987, London SE23 3XS
Website: www.man-mela.dircon.co.uk
e-mail: man-mela@dircon.co.uk
Mobile: 07973 349101   Mobile: 07966 215090

MANCHESTER ACTORS COMPANY
PO BOX 54, Manchester M60 7AB
Website: manactors@cs.com
e-mail: stephenboyes@amserve.net
Tel: 0161-227 8702

MAYA PRODUCTIONS Ltd
156 Richmond Road, London E8 3HN
e-mail: mayachris@aol.com   Tel/Fax: 020-7923 0675

**MERSEYSIDE YOUNG PEOPLE'S
THEATRE COMPANY**
13 Hope Street, Liverpool L1 9BH
e-mail: mail@mypt.co.uk   Tel/Fax: 0151-708 0877

MIKRON THEATRE COMPANY Ltd
(Canal Touring Nationally)
Marsden Mechanics
Peel Street, Marsden, Huddersfield HD7 6BW
Website: www.mikron.org.uk
e-mail: admin@mikron.org.uk   Tel: 01484 843701

MONTAGE THEATRE
(Director Judy Gordon)
59 Embleton Road, London SE13 7DQ
Website: www.montagetheatre.com
e-mail: info@montagetheatre.com
Tel: 020-8314 5036

MOVING THEATRE
16 Laughton Lodge
Laughton, Nr Lewes
East Sussex BN8 6BY
Website: www.movingtheatre.com
e-mail: info@movingtheatre.com
Fax: 01323 815736   Tel: 01323 815726

MUZIKANSKY YOUTH & COMMUNITY
The Forum, Fonthill
The Common, Tunbridge Wells
Kent TN4 9NQ
Website: www.mzky.co.uk
e-mail: admin@mzky.co.uk   Tel/Fax: 01892 542260

NATIONAL ASSOCIATION OF YOUTH THEATRES (NAYT)
Arts Centre, Vane Terrace, Darlington
County Durham DL3 7AX
Website: www.nayt.org.uk
e-mail: naytuk@aol.com
Fax: 01325 363313   Tel: 01325 363330

NATIONAL STUDENT THEATRE COMPANY
20 Lansdowne Road
London N10 2AU
Website: www.studentdrama.org.uk/nstc
e-mail: clive@nsdf.org.uk
Fax: 020-8883 7142   Tel: 020-8883 4586

NATIONAL YOUTH MUSIC THEATRE
5th Floor, The Palace Theatre
Shaftesbury Avenue, London W1D 5AY
Website: www.nymt.org.uk
e-mail: enquiries@nymt.org.uk
Fax: 020-7734 7515   Tel: 020-7734 7478

NATIONAL YOUTH THEATRE OF GREAT BRITAIN
443-445 Holloway Road, London N7 6LW
Website: www.nyt.org.uk
e-mail: info@nyt.org.uk
Fax: 020-7281 8246   Tel: 020-7281 3863

NATURAL THEATRE COMPANY
Widcombe Institute
Widcombe Hill, Bath BA2 6AA
Website: www.naturaltheatre.co.uk
e-mail: info@naturaltheatre.co.uk
Fax: 01225 442555   Tel: 01225 469131

NETI-NETI THEATRE COMPANY
Whitefield School, Claremont Road
London NW2 1TR   Tel/Fax: 020-8881 9336

NETTLEFOLD The
West Norwood Library Centre
1 Norwood High Street
London SE27 9JX
Fax: 020-7926 8071   Tel: 020-7926 8070

NEW PECKHAM VARIETIES@MAGIC EYE THEATRE
Havil Street, London SE5 7SD
e-mail: npv-arts@easynet.co.uk   Tel: 020-7708 5401

NEW PERSPECTIVES THEATRE COMPANY
(Touring & Community Theatre Projects)
The Old Library, Leeming Street, Mansfield
Nottinghamshire NG18 1NG
Website: www.newperspectives.co.uk
e-mail: info@newperspectives.co.uk
Tel: 01623 635225

NORTHERN STAGE THEATRICAL PRODUCTIONS Ltd
Newcastle Playhouse, Barras Bridge, Haymarket
Newcastle upon Tyne NE1 7RH
Website: www.northernstage.com
e-mail: info@northernstage.com
Fax: 0191-261 8093   Tel: 0191-232 3366

NTC TOURING THEATRE COMPANY
(Touring Regionally & Nationally)
The Playhouse, Bondgate Without, Alnwick
Northumberland NE66 1PQ
Website: www.ntc-touringtheatre.co.uk
e-mail: admin@ntc-touringtheatre.co.uk
Fax: 01665 605837   Tel: 01665 602586

NUFFIELD THEATRE
(Touring & Projects)
University Road, Southampton SO17 1TR
e-mail: theatrefirst@nuffieldtheatre.co.uk
Fax: 023-8031 5511   Tel: 023-8034 4515

OLD TYME PLAYERS The
140 Manor Road, New Milton, Hampshire BH25 5ED
Website: www.fliteuk.com
e-mail: fliteuk@hotmail.com   Tel: 01425 612830

ONATTI THEATRE COMPANY
9 Field Close, Warwick, Warwickshire CV34 4QD
Website: www.onatti.co.uk
e-mail: info@onatti.co.uk
Fax: 0870 1643629   Tel: 01926 495220

OPEN STAGE PRODUCTIONS
49 Springfield Road, Moseley
Birmingham B13 9NN   Tel/Fax: 0121-777 9086

OXFORDSHIRE TOURING THEATRE COMPANY
Isis C of E Middle School
Meadow Lane, Oxford OX4 1JJ
Website: www.ottc.org.uk
e-mail: manager@ottc.oxfordshire.co.uk
Tel: 01865 249444

PANDEMONIUM TOURING PARTNERSHIP
228 Railway Street
Cardiff CF24 2NJ   Tel: 029-2047 2060

PASCAL THEATRE COMPANY
35 Flaxman Court, Flaxman Terrace, Bloomsbury
London WC1H 9AR
Website: www.pascal-theatre.com
e-mail: pascaltheatreco@aol.com
Fax: 020-7419 9798   Tel: 020-7383 0920

PAUL'S THEATRE COMPANY
Fairkytes Arts Centre
51 Billet Lane, Hornchurch, Essex RM11 1AX
e-mail: paul@the-theatreschool.fsnt.co.uk
Fax: 01708 475286   Tel: 01708 447123

PEOPLE'S THEATRE COMPANY The
12E High Street, Egham, Surrey TW20 9EA
Website: www.ptc.org.uk
e-mail: admin@ptc.org.uk   Tel: 01784 470439

PERFORMANCE PROJECT The
32 Kenbrook House, Leighton Road
London NW5 2QN   Tel: 020-7482 1850

PHANTOM CAPTAIN The
618B Finchley Road, London NW11 7RR
Website: www.phantomcaptain.netfirms.com
e-mail: ziph@macunlimited.net
Tel/Fax: 020-8455 4564

PIED PIPER COMPANY (TIE)
(In association with The Yvonne Arnaud
Theatre Guildford)
1 Lilian Place
Coxcombe Lane, Chiddingfold, Surrey GU8 4QA
e-mail: twpiedpiper@aol.com
Tel/Fax: 01428 684022

PILOT THEATRE COMPNAY
Production Office: c/o York Theatre Royal
St Leonards Place, York YO1 7HD
Website: www.pilot-theatre.com
e-mail: info@pilot-theatre.com
Fax: 01904 656378   Tel: 01904 635755

PLAYTIME THEATRE COMPANY
18 Bennells Avenue, Whitstable, Kent CT5 2HP
Website: www.playtime.dircon.co.uk
e-mail: playtime@dircon.co.uk
Fax: 01227 266648   Tel: 01227 266272

PRAXIS THEATRE COMPANY Ltd
24 Wykeham Road, London NW4 2SU
e-mail: praxisco@globalnet.com
                    Tel/Fax: 020-8203 1916

PRIME PRODUCTIONS
54 Hermiston Village, Currie EH14 4AQ
Website: www.primeproductions.co.uk
e-mail: mheller@primeproductions.fsnet.co.uk
                    Tel/Fax: 0131-449 4055

PROTEUS THEATRE COMPANY
Queen Mary's College, Cliddesden Road
Basingstoke, Hampshire RG21 3HF
Website: www.proteustheatre.com
e-mail: info@proteustheatre.com
                    Tel: 01256 354541

PURSUED BY A BEAR PRODUCTIONS
6 Glenluce Road, Blackheath, London SE3 7SB
Website: www.pbab.org
e-mail: pbab@pbab.org   Tel/Fax: 020-8480 9514

Q20 THEATRE COMPANY
19 Wellington Crescent, Shipley
West Yorkshire BD18 3PH
e-mail: info@q20theatre.co.uk   Tel: 0845 1260632

QUAKER YOUTH THEATRE
Ground Floor, 1 The Lodge, 1046 Bristol Road
Birmingham B29 6LJ
Website: www.leaveners.org
e-mail: qyt@leaveners.org
Fax: 0121-414 0090   Tel: 0121-414 0099

QUANTUM THEATRE FOR SCIENCE
The Old Button Factory, 1-11 Bannockburn Road
Plumstead, London SE18 1ET
Website: www.quantumtheatre.co.uk
e-mail: quantumtheatre@btinternet.com
                    Tel: 020-8317 9000

QUEST THEATRE COMPANY
(Artistic Director David Craik)
3C Mecklenburgh Street, Bloomsbury
London WC1N 2AH   Tel/Fax: 020-7713 0342

QUICKSILVER THEATRE
The Glasshouse, 4 Enfield Road, London N1 5AZ
Website: www.quicksilvertheatre.org
e-mail: talktous@quicksilvertheatre.org
Fax: 020-7254 3119   Tel: 020-7241 2942

RED LADDER THEATRE COMPANY Ltd
3 St Peter's Buildings, York Street, Leeds LS9 8AJ
Website: www.redladder.co.uk
e-mail: wendy@redladder.co.uk
Fax: 0113-245 5351   Tel: 0113-245 5311

RIDING LIGHTS THEATRE COMPANY
Friargate Theatre, Lower Friargate, York YO1 9SL
Website: www.ridinglights.org
e-mail: info@rltc.org
Fax: 01904 651532   Tel: 01904 655317

ROSE THEATRE COMPANY The
10 Riverside Forest Row, East Sussex RH18 5HB
e-mail: dan.skinner@btinternet.com
                    Tel: 01342 825639

ROYAL COURT YOUNG WRITERS PROGRAMME
The Site, Royal Court Theatre, Sloane Square
London SW1W 8AS
Website: www.royalcourttheatre.com
e-mail: ywp@royalcourttheatre.com
Fax: 020-7565 5001   Tel: 020-7565 5050

SALTMINE THEATRE COMPANY
St James House
Trinity Road, Dudley
West Midlands DY1 1JB
Website: www.saltmine.org
e-mail: stc@saltmine.org   Tel: 01384 454807

SCARLET THEATRE
Studio 4, The Bull, 68 High Street, Barnet
Hertfordshire EN5 5SJ
Website: www.scarlettheatre.co.uk
e-mail: admin@scarlettheatre.co.uk
Fax: 020-8447 0075   Tel: 020-8441 9779

SCOTTISH YOUTH THEATRE
Third Floor, Forsyth House, 111 Union Street
Glasgow G1 3TA
Website: www.scottishyouththeatre.org
e-mail: info@scottishyouththeatre.org
Fax: 0141-221 9123   Tel: 0141-221 5127

SGRIPT CYMRU
CONTEMPORARY DRAMA WALES
Chapter, Market Road, Canton, Cardiff CF5 1QE
Website: www.sgriptcymru.com
e-mail: sgriptcymru@sgriptcymru.com
Fax: 08712 421481   Tel: 029-2023 6650

SHARED EXPERIENCE YOUTH THEATRE
The Soho Laundry, 9 Dufours Pl, London W1F 7SJ
e-mail: youththeatre@setheatre.com
Fax: 020-7287 8763   Tel: 020-7434 9248

SKINNING THE CAT, CIRCUS OF THE SKY
163 Washington Street
Girlington, Bradford BD8 9QP
Website: www.skinningthecat.com
e-mail: skats@globalnet.co.uk   Tel: 01274 770300

SNAP THEATRE COMPANY
29 Raynham Road, Bishops Stortford
Hertfordshire CM23 5PE
Website: www.snaptheatre.co.uk
Fax: 01279 506694   Tel: 01279 461607

SPANNER IN THE WORKS
155 Station Road, Sidcup, Kent DA15 7AA
Website: members.netscapeonline.co.uk/spintheworks
e-mail: rapieruk@aol.com   Tel: 020-8304 7660

SPARE TYRE THEATRE COMPANY
(Community Drama & Music Projects)
Hampstead Town Hall, 213 Haverstock Hill
London NW3 4QP   Tel: 020-7419 7007

SPECTACLE THEATRE
Coleg Morgannwg, Rhondda Campus
Llwynypia, Tonypandy CF40 2TQ
Website: www.spectacletheatre.co.uk
e-mail: info@spectacletheatre.co.uk
Fax: 01443 423080   Tel: 01443 430700

SPRINGBOARD THEATRE COMPANY
20 Lansdowne Road, London N10 2AU
e-mail: clive@nsdf.org.uk   Tel: 020-8883 4586

TAG THEATRE COMPANY
18 Albion Street, Glasgow G1 1LH
Website: www.tag-theatre.co.uk
e-mail: info@tag-theatre.co.uk
Fax: 0141-552 0666   Tel: 0141-552 4949

TARA ARTS GROUP
356 Garratt Lane, London SW18 4ES
Fax: 020-8870 9540   Tel: 020-8333 4457

THEATR NA N'OG
Unit 3, Milland Road Industrial Estate, Neath
West Glamorgan SA11 1NJ
Website: www.theatr-nanog.co.uk
e-mail: cwmni@theatr-nanog.co.uk
Fax: 01639 647941   Tel: 01639 641771

THEATR POWYS
The Drama Centre, Tremont Road
Llandrindod Wells, Powys LD1 5EB
Website: www.theatrpowys.co.uk
e-mail: theatr.powys@powys.gov.uk
Fax: 01597 824381   Tel: 01597 824444

THEATRE BABEL
11 Sandyford Place, Glasgow G3 7NB
Website: wwwtheatrebabel.co.uk
e-mail: admin@theatrebabel.co.uk
Fax: 0141-249 9900   Tel: 0141-226 8806

THEATRE CENTRE
(National Touring & New Writing for Young
Audiences)
Units 7 & 8, Toynbee Workshops
3 Gunthorpe Street, London E1 7RQ
Website: www.theatre-centre.co.uk
e-mail: admin@theatre-centre.co.uk
Fax: 020-7377 1376   Tel: 020-7377 0379

THEATRE EXPRESS
(Write)
PO Box 97, Cleveleys FY5 5XA
e-mail: perform@theatre-express.com

THEATRE IN EDUCATION TOURS (TIE TOURS)
Holloway School
Hilldrop Road, Islington, London N7 0JG
Website: www.tietours.com
e-mail: tie@tietours.com
Fax: 020-7700 3697   Tel: 020-7354 4067

THEATRE OF LITERATURE The
(Dramatised Readings)
51 The Cut, London SE1 8LF
e-mail: info@calderpublications.com
Fax: 020-7928 5930   Tel: 020-7633 0599

THEATRE RE:PUBLIC
1 Mellor Road, Leicester LE3 6HN
e-mail: theatrerepublic@hotmail.com
                           Tel: 0116-233 8432

THEATRE WORKSHOP
34 Hamilton Place, Edinburgh EH3 5AX
Website: www.theatre-workshop.com
Fax: 0131-220 0112   Tel: 0131-225 7942

THEATRE WORKSHOP Ltd
18 Weston Lane, Crewe, Cheshire CW2 5AN
Website: www.theatreworkshop.co.uk
e-mail: tw4kids@globalnet.co.uk
Fax: 07020 982098   Tel: 07020 962096

THIRD PARTY PRODUCTIONS Ltd
87 St Thomas' Road
Hastings, East Sussex TN34 3LD
Website: www.thirdparty.demon.co.uk
e-mail: agleave@thirdparty.demon.co.uk
                           Tel: 01424 719320

TIME OF OUR LIVES MUSIC THEATRE Ltd
(Formerly Gilt & Gaslight Music Theatre Ltd)
5 Monkhams Drive
Woodford Green, Essex IG8 0LG
Website: www.toolmusictheatre.co.uk
e-mail: dympna@toolmusictheatre.co.uk
                           Tel/Fax: 020-8491 6695

TITHE BARN MUSIC & DRAMA SOCIETY
Shiplake College
Henley-on-Thames RG9 4BW
Website: www.shiplake.org.uk
e-mail: tithe@shiplake.org.uk   Tel: 0118-940 2455

TOBACCO FACTORY
Raleigh Road, Southville, Bristol BS3 1TF
Website: www.tobaccofactory.com
e-mail: admin@tobaccofactory.com
Fax: 0117-902 0162   Tel: 0117-902 0345

TRICYCLE THEATRE
269 Kilburn High Road
London NW6 7JR
Website: www.tricycle.co.uk
e-mail: admin@tricycle.co.uk
Fax: 020-7328 0795   Tel: 020-7372 6611

WAREHOUSE THEATRE COMPANY
Dingwall Road,
Croydon CR0 2NF
Website: www.warehousetheatre.co.uk
e-mail: info@warehousetheatre.co.uk
Fax: 020-8688 6699   Tel: 020-8681 1257

WIGAN PIER THEATRE COMPANY
The 'Way We Were' Museum
Wigan Pier
Trencherfield Mill, Wigan
Lancashire WN3 3JQ
Website: www.wiganpier.net
e-mail: s.aitken@wlct.org   Tel: 01942 709305

WINCHESTER HAT FAIR
FESTIVAL OF STREET THEATRE
5A Jewry Street
Winchester
Hampshire SO23 8RZ
Website: www.hatfair.co.uk
e-mail: info@hatfair.co.uk
Fax: 01962 868957   Tel: 01962 849841

WOMEN & THEATRE BIRMINGHAM Ltd
220 Moseley Road
Highgate
Birmingham B12 0DG
e-mail: womenandtheatre@btinternet.com
Fax: 0121-446 4280   Tel: 0121-440 4203

Y TOURING THEATRE COMPANY
8-10 Lennox Road
Finsbury Park
London N4 3JQ
Website: www.ytouring.org.uk
e-mail: d.jackson@ytouring.org.uk
Fax: 020-7272 8413   Tel: 020-7272 5755

YELLOW EARTH THEATRE
Diorama Arts Centre
34 Osnaburgh Street
London NW1 3ND
Website: www.yellowearth.org
e-mail: admin@yellowearth.org
Fax: 020-7209 2327   Tel: 020-7209 2326

YORICK INTERNATIONALIST THEATRE ENSEMBLE
(Yorick Theatre & Film)
4 Duval Court
36 Bedfordbury
Covent Garden, London WC2N 4DQ
e-mail: yorickx@hotmail.com
                           Tel/Fax: 020-7836 7637

YORKSHIRE WOMEN'S THEATRE COMPANY
(Touring Theatre in Health Education)
Host Media Centre
21 Savile Mount, Leeds LS7 3HZ
e-mail: admin@ywtheatre.com   Tel: 0113-200 7200

YOUNG VIC
66 The Cut, London SE1 8LZ
Website: www.youngvic.org
e-mail: info@youngvic.org
Fax: 020-7922 8401   Tel: 020-7922 8400

ZIP THEATRE
Newhampton Arts Centre
Dunkley Street
Wolverhampton WV1 4AN
Website: www.ziptheatre.co.uk
e-mail: cathy@ziptheatre.co.uk
Fax: 01902 572251   Tel: 01902 572250

ARC ENTERTAINMENTS
10 Church Lane, Redmarshall, Stockton on Tees
Cleveland TS21 1EP
e-mail: cmlittlefair@fsbdial.co.uk   Tel: 0870 7418789

BAC
(Constant Workshops & Theatre on Saturdays)
Lavender Hill, Battersea, London SW11 5TF
Website: www.bac.org.uk
e-mail: mailbox@bac.org.uk
Fax: 020-7978 5207   Tel: 020-7223 6557

BARKING DOG THEATRE COMPANY
18 Hayley Bell Grdns, Bishop's Stortford, CM23 3HB
Website: www.barkingdog.co.uk
e-mail: pat@barkingdog.co.uk
Fax: 01279 465386   Tel: 01279 465550

BECK THEATRE
Grange Road, Hayes
Middlesex UB3 2UE   Tel: 020-8561 7506

BIRMINGHAM STAGE COMPANY The
Suite 228 The Linen Hall, 162 Regent St W1B 5TG
Website: www.birminghamstage.net
e-mail: info@birminghamstage.net
Fax: 020-7437 3395   Tel: 020-7437 3391

BITESIZE THEATRE COMPANY
8 Green Meadows, New Broughton
Wrexham LL11 6SG
Website: www.bitesizetheatre.co.uk
Fax: 01978 358315   Tel: 01978 358320

BLUE HAT PRODUCTIONS
43 Radwinter Rd, Essex CB11 3HU
e-mail: ksweeney@ntlworld.com
Mobile: 07811 175351   Tel: 01799 502569

BLUNDERBUS THEATRE COMPANY
The Mick Jagger Centre
Shepherds Lane, Dartford, Kent DN1 2JZ
Website: www.blunderbus.co.uk
e-mail: admin@blunderbus.co.uk
Fax: 01322 286285   Tel: 01322 286284

BOOSTER CUSHION THEATRE COMPANY
1st Floor, Building B, Chocolate Factory
Clarendon Road, London N22 6JX
e-mail: boostercushion@hotmail.com
Fax: 020-8365 8686   Tel: 020-8888 4545

DANCE FOR EVERYONE Ltd
30 Sevington Road, London NW4 3RX
Website: www.dfe.org.uk
e-mail: orders@dfe.org.uk   Tel: 020-8202 7863

DAYLIGHT THEATRE
66 Middle Street, Stroud
Gloucestershire GL5 1EA   Tel: 01453 763808

DONNA MARIA COMPANY
16 Bell Meadow, Dulwich, London SE19 1HP
Website: www.donna-marias-world.co.uk
e-mail: info@donna-marias-world.co.uk
        Tel: 020-8670 7814

DRAGON DRAMA
(Theatre Company, Tuition, Workshops, Parties)
1B Station Rd, Hampton Wick, Kingston KT1 4HG
Website: www.dragondrama.co.uk
e-mail: info@dragondrama.co.uk
        Tel/Fax: 020-8943 1504

EUROPA CLOWN THEATRE SHOW
36 St Lukes Road, Tunbridge Wells, Kent TN4 9JH
Website: www.clownseuropa.co.uk   Tel: 01892 537964

IMAGE MUSICAL THEATRE
23 Sedgeford Rd, Shepherd's Bush W12 0NA
Website: www.imagemusicaltheatre.co.uk
e-mail: brianthresh@image-theatre-co.demon.uk
Fax: 020-8749 9294   Tel: 020-8743 9380

INTERPLAY THEATRE COMPANY
Armley Ridge Road, Leeds LS12 3LE
Website: www.interplaytheatre.org
e-mail: info@interplaytheatre.org   Tel: 0113-263 8556

KOMEDIA
44-47 Gardner Street, Brighton BN1 1UN
Website: www.komedia.co.uk   e-mail: info@komedia.co.uk
Fax: 01273 647102   Tel: 01273 647101

LITTLE ACTORS THEATRE COMPANY
12 Hardy Close
Surrey Quays, London SE16 6RT
e-mail: littleactorstheatrecompany@hotmail.com
Fax: 0870 1645895   Tel: 020-7231 6083

MAGIC CARPET THEATRE
18 Church Street, Sutton-on-Hull HU7 4TS
Website: www.magiccarpettheatre.com
e-mail: admin@magiccarpettheatre.com
Fax: 01482 787362   Tel: 01482 709939

NETTLEFOLD The
The Nettlefold
West Norwood Library Centre
1 Norwood High Street, SE27 9JX
Fax: 020-7926 8071   Tel: 020-7926 8070

OILY CART COMPANY
Smallwood School Annexe, Smallwood Road
London SW17 0TW
Website: www.oilycart.org.uk
e-mail: oilies@oilycart.org.uk
Fax: 020-8672 0792   Tel: 020-8672 6329

PANDEMONIUM TOURING PARTNERSHIP
228 Railway Street
Cardiff CF24 2NJ   Tel: 029-2047 2060

PARASOL THEATRE FOR CHILDREN
Artistic Director: Richard Gill
Garden Hse, 4 Sunnyside, Wimbledon SW19 4SL
Website: www.parasoltheatre.co.uk
e-mail: parasoltheatre@waitrose.com
Fax: 020-8946 0228   Tel: 020-8946 9478

PAUL'S THEATRE COMPANY
Fairkytes Arts Centre
51 Billet Lane, Hornchurch, Essex RM11 1AX
e-mail: paul@the-theatreschool.fsnet.co.uk
Fax: 01708 475286   Tel: 01708 447123

PIED PIPER THEATRE COMPANY
(In Association with The Yvonne Arnaud Theatre
Guildford)
1 Lilian Place, Coxcombe Lane
Chiddingfold, Surrey GU8 4QA
e-mail: twpiedpiper@aol.com   Tel/Fax: 01428 684022

PLAYTIME THEATRE COMPANY
18 Bennells Avenue, Whitstable, Kent CT5 2HP
Website: www.playtime.dircon.co.uk
e-mail: playtime@dircon.co.uk
Fax: 01227 266648   Tel: 01227 266272

POLKA THEATRE FOR CHILDREN
240 The Broadway, Wimbledon
London SW19 1SB
Website: www.polkatheatre.com
e-mail: admin@polkatheatre.com
Fax: 020-8545 8365   Tel: 020-8545 8320

Q20 THEATRE COMPANY
19 Wellington Crescent, Shipley
West Yorkshire BD18 3PH
e-mail: info@q20theatre.co.uk   Tel: 0845 1260632

QUANTUM THEATRE FOR SCIENCE
The Old Button Factory, 1-11 Bannockburn Road
Plumstead, London SE18 1ET
Website: www.quantumtheatre.co.uk
e-mail: quantumtheatre@btinternet.com
        Tel: 020-8317 9000

QUERCUS THEATRE COMPANY
33 Broadlands Ave, Shepperton, Middx TW17 9DJ
Website: www.quercustheatrecompany.org.uk
e-mail: quercus@quercustheatrecompany.org.uk
        Tel: 01932 252182

QUICKSILVER THEATRE COMPANY
(National Touring - New Writing for the under 12's)
4 Enfield Road, London N1 5AZ
Website: www.quicksilvertheatre.org.uk
e-mail: talktous@quicksilvertheatre.org
Fax: 020-7254 3119   Tel: 020-7241 2942

REDROOFS THEATRE COMPANY
The Novello Theatre, Sunninghill, Nr Ascot
Berkshire SL5 9NE   Tel: 01344 620881

SCOTTISH YOUTH THEATRE
3rd Floor, Forsyth House, 111 Union Street
Glasgow G1 3TA
Website: www.scottishyouththeatre.org
e-mail: info@scottishyouththeatre.org
Fax: 0141-221 9123   Tel: 0141-221 5127

SEAGULL THEATRE OF THE GORGE Ltd
(Theatre in Education)
Artistic Directors: Margo Cooper & Sian Murray
16 Victoria Road, Much Wenlock, Salop TF13 6AL
Tel/Fax: 01952 727803

SEAHORSE THEATRE COMPANY The
Ealing House, 33 Hanger Lane, London W5 3HJ
e-mail: seahorseparties@vampevents.com
Fax: 020-8932 6169   Tel: 020-8997 3355

SHAKESPEARE 4 KIDZ THEATRE COMPANY The
42 Station Road East, Oxted, Surrey RH8 0PG
Website: www.shakespeare4kidz.com
e-mail: office@shakepeare4kidz.com
Fax: 01883 730384   Tel: 01883 723444

THE GOOD THE BAD & THE CUDDLY THEATRE COMPANY
140 Manor Road, New Milton, Hampshire BH25 5ED
Website: www.fliteuk.com
e-mail: fliteuk@hotmail.com   Tel: 01425 612830

TICKLISH ALLSORTS SHOW
Cremyll, Marshmead Close, Clarendon
Salisbury, Wiltshire SP5 3DD
Website: www.ticklishallsorts.co.uk
e-mail: garynunn@lineone.net   Tel/Fax: 01722 711800

TIEBREAK THEATRE COMPANY
42-58 St George's Street, Norwich NR3 1AB
Website: www.tiebreak-theatre.com
e-mail: info@tiebreak-theatre.com
Fax: 01603 666096   Tel: 01603 665899

TRICYCLE THEATRE
269 Kilburn High Road, London NW6 7JR
Website: www.tricycle.co.uk
e-mail: admin@tricycle.co.uk   Tel: 020-7372 6611

UNICORN
St Mark's Studios, Chillingworth Road, N7 8QJ
Website: www.unicorntheatre.com
e-mail: admin@unicorntheatre.com
Fax: 020-7700 3870   Tel: 020-7700 0702

WHIRLIGIG THEATRE
(National Touring Company)
14 Belvedere Drive, Wimbledon SW19 7BY
e-mail: whirligig.theatre@virgin.net
Fax: 020-8879 7648   Tel: 020-8947 1732

Theatre - English Speaking in Europe

■ **AUSTRIA**
Vienna's English Theatre
UK Representative: VM Theatre Productions Ltd
16 The Street, Ash
Kent CT3 2HJ   Tel/Fax: 01304 813330

■ **DENMARK**
The English Theatre of Copenhagen
London Toast Theatre, Kochsvej 18
1812 Fred C. Copenhagen Denmark
Website: www.londontoast.dk
e-mail: mail@londontoast.dk   Tel: + 45 33 22 8686
Artistic Director: Vivienne McKee
Administrator: Soren Hall

■ **FRANCE**
ACT Company
51 rue Hoche, 92240 Malakoff, France
Website: www.actheatre.com
e-mail: andrew.wilson@wanadoo.fr
Fax: + 33 1 46 56 23 18   Tel: + 33 1 46 56 20 50
Artistic Director: Andrew Wilson
Administrator: Anne Wilson

■ **FRANCE**
Amandla Theatre Company (Bilingual Touring Theatre Company)
179 rue de Vaugirard, 75015 Paris, France
e-mail: amandlatheatreco@aol.com
                    Mobile: + 33 6 30 89 88 81
Artistic Director: Caroline Benamza
Administrator: Jean-Marie Degove

■ **FRANCE**
Dear Conjunction Theatre Company
6 rue Arthur Rozier, 75019, Paris
e-mail: dearconjunction@wanadoo.fr
                    Tel: + 33 1 42 41 69 65
A D's: Barbara Bray, Leslie Clack, Patricia Kessler

■ **GERMANY**
The English Theatre of Hamburg
Lerchenfeld 14, 22081 Hamburg, Germany
Website: www.englishtheatre.de
Fax: + 49 40 229 5040   Tel: + 49 40 227 7089
Contact: Robert Rumpf, Clifford Dean

■ **GERMANY**
White Horse Theatre
Boerdenstrasse 17, 59494 Soest-Muellingsen,
Germany   e-mail: theatre@whitehorse.de
Fax: + 49 29 21 339336   Tel: + 49 29 21 339339
Contact: Peter Griffith, Michael Dray

■ **HUNGARY**
Merlin International Theatre
Gerloczy Utca 4, 1052 Budapest, Hungary
e-mail: angol@merlinszinhaz.hu
Fax: + 36 1 2660904   Tel: + 36 1 3179338
Contact: Laszlo Magacs

■ **ICELAND**
Light Nights - The Summer Theatre
The Travelling Theatre, Baldursgata 37
IS-101 Reykjavik, Iceland
Fax: + 354 551 5015   Tel: + 354 551 9181
Artistic Director: Kristine G Magnus

■ **NORWAY**
The English Speaking Theatre Oslo
Jacob Aalls Gate 30, 0364 Oslo, Norway
e-mail: testo-no@online.no   Tel: + 47 22 46 62 48
Artistic Director: Simon Lay   Director: Kristin Zachariassen

■ **SWEDEN**
The English Theatre Company Ltd
(TMA Member), Nybrogatan 35
114 39 Stockholm, Sweden
Website: www.englishtheatre.se
e-mail: etc.ltd@telia.com
Fax: + 46 8 660 1159   Tel: + 46 8 662 4133
Artistic Director: Christer Berg

■ **UNITED KINGDOM**
Onatti Theatre Company
9 Field Close, Warwick, Warwickshire CV34 4QD
Website: www.onatti.co.uk   e-mail: info@onatti.co.uk
Fax: 0870 1643629   Tel: 01926 495220
Contact: Andrew Bardwell

■ **UNITED KINGDOM**
Theatre From Oxford (Touring Europe & Beyond)
69-71 Oxford Street, Woodstock
Oxford OX20 1TJ, Contact: Robert Southam (Write)

T

ADELPHI
Strand, London WC2R 0NS
Manager: 020-7836 1166
Stage Door: 020-7836 1166
Box Office: 020-7836 1166

ALBERY
85 St Martin's Lane, London WC2N 4AU
Manager: 020-7438 9700
Stage Door: 020-7438 9700
Box Office: 020-7369 1730

ALDWYCH
Aldwych, London WC2B 4DF
Manager: 020-7836 5537
Stage Door: 020-7836 5537
Box Office: 0870 4000805
Website: www.aldwychtheatre.com

ALMEIDA
Almeida Street, London N1 1TA
Manager: 020-7288 4900
Stage Door: -------------
Box Office: 020-7359 4404

APOLLO
Shaftesbury Avenue, London W1D 7EZ
Manager: 020-7850 8701
Stage Door: 020-7850 8700
Box Office: 0870 8901101

APOLLO VICTORIA
17 Wilton Road, London SW1V 1LG
Manager: 020-7834 6318
Stage Door: 020-7834 7231
Box Office: 0870 4000650
Website: www.ticketmaster.co.uk

ARTS THEATRE
6-7 Great Newport Street, London WC2H 7JB
Manager: 020-7836 2132
Stage Door: 020-7836 2132
Box Office: 020-7836 3334
Website: www.artstheatre.com
e-mail: info@artstheatre.com

BARBICAN
Barbican, London EC2Y 8DS
Manager: 020-7628 3351
Stage Door: 020-7628 3351
Box Office: 020-7638 8891
Website: www.barbican.org.uk

CAMBRIDGE
Earlham Street
Seven Dials, Covent Garden
London WC2 9HU
Manager: 020-7850 8711
Stage Door: 020-7850 8710
Box Office: 0870 8901102

CARLING APOLLO HAMMERSMITH
Queen Caroline Street, London W6 9QH
Manager: 020-8563 3800
Stage Door: -------------
Box Office: 0870 6063400

COLISEUM (English National Opera)
St Martin's Lane, London WC2N 4ES
Manager: 020-7836 0111
Stage Door: 020-7836 1416
Box Office: 020-7632 8300

COMEDY
Panton Street, London SW1Y 4DN
Manager: 020-7321 5310
Stage Door: 020-7321 5300
Box Office: 020-7369 1731

CRITERION
Piccadilly, London W1V 9LB
Manager: 020-7839 8811
Stage Door: 020-7839 8811
Box Office: 020-7839 4489

DOMINION
268-269 Tottenham Court Road
London W1T 7AQ
Manager: -------------
Stage Door: 020-7927 0900
Box Office: 0870 1690116
Website: www.london-dominion.co.uk

DONMAR WAREHOUSE
41 Earlham Street, London WC2H 9LX
Manager: 020-7845 5800
Stage Door: 020-7438 9200
Box Office: 020-7369 1732
Website: www.donmarwarehouse.com
e-mail: office@donmarwarehouse.com

DUCHESS
Catherine Street, London WC2B 5LA
Manager: 020-7850 8721
Stage Door: 020-7850 8720
Box Office: 020-7850 8725

DUKE OF YORK'S
St Martin's Lane, London WC2N 4BG
Manager: 020-7836 4615
Stage Door: 020-7836 4615
Box Office: 020-7369 1791

FORTUNE
Russell Street
Covent Garden, London WC2B 5HH
Manager: 020-7010 7900
Stage Door: 020-7010 7900
Box Office: 020-7369 1737

GARRICK
Charing Cross Road, London WC2H 0HH
Manager: 020-7850 8731
Stage Door: 020-7850 8730
Box Office: 020-7494 5085

GIELGUD
Shaftesbury Avenue, London W1D 6AR
Manager: 020-7850 8741
Stage Door: 020-7850 8740
Box Office: 0870 8901105

HACKNEY EMPIRE
291 Mare Street, London E8 1EJ
Manager:	020-8510 4500
Stage Door:	020-8510 4515
Box Office:	020-8985 2424
Website:	www.hackneyempire.co.uk
e-mail:	info@hackneyempire.co.uk

HAMPSTEAD THEATRE
Eton Avenue, Swiss Cottage, London NW3 3EU
Manager:	020-7449 4200
Stage Door:	------------
Box Office:	020-7722 9301
Website:	www.hampsteadtheatre.com
e-mail:	info@hampsteadtheatre.com

HER MAJESTY'S
Haymarket, London SW1Y 4QL
Manager:	020-7850 8750
Stage Door:	020-7850 8750
Box Office:	0870 8901106

LYCEUM THEATRE
21 Wellington Street, London WC2E 7RQ
Manager:	020-7420 8191
Stage Door:	020-7420 8100
Box Office:	020-7420 8114

LYRIC
Shaftesbury Avenue, London W1D 7ES
Manager:	020-7850 8761
Stage Door:	020-7850 8760
Box Office:	0870 8901107

LYRIC THEATRE HAMMERSMITH
King Street, London W6 0QL
Manager:	020-8741 0824
Stage Door:	020-8741 0824
Box Office:	08700 5005811
Website:	www.lyric.co.uk
e-mail:	enquiries@lyric.co.uk

NEW AMBASSADORS
West Street, London WC2H 9ND
Manager:	020-7395 5400
Stage Door:	020-7395 5400
Box Office:	020-7369 1761
Website:	www.newambassadors.com
e-mail:	newambassadors@theambassadors.com

NEW LONDON
Drury Lane, London WC2B 5PW
Manager:	020-7242 9802
Stage Door:	020-7242 9802
Box Office:	0870 8900141

OLD VIC The
Waterloo Road, London SE1 8NB
Manager:	020-7928 2651
Stage Door:	020-7928 2651
Box Office:	020-7369 1722
Website:	www.oldvictheatre.com
e-mail:	old.vic@pobox.com

OPEN AIR THEATRE
Inner Circle, Regent's Park
London NW1 4NR
Manager:	020-7935 5756
Stage Door:	020-7935 5756
Box Office:	020-7486 2431

PALACE
Shaftesbury Avenue
London W1D 5AY
Manager:	020-7434 0088
Stage Door:	020-7434 0088
Box Office:	020-7434 0909
Website:	www.rutheatres.com
e-mail:	thepalacetheatre@hotmail.com

PALLADIUM
Argyll Street, London W1F 7TF
Manager:	020-7850 8771
Stage Door:	020-7850 8770
Box Office:	020-7494 5572

PEACOCK
(See SADLER'S WELLS IN THE WEST END)

PHOENIX
Charing Cross Road
London WC2H 0JP
Manager:	------------
Stage Door:	020-7438 9600
Box Office:	020-7438 9605

PICCADILLY
Denman Street
London W1D 7DY
Manager:	020-7478 8810
Stage Door:	020-7478 8800
Box Office:	020-7478 8805

PLAYHOUSE
Northumberland Avenue
London WC2N 5DE
Manager:	020-7839 4292
Stage Door:	020-7839 4292
Box Office:	020-7839 4401

PRINCE EDWARD
Old Compton Street
London W1D 4HS
Manager:	020-7437 2024
Stage Door:	020-7439 3041
Box Office:	0870 8500393
Website:	www.delfont-mackintosh.com

PRINCE OF WALES
Coventry Street, London W1D 6AS
Manager:	020-7930 1867
Stage Door:	020-7930 1432
Box Office:	020-7839 5972

QUEEN'S
51 Shaftesbury Avenue
London W1D 6BA
Manager:	020-7850 8781
Stage Door:	020-7850 8780
Box Office:	0870 890110

ROYAL COURT THEATRE
Sloane Square
London SW1W 8AS
Manager:	020-7565 5050
Stage Door:	020-7565 5050
Box Office:	020-7565 5000
Website:	www.royalcourttheatre.com
e-mail:	info@royalcourttheatre.com

T

ROYAL NATIONAL
South Bank, London SE1 9PX
Admin:	020-7452 3333
Stage Door:	020-7452 3333
Box Office:	020-7452 3000
Website:	www.nationaltheatre.org.uk

ROYAL OPERA HOUSE
Covent Garden, London WC2E 9DD
Manager:	020-7240 1200
Stage Door:	-------------
Box Office:	020-7304 4000

SADLER'S WELLS
Rosebery Avenue
London EC1R 4TN
Manager:	-------------
Stage Door:	020-7863 8198
Box Office:	020-7863 8000
Website:	www.sadlerswells.com
e-mail:	info@sadlerswells.com

SADLER'S WELLS IN THE WEST END
Peacock Theatre
Portugal Street, Kingsway
London WC2A 2HT
Manager:	020-7863 8204
Stage Door:	020-7863 8268
Box Office:	020-7863 8222

SAVOY
Strand, London WC2R 0ET
Manager:	020-7240 1649
Stage Door:	020-7836 8117
Box Office:	020-7836 8888

SHAFTESBURY
210 Shaftesbury Avenue
London WC2H 8DP
Manager:	020-7379 3345
Stage Door:	020-7379 3345
Box Office:	020-7379 5399
e-mail:	mhone@toc.dltentertainment.co.uk

SHAKESPEARE'S GLOBE
21 New Globe Walk
Bankside, London SE1 9DT
Manager:	020-7902 1400
Stage Door:	020-7902 1400
Box Office:	020-7401 9919
Website:	www.shakespeares-globe.org
e-mail:	info@shakespeares-globe.com

SOHO THEATRE
21 Dean Street, London W1D 3NE
Manager:	020-7287 5060
Stage Door:	-------------
Box Office:	020-7478 0100
Website:	www.sohotheatre.com
e-mail:	mail@sohotheatre.com

ST MARTIN'S
West Street, London WC2H 9NZ
Manager:	020-7497 0578
Stage Door:	020-7836 1086
Box Office:	020-7836 1443

STRAND
Aldwych
London WC2B 5LD
Manager:	020-7836 4144
Stage Door:	020-7836 4144
Box Office:	0870 0602335

THEATRE ROYAL
(Haymarket)
London SW1Y 4HT
Manager:	020-7930 8890
Stage Door:	-------------
Box Office:	0870 9013356

THEATRE ROYAL DRURY LANE
Catherine Street
London WC2B 5JF
Manager:	020-7850-8793
Stage Door:	020-7850 8790
Box Office:	0870 8901109

UCL BLOOMSBURY
15 Gordon Street
London WC1H 0AH
Manager:	020-7679 2777
Stage Door:	020-7679 2922
Box Office:	020-7388 8822
Website:	www.thebloomsbury.com
e-mail:	blooms.theatre@ucl.ac.uk

VAUDEVILLE
404 Strand
London WC2R 0NH
Manager:	020-7836 1820
Stage Door:	020-7836 3191
Box Office:	020-7836 9987

VICTORIA PALACE
Victoria Street
London SW1E 5EA
Manager:	020-7828 0600
Stage Door:	020-7834 2781
Box Office:	0870 1658787

WHITEHALL
14 Whitehall
London SW1A 2DY
Manager:	020-7321 5400
Stage Door:	020-7321 5400
Box Office:	020-7321 5405
e-mail:	whitehall@theambassadors.com

WYNDHAM'S
Charing Cross Road
London WC2H 0DA
Manager:	020-7438 9700
Stage Door:	020-7438 9700
Box Office:	020-7438 9755

YOUNG VIC
66 The Cut, London SE1 8LZ
Manager:	020-7922 8400
Stage Door:	020-7922 8400
Box Office:	020-7928 6363
Website:	www.youngvic.org
e-mail:	info@youngvic.org

ALBANY The
Douglas Way, Deptford, London SE8 4AG
Fax: 020-8469 2253   Tel: 020-8692 4446

ARCOLA THEATRE
(Artistic Director - Mehmet Ergen)
27 Arcola Street, Dalston
(Off Stoke Newington Road), London E8 2DJ
e-mail: info@arcolatheatre.com
Fax: 020-7503 1645
BO: 020-7503 1646   Admin: 020-7503 1645
Route: Victoria Line to Highbury & Islington, then
North London Line to Dalston Kingsland BR - 5 min
walk. Buses: 38 from West End, 149 from London
Bridge or 30, 67, 76, 243

ARTSDEPOT
At The Bull Theatre, 68 High Street, Barnet EN5 5SJ
e-mail: admin@artsdepot.co.uk   BO: 020-8449 0048

ASHCROFT THEATRE
Fairfield Halls, Park Lane, Croydon CR9 1DG
Website: www.fairfield.co.uk
e-mail: dbarr@fairfield.co.uk
BO: 020-8688 9291   Admin & SD: 020-8681 0821
Route: Victoria (BR) to East Croydon then 5 min
walk

BAC
Lavender Hill, London SW11 5TN
Website: www.bac.org.uk
e-mail: mailbox@bac.org.uk
Fax: 020-7978 5207
BO: 020-7223 2223   Admin: 020-7223 6557
Route: Victoria or Waterloo (BR) to Clapham
Junction then 5 min walk or Northern Line to
Clapham Common then 20 min walk

BARONS COURT THEATRE
'The Curtain's Up'
28A Comeragh Road
West Kensington, London W14 9RH
Fax: 020-7603 8935   Admin/BO: 020-8932 4747
Route: West Kensington or Barons Court tube

BECK THEATRE
Grange Road, Hayes, Middlesex UB3 2UE
BO: 020-8561 8371   Admin: 020-8651 7506
Route: Metropolitan Line to Uxbridge then buses
207 or 607 (10 min) to Theatre or Paddington (BR)
to Hayes Harlington then buses 90, H98 or 195
(10 min)

BEDLAM THEATRE
11B Bristo Place, Edinburgh EH1 1EZ
Website: www.bedlamfringe.co.uk
e-mail: info@bedlamtheatre.co.uk
     Tel: 0131-225 9873

BELLAIRS PLAYHOUSE
Millmead Terrace, Guildford GU2 4YT
e-mail: enquiries@conservatoire.org
BO: 01483 565787 (12-4pm)   Admin: 01483 560701

BRENTWOOD THEATRE
(Theatre Administrator - Mark P Reed)
15 Shenfield Road, Brentwood, Essex CM15 8AG
Website: www.brentwood-theatre.co.uk
BO: 01277 200300
Stage Door: 01277 226658   Admin/Fax: 01277 230833
Liverpool Street (BR) to Brentwood, then 15 min
walk

BRIDEWELL THEATRE The
Bride Lane, (Off Fleet Street), London EC4Y 8EQ
Website: www.bridewelltheatre.co.uk
e-mail: admin@bridewelltheatre.co.uk
Fax: 020-7583 5289
BO: 020-7936 3456   Admin: 020-7353 0259
Route: Blackfriars, St Paul's: City Thameslink. Fifteen
different bus routes

BUSH THEATRE
(Artistic Director - Mike Bradwell)
Shepherd's Bush Green, London W12 8QD
Production: 020-8743 5050
BO: 020-7610 4224   Admin: 020-7602 3703
Route: Central Line to Shepherd's Bush or
Hammersmith & City Line to Goldhawk Road or
buses 12, 49, 94, 207 or 220

CAMDEN PEOPLE'S THEATRE
(Artistic Director - Chris Goode)
58-60 Hampstead Road, London NW1 2PY
Website: www.cpt.dircon.co.uk
e-mail: cpt@dircon.co.uk
Fax: 020-7813 3889   Tel: 020-7916 5878
Route: Victoria or Northern Line to Warren Street,
Metropolitan or Circle Line to Euston Square (1 min
walk either way)

CANAL CAFE THEATRE The
(Artistic Director - Emma Taylor)
The Bridge House
Delamere Terrace
Little Venice, London W2 6ND
Website: www.newsrevue.com
e-mail: mail@canalcafetheatre.com
Fax: 020-7266 1717
BO: 020-7289 6054   Admin: 020-7289 6056

CAPITAL ARTS THEATRE COMPANY
Capital Arts
Wyllyotts Centre, Darkes Lane
Potters Bar, Hertfordshire EN6 2HN
e-mail: capitalartstheatre@o2.co.uk
Mobile: 07885 232414   Tel/Fax: 020-8449 2342

CHANTICLEER THEATRE
(Webber Douglas Academy)
30 Clareville Street
London SW7 5AP
e-mail: webberdouglas@btclick.com
Fax: 020-7373 5639   Tel: 020-7370 4154
Route: Piccadilly, District or Circle Line to
Gloucester Road, turn right, walk 300 yards then
turn left into Clareville Street

CHATS PALACE ARTS CENTRE
(Nick Reed)
42-44 Brooksby's Walk
Hackney, London E9 6DF
e-mail: chatspalace@hotmail .com
Fax: 020-8985 6878   Tel: 020-8533 0227

CHELSEA THEATRE
World's End Place
King's Road, London SW10 0DR
e-mail: admin@chelseatheatre.org.uk
Fax: 020-7352 2024   Tel: 020-7352 1967
Route: District or Circle Line to Sloane Square then
short bus ride 11 or 22 down King's Road

CHICKEN SHED THEATRE
(Artistic Director: Mary Ward MBE)
Chase Side, Southgate, London N14 4PE
Website: www.chickenshed.org.uk
e-mail: info@chickenshed.org.uk
Fax: 020-8292 0202   Minicom: 020-8350 0676
BO: 020-8292 9222   Admin: 020-8351 6161
Route: Piccadilly Line to Oakwood, turn left outside
tube & walk 8 min down Bramley Road or take 307
bus. Buses 298, 299, 699 or N19 Car parking
available & easy access parking by reservation.

CHRIST'S HOSPITAL THEATRE
(Director - Jeff Mayhew)
Horsham, West Sussex RH13 7LW
e-mail: jm@christs-hospital.org.uk
BO: 01403 247434   Admin: 01403 247435

CLUB FOR ACTS & ACTORS The
(Concert Artistes Association)
(Gerald Moon, Barbara Daniels)
20 Bedford Street
London WC2E 9HP   Admin: 020-7836 3172
Route: Piccadilly or Northern Line to Leicester
Square then few mins walk

COCHRANE THEATRE
(Deirdre Malynn)
Southampton Row, London WC1B 4AP
e-mail: info@cochranetheatre.co.uk
BO: 020-7269 1606   Admin: 020-7269 1600
Route: Central or Piccadilly Line to Holborn then 3
min walk

COCKPIT THEATRE
(Artistic Director - June Abbott)
Gateforth Street, London NW8 8EH
e-mail: dave.wybrow@awc.ac.uk
Fax: 020-7258 2921
BO: 020-7258 2925   Admin: 020-7258 2920
Route: Tube to Marylebone/Edgware Road then
short walk or bus 139 to Lisson Grove & 6, 8 or 16 to
Edgware Road

CORBETT THEATRE
(East 15 Acting School)
Rectory Lane, Loughton, Essex IG10 3RY
Website: www.east15.ac.uk
e-mail: east15@essex.ac.uk
Fax: 020-8508 7521   BO & Admin: 020-8508 5983
Route: Central Line (Epping Branch) to Debden
then 6 min walk

COURTYARD THEATRE The
(Artistic Director - June Abbott)
10 York Way, King's Cross, London N1 9AA
Website: www.thecourtyard.org.uk
e-mail: info@thecourtyard.org.uk
BO: 020-7833 0876   Admin/Fax: 020-7833 0870
Route: Side of King's Cross Station

CUSTARD FACTORY
Gibb Street, Digbeth, Birmingham B9 4AA
Website: www.custardfactory.com
e-mail: custardfactory@clara.net
Fax: 0121-604 8888   Tel: 0121-693 7777

DARTFORD ORCHARD THEATRE
(Vanessa Hart)
Home Gardens, Dartford, Kent DA1 1ED
Website: www.orchardtheatre.co.uk
Fax: 01322 227122
BO: 01322 220000   Admin: 01322 220099
Route: Charing Cross (BR) to Dartford

DENCH Judi THEATRE
(See MOUNTVIEW THEATRE)

DIORAMA STUDIO THEATRE
(Mark Ross)
34 Osnaburgh Street, London NW1 3ND
Website: www.diorama-arts.org.uk
e-mail: admin@diorama-arts.org.uk
Fax: 020-7813 3116   Admin: 020-7916 5467
Route: Circle & District Line to Great Portland
Street then 1 min walk, or Victoria/Northern line to
Warren Street then 5 min walk

DRILL HALL The
16 Chenies Street, London WC1E 7EX
Website: www.drillhall.co.uk
e-mail: admin@drillhall.co.uk
Fax: 020-7307 5062
BO: 020-7307 5060   Admin: 020-7307 5061
Route: Northern Line to Goodge Street then 1 min
walk

EDINBURGH FESTIVAL FRINGE
180 High Street, Edinburgh EH1 1QS
Website: www.edfringe.com
e-mail: admin@edfringe.com
Fax: 0131-226 0016   Tel: 0131-226 0026

EDINBURGH UNIVERSITY THEATRE COMPANY
(See BEDLAM THEATRE)

EMBASSY THEATRE & STUDIOS
(Central School of Speech & Drama)
64 Eton Avenue
Swiss Cottage, London NW3 3HY
Website: www.cssd.ac.uk
BO: 020-7559 3935   Admin: 020-7559 3999
Route: Jubilee Line to Swiss Cottage then 1 min walk

ETCETERA THEATRE CLUB
(Director - Kirsty Housley)
Oxford Arms, 265 Camden High Street
London NW1 7BU
Website: www.etcetera-theatre.co.uk
e-mail: etceteratheatre@hotmail.com
Fax: 020-7482 0378   Admin/BO: 020-7482 4857

FINBOROUGH THEATRE
(Artistic Director - Neil McPherson)
The Finborough, 118 Finborough Road
London SW10 9ED
Website: www.finboroughtheatre.co.uk
e-mail: admin@finboroughtheatre.co.uk
Fax: 020-7835 1853
BO: 020-7373 3842   Admin: 020-7244 7439
Route: District or Piccadilly Line to Earls Court then 5
min walk. Buses 74, 328, C1, C3, 74 then 3 min walk

GATE THEATRE
(Erica Whyman)
Above Prince Albert Pub
11 Pembridge Road, London W11 3HQ
Website: www.gatetheatre.co.uk
e-mail: gate@gatetheatre.freeserve.co.uk
Fax: 020-7221 6055
BO: 020-7229 0706   Admin: 020-7229 5387
Route: Central, Circle or District Line to Notting Hill
Gate then 1 min walk

GREENWICH PLAYHOUSE
(Alice De Sousa)
Greenwich BR Station Forecourt
189 Greenwich High Road, London SE10 8JA
Website: www.galleontheatre.co.uk
e-mail: alice@galleontheatre.co.uk
Fax: 020-8969 2910   Tel: 020-8858 9256
Route: BR from Charing Cross, Waterloo East or
London Bridge, DLR to Greenwich

GREENWICH THEATRE
(Executive Director - Hilary Strong)
Crooms Hill, Greenwich, London SE10 8ES
Website: www.greenwichtheatre.org.uk
e-mail: info@greenwichtheatre.org.uk
Fax: 020-8858 8042
BO: 020-8858 7755   Admin: 020-8858 4447
Route: Jubilee Line (change Canary Wharf) then
DLR to Greenwich Cutty Sark, 3 min walk or
Charing Cross (BR) to Greenwich, 5 min walk

GUILDHALL SCHOOL OF MUSIC & DRAMA
Silk Street, Barbican, London EC2Y 8DT
e-mail: info@gsmd.ac.uk
Fax: 020-7256 9438   Tel: 020-7628 2571
Route: Hammersmith & City, Circle or Metropolitan
line to Barbican or Moorgate (also served by
Northern line) then 5 min walk

HACKNEY EMPIRE THEATRE
291 Mare Street
Hackney, London E8 1EJ
BO: 020-8985 2424   Press/Admin: 020-8510 4500

HEN & CHICKENS THEATRE
Unrestricted View
Above Hen & Chickens Theatre Bar
109 St Paul's Road, Islington, London N1 2NA
Website: www.henandchickens.com
e-mail: james@henandchickens.com Tel: 020-7704 2001
Route: Victoria Line or Main Line to Highbury &
Islington directly opposite station

HORLA
The Rose & Crown Theatre
59-61 High Street
Hampton Wick, Surrey KT1 4DG
Website: www.horla.co.uk
e-mail: info@horla.co.uk
BO: 020-8296 9100   Admin/Fax: 020-8296 0242

HUNT THEATRE
Felsted School
Felsted, Nr Dunmow, Essex CM6 3JG
e-mail: crsl@felsted.essex.sch.uk
Fax: 01371 822607   Tel: 01371 821191

ICA THEATRE
The Mall, London SW1Y 5AH
Website: www.ica.org.uk
Fax: 020-7873 0051
BO: 020-7930 3647   Admin: 020-7930 0493
Route: Nearest stations Piccadilly & Charing Cross

INVENTION ARTS
Lower Borough Walls
Bath BA1 1QR
e-mail: info@inventionarts.org   Tel: 01225 421700

JACKSONS LANE THEATRE
269A Archway Road, London N6 5AA
Website: www.jacksonslane.co.uk
e-mail: mail@jacksonslane.co.uk   Tel: 020-8340 5226

JERMYN STREET THEATRE
(Administrator - Penny Horner)
16B Jermyn Street
London SW1Y 6ST
Website: www.jermynstreettheatre.co.uk
Fax: 020-7287 3232
BO: 020-7287 2875   Admin: 020-7434 1443

KING'S HEAD THEATRE
(Artistic Director - Dan Crawford)
115 Upper Street, Islington, London N1 1QN
BO: 020-7226 1916   Admin: 020-7226 8561
Route: Northern Line to Angel then 5 min walk.
Approx halfway between Angel and Highbury &
Islington tube stations

KING'S LYNN CORN EXCHANGE
Tuesday Market Place
King's Lynn, Norfolk PE30 1JW
Website: www.kingslynncornexchange.co.uk
e-mail: entertainment_admin@west-norfolk.gov.uk
Fax: 01553 762141
BO: 01553 764864   Admin: 01553 765565

KOMEDIA
(Artistic Directors: Theatre & Comedy -
David Lavender. Music, Cabaret & Children's
Theatre - Marina Kobler)
44-47 Gardner Street, Brighton BN1 1UN
Website: www.komedia.co.uk
e-mail: info@komedia.co.uk
Fax: 01273 647102
BO: 01273 647100   Tel: 01273 647101

LANDMARK ARTS CENTRE
Ferry Road
Teddington Lock, Middlesex TW11 9NN
Website: www.landmarkartscentre.org
e-mail: landmarkinfo@aol.com
Fax: 020-8977 4830   Tel: 020-8977 7558

LANDOR THEATRE The
(Artistic Director/Founder - Linda Edwards, Artistic
Director/General Manager - Robert Mcwhir)
70 Landor Road
London SW9 9PH
Website: www.landortheatre.co.uk
e-mail: info@landortheatre.co.uk
                            Admin/BO: 020-7737 7276
Route: Northern Line Clapham North then 2 min walk

LATCHMERE THEATRE
503 Battersea Park Road
London SW11 3BW
Website: www.latchmeretheatre.com
e-mail: info@latchmeretheatre.com
BO: 020-7978 7040   Admin/Fax: 020-7978 7041
Route: Victoria or Waterloo (BR) to Clapham
Junction then 10 min walk or buses 44, 219, 319,
344, 345 or tube to South Kensington then buses 49
or 345 or tube to Sloane Square then Bus 319

LEIGHTON BUZZARD
(Development Manager - Lois Wright)
Leighton Buzzard Theatre, Lake Street
Leighton Buzzard LU7 1RX   Tel: 01525 850290

LILIAN BAYLIS THEATRE
(Information: Sadler's Wells Theatre)
Rosebery Avenue
London EC1R 4TN
Website: www.sadlerswells.com
e-mail: info@sadlerswells.com
BO: 020-7863 8000   SD: 020-7863 8198

LIVE THEATRE
27 Broad Chare, Quayside
Newcastle upon Tyne NE1 3DQ
Website: www.live.org.uk
e-mail: info@live.org.uk   Fax: 0191-232 2224
BO: 0191-232 1232   Admin: 0191-261 2694

MACOWAN THEATRE
(LAMDA)
1-2 Logan Place, London W8 6QN
Website: www.lamda.org.uk
Fax: 020-7370 1980   Tel: 020-8834 0500
Route: District or Piccadilly Line to Earl's Court then
6 min walk

MADDERMARKET THEATRE
(Artistic Director - Clare Goddard
General Manager - Michael Lyas)
St John's Alley, Norwich NR2 1DR
Website: www.maddermarket.co.uk
e-mail: theatre@maddermarket.co.uk
Fax: 01603 661357
BO: 01603 620917   Admin: 01603 626560

MAN IN THE MOON THEATRE
392 King's Road, London SW3 5UZ
Fax: 020-7351 1873
BO: 020-7351 2876   Admin: 07801 932321
Route: Tube to Sloane Square then short bus ride
11, 22 or 19 down King's Road or tube to South
Kensington then bus 49 or 345 to junction of
Beaufort Street & King's Road

MENIER THEATRE
Menier Arts Centre
51-53 Southwark Street, London SE1 1TE
Website: www.menier.org.uk
e-mail: meniertheatre@hotmail.com
Fax: 020-7357 0544   Tel: 020-7407 5388

MERMAID THEATRE
(Conference & Events Centre)
Puddle Dock, Blackfriars, London EC4V 3DB
Website: www.the-mermaid.co.uk
e-mail: info@the-mermaid.co.uk   Tel: 020-7236 1919
Route: Tube to Blackfriars or St Paul's, buses 45 or
63, or Thameslink to Blackfriars

MILLFIELD THEATRE
Silver Street, London N18 1PJ
Website: www.millfieldtheatre.co.uk
e-mail: info@millfieldtheatre.co.uk
Fax: 020-8807 3892
BO: 020-8807 6680   Admin: 020-8803 5283
Route: Liverpool Street (BR) to Silver Street or tube
to Turnpike Lane then buses 144A, 217, 231 or 444.
10 min to Cambridge roundabout

MOUNTVIEW THEATRE
104 Crouch Hill
London N8 9EA   BO: 020-8829 0035
Route: Piccadilly or Victoria Line to Finsbury Park
then W7 bus to Dickenson Road (5 min)

MYERS STUDIO THEATRE The
(Venues Manager - Trevor Mitchell)
The Epsom Playhouse, Ashley Avenue
Epsom, Surrey KT18 5AL
Website: www.epsomplayhouse.co.uk
e-mail: tmitchell@epsom-ewell.gov.uk
Fax: 01372 726228
BO: 01372 742555   Tel: 01372 742226

NETHERBOW SCOTTISH STORYTELLING CENTRE The
(Donald Smith)
43-45 High Street
Edinburgh EH1 1SR
Website: www.scottishstorytellingcentre.co.uk
          Tel: 0131-556 9579

NETTLEFOLD The
West Norwood Library Centre
1 Norwood High Street, London SE27 9JX
Fax: 020-7926 8071   Admin/BO: 020-7926 8070
Route: Victoria, West Croydon or London Bridge
(BR) to West Norwood then 2 min walk, or tube to
Brixton then buses 2, 196, 322 or 432, or buses 68 or
468

NEW END THEATRE
27 New End
Hampstead, London NW3 1JD
Website: www.newendtheatre.co.uk
Fax: 020-7472 5808
BO: 020-7794 0022   Admin: 020-7472 5800
Route: Northern Line to Hampstead then 2 min
walk off Heath Street

NORTHBROOK THEATRE The
Littlehampton Road
Goring-by-Sea, Worthing
West Sussex BN12 6NU
Website: www.northbrooktheatre.co.uk
e-mail: box.office@nbcol.ac.uk
Fax: 01903 606316
Marketing & Publicity: 01903 606230
BO: 01903 606162   Theatre Manager: 01903 606287

NOVELLO THEATRE The
(Redroofs Theatre Company
2 High Street, Sunninghill
Nr Ascot Berkshire   Tel: 01344 620881
Route: Waterloo (BR) to Ascot then 1 mile from
station

OLD RED LION THEATRE PUB
(Artistic Director - Melanie Tait)
418 St John Street, Islington
London EC1V 4NJ
BO: 020-7837 7816   Admin/Fax: 020-7833 3053
Route: Northern Line to Angel then 1 min walk

ORANGE TREE
(Artistic Director - Sam Walters)
1 Clarence Street
Richmond TW9 2SA
e-mail: admin@orange-tree.demon.co.uk
Fax: 020-8332 0369
BO: 020-8940 3633   Admin: 020-8940 0141
Route: District Line, Waterloo (BR) or North London
Line then virtually opposite station

OVAL HOUSE THEATRE
52-54 Kennington Oval
London SE11 5SW
Website: www.ovalhouse.com
e-mail: admin@ovalhouse.com
Fax: 020-7820 0990   BO: 020-7582 7680
Admin: 020-7582 0080
Route: Northern Line to Oval then 1 min walk,
Victoria Line & BR to Vauxhall then 10 min walk

PAVILION THEATRE
Marine Road
Dun Laoghaire, County Dublin, Eire
Website: www.paviliontheatre.ie
e-mail: info@paviliontheatre.ie
Fax: 353 1 663 6328   Tel: 353 1 231 2929

PENTAMETERS
Three Horseshoes, 28 Heath Street
London NW3 6TE   BO/Admin: 020-7435 3648
Route: Northern Line to Hampstead then 1 min
walk

PLACE The
(Main London Venue for Contemporary Dance)
17 Duke's Road, London WC1H 9PY
Website: www.theplace.org.uk
e-mail: theatre@theplace.org.uk
BO: 020-7387 0031   Admin: 020-7380 1268
Route: Northern or Victoria Lines to Euston or King's
Cross then 5 min walk (Opposite rear of St Pancras
Church)

PLEASANCE LONDON
(Christopher Richardson)
Carpenters Mews, North Road
(Off Caledonian Road), London N7 9EF
Website: www.pleasance.co.uk
e-mail: info@pleasance.co.uk
Fax: 020-7700 7366
BO: 020-7609 1800   Admin: 020-7619 6868
Route: Piccadilly Line to Caledonian Road, turn
left, walk 50 yds, turn left into North Road, 2 min
walk. Buses 10, 17, 91, 259 or N91

POLISH THEATRE
(Polish Social & Cultural Association Ltd)
238-246 King Street, London W6 0RF
BO: 020-8741 0398   Admin: 020-8741 1940
Route: District Line to Ravenscourt Park, or District,
Piccadilly or Metropolitan Lines to Hammersmith
then 7 min walk. Buses 27, 267, 190, 391 or H91

POLKA THEATRE FOR CHILDREN
240 The Broadway, Wimbledon SW19 1SB
Website: www.polkatheatre.com
e-mail: info@polkatheatre.com
Fax: 020-8545 8365
BO: 020-8543 4888   Admin: 020-8545 8320
Route: Waterloo (BR) or District Line to Wimbledon
then 10 min walk. Northern Line to South
Wimbledon then 10 min walk

PRINCESS THEATRE HUNSTANTON
The Green
Hunstanton, Norfolk PE36 5AH
Fax: 01485 534463
BO: 01485 532252   Admin: 01485 535937

QUEEN'S THEATRE
(Artistic Director - Bob Carlton
Administrator - Henrietta Duckworth)
Billet Lane, Hornchurch, Essex RM11 1QT
Website: www.queens-theatre.co.uk
e-mail: info@queens-theatre.co.uk
Fax: 01708 452348   SD: 01708 442078
BO: 01708 443333   Admin: 01708 456118
Route: District Line to Hornchurch, BR to
Romford/Gidea Park. 15 miles from West End take
A13, A1306 then A125 or A12 then A127

QUESTORS THEATRE EALING The
12 Mattock Lane, London W5 5BQ
Website: www.questors.org.uk
e-mail: enquiries@questors.org.uk
Fax: 020-8567 8736
BO: 020-8567 5184   Admin: 020-8567 0011
Route: Central or District Line to Ealing Broadway
then 5 min walk

RICHMOND THEATRE
(Karin Gartzke)
The Green, Richmond, Surrey TW9 1QJ
Website: www.richmondtheatre.net
e-mail: richmondtheatre@theambassadors.com
Fax: 020-8948 3601
BO: 020-8940 0088   Admin & SD: 020-8940 0220
Route: 20 minutes from Waterloo (South West
Trains) or District Line or Silverlink to Richmond then
2 min walk

RIDWARE THEATRE
(Alan & Margaret Williams)
Wheelwright's House, Pipe Ridware
Rugeley, Staffordshire WS15 3QL
e-mail: alan@christmas-time.com   Tel: 01889 504380

RIVERSIDE STUDIOS
Crisp Road, London W6 9RL
Website: www.riversidestudios.co.uk
e-mail: info@riversidestudios.co.uk
BO: 020-8237 1111   Admin: 020-8237 1000
Route: District, Piccadilly or Hammersmith & City
Line to Hammersmith Broadway then 5 min walk.
Buses 9, 11, 27, 73, 91, 220, 283 or 295

ROSEMARY BRANCH THEATRE
2 Shepperton Road, London N1 3DT
Website: www.rosemarybranch.co.uk
e-mail: cecilia@rosemarybranch.co.uk
                                    Tel: 020-7704 6665

SETTLE FESTIVAL OF THEATRE
(Artistic Director - Martin Lewton)
('A Theatre in The Dales')
The Mains, Giggleswick, Settle
North Yorkshire BD24 0AY
e-mail: sft@giggleswick301.fsnet.co.uk
                                    Tel/Fax: 01729 822058

SEVENOAKS STAG THEATRE
London Road, Sevenoaks, Kent TN13 1ZZ
Website: www.stagtheatre.co.uk
BO: 01732 450175   Admin: 01732 451548
Route: Charing Cross (BR) to Sevenoaks then 15
min up the hill from station

SHAW THEATRE The
The Novotel Hotel, 100-110 Euston Road
London NW1 2AJ
Website: www.shawtheatre.com
e-mail: nina@shawtheatre.com
Fax: 020-7383 7708   BO: 020-7387 6864

SOHO THEATRE & WRITERS' CENTRE
21 Dean Street, London W1D 3NE
Website: www.sohotheatre.com
Fax: 020-7287 5061   BO: 020-7478 0100
Route: Tube to Tottenham Court Road then
second left up Oxford Street

SOUTH HILL PARK ARTS CENTRE
Bracknell, Berkshire RG12 7PA
Website: www.southhillpark.org.uk
e-mail: admin@southhillpark.org.uk
BO: 01344 484123   Admin & SD: 01344 484858
Route: Waterloo (BR) to Bracknell then 10 min bus
ride or taxi rank at station

SOUTH LONDON THEATRE
(Bell Theatre & Prompt Corner)
2A Norwood High Street, London SE27 9NS
Website: www.southlondontheatre.co.uk
e-mail: southlondontheatre@yahoo.co.uk
                                    Tel: 020-8670 3474
Route: Victoria or London Bridge (BR) to West
Norwood then 2 min walk, or Victoria Line to
Brixton then buses 2, 68, 196 or 322

SOUTHWARK PLAYHOUSE
(Artistic Director - Thea Sharrock, Chief Executive -
Juliet Alderdice, Education Director - Tom Wilson)
62 Southwark Bridge Road, London SE1 0AT
Website: www.southwarkplayhouse.co.uk
e-mail: admin@southwarkplayhouse.co.uk
BO: 020-7620 3494   Admin: 020-7652 2224
Route: Northern Line to Borough or Jubilee Line to
Southwark (BR) & London Bridge. Buses 133, 35,
344, 40, P3

TABARD THEATRE
(Artistic Director - Hamish Gray)
2 Bath Road, Turnham Green, London W4 1LW
BO: 020-8995 6035   Admin: 020-8994 5985
Route: District Line to Turnham Green then 1 min walk

THEATRE OF ALL POSSIBILITIES
(Artistic Director - Kathlin Gray)
24 Old Gloucester Street
London WC1N 3AL
Website: www.allpossibilities.org
e-mail: engage@allpossibilities.org
Tel: 020-7242 9831

THEATRE ROYAL STRATFORD EAST
(Artistic Director - Philip Hedley)
Gerry Raffles Square
London E15 1BN
Website: www.stratfordeast.com
e-mail: theatreroyal@stratfordeast.com
Fax: 020-8534 8381
BO: 020-8534 0310   Admin: 020-8534 7374
Route: Central or Jubilee Line to Stratford then 2 min
walk

THEATRO TECHNIS
(Artistic Director - George Eugeniou)
26 Crowndale Road
London NW1   BO & Admin: 020-7387 6617
Route: Northern Line to Mornington Crescent then 3
min walk

TRICYCLE THEATRE
(Artistic Director - Nicolas Kent
General Manager - Mary Lauder)
269 Kilburn High Road
London NW6 7JR
Website: www.tricycle.co.uk
e-mail: admin@tricycle.co.uk
Fax: 020-7328 0795
BO: 020-7328 1000   Admin: 020-7372 6611
Route: Jubilee Line to Kilburn then 5 min walk or buses
16, 189 or 32 pass the door, 98, 31, 206 & 316 pass
nearby

TRON THEATRE
(Director - Neil Murray)
63 Trongate, Glasgow G1 5HB
Website: www.tron.co.uke-mail: admin@tron.co.uk
Fax: 0141-552 6657
BO: 0141-552 4267   Admin: 0141-552 3748

UCL BLOOMSBURY THEATRE
15 Gordon Street
Bloomsbury
London WC1H 0AH
Website: www.thebloomsbury.com
e-mail: blooms.theatre@ucl.ac.uk
BO: 020-7388 8822   Admin: 020-7679 2777
Route: Tube to Euston, Euston Square or Warren Street

UNION THEATRE The
(Artisrtic Director: Sasha Regan)
(All Casting Enquiries - Paul Flynn)
204 Union Street
Southwark, London SE1 0LX
Website: www.uniontheatre.freeserve.co.uk
e-mail: sasha@uniontheatre.freeserve.co.uk
Tel/Fax: 020-7261 9876
Route: Jubilee line to Southwark then 2 min walk

UPSTAIRS AT THE GATEHOUSE
(Ovation Theatres Ltd)
The Gatehouse Pub
North Road, London N6 4BD
Website: www.upstairsatthegatehouse.com
e-mail: events@ovationproductions.com
BO: 020-8340 3488   Admin: 020-8340 3477

WAREHOUSE THEATRE
(Artistic Director - Ted Craig)
Dingwall Road
Croydon CR0 2NF
Website: www.warehousetheatre.co.uk
e-mail: info@warehousetheatre.co.uk
Fax: 020-8688 6699
BO: 020-8680 4060   Admin: 020-8681 1257
Adjacent to East Croydon (BR). Direct from
Victoria (15 mins), Clapham Junction (10 mins) or
by Thameslink from West Hampstead, Kentish
Town, Kings Cross, Blackfriars & London Bridge

WATERMANS
40 High Street
Brentford TW8 0DS
e-mail: info@watermans.org.uk
Fax: 020-8232 1030
BO: 020-8232 1010   Admin: 020-8232 1020
Route: Buses: 237, 267, 65 or N97 Tube:
Gunnersbury or South Ealing BR: Kew Bridge then 5
min walk, Gunnersbury then 10 min walk, or
Brentford

WESTRIDGE OPEN CENTRE
Star Lane, Andover Road
Highclere, Nr Newbury
Berkshire RG20 9PJ   Tel: 01635 253322

WHITE BEAR THEATRE
(Favours New Writing)
138 Kennington Park Road
London SE11 4DJ
e-mail: mkwbear@hotmail.com
Admin/BO: 020-7793 9193

WILTONS MUSIC HALL
Graces Alley
Off Ensign Street
London E1 8JB
e-mail: opera@broomhill.demon.co.uk
Fax: 020-7702 1414   Tel: 020-7702 9555
Route Tube: Under 10 minutes walk from Aldgate
East (exit for Leman Street)/Tower Hill/Shadwell.
DLR: Shadwell & Tower Gateway. Car: Look out for
the yellow AA signs to Wiltons Music Hall from the
Highway, Aldgate & Tower Hill.

WIMBLEDON STUDIO THEATRE
(Wimbledon Theatre)
103 The Broadway
London SW19 1QG
Website: www.wimbledontheatre.com
Fax: 020-8543 6637
BO: 020-8540 0362   Admin: 020-8543 4549
Route: BR or District Line to Wimbledon BR, Tube &
Tramlink, then 3 min walk. Buses 57,93,155

WIMBLEDON THEATRE
The Broadway
London SW19 1QG
Fax: 020-8543 6637
BO: 020-8540 0362   Admin: 020-8543 4549
Route: BR or District Line to Wimbledon BR & Tube,
then 3 min walk. Buses 57, 93, 155

WYCOMBE SWAN
St Mary Street
High Wycombe
Buckinghamshire HP11 2XE
Website: www.wycombeswan.co.uk
e-mail: enquiries@wycombeswan.co.uk
BO: 01494 512000   Admin: 01494 514444

ABERDEEN

His Majesty's Theatre
Rosemount Viaduct, Aberdeen AB25 1GL
Box Office: 01224 641122
Stage Door: 01224 638677
Admin: 01224 637788
Website: www.hmtheatre.com
e-mail: info@hmtheatre.com

ABERYSTWYTH

Aberystwyth Arts Centre
University of Wales, Aberystwyth SY23 3DE
Box Office: 01970 623232
Stage Door: 01970 624239
Admin: 01970 622882
Website: www.aber.ac.uk/artscentre
e-mail: lla@aber.ac.uk

ASHTON-UNDER-LYNE

Tameside Hippodrome
Oldham Road, Ashton-under-Lyne OL6 7SE
Box Office: 0161-308 3223
Stage Door: ---------------
Admin: 0161-330 2095

AYR

Gaiety Theatre
Carrick Street, Ayr KA7 1NU
Box Office: 01292 611222
Stage Door: 01292 617414
Admin: 01292 617400

BACUP

Royal Court Theatre
Rochdale Road, Bacup OL13 9NR
Box Office: 01706 874080
Stage Door: ---------------
Admin: ---------------

BASINGSTOKE

Haymarket Theatre
Wote Street, Basingstoke RG21 7NW
Box Office: 01256 465566
Stage Door: 01256 323073
Admin: 01256 323073
Website: www.haymarket.org.uk
e-mail: info@haymarket.org.uk

BATH

Theatre Royal
Sawclose, Bath BA1 1ET
Box Office: 01225 448844
Stage Door: 01225 448815
Admin: 01225 448815
Website: www.theatreroyal.org.uk
e-mail: forename.surname@theatreroyal.org.uk

BELFAST

Grand Opera House
Great Victoria Street, Belfast BT2 7HR
Box Office: 028-9024 1919
Stage Door: 028-9024 0411
Admin: 028-9024 0411
Website: www.goh.co.uk
e-mail: info@goh.co.uk

BILLINGHAM

Forum Theatre
Town Centre, Billingham TS23 2LJ
Box Office: 01642 552663
Stage Door: ---------------
Admin: 01642 551389

BIRMINGHAM

Alexandra Theatre
Station Street, Birmingham B5 4DS
Box Office: 0870 6077533
Stage Door: 0121-230 9102
Admin: 0121-643 5536
Website: www.ticketmaster.co.uk

BIRMINGHAM

Hippodrome
Hurst Street, Birmingham B5 4TB
Box Office: 0870 7301234
Stage Door: ---------------
Admin: 0870 7305555

BLACKPOOL

Grand Theatre
33 Church Street, Blackpool FY1 1HT
Box Office: 01253 290190
Stage Door: 01253 743218
Admin: 01253 290111
Website: www.blackpoolgrand.co.uk
e-mail: geninfo@blackpoolgrand.co.uk

BLACKPOOL

Opera House
Church Street, Blackpool FY1 1HW
Box Office: 01253 292029
Stage Door: 01253 625252 ext 148
Admin: 01253 625252

BOURNEMOUTH

Pavilion Theatre
Westover Road, Bournemouth BH1 2BU
Box Office: 01202 456456
Stage Door: 01202 451863
Admin: 01202 456400

BRADFORD

Alhambra Theatre
Morley Street, Bradford BD7 1AJ
Box Office: 01274 752000
Stage Door: 01274 752375
Admin: 01274 752375
Website: www.bradford-theatres.co.uk
e-mail: administration@ces.bradford.gov.uk

BRADFORD

Theatre in the Mill
University of Bradford, Shearbridge Road
Bradford BD7 1DP
Box Office: 01274 233200
Stage Door: ---------------
Admin: 01274 233188
Website: www.bradford.ac.uk/theatre
e-mail: theatre-manager@brad.ac.uk

BRIGHTON

The Dome, Corn Exchange & Pavilion Theatres
29 New Road, Brighton BN1 1UG
Box Office: 01273 709709
Stage Door: 01273 261550
Admin: 01273 700747
e-mail: info@brighton-dome.org.uk

BRIGHTON

Theatre Royal
New Road, Brighton BN1 1SD
Box Office: 01273 328488
Stage Door: 01273 764400
Admin: 01273 764400
e-mail: brightontheatremanager@theambassadors.com

BRISTOL

Hippodrome
St Augustines Parade
Bristol BS1 4UZ
Box Office: 0870 6077500
Stage Door: 0117-927 3077
Admin: 0117-302 3310
Website: www.ticketmaster.co.uk

BROXBOURNE (Herts)

Broxbourne Civic Hall
High Street, Hoddesdon
Hertfordshire EN11 8BE
Box Office: 01992 441946
Stage Door: ---------------
Admin: 01992 441931
Website: www.broxbourne.gov.uk
e-mail: civic.leisure@broxbourne.gov.uk

BURY ST EDMUNDS

Theatre Royal
Westgate Street, Bury St Edmunds IP33 1QR
Box Office: 01284 769505
Stage Door: 01284 755127
Admin: 01284 755127
Website: www.theatreroyal.org
e-mail: admin@theatreroyal.org

BUXTON

Opera House
Water Street, Buxton SK17 6XN
Box Office: 0845 1272190
Stage Door: 01298 71382
Admin: 01298 72050
Website: www.buxton-opera.co.uk
e-mail: admin@buxtonopera.co.uk

CAMBERLEY

The Camberley Theatre
Knoll Road, Camberley, Surrey GU15 3SY
Box Office: 01276 707600
Stage Door: ---------------
Admin: 01276 707612
Website: www.camberleytheatre.biz
e-mail: camberleytheatre@surreyheath.gov.uk

CAMBRIDGE

Cambridge Arts Theatre
6 St Edward's Passage, Cambridge CB2 3PJ
Box Office: 01223 503333
Stage Door: 01223 578933
Admin: 01223 578933
Website: www.cambridgeartstheatre.com
e-mail: info@cambridgeartstheatre.com

CAMBRIDGE

Mumford Theatre
Anglia Polytechnic University, East Road
Cambridge CB1 1PT
Box Office: 01223 352932
Stage Door: 01223 352932
Admin: 01223 352932
e-mail: mumford@apu.ac.uk

CANTERBURY

Gulbenkian Theatre
University of Kent, Canterbury CT2 7NB
Box Office: 01227 769075
Stage Door: 01227 769565
Admin: 01227 827861
Website: www.kent.ac.uk/gulbenkian
e-mail: gulbenkian@kent.ac.uk

CANTERBURY

The Marlowe Theatre
The Friars, Canterbury CT1 2AS
Box Office: 01227 787787
Stage Door: 01227 786867
Admin: 01227 763262
Website: www.marlowetheatre.com
e-mail: markeverett@canterbury.gov.uk

CARDIFF

New Theatre
Park Place, Cardiff CF10 3LN
Box Office: 029-2087 8889
Stage Door: 029-2087 8900
Admin: 029-2087 8787

CHELTENHAM

Everyman Theatre
Regent Street, Cheltenham GL50 1HQ
Box Office: 01242 572573
Stage Door: 01242 512515
Admin: 01242 512515
Website: www.everymantheatre.org.uk
e-mail: admin@everymantheatre.org.uk

CHESTER

Gateway Theatre
Hamilton Place, Chester, Cheshire CH1 2BH
BO: 01244 340392
Admin: 01244 318603
Fax: 01244 317277
Website: www.chestergateway.co.uk
e-mail: admin@gateway-theatre.org

CHICHESTER

Festival Theatre
Oaklands Park, Chichester PO19 6AP
Box Office: 01243 781312
Stage Door: 01243 784437
Admin: 01243 784437
Website: www.cft.org.uk
e-mail: admin@cft.org.uk

CRAWLEY

The Hawth
Hawth Avenue, Crawley RH10 6YZ
Box Office: 01293 553636
Stage Door: -----------------
Admin: 01293 552941
Website: www.hawth.co.uk
e-mail: info@hawth.co.uk

CREWE

Lyceum Theatre
Heath Street, Crewe CW1 2DA
Box Office: 01270 537333
Stage Door: 01270 537336
Admin: 01270 537243

DARLINGTON

Civic Theatre
Parkgate, Darlington DL1 1RR
Box Office: 01325 486555
Stage Door: 01325 467743
Admin: 01325 387775
Website: www.darlington-arts.co.uk

DUBLIN

Gaiety Theatre
South King Street, Dublin 2
Box Office: 00 353 1 6771717
Stage Door: 00 353 1 6795622
Admin: 00 353 1 6795622

T

DUBLIN

Gate Theatre
1 Cavendish Row, Dublin 1
Box Office: 00 353 1 8744045
Stage Door: ---------------
Admin: 00 353 1 8744368
Website: www.gate-theatre.ie
e-mail: info@gate-theatre.ie

DUBLIN

Olympia Theatre
72 Dame Street, Dublin 2
Box Office: 00 353 1 6793323
Stage Door: 00 353 1 6771400
Admin: 00 353 1 6725883
Website: www.mcd.ie
e-mail: info@olpmpia.ie

EASTBOURNE

Congress Theatre
Admin: Winter Garden, Compton Street
Eastbourne BN21 4BP
Box Office: 01323 412000
Stage Door: 01323 410048
Admin: 01323 415500
Website: www.eastbournetheatres.co.uk
e-mail: theatres@eastbourne.gov.uk

EASTBOURNE

Devonshire Park Theatre
Admin: Winter Garden, Compton Street
Eastbourne BN21 4BP
Box Office: 01323 412000
Stage Door: 01323 410074
Admin: 01323 415500
Website: www.eastbournetheatres.co.uk
e-mail: theatres@eastbourne.gov.uk

EDINBURGH

King's Theatre
2 Leven Street, Edinburgh EH3 9LQ
Box Office: 0131-529 6000
Stage Door: 0131-229 3416
Admin: 0131-662 1112
Website: www.eft.co.uk
e-mail: admin@eft.co.uk

EDINBURGH

Playhouse Theatre
18-22 Greenside Place, Edinburgh EH1 3AA
Box Office: 0870 6063424
Stage Door: 0131-524 3324
Admin: 0131-524 3333
Website: www.ticketmaster.co.uk

GLASGOW

King's Theatre
297 Bath Street, Glasgow G2 4JN
Box Office: 0141-240 1111
Stage Door: 0141-240 1300
Admin: 0141-240 1300

GLASGOW

Theatre Royal
282 Hope Street, Glasgow G2 3QA
Box Office: 0141-332 9000
Stage Door: 0141-332 3321
Admin: 0141-332 3321
Website: www.theatreroyalglasgow.com

GRAYS THURROCK

Thameside Theatre
Orsett Road, Grays Thurrock RM17 5DX
Box Office: 01375 383961
Stage Door: ---------------
Admin: 01375 382555
Website: www.thurrock.gov.uk/theatre
e-mail: mallinson@thurrock.gov.uk

HARLOW

The Playhouse
Playhouse Square, Harlow CM20 1LS
Box Office: 01279 431945
Stage Door: ---------------
Admin: 01279 446760
Website: www.playhouseharlow.com
e-mail: philip.dale@harlow.gov.uk

HARROGATE

Harrogate International Centre
Kings Road, Harrogate HG1 5LA
Box Office: 01423 537230
Stage Door: 01423 537222
Admin: 01423 537200

HARROGATE

Royal Hall
Ripon Road, Harrogate HG1 2RD
Box Office: 01423 537230
Stage Door: ---------------
Admin: 01423 537200

HASTINGS

White Rock Theatre
White Rock, Hastings TN34 1JX
Box Office: 01424 781000
Stage Door: ---------------
Admin: 01424 781010

HAYES (Middlesex)

Beck Theatre
Grange Road, Hayes, Middlesex UB3 2UE
Box Office: 020-8561 8371
Stage Door: ---------------
Admin: 020-8561 7506

HIGH WYCOMBE

Wycombe Swan
St Mary Street, High Wycombe HP11 2XE
Box Office: 01494 512000
Stage Door: 01494 514444
Admin: 01494 514444
Website: www.wycombeswan.co.uk
e-mail: enquiries@wycombeswan.co.uk

HUDDERSFIELD

Cragrats Ltd
The Mill, Dunford Road, Holmfirth
Huddersfield HD9 2AR
Tel: 01484 686451
Website: www.cragrats.com
e-mail: jill@cragrats.com

HUDDERSFIELD

Lawrence Batley Theatre
Queen Street, Huddersfield HD1 2SP
Box Office: 01484 430528
Stage Door: ---------------
Admin: 01484 425282
e-mail: theatre@lbt-uk.org

HULL

Hull New Theatre
Kingston Square, Hull HU1 3HF
Box Office: 01482 226655
Stage Door: 01482 320244
Admin: 01482 613818
e-mail: theatre.management@hullcc.gov.uk

HULL

Hull Truck Theatre
Spring Street, Hull HU2 8RW
Box Office: 01482 323638
Stage Door: ---------------
Admin: 01482 224800
Website: www.hulltruck.co.uk
e-mail: admin@hulltruck.co.uk

ILFORD

Kenneth More Theatre
Oakfield Road, Ilford IG1 1BT
Box Office: 020-8553 4466
Stage Door: 020-8553 4465
Admin: 020-8553 4464
Website: www.kenneth-more-theatre.co.uk
e-mail: kmtheatre@aol.com

IPSWICH

Sir John Mills Theatre (Hire Only)
Gatacre Road, Ipswich IP1 2LQ
Box Office: 01473 211498
Stage Door: ---------------
Admin: 01473 218202
Website: www.easternangles.co.uk
e-mail: admin@easternangles.co.uk

JERSEY

Opera House
Gloucester Street, St Helier, Jersey JE2 3QR
Box Office: 01534 511115
Stage Door: ---------------
Admin: 01534 511100
e-mail: ian@jerseyoperahouse.co.uk

KIRKCALDY

Adam Smith Theatre
Bennochy Road, Kirkaldy KY1 1ET
Box Office: 01592 412929
Stage Door: ---------------
Admin: 01592 412567

LEEDS

City Varieties Music Hall
Swan Street, Leeds LS1 6LW
Box Office: 0113-243 0808
Stage Door: ---------------
Admin: 0113-391 7777
Website: www.cityvarieties.co.uk
e-mail: info@cityvarieties.co.uk

LEEDS

Grand Theatre & Opera House
46 New Briggate, Leeds LS1 6NZ
Box Office: 0113-222 6222
Stage Door: ---------------
Admin: 0113-245 6014

LICHFIELD

The Lichfield Garrick
Castle Dyke
Lichfield WS13 6HR
Box Office: 01543 412121
Stage Door: ---------------
Admin: 01543 412110

LINCOLN

Theatre Royal
Clasketgate, Lincoln LN2 1JJ
Box Office: 01522 525555
Stage Door: 01522 523303
Admin: 01522 523303
Website: www.theatreroyallincoln.com
e-mail: theatre.royal@dial.pipex.com

LIVERPOOL

Empire Theatre
Lime Street, Liverpool L1 1JE
Box Office: 0870 6063536
Stage Door: 0151-708 3200
Admin: 0151-708 3200

LIVERPOOL

Neptune Theatre
Hanover Street, Liverpool L1 3DY
Box Office: 0151-709 7844
Stage Door: 0151-709 7844
Admin: 0151-709 7844
Website: www.neptunetheatre.co.uk
e-mail: neptune.theatre@liverpool.gov.uk

MALVERN

Malvern Theatres (Festival & Forum Theatres)
Grange Road, Malvern WR14 3HB
Box Office: 01684 892277
Stage Door: ---------------
Admin: 01684 569256
Website: www.malvern-theatres.co.uk
e-mail: post@malvern-theatres.co.uk

MANCHESTER

Carling Apollo
Stockport Road, Ardwick Green
Manchester M12 6AP
Box Office: 0870 4018000
Stage Door: 0161-273 2416
Admin: 0161-273 6921
Website: www.cclive.co.uk

MANCHESTER

Opera House
Quay Street, Manchester M3 3HP
Box Office: 0870 4019000
Stage Door: 0161-834 1787
Admin: 0161-834 1787

MANCHESTER

Palace Theatre
Oxford Street, Manchester M1 6FT
Box Office: 0870 401300
Stage Door: 0161-228 6255
Admin: 0161-228 6255

MARGATE

Theatre Royal
Addington Street, Margate, Kent CT9 1PW
Box Office: 01843 293877
Stage Door: 01843 293397
Admin: 01843 293397

MILTON KEYNES

Milton Keynes Theatre
500 Marlborough Gate,
Central Milton Keynes MK9 3NZ
Box Office: 01908 606090
Stage Door: 01908 547500
Admin: 01908 547500

NEWARK

Palace Theatre
Appletongate, Newark NG24 1JY
Box Office: 01636 655755
Stage Door: ---------------
Admin: 01636 655750
Website: www.palacenewark.com
e-mail: david.piper@nsdc.info

NEWCASTLE UPON TYNE

Newcastle Opera House
111 Westgate Rd, Newcastle upon Tyne NE1 4AG
Box Office: 0191-232 0899
Stage Door: 0191-232 1551
Admin: 0191-261 1725
Website: www.newcastleopera.org
e-mail: operahouse@virgin.net

NEWCASTLE UPON TYNE

Playhouse & Gulbenkian Studio Theatre
Barras Bridge, Haymarket
Newcastle upon Tyne NE1 7RH
Box Office: 0191-232 5151
Stage Door: --------------
Admin: 0191-232 3366
Website: www.northernstage.com
e-mail: info@northernstage.com

NEWCASTLE UPON TYNE

Theatre Royal
Grey Street, Newcastle upon Tyne NE1 6BR
Box Office: 0870 9055060
Stage Door: 0191-244 2500
Admin: 0191-232 0997

NORTHAMPTON

Royal & Derngate Theatres, Northampton
19-21 Guildhall Road
Northampton NN1 1DP
Box Office: 01604 624811
Stage Door: 01604 626289
Admin: 01604 626222
Website: www.royalandderngate.com
e-mail: postbox@ntt.org.uk

NORWICH

Theatre Royal
Theatre Street, Norwich NR2 1RL
Box Office: 01603 630000
Stage Door: 01603 598500
Admin: 01603 598500
Website: www.theatreroyalnorwich.co.uk

NOTTINGHAM

Theatre Royal & Royal Concert Hall
Theatre Square, Nottingham NG1 5ND
Box Office: 0115-989 5555
Stage Door: 0115-989 5500
Admin: 0115-989 5500
Website: www.royalcentre-nottingham.co.uk
e-mail: enquiry@royalcentre-nottingham.co.uk

OXFORD

New Theatre
George Street, Oxford OX1 2AG
Box Office: 0870 6063500
Stage Door: 01865 320760
Admin: 01865 320761
Website: www.cclive.co.uk

OXFORD

Oxford Playhouse
Beaumont Street, Oxford OX1 2LW
Box Office: 01865 305305
Stage Door: 01865 305301
Admin: 01865 305300
Website: www.oxfordplayhouse.co.uk
e-mail: admin@oxfordplayhouse.com

PAIGNTON

Palace Theatre
Palace Avenue, Paignton TQ3 3HF
Box Office: 01803 665800
Stage Door: --------------
Admin: 01803 558367
Website: www.torbay.gov.uk/palacetheatre
e-mail: palace.theatre@torbay.gov.uk

PLYMOUTH

Athenaeum
Derry's Cross, Plymouth PL1 2SW
Box Office: 01752 266104
Stage Door: --------------
Admin: 01752 266079

POOLE

Lighthouse, Poole's Centre for The Arts
Kingland Road, Poole BH15 1UG
Box Office: 01202 685222
Stage Door: --------------
Admin: 01202 665334

READING

The Hexagon
Queen's Walk, Reading RG1 7UA
Box Office: 0118-960 6060
Stage Door: 0118-939 0018
Admin: 0118-939 0390

RICHMOND (N Yorks)

Georgian Theatre Royal
Victoria Road, Richmond
North Yorkshire DL10 4DW
Box Office: 01748 825252
Stage Door: --------------
Admin: 01748 823710
Website: www.georgiantheatreroyal.co.uk

RICHMOND (Surrey)

Richmond Theatre
The Green, Richmond, Surrey TW9 1QJ
Box Office: 020-8940 0088
Stage Door: 020-8940 0220
Admin: 020-8940 0220
Website: www.richmondtheatre.net

SHEFFIELD

Sheffield Theatres - Crucible, Lyceum & Crucible Studio
55 Norfolk Street, Sheffield S1 1DA
Box Office: 0114-249 6000
Stage Door: 0114-249 5999
Admin: 0114-249 5999
Website: www.sheffieldtheatres.co.uk

SOUTHAMPTON

Mayflower Theatre
Commercial Road, Southampton SO15 1GE
Box Office: 023-8071 1811
Stage Door: 023-8033 0071
Admin: 023-8071 1800
Website: www.the-mayflower.com
e-mail: info@the-mayflower.com

ST ALBANS

Abbey Theatre
Holywell Hill, St Albans AL1 2DL
Admin: 01727 847472
Box Office: 01727 857861
Website: www.abbeytheatre.org.uk
e-mail: manager@abbeytheatre.org.uk

ST ALBANS

Alban Arena
Civic Centre, St Albans AL1 3LD
Box Office: 01727 844488
Stage Door: -----------------
Admin: 01727 861078
Website: www.alban-arena.co.uk
e-mail: info@alban-arena.co.uk

ST HELENS

Theatre Royal
Corporation Street, St Helens WA10 1LQ
Box Office: 01744 756000
Stage Door: ---------------
Admin: 01744 756333

STAFFORD

Stafford Gatehouse Theatre
Eastgate Street, Stafford ST16 2LT
Box Office: 01785 254653
Stage Door: ---------------
Admin: 01785 253595
e-mail: gatehouse@staffordbc.gov.uk

STEVENAGE

Gordon Craig Theatre
Arts & Leisure Centre, Lytton Way, Stevenage SG1 1LZ
Box Office: 08700 131030
Stage Door: 01438 242629
Admin: 01438 242642
Website: www.stevenage-leisure.co.uk
e-mail: gordoncraig@stevenage-leisure.co.uk

STOCKPORT

The Peter Barkworth Theatre
Stockport College, Wellington Rd, Stockport SK1 3UQ
Box Office: 0161-958 3114
Stage Door: 0161-958 3429
Admin: 0161-429 7413

STRATFORD-UPON-AVON

Royal Shakespeare Theatre
Waterside, Stratford-upon-Avon CV37 6BB
Box Office: 01789 403403
Stage Door: 01789 296655
Admin: 01789 296655
Website: www.rsc.org.uk
e-mail: info@rsc.org.uk

STRATFORD-UPON-AVON

The Other Place
Southern Lane, Stratford-upon-Avon CV37 6BH
Box Office: 0870 6091110
Stage Door: 01789 296655
Admin: 01789 296655

SUNDERLAND

Empire Theatre
High Street West, Sunderland SR1 3EX
Box Office: 0191-514 2517
Stage Door: 0191-565 6750
Admin: 0191-510 0545

SWANAGE

Mowlem Theatre
Shore Road, Swanage BH19 1DD
Box Office: 01929 422239
Stage Door: ---------------
Admin: 01929 422229

TAMWORTH

Assembly Rooms
Corporation Street, Tamworth B79 7BX
Box Office: 01827 709618
Stage Door: ---------------
Admin: 01827 709620

TEWKESBURY

The Roses
Sun Street, Tewkesbury GL20 5NX
Box Office: 01684 295074
Stage Door: ---------------
Admin: 01684 290734
e-mail: arts@rosestheatre.org.uk

TORQUAY

Babbacombe Theatre
Babbacombe Downs, Torquay TQ1 3LU
Box Office: 01803 328385
Stage Door: 01803 328385
Admin: 01803 322233
Website: www.babbacombe-theatre.com
e-mail: mail@matpro-show.biz

TORQUAY

Princess Theatre
Torbay Road, Torquay TQ2 5EZ
Box Office: 0870 2414120
Stage Door: 01803 290068
Admin: 01803 290288
Website: www.ticketmaster.co.uk
e-mail: princess@clearchannel.co.uk

WATFORD

Palace Theatre
Clarendon Road, Watford WD17 1JZ
Box Office: 01923 225671
Stage Door: ---------------
Admin: 01923 235455
Website: www.watfordtheatre.co.uk
e-mail: enquiries@watfordtheatre.co.uk

WINCHESTER

Theatre Royal
21-23 Jewry Street, Winchester SO23 8SB
Box Office: 01962 840440
Stage Door: ---------------
Admin: 01962 844600
e-mail: marketing@theatre-royal-winchester.co.uk

WOLVERHAMPTON

Grand Theatre
Lichfield Street, Wolverhampton WV1 1DE
Box Office: 01902 429212
Stage Door: 01902 573320
Admin: 01902 573300
Website: www.grandtheatre.co.uk
e-mail: marketing@grandtheatre.co.uk

WORTHING

Connaught Theatre
Union Place, Worthing BN11 1LG
Box Office: 01903 206206
Stage Door: ---------------
Admin: 01903 231799

YEOVIL

Octagon Theatre
Hendford, Yeovil BA20 1UX
Box Office: 01935 422884
Stage Door: 01935 845926
Admin: 01935 845900
Website: www.octagon-theatre.co.uk
e-mail: octagontheatre@southsomerset.gov.uk

YORK

Grand Opera House
Cumberland Street, York YO1 9SW
Box Office: 01904 671818
Stage Door: ---------------
Admin: 01904 678700

AUTHENTIC PUNCH & JUDY
Puppets, Booths & Presentations (John Styles)
42 Christchurch Road
Sidcup, Kent DA15 7HQ
Website: www.johnstylesentertainer.co.uk
Tel/Fax: 020-8300 3579

BROOKER David
(Punch & Judy)
75 Northcote Road
New Malden
Surrey KT3 3HF
Tel: 020-8949 5035

BUCKLEY Simon
(Freelance Puppeteer/Presenter)
c/o Talent Artists Ltd
59 Sydner Road
London N16 7UF
Website: www.simonbuckley.co.uk
e-mail: puppet.buckley@virgin.net
Tel: 020-7923 1119

COMPLETE WORKS THEATRE COMPANY Ltd The
12 Willowford
Bancroft Park, Milton Keynes
Buckinghamshire MK13 0RH
Website: www.tcw.org.uk
e-mail: info@tcw.org.uk
Fax: 01908 320263
Tel: 01908 316256

CORNELIUS & JONES
49 Carters Close
Sherington, Newport Pagnell
Buckinghamshire MK16 9NW
Website: www.corneliusjones.com
e-mail: admin@corneliusjones.com
Fax: 01908 216400
Tel: 01908 612593

DYNAMIC NEW ANIMATION
19 Royal Close
Manor Road, London N16 5SE
Website: www.dynamicnewanimation.co.uk
e-mail: dna@dynamicnewanimation.co.uk
Mobile: 07976 946003

GRIFFITHS Marc
(Ventriloquist)
The Mega Centre
Bernard Road
Sheffield S2 5BQ
Tel: 0114-272 5077

JACOLLY PUPPET THEATRE
Kirkella Road
Yelverton
West Devon PL20 6BB
Website: www.jacolly-puppets.co.uk
e-mail: theatre@jacolly-puppets.co.uk
Tel: 01822 852346

LITTLE ANGEL THEATRE
14 Dagmar Passage
Cross Street, London N1 2DN
Website: www.littleangeltheatre.com
e-mail: info@littleangeltheatre.com
Fax: 020-7359 7565
Tel: 020-7226 1787

MAJOR MUSTARD'S TRAVELLING SHOW
1 Carless Avenue
Harborne, Birmingham B17 9EG
e-mail: majormustard@bnum.com
Fax: 0121-427 2358
Tel: 0121-426 4329

NORWICH PUPPET THEATRE
St James, Whitefriars
Norwich NR3 1TN
Website: www.geocities.com/norwichpuppets
e-mail: norpuppet@hotmail.com
Fax: 01603 617578
Tel: 01603 615564

PARASOL PUPPET THEATRE
Garden House
4 Sunnyside, Wimbledon SW19 4SL
Website: www.parasoltheatre.co.uk
e-mail: parasoltheatre@waitrose.com
Fax: 020-8946 0228
Tel: 020-8946 9478

PEKKO'S PUPPETS
(Director - Stephen Novy)
92 Stanley Avenue, Greenford
Middlesex UB6 8NP
Tel: 020-8575 2311

PICCOLO PUPPET COMPANY
Maythorne, Higher Park Road, Braunton
North Devon EX33 2LF
e-mail: angiepassmore@onetel.net.uk
Tel: 01271 815984

PLAYBOARD PUPPETS
94 Ockendon Road, London N1 3NW
e-mail: thebuttonmoon@aol.com
Fax: 020-7704 1081
Tel: 020-7226 5911

POM POM PUPPETS
9 Fulham Park Gardens, London SW6 4JX
Website: www.pompompuppets.co.uk
Mobile: 07974 175247
Tel: 020-7736 6532

PROFESSOR PATTEN'S PUNCH & JUDY
(Puppetry & Magic)
14 The Crest, Goffs Oak
Hertforshire EN7 5NP
Website: www.dennispatten.co.uk
Tel: 01707 873262

PUNCH & JUDY
(Des Turner, President Punch & Judy Fellowship)
Richmond House
2 Benington Road
Aston, Stevenage, Hertfordshire SG2 7DX
Website: www.punchandjudy.org.uk
e-mail: desturner@aol.com
Tel: 01438 880376

PUPPET CENTRE TRUST
BAC Lavender Hill, London SW11 5TN
Website: www.puppetcentre.com
e-mail: pct@puppetcentre.demon.co.uk
Fax: 020-7228 8863
Tel: 020-7228 5335

THE GOOD THE BAD & THE CUDDLY THEATRE COMPANY
140 Manor Road
New Milton
Hampshire BH25 5ED
Website: www.fliteuk.com
e-mail: fliteuk@hotmail.com
Tel: 01425 612830

THEATR BYPEDAU SBLOT
(Splott Puppet Theatre)
22 Starling Road, St Athan
Vale of Glamorgan CF62 4NJ
e-mail: splottpuppets02@aol.com
Tel: 01446 790634

TICKLISH ALLSORTS SHOW
Cremyll, Marshmead Close
Clarendon
Salisbury, Wiltshire SP5 3DD
Website: www.ticklishallsorts.co.uk
e-mail: garynunn@lineone.net
Tel/Fax: 01722 711800

TOPPER Chris PUPPETS
(Puppets Created & Performed)
75 Barrows Green Lane
Widnes, Cheshire WA8 3JH
Website: www.christopperpuppets.com
Tel: 0151-424 8692

Where appropriate, Rep periods are indicated,
e.g. (4 Weekly) and matinee times e.g. Th 2.30 for
Thursday 2.30pm.

SD - Stage Door
BO - Box Office
TIE - Theatre in Education (For further details of TIE/YPT
See Theatre - TIE/YPT Companies).

ALDEBURGH
Summer Theatre (July & August) The Jubilee Hall
Crabbe Street, Aldeburgh IP15 5BW
Admin: (Oct-May) 020-7724 5432
Admin: (June-Sept) 01502 723077
Mon-Fri: 11-4 & Sat 11-2.30 BO: 01728 453007
Mon-Fri: 6-9 & Sat 4-8.30 BO: 01728 454022
Website: www.southworldtheatre.org

BASINGSTOKE
Haymarket Theatre Company
Wote Street, Basingstoke RG21 7NW
Fax: 01256 357130
BO: 01256 465566   Admin: 01256 323073
Website: www.haymarket.org.uk
e-mail: info@haymarket.org.uk
Theatre Director: Alasdair Ramsay
Executive Director: Zoë Curnow

BELFAST
Lyric Theatre
55 Ridgeway Street, Belfast BT9 5FB
Fax: 028-9038 1395
BO: 028-9038 1081   Admin: 028-9038 5685
Website: www.lyrictheatre.co.uk
e-mail: info@lyrictheatre.co.uk
General Manager: Mike Blair

BIRMINGHAM
Birmingham Stage Company
The Old Rep Theatre, Station Street
Birmingham B5 4DY
BO: 0121-236 5622   Admin: 0121-643 9050
Actor/Manager: Neal Foster
Administrator: Philip Compton

London Office:
Suite 228, The Linen Hall, 162 Regent Street W1B 5TG
Fax: 020-7437 3395   Admin: 020-7437 3391

Website: www.birminghamstage.net
e-mail: info@birminghamstage.net

BIRMINGHAM
Repertory Theatre
Centenary Square, Broad St, Birmingham B1 2EP
BO: 0121-236 4455
Press Office: 0121-245 2075   Tel: 0121-245 2000
e-mail: info@birmingham-rep.co.uk
Artistic Director: Jonathan Church
Executive Director: Stuart Rogers

BOLTON
Octagon Theatre
Howell Croft South, Bolton BL1 1SB
Fax: 01204 556502
BO: 01204 520661   Admin: 01204 529407
Artistic Director: Mark Babych
Executive Director: John Blackmore

BRISTOL
Theatre Royal & New Vic Studio
(3/4 Weekly) Eves 7.30pm Thurs & Sat Mats 2.00pm
(Bristol Old Vic Trust Ltd), King Street, Bristol BS1 4ED
Fax: 0117-949 3996
BO: 0117-987 7877   Tel: 0117-949 3993
e-mail: admin@bristol-old-vic.co.uk
Executive Director: Sarah Smith

BROMLEY
Churchill Theatre (Administration)
High Street, Bromley, Kent BR1 1HA
Fax: 020-8290 6968
BO: 020-8460 6677   Tel: 020-8464 7131
Website: www.churchilltheatre.co.uk
Chief Executive: Derek Nicholls

CARDIFF
Sherman Theatre & Sherman Studio
Senghennydd Road CF24 4YE
Fax: 029-2064 6902
BO: 029-2064 6900   Tel: 029-2064 6901
Director: Phil Clark
General Manager: Margaret Jones

CHELMSFORD
Civic Theatre
(2 Weekly) (Oct-Mar) Sat 5.00pm
Fairfield Road, Chelmsford, Essex CM1 1JG
Tel: 020-8349 0802 (London)   Admin: 01245 268998
Artistic Director: John Newman (Newpalm Prods)

CHICHESTER
Chichester Festival Theatre
(May-Oct & Touring)
Eves 7.30pm Thurs & Sat Mats 2.30pm
Oaklands Park, Chichester, West Sussex PO19 6AP
Fax: 01243 787288
BO: 01243 781312   SD & Admin: 01243 784437
Website: www.cft.org.uk
e-mail: admin@cft.org.uk
Theatre Manager: Janet Burton
Artistic Director: Ruth MacKenzie

CHICHESTER
Minerva Theatre at Chichester Festival Theatre
(June-Oct) Eves 7.45pm Weds & Sat Mats 2.45pm
Oaklands Park, Chichester, West Sussex PO19 6AP
Fax: 01243 787288
BO: 01243 781312   SD & Admin: 01243 784437
Website: www.cft.org.uk
e-mail: admin@cft.org.uk
Theatre Manager: Janet Burton
Artistic Director: Ruth MacKenzie

COLCHESTER
Mercury Theatre
(3-4 Weekly) Thurs & Sat Mats 2.30pm
Balkerne Gate, Colchester, Essex CO1 1PT
Fax: 01206 769607
BO: 01206 573948   Admin: 01206 577006
Website: www.mercurytheatre.co.uk
e-mail: info@mercurytheatre.co.uk
Chief Executive: Dee Evans

COVENTRY
Belgrade Theatre & Belgrade Studio
Belgrade Square, Coventry, West Midlands CV1 1GS
BO: 024-7655 3055   Admin: 024-7625 6431
Website: www.belgrade.co.uk
e-mail: admin@belgrade.co.uk
Theatre Director: Hamish Glen
Associate Producer: Jane Hytch
Executive Director: Joanna Reid
Head of Marketing: tba

DERBY
Derby Playhouse
(3½ Weekly)
Theatre Walk, Eagle Centre, Derby DE1 2NF
Fax: 01332 547200   BO: 01332 363275
SD: 01332 363271   Admin: 01332 363271
Website: www.derbyplayhouse.co.uk
e-mail: admin@derbyplayhouse.demon.co.uk
Creative Producer: Stephen Edwards
Chief Executive: Karen Hebden

DUBLIN
Abbey Theatre & Peacock Theatre
The National Theatre Society Limited
26 Lower Abbey Street, Dublin 1, Eire
Fax: 00 353 1 872 9177
BO: 00 353 1 878 7222   Admin: 00 353 1 887 2200
Website: www.abbeytheatre.ie
e-mail: mail@abbeytheatre.ie
General Manager: Brian Jackson

DUNDEE
Dundee Repertory Theatre
Tay Square, Dundee DD1 1PB
Fax: 01382 228609
BO: 01382 223530   Admin: 01382 227684
Website: www.dundeereptheatre.co.uk
Artistic Directors: James Brining, Dominic Hill
Executive Director: tba

EDINBURGH
Royal Lyceum Theatre Company
30B Grindlay Street, Edinburgh EH3 9AX
Fax: 0131-228 3955
BO: 0131-248 4848   SD & Admin: 0131-248 4800
Website: www.lyceum.org.uk
e-mail: info@lyceum.org.uk
Artistic Director: Mark Thomson

EDINBURGH
Traverse Theatre
(New Writing, Own Productions & Visiting
Companies)
Cambridge Street, Edinburgh EH1 2ED
Fax: 0131-229 8443
BO: 0131-228 1404   Admin: 0131-228 3223
Website: www.traverse.co.uk
e-mail: admin@traverse.co.uk
Artistic Director: Philip Howard
Administrative Director: Mike Griffiths

EXETER
Northcott Theatre
(3/4 Weekly)
Stocker Road, Exeter, Devon EX4 4QB
Fax: 01392 223996
BO: 01392 493493   Admin: 01392 223999
Website: www.northcott-theatre.co.uk
Artistic Director: Ben Crocker
Executive Director: Shea Connolly

EYE THEATRE
Eye Theatre
(4 Weekly) Sat 4.00pm
Broad Street, Eye, Suffolk IP23 7AF
Fax: 01379 871142   Tel: 01379 870519
e-mail: tomscott@eyetheatre.freeserve.co.uk
Artistic Director: Tom Scott
Associate Director: Janeena Sims

FRINTON
Frinton Summer Theatre
(July-Sept)
Ashlyns Road, Frinton, Essex
(During Season Only)   Admin: 01255 674443
Producer: Seymour Matthews

GLASGOW
Citizens Theatre
Gorbals, Glasgow G5 9DS
Fax: 0141-429 7374
BO: 0141-429 0022   Admin: 0141-429 5561
Website: www.citz.co.uk
e-mail: anna@citz.co.uk
Artistic Director: Jeremy Raison
General Manager: Anna Stapleton

GUILDFORD
Yvonne Arnaud Theatre
Millbrook, Guildford, Surrey GU1 3UX
Fax: 01483 564071
BO: 01483 440000   Admin: 01483 440077
Website: www.yvonne-arnaud.co.uk
e-mail: yat@yvonne-arnaud.co.uk
Director: James Barber

HARROGATE
Harrogate Theatre
(3-4 weekly) 2.30pm Sat
Oxford Street, Harrogate HG1 1QF
Fax: 01423 563205
BO: 01423 502116   Admin: 01423 502710
e-mail: christianname.surname@harrogatetheatre.demon.co.uk
Artistic Director: Hannah Chissick
Executive Director: Sheena Wrigley

IPSWICH
The New Wolsey Theatre
Civic Drive, Ipswich, Suffolk IP1 2AS
Admin Fax: 01473 295910
BO: 01473 295900   Admin: 01473 295911
Website: www.wolseytheatre.co.uk
e-mail: info@wolseytheatre.co.uk
Artistic Director: Peter Rowe
Chief Executive: Sarah Holmes

KESWICK
Theatre by The Lake
Lakeside, Keswick, Cumbria CA12 5DJ
Fax: 017687 74698
BO: 017687 74411   Admin: 017687 72282
Website: www.theatrebythelake.com
e-mail: enquiries@theatrebythelake.com
Artistic Director: Ian Forrest

LANCASTER
The Dukes
Moor Lane, Lancaster, Lancashire LA1 1QE
Fax: 01524 598519
BO: 01524 598500   Admin: 01524 598505
Website: www.dukes-lancaster.org
Artistic Director: Ian Hastings
Chief Executive: Amanda Belcham

LEEDS
The West Yorkshire Playhouse
Inc Schools Company
Playhouse Square, Quarry Hill, Leeds LS2 7UP
Fax: 0113-213 7250
BO: 0113-213 7700   Admin: 0113-213 7800
Website: www.wyp.org.uk
Artistic Director (Chief Executive): Ian Brown
Executive Director: Dan Bates
Casting Director: Kay Magson
Producer: Paul Crewes

LEICESTER
Leicester Haymarket Theatre & Studio
Belgrave Gate, Leicester LE1 3YQ
Fax: 0116-251 3310
BO: 0116-253 9797   Admin: 0116-253 0021
Website: www.leicesterhaymarkettheatre.co.uk
e-mail: enquiry@leicesterhaymarkettheatre.org
Artistic Director: Paul Kerryson, Kully Thiarai
Chief Executive: Mandy Stewart

LIVERPOOL
Everyman & Playhouse Theatres
Everyman: 13 Hope Street, Liverpool L1 9BH,
Playhouse: Williamson Square, Liverpool L1 1EL
Fax: 0151-709 0398
BO: 0151-709 4776   Admin: 0151-708 0338
Website: www.everymanplayhouse.com
e-mail: reception@everymanplayhouse.com
Artistic Director: Gemma Bodinetz
Executive Director: Deborah Aydon

MANCHESTER
Contact Theatre Company
(3/4 Weekly)
Oxford Road, Manchester M15 6JA
Fax: 0161-274 0640
BO: 0161-274 0600   Admin: 0161-274 3434
Website: www.contact-theatre.org
e-mail: info@contact-theatre.org.uk
Chief Executive/Artistic Director:
John Edward McGrath

MANCHESTER
Library Theatre Company
St Peter's Square, Manchester M2 5PD
Fax: 0161-228 6481
BO: 0161-236 7110   Admin: 0161-234 1913
Website: www.librarytheatre.com
e-mail: ltc@libraries.manchester.gov.uk
Artistic Director: Chris Honer
General Manager: Adrian J. P. Morgan

MANCHESTER
Royal Exchange Theatre
St Ann's Square, Manchester M2 7DH
Fax: 0161-832 0881
BO: 0161-833 9833   SD & Admin: 0161-833 9333
Website: www.royalexchange.co.uk
Artistic Directors: Braham Murray, Gregory Hersov
Executive Director: Patricia Weller
General Manager: Richard Morgan
Casting Director: Sophie Marshall

MILFORD HAVEN
Torch Theatre
St Peter's Road
Milford Haven, Pembrokeshire SA73 2BU
Fax: 01646 698919
BO: 01646 695267   Admin: 01646 694192
Website: www.torchtheatre.org.uk
e-mail: info@torchtheatre.co.uk
Artistic Director: Peter Doran

MOLD
Clwyd Theatr Cymru
(Repertoire, 4 Weekly, also touring)
Mold, Flintshire, North Wales CH7 1YA
Fax: 01352 701558
BO: 0845 3303565   Admin: 01352 756331
Website: www.clwyd-theatr-clwyd.co.uk
e-mail: drama@celtic.co.uk

MUSSELBURGH
The Brunton Theatre
(Annual programme of theatre, dance, music,
comedy & children's work)
Ladywell Way, Musselburgh EH21 6AA
Fax: 0131-665 3665
BO: 0131-665 2240   Admin: 0131-665 9900
General Manager: Lesley Smith

NEWBURY
Watermill Theatre
(4-7 Weekly) (Feb-Jan)
Bagnor, Nr Newbury, Berkshire RG20 8AE
Fax: 01635 523726   BO: 01635 46044
SD: 01635 44532   Admin: 01635 45834
Website: www.watermill.org.uk
e-mail: admin@watermill.org.uk
Artistic Director: Jill Fraser

NEWCASTLE UPON TYNE
Northern Stage (Theatrical Productions) Ltd
Newcastle Playhouse, Barras Bridge
Haymarket NE1 7RH
Fax: 0191-261 8093
BO: 0191-230 5151   Admin: 0191-232 3366
Website: www.northernstage.com
e-mail: info@northernstage.com
Artistic Director: Alan Lyddiard
Executive Director: Caroline Routh

NEWCASTLE-UNDER-LYME
New Vic Theatre
(3-4 Weekly)
Theatre in the Round, Etruria Road
Newcastle-under-Lyme, Staffordshire ST5 0JG
Fax: 01782 712885
BO: 01782 717962   Tel: 01782 717954
e-mail: admin@newvictheatre.org.uk
Artistic Director: Gwenda Hughes

NORTHAMPTON
Royal & Derngate Theatres
Guildhall Road, Northampton
Northamtonshire NN1 1DP
TIE: 01604 627566
BO: 01604 624811   Admin: 01604 626222
Chief Executive: Donna Mundy
Artistic Director: Rupert Goold
Associate Director: Simon Godwin

NOTTINGHAM
Nottingham Playhouse
(3/4 Weekly)
(Nottingham Theatre Trust Ltd)
Wellington Circus, Nottingham NG1 5AF
Fax: 0115-947 5759
BO: 0115-941 9419   Admin: 0115-947 4361
Chief Executive: Stephanie Sirr
Artistic Director: Giles Croft
Roundabout TIE Director: Andrew Breakwell

OLDHAM
Coliseum Theatre
(3-4 Weekly)
Fairbottom Street, Oldham, Lancashire OL1 3SW
Fax: 0161-624 5318
BO: 0161-624 2829   Admin: 0161-624 1731
Website: www.coliseum.org.uk
e-mail: mail@coliseum.org.uk
Chief Executive: Kevin Shaw

PERTH
Perth Repertory Theatre
(2-3 Weekly)
185 High Street, Perth PH1 5UW
Fax: 01738 624576   BO: 01738 621031
SD: 01738 621435   Admin: 01738 472700
Website: www.perththeatre.co.uk
e-mail: info@perththeatre.co.uk
Artistic Director: Michael Winter
General Manager: Paul Hackett

PETERBOROUGH
Key Theatre
(Touring & Occasional Seasonal)
Embankment Road, Peterborough
Cambridgeshire PE1 1EF
Fax: 01733 567025
BO: 01733 552439   Admin: 01733 552437
e-mail: keytheatre@freenetname.co.uk

PITLOCHRY
Pitlochry Festival Theatre
Pitlochry, Perthshire PH16 5DR
Fax: 01796 484616
BO: 01796 484626   Admin: 01796 484600
Website: www.pitlochry.org.uk
e-mail: admin@pitlochry.org.uk
Chief Executive: Nikki Axford
Artistic Director: John Durnin

PLYMOUTH
Theatre Royal & Drum Theatre
Royal Parade, Plymouth, Devon PL1 2TR
Fax: 01752 230499   Admin: 01752 668282
e-mail: s.stokes@theatreroyal.com
Artistic Director: Simon Stokes
Chief Executive: Adrian Vinken

SALISBURY
Playhouse & Salberg Studio
(3-4 Weekly)
Malthouse Lane, Salisbury, Wiltshire SP2 7RA
Fax: 01722 421991
BO: 01722 320333   Admin: 01722 320117
Website: www.salisburyplayhouse.com
e-mail: info@salisburyplayhouse.com
Artistic Director: Joanna Read
Executive Director: Rebecca Morland

SCARBOROUGH
Stephen Joseph Theatre
(Repertoire/Repertory)
Westborough, Scarborough
North Yorkshire YO11 1JW
Fax: 01723 360506   BO: 01723 370541
SD: 01723 507047   Admin: 01723 370540
e-mail: enquiries@sjt.uk.com
Artistic Director: Alan Ayckbourn
General Administrator: Stephen Wood

SHEFFIELD
Crucible, Studio & Lyceum Theatres
55 Norfolk Street, Sheffield S1 1DA
Fax: 0114-249 6003
BO: 0114-249 6000   Admin: 0114-249 5999
Website: www.sheffieldtheatres.co.uk
e-mail: initial.surname@sheffieldtheatres.co.uk
Associate Directors: Michael Grandage
& Anna Mackmin
Chief Executive: Grahame Morris

SIDMOUTH
Manor Pavilion
(Weekly) (July-Sept)
Manor Road, Sidmouth, Devon EX10 8RP
BO: 01395 579977 (Season Only)
                    Tel: 020-7636 4343 Charles Vance

SONNING THEATRE
The Mill at Sonning Theatre
(5-6 Weekly)
Sonning Eye, Reading RG4 6TY
SD: 0118-969 5201
BO: 0118-969 8000   Admin: 0118-969 6039
Artistic Director: Sally Hughes
Assistant Administrator: Ann Seymour

SOUTHAMPTON
Nuffield Theatre
(Sept-July, Sunday Night Concerts, Occasional
Tours)
University Road, Southampton SO17 1TR
Fax: 023-8031 5511
BO: 023-8067 1771   Admin: 023-8031 5500
Website: www.nuffieldtheatre.co.uk
Artistic Director: Patrick Sandford
Administrative Director: Kate Anderson

SOUTHWOLD
Summer Theatre
(July-Sept)
St Edmund's Hall, Cumberland Road
Southwold IP18 6JP   Admin: 020-7724 5432
Website: www.southwoldtheatre.org
e-mail: jill@southwoldtheatre.org

ST ANDREWS
Byre Theatre
Abbey Street, St Andrews KY16 9LA
Fax: 01334 475370
BO: 01334 475000   Admin: 01334 476288
Website: www.byretheatre.com
e-mail: enquiries@byretheatre.com
Artistic Director: Ken Alexander
Managing Director: Tom Gardner

STRATFORD-UPON-AVON
Swan Theatre & Royal Shakespeare Theatre
Waterside, Stratford-upon-Avon CV37 6BB
Fax: 01789 294810
BO: 01789 403403   Admin: 01789 296655
Website: www.rsc.org.uk
e-mail: info@rsc.org.uk

WATFORD
Palace Theatre
(3-4 Weekly) Weds 2.30pm, Sat 3pm
Clarendon Road, Watford
Hertfordshire WD17 1JZ
Fax: 01923 819664
BO: 01923 225671   Admin: 01923 235455
Website: www.watfordtheatre.co.uk
e-mail: enquiries@watfordtheatre.co.uk
Artistic Director: Lawrence Till
Administrative Director: Mary Caws
Casting: Andrea Bath

WESTCLIFF
Southend Theatres
Palace & Dixon Theatres:
London Road
Westcliff-on-Sea, Essex SS0 9LA
Fax: 01702 391573
BO: 01702 351135   Admin: 01702 390657

Cliffs Pavilion:
Station Raod, Westcliff-on-Sea
Essex SS0 7RA
Fax: 01702 391573
BO: 01702 351135   Admin: 01702 390657
Website: www.palacetheatrewestcliff.org.uk
e-mail: palacetheatre@hotmail.com

WINDSOR
Theatre Royal
(2-3 Weekly) (Thurs 2.30 Sat 4.45pm)
Thames Street
Windsor, Berkshire SL4 1PS
Fax: 01753 831673
BO: 01753 853888   Admin/SD: 01753 863444
Website: www.theatreroyalwindsor.co.uk
e-mail: info@theatreroyalwindsor.co.uk
Executive Director: Mark Piper

WOKING
New Victoria Theatre,
The Ambassadors
Peacocks Centre, Woking GU21 6GQ
BO: 01483 545900
SD: 01483 545855   Admin: 01483 545800
Website: www.theambassadors.com/woking
e-mail: boxoffice@theambassadors.com

WORCESTER
Swan Theatre
The Moors, Worcester WR1 3EF
Fax: 01905 723738
BO: 01905 27322   Admin: 01905 726969
Website: www.worcesterswantheatre.co.uk
e-mail: swan_theatre@lineone.net
Artistic Director: Jenny Stephens
General Manager: Deborah Rees

YORK
Theatre Royal
St Leonard's Place, York YO1 7HD
Fax: 01904 611534
BO: 01904 623568   Admin: 01904 658162
Website: www.yorktheatreroyal.co.uk
e-mail: admin@theatreroyalyork.fsnet.co.uk
Artistic Director: Damian Cruden
Chief Executive: Ludo Keston

6:15 THEATRE COMPANY
22 Brookfield Mansions, Highgate West Hill
London N6 6AS
Website: www.six15.dircon.co.uk
e-mail: six15@dircon.co.uk
Fax: 020-8340 5696   Tel: 020-8342 8239

ACTION TRANSPORT THEATRE COMPANY
Whitby Hall, Stanney Lane, Ellesmere Port
South Wirral CH65 9AE
Website: www.actiontransporttheatre.co.uk
e-mail: info@actiontransporttheatre.co.uk
Tel: 0151-357 2120

BLAH BLAH BLAH THEATRE COMPANY The
East Leeds Family Learning Centre
Brooklands View
Leeds LS14 6SA
Website: www.blahs.co.uk
e-mail: admin@blahs.co.uk
Fax: 0113-224 3685   Tel: 0113-224 3171

BLUNDERBUS THEATRE COMPANY Ltd
The Mick Jagger Centre
Shepherd's Lane, Dartford, Kent DA1 2JZ
Website: www.blunderbus.co.uk
e-mail: admin@blunderbus.co.uk
Fax: 01322 286285   Tel: 01322 286284

BORDERLINE THEATRE COMPANY
North Harbour Street, Ayr KA8 8AA
Website: www.borderlineartre.co.uk
e-mail: enquiries@borderlinetheatre.co.uk
Fax: 01292 263825   Tel: 01292 281010
Producer: Eddie Jackson

CHALKFOOT THEATRE ARTS
Central Studios
36 Park Place, Margate, Kent CT9 1LE
Website: www.chalkfoot.org.uk
e-mail: info@chalkfoot.org.uk   Tel: 01843 280077
Artistic Director: Philip Dart

CHICKEN SHED THEATRE
Chase Side, Southgate, London N14 4PE
Website: www.chickenshed.org.uk
e-mail: info@chickenshed.org.uk
Minicom: 020-8350 0676   Tel: 020-8351 6161
Artistic Director: Mary Ward MBE

CLWYD THEATRE/CYMRU THEATR FOR YOUNG PEOPLE
(Contact - Education Administator)
Mold, Flintshire CH7 1YA
Website: www.clywd-theatr-cymru.co.uk
e-mail: education@clwyd-theatre-cymru.co.uk
Fax: 01352 701558   Tel: 01352 701575

COMPLETE WORKS THEATRE COMPANY Ltd The
12 Willowford, Bancroft Park, Milton Keynes
Buckinghamshire MK13 0RH
Website: www.tcw.org.uk
e-mail: info@tcw.org.uk
Fax: 01908 320263   Tel: 01908 316256
Artistic Director: Phil Evans

CRAGRATS Ltd
The Mill, Dunford Road, Holmfirth
Huddersfield HD9 2AR
Website: www.cragrats.com
e-mail: jill@cragrats.com
Fax: 01484 686212   Tel: 01484 686451

CTC THEATRE
Arts Centre, Vane Terrace, Darlington
County Durham DL3 7AX
Website: www.ctctheatre.org.uk
e-mail: ctc@ctctheatre.org.uk
Fax: 01325 369404   Tel: 01325 352004

EUROPEAN THEATRE COMPANY The
39 Oxford Avenue, London SW20 8LS
Website: www.europeantheatre.co.uk
e-mail: admin@europeantheatre.co.uk
Fax: 020-8544 1999   Tel: 020-8544 1994

GAZEBO TIE COMPANY Ltd
The Multipurpose Centre, Victoria Road, Darlaston
West Midlands WS10 8AP
Website: www.gazebotie.com
e-mail: gazebo@ukgateway.net
Tel/Fax: 0121-526 6877

GWENT TIE COMPANY
The Drama Centre Pen-y-pound
Abergavenny
Monmouthshire NP7 5UD
Website: www.gwenttie.co.uk
e-mail: gwenttie@aol.com
Fax: 01873 853910   Tel: 01873 853167

IMPACT UK Ltd
Hope Bank House, Woodhead Road, Honley
Huddersfield HD9 6PF
Fax: 08700 111266   Tel: 08700 111288

JOE PUBLIC THEATRE COMPANY
(Nick Rawling)
c/o New College Telford, King Street
Wellington Telford TF1 1NY
Website: www.newcollagetelford.ac.uk
e-mail: info@nct.ac.uk   Tel: 01952 641892

KINETIC THEATRE COMPANY Ltd
Suite H, The Jubilee Centre, Lombard Road
Wimbledon, London SW19 3TZ
Website: www.kinetictheatre.co.uk
e-mail: sarah@kinetictheatre.co.uk
Fax: 020-8286 2645   Tel: 020-8286 2613
Contact: Dr Oliver Thalmann

LANGUAGE ALIVE!
The Playhouse, Longmore St, Birmingham B12 9ED
e-mail: theplayhouse@btconnect.com
Fax: 0121-440 6263   Tel: 0121-446 4301

M6 THEATRE COMPANY
Hamer CP School, Albert Royds Street
Rochdale OL16 2SU
e-mail: info@m6theatre.co.uk
Fax: 01706 711700   Tel: 01706 355898

NATIONAL TRUST THEATRE The
(TMA Member)
Sutton House, 2 & 4 Homerton High Street
Hackney, London E9 6JQ
Website: www.nationaltrust.org.uk/learning
e-mail: theatre@nationaltrust.org.uk
Fax: 020-8985 2343   Tel: 020-8986 0242

ONATTI THEATRE COMPANY
9 Field Close, Warwick, Warwickshire CV34 4QD
Website: www.onatti.co.uk
e-mail: info@onatti.co.uk
Fax: 0870 1643629   Tel: 01926 495220
Artistic Director: Andrew Bardwell

QUANTUM THEATRE FOR SCIENCE
The Old Button Factory, 1-11 Bannockburn Road
Plumstead, London SE18 1ET
Website: www.quantumtheatre.co.uk
e-mail: quantumtheatre@btinternet.com
Tel: 020-8317 9000
Artistic Directors: Michael Whitmore, Jessica Selous

QUERCUS THEATRE COMPANY
33 Broadlands Avenue, Shepperton
Middlesex TW17 9DJ
Website: www.quercustheatrecompany.org.uk
e-mail: quercus@quercustheatrecompany.org.uk
Tel: 01932 252182
Director: Therese Kitchin

ROUNDABOUT THEATRE IN EDUCATION
Nottingham Playhouse, Wellington Circus
Nottingham NG1 5AF
e-mail: info@nottinghamplayhouse.co.uk
Fax: 0115-953 9055   Tel: 0115-947 4361

ROYAL & DERNGATE THEATRE IN EDUCATION
19-21 Guildhall Road
Northampton NN1 1DP
e-mail: education@ntt.org   Tel: 01604 627566

SHEFFIELD THEATRES EDUCATION COMPANY
55 Norfolk Street
Sheffield S1 1DA
Website: www.sheffieldtheatres.co.uk/education
Fax: 0114-249 6003   Tel: 0114-249 5999
Education Administator: Sue Burley
Education Director: Karen Simpson

SNAP THEATRE COMPANY
29 Raynham Road, Bishop's Stortford
Hertfordshire CM23 5PE
Website: www.snaptheatre.co.uk
e-mail: info@snaptheatre.co.uk
Fax: 01279 506694   Tel: 01279 461607

SPECTACLE THEATRE
Coleg Morgannwg, Rhondda Campus, Llwynypia
Tonypandy CF40 2TQ
Website: www.spectacletheatre.co.uk
e-mail: info@spectacletheatre.co.uk
Fax: 01443 423080   Tel: 01443 430700

TEAM PLAYERS THEATRE COMPANY
Lingfield Countryside Centre, Mount Pleasant Way
Coulby Newham, Middlesborough TS8 0XF
Website: www.companytraining.co.uk
e-mail: terry.wilkinson@talk21.com
Fax: 01642 577121   Tel: 01642 592648

THEATR IOLO Ltd
The Old School Building, Cefn Road, Mynachdy
Cardiff CF14 3HS
Website: www.theatriolo.com
e-mail: admin@theatriolo.com
Fax: 029-2052 2225   Tel: 029-2061 3782

THEATRE IN EDUCATION TOURS (TIE TOURS)
Holloway School, Hilldrop Road, Islington
London N7 0JG
Website: www.tietours.com
e-mail: tie@tietours.com
Fax: 020-7700 3697   Mobile: 07815 855672

TIEBREAK THEATRE COMPANY
42-58 St George's Street, Norwich NR3 1AB
Website: www.tiebreak-theatre.com
e-mail: info@tiebreak-theatre.com
Fax: 01603 666096   Tel: 01603 665899

WEST YORKSHIRE PLAYHOUSE SCHOOLS TOURING COMPANY
West Yorkshire Playhouse, Playhouse Square
Quarry Hill, Leeds LS2 7UP
e-mail: gail.mcintyre@wyp.org.uk   Tel: 0113-213 7800

Vehicles & Transport

ACTION CARS Ltd
(Steven Royffe)
Units 3 & 4 Rosslyn Crescent, Harrow
Middlesex HA1 2RZ
e-mail: info@actioncars.co.uk
Fax: 020-8861 4876   Tel: 020-8863 6889

ANCHOR MARINE FILM & TELEVISION
(Boat Location, Charter, Marine Co-ordinators)
Spike Mead Farm, Poles Lane, Lowfield Heath
West Sussex RH11 0PX
e-mail: amsfilms@aol.com
Fax: 01293 551558   Tel: 01293 538188

ANGLO PACIFIC INTERNATIONAL Plc
(Freight Forwarders to the Performing Arts)
Unit 1, Bush Industrial Estate, Standard Road
North Acton, London NW10 6DF
Website: www.anglopacific.co.uk
e-mail: info@anglopacific.co.uk
Fax: 020-8965 4954   Tel: 020-8965 1234

AUTOMOTIVE ACTION TRACKING DIVISION
(Supplier)
2 Sheffield House, Park Road, Hampton Hill
Middlesex TW12 1HA
Website: www.cameratrackingvehicle.com
Mobile: 07974 919589   Tel: 020-8977 6186

AZTEC OF BRISTOL
20 Walnut Lane, Kingswood
Bristol BS15 4JG   Tel/Fax: 0117-940 7712

BIANCHI AVIATION FILM SERVICES
(Historic & Other Aircraft)
Wycombe Air Park, Booker, Nr Marlow
Buckinghamshire SL7 3DP
e-mail: info@bianchiaviation.com
Fax: 01494 461236   Tel: 01494 449810

BICYCLES UNLIMITED
(D Pinkerton)
522 Holly Lane, Erdington
Birmingham B24 9LY   Tel/Fax: 0121-350 0685

BLUEBELL RAILWAY Plc
(Steam Locomotives, Pullman Coaches, Period
Stations. Much Film Experience)
Sheffield Park Station, East Sussex TN22 3QL
Website: www.bluebell-railway.co.uk
Fax: 01825 720804   Tel: 01825 720800

BRUNEL'S THEATRICAL SERVICES
Unit 4, Crown Industrial Estate, Crown Road
Warmley, Bristol BS30 8JB
Fax: 0117-907 7856   Tel: 0117-907 7855

BURLINGTON SERVICES
(Online database and period vehicles)
PO Box 7484, Epping, Essex, CM16 7WB
Website: www.classicstars.co.uk
e-mail: contact@classicstars.co.uk   Tel: 01992 575720

CARLINE & CREW TRANSPORTATION
(Celebrity Services)
12A Bridge Industrial Estate, Balcombe Road
West Sussex RH6 9HU
e-mail: carlinehire@btconnect.com
Fax: 01293 400508   Tel: 01293 400505

CLASSIC CAR AGENCY The
(Film, Promotional, Advertising, Publicity)
PO Box 427, Dorking, Surrey RH5 6WP
Website: www.theclassiccaragency.com
e-mail: theclassiccaragency@btopenworld.com
Mobile: 07788 977655   Tel: 01306 731052

CLASSIC CAR HIRE
(Rolls Royce Phantoms, Bentleys, a Lagonda &
Daimlers for hire 1920-70)
Unit 2 Hampton Court Estate, Summer Road
Thames Ditton, KT7 0RG
Website: www.classic-hire.com
e-mail: classic-wedding@supemet.com
          Tel: 020-8398 8304

CLASSIC OMNIBUS
(Vintage Open-Top Buses & Coaches)
44 Welson Road, Folkestone, Kent CT20 2NP
Website: www.opentopbus.co.uk
Fax: 01303 241245   Tel: 01303 248999

DEVEREUX K. W. & SONS
(Removals)
Daimler Drive, Cowpen Industrial Estate, Billingham
Cleveland TS23 4JD
e-mail: devereux@onyxnet.co.uk
Fax: 01642 566664   Tel: 01642 560854

EASYBIKES
1-3 Leeke Street, London WC1X 9HZ
Fax: 020-7833 4613   Tel: 020-7833 4607

EST Ltd
(Trucking - Every Size & Country)
Marshgate Sidings
Marshgate Lane, London E15 2PB
Website: www.yourockweroll.com
e-mail: info@edwin-shirley-trucking.co.uk
Fax: 020-8522 1002   Tel: 020-8522 1000

FELLOWES Mark TRANSPORT SERVICES
(Transport/Personal Storage)
59 Sherbrooke Road, London SW6 7QL
Website: www.fellowesproductions.com
Mobile: 07850 332818   Tel: 020-7386 7005

FRANKIE'S YANKEES
(Classic 1950s American Cars, Memorabilia & New
Superstretch Limos)
283 Old Birmingham Road
Bromsgrove B60 1HQ   Tel: 0121-445 5522

IMPACT
(Private & Contract Hire of Coaches)
1 Leighton Road, Ealing, London W13 9EL
Fax: 020-8840 4880   Tel: 020-8579 9922

JASON'S LADY ROSE
(Up-market Cruising Canal Wideboat, Daily
Scheduled Trips to Camden Lock)
Opposite. 42 Blomfield Road, Little Venice
London W9 2PD
Website: www.jasons.co.uk
e-mail: enquiries@jasons.co.uk
Fax: 020-7266 4332   Tel: 020-7286 3428

KEIGHLEY & WORTH VALLEY LIGHT RAILWAY Ltd
(Engines, Stations, Carriages, Props & Crew)
The Railway Station, Haworth, Keighley
West Yorkshire BD22 8NJ
Website: www.kwvr.co.uk
e-mail: admin@kwvr.co.uk
Fax: 01535 647317   Tel: 01535 645214

LUCKING G. H. & SONS
(Transporters/Storage/Stage Hands)
NTS House, Headley Road East, Woodley
Reading, Berkshire RG5 4SZ
e-mail: enquiries@luckings.co.uk
Fax: 0118-969 6881   Tel: 0118-969 7878

M V DIXIE QUEEN
Thames Luxury Charters
5 The Mews
6 Putney Common, London SW15 1HL
Website: www.thamesluxurycharters.co.uk
e-mail: sales@thamesluxurycharters.co.uk
Fax: 020-8788 0072   Tel: 020-8780 1562

MAINSTREAM LEISURE GROUP
(Riverboat/Canal Boat Hire)
5 The Mews, 6 Putney Common, London SW15 1HL
Website: www.mainstreamleisure.co.uk
Fax: 020-8788 0073   Tel: 020-8788 2669

McNEILL Brian
(Vintage Truck & Coaches)
Hawk Mount, Kebcote, Todmorden
Lancashire OL14 8SB
Website: www.rollingpast.com
e-mail: autotrams@currantbun.com
Fax: 01706 812292   Tel: 01706 812291

MOTORHOUSE HIRE Ltd
(Period Vehicles 1900-80)
Weston Underwood, Olney
Buckinghamshire MK46 5LD
e-mail: john@motorhouseltd.co.uk
Fax: 01234 240393   Tel: 020-7495 1618

NATIONAL MOTOR MUSEUM
John Montagu Building, Beaulieu
Nr Brockenhurst, Hampshire SO42 7ZN
Website: www.beaulieu.co.uk
e-mail: info@beaulieu.co.uk
Fax: 01590 612624   Tel: 01590 612345

NINE-NINE CARS Ltd
Hyde Meadow Farm, Hyde Lane
Hemel Hempstead HP3 8SA
e-mail: david@nineninecars.com   Tel: 01923 266373

PICKFORDS REMOVALS Ltd
Heritage House
345 Southbury Road, Enfield
Middlesex EN1 1UP
Website: www.pickfords.com
Fax: 020-8219 8001   Tel: 020-8219 8000

PLUS FILM SERVICES Ltd
(All Periods Vehicle Hire)
1 Mill House Cottages
Winchester Road
Bishop's Waltham SO32 1AH
e-mail: stephen@plusfilms7.freeserve.co.uk
                              Tel/Fax: 01489 895559

RADCLIFFE'S TRANSPORT
(see LUCKING G. H. & SONS)

STOKE BRUERNE BOAT COMPANY Ltd
(Passenger & Commercial Boats)
29 Main Road, Shutlanger
Northamptonshire NN12 7RU
Website: www.stokebruerneboats.co.uk
Fax: 01604 864098   Tel: 01604 862107

THAMES LUXURY CHARTERS Ltd
5 The Mews
6 Putney Common
London SW15 1HL
Website: www.thamesluxurycharters.co.uk
e-mail: sales@thamesluxurycharters.co.uk
Fax: 020 8788 0072   Tel: 020 8780 1562

TOWN TYRE SERVICES Ltd
(Tug Boat for Hire)
Valley Way
Swansea Enterprise Park, Llansamcet
Swansea SA6 8QP   Tel: 01792 773431

VINTAGE CARRIAGES TRUST
(Owners of the Museum of Rail Travel at Ingrow
Railway Centre)
Keighley, West Yorkshire BD22 8NJ
Website: www.vintagecarriagestrust.org
e-mail: admin@vintagecarriagestrust.org
Fax: 01535 610796   Tel: 01535 680425

VIRGIN ATLANTIC AIRWAYS
(Reservations)
The Office, Crawley Business Quarter
Manor Royal, West Sussex RH10 9NU
Website: www.virgin.com/atlantic
                              Tel: 01293 747747

**WOFFORD INTERNATIONAL HORSE
TRANSPORT Ltd**
Abnalls Farm
Cross-In-Hand Lane, Lichfield
Staffordshire WS13 8DZ
Website: www.wofford.co.uk
Fax: 01543 417226   Tel: 01543 417225

INDEX TO ADVERTISERS CONTACTS 2004

PROPERTIES & TRADES

PUBLICATIONS & PUBLISHERS

REHEARSAL/AUDITION ROOMS/CASTING SUITES

REPRO COMPANIES & PHOTOGRAPHIC RETOUCHING

SCRIPT SERVICES

SHOWREELS, VOICE TAPES, CV's, LABELS, etc

TRAINING (Private Coaches)

TRAINING (Schools, Companies & Workshops)

TRANSPORT

WIG SUPPLIERS

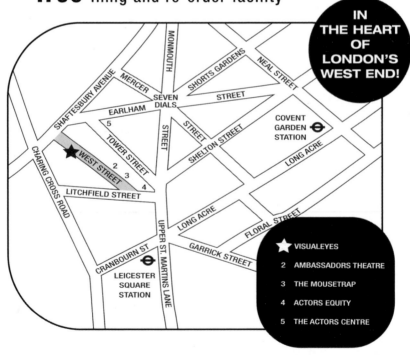